ACCOUNTANTS'
HANDBOOK

ELEVENTH EDITION
2011 CUMULATIVE SUPPLEMENT

Update Service

BECOME A SUBSCRIBER!

Did you purchase this product from a bookstore?

If you did, it's important for you to become a subscriber. John Wiley & Sons, Inc. may publish, on a periodic basis, supplements and new editions to reflect the latest changes in the subject matter that you **need to know** in order to stay competitive in this ever-changing industry. By contacting the Wiley office nearest you, you'll receive any current update at no additional charge. In addition, you'll receive future updates and revised or related volumes on a 30-day examination review.

If you purchased this product directly from John Wiley & Sons, Inc., we have already recorded your subscription for this update service.

To become a subscriber, please call **1-877-762-2974** or send your name, company name (if applicable), address, and the title of the product to:

mailing address: **Supplement Department**
                    John Wiley & Sons, Inc.
                    One Wiley Drive
                    Somerset, NJ 08875
e-mail: **subscriber@wiley.com**
fax: **1-732-302-2300**

For customers outside the United States, please contact the Wiley office nearest you:

Professional & Reference Division
John Wiley & Sons Canada, Ltd.
22 Worcester Road
Etobicoke, Ontario M9W 1L1
CANADA
Phone: 416-236-4433
Phone: 1-800-567-4797
Fax: 416-236-4447
Email: canada@wiley.com

John Wiley & Sons Australia, Ltd.
33 Park Road
P.O. Box 1226
Milton, Queensland 4064
AUSTRALIA
Phone: 61-7-3859-9755
Fax: 61-7-3859-9715
Email: brisbane@johnwiley.com.au

John Wiley & Sons, Ltd.
The Atrium
Southern Gate, Chichester
West Sussex PO 19 8SQ
ENGLAND
Phone: 44-1243-779777
Fax: 44-1243-775878
Email: customer@wiley.co.uk

John Wiley & Sons (Asia) Pte., Ltd.
2 Clementi Loop #02-01
SINGAPORE 129809
Phone: 65-64632400
Fax: 65-64634604/5/6
Customer Service: 65-64604280
Email: enquiry@wiley.com.sg

ACCOUNTANTS' HANDBOOK

ELEVENTH EDITION

2011 CUMULATIVE SUPPLEMENT

LYNFORD GRAHAM

WILEY

John Wiley & Sons, Inc.

For general information on our other products and services, or technical support, please contact our
Customer Care Department within the United States at 800-762-2974, outside the United States at
317-572-3993 or fax 317-572-4002.

Wiley also publishes its books in a variety of electronic formats. Some content that appears in print may
not be available in electronic books.

For more information about Wiley products, visit our web site at www.wiley.com.

ISBN 978-0-470-61080-0 (supplement)

Printed in the United States of America

10   9   8   7   6   5   4   3   2   1

ABOUT THE EDITOR

Lynford Graham, CPA, PhD, CFE, is a Certified Public Accountant with more than 25 years of public accounting experience in audit practice and national policy development groups. He is currently Visiting Professor of Accountancy and Executive in Residence at Bentley University in Waltham, Massachusetts. He was a Partner and the Director of Audit Policy for BDO Seidman LLP, and was a National Accounting & SEC Consulting Partner for Coopers & Lybrand, responsible for the technical issues research function and database, auditing research, audit automation, and audit sampling techniques. Prior to joining BDO Seidman LLP, Dr. Graham was an Associate Professor of Accounting and Information Systems and a Graduate Faculty Fellow at Rutgers University in Newark, New Jersey, where he taught primarily financial accounting courses. Dr. Graham is a member of the American Institute of Certified Public Accountants and a recent past member of the AICPA Auditing Standards Board. He is a Certified Fraud Examiner and a member of the Association of Certified Fraud Examiners. Throughout his career he has maintained an active profile in the academic as well as the business community. In 2002 he received the Distinguished Service Award of the Auditing Section of the AAA. His numerous academic and business publications span a variety of topical areas including information systems, internal controls, expert systems, audit risk, audit planning, fraud, sampling, analytical procedures, audit judgment, and international accounting and auditing. Dr. Graham holds an MBA in Industrial Management and PhD in Business and Applied Economics from the University of Pennsylvania (Wharton School).

ABOUT THE CONTRIBUTORS

Antonetti, Michael A., CPA, CMA, is a partner with Crowe Horwath LLP. Mr. Antonetti has over 20 years of experience providing assurance and business advisory services to clients in many industries including manufacturing, distribution, banking, professional services, transportation, and hospitality. Mr. Antonetti's experience also includes assisting clients with merger, acquisition, and divestiture transactions, and application of the related accounting standards. Mr. Antonetti also serves clients with international operations in Europe, Asia, and North and South America.

Bahl, Yogesh, is a partner in our Deloitte Financial Advisory Services LLP practice and is the Northeast leader of the Antifraud Programs and Controls practice. Mr. Bahl has more than 14 years of experience in performing forensic investigations and providing dispute consulting services. He also provides advisory services to companies in various industries with respect to structuring collaboration, distribution, co-promotion, and licensing agreements. Mr. Bahl earned his MBA in Finance and Statistics and BS in Accounting and International Business from New York University's Stern School of Business.

Beaton, Neil J., CPA/ABV, CFA, ASA, is the partner in charge of Grant Thornton LLP's national valuation services group. He has over 25 years of experience analyzing both closely held and publicly traded companies. Mr. Beaton has appeared as an expert witness in numerous courts across the country, lectures at local universities, is an instructor for the AICPA's business valuation courses, and speaks nationally on business valuation topics with a special emphasis on early-stage and high-technology companies. He has served on the AICPA's National Accreditation Commission and the FASB's Valuation Resource Group. He has a Bachelor of Arts degree in Economics from Stanford University and a Master of Business Administration in Finance from National University. In addition to his formal education, Mr. Beaton is a Certified Public Accountant, accredited in Business Valuation, a Chartered Financial Analyst, and an Accredited Senior Appraiser in business valuation from the American Society of Appraisers.

Grant Thornton LLP is the U.S. member firm of Grant Thornton International, one of the six global accounting, tax, and business advisory organizations. Through member firms in 112 countries, including 51 offices in the United States, the partners and employees of Grant Thornton member firms provide personalized attention and the highest quality service to public and private clients around the globe. Visit Grant Thornton LLP at www.GrantThornton.com.

Bongiorno, Benedetto, CPA, CRE, has more than 40 years of public accounting experience providing auditing, accounting, and consulting services to both public and private real estate companies. Having served as National Director of Real Estate for Deloitte & Touche, coupled with many years of research and practical application of specially developed substantive analytical audit procedures and technologically based tools, he has made major contributions in both real estate audits and the field of continuous audit. He is also a cofounder of Natural Decision Systems, Inc., a developer and provider of audit technology tools.

Epstein, Barry Jay, PhD, CPA, is a partner at Russell Novak & Company LLP. With almost 40 years' experience in the public accounting profession as auditor and technical director/partner for several national and local firms, Dr. Epstein's current practice is concentrated on providing technical consultations to CPA firms and corporations on U.S. GAAP and IFRS accounting and financial reporting matters; U.S. and international auditing standards; financial analysis; forensic accounting investigations; and corporate governance. A widely published authority on accounting and auditing, his current publications include *Wiley GAAP*, now in its 22nd edition, and *Wiley IFRS*, for both of which he is the lead coauthor. He previously chaired the Audit Committee of the AICPA's Board of Examiners, responsible for the Uniform CPA Examination, and has served on other professional panels at state and national levels. Dr. Epstein holds degrees from DePaul University, Chicago (BSC, Accounting and Finance, 1967), University of Chicago (MBA, Economics and Industrial Relations, 1969), and University of Pittsburgh (PhD, Information Systems and Finance, 1979).

Gini, Ernest J., CPA, CGFM, is a partner with Macias Gini & O'Connell LLP (MGO) with 33 years of experience as a CPA. An expert in the field of governmental and nonprofit accounting, Mr. Gini was appointed to the 2006–2007 AICPA Virtual Grassroots Panel, formerly known as the Group of 100. He is a Certified Government Financial Manager with the Association of Government Accountants and has conducted seminars for public finance officials on the New Financial Reporting Model (GASB 34), Changes to OMB Circular A-133, Accounting for Redevelopment Agencies, Single Audit Applications, Changes in Government Auditing Standards, GASB Statement Updates, Program-Specific Audits, and other topics. He also served on the GASB Advisory Committee on the *User Guide to Local Government Financial Statements* and was a contributor to *What You Should Know about Your Local Government's Finances: A Guide to Financial Statements.*

Hydoski, Frank, PhD, is a director in the New York Forensics & Dispute Services practice of Deloitte Financial Advisory Services LLP. He is responsible for developing new products and approaches in forensic accounting and investigations for clients in both the private and public sector. Mr. Hydoski is internationally recognized for his work in complex investigations, especially those requiring information technologies to facilitate forensic analysis. He was the chief investigator examining the United Nations Oil-for-Food Programme, and he also led a crucial part of the massive forensic effort in the investigation of Holocaust-era accounts held by Swiss banks.

The authors wish to acknowledge the contributions of Donald F. Andersen, Daniel L. Collins, Stephen Doka, Daniel Krittman, Satish Lalchand, and Michael Shepard, all part of Deloitte FAS LLP.

Leisner, Christopher J., CPA, CMC, is founder of Creative IP Solutions LLC, an intellectual property consulting firm that specializes in managing and monetizing intellectual property for a diverse domestic and international client base, from Fortune 100 companies to privately held companies. A speaker at several IP management and patent securitization conferences, Mr. Leisner has authored several articles and white papers on IP value extraction techniques and has served as an expert witness on accounting malpractice, fraud, and damages. He was previously Midwest Partner in Charge of Litigation Consulting Services and Regional Business Line Leader for Specialty Consulting Services at BDO Seidman LLP. A certified management consultant, Mr. Leisner has assisted clients in resolving various business issues relating to strategic planning, equity and debt financing, mergers and acquisitions support, management reporting systems, and internal control procedures.

O'Connell, Kevin J., CPA, is the managing partner of Macias Gini & O'Connell LLP (MGO), a leading California certified public accounting and consulting firm. He has over 15 years of experience in federal, state, and local financial compliance auditing at all levels of government, including California's largest cities and counties and governmental component organizations in the airport, mass transit, utilities, and healthcare industries. Mr. O'Connell has served on the AICPA State and Local Government Expert Panel and contributed to the AICPA guide *Audits of State and Local Governments (GASB 34 Edition)*. In 2007, he was recognized by *CPA Technology Advisor* magazine as one of the nation's top 40 tax and accounting professionals under the age of 40 who will help lead the professions of public accounting and professional tax preparation into the future.

Pon, Cynthia, CPA, has over 15 years of professional experience providing auditing, accounting, and consulting services to the private and public sectors. She leads the San Francisco Bay Area public sector assurance practice of Macias Gini & O'Connell LLP (MGO), bringing extensive experience in federal, state, and local financial and compliance auditing. Ms. Pon is an expert in the application of governmental GAAP and has been recognized by the Governmental Accounting Standards Board for her leadership in assisting large California governments with early implementation of its standards. She also serves on the Government Finance Officers Association Special Review Committee for Comprehensive Annual Financial Report awards and has instructed numerous governmental clients on a variety of audit issues and challenges.

Rezaee, Zabihollah, PhD, is the Thompson-Hill Chair of Excellence and professor of accountancy at the University of Memphis. He served a two-year term on the Standing Advisory Group (SAG) of the Public Company Accounting Oversight Board (PCAOB). Professor Rezaee received his BS degree from the Iranian Institute of Advanced Accounting, his MBA from Tarleton State University in Texas, and his PhD from the University of Mississippi. He holds several certifications, including Certified Public Accountant (CPA), Certified Fraud Examiner (CFE), Certified Management Accountant (CMA), Certified Internal Auditor (CIA), and Certified Government Financial Manager (CGFM), Certified Sarbanes-Oxley Professional (CSOXP), Certified Corporate Governance Professional (CGOVP) and Certified Governance Risk Compliance Professional (CGRCP). He was a finalist for SOX Institute's SOX MVP 2007 Award. Professor Rezaee has published over 180 articles in a variety of accounting and business journals and made more than 180 presentations at national and international conferences. He has also published six books: *Financial Institutions, Valuations, Mergers, and Acquisitions: The Fair Value Approach*; *Financial Statement Fraud: Prevention and Detection*; *U.S. Master Auditing Guide,* 3rd edition; *Audit Committee Oversight Effectiveness Post-Sarbanes-Oxley Act*; *Corporate Governance Post-Sarbanes-Oxley: Regulations, Requirements, and Integrated Processes*; and *Corporate Governance and Business Ethics*. Two new books, *Corporate and Sustainability Reporting* and *Integrated Financial and Internal Control Reporting*, are scheduled to be published in 2010.

Shim, Jae K., PhD, is a professor of accounting and finance at California State University, Long Beach, and CEO of Delta Consulting Company, a financial consulting and training firm. Dr. Shim received his MBA and PhD degrees from the University of California at Berkeley (Haas School of Business). He has been a consultant to commercial and nonprofit organizations for over 30 years. Dr. Shim has also published numerous articles in professional and academic journals and has over 50 college and professional books to his credit.

Victor, George I., CPA, is the Director of Quality Control at Giambalvo, Giammarese & Stalzer, CPAs, P.C., responsible for the development and maintenance of quality control, staff training, technical research, consulting, and review of completed engagements. Mr. Victor has extensive experience in providing accounting and advisory services to both privately held and SEC reporting companies, including audits of financial statements, SEC filings for public offerings and periodic reporting, private placements, and complex business combinations. He provides consulting services in the areas of quality control and technical matters to other CPA firms, traveling domestically as well as to Latin America, India, and the United Kingdom. He is a member of the American Institute of CPAs (AICPA), the New York State Society of CPAs (NYSSCPA), and has chaired the NYSSCPA's Accounting and Auditing Oversight Committee and SEC Practice Committee. He is also a member of the Editorial Board of the *CPA Journal*. A frequent author and lecturer, Mr. Victor has been published or quoted in various international and national publications and professional journals, and lectures on SEC, accounting, and auditing related topics.

Zyla, Mark L., CPA/ABV, CFA, ASA, is Managing Director of Acuitas, Inc., an Atlanta, Georgia–based valuation and litigation consultancy firm. As a valuation specialist, he has provided consulting for numerous valuations in financial reporting and other types of engagements. Mr. Zyla is a member of the AICPA Fair Value Resource Panel and was named as the vice chairman of the Appraisal Foundation's first Business Valuation Best Practices Working Group. He is also the chairman of the conference committee of the AICPA's first annual Fair Value Measurements conference. He is the author of *Fair Value Measurements: Practical Guidance and Implementation,* published by John Wiley & Sons.

CONTENTS

Note to the Reader: Sections not in the main bound volume, *Accountants' Handbook Eleventh Edition* (978-0-471-79041-9), are indicated by "(New)" after the title. Material from the main bound volume that has been updated for *this* supplement is indicated by "(Revised)" after the title. Material new to or modified in *this* supplement is indicated by an asterisk (*) in the left margin in the contents and throughout the supplement.

PREFACE

This is the 2011 cumulative supplement to the 11th edition of the *Accountant's Handbook*. Annual updates to this work provide important revisions and new topics that update the *Handbook* between editions. In addition, reader feedback suggests additional topical areas that are of interest to our readers. We are pleased to expand the *Handbook* to include those topical areas of significant interest. This cumulative supplement provides significantly revised and enhanced chapters. Of special note in this supplement is the revised Chapter 31 on Financial Institutions.

Chapter 4. Introduction to Internal Control Assessment and Reporting (Revised) provides an update that includes the continuing SEC reporting requirements for accelerated filers and smaller public companies, as stated and clarified in the Dodd–Frank Wall Street Reform Act of 2010. Under the Act, all public companies will continue to publicly report on the effectiveness of their internal controls over financial reporting.

Chapter 21: Property, Plant, Equipment, and Depreciation is a slightly revised chapter regarding a topic relevant to most business entities.

Chapter 31: Financial Institutions is a replacement of an existing chapter on this subject by a new author. Included are insights into the implications of the Dodd–Frank Wall Street Reform Act of 2010 on the institutions so intimately involved in the financial services meltdown in 2008-2009.

Previously updated chapters since the publication of the 11th edition that have not otherwise been revised in this edition continue to be included as part of the annual cumulative supplement.

ACCOUNTANTS' HANDBOOK

ELEVENTH EDITION

FINANCIAL ACCOUNTING AND GENERAL TOPICS

CHAPTER 4

INTRODUCTION TO INTERNAL CONTROL ASSESSMENT AND REPORTING (REVISED)

LYNFORD GRAHAM, CPA, PHD, CFE
Bentley University

4.1 INTRODUCTION

The Sarbanes-Oxley Act of 2002[1] made significant changes to many aspects of the financial reporting process. One of those changes is a requirement that management evaluate the effectiveness of its internal control over financial reporting and provide a report on this evaluation. Additionally, the company's independent auditors are required to report on the effectiveness of internal control in conjunction with their traditional audit of the company's financial statements.

The motivation for this requirement arose out of the business and audit failures in the early 2000s. Corporate names such as Enron, WorldCom, and Global Crossing dominated the news with tales of financial reporting shenanigans and corporate executive misdirections. The root foundation for this requiring the controls reporting remedy is a long trail of academic and professional research that concluded time and time again that weaknesses in internal controls were an underlying cause of these types of problems. In addition, a rising proportion of restatements of previously issued financial reports was also observed. These factors contributed to a conclusion that investor confidence in the U.S. securities market was at risk. In light of recent emerging strengths in international securities markets, the trend had to be reversed.

While a much-discussed aspect of the Sarbanes-Oxley Act has been the requirement for corporations to report publicly on internal controls, other provisions of the act have had significance for the business community and the auditing profession. Those provisions include:

- Establishment of the Public Company Accounting Oversight Board (PCAOB) as the auditing standards setting and inspection body over public company audits
- Strengthened independence rules for independent auditors and limitations on providing certain nonaudit services for audit clients
- Strengthened penalties for corporate executive misconduct
- More accountability for corporate financial executives for establishing, maintaining, and monitoring internal controls and quarterly certifications regarding significant changes in internal controls
- Additional penalties for corporate executives not complying with the rules

In years subsequent to 2004, the Securities and Exchange Commission (SEC) and the PCAOB issued revised guidance to companies and auditors, designed to ease the burdens of compliance as a result of cost concerns. Nonaccelerated filer entities (capitalization under $75 million) finally began reporting on the effectiveness of their controls in 2008. In July 2010, the Dodd–Frank Wall Street Reform and Consumer Protection Act (Pub.L. 111-203, July 21) suspended the requirement that auditors separately assess, test, and report on the internal controls reports of nonaccelerated filer public companies. All public companies will, however, continue to report on the effectiveness of their internal controls following SEC guidelines. Auditors of nonaccelerated filers will read and assess the disclosures made by companies regarding their internal controls under other auditing standards (AU Section 550).

(a) THE EFFECTIVENESS OF SARBANES-OXLEY REQUIREMENTS TO DATE   It is difficult to quantitatively assess the success of the Sarbanes-Oxley Act at this time. We are aware that fraud and financial statement misstatement have not ended, but the extent to which

---

1.   United States Congress. *The Public Company Accounting Reform and Investor Protection Act of 2002* (The Sarbanes-Oxley Act). Pub. L. No. 107-204, 116 Stat. 745, July 30, 2002.

they would be higher in the absence of the requirements is not easily measured. Anecdotal evidence and information gathered for an academic research study[2] indicate the identification of many deficiencies in internal control in even the largest and most well controlled entities. In a study of 44 accelerated filer audit engagements over two years (2004 and 2005) that yielded 76 data observations, nearly 4,000 deficiencies of various magnitudes were identified and documented by entities and auditors. It was found that management's classifications of the severity of deficiencies that were also assessed by the auditor were often understated, adding credence to the value of independent auditor involvement. More than 65% of the time, companies underrated the severity of deficiencies they found, relative to the way the auditor assessed these deficiencies. Also, the auditor seems to have been the primary source of deficiency identification (over 70 percent of the total deficiencies), and control tests were the predominant discovery vehicle for uncovering the deficiencies (again over 70 percent). The remediation of material weaknesses identified during the year resulted in a more modest reported number of ineffective control opinions than would have been the case if all weaknesses (and not just those remaining at year-end) were determinant of controls effectiveness. By that measure, the requirements seem to be identifying issues that should result in fewer financial statement misstatements and restatements. In light of the importance of auditor procedures in identifying and classifying control deficiencies, it is surprising that the Dodd–Frank Financial Wall Street Reform and Consumer Protection Act suspended the auditor attestation provision. Instead, Dodd–Frank places considerable reliance on company performance of control assessment and evaluation procedures, which have not been shown to be sufficient in earlier years.

Evidence also shows that after an initial rise in restatements after the introduction of the internal controls requirements (i.e., a number of past misstatements were uncovered by the procedures), subsequent years show a decline and leveling off of the upward trends of pre-Sarbanes years. Also, some studies show that a lower cost of capital is associated with companies with effective internal controls. A 2008 report of the Association of Certified Fraud Examiners noted that companies that implemented such antifraud controls as a fraud hotline experienced over 60 percent lower loss due to fraud. The implementation of other controls and audit-related procedures also revealed significant reductions in the losses due to fraud. Clearly gains are being made. But the cost-benefit remains in debate. While the lessened requirements of the SEC's guidance[3] and the new PCAOB Auditing Standard Number 5, *An Audit of Internal Control over Financial Reporting That Is Integrated with an Audit of Financial Statements*,[4] are designed to enhance efficiency, the intent is to not lessen the effectiveness of the intended legislation for companies and auditors.

---

2. Jean C. Bedard and Lynford Graham, "Detection and Severity Classification of Sarbanes-Oxley Section 404 Internal Control Deficiencies, and Archival Evidence on Remediation of Sarbanes-Oxley Section 404 Internal Control Deficiencies." Forthcoming in 2011 in The Accounting Review.

3. Securities and Exchange Commission, *Commission Guidance Regarding Management's Report on Internal Control over Financial Reporting under Section 13(a) or 15(d) of the Securities Exchange Act of 1934*. Release Nos. 33-8810; 34-55929; FR-77; File No. S7-24-06.

4. Public Company Accounting Oversight Board, Auditing Standard Number 5, *An Audit of Internal Control over Financial Reporting That Is Integrated with an Audit of Financial Statements*. PCAOB Release No. 2007-005, May 24, 2007.

There have been some studies of factors that influence the costs of Sarbanes-Oxley compliance. In one study of 2,451 accelerated filers that reported on their internal controls in both 2004 and 2005,[5] some findings are worthy of note:

- The smaller of the filers in this group reported a greater proportion of the material weaknesses. This may have implications for the nonaccelerated filers that may become subject to auditor assessment and testing in 2010.
- Audit fees were relatively higher for companies reporting a material weakness.
- Audit fees generally declined in the second year of implementation. Greater reductions were found in companies with effective internal controls.
- The audit fees for companies reporting a material weakness in the second year increased.

Because many of the documentation costs and project organizational costs are first-year costs, a general reduction in audit and compliance costs in the second year of implementation can be expected. However, the message here is that establishing effective company internal controls is one controllable factor in reducing compliance costs, even before considering the possible effects of the revised SEC or auditing guidance.

4.2 DEFINITION OF INTERNAL CONTROL

For the purposes of complying with the internal control reporting requirements of the Sarbanes-Oxley Act, the SEC rules provide the working definition of the term *internal control over financial reporting*. Rule 13a-15(f) defines internal control over financial reporting as follows:

> The term internal control over financial reporting is defined as a process designed by, or under the supervision of, the issuer's principal executive and principal financial officers, or persons performing similar functions, and effected by the issuer's board of directors, management and other personnel, to provide reasonable assurance regarding the reliability of financial reporting and the preparation of financial statements for external purposes in accordance with generally accepted accounting principles and includes those policies and procedures that:
>
> 1. Pertain to the maintenance of records that in reasonable detail accurately and fairly reflect the transactions and dispositions of the assets of the issuer;
> 2. Provide reasonable assurance that transactions are recorded as necessary to permit preparation of financial statements in accordance with generally accepted accounting principles, and that receipts and expenditures of the issuer are being made only in accordance with authorizations of management and directors of the issuer; and
> 3. Provide reasonable assurance regarding prevention or timely detection of unauthorized acquisition, use or disposition of the issuer's assets that could have a material effect on the financial statements.

When considering the SEC's definition, you should note the following:

- The term *internal control* is a broad concept that extends to all areas of the management of an enterprise. The SEC definition narrows the scope of an entity's consideration of internal control to the preparation of the financial statements—hence the use of the term *internal control over financial reporting*.

---

5. Jean C. Bedard, Lynford Graham, Rani Hoitashi, and Udi Hoitashi, "Sarbanes-Oxley Section 404 and Internal Controls," *CPA Journal*, October 2007.

- The SEC intends its definition to be consistent with the definition of internal controls that pertains to financial reporting objectives that was provided in the Committee of Sponsoring Organizations (COSO) of the Treadway Commission 1992 COSO Report[6]: The rule makes explicit reference to the use or disposition of the entity's assets—that is, the safeguarding of assets.

4.3 MANAGEMENT'S REQUIRED REPORTS ON INTERNAL CONTROL

(a) ANNUAL REPORTING REQUIREMENTS   Section 404 of the Sarbanes-Oxley Act (SOX 404) requires chief executive officers (CEOs) and chief financial officers (CFOs) to annually evaluate and report on the effectiveness of the entity's internal control over financial reporting. This report is contained in the company's Form 10-K, which is filed annually with the SEC. The SEC has adopted rules for its registrants that effectively implement the requirements of the Sarbanes-Oxley Act, Section 404.

Under the SEC rules (final rule adopted by the SEC in 2003),[7] the company's 10-K must include[8]:

A. *Management's Annual Report on Internal Control over Financial Reporting.* Provide a report on the company's internal control over financial reporting that contains:
  1. A statement of management's responsibilities for establishing and maintaining adequate internal control over financial reporting
  2. A statement identifying the framework used by management to evaluate the effectiveness of the company's internal control over financial reporting
  3. Management's assessment of the effectiveness of the company's internal control over financial reporting as of the end of the most recent fiscal year, including a statement as to whether or not internal control over financial reporting is effective. This discussion must include disclosure of any material weakness in the company's internal control over financial reporting identified by management. Management is not permitted to conclude that the registrant's internal control over financial reporting is effective if there are one or more material weaknesses in the company's internal control over financial reporting.

B. *Changes in Internal Control over Financial Reporting.* Disclose any change in the company's internal control over financial reporting that has materially affected, or is reasonably likely to materially affect, the company's internal control over financial reporting.

The company's annual report filed with the SEC also should include management's fourth-quarter report on the effectiveness of the entity's disclosure controls and procedures, as described section 4.3(b). The SEC final rules also require a company to file, as part of the company's annual report, the attestation report of the registered public accounting firm that audited the company's financial statements.

(i) Effective Dates   The requirement to disclose material changes in the entity's internal control became effective on August 14, 2003. The effective date for the other provisions of the

---

6. Committee of Sponsoring Organizations (COSO), *Internal Control—Integrated Framework* (New York: American Institute of Certified Public Accountants, 1992).
7. Securities and Exchange Commission, *Final Rule: Management's Report on Internal Control over Financial Reporting and Certification of Disclosure in Exchange Act Periodic Reports.* Release Nos. 33-8238; 34-47986; IC-26068; File Nos. S7-40-02; S7-06-03.
8. *See* Regulation S-K, Item 308 (17 CFR §229.308).

rules described—that is, management's report on the effectiveness of internal control and the related auditor attestation—become effective at different times, depending on the filing status of the company.

- *Accelerated filer.* A company that is an accelerated filer as of the end of its first fiscal year ending on or after November 15, 2004, must begin to comply with the internal control reporting and attestation requirements in its annual report for that fiscal year.[9]
- *Nonaccelerated filer.* Smaller companies are required to comply with the new rules for their first fiscal year ending on or after December 15, 2008, with independent auditor reports on the effectiveness of internal control scheduled to begin the following year.[10]

(b) QUARTERLY REPORTING REQUIREMENTS   Section 302 of the Sarbanes-Oxley Act requires quarterly reporting on the effectiveness of an entity's "disclosure controls and procedures." Item 307 of SEC Regulation S-K implements this requirement for the company's quarterly Form 10-Q filings by requiring management to:

> [d]isclose the conclusions of the company's principal executive and principal financial officers, or persons performing similar functions, regarding the effectiveness of the company's disclosure controls and procedures as of the end of the period covered by the report, based on the evaluation of these controls and procedures.

In addition to reporting on disclosure controls, the company's quarterly reports also must disclose material changes in the entity's internal control over financial reporting.

Note that for these quarterly filings management is *not* required to evaluate or report on internal control over financial reporting. That evaluation is required on an *annual basis only.*

(i) Disclosure Controls and Procedures   With these rules, the SEC introduces a new term, *disclosure controls and procedures,* which is different from *internal controls over financial reporting* defined earlier. SEC Rule 13a-15(e) defines disclosure controls and procedures as those that are:

> [d]esigned to ensure that information required to be disclosed by the issuer in the reports that it files or submits under the Act is

- recorded,
- processed,
- summarized, and
- reported

within the time periods specified in the Commission's rules and forms. Disclosure controls and procedures include, without limitation, controls and procedures designed to ensure that information required to be disclosed by an issuer in the reports that it files or submits under the Act is accumulated and communicated to the issuer's management, including its principal executive and principal financial officers, or persons performing similar functions, as appropriate to allow timely decisions regarding required disclosure.

---

9. *Accelerated filer* is defined in Exchange Act Rule 12b-2. Generally, companies with a market capitalization of $75 million or more are considered accelerated filers.
10. In October 2009, the SEC granted another extension on the requirement for companies to include an auditor report regarding the effectiveness of internal controls.

Thus, "disclosure controls and procedures" would encompass the controls over all material financial and nonfinancial information in Exchange Act reports. Information that would fall under this definition that would not be part of an entity's internal control over financial reporting might include the signing of a significant contract, changes in a strategic relationship, management compensation, or legal proceedings.

In relation to its rule requiring an assessment of disclosure controls and procedures, the SEC also advised all public companies to create a disclosure committee to oversee the process by which disclosures are created and reviewed, including:

- Review of 10-Q, 10-K, and other SEC filings; earnings releases; and other public information for the appropriateness of disclosure
- Determination of what constitutes a significant transaction or event that requires disclosure
- Determination and identification of significant deficiencies and material weaknesses in the design or operating effectiveness of disclosure controls and procedures
- Assessment of CEO and CFO awareness of material information that could affect disclosure

The existence and effective operation of an entity's disclosure committee can have a significant effect on the nature and scope of management's work to evaluate the effectiveness of the entity's internal control. For example:

- The effective functioning of a disclosure committee may be viewed as an element that strengthens the entity's control environment.
- The work of the disclosure committee may create documentation that engagement teams can use to reduce the scope of their work.

4.4 MANAGEMENT CERTIFICATIONS

In addition to providing a report on the effectiveness of its disclosure controls and internal control over financial reporting, the company's principal executive officer and principal financial officer are required to sign two certifications, which are included as exhibits to the entity's 10-Q and 10-K. These two certifications are required by the Sarbanes-Oxley Act:

1. Section 302, which requires a certification to accompany each quarterly and annual report filed with the SEC.
2. Section 906, which added a new Section 1350 to Title 18 of the U.S. Code, and which contains a certification requirement subject to specific federal criminal provisions. This certification is separate and distinct from the Section 302 certification requirement.

Exhibit 4.1 provides the text of the Section 302 certification. This text is provided in SEC Rule 13a-14(a) and should be used exactly as set forth in the rule.

Exhibit 4.2 provides an example of the Section 906 certification. Note that some certifying officers may choose to include a "knowledge qualification," as indicated by the optional language within the parentheses. Officers who choose to include this language should do so only after consulting with their SEC counsel. Unlike the Section 302 certification, which requires a separate certification for both the CEO and CFO, the company can provide only one 906 certification, which is then signed by both individuals.

An initial concern was that the required certification process would result in a mass exodus of company executives, reluctant to make the explicit disclosures and certifications required. While there is evidence that some executives did feel strongly enough about the new risks to change positions, there has been no observed mass exodus. In this period of time the increased focus on the responsibilities and liabilities of the boards of directors and audit committees has made it more difficult to recruit directors, but again, there is no evidence of a crisis in oversight.

I, [identify the certifying individual], certify that:

1. I have reviewed this [specify report] of [identify registrant];

2. Based on my knowledge, this report does not contain any untrue statement of a material fact or omit to state a material fact necessary to make the statements made, in light of the circumstances under which such statements were made, not misleading with respect to the period covered by this report;

3. Based on my knowledge, the financial statements, and other financial information included in this report, fairly present in all material respects the financial condition, results of operations, and cash flows of the registrant as of, and for, the periods presented in this report;

4. The registrant's other certifying officer(s) and I are responsible for establishing and maintaining disclosure controls and procedures (as defined in Exchange Act Rules 13a-15(e) and 15 d-15(e)) and internal control over financial reporting (as defined in Exchange Act Rules 13a-15(f) and 15 d-15(f)) for the registrant and have:

    a. Designed such disclosure controls and procedures, or caused such disclosure controls and procedures to be designed under our supervision, to ensure that material information relating to the registrant, including its consolidated subsidiaries, is made known to us by others within those entities, particularly during the period in which this report is being prepared;

    b. Designed such internal control over financial reporting, or caused such internal control over financial reporting to be designed under our supervision, to provide reasonable assurance regarding the reliability of financial reporting and the preparation of financial statements for external purposes in accordance with generally accepted accounting principles;

    c. Evaluated the effectiveness of the registrant's disclosure controls and procedures and presented in this report our conclusions about the effectiveness of the disclosure controls and procedures, as of the end of the period covered by this report based on such evaluation; and

    d. Disclosed in this report any change in the registrant's internal control over financial reporting that occurred during the registrant's most recent fiscal quarter (the registrant's fourth fiscal quarter in the case of an annual report) that has materially affected, or is reasonably likely to materially affect, the registrant's internal control over financial reporting;

5. The registrant's other certifying officer(s) and I have disclosed, based on our most recent evaluation of internal control over financial reporting, to the registrant's auditors and the audit committee of the registrant's board of directors (or persons performing the equivalent functions):

    a. All significant deficiencies and material weaknesses in the design or operation of internal control over financial reporting which are reasonably likely to adversely affect the registrant's ability to record, process, summarize, and report financial information; and

    b. Any fraud, whether or not material, that involves management or other employees who have a significant role in the registrant's internal control over financial reporting.

Exhibit 4.1   Section 302 Certification, SEC Rule 13a-14(a)/15d-14(a)

In connection with the [annual/quarterly] report of [name of registrant] (the "Company") on Form (10-K/10-Q] for the period ended (the "Report"), the undersigned in the capacities listed below, hereby certify, pursuant to 18 U.S.C. ss. 1350, as adopted pursuant to Section 906 of the Sarbanes-Oxley Act of 2002, that

    i. The Report fully complies with the requirements of Section 12(a) or 15(d) of the Securities Exchange Act of 1934; and

    ii. The information contained in the Report fairly presents, in all material respects, the financial condition and results of operations of the company.

EXHIBIT 4.2 SECTION 906 CERTIFICATION, 18 U.S.C. SECTION 1350

In the view of many, the increased focus on governance and competence at the board level seems to have strengthened corporate governance.

A great deal of the information included in financial statements and other reports filed with the SEC originates in areas of the company that are outside the day-to-day or direct control of the CEO and CFO. Because of the significance of information prepared by others, it is becoming common for the CEO and CFO to request those individuals who are directly responsible for supplying this information to certify it. This process is known as *subcertification*, and it usually involves providing a written affidavit to the CEO and CFO that will in turn allow them to sign their certifications in good faith.

Items that may be the subject of subcertification affidavits include:

- Adequacy of specific disclosures in the financial statements or other reports filed with the SEC, such as Management's Disclosure and Analysis included in the entity's 10-Q or 10-K
- Accuracy of specific account balances
- Compliance with company policies and procedures, including the company's code of conduct
- Adequacy of the design and/or operating effectiveness of departmental internal controls and disclosure controls
- Accuracy of reported financial results of the department, subsidiary, or business segment

4.5 THE INDEPENDENT AUDITOR'S RESPONSIBILITIES

Exhibit 4.3 describes the relationship between the various rule-making bodies, companies, and their auditors regarding the reporting on internal control. As described previously, management of a public company is required to report on the effectiveness of the entity's internal control on an annual basis, and the company's independent auditors are required to audit this report. The SEC is responsible for setting rules to implement the Sarbanes-Oxley Act requirements. Those rules include guidance for reporting by the CEO and CFO on the entity's internal control over financial reporting and disclosure controls, but they do not provide any guidance or set standards for the independent auditors. The Public Company Accounting Oversight Board (PCAOB) sets the auditing standards, which have a direct effect on auditors and how they plan and perform their engagements.

In addition, the auditing standards will have an *indirect effect* on the company as it prepares for the audit of the internal control report. Just as in a financial statement audit,

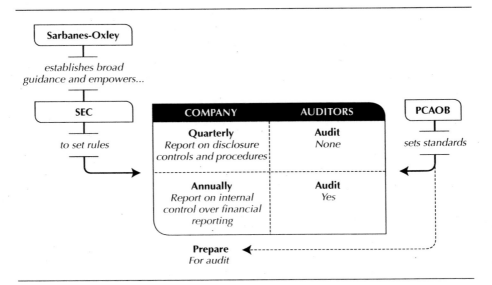

EXHIBIT 4.3   RELATIONSHIP OF THE RULES, REGULATIONS, AND STANDARDS

the company should be able to support its conclusions about internal control and provide documentation that is sufficient for the auditor to perform an audit. Thus, in preparing for the audit of its internal control report, it is vital for management, and those who assist managers, to have a good understanding of what the independent auditors will require.

4.6 THE AUDIT STANDARDS

In June 2004, the SEC approved PCAOB Auditing Standard No. 2, *An Audit of Internal Control over Financial Reporting Performed in Conjunction with an Audit of Financial Statements*. That standard required auditors for the first time to conduct two audits of their publicly traded clients: the traditional audit of financial statements and a new audit of internal control. The standard was revised and reissued as Auditing Standard No. 5 in response to concerns that the original standard required unnecessary procedures without corresponding benefits, and to take advantage of the experience gained in the first several years of implementation. There was no intent to lessen the effectiveness of the standard.

The Auditing Standard can have a significant effect on the way in which company management conducts its own required assessment in internal control effectiveness. For example, the standard:

- Requires auditors to makes their own assessment of the effectiveness of the company's internal control. Since management and the auditor are seeking to arrive at the same conclusion, careful consideration should be made of both the SEC and the PCAOB guidance by both companies and auditors. Auditors will read management's disclosures regarding internal control. If management makes a misstatement in its disclosures or fails to have an adequate basis for its statements and conclusions about internal controls, the auditors will need to note this in their opinion if the issue cannot be resolved.

- Allows the auditor to rely on the work performed by the company in its self-assessment process to support his or her conclusion on internal control effectiveness. However, to rely on this work to the maximum extent, certain conditions regarding the objectivity and competence of the work performed and the people who performed it must be met.
- Establishes the definition of a *material weakness* in internal control. To conclude that internal control is effective, management should have reasonable assurance that there were no material weaknesses in internal control in any of the five COSO components as of the reporting date.

Subsequent to the original auditing standard, both the PCAOB and the SEC released interpretive guidance that today has for the most part been folded into the most recent guidance issued. An important step in planning a SOX 404 compliance engagement is for management to have read the most current guidance and any outstanding staff positions issued by the PCAOB and the SEC.

(a) RELATIONSHIP WITH MANAGEMENT'S ASSESSMENT   The SEC rules relating to the scope of management's assessment of internal control effectiveness remain rather conceptual. In practice, companies frequently encounter situations for which the SEC has not provided guidance. In those situations, companies may look to the Auditing Standard to help determine which business units or controls should be included in their assessment.

Auditing Standard No. 5 provides conceptual guidance on the required scope of the auditor's assessment of the company's internal control. This guidance is in the context of the independent auditor's responsibilities, but of course the nature and extent of procedures performed by management may shape the nature and extent of procedures the auditor performs to achieve his or her required high level of assurance that the controls are operating effectively.

If the company's self-assessment process does *not* include the required elements or it does not gather sufficient evidence to support its conclusions, the auditor should discuss the situation with management. If the independent auditor concludes that the company process was inadequate to support the assertion, the auditor would need to point that out in a modification of his or her audit report. It is a general audit requirement whenever the independent auditor believes a disclosure in the financial statements or in accompanying materials is misleading or unsupported that the auditor needs to point this out, even if it is not directly a part of the financial statements and disclosures. As a practical matter, most companies take steps to ensure that their assessment process provides support for their assertion on internal controls.

(b) DOCUMENTATION   The independent auditors will evaluate the adequacy of management's support for their assertion regarding internal control. That support includes documentation of the design of management's process to assess the effectiveness of its controls as well as documentation of the existing controls and procedures performed to confirm the effective operation of its controls. Without adequate documentation on the part of the company of its assessment process, the auditor is hampered in his or her assessment, or may be unable to conclude that management has support for its disclosed assertion. Lack of, or deficient controls documentation in itself is considered a control deficiency.

The SEC guidance on management's responsibilities includes general conceptual documentation guidance. Companies are well advised to discuss with the independent auditors the nature and extent of their planned documentation to anticipate in advance any differing views or differing expectations regarding company documentation.

More robust documentation of the company process can lead to efficiencies in the required audit work. Since under Auditing Standard No. 5 more reliance can be placed on company procedures when they are objectively and competently performed, better company documentation and attention to the assessment process can enhance the ability of auditors to rely on procedures already performed by management.

(c) SCOPE OF TEST WORK   The Auditing Standard provides limited guidance on the nature, timing, and extent of the auditor's procedures for a number of situations, including:

- Extent of testing of manual and automated controls
- Required procedures when the entity uses a service organization to process transactions
- Required procedures when the entity engages others, including internal auditors, to perform procedures as part of the company assessment process
- Updated test work that may be required when the original testing was performed at an interim date, well in advance of the reporting date

(d) USE OF WORK OF INTERNAL AUDITORS AND OTHERS   Both the Sarbanes-Oxley Act and the PCAOB Auditing Standard describe a two-pronged approach for providing financial statement users with useful information about the reliability of a company's internal control:

1. Management assesses and reports on the effectiveness of the entity's internal control.
2. Next, the company's independent auditors issue a separate, independent opinion on the effectiveness of the company's internal control.

In this scheme, it is vital that the two participants perform their duties independently of each other. While auditors may sometimes rely on the company's procedures, companies cannot use any auditor-performed procedures as a basis for their required attestation. The company attestation should stand on its own. COSO makes it clear that the independent auditor is not an element of the internal control system of a company, and it is that control system that is the focus of the controls attestation.

Keep in mind that the company is required to perform a thorough assessment of the company's internal control that is prioritized by a risk assessment. As much as possible, management will want to provide the results of its work to the independent auditors, so the auditors will have a clear understanding of management's assessment and will not have to duplicate the company's efforts.

(i) *The Independent Auditor's Use of the Company's Internal Control Work*   An important efficiency concession in recent guidance on the performance of the audit of internal controls is the relaxation on the limitations on the reliance the independent auditor can place on the work of others that is objective and competently performed. The work of others includes the relevant work performed by:

- Internal auditors
- Other company personnel
- Third parties such as consultants working under the direction of management or the audit committee

The independent auditor's ability to rely on the work of others has some limits. For example, in identified high-risk areas or in areas requiring significant subjective judgment, the independent auditor will often perform more of the procedures supporting the auditor opinion.

(ii) Using the Work of Others   To determine the extent to which the independent auditor may use the company's work, the independent auditor:

- Considers the nature of the controls subjected to the work of others. In general, auditors will probably want to perform some of their own tests on the controls related to accounts that have a high risk of material misstatement.
- Evaluates the objectivity of the individuals who performed the work. The more objective the company's project team, the more likely the independent auditors will be to rely on their work.
- Tests some of the work performed by others to evaluate the quality and competence of their work.

Auditors cannot rely on procedures performed by individuals who are not objective (e.g., employees self-assessing their own work) nor on work not competently performed. Both characteristics (objectivity and competence) are necessary.

To encourage the company's independent auditors to make as much use as possible of the company's own assessment of internal control, company management should have a clear understanding of the conditions that must be met for the independent auditors to use the work. To help the independent auditors determine that those criteria have been met, companies may wish to ensure their documentation includes information relevant to compliance with the key requirements of the Auditing Standard and make this documentation available to the independent auditors early on in their audit planning process. For example, such information might include:

- Obtaining the resumes of project team members showing their education level, experience, professional certifications, and continuing education
- Documenting the company's policies regarding the assignment of individuals to work areas
- Documenting the organizational status of the project team and how they have been provided access to the board of directors and audit committee
- Determining that the internal auditors follow the relevant internal auditing standards
- Establishing policies that ensure that the *documentation* of the work performed includes:
  - A description of the scope of the work
  - Work programs that document when and by whom the work is to be completed
  - Evidence of supervision and review
  - Conclusions about the work performed

(e) DETERMINATION OF MATERIAL WEAKNESSES   The SEC reporting rules require entity management to disclose any material weaknesses in internal control. A company cannot assess its controls as effective if one or more material weaknesses remain as of the reporting date of the assertion regarding the effectiveness of internal control. Weaknesses and deficiencies identified in the course of the assessment and satisfactorily remediated before the reporting date are not considered in the final assessment of the effectiveness of the internal controls. For example, numerous material weaknesses might be identified in the course of the assessment of controls, and if successfully remediated the company and auditor can state that internal controls are effective as of the reporting date. However, weaknesses discovered in a financial statement quarter during the year are likely to trigger disclosures as part of the Section 302 quarterly reporting requirements. Engagements to assess the effectiveness of internal controls should be planned and performed in a way that will detect material misstatements. Thus, it is critical that you have a working definition of the term. The Auditing Standard provides the following definitions:

- A control deficiency exists when the design or operation of a control does not allow management or employees, in the normal course of performing their assigned functions, to prevent or detect misstatements on a timely basis.
- A material weakness is a deficiency, or a combination of deficiencies, in internal control over financial reporting, such that there is a reasonable possibility that a material misstatement of the company's annual or interim financial statements will not be prevented or detected on a timely basis. The term *reasonable possibility* is related to the use of that term in FASB Statement No. 5, *Accounting for Contingencies*, and refers to a likelihood assessment that is more than remote.
- A significant deficiency is a deficiency, or a combination of deficiencies, in internal control over financial reporting that is less severe than a material weakness, yet important enough to merit attention by those responsible for oversight of a registrant's financial reporting.

An issue relevant to the material weakness determination is that it remains a subjective judgment and reasonable persons might disagree on the severity assessment in some situations. In assessing the severity of a deficiency, related compensating, redundant, or monitoring controls should be considered to see if they would be sufficiently effective to limit the severity of any controls deficiency to less than a material weakness or significant deficiency. The SEC and PCAOB agree that there are at least four situations that are indicators of a material weakness; however, there is no "automatic" classification.

1. Identification of fraud, whether or not material, on the part of senior management
2. Restatement of previously issued financial statements to reflect the correction of a material misstatement
3. Identification of a material misstatement of the financial statements in the current period in circumstances that indicate the misstatement would not have been detected by the company's internal control over financial reporting (ICFR)
4. Ineffective oversight of the company's external financial reporting and internal control over financial reporting by the company's audit committee

As a final check on the reasonableness of a weakness classification, the PCAOB states, "If the auditor determines that a deficiency, or combination of deficiencies, might prevent prudent officials in the conduct of their own affairs from concluding that they have reasonable assurance that transactions are recorded as necessary to permit the preparation of financial statements in conformity with generally accepted accounting principles, then the auditor should treat the deficiency, or combination of deficiencies, as an indicator of a material weakness." This final check is a sort of plausibility test that asks if it would make sense to a businessperson that the classification is less than a material weakness (or significant deficiency). All material weaknesses are not created equal. Investors and financial experts usually consider both the existence of a weakness as well as the nature of a material weakness when assessing the implications of the disclosure. A material weakness in the control environment due to an ineffective governance function or a poor tone at the top is likely to generate a more significant response than a weakness in a transaction-related control or as a result of an infrequently encountered transaction such as a merger. This is why management must identify the nature of any material weaknesses in their report on the effectiveness of internal control.

(f) WORKING WITH THE INDEPENDENT AUDITORS To render an opinion on either the financial statements or the effectiveness of internal control, the company's independent auditors are required to maintain their independence, in accordance with applicable SEC rules. These rules are guided by certain underlying principles, which include:

- The audit firm must not be in a position where it audits its own work.
- The auditor must not act as management or as an employee of the client.

Although maintaining independence is primarily the responsibility of the auditors, several of the PCAOB independence requirements impose certain responsibilities on management and the audit committee. These requirements include:

- *Preapproval by the audit committee.* Each internal control-related service to be provided by the auditor must be preapproved by the audit committee. The PCAOB clarifies that "the audit committee cannot pre-approve internal control-related services as a category, but must approve each service."
- *Independence in fact and appearance.* The company's audit committee and independent auditors must be diligent to ensure that independence is maintained both in fact and in appearance.

No matter how detailed the independence rules may become, they cannot possibly address every possible interaction between the company and its auditors. During the initial implementation of SOX 404, many situations arose that called into question whether the auditor could interact with the company in a particular way and still maintain its independence.

For example, if the company was unsure whether its documentation of internal control would be acceptable, could it approach its auditors for advice? If the auditors made recommendations on how to improve the documentation and the company then incorporated those recommendations, would that put the audit firm in the position of auditing its own work when it reviewed that documentation? The form and content of the company's documentation of its internal control is the responsibility of management. If the auditor becomes significantly involved in that decision, does that imply that it is acting in the capacity of management?

In the initial implementation of SOX 404, it became common for auditors to provide little advice to their clients on internal control matters. Concerned about possibly violating the independence rules, they chose to largely remove themselves from their clients' efforts.

As a practical matter, both the SEC and the PCAOB understood that the public interest is not well served if the independent auditors are completely uninvolved with the company's efforts to understand and assess its internal control. There must be some sharing of information between the company and its auditors, and the auditors must be able to provide help and advice on some matters without dictating company practices and approaches.

In June 2004 the SEC and the PCAOB issued guidance allowing the auditor to provide "limited assistance to management in documenting internal controls and making recommendations for changes to internal controls. However, management has the ultimate responsibility for the assessment, documentation, and testing of the company's internal control." This was broadly interpreted by many at the time as limiting the independent auditor role to that of a scribe in the company documentation process.

The PCAOB later provided more extensive guidance on how company management may solicit advice from and share advice with its auditors on internal control matters. The guidance from the staff was in answer to a question directed specifically to an auditor's review of the company's draft financial statements or its providing advice on the adoption of a new accounting principle or emerging issue—services that historically have been considered a routine part of a quality audit.

The PCAOB staff stated that "some type of information-sharing on a timely basis between management and the auditor is necessary." However, when management seeks the assistance of the company's auditors to help with its internal control assessment, it should make it clear that management retains the ultimate responsibility for internal control. The PCAOB places the burden on management to clearly communicate with the auditor the nature of the advice it is seeking and the purpose for which the auditor is being involved.

4.7 A TOP-DOWN, RISK-BASED APPROACH FOR EVALUATING INTERNAL CONTROL

As indicated previously, both the SEC and the PCAOB periodically issue staff position papers to clarify how to address specific circumstances. On May 16, 2005, in response to information that was gathered about the first year of implementation, both the SEC and the PCAOB issued guidance that addressed the most significant problems encountered with the implementation of Auditing Standard No. 2. Of the five main areas addressed in the guidance, the following are the most relevant to company management:

- Use a risk-based, top-down approach. The PCAOB emphasized that auditors should use a top-down approach, and company management would be wise to use this same approach. In a top-down approach, you begin with an evaluation of entity-level controls such as the control environment and shared software and information technology controls and from there move to the testing of detailed activity-level controls.

  One of the key principles of the top-down approach is that the decision of which controls to document and test is based an assessment of risk as well as materiality. Controls that mitigate significant risks should be documented and assessed. Those that mitigate less significant risks would be subject to considerably less, if any, testing and evaluation.

- Auditors and company management should engage in direct and timely communication with each other. As described in the previous section of this chapter, during the first year of compliance, there was often a lack of communication between the two.

Ultimately the PCAOB made it clear that the auditor should be responsive to client requests for advice, provided that company management would take final responsibility for internal control.

- Auditors should make as much use as possible of quality work on internal control performed by the company. This guidance should help companies keep down the cost of compliance, but it also means that companies have to perform their assessment with objective and qualified individuals in a way that is consistent with the requirements of Auditing Standard No. 5.

(a) PRINCIPLES OF A TOP-DOWN, RISK-BASED APPROACH   Controls in the COSO *Internal Control Integrated Framework* are comprised of five components. Some of those components often involve the entity as a whole, such as the control environment and risk assessment. Other components, like activity controls, operate more at the transaction level. Entity-level controls are generally pervasive and can affect many different financial statement accounts. For example, the tone at the top of an organization can establish an environment of honesty and ethics, which can set the tone for employee expected behavior and adherence to policies. Since management override has been so often identified as an underlying fraud characteristic, the risk of management override is an important "top-side" consideration. As another example, a company's hiring and training policies will affect the way in which individual control procedures are performed. Companies that hire qualified people, train them properly, and evaluate them fairly will have much greater success when it comes time for those people to perform their jobs. The converse also is true. In that sense, hiring and training policies can have an effect on many different financial statement accounts. A less than fully competent controller or financial officer can unwittingly make errors that auditors will need to catch to prevent misstatements. That lack of competence is a control environment issue, and may require the auditor to assign staff with stronger accounting backgrounds and test more period transactions. Failures in the control environment or certain other far-reaching or overarching controls can render tests of the underlying transaction controls less meaningful.

Activity-level controls, however, may often be restricted to transactions. Controls over cash disbursements generally will affect cash disbursements only and will have no impact on other specific noncash accounts, such as goodwill or the depreciation of fixed assets.

In the first year of implementation, many companies and their auditors adopted a bottom-up approach in which they started by identifying all of the companies' activity-level controls and then documenting and testing each of these to determine whether internal control as a whole was effective. This was because companies and auditors were more familiar with transaction controls than, say, the information and communication and monitoring components of COSO. As you can imagine, when fundamental, pervasive, or entity-level controls were identified as deficient late in the audit, the prior tests of any underlying controls that had already been tested became suspect, and in some cases needed to be repeated after redesigns and remediations of the deficient controls. As such, this strategy was highly inefficient. As later clarified, "top-down" also means testing the highest-level control that meets the required precision of the control effectiveness, so if there are detailed controls over each stage of processing an invoice for payment as well as a final detailed supervisory review of the payment support before payment, then testing the supervisory review may be sufficient to meet the objectives of the control, and the underlying controls may not need to be evaluated or tested. That assumes the identified supervisory review covers all the relevant assertions that are covered by the other controls.

In a top-down approach, one begins at the risk assessment and then goes to the top, at the entity level. You then identify the most significant accounts and transaction types and risks of the organization and the control objectives for those accounts and transactions. Once you determine the control objectives, you identify those controls, starting with the entity and top-side controls that are in place to meet those objectives. Those controls are then tested and evaluated.

By using a top-down approach the company:

- Tests only those controls related to significant risks of misstatement in the accounts and transactions. This eliminates the need to focus attention on other controls in those areas that do not pose a risk that the company's financial statements could be materially misstated.
- Tests the minimum number of controls necessary to meet the control objective. Redundant controls or controls operating at a level lower than other effective controls (and there are many of these) need not be tested.

Implementing a top-down approach requires company management to exercise its judgment. How do you decide which accounts and transactions are significant and which are insignificant? If you are not going to test all the control activities for significant accounts and transactions, how do you determine which ones to test?

To make these and other decisions, you should consider the related risk of material misstatement of the financial statements. Control activities are designed to meet identified risks of misstatement. For example, one of the risks of misstatement is that the company may fail to record all of its accounts payable as of year-end. To mitigate this risk, management will design and implement procedures at the company to make sure that that all payables get recorded in the proper period.

Do these controls need to be documented and tested? It depends on the relative significance of the risk of failing to record all accounts payable. What is the likelihood that the failure to record all accounts payable would result in a material misstatement of the company's financial statements? If material amounts are or could be outstanding at year-end, then the risk is probably not negligible. In a business where cash is used for most transactions, then the misstatement risk posed by accounts payable might be negligible. The question needs to be resolved on a company-by-company and account-by-account basis. While the guidance seems to imply to some that only a few significant controls will be identified and need to be tested, in practice a good risk assessment will identify many significant controls. More controls will be identified when estimates and judgments are involved, when few entity-level controls are present, and when the company is comprised of more locations and business segments. Few material accounts are without risk of misstatement when the effectiveness of internal controls is not considered in making the risk assessment. There have been major frauds and misstatements of financial statements associated with just about every account in the balance sheet and income statement, including even the supposedly safe ones (e.g., fixed assets).

Performing an assessment of internal control is not a paint-by-numbers exercise. It is a process that requires a great deal of objective judgment. The primary benchmark for making these judgments is the risk that the financial statements would be materially misstated if a material misstatement is introduced through an account and an effective control is not in place to identify and correct the misstatement.

4.8 COORDINATING WITH THE INDEPENDENT AUDITORS

The SEC makes clear in its guidance that the company is not obligated to follow any specific course in meeting its requirements, and the auditor cannot dictate the way the company goes about its assessment. Nevertheless, it is recommended that companies consider the needs and expectations of the entity's independent auditors when planning their project to assess internal controls. Proper understanding between the company and the independent auditors will facilitate an effective and efficient audit. A lack of coordination with the auditors could result in a variety of negative unforeseen consequences, including:

- A lack of sufficient support for management's assertion, which will prompt a comment by the auditor in its report (and probably a comment to the company by the SEC)
- Duplication of effort
- Reperformance of certain tests
- Performance of additional tests or expansion of the scope of the engagement
- Misunderstandings relating to the definition or reporting of material weaknesses

Some of the key areas where consideration on SEC and PCAOB requirements will be useful include:

- The overall engagement process and approach
- The scope of the project, including locations or business units to be included, based on a risk assessment
- Preliminary identification of significant controls in meeting the risks
- The nature of any internal control deficiencies noted by the auditors during past audits of the entity's financial statements
- An understanding about what will constitute a significant deficiency or material weakness
- The nature and extent of the documentation of controls
- The nature and extent of the documentation of tests of controls
- The degree to which the auditors might be able to rely on the results of your test work to reach their conclusion
- The identification and evaluation of the monitoring component of the COSO framework

4.9 A NEW ERA

The passage of the Sarbanes-Oxley Act signaled the start of a new era in financial reporting, on par with the requirement of 70 years ago that the company's financial statements be audited by an independent Certified Public Accountant (CPA). Then, the capital markets looked to the CPA profession for help in implementing this new requirement. Now members of the profession—whether in public practice or employed in industry—seem equally well positioned to make a significant contribution as our country's financial reporting process embarks on another new direction.

CHAPTER 18

CASH, LOANS, AND INVESTMENTS (REVISED)

MICHAEL A. ANTONETTI, CPA, CMA
Crowe Horwath LLP†

† The information contained in this chapter does not necessarily represent the views of Crowe Horwath LLP.

18.1   INTRODUCTION TO CASH

(a) NATURE AND IMPORTANCE OF CASH   Cash is both the beginning and the end of the operating cycle (cash–inventory–sales–receivables–cash) in the typical business enterprise, and almost all transactions affect cash either directly or indirectly. Cash transactions are probably the most frequently recurring type entered into by a business because (except for barter transactions) every sale leads to a cash receipt and every expense to a cash disbursement. Cash is recognized as the most liquid of assets, and thus has prominence for users who are focusing on issues of liquidity.

Cash derives its primary importance from its dual role as a medium of exchange and a unit of measure. As a medium of exchange, it has a part in the majority of transactions entered into by an enterprise. Assets are acquired and realized, and liabilities are incurred and liquidated, in terms of cash. Thus, cash is generally the most active asset possessed by a company. As a unit of measure, it sets the terms in which all properties and claims against the company are stated in its financial statements. Price-change reporting, which addresses disclosures for fluctuations in value as general and specific price levels rise and fall, is discussed in another chapter in the *Accountants' Handbook.*

(b) CASH ACCOUNTING AND CONTROL   The major challenge in accounting for cash is maintaining adequate control over the great variety and quantity of cash transactions. Cash receipts may come from such diverse sources as cash sales, cash on delivery (COD) transactions, collections on accounts and notes receivable, loans, security issues, income from investments, and sales of such properties as retired assets, scrap, and investments. Disbursements may be made for a variety of expense items, for cash purchases and in payment of various liabilities, for dividends and for taxes. Thus, the variety of cash transactions in itself presents inherent problems.

The quantity of cash transactions constitutes another source of difficulty. To handle expeditiously the volume of cash transactions calls for appropriate equipment, careful organization and segregation of duties, planning of procedures, and design of appropriate forms. Information as to available cash balances is of daily interest to the management of every company, and this information must be accurate and prompt if it is to be useful.

(c) MISREPRESENTED CASH BALANCES   Companies sometimes misrepresent their cash balance to improve the appearance of their financial liquidity. This practice is sometimes called *window dressing.* Smith and Skousen describe this practice as follows:

> Certain practices designed to present a more favorable financial condition than is actually the case may be encountered. For example, cash records may be held open for a few days after the close of a fiscal period and cash received from customers during this period reported as receipts of the preceding period. An improved cash position is thus reported. If this balance is then used as a basis for drawing predated checks in payment of accounts payable, the ratio of current assets to current liabilities is improved. The current ratio may also be improved by writing checks in payment of obligations and entering these on the books even though checks are not to be mailed until the following period.[1]

---

1.   Jay M. Smith, Jr. and K. Fred Skousen, *Intermediate Accounting, Tenth Edition* (Cincinnati: South-Western Publishing, 1990).

18.2 ACCOUNTING FOR AND REPORTING CASH

(a) CLASSIFICATION AND PRESENTATION   The presentation of cash in the balance sheet is largely an issue of appropriate classification and description. Because of its importance in evaluating an entity's financial condition, cash must be stated as accurately as possible. This calls for careful analysis of each component of cash so that no items will improperly be included in, or excluded from, current assets. In this connection, paragraphs 4–6 of Chapter 3 of Accounting Research Bulletin (ARB) No. 43, *Restatement and Revision of Accounting Research Bulletins*, state, in part:

> For accounting purposes, the term current assets is used to designate cash and other assets or resources commonly identified as those which are reasonably expected to be realized in cash or sold or consumed during the normal operating cycle of the business. Thus the term comprehends in general such resources as (a) cash available for current operations and items which are the equivalent of cash. . . .
>
> The ordinary operations of a business involve a circulation of capital within the current asset group. Cash is expended for materials, finished parts, operating supplies, labor, and other factory services, and such expenditures are accumulated as inventory cost. Inventory costs, upon sale of the products to which such costs attach, are converted into trade receivables and ultimately into cash again. The average time intervening between the acquisition of materials or services entering this process and the final cash realization constitutes an operating cycle. . . .
>
> This concept of the nature of current assets contemplates the exclusion from that classification of such resources as: (a) cash and claims to cash which are restricted as to withdrawal or use for other than current operations, are designated for expenditure in the acquisition or construction of noncurrent assets, or are segregated for the liquidation of long-term debts. . . .

As the one asset that is liquid, that is, expendable with no intermediary transactions or conversions, cash assumes the position of prime importance in the balance sheet and is generally presented as the first item among the assets of the enterprise. Four examples of presentation are:

1. Cash and cash equivalents
2. Cash
3. Cash and equivalents
4. Cash combined with marketable securities

Generally, the form shown in example 1 above is widely used, but the important point is that cash subject to withdrawal restrictions should not be combined with cash of immediate availability. In this regard, O'Reilly et al. state in *Montgomery's Auditing*: "The cash caption on the balance sheet should include cash on hand and balances with financial institutions that are immediately available for any purpose and cash equivalents."

Paragraph 8 of FASB Statement No. 95, *Statement of Cash Flows*, states that cash equivalents are short-term highly liquid investments that are both:

- Readily convertible to known amounts of cash
- So near their maturity that they present insignificant risk of changes in value because of changes in interest rates

Paragraph 8 also states that "generally only investments with original maturities of three months or less qualify under that definition." Original maturity is further defined as maturity to the entity holding the investment. Statement 95 clarifies that the maturity date must be three months from the date of its acquisition by the entity. Thus, a Treasury note purchased three years ago and held does not become a cash equivalent when its remaining maturity is three months. Cash equivalents include Treasury bills, commercial paper, and money market funds.

(b) DEFINITION OF CASH   Cash exists both in physical and book entry forms: physical in the form of coin and paper currency as well as other negotiable instruments of various kinds, and book entry in various forms such as commercial bank deposits and savings deposits. In addition to coin and paper currency, other kinds of physical cash instruments that are commonly reported as cash for financial accounting purposes include certificates of deposit, bank checks, demand bills of exchange (in some cases), travelers' checks, post office or other money orders, bank drafts, cashiers' checks, certain short-term Treasury bills, and money market funds.

All these forms of cash involve credit and depend for their ready acceptance on the integrity and liquidity of some person or institution other than those offering or accepting them as cash. This is true even for coin and paper currency, which is ultimately dependent on the credit of the government issuing it. Given this integrity and liquidity, the book entry forms and other physical instruments are properly viewed as cash because of their immediate convertibility into cash in its currency form at the will of the holder. Convertibility in the case of savings accounts, certificates of deposit, and other time deposits may be something less than immediate depending on stipulated conditions imposed by the depository, but the assurance of such convertibility makes these items a generally accepted form of cash. However, only investments with original maturities of three months or less qualify for presentation as cash equivalents, as described earlier.

(c) RESTRICTED CASH   Cash restricted as to use by agreement, such as amounts deposited in escrow or for a specified purpose subject to release only at the order of a person other than the depositor, should not be classified in the balance sheet as cash and, unless deposited to meet an existing current liability, should presumably be excluded from current assets. Cash is sometimes received from customers in advance payment for work being performed under contract or under similar circumstances. Such cash is properly designated as cash in the balance sheet, but may be properly classified as a current asset only if the resulting customer's deposit is classified as a current liability. Cash restricted as to withdrawal because of inability of the depository to meet demands for withdrawal (such as deposits in banks in receivership) is not a current asset and should not be designated in the balance sheet as cash without an appropriate qualifying caption.

In regard to cash awaiting use for construction or other capital purposes or held for the payment of long-term debt, O'Reilly et al. state:

> Cash sometimes includes balances with trustees, such as sinking funds or other amounts not immediately available, for example, those restricted to uses other than current operations, designated for acquisition or construction of noncurrent assets, or segregated for the liquidation of long-term debt. Restrictions are considered effective if the company clearly intends to observe them, even though the funds are not actually set aside in special bank accounts. The facts pertaining to

those balances should be adequately disclosed, and the amounts should be properly classified as current or noncurrent.[2]

(d) BANK OVERDRAFTS   Overdrafts may be of two kinds: (1) an actual bank overdraft, resulting from payment by the bank of checks in an amount exceeding the balance available to cover such checks; (2) a book overdraft, arising from issuance of checks in an amount in excess of the balance in the account on which drawn, although such checks have not cleared through the bank in an amount sufficient to exhaust the account.

Actual bank overdrafts represent the total of checks honored by the bank without sufficient funds in the account to cover them; such an overdraft is the bank's way of temporarily loaning funds to its customer. Accordingly, bank overdrafts (other than those that arise in connection with a "zero-balance" or similar arrangement with a bank) represent short-term loans and should be classified as liabilities if the right of offset does not exist.

Book overdrafts representing outstanding checks in excess of funds on deposit should generally be classified as liabilities and cash reinstated at the balance sheet date. Such credit book balances should not be viewed as offsets to other cash accounts except where the legal right of setoff exists within the same bank due to the existence of other positive balances in that bank.

FASB Interpretation (FIN) No. 39, *Offsetting of Amounts Related to Certain Contracts (An Interpretation of APB Opinion No. 10 and FASB Statement No. 105)*, provides guidance on whether the right of offset has been met. Where right of offset does not exist, the credit balance can be viewed as a reinstatement of the liabilities that were cleared in the bookkeeping process. When outstanding checks in excess of funds on deposit are reclassified, it is preferable that they be separately classified; if they are included in accounts payable, the amounts so included should be disclosed, if material. Reclassifying as a liability all outstanding checks (including those covered by funds on deposit in the bank account concerned) is generally not considered acceptable.

(e) FOREIGN BALANCES   Cash in foreign countries may properly be included in the balance sheet as cash if stated at its equivalent in U.S. currency at the prevailing rate of exchange and if no exchange restrictions exist to prevent the transfer of such monies to the domicile of the owner. Depending on circumstances and the extent to which such cash balances may be subject to exchange control or other restrictions, the amount of cash so included should be considered for disclosure, by being stated either separately, parenthetically, or otherwise. The question of exchange restrictions (or economic conditions) preventing transfer of cash across national boundaries is of prime importance, and cash in foreign countries should be classified as a current asset only if appropriate review establishes that no significant restrictions or conditions exist with respect to the amounts involved. If restrictions exist but ultimate transfer seems probable, the cash may be included in the balance sheet in a noncurrent classification.

Difficulty in stating foreign cash balances at their equivalent in U.S. currency occurs when more than one rate of exchange exists. In this situation, the use of an exchange rate related to earnings received from the foreign subsidiary for the purpose of translating foreign currency accounts is recommended. Paragraphs 26–28 of FASB Statement No. 52, *Foreign Currency Translation*, provide guidance on the selection of exchange rates.

---

2.   Vincent M. O'Reilly et al., *Montgomery's Auditing, Twelfth Edition* (New York: John Wiley & Sons, 1998), Section 17.17.

(f) COMPENSATING CASH BALANCES   It is not uncommon for banks to require that a current or prospective borrower maintain a compensating balance on deposit with the bank. Frequently, the required compensating balance is based on the average outstanding loan balance. A compensating deposit balance may also be required to assure future credit availability (including maintenance of an unused line of credit). The compensating balance requirement may be (1) written into a loan or line of credit agreement, (2) the subject of a supplementary written agreement, or (3) based on an oral understanding. In some instances, a fee is paid on an unused line of credit (or commitment) to ensure credit availability.

The Securities and Exchange Commission (SEC) originally defined compensating balances in Accounting Series Release (ASR) No. 148 as follows:

> A compensating balance is defined as that portion of any demand deposit (or any time deposit or certificate of deposit) maintained by a corporation (or by any other person on behalf of the corporation) which constitutes support for existing borrowing arrangements of the corporation (or any other person) with a lending institution. Such arrangements would include both outstanding borrowings and the assurance of future credit availability.

For SEC registrants, requirements for the disclosure of restrictions on the withdrawal or use of cash and cash items, such as compensating balance arrangements, are set forth in Rule 5-02.1 of Regulation S-X as follows:

> CASH AND CASH ITEMS.
> Separate disclosure shall be made of the cash and cash items which are restricted as to withdrawal or usage. The provisions of any restrictions shall be described in a note to the financial statements. Restrictions may include legally restricted deposits held as compensating balances against short-term borrowing arrangements, contracts entered into with others, or company statements of intention with regard to particular deposits; however, time deposits and short-term certificates of deposit are not generally included in legally restricted deposits. In cases where compensating balance arrangements exist but are not agreements which legally restrict the use of cash amounts shown on the balance sheet, describe in the notes to the financial statements these arrangements and the amount involved, if determinable, for the most recent audited balance sheet required and for any subsequent unaudited balance sheet required in the notes to the financial statements. Compensating balances that are maintained under an agreement to assure future credit availability shall be disclosed in the notes to the financial statements along with the amount and terms of such agreement.

Guidelines and interpretations for disclosure of compensating balance arrangements are described within SEC Financial Reporting Release (FRR) No. 203 and SEC Staff Accounting Bulletin (SAB) Topic 6H. These provide useful information in evaluating the need for segregation and disclosure of compensating balance arrangements, including determination of the amount to be disclosed. Cash float and other factors should be considered.

Although no other authoritative literature requires compensating balance disclosures in the financial statements of non-SEC registrants, disclosure of material compensating balances will usually be necessary for fair presentation of the financial statements in accordance with generally accepted accounting principles (GAAP). Consequently, the disclosure of material compensating balance arrangements in financial statements of non-SEC reporting companies, whether maintained under a written agreement or under an informal agreement confirmed by the bank, is usually considered necessary as an "informative disclosure" under the third standard of reporting. It should be noted that compensating balances may also relate to an agreement or an understanding relative to future credit availability (including unused lines of credit). Compensating balances related to future credit availability should be disclosed as well as those related to outstanding borrowings.

(i) Disclosure   In circumstances where compensating balances relative to outstanding loans and future credit availability are not legally restricted as to withdrawal, note disclosure is appropriate.

(ii) Segregation in the Balance Sheet   Cash that is not subject to withdrawal should be classified as a noncurrent asset to the extent such cash relates to the noncurrent portion of the debt that causes its restriction. To the extent legally restricted cash relates to short-term borrowings, it may be included with unrestricted amounts on one line in financial statements of non-SEC reporting companies, provided the caption is appropriate and there is disclosure of the restricted amounts in the notes, for example, "Cash and restricted cash (Note 3)." Rule 5-02.1 of Regulation S-X requires SEC-reporting companies to disclose separately funds legally restricted as to withdrawal, but FRR No. 203.02.b is more specific in its requirement to segregate all legally restricted cash in the balance sheet.

No single example is appropriate for the disclosure of all compensating balance arrangements and future credit availability (including unused lines of credit) because the terms of loan agreements vary greatly. However, the following hypothetical examples illustrate methods of disclosing the details of compensating balance agreements and future credit availability.

The following is an example of disclosure where withdrawal of the compensating balance was legally restricted at the date of the balance sheet.

CASH ITEMS DISCLOSED ON BALANCE SHEET
SEC-Reporting Companies
Current assets

Cash	$3,500,000
Restricted cash compensating balances (Note X)	$6,000,000

Non-SEC Reporting Companies
Current assets $9,500,000
Cash and restricted cash (Note X)
Note X. Compensating Balances

A maximum of $100,000,000 is available to the company under a revolving credit agreement. Under the terms of the agreement, the company is required to maintain on deposit with the bank a compensating balance, restricted as to use, of 10 percent of the outstanding loan balance. At December 31, 20XX, $6,000,000 of the cash balance shown in the balance sheet was so restricted after adjusting for differences of "float" between the balance shown by the books of the company and the records of the bank.

For SEC-reporting companies, the following disclosure should be added to the above note:

This "float" amount consisted of $3,000,000 of unpresented checks less $500,000 of deposits of delayed availability at the agreed-upon schedule of 1.5 days' deposits.

The following is an example of disclosure for both SEC and non-SEC reporting companies where withdrawal of the compensating balance was not legally restricted at the date of the balance sheet.

Current assets
      Cash (Note X) $10,000,000
    Note X. Compensating Balances

Under an informal agreement with a lending bank, the company maintains on deposit with the bank a compensating balance of 5 percent of an unused line of credit and 10 percent of the outstanding loan balance. At December 31, 20XX, approximately $5,800,000 of the cash balance shown in the balance sheet represented a compensating balance.

(g) UNUSED LINES OF CREDIT   Rules 5-02.19 and 22 of Regulation S-X require that the amount and terms (including commitment fees and the conditions under which commitments may be withdrawn) of unused lines of credit or unused commitments for financing arrangements be disclosed. The term *unused lines of credit* is used for short-term financing arrangements; the term *unused commitments* refers to long-term financing arrangements. The requirements of Regulation S-X are as follows:

5.02.19 ACCOUNTS AND NOTES PAYABLE. (b) The amount and terms (including commitment fees and the conditions under which lines may be withdrawn) of unused lines of credit for short-term financing shall be disclosed, if significant, in the notes to the financial statements. The weighted average interest rate on short-term borrowings outstanding as of the date of each balance sheet presented shall be furnished in a note. The amount of these lines of credit which support a commercial paper borrowing arrangement or similar arrangements shall be separately identified.

5.02.22 BONDS, MORTGAGES, AND OTHER LONG-TERM DEBT, INCLUDING CAPITALIZED LEASES. (b) The amount and terms (including commitment fees and the conditions under which commitments may be withdrawn) of unused commitments for long-term financing arrangements that would be disclosed under this rule if used shall be disclosed in the notes to the financial statements if significant.

Many future credit arrangements are informal. Even formal arrangements may be withdrawn by lending institutions on very short notice, usually resulting from an adverse change in the financial position of a company. Therefore, limitations relating to the subsequent use of such lines of credit make it particularly difficult to provide informative and adequate disclosure so that the reader does not get a more favorable picture than is warranted. Because of the uncertainty of the duration of some lines of credit, disclosure of these types of lines of credit in financial statements requires the exercise of individual judgment based on the facts of the particular situation, and disclosures should include the limitations and conditions of subsequent use. Unused lines of credit or commitments that may be withdrawn at the mere option of the lender need not be disclosed but, if disclosed, the nature of the arrangement should be disclosed as well.

(i) Fee Paid for Future Credit Availability   A commitment fee has an effect on the cost of borrowing that is similar to that of a compensating balance. If a fee is paid to a lending bank for an unused line of credit or commitment, such fee should be disclosed if significant (Rule 502.19b of Regulation S-X).

(ii) Disclosure   The following is an example of disclosure of binding bank credit arrangements. Information of this nature may be combined with note disclosure of indebtedness.

> NOTE X. UNUSED LINES OF CREDIT
> Bank lines of credit under which notes payable of $105,000,000 were outstanding at December 31, 20XX, aggregated $152,500,000. The use of these lines generally is restricted to the extent that the Company is required periodically to liquidate its indebtedness to individual banks for 30 to 60 days each year. Borrowings under such agreements are at interest rates ranging from 1/4 to 1/2 of 1 percent above the prime rate, plus a commitment fee of 1/4 to 1/2 of 1 percent on the unused available credit. Commitments by the banks generally expire one year from the date of the agreement and are generally renewed.

For SEC-reporting companies, the following disclosure should be added to the above note:

> Total commitment fees paid on the unused lines of credit amounted to $175,000 for 20XX, $195,000 for 20XX, and $180,000 for 20XX.

(h) CONCENTRATION OF CREDIT RISK   Disclosures related to cash balances should include the existence of uninsured cash balances that represent a significant concentration of credit risk. American Institute of Certified Public Accountants (AICPA) Technical Practice Aid No. 2110.06, *Disclosure of Cash Balances in Excess of Federally Insured Amounts*, provides the following guidance:

> **Inquiry.** Should the existence of cash on deposit with banks in excess of Federal Deposit Insurance Corporation (FDIC)–insured limits be disclosed in the financial statements?
> **Reply.** The existence of uninsured cash balances should be disclosed if the uninsured balances represent a significant concentration of credit risk. Credit risk is defined in FASB Statement No. 105, *Disclosure of Information about Financial Instruments with Off-Balance-Sheet Risk and Financial Instruments with Concentrations of Credit Risk*, Paragraph 7 (AC F25.107), as "the possibility that a loss may occur from the failure of another party to perform according to the terms of the contract." As a result, bank statement balances in excess of FDIC-insured amounts represent credit risk.
> An example of disclosure for this circumstance might be:
> The Company maintains its cash in bank deposit accounts which, at times, may exceed federally insured limits. The Company has not experienced any losses in such account. The Company believes it is not exposed to any significant credit risk on cash and cash equivalents.

(i) Fair Value Disclosures   FASB Statement No. 107, *Disclosures about Fair Value of Financial Instruments*, requires disclosure of fair values of all financial instruments. The disclosure should include the method and significant assumptions used to estimate fair value. Due to the short-term maturity of cash and cash equivalents, this requirement is often met by the following sample disclosure:

> *Cash and Cash Equivalents.* The carrying amount approximates fair value because of the short-term maturity of those instruments.

18.3   LOANS

(a) INTRODUCTION   Although not the primary focus of their business, manufacturers, wholesalers, retailers, and service companies may nevertheless originate loans in connection with their revenue-generating activities. FASB Statement No. 114, *Accounting by Creditors for Impairment of a Loan*, applies to all creditors and defines a loan, in paragraph 4, as:

> a contractual right to receive money on demand or on fixed or determinable dates that is recognized as an asset in the creditor's statement of financial position. Examples include but are not limited to accounts receivable (with terms exceeding one year) and notes receivable.

However, there are certain requirements, as discussed below, for any type of credit arrangement, including trade receivables. In contrast, one of the most significant activities for financial institutions is the origination and acquisition of loans in order to generate interest revenue. Chapter 31 discusses matters of interest to financial institutions and entities involved in lending and deposit taking activities.

(b) INITIAL RECOGNITION AND MEASUREMENT   Paragraph 8a of Statement of Position (SOP) 01-6, *Accounting by Certain Entities (Including Entities with Trade Receivables) That Lend to or Finance the Activities of Others*, states that:

> Loans and trade receivables that management has the intent and ability to hold for the foreseeable future or until maturity or payoff should be reported in the balance sheet at outstanding principal adjusted for any chargeoffs, the allowance for loan losses (or the allowance for doubtful accounts), any deferred fees or costs on originated loans, and any unamortized premiums or discounts on purchased loans.

Generally, interest income on loans is accrued at the contractual rate, and premiums and discounts are amortized using the interest method in accordance with FASB Statement No. 91, *Accounting for Nonrefundable Fees and Costs Associated with Originating or Acquiring Loans and Initial Direct Costs of Leases.*

Accounting Principles Board (APB) Opinion No. 21, *Interest on Receivables and Payables*, discusses the appropriate accounting when the face amount of a note does not reasonably represent the present value of the consideration given or received in the exchange. APB 21 (par. 3) excludes from its scope "receivables and payables arising from transactions with customers or suppliers in the normal course of business which are due in customary trade terms not exceeding approximately one year" and "transactions between parent and subsidiary companies and between subsidiaries of a common parent."

Non-interest-bearing loans, loans with unrealistic interest rates, and loans obtained in exchange for property, goods, or services with fair values materially different from the principal amount of the loan lead to the recognition of premiums and discounts. APB 21 (par. 16) requires discounts and premiums to be reported "as a direct deduction from or addition to the face amount of the [loan]." Appendix A of APB 21 provides illustrations of the appropriate balance sheet presentation.

Nonrefundable fees and costs associated with an entity's lending activities are discussed in Statement 91. Such considerations are most prevalent for financial institutions, and the accounting for these fees and costs is discussed in Chapter 31.

Some acquired loans may have experienced a decline in credit quality. SOP 03-3, *Accounting for Certain Loans or Debt Securities Acquired in a Transfer*, addresses the accounting and reporting for those loans. Loans that have been acquired should be evaluated to determine whether the provisions of SOP 03-3 should be applied.

(c) LOAN IMPAIRMENT AND INCOME RECOGNITION   FASB Concepts Statement No. 6, *Elements of Financial Statements* (par. 25), defines assets as "probable future economic benefits obtained or controlled by a particular entity as a result of past transactions or events." FASB Statement No. 5, *Accounting for Contingencies*, and Statement 114 address the accounting by creditors for impairment of certain loans. These Statements indicate that "a loan is impaired when, based on current information and events, it is probable that a creditor will be unable to collect all amounts due according to the contractual terms of the loan agreement." It applies to all creditors. While both Statements address loan impairment, Statement 5 generally addresses smaller-balance homogeneous loans while Statement 114 addresses all loans except those specifically excluded (par. 6):

- Large groups of smaller-balance homogeneous loans that are collectively evaluated for impairment. Those loans may include but are not limited to credit card, residential mortgage, and consumer installment loans.
- Loans that are measured at fair value or at the lower of cost or fair value, for example, in accordance with FASB Statement No. 65, *Accounting for Certain Mortgage Banking Activities*, or other specialized industry practice.
- Leases as defined in FASB Statement No. 13, *Accounting for Leases*.
- Debt securities as defined in FASB Statement No. 115, *Accounting for Certain Investments in Debt and Equity Securities*.

Statement 114 does not specify how a creditor should identify loans that are to be evaluated for impairment. However, in practice, a number of different mechanisms are employed to identify loans for impairment evaluation. These mechanisms include but are not limited to past-due reports, reports from regulatory examiners, reviews of incomplete loan files of financial institutions, identification of those borrowers facing financial difficulties or operating in industries facing such difficulties, and loss statistics pertaining to certain categories of loans.

(i) Impairment Measurement Guidelines   The measurement of impairment should take into account both contractual interest payments and contractual principal payments consistent with the original payment terms of the loan agreement. For loans within the scope of Statement 114, the creditor should measure impairment based on the present value of expected future cash flows discounted at the loan's effective interest rate. A loan's effective interest rate is defined as "the rate of return implicit in the loan (i.e., the contractual interest rate adjusted

for any net deferred loan fees or costs, premium, or discount existing at the origination or acquisition of the loan)" (par. 14).

Statement 114 provides that, as a practical expedient, creditors may alternatively measure impairment based on a loan's observable market price or the fair value of the collateral if the loan is collateral dependent. If the latter approach is used, the measurement of impairment should take into account estimated costs to sell the collateral, on a discounted basis. Furthermore, when a creditor determines that foreclosure is probable, impairment must be measured based on the fair value of the collateral.

When valuations are based on appraisals, particular attention should be given to the objectivity and competence of the specialist providing the appraisal and the methods and assumptions used to develop the appraised fair value. Additionally, the appraisal should be assessed as to its suitability for the purpose. For example, "appraisals" are sometimes obtained to assess the feasibility of a commercial development project (e.g., a golf course and condominium complex) and assume the existence of the completed project. Such an "appraisal" might not be useful in assessing the *as-is* fair value of a property comprised mostly of raw land in foreclosure. While companies are not precluded from internally appraising collateral, the increased objectivity of third-party appraisals may provide more objective valuations to assist management in decision making and also permit auditors to rely on the work of a specialist performing the appraisal. Valuations are the subject of a separate chapter in the *Accountants' Handbook*.

In any event, a valuation allowance should be established if the recorded investment in the loan (including accrued interest, net deferred loan fees or costs, and unamortized discount or premium) exceeds the impaired measure. The recognition of such an allowance is accompanied by a corresponding charge to bad debt expense.

(ii) Income Recognition   Once a loan has been impaired, some entities, particularly financial institutions, suspend the accrual of interest because such accruals do not in those circumstances reflect economic reality.

The recognition of interest income on impaired loans was initially addressed by Statement 114 (pars. 17–19). Subsequent to its issuance, however, a number of commentators requested an extension of the effective date of the Statement due to the difficulty of applying the new guidelines. As a result, the FASB issued Statement No. 118, *Accounting by Creditors for Impairment of a Loan—Income Recognition and Disclosures*, to "allow a creditor to use existing methods for recognizing interest income on impaired loans" (par. 3). Statement 118 eliminated the original income recognition provisions of paragraphs 17–19 of Statement 114. However, Statement 114 (par. 17), as amended, recognizes that accounting methods for the recognition of interest income include using "a cost-recovery method, a cash-basis method, or some combination of those methods." While the decision to recognize interest income on impaired or defaulted loans requires judgment and consideration of the facts and circumstances, oftentimes companies do not recognize as income the interest on loans defaulted more than 90 days.

(d) TROUBLED DEBT RESTRUCTURINGS   Occasionally, a loan may be restructured to meet a borrower's changing circumstances, and a new loan is recognized. However, if "the creditor for economic or legal reasons related to the debtor's financial difficulties grants a concession to the debtor that it would not otherwise consider" (par. 2 of Statement 15), the transaction should be accounted for in accordance with FASB Statement No. 15, *Accounting* *by Debtors and Creditors for Troubled Debt Restructurings.* The following types of restructuring arrangements are discussed in Statement 15:

- Transfers of assets of the debtor or an equity interest in the debtor to fully or partially satisfy the debt
- Modification of debt terms, including reduction of one or more of the following: (1) interest rates with or without extension of maturity date(s), (2) face or maturity amounts, and (3) accrued interest

Creditors that receive assets or an equity interest in the debtor in full satisfaction of the loan should account for the restructuring at the fair value of the assets or equity interest received or the fair value of the loan, whichever is more clearly determinable. In the case of a partial satisfaction of the loan, the fair value of the loan may not be used (Statement 15, par. 28, fn. 16).

Statement 114 amended Statement 15 to require that a creditor account for a troubled debt restructuring involving a modification of terms in accordance with Statement 114. However, the effective interest rate to be used in these situations is the original contractual rate and not the rate specified in the restructuring agreement. Furthermore, creditors must disclose "the amount of commitments, if any, to lend additional funds to debtors owing receivables whose terms have been modified in troubled debt restructurings" (Statement 15, par. 40b).

(e) NOTES RECEIVED FOR CAPITAL STOCK   An entity may sometimes receive a note from the sale of capital stock or as a contribution to paid-in capital. The Emerging Issues Task Force (EITF), in EITF 85-1, *Classifying Notes Received for Capital Stock,* addressed the issue of whether an entity should report the note receivable as a reduction of shareholders' equity or as an asset. The EITF "reached a consensus that reporting the note as an asset is generally not appropriate, except in very limited circumstances when there is substantial evidence of ability and intent to pay within a reasonably short period of time." One situation where such a note receivable may be reported as an asset is the payment of the note prior to issuance of the financial statements.

(f) DISCLOSURES   There are a number of standards that require disclosures related to loans as follows:

- APB Opinion No. 22, *Disclosure of Accounting Policies,* paragraphs 8 and 12
- SOP 01-6, paragraphs 13–17
- APB Opinion No. 12, *Omnibus Opinion—1967—Classification and Disclosure of Allowances; Disclosure of Depreciable Assets and Depreciation; Deferred Compensation Contracts; Capital Changes; Convertible Debt and Debt Issued with Stock Warrants; Amortization of Debt Discount and Expense or Premium,* paragraphs 2 and 3
- Statement 5, paragraphs 9–11
- SOP 94-6, *Disclosure of Certain Significant Risks and Uncertainties,* paragraphs 13 and 14
- FSP-SOP 94-6-1, *Terms of Loan Products That May Give Rise to a Concentration of Credit Risk*
- Statement 114 as amended by Statement 118, paragraph 20A
- SOP 03-3, paragraphs 14–16
- Statement 107

18.4   DEBT SECURITIES

(a) INTRODUCTION   An entity may invest in debt securities (e.g., bonds) to generate interest revenue and/or to realize gains from their sale at increased market prices. Statement 115 is the primary standard applicable to investments in debt securities. The FASB has also issued a special report entitled, *A Guide to Implementation of Statement 115 on Accounting for Certain Investments in Debt and Equity Securities*, which contains a series of questions and answers (herein referred to by question number as FASB Q&A) useful in understanding and implementing the Statement. Paragraph 137 of Statement 115 defines, in part, debt securities as those securities that represent "a creditor relationship with an enterprise." These securities include:

- U.S. Treasury securities; U.S. government agency securities; municipal securities; corporate bonds; convertible debt; commercial paper; all securitized debt instruments, such as collateralized mortgage obligations (CMOs) and real estate mortgage investment conduits (REMICs); and interest-only and principal-only strips
- A CMO (or other instrument) that is issued in equity form but is required to be accounted for as a nonequity instrument regardless of how that instrument is classified (i.e., whether equity or debt) in the issuer's statement of financial position
- Preferred stock that by its terms either must be redeemed by the issuing enterprise or is redeemable at the option of the investor

Except as mentioned below, Statement 115 "applies to all debt securities, including securities that have been grouped with loans in the statement of financial position" (EITF Topic No. D-39, *Questions Related to the Implementation of FASB Statement No. 115*). These include (1) a bank's originated and securitized mortgage loans that continue to be reported as loans in the Call Report, (2) bank investments in unrated industrial development bonds classified as loans in the Call Report, and (3) "Brady Bonds." In addition, FASB Technical Bulletin No. 94-1, *Application of Statement 115 to Debt Securities Restructured in a Troubled Debt Restructuring*, indicates that "Statement 115 applies to all loans that meet the definition of a security in that Statement. Thus, any loan that was restructured in a troubled debt restructuring involving a modification of terms, including those restructured before the effective date of Statement 114, would be subject to the provisions of Statement 115 if the debt instrument meets the definition of a security" (par. 3).

Excluded from the definition of debt securities are unsecuritized loans, options on debt securities, accounts receivable, option contracts, financial futures contracts, forward contracts, and lease contracts. In addition, since Statement 115 generally requires that investments in debt securities be presented at fair value, enterprises that already use similar measurement guidelines in accounting for these investments—for example, brokers and dealers in securities, defined benefit pension plans, and investment companies—need not apply the requirements of the Statement. In this regard, Statement 115 (par. 4) states, in part, "This Statement does not apply to enterprises whose specialized accounting practices include accounting for substantially all investments in debt and equity securities at market value or fair value, with changes in value recognized in earnings (income) or in the change in net assets. . . ."

Not-for-profit organizations are also excluded from the Statement's provisions. However, the Statement applies "to cooperatives and mutual enterprises, including credit unions and mutual insurance companies" (par. 4).

As discussed in Chapter 18A in this supplement, "Transfers of Financial Assets," certain financial assets subject to prepayment are measured like investment in debt securities. Those assets include interest-only strips, retained interests in securitizations, loans, other receivables, or other financial assets that can contractually be prepaid or otherwise settled in such a way that the holder would not recover substantially all of its recorded investment, except for instruments that are within the scope of FASB Statement No. 133, *Accounting for Derivative Instruments and Hedging Activities.*

EITF 99-20, *Recognition of Interest Income and Impairment on Purchased and Retained Beneficial Interests in Securitized Financial Assets*, provides interest income recognition and measurement guidance for interests retained in a securitization transaction accounted for as a sale. The scope of EITF 99-20 includes retained beneficial interests in securitization transactions that are accounted for as sales under Statement 140 and certain purchased beneficial interests in securitized financial assets. The scope includes beneficial interests that (par. 5):

- Are either debt securities under Statement 115 or required to be accounted for like debt securities under Statement 115 pursuant to paragraph 14 of Statement 140.
- Involve securitized financial assets that have contractual cash flows (e.g., loans, receivables, debt securities, and guaranteed lease residuals, among other items). Thus, the consensus in this issue does not apply to securitized financial assets that do not involve contractual cash flows (e.g., common stock equity securities, among other items). The Task Force observed that the guidance in EITF Issue No. 96-12, *Recognition of Interest Income and Balance Sheet Classification of Structured Notes*, may be applied to those beneficial interests involving securitized financial assets that do not involve contractual cash flows.
- Do not result in consolidation of the entity issuing the beneficial interest by the holder of the beneficial interests.

Under EITF 99-20, when an adverse change in the expected cash flows (principal or interest) to be received occurs and the fair value of the beneficial interest is less than its carrying amount, an other-than-temporary impairment has occurred. In determining whether an adverse change in cash flows has occurred, the present value of the remaining cash flows, as estimated at the initial transaction date (or the last date previously revised), which will be the book value if there is no premium or discount, should be compared to the present value of the expected cash flows at the current reporting date. The estimated cash flows should be reflective of those a market participant would use and should be discounted at a rate equal to the current effective yield. If an other-than-temporary impairment is recognized as a result of this analysis, the yield is changed to the market rate. The last revised estimated cash flows would be used for future impairment analysis purposes.

Under EITF 99-20, when an adverse change in the expected cash flows to be received occurs, but the fair value of the beneficial interest is still greater than the carrying value, then the investor should recalculate the amount of accretable yield for the beneficial interest on the date of evaluation as the excess of estimated cash flows over the beneficial interest's reference amount (the reference amount is equal to (1) the initial investment less (2) cash received to date less (3) other than temporary impairments recognized to date plus (4) the yield accreted to date). The adjustment should be accounted for prospectively as a change in estimate in conformity with APB Opinion No. 20, *Accounting Changes*, with the amount of periodic accretion adjusted over the remaining life of the beneficial interest.

(b) INITIAL RECOGNITION AND MEASUREMENT   Upon acquisition, debt securities are classified into one of three categories: (1) held-to-maturity, (2) trading, or (3) available-for-sale. Generally, these securities are initially recorded at cost with appropriate identification of premium or discounts. EITF Issue No. 94-8, *Accounting for Conversion of a Loan into a Debt Security in a Debt Restructuring*, states that "the initial cost basis of a debt security of the original debtor received as part of a debt restructuring should be the security's fair value at the date of the restructuring."

(i) Held-to-Maturity   An entity that has the positive intent and ability to hold a debt security to maturity should classify such security as a held-to-maturity security. Otherwise, the security should be classified as trading or available-for-sale. A positive intent and ability to hold a security to maturity does not exist if management's intent to hold the security to maturity is uncertain, if the intent is "to hold the security for only an indefinite period" (par. 9), or if there is a "mere absence of an intent to sell" (par. 59). FASB Q&A No. 18 states that "given the unique opportunities for profit embedded in a convertible security, it generally would be contradictory to assert the positive intent and ability to hold a convertible debt security to maturity and forego [*sic*] the opportunity to exercise the conversion feature." In determining positive intent and ability, the following additional guidance is available:

- Statement 115 (par. 9) states that "a debt security should not, for example, be classified as held-to-maturity if the enterprise anticipates that the security would be available to be sold in response to . . . needs for liquidity (e.g., due to the withdrawal of deposits, increased demands for loans, surrender of insurance policies, or payment of insurance claims)," or changes in (1) "market interest rates and related changes in the security's prepayment risk," (2) "the availability of and the yield on alternative investments," (3) "funding sources and terms," or (4) "foreign currency risk."
- Statement 115 (par. 7), as amended, provides that "a security may not be classified as held-to-maturity if that security can contractually be prepaid or otherwise settled in such a way that the holder of the security would not recover substantially all of its recorded investment."
- FASB Statement No. 140, *Accounting for Transfers and Servicing of Financial Assets and Extinguishments of Liabilities—A Replacement of FASB Statement 125* (par. 14), also requires that "interest-only strips, other interests that continue to be held by a transferor in securitizations, loans, other receivables, or other financial assets that can contractually be prepaid or otherwise settled in such a way that the holder would not recover substantially all of its recorded investment, except for instruments within the scope of Statement 133, shall be subsequently measured like investments in debt securities classified as available-for-sale or trading under Statement 115, as amended."

(ii) Trading   Debt securities classified as trading securities are those that are "bought and held principally for the purpose of selling them in the near term (thus held for only a short period of time)" (par. 12a). These include mortgage-backed securities held for sale in conjunction with mortgage banking activities.

(iii) Available-for-Sale   Debt securities that are not classified as held-to-maturity or trading securities are classified as available-for-sale securities.

(c) ACCOUNTING AFTER ACQUISITION   Gains and losses realized upon the sale of debt securities are included in earnings. As discussed in Chapter 18A of this supplement, "Transfers of Financial Assets," sale accounting is appropriate only for transfers of financial assets in which the transferor surrenders control over those financial assets pursuant to the provisions of Statement 140, paragraph 9. Otherwise, the transferor should account for the transfer as a secured borrowing with pledge of collateral pursuant to Statement 140, paragraph 15.

Generally, interest income is recognized at the contractual rate and premiums and discounts are amortized using the interest method. As discussed above, certain beneficial interests should follow the guidance in EITF 99-20. In addition, the retrospective interest method should be used for recognizing income on structured note securities that are classified as available-for-sale or held-to-maturity and that meet one or more of the conditions set forth in EITF 96-12. Structured notes are debt instruments whose cash flows are linked to the movement in one or more indexes, interest rates, foreign exchange rates, commodities prices, prepayment rates, or other market variables.

The amount at which a debt security is presented in the statement of financial position depends on its classification, as discussed below. This will require a determination of fair value: "the amount at which a financial instrument could be exchanged in a current transaction between willing parties, other than in a forced or liquidation sale. If a quoted market price is available for an instrument, the fair value to be used in applying [the] Statement is the product of the number of trading units of the instrument times its market price" (par. 137). If a quoted market price is not available for a debt security, pricing techniques such as "discounted cash flow analysis, matrix pricing, option-adjusted spread models, and fundamental analysis" (par. 111) can be used to obtain an estimate of fair value.

The appropriateness of a security's classification must be reassessed at each reporting date. In making this assessment, prior sales and transfers should be considered. Transfers to another category are discussed in section (iv).

(i) Held-to-Maturity   Debt securities classified as held-to-maturity are carried at amortized cost. As with loans, premiums and discounts pertaining to these securities are generally amortized using the interest method in accordance with Statement 91.

In assessing the appropriateness of the held-to-maturity designation at each reporting date, Statement 115 (par. 8) provides that transfers or sales due to the following changes in circumstances do not refute the held-to-maturity classification of other debt securities:

- Evidence of a significant deterioration in the issuer's creditworthiness
- A change in tax law that eliminates or reduces the tax-exempt status of interest on the debt security (but not a change in tax law that revises the marginal tax rates applicable to interest income)
- A major business combination or major disposition (such as sale of a components of an entity) that necessitates the sale or transfer of held-to-maturity securities to maintain the enterprise's existing interest rate risk position or credit risk policy
- A change in statutory or regulatory requirements significantly modifying either what constitutes a permissible investment or the maximum level of investments in certain kinds of securities, thereby causing an enterprise to dispose of a held-to-maturity security
- A significant increase by the regulator in the industry's capital requirements that causes the enterprise to downsize by selling held-to-maturity securities

- A significant increase in the risk weights of debt securities used for regulatory risk-based capital purposes

It is not appropriate to apply these exceptions to situations that are similar, but not the same as, those listed above. However, the Statement indicates that "in addition to the foregoing changes in circumstances, other events that are isolated, nonrecurring, and unusual for the reporting enterprise that could not have been reasonably anticipated may cause the enterprise to sell or transfer a held-to-maturity security without necessarily calling into question its intent to hold other debt securities to maturity" (par. 8).

FASB Q&A No. 29 indicates that "the sale of a held-to-maturity security in response to a tender offer will call into question an investor's intent to hold other debt securities to maturity in the future." In addition, FASB Q&A No. 24 notes that "sales of held-to-maturity securities to fund an acquisition (or a disposition, for example, if deposit liabilities are being assumed by the other party) are inconsistent with [Statement 115] paragraph 8."

(ii) Trading   Debt securities classified as trading securities are carried at fair value. The resulting unrealized gain or loss is reflected in earnings.

(iii) Available-for-Sale   Debt securities classified as available-for-sale are, like debt securities classified as trading, carried at fair value. Unrealized holding gains and losses for available-for-sale securities (including those classified as current assets) are excluded from earnings and reported in Other Comprehensive Income (OCI), net of related deferred income taxes. These unrealized gains and losses should include the entire change in the fair value of foreign currency–denominated available-for-sale debt securities, and not just the portion attributable to changes in exchange rates.

The FASB staff has announced that "when an entity has decided to sell an available-for-sale security whose fair value is less than its cost and the entity does not expect the fair value of the security to recover prior to the expected time of sale, a write-down for other-than-temporary impairment should be recognized in earnings in the period in which the decision to sell is made" (EITF Topic No. D-44, *Recognition of Other-Than-Temporary Impairment upon the Planned Sale of a Security Whose Cost Exceeds Fair Value*, which was superseded with the issuance of FSP FAS 115-1 and FAS 124-1, *The Meaning of Other-Than-Temporary Impairment and Its Application to Certain Investments*).

(iv) Transfers between Categories   Changes in the classification of investments in debt securities are accounted for at fair value. The following table summarizes the proper accounting for transfers:

Transfer From	Transfer To	Accounting Principles
Trading	Available-for-Sale	The unrealized holding gain or loss at the date of the transfer will have already been recognized in earnings and shall not be reversed.
	Held-to-Maturity	The unrealized holding gain or loss at the date of the transfer will have already been recognized in earnings and shall not be reversed.

Transfer From	Transfer To	Accounting Principles
Available-for-Sale	Trading	The portion of the unrealized holding gain or loss at the date of the transfer that has not been previously recognized in earnings shall be recognized in earnings immediately.
	Held-to-Maturity	The unrealized holding gain or loss at the date of the transfer shall continue to be reported in a separate component of shareholders' equity, such as accumulated other comprehensive income, but shall be amortized over the remaining life of the security as an adjustment of yield in a manner consistent with the amortization of any premium or discount.
Held-to-Maturity	Trading	The portion of the unrealized holding gain or loss at the date of the transfer that has not been previously recognized in earnings shall be recognized in earnings immediately.
	Available-for-Sale	The unrealized holding gain or loss at the date of the transfer shall be reported in other comprehensive income.

(d) IMPAIRMENT   Temporary declines in the fair value of securities below amortized cost are not recognized since it is generally held that such declines will ultimately reverse. However, the evaluation of whether an impairment is considered other-than-temporary has been a long-standing practice issue. In order to provide some guidance on evaluating other-than-temporary impairment, the FASB issued FSP FAS 115-1 and FAS 124-1 in November 2005. While the FSP clarifies the accounting in a few areas, it largely refers to existing accounting literature and incorporates the existing guidance from the SEC. The FSP refers to a basic three-step model:

Step 1:   Determine whether an investment is impaired (i.e., fair value is less than cost). Generally, cost equals amortized cost less any previous write-downs.

Step 2:   Determine whether the impairment is other-than-temporary. Other-than-temporary does not mean permanent, and an investment does not have to be deemed permanently impaired in order to require a write-down.

Step 3:   If the impairment is deemed to be other-than-temporary, recognize an impairment loss equal to the difference between the carrying amount and its fair value, measured as of the balance sheet date. Further, the fair value becomes the new cost basis of the investment and should not be adjusted for subsequent recoveries in fair value.

Step 1:   Determine Whether an Investment Is Impaired
Paragraphs 7 to 12 of FSP FAS 115-1 and FAS 124-1 state the following:

Impairment shall be assessed at the individual security level (herein referred to as "an investment"). An investment is impaired if the fair value of the investment is less than its cost. Except as provided in paragraph 10, an investor shall assess whether an investment is impaired in each reporting period. For entities that issue interim financial statements, each interim period is a reporting period.

An investor shall not combine separate contracts (a debt security and a guarantee or other credit enhancement) for purposes of determining whether a debt security is impaired or can contractually be prepaid or otherwise settled in such a way that the investor would not recover substantially all of its cost.

For investments other than cost-method investments (see paragraph 4(c)), if the fair value of the investment is less than its cost, proceed to Step 2.

Because the fair value of cost-method investments is not readily determinable, the evaluation of whether an investment is impaired shall be determined as follows:

(a) If an investor has estimated the fair value of a cost-method investment (for example, for disclosure under FASB Statement No. 107, *Disclosures about Fair Value of Financial Instruments*), that estimate shall be used to determine if the investment is impaired for the reporting periods in which the investor estimates fair value. If the fair value of the investment is less than its cost, proceed to Step 2.

(b) For reporting periods in which an investor has not estimated the fair value of a cost-method investment, the investor shall evaluate whether an event or change in circumstances has occurred in that period that may have a significant adverse effect on the fair value of the investment (an "impairment indicator"). Impairment indicators include, but are not limited to:

1. A significant deterioration in the earnings performance, credit rating, asset quality, or business prospects of the investee
2. A significant adverse change in the regulatory, economic, or technological environment of the investee
3. A significant adverse change in the general market condition of either the geographic area or the industry in which the investee operates
4. A bona fide offer to purchase (whether solicited or unsolicited), an offer by the investee to sell, or a completed auction process for the same or similar security for an amount less than the cost of the investment
5. Factors that raise significant concerns about the investee's ability to continue as a going concern, such as negative cash flows from operations, working capital deficiencies, or noncompliance with statutory capital requirements or debt covenants.

In addition, if an investment was previously tested for impairment under Step 2 and the investor concluded that the investment was not other-than-temporarily impaired, the investor shall continue to evaluate whether the investment is impaired (that is, shall estimate the fair value of the investment) in each subsequent reporting period until either (a) the investment experiences a recovery of fair value up to (or beyond) its cost or (b) the investor recognizes an other-than-temporary impairment loss.

If an impairment indicator is present, the investor shall estimate the fair value of the investment. If the fair value of the investment is less than its cost, proceed to Step 2.

Step 2: Evaluate Whether an Impairment Is Other Than Temporary

Paragraphs 13 and 14 of FSP FAS 115-1 and FAS 124-1 state the following:

When the fair value of an investment is less than its cost at the balance sheet date of the reporting period for which impairment is assessed, the impairment is either temporary or other than temporary. An investor shall apply other guidance that is pertinent to the determination of whether an impairment is other than temporary, such as paragraph 16 of Statement 115 (which references SEC Staff Accounting Bulletin Topic 5M, Other-Than-Temporary Impairment of Certain Investments in Debt and Equity Securities), paragraph 6 of APB Opinion No. 18, The Equity Method of Accounting for Investments in Common Stock, and EITF 99-20.

In applying that guidance, questions sometimes arise about whether an investor shall recognize an other-than-temporary impairment only when it intends to sell a specifically identified available-for-sale debt or equity security at a loss shortly after the balance sheet date. When an investor has decided to sell an impaired available-for-sale security and the investor does not expect the fair value of the security to fully recover prior to the expected time of sale, the security shall be deemed other-than-temporarily impaired in the period in which the decision to sell is made. However, an investor shall recognize an impairment loss when the impairment is deemed other than temporary even if a decision to sell has not been made.

Step 3: If the Impairment Is Other Than Temporary, Recognize an Impairment Loss Equal to the Difference between the Investment's Cost and Its Fair Value

Paragraph 15 of FSP FAS 115-1 and FAS 124-1 states the following:

If it is determined in Step 2 that the impairment is other than temporary, then an impairment loss shall be recognized in earnings equal to the entire difference between the investment's cost and its fair value at the balance sheet date of the reporting period for which the assessment is made. The measurement of the impairment shall not include partial recoveries subsequent to the balance sheet date. The fair value of the investment would then become the new cost basis of the investment and shall not be adjusted for subsequent recoveries in fair value.

FSP FAS 115-1 refers to paragraph 16 of Statement 115 for determining whether an impairment is other than temporary:

For individual securities classified as either available-for-sale or held-to-maturity, an enterprise shall determine whether a decline in fair value below the amortized cost basis is other than temporary. (If a security has been the hedged item in a fair value hedge, the security's "amortized cost basis" shall reflect the effect of the adjustments of its carrying amount made pursuant to paragraph 22(b) of Statement 133.) For example, if it is probable that the investor will be unable to collect all amounts due according to the contractual terms of a debt security not impaired at acquisition, an other-than-temporary impairment shall be considered to have occurred. [Footnote 4] If the decline in fair value is judged to be other than temporary, the cost basis of the individual security shall be written down to fair value as a new cost basis and the amount of the write-down shall be included in earnings (that is, accounted for as a realized loss). The new cost basis shall not be changed for subsequent recoveries in fair value. Subsequent increases in the fair value of available-for-sale securities shall be included in other comprehensive income pursuant to paragraph 13; subsequent decreases in fair value, if not an other-than-temporary impairment, also shall be included in other comprehensive income.

Footnote 4: A decline in the value of a security that is other than temporary is also discussed in FSP FAS 115-1 and FAS 124-1, AICPA Statement on Auditing Standards No. 92, *Auditing Derivative Instruments, Hedging Activities, and Investments in Securities*, and in SEC Staff Accounting Bulletin No. 59, *Accounting for Noncurrent Marketable Equity Securities.*

As referenced in Statement 115, paragraph 47 of SAS 92 provides the following guidance:

Impairment Losses. Regardless of the valuation method used, generally accepted accounting principles might require recognizing in earnings an impairment loss for a decline in fair value that is other than temporary. Determinations of whether losses are other than temporary often involve estimating the outcome of future events. Accordingly, judgment is required in determining whether factors exist that indicate that an impairment loss has been incurred at the end of the reporting period. These judgments are based on subjective as well as objective factors, including knowledge and experience about past and current events and assumptions about future events. The following are examples of such factors.

(a) Fair value is significantly below cost and

- The decline is attributable to adverse conditions specifically related to the security or to specific conditions in an industry or in a geographic area.
- The decline has existed for an extended period of time.
- Management does not possess both the intent and the ability to hold the security for a period of time sufficient to allow for any anticipated recovery in fair value.

(b) The security has been downgraded by a rating agency.
(c) The financial condition of the issuer has deteriorated.
(d) Dividends have been reduced or eliminated, or scheduled interest payments have not been made.
(e) The entity recorded losses from the security subsequent to the end of the reporting period.

As referenced in Statement 115, SAB 59 (as amended by SAB No. 103, *Update of Codification of Staff Accounting Bulletins*) provides the following guidance as Topic 5: "Miscellaneous Accounting, Other Than Temporary Impairment of Certain Investments in Debt and Equity Securities":

M. Other Than Temporary Impairment of Certain Investments in Debt and Equity Securities
Facts: Paragraph 16 of Statement 115 specifies that "[f]or individual securities classified as either available-for-sale or held-to-maturity, an enterprise shall

determine whether a decline in fair value below the amortized cost basis is other than temporary. . . . If the decline in fair value is judged to be other than temporary, the cost basis of the individual security shall be written down to fair value as a new cost basis and the amount of the write-down shall be included in earnings (that is, accounted for as a realized loss)."

Statement 115 does not define the phrase "other than temporary." In applying this guidance to its own situation, Company A has interpreted "other than temporary" to mean permanent impairment. Therefore, because Company A's management has not been able to determine that its investment in Company B is permanently impaired, no realized loss has been recognized even though the market price of B's shares is currently less than one-third of A's average acquisition price.

Question: Does the staff believe that the phrase "other than temporary" should be interpreted to mean "permanent"?

Interpretive Response: No. The staff believes that the FASB consciously chose the phrase "other than temporary" because it did not intend that the test be "permanent impairment," as has been used elsewhere in accounting practice. [Footnote 12]

Footnote 12: Footnote 4 to Statement 115 refers to this SAB for a discussion of considerations applicable to a determination as to whether a decline in market value below cost, at a particular point in time, is other than temporary. FASB's implementation guide, *A Guide to Implementation of Statement 115 on Accounting for Certain Investments in Debt and Equity Securities*, SAS 92, *Auditing Derivative Instruments, Hedging Activities, and Investments in Securities*, AICPA's Audit Guide, *Auditing Derivative Instruments, Hedging Activities, and Investments in Securities*, and EITF Topic D-44 also address issues related to the determination of whether a decline in fair value of a investment security is other than temporary.

The value of investments in marketable securities classified as either available-for-sale or held-to-maturity may decline for various reasons. The market price may be affected by general market conditions which reflect prospects for the economy as a whole or by specific information pertaining to an industry or an individual company. Such declines require further investigation by management. Acting upon the premise that a write-down may be required, management should consider all available evidence to evaluate the realizable value of its investment.

There are numerous factors to be considered in such an evaluation, and their relative significance will vary from case to case. The staff believes that the following are only a few examples of the factors which, individually or in combination, indicate that a decline is other than temporary and that a write-down of the carrying value is required:

(a) The length of the time and the extent to which the market value has been less than cost;
(b) The financial condition and near-term prospects of the issuer, including any specific events which may influence the operations of the issuer, such as changes in technology that may impair the earnings potential of the

investment or the discontinuance of a segment of the business that may affect the future earnings potential; or

(c) The intent and ability of the holder to retain its investment in the issuer for a period of time sufficient to allow for any anticipated recovery in market value.

Unless evidence exists to support a realizable value equal to or greater than the carrying value of the investment, a write-down to fair value accounted for as a realized loss should be recorded. In accordance with the guidance of paragraph 16 of Statement 115, such loss should be recognized in the determination of net income of the period in which it occurs and the written-down value of the investment in the company becomes the new cost basis of the investment.

In addition to retaining the disclosure requirements of the superseded EITF 03-1, *The Meaning of Other-Than-Temporary Impairment and Its Application to Certain Investments*, and referring to existing GAAP and SEC guidance, FSP FAS 115-1 and FAS 124-1 also clarifies the following:

- If the impairment is considered other-than-temporary, then the impairment should be measured as the difference between fair value and cost basis at the balance sheet date (paragraph 15 of the FSP FAS 115-1 and FAS 124-1).
- For post-impairment income recognition, income must be recognized on expected, not contractual, cash flows (paragraph 16 of the FSP FAS 115-1 and FAS 124-1).
- If the decision is made to sell an investment in a loss position, the loss should be recorded in the period the decision is made rather than when the actual sale occurs, incorporating existing guidance in EITF Topic 0-44 (paragraph 14 of the FSP FAS 115-1 and FAS 124-1).

(e) DISCLOSURES   The references applicable to disclosure requirements are:

- Statement 105, paragraph 20
- Statement 115, paragraphs 19–22
- SOP 03-3, paragraphs 14–16
- FSP FAS 115-1 and FAS 124-1, paragraph 17

18.5   EQUITY SECURITIES

(a) INTRODUCTION   Equity securities are often purchased to generate dividend income, to realize gains from their sale to other parties, and/or to achieve control over another enterprise. Except as discussed below, Statement 115, as amended, is the primary standard applicable to investments in equity securities that have readily determinable fair values. As mentioned earlier, the FASB has also issued a special report entitled *A Guide to Implementation of Statement 115 on Accounting for Certain Investments in Debt and Equity Securities*, which contains a series of questions and answers useful in understanding and implementing the Statement.

Statement 115 (par. 137) defines an equity security as "any security representing an ownership interest in an enterprise (e.g., common, preferred, or other capital stock) or the right to acquire (e.g., warrants, rights, and call options) or dispose of (e.g., put options) an ownership interest in an enterprise at fixed or determinable prices." This definition excludes "convertible debt or preferred stock that by its terms either must be redeemed by the issuing enterprise or is redeemable at the option of the investor." FASB Q&A No. 3 indicates that this "definition does not include written equity options because they represent *obligations* of the writer, not investments. Is also does not include cash-settled options on equity securities or options on equity-based indexes, because those instruments do not represent ownership interests in an enterprise. Options on debt securities are not within the scope of the Statement." In addition, the Statement does not apply to:

- "Enterprises whose specialized accounting practices include accounting for substantially all investments in debt and equity securities at market value or fair value, with changes in value recognized in earnings (income) or in the change in net assets" (par. 4).
- Not-for-profit organizations. However, the Statement applies "to cooperatives and mutual enterprises, including credit unions and mutual insurance companies" (par. 4).
- "Investments in equity securities accounted for under the equity method nor to investments in consolidated subsidiaries" (par. 4). Consolidation and the equity method of accounting are discussed in Chapter 11 of this *Handbook*.
- Equity securities that do not have readily determinable fair values (e.g., restricted stock).

FASB Q&A No. 4 notes that "APB Opinion No. 18, *The Equity Method of Accounting for Investments in Common Stock*, describes the cost method and the equity method of accounting for investments in common stock and specifies the criteria for determining when to use the equity method. Equity securities that do not have readily determinable fair values that are not required to be accounted for by the equity method are typically carried at cost, as described in paragraph 6 of Opinion 18, adjusted for other-than-temporary impairment."

(b) INITIAL RECOGNITION AND MEASUREMENT   Upon acquisition, equity securities are generally recorded at cost, presumably fair value at acquisition, and classified into one of two categories: (1) available-for-sale or (2) trading. FASB Q&A No. 38 provides that the initial basis under Statement 115 of a marketable equity security that should no longer be accounted for under the equity method would be the previous carrying amount of the investment. The Q&A notes that "paragraph 19(1) of APB Opinion No. 18, *The Equity Method of Accounting for Investments in Common Stock*, states that the earnings or losses that relate to the stock retained should remain as a part of the carrying amount of the investment and that the investment account should not be adjusted retroactively."

(c) ACCOUNTING AFTER ACQUISITION   Gains and losses realized on the sale of equity securities are included in earnings and dividend income is recognized upon declaration. As previously discussed in the section, sale accounting is appropriate only for transfers of financial assets in which the transferor surrenders control over those financial assets pursuant to the provisions of Statement 140, paragraph 9. Otherwise, the transferor should account for the transfer as a secured borrowing with pledge of collateral pursuant to Statement 140, paragraph 15.

Equity securities are carried at fair value. As with debt securities, the accounting for the resulting unrealized gain or loss depends on the equity security's classification. Changes in the fair value of equity securities classified as trading are reflected in earnings while changes in the fair value of equity securities classified as available-for-sale are reflected in a separate component of shareholder's equity (or other comprehensive income), net of the related deferred income tax effects.

(d) IMPAIRMENT   Declines in fair value that are deemed to be "other than temporary" should be accounted for as realized losses, resulting in a new cost basis for the security. Impairment is discussed earlier. For equity securities with readily determinable market values, the impairment guidance in paragraph 16 of Statement 115 (see earlier section) should be followed. For investments in equity securities that are carried on the cost method, FSP FAS 115-1 and FAS 124-1 refers to Paragraph 6 of APB 18 for determining whether an impairment is other than temporary:

> a. THE COST METHOD. An investor records an investment in the stock of an investee at cost, and recognizes as income dividends received that are distributed from net accumulated earnings of the investee since the date of acquisition by the investor. The net accumulated earnings of an investee subsequent to the date of investment are recognized by the investor only to the extent distributed by the investee as dividends. Dividends received in excess of earnings subsequent to the date of investment are considered a return of investment and are recorded as reductions of cost of the investment. A series of operating losses of an investee or other factors may indicate that a decrease in value of the investment has occurred which is other than temporary and should accordingly be recognized. [Footnote 3a]
>
> Footnote 3a: FSP FAS 115-1 and FAS 124-1 discusses the methodology for determining impairment and evaluating whether the impairment is other than temporary.

Paragraph 10 of FSP FAS 115-1 and FAS 124-1 discusses the impairment considerations for cost-method investments for which the fair value is not readily determinable.

(e) TRANSFERS BETWEEN CATEGORIES   The transfer of equity securities between categories is accounted for in the same manner as the transfer of debt securities discussed earlier. Of course, transfers to or from the held-to-maturity category do not apply.

(f) DISCLOSURES   The references applicable to disclosure requirements are:

- Statement 105, paragraph 20
- Statement 115, paragraphs 19, 21–22
- FSP FAS 115-1 and FAS 124-1, paragraph 18

18.6   SOURCES AND SUGGESTED REFERENCES

American Institute of CPAs, "Accounting by Certain Entities (Including Entities with Trade Receivables) That Lend to or Finance the Activities of Others," Statement of Position 01-6, AICPA, New York.

American Institute of CPAs, "Accounting for Certain Purchased Loans or Debt Securities Acquired in a Transfer," Statement of Position 03-3, AICPA, New York.

American Institute of CPAs, "Disclosure of Certain Significant Risks and Uncertainties," Statement of Position 94-6, AICPA, New York.

Bort, Richard, *Corporate Cash Management Handbook*, Warren, Gorham & Lamont, Boston, 1989.

Committee on Accounting Procedure, "Restatement and Revision of Accounting Research Bulletins," Accounting Research Bulletin No. 43, AICPA, New York, 1953.

Financial Accounting Standards Board, "A Guide to Implementation of Statement 115 on Accounting for Certain Investments in Debt and Equity Securities," Special Report FASB, Norwalk, CT, 1995.

Financial Accounting Standards Board, "Accounting by Debtors and Creditors for Troubled Debt Restructurings," Statement of Financial Accounting Standards No. 15, FASB, Stamford, CT, 1977.

Financial Accounting Standards Board, "Accounting by Creditors for Impairment of a Loan," Statement of Financial Accounting Standards No. 114, FASB, Norwalk, CT, 1993.

Financial Accounting Standards Board, "Accounting by Creditors for Impairment of a Loan—Income Recognition and Disclosures," Statement of Financial Accounting Standards No. 118, FASB, Norwalk, CT, 1994.

Financial Accounting Standards Board, "Accounting for Certain Investments in Debt and Equity Securities," Statement of Financial Accounting Standards No. 115, FASB, Norwalk, CT, 1993.

Financial Accounting Standards Board, "Accounting for Changes That Result in a Transferor Regaining Control of Financial Assets Sold," EITF Issue No. 02-9, FASB, Norwalk, CT.

Financial Accounting Standards Board, "Accounting for Contingencies," Statement of Financial Accounting Standards No. 5, FASB, Stamford, CT, 1975.

Financial Accounting Standards Board, "Accounting for Conversion of a Loan into a Debt Security in a Debt Restructuring," EITF Issue No. 94-8, FASB, Norwalk, CT, 1997.

Financial Accounting Standards Board, "Accounting for Nonrefundable Fees and Costs Associated with Originating or Acquiring Loans and Initial Direct Costs of Leases," Statement of Financial Accounting Standards No. 91, FASB, Norwalk, CT.

Financial Accounting Standards Board, "Accounting for Transfers and Servicing of Financial Assets and Extinguishments of Liabilities," Statement of Financial Accounting Standards No. 140, FASB, Norwalk, CT, 2000.

Financial Accounting Standards Board, "Accounting for Transfers and Servicing of Financial Assets and Extinguishment of Liabilities," Statement of Financial Accounting Standards No. 140, FASB, Norwalk, CT, 2001.

Financial Accounting Standards Board, "Balance Sheet Treatment of a Sale of Mortgage Servicing Rights with a Subservicing Agreement," EITF Issue 90-21, FASB, Norwalk, CT.

Financial Accounting Standards Board, "Classifying Notes Received for Capital Stock," EITF Issue 85-1, FASB, Norwalk, CT.

Financial Accounting Standards Board, "Consolidation of All Majority-Owned Subsidiaries," Statement of Financial Accounting Standards No. 94, FASB, Stamford, CT, 1987.

Financial Accounting Standards Board, "Determination of What Risks and Rewards, If Any, Can Be Retained and Whether Any Unresolved Contingencies May Exist in a Sale of Mortgage Loan Servicing Rights," EITF Issue 95-5, FASB, Norwalk, CT.

Financial Accounting Standards Board, "Financial Reporting and Changing Prices," Statement of Financial Accounting Standards No. 89, FASB, Stamford, CT, 1986.

Financial Accounting Standards Board, "Foreign Currency Translation," Statement of Financial Accounting Standards No. 52, FASB, Stamford, CT, 1981.

Financial Accounting Standards Board, "Questions and Answers Related to Servicing Activities in a Qualifying Special-Purpose Entity under FASB Statement No. 140," Topic D-99, FASB, Norwalk, CT.

Financial Accounting Standards Board, "Questions Related to the Implementation of FASB Statement No. 115," EITF Topic No. D-39, FASB, Norwalk, CT.

Financial Accounting Standards Board, "Recognition of Interest Income and Impairment on Purchased and Retained Beneficial Interests in Securitized Financial Assets," EITF Issue No. 99-20, FASB, Norwalk, CT.

Financial Accounting Standards Board, "Reporting Comprehensive Income," Statement of Financial Accounting Standards No. 130, FASB, Norwalk, CT, 1997.

Financial Accounting Standards Board, "Terms of Loan Products That May Give Rise to a Concentration of Credit Risk," FASB Staff Position-SOP 94-6-1.

Financial Accounting Standards Board, "The Applicability of FASB Statement No. 115 to Desecuritizations of Financial Assets," EITF Topic No. D-51, FASB, Norwalk, CT.

Financial Accounting Standards Board, "The Meaning of Other-Than-Temporary Impairment and Its Application to Certain Investments," EITF Issue 03-1, FASB, Norwalk, CT.

Keiso, Donald E., Weygandt, Jerry D., and Warfield, Terry D., *Intermediate Accounting, Twelfth Edition,* John Wiley & Sons, Hoboken, NJ, 2006.

Meigs, Walter B., Larsen, E. John, and Meigs, Robert F., *Principles of Auditing, Ninth Edition,* Irwin, Homewood, IL, 1988.

O'Reilly, Vincent M., McDonnell, Patrick J., Winograd, Barry N., Gerson, James, S., and Jaenicke, Henry R., *Montgomery's Auditing, Twelfth Edition,* John Wiley & Sons, New York, 1998.

Securities and Exchange Commission, "Notice of Adoption of Amendments to Regulation S-X and Related Interpretations and Guidelines Regarding Disclosure of Compensating Balances and Short-Term Borrowing Arrangements," Accounting Series Release No. 148, SEC, Washington, DC, November 1973.

Smith, Jay M., Jr., and Skousen, K. Fred, *Intermediate Accounting, Tenth Edition,* South-Western Publishing, Cincinnati, OH, 1990.

TRANSFERS OF FINANCIAL ASSETS (NEW)

MICHAEL A. ANTONETTI, CPA, CMA
Crowe Horwath LLP†

---

† The information contained in this chapter does not necessarily represent the views of Crowe Horwath LLP.

18A.1   INTRODUCTION

Transfers of financial assets take many forms. Accounting for transfers in which the transferor has no continuing involvement with the transferred assets or with the transferee has not been controversial. However, transfers of financial assets often occur in which the transferor has some continuing involvement either with the assets transferred or with the transferee. Examples of continuing involvement are recourse, servicing, agreements to reacquire, options written or held, and pledges of collateral. Transfers of financial assets with continuing involvement raise issues about the circumstances under which the transfers should be considered as sales of all or part of the assets or as secured borrowings and about how transferors and transferees should account for sales and secured borrowings.[1] During September 2000, the Financial Accounting Standards Board (FASB) issued Statement No. 140, *Accounting for Transfers and Servicing of Financial Assets and Extinguishments of Liabilities—A Replacement of FASB Statement 125*, to address the accounting for transfers of financial assets.

As discussed later in this chapter, Statement 140 provides accounting and reporting standards for transfers and servicing of financial assets and extinguishment of liabilities. Those standards are based on consistent application of a financial-components approach that focuses on control. Under that approach, after a transfer of financial assets, an entity recognizes the financial and servicing assets it controls and the liabilities it has incurred, derecognizes financial assets when control has been surrendered, and derecognizes liabilities when extinguished. Statement 140 provides consistent standards for distinguishing transfers of financial assets that are sales from transfers that are secured borrowings.[2] Statement 140 was effective for most transfers and servicing of financial assets and extinguishments of liabilities occurring after March 31, 2001.

In recent years, additional guidance has been issued to clarify or amend some of the provisions contained within Statement 140, such as the following:

- FASB Statement No. 155, *Accounting for Certain Hybrid Financial Instruments—An Amendment of FASB Statements No. 133 and 140*, issued in February 2006 and effective for all financial instruments acquired or issued after the beginning of an entity's first fiscal year that begins after September 15, 2006
- FASB Statement No. 156, *Accounting for Servicing of Financial Assets—An Amendment of FASB Statement No. 140*, issued in March 2006 and effective as of the beginning of an entity's first fiscal year that begins after September 15, 2006
- FASB Statement No. 157, *Fair Value Measurements*, issued in September 2006 and effective for financial statements issued for fiscal years beginning after November 15, 2007, and interim periods within those fiscal years
- FASB Staff Position No. 140-1, *Accounting for Accrued Interest Receivable Related to Securitized and Sold Receivables under Statement 140*, issued on April 14, 2003, and effective for fiscal quarters beginning after March 31, 2003
- FASB Staff Position No. 140-2, *Clarification of the Application of Paragraphs 40(b) and 40(c) of FASB Statement No. 140*, issued on November 9, 2005, and effective immediately

---

1. FASB Statement No. 140, *Accounting for Transfers and Servicing of Financial Assets and Extinguishments of Liabilities—A Replacement of FASB Statement 125*, September 2000 (from Summary page).
2. Statement 140 (from Summary page).

- FASB Staff Position No. 140-3, *Accounting for Transfers of Financial Assets and Repurchase Financing Transactions*, issued on February 20, 2008, and effective for financial statements issued for fiscal years beginning after November 15, 2008 and interim periods within those fiscal years

The information contained within this chapter includes the effects of the additional guidance that has amended Statement 140.

18A.2   WHAT ARE FINANCIAL ASSETS?

Statement 140 defines a **financial asset** as "cash, evidence of an ownership interest in an entity, or a contract that conveys to [one] entity a right (a) to receive cash or another financial instrument from a [second] entity or (b) to exchange other financial instruments on potentially favorable terms with the [second] entity."[3] Some common financial assets include trade receivables, credit card receivables, residential mortgage receivables, government bonds, and corporate bonds. Transfers of financial assets are discussed later in this chapter.

18A.3   WHAT ARE BENEFICIAL INTERESTS?

As discussed further later in this chapter, many financial asset transfers utilize a qualifying special-purpose entity. A qualifying special-purpose entity issues to third parties interests in the cash flows generated by the financial assets that it holds. These interests are often referred to as *beneficial interests*. Statement 140 defines **beneficial interests** as "rights to receive all or portions of specified cash inflows to a trust or other entity, including senior and subordinated shares of interest, principal, or other cash inflows to be 'passed-through' or 'paid-through,' premiums due to guarantors, commercial paper obligations, and residual interests, whether in the form of debt or equity."[4] Common investors in beneficial interests include banks, insurance companies, brokers and dealers, hedge funds, and pension funds.

18A.4   WHAT IS A FINANCIAL ASSET TRANSFER?

Statement 140 defines a **transfer** as "the conveyance of a noncash financial asset by and to someone other than the issuer of that financial asset. Thus, a transfer includes selling a receivable, putting it into a securitization trust, or posting it as collateral but excludes the origination of that receivable, the settlement of that receivable, or the restructuring of that receivable into a security in a troubled debt restructuring."[5] A **transferor** is "an entity that transfers a financial asset, a portion of a financial asset, or a group of financial assets that it controls to another entity,"[6] while a **transferee** is "an entity that receives a financial asset, a portion of a financial asset, or a group of financial assets from a transferor."[7]

Companies wish to transfer and derecognize financial assets for a variety of reasons. Most importantly, a transfer of financial assets improves a company's liquidity. Other benefits from

---

3.   Statement 140 (Appendix E).
4.   Id.
5.   Id.
6.   Id.
7.   Id.

transferring financial assets include improved balance sheet ratios, increased return on assets and equity, and an ability to manage interest rate and credit risks.

18A.5   WHAT ARE THE CONTROL CRITERIA THAT MUST BE MET FOR A TRANSFER OF FINANCIAL ASSETS TO BE RECORDED AS A SALE?

Paragraph 9 of Statement 140 states,

A transfer of financial assets (or all or a portion of a financial asset) in which the transferor surrenders control over those financial assets shall be accounted for as a sale to the extent that consideration other than beneficial interests in the transferred assets is received in exchange. The transferor has surrendered control over transferred assets if and only if *all of the following conditions* are met:

a. The transferred assets have been isolated from the transferor—put presumptively beyond the reach of the transferor and its creditors, even in bankruptcy or other receivership.

b. Each transferee (or if the transferee is a qualifying special purpose entity, each holder of its beneficial interests) has the right to pledge or exchange the assets (or beneficial interests) it received, and no condition both constrains the transferee (or holder) from taking advantage of its right to pledge or exchange and provides more than a trivial benefit to the transferor.

c. The transferor does not maintain effective control over the transferred assets through either (1) an agreement that both entitles and obligates the transferor to repurchase or redeem them before their maturity or (2) the ability to unilaterally cause the holder to return specific assets, other than through a cleanup call.[8]

If the transferor maintains control of the financial assets after the transfer, then the transfer is considered a secured borrowing arrangement.

In recent years, many mortgage stakeholders such as banks and government-sponsored entities have had to restate their financial statements. Often, one company will discover an accounting issue related to Statement 140 and, when the details become public, another company will find that they, too, have the same issue. Below are excerpts from restatements discussed in annual reports on Form 10-K as filed with the Securities and Exchange Commission:

Doral Financial Corporation Annual Report on Form 10-K/A for the year ended December 31, 2004 as filed with the SEC on February 27, 2006:

In October 2005, new information came to the attention of the Audit Committee regarding the possible existence of certain recourse provisions in the Company's mortgage loan sales to local financial institutions that were not captured by the Company's financial reporting process. The Audit Committee promptly asked Latham to investigate this issue. On December 14, 2005, Latham informed the Audit Committee that, based on its investigation, it is likely that there were oral agreements or understandings between the former treasurer and the former director emeritus of the Company and FirstBank Puerto Rico, a wholly owned banking

---

8.   Statement 140 (paragraph 9).

subsidiary of First BanCorp ("FirstBank"), providing recourse beyond the limited recourse established in the written contracts. Based on an analysis of these findings and other evidence reviewed by the Company, the Company concluded that the mortgage loan sales to FirstBank did not qualify as sales under Statement of Financial Accounting Standard ("SFAS") 140, "Accounting for Transfers and Servicing of Financial Assets and Extinguishments of Liabilities" ("SFAS 140"), because these sales did not satisfy the "reasonable assurance" standard of SFAS 140 regarding the isolation of assets in bankruptcy. In addition, the former treasurer entered into side letters guaranteeing the yield to an investor in connection with certain sales of IOs. Neither the oral recourse agreements or understandings nor the side letters were captured by the Company's financial reporting process or communicated to the Audit Committee, PwC or the Company's internal and external counsel. This resulted in the misapplication of generally accepted accounting principles in the United States of America ("GAAP") to several transactions and had a material impact on the Company's consolidated financial statements.

In addition, on December 14, 2005, based on the results of the independent investigation, the Audit Committee concluded that it was necessary to reverse a number of transactions, including a transaction occurring during the fourth quarter of 2004, involving generally contemporaneous purchases and sales of mortgage loans from and to local financial institutions where the amounts purchased and sold, and other terms of the transactions, were similar. The decision followed a determination that there was insufficient contemporaneous documentation to substantiate the business purpose for these transactions in light of the timing and similarity of the purchase and sale amounts and other terms of the transactions. For some periods, the gains on sale previously recorded in connection with such transactions had a material impact on the Company's consolidated financial statements.

Bluegreen Corp. Annual Report on Form 10-K for the year ended December 31, 2005 as filed with the SEC on March 16, 2006:

In connection with the securitization of certain of its receivables in December 2005, the Company undertook a review of the prior accounting treatment for certain of its existing and prior notes receivable purchase facilities (together the "Purchase Facilities"). As a result of that review, on December 15, 2005, the Company determined that it would restate its consolidated financial statements for the first three quarters of fiscal 2005 and the fiscal years ended December 31, 2003 and 2004 due to certain misapplications of GAAP in the accounting for sales of the Company's vacation ownership notes receivable and other related matters. The following sections describe the restatement matters in more detail.

The restatement reflects the sales of notes receivable under three separate Purchase Facilities as on-balance-sheet financing transactions as opposed to off-balance-sheet sales transactions as the Company had originally accounted for these transactions pursuant to Statement of Financial Accounting Standards No. 140, "Accounting for Transfers and Servicing of Financial Assets and Extinguishments of Liabilities" ("SFAS 140"). Accordingly, the consolidated financial statements have been restated to (1) remove the gain on sale of notes receivable and retained interest in notes receivable sold previously recognized, (2) re-recognize the original notes receivable sold and the related interest income for the periods outstanding, (3) and recognize debt for the cash proceeds received from the Purchase Facilities and the related interest expense for the periods outstanding.

The Company consummated two term securitization transactions, one in December 2002 and one in July 2004, which included substantially all of the notes receivable that had been previously accounted for as having been sold under the Purchase Facilities. Both of these term securitization transactions have been accounted for as sales pursuant to SFAS 140, and therefore the notes receivable financed under the Purchase Facilities are considered to be sold in the term securitization transactions, with resulting gains on sale recognized at that time.

In connection with the sales of notes receivable, we retain servicing rights. Receivables servicing includes processing payments from borrowers, accounting for principal and interest on such receivables, making advances when required, performing collections efforts with delinquent borrowers, processing defaults, reporting to investors and lenders on portfolio activity, and performing other administrative duties. During the review of our accounting policies related to the sales of notes receivables, the Company determined that the servicing fees earned for servicing the sold notes receivable reflected fair value (i.e., adequate compensation) at the time of the transaction. Pursuant to SFAS 140, a servicing asset exists when the benefits of servicing are more than adequate compensation. Accordingly, the consolidated financial statements have been restated to remove the original values recognized as servicing assets as well as the related servicing asset amortization expense.

Also, as a part of its re-evaluation of these transactions, the Company determined that the computation of the gains on sales of receivables in the December 2002 and July 2004 term securitization transactions did not take into account the fair value allocation of financial components methodology for recording its retained interest as prescribed by SFAS 140. The impact of the fair value allocation of financial components methodology is to reduce the gain on sale, but once the retained interest is marked to market value immediately thereafter, the impact will be to increase other comprehensive income in the balance sheet.

As part of the restatement, the company recorded, as of the beginning of fiscal 2004, a cumulative charge of $7.8 million to retained earnings and a $4.0 million increase to beginning other comprehensive income reflecting the impact of the change in accounting for the above mentioned transactions originating in prior periods. Also, the restatement resulted in a reduction of net income of $6.0 million for fiscal 2003 and an increase of $6.1 million for fiscal 2004.

(a) THE TRANSFERRED ASSETS HAVE BEEN ISOLATED FROM THE TRANSFEROR

Generally, a transfer of financial assets directly to third parties with no continuing involvement by the transferor will qualify for sale accounting provided the other Statement 140 criteria are met; however, a transfer can still qualify for sale accounting even though the transferor may have some continuing involvement (e.g., providing recourse for credit risk, servicing the financial assets, etc.) with the financial assets. Sale accounting is not based on whether the transferor has continuing involvement with the financial assets, but rather whether the transferor has given up effective control of the financial assets to the transferee. See the discussion later regarding the use of qualifying special-purpose entities to legally isolate the financial assets from the transferor.

(b) EACH TRANSFEREE HAS THE RIGHT TO PLEDGE OR EXCHANGE THE ASSETS IT RECEIVED
"Sale accounting is allowed . . . only if each transferee has the right to pledge, or the right to exchange, the transferred assets or beneficial interests it received, but constraints on that right also matter. Many transferor-imposed or other conditions on a transferee's right to pledge or exchange a transferred asset both constrain a transferee from pledging or exchanging the transferred assets and, through that constraint, provide more than a trivial benefit to the transferor."[9] Some conditions that constrain a transferee's ability to control a financial asset include (1) a transferor prohibiting a subsequent sale of the financial assets by the transferee, (2) a call option held by the transferor on the financial assets, and (3) other transferor-imposed terms that limit a transferee's ability to exchange, sell, or pledge the financial assets. Generally, most restrictions imposed by a transferor would prevent sale accounting because they would be deemed to provide "more than a trivial benefit" to the transferor.

"Some conditions do not constrain a transferee from pledging or exchanging the asset and therefore do not preclude a transfer subject to such a condition from being accounted for as a sale. For example, a transferor's right of first refusal on the occurrence of a bona fide offer to the transferee from a third party presumptively would not constrain a transferee, because that right in itself does not enable the transferor to compel the transferee to sell the assets and the transferee would be in a position to receive the sum offered by exchanging the asset, albeit possibly from the transferor rather than the third party."[10]

(c) THE TRANSFEROR DOES NOT MAINTAIN EFFECTIVE CONTROL OVER THE TRANSFERRED ASSETS THROUGH EITHER A REPURCHASE AGREEMENT OR THE ABILITY TO UNILATERALLY CAUSE THE HOLDER TO RETURN SPECIFIC ASSETS
Financial asset transfers that include a right for the transferor to repurchase, redeem, or require the transferee to return the financial assets to the transferor prior to maturity would not qualify for sale accounting because the transferor never gave up effective control of the financial assets. Whether or not a transferor exercises one of these rights is irrelevant in the determination of sale accounting. The mere existence of these rights creates effective control over the transferred financial assets. As such, the transferor would have to account for the transfer as a secured borrowing.

If the transferor's right to reclaim transferred assets is contingent on an event that is outside of the transferor's control, then this right would not preclude sale accounting as long as the other conditions within paragraph 9 of Statement 140 are met. If such an outside event were to occur, then the transferor would have to again recognize the transferred financial assets as it would once again have effective control.

As noted within paragraph 9 of Statement 140, a cleanup call does not preclude sale accounting. Statement 140 defines a *cleanup call* as "an option held by the servicer or its affiliate, which may be the transferor, to purchase the remaining transferred financial assets, or the remaining beneficial interests not held by the transferor, its affiliates, or its agents in a qualifying SPE [special-purpose entity] (or in a series of beneficial interests in transferred assets within a qualifying SPE), if the amount of outstanding assets or beneficial interests falls

---

9.   Statement 140 (paragraph 29).
10.   Statement 140 (paragraph 30).

to a level at which the cost of servicing those assets or beneficial interests becomes burdensome in relation to the benefits of servicing."[11]

The right of a servicer, which may also be the transferor, to initiate a cleanup call would not cause the servicer to maintain effective control over the transferred assets, provided the servicer may only call a *de minimis* level of outstanding financial assets or beneficial interests.

18A.6 WHAT IS A QUALIFYING SPECIAL-PURPOSE ENTITY?

Many companies create *special-purpose entities* to facilitate the sale accounting treatment for a transfer of financial assets because such entities help isolate the financial assets from the transferor and its creditors. Paragraph 35 of Statement 140 describes the conditions under which a company may transfer financial assets to a trust or other legal vehicle that is deemed to be a qualifying special-purpose entity (SPE). A qualifying SPE is significantly limited in the activities it may perform, the types of assets it may own, and the situations in which it may dispose of assets. If a transfer of financial assets to a qualifying SPE meets the sale criteria specified in paragraph 9 of Statement 140, then the qualifying SPE does not have to be consolidated by the transferor.

Paragraph 35 of Statement 140 states,

> A qualifying SPE is a trust or other legal vehicle that meets *all* of the following conditions:
>
> **a.** It is demonstrably distinct from the transferor.
> **b.** Its permitted activities (1) are significantly limited, (2) were entirely specified in the legal documents that established the SPE or created the beneficial interests in the transferred assets that it holds, and (3) may be significantly changed only with the approval of the holders of at least a majority of the beneficial interests held by entities other than any transferor, its affiliates, and its agents.
> **c.** It may hold only:
>
> > **(i)**   Financial assets transferred to it that are passive in nature
> > **(ii)** Passive derivative financial instruments that pertain to beneficial interests issued or sold to parties other than the transferor, its affiliates, or its agents
> > **(iii)** Financial assets (for example, guarantees or rights to collateral) that would reimburse it if others were to fail to adequately service financial assets transferred to it or to timely pay obligations due to it and that it entered into when it was established, when assets were transferred to it, or when beneficial interests (other than derivative financial instruments) were issued by the SPE
> > **(iv)** Servicing rights related to financial assets that it holds
> > **(v)**   Temporarily, nonfinancial assets obtained in connection with the collection of financial assets that it holds
> > **(vi)** Cash collected from assets that it holds and investments purchased with that cash pending distribution to holders of beneficial interests that are appropriate for that purpose (that is, money-market or other relatively risk-free instruments without options and with maturities no later than the expected distribution date).

---

11.   Statement 140 (Appendix E).

d. If it can sell or otherwise dispose of noncash financial assets, it can do so only in automatic response to one of the following conditions:

   (i) Occurrence of an event or circumstance that (a) is specified in the legal documents that established the SPE or created the beneficial interests in the transferred assets that it holds; (b) is outside the control of the transferor, its affiliates, or its agents; and (c) causes, or is expected at the date of transfer to cause, the fair value of those financial assets to decline by a specified degree below the fair value of those assets when the SPE obtained them

   (ii) Exercise by a BIH ("beneficial interest holder") (other than the transferor, its affiliates, or its agents) of a right to put that holder's beneficial interest back to the SPE

   (iii) Exercise by the transferor of a call or ROAP ("removal-of-accounts provision") specified in the legal documents that established the SPE, transferred assets to the SPE, or created the beneficial interests in the transferred assets that it holds

   (iv) Termination of the SPE or maturity of the beneficial interests in those financial assets on a fixed or determinable date that is specified at inception

(a) IT IS DEMONSTRABLY DISTINCT FROM THE TRANSFEROR   A qualifying SPE is demonstrably distinct from the transferor only if it cannot be unilaterally dissolved by any transferor, its affiliates, or its agents and either (1) at least 10 percent of the fair value of its beneficial interests is held by parties other than any transferor, its affiliates, or its agents or (2) the transfer is a guaranteed mortgage securitization.[12] If a transferor retains more than 90 percent of the fair value of beneficial interests of the qualifying SPE, the transferor is deemed to have control of the transferred financial assets and, therefore, sale accounting would be precluded. "An ability to unilaterally dissolve an SPE can take many forms, including but not limited to holding sufficient beneficial interests to demand that the trustee dissolve the SPE, the right to call all the assets transferred to the SPE, and a right to call or a prepayment privilege on the beneficial interests held by other parties."[13]

A guaranteed mortgage securitization is a securitization of a mortgage loan that includes a substantive guarantee by a third party. Guaranteed mortgage securitizations are exempt from the 10 percent holding threshold described above. Mortgage-backed securities that continue to be held by a transferor in a guaranteed mortgage securitization in which the SPE meets all conditions for being a qualifying SPE are classified in the financial statements of the transferor as securities that are subsequently measured under FASB Statement No. 115, *Accounting for Certain Investments in Debt and Equity Securities.*

(b) ITS PERMITTED ACTIVITIES ARE SIGNIFICANTLY LIMITED, WERE ENTIRELY SPECIFIED IN THE LEGAL DOCUMENTS THAT CREATED IT, AND MAY BE SIGNIFICANTLY CHANGED ONLY WITH THE APPROVAL OF A MAJORITY OF THE HOLDERS OTHER THAN THE TRANSFEROR   The powers of the SPE must be limited to those activities allowed by paragraph 35 of Statement 140 for it to be a qualifying SPE. In addition, the qualifying SPE's activities must be entirely specified in the legal documents that created it.

---

12.   Statement 140 (paragraph 36).
13.   Id.

The beneficial interest holders other than any transferor, its affiliates, or its agents may have the ability to change the powers of a qualifying SPE (QSPE). If a QSPE's activities change such that it no longer meets the conditions specified in paragraph 35 of Statement 140, then the QSPE would lose its qualifying status and the transferred financial assets would no longer qualify for sale accounting. In these instances, paragraph 55 of Statement 140 requires the transferor to re-recognize the transferred assets on the date in which the QSPE became disqualified. The transferor initially measures the financial assets and any liabilities at fair value on the date of the change, as if the transferor purchased the assets and assumed the liabilities on that date.

(c) IT MAY HOLD PASSIVE FINANCIAL INSTRUMENTS   A qualifying SPE may hold passive financial instruments, including passive derivative financial instruments. Financial instruments are passive only if holding the instrument does not involve its holder in making decisions other than the decisions inherent in servicing.

Typical passive financial instruments transferred to a QSPE include residential mortgage loans, credit card receivables, and trade receivables. A QSPE can only hold financial assets that were transferred to it by the transferor. A QSPE cannot create financial assets, such as loans, nor can it actively purchase financial assets or manage an asset portfolio.

(d) IT MAY SELL OR DISPOSE OF NONCASH FINANCIAL ASSETS ONLY IN RESPONSE TO CERTAIN CONDITIONS   If a sale of assets from a qualifying SPE occurs, it must be an automatic response to one of the conditions described in paragraph 35(d) of Statement 140. The QSPE cannot have discretion to choose which assets to be disposed of or when the disposal may occur because such discretion would make the SPE an active rather than a passive entity and, thereby, jeopardize its qualifying status.

Examples of requirements to sell, exchange, put, or distribute (hereinafter referred to collectively as *dispose of*) noncash financial assets that *are* **permitted** activities of a QSPE include requirements to dispose of transferred assets in response to:

1.   A failure to properly service transferred assets that could result in the loss of a substantial third-party credit guarantee
2.   A default by the obligor
3.   A downgrade by a major rating agency of the transferred assets or of the underlying obligor to a rating below a specified minimum rating
4.   The involuntary insolvency of the transferor
5.   A decline in the fair value of the transferred assets to a specified value less than their fair value at the time they were transferred to the SPE

The following are examples of powers or requirements to dispose of noncash financial assets that *are not* **permitted** activities of a QSPE, because they do not respond automatically to the occurrence of a specified event or circumstance outside the control of the transferor, its affiliates, or its agents that causes, or is expected to cause, the fair value of those transferred assets to decline by a specified degree below the fair value of those assets when the SPE obtained them:

1.   A power that allows an SPE to choose to either dispose of transferred assets or hold them in response to a default, a downgrade, a decline in fair value, or a servicing failure

2. A requirement to dispose of marketable equity securities upon a specified decline from their "highest fair value" if that power could result in disposing of the asset in exchange for an amount that is more than the fair value of those assets at the time they were transferred to the SPE

3. A requirement to dispose of transferred assets in response to the violation of a non-substantive contractual provision (i.e., a provision for which there is not a sufficiently large disincentive to ensure performance)[14]

18A.7   WHAT ARE SECURITIZATIONS?

Securitization is "the process by which financial assets are transformed into securities."[15] "Financial assets such as mortgage loans, automobile loans, trade receivables, credit card receivables, and other revolving charge accounts are assets commonly transferred in securitizations."[16]

Securitization often begins with the creation of a legal entity (e.g., a corporation or trust) to own the portfolio of financial assets. The legal entity's capital structure (used to fund the purchase of the portfolio) is designed in ways to attract investors to the repackaged cash flows. Credit enhancement (e.g., a guarantee by the transferor or a third party) is added and the resulting securities often are rated by a third-party rating agency (e.g., Moody's). Proceeds from the sale of the resulting securities are used to acquire the portfolio of financial assets. The transferor may continue in the role of servicer, collecting and remitting payments from obligors on the transferred assets, or may have other continuing involvement with the transaction.

"A securitization carried out in one transfer or a series of transfers may or may not isolate the transferred assets beyond the reach of the transferor and its creditors. Whether it does depends on the structure of the securitization transaction taken as a whole, considering such factors as the type and extent of further involvement in arrangements to protect investors from credit and interest rate risks, the availability of other assets, and the powers of bankruptcy courts or other receivers."[17] Securitizations that meet the criteria in paragraph 9 of Statement 140 qualify for sale accounting.

Many securitizations use two transfers intended to isolate transferred assets beyond the reach of the transferor and its creditors, even in bankruptcy. In those "two-step" structures:

1. The corporation transfers financial assets to a special-purpose corporation that, although wholly owned, is so designed that the possibility that the transferor or its creditors could reclaim the assets is remote. This first transfer is designed to be judged to be a true sale at law, in part because the transferor does not provide "excessive" credit or yield protection to the special-purpose corporation. Additionally, the transferred assets are likely to be judged beyond the reach of the transferor or the transferor's creditors even in bankruptcy.

2. The special-purpose corporation transfers the assets to a trust or other legal vehicle with a sufficient increase in the credit or yield protection on the second transfer (provided by a junior beneficial interest that continues to be held by the transferor or other means) to merit the high credit rating sought by third-party investors who

---

14.   Statement 140 (paragraphs 42–43).
15.   Statement 140 (Appendix E).
16.   Statement 140 (paragraph 73).
17.   Statement 140 (paragraph 80).

buy senior beneficial interests in the trust. Because of that aspect of its design, that second transfer might not be judged to be a true sale at law and, thus, the transferred assets could at least in theory be reached by a bankruptcy trustee for the special-purpose corporation.

However, the special-purpose corporation is designed to make remote the possibility that it would enter bankruptcy, either by itself or by substantive consolidation into a bankruptcy of its parent, should that occur. For example, its charter forbids it from undertaking any other business or incurring any liabilities, so that there can be no creditors to petition to place it in bankruptcy. Furthermore, its dedication to a single purpose is intended to make it extremely unlikely, even if it somehow entered bankruptcy, that a receiver under the U.S. Bankruptcy Code could reclaim the transferred assets because it has no other assets to substitute for the transferred assets.[18]

18A.8   WHAT IS A REMOVAL-OF-ACCOUNTS PROVISION IN A SECURITIZATION?[19]

Many transfers of financial assets in securitizations empower the transferor to reclaim assets subject to certain restrictions. Such a power is sometimes called a *removal-of-accounts provision* (ROAP). Whether a ROAP precludes sale accounting depends on whether the ROAP results in the transferor's maintaining effective control over specific transferred assets.

The following are examples of ROAPs that preclude transfers from being accounted for as sales:

1.   An unconditional ROAP or repurchase agreement that allows the transferor to specify the assets that may be removed, because such a provision allows the transferor unilaterally to remove specific assets

2.   A ROAP conditioned on a transferor's decision to exit some portion of its business, because whether it can be triggered by canceling an affinity relationship, spinning off a business segment, or accepting a third party's bid to purchase a specified (e.g., geographic) portion of the transferor's business, such a provision allows the transferor unilaterally to remove specific assets

The following are examples of ROAPs that *do not* preclude transfers from being accounted for as sales:

1.   A ROAP for random removal of excess assets, if the ROAP is sufficiently limited so that the transferor cannot remove specific transferred assets, for example, by limiting removals to the amount of the interests that continue to be held by the transferor and to one removal per month

2.   A ROAP for defaulted receivables, because the removal would be allowed only after a third party's action (default) and could not be caused unilaterally by the transferor

3.   A ROAP conditioned on a third-party cancellation, or expiration without renewal, of an affinity or private-label arrangement, because the removal would be allowed only after a third party's action (cancellation) or decision not to act (expiration) and could not be caused unilaterally by the transferor

---

18.   Statement 140 (paragraph 83).
19.   Section taken from Statement 140 (paragraphs 85–88).

A ROAP that can be exercised only in response to a third party's action that has not yet occurred does not maintain the transferor's effective control over assets potentially subject to that ROAP. However, when a third party's action (such as default or cancellation) or decision not to act (expiration) occurs that allows removal of assets to be initiated solely by the transferor, the transferor must recognize any assets subject to the ROAP, whether the ROAP is exercised or not. If the ROAP is exercised, the assets are recognized because the transferor has reclaimed the assets. If the ROAP is not exercised, the assets are recognized because the transferor now can unilaterally cause the qualifying SPE to return those specific assets and, therefore, the transferor once again has effective control over those transferred assets.

18A.9 HOW SHOULD A TRANSFEROR ACCOUNT FOR A TRANSFER OF FINANCIAL ASSETS THAT QUALIFIES FOR SALE ACCOUNTING?

Paragraphs 10 and 11 of Statement 140 (as amended by Statement 157) summarize the accounting that a transferor must follow related to a sale of financial assets.

Upon completion of any transfer of financial assets, the transferor shall:

- Initially recognize and measure at fair value, if practicable, servicing assets and servicing liabilities that require recognition under the provisions of paragraph 13 of Statement 140 (discussed further below).
- Allocate the previous carrying amount between the assets sold, if any, and the interests that continue to be held by the transferor, if any, based on their relative fair values at the date of transfer.
- Continue to carry in its statement of financial position any interest it continues to hold in the transferred assets, including, if applicable, beneficial interest in assets transferred to a qualifying SPE in a securitization, and any undivided interests.

Upon completion of a transfer of financial assets that satisfies the conditions to be accounted for as a sale, the transferor (seller) shall:

- Derecognize all assets sold.
- Recognize all assets obtained and liabilities incurred in consideration as proceeds of the sale, including cash, put or call options held or written (e.g., guarantee or recourse obligations), forward commitments (e.g., commitments to deliver additional receivables during the revolving periods of some securitizations), swaps (e.g., provisions that convert interest rates from fixed to variable), and servicing assets and servicing liabilities, if applicable.
- Initially measure at fair value assets obtained and liabilities incurred in a sale or, if it is not practicable to estimate the fair value of an asset or a liability, apply alternative measures.
- Recognize in earnings any gain or loss on the sale.

A gain or loss on the transfer of financial assets is calculated as the difference between the net proceeds received from the sale and the carrying value of the assets transferred. Paragraph 56 of Statement 140 states,

> The proceeds from a sale of financial assets consist of the cash and any other assets obtained, including separately recognized servicing assets, in the transfer less any liabilities incurred, including separately recognized servicing liabilities. Any asset obtained that is not an interest in the transferred asset is part of the proceeds from the

sale. Any liability incurred, even if it is related to the transferred assets, is a reduction of the proceeds. Any derivative financial instrument entered into concurrently with a transfer of financial assets is either an asset obtained or a liability incurred and part of the proceeds received in the transfer. All proceeds and reductions of proceeds from a sale shall be initially measured at fair value, if practicable.

For transfers of financial assets recorded as sales, the transferee should recognize all assets obtained and any liabilities incurred and initially measure them at fair value.

"If a transfer of financial assets in exchange for cash or other consideration (other than beneficial interests in the transferred assets) does not meet the criteria for a sale in paragraph 9, the transferor and transferee shall account for the transfer as a secured borrowing with pledge of collateral."[20] See below for further discussion regarding secured borrowings.

18A.10 HOW SHOULD A TRANSFEROR SUBSEQUENTLY ACCOUNT FOR FINANCIAL INSTRUMENTS OBTAINED OR CREATED AS PART OF A SALE OF FINANCIAL ASSETS?

Statement 140 does not address how assets and liabilities should be accounted for subsequent to a sale transaction. Those assets and liabilities should be accounted for using the accounting guidance that would otherwise be applicable, regardless of the method of acquisition. For instance, derivatives and forward sales agreements should be accounted for in accordance with SFAS 133, *Accounting for Derivative Instruments and Hedging Activities.*

Statement 156 was issued in March 2006 and amended Statement 140 with respect to the accounting for separately recognized servicing assets and servicing liabilities. See below for further discussion regarding the accounting for servicing rights.

18A.11 HOW SHOULD A TRANSFEROR ACCOUNT FOR THE RE-RECOGNITION OF PREVIOUSLY SOLD ASSETS?

Certain events may occur that result in a transferor reacquiring control of previously derecognized financial assets. For instance, a QSPE might lose its qualifying status if at least 90 percent of the fair value of the beneficial interests issued by the QSPE is no longer held by third parties. Paragraph 55 of Statement 140 states,

A change in law, status of the transferee as a qualifying SPE, or other circumstance may result in the transferor's regaining control of assets previously accounted for appropriately as having been sold, because one or more of the conditions in paragraph 9 are no longer met. Such a change, unless it arises solely from either the initial application of this Statement or a change in market prices (for example, an increase in price that moves into-the-money a freestanding call that was originally sufficiently out-of-the money that it was judged not to constrain the transferee), is accounted for in the same manner as a purchase of the assets from the former transferee(s) in exchange for liabilities assumed (paragraph 11). After that change, the transferor recognizes in its financial statements those assets together with liabilities to the former transferee(s) or beneficial interest holders (BIHs) in those assets (paragraph 38). The transferor initially

---

20. Statement 140 (paragraph 12).

measures those assets and liabilities at fair value on the date of the change, as if the transferor purchased the assets and assumed the liabilities on that date. The former transferee would derecognize the assets on that date, as if it had sold the assets in exchange for a receivable from the transferor.

(a) EXAMPLE OF FINANCIAL ASSET TRANSFER RECORDED AS A SALE   The following example illustrates the accounting for a financial asset transfer recorded as a sale that includes cash proceeds, derivatives, and other liabilities.

(i) Facts[21]   Company A sells loans with a fair value of $1,100 and a carrying amount of $1,000. Company A undertakes no servicing responsibilities but obtains an option to purchase from the transferee loans similar to the loans sold (which are readily obtainable in the

Fair Values		
Cash proceeds	$1,050	
Interest rate swap	40	
Call option	70	
Recourse obligation	60	
Net Proceeds		
Cash received	$1,050	
Plus: Call option	70	
Plus: Interest rate swap	40	
Less: Recourse obligation	(60)	
Net proceeds	$1,100	
Gain on Sale		
Net proceeds	$1,100	
Carrying amount of loans sold	1,000	
Gain on sale	$ 100	
Journal Entry to Record Transfer		
Cash	$1,050	
Interest rate swap	40	
Call option	70	
Loans		$1,000
Recourse obligation		60
Gain on sale		100

---

21.   Example taken from Statement 140 (paragraph 57).

marketplace) and assumes a limited recourse obligation to repurchase delinquent loans. Company A agrees to provide the transferee a return at a floating rate of interest even though the contractual terms of the loan are fixed in nature (that provision is effectively an interest rate swap).

18A.12 WHAT ARE SERVICING ASSETS AND LIABILITIES?

"Servicing of mortgage loans, credit card receivables, or other financial assets commonly includes, but is not limited to, collecting principal, interest, and escrow payments from borrowers; paying taxes and insurance from escrowed funds; monitoring delinquencies; executing foreclosure if necessary; temporarily investing funds pending distribution; remitting fees to guarantors, trustees, and others providing services; and accounting for and remitting principal and interest payments to the holders of beneficial interests in the financial assets. Servicing is inherent in all financial assets."[22]

Paragraph 13 of Statement 140 states,

> An entity shall recognize and initially measure at fair value, if practicable, a servicing asset or servicing liability each time it undertakes an obligation to service a financial asset by entering into a servicing contract in any of the following situations:
>
> a. A transfer of the servicer's financial assets that meets the requirements for sale accounting
> b. A transfer of the servicer's financial assets to a qualifying SPE in a guaranteed mortgage securitization in which the transferor retains all of the resulting securities and classifies them as either available-for-sale securities or trading securities in accordance with FASB Statement No. 115, *Accounting for Certain Investments in Debt and Equity Securities*
> c. An acquisition or assumption of a servicing obligation that does not relate to financial assets of the servicer or its consolidated affiliates
>
> An entity that transfers its financial assets to a qualifying SPE in a guaranteed mortgage securitization in which the transferor retains all of the resulting securities and classifies them as debt securities held-to-maturity in accordance with Statement 115 may either separately recognize its servicing assets or servicing liabilities or report those servicing assets or servicing liabilities together with the asset being serviced.

"A servicer of financial assets commonly receives the benefits of servicing—revenues from contractually specified servicing fees, a portion of the interest from the financial assets, late charges, and other ancillary sources, including 'float' (income earned on balances held in trust by servicers from the date a loan payment is received from the borrower to the date funds are forwarded to investors), all of which it is entitled to receive only if it performs the servicing—and incurs the costs of servicing the assets. Typically, the benefits of servicing are expected to be more than adequate compensation to a servicer for performing the servicing, and the contract results in a servicing asset. However, if the benefits of servicing are not expected to adequately compensate a servicer for performing the servicing, the contract results in a

---

22. Statement 140 (paragraph 61).

servicing liability. (A servicing asset may become a servicing liability, or vice versa, if circumstances change, and the initial measure for servicing may be zero if the benefits of servicing are just adequate to compensate the servicer for its servicing responsibilities.) A servicer would account for its servicing contract that qualifies for separate recognition as a servicing asset or a servicing liability initially measured at its fair value regardless of whether explicit consideration was exchanged."[23]

Statement 140 defines *adequate compensation* as "The amount of benefits of servicing that would fairly compensate a substitute servicer should one be required, which includes the profit that would be demanded in the marketplace."[24] The determination of adequate compensation should be made independent of a servicer's internal cost structure.

"A servicer that transfers or securitizes financial assets in a transaction that does not meet the requirements for sale accounting and is accounted for as a secured borrowing with the underlying assets remaining on the transferor's balance sheet shall not recognize a servicing asset or a servicing liability. However, if a transferor enters into a servicing contract when the transferor transfers mortgage loans in a guaranteed mortgage securitization, retains all the resulting securities, and classifies those securities as either available-for-sale securities or trading securities in accordance with Statement 115, the transferor shall separately recognize a servicing asset or a servicing liability."[25]

18A.13   HOW SHOULD SERVICING ASSETS AND SERVICING LIABILITIES BE ACCOUNTED FOR UNDER STATEMENT 156?

Statement 156 was issued in March 2006 and amended Statement 140 with respect to the accounting for separately recognized servicing assets and servicing liabilities. Specifically, Statement 156:

1. Requires an entity to recognize a servicing asset or servicing liability each time it undertakes an obligation to service a financial asset by entering into a servicing contract in any of the following situations:

    a. A transfer of the servicer's financial assets that meets the requirements for sale accounting.

    b. A transfer of the servicer's financial assets to a qualifying special-purpose entity in a guaranteed mortgage securitization in which the transferor retains all of the resulting securities and classifies them as either available-for-sale securities or trading securities in accordance with Statement 115.

    c. An acquisition or assumption of an obligation to service a financial asset that does not relate to financial assets of the servicer or its consolidated affiliates.

2. Requires all separately recognized servicing assets and servicing liabilities to be initially measured at fair value, if practicable.

---

23.   Statement 140 (paragraph 62).
24.   Statement 140 (Appendix E).
25.   Statement 140 (paragraph 62A).

3. Permits an entity to choose either of the following subsequent measurement methods for each class of separately recognized servicing assets and servicing liabilities:

   a. *Amortization method*—Amortize servicing assets or servicing liabilities in proportion to and over the period of estimated net servicing income or net servicing loss and assess servicing assets or servicing liabilities for impairment or increased obligation based on fair value at each reporting date.

   b. *Fair value measurement method*—Measure servicing assets or servicing liabilities at fair value at each reporting date and report changes in fair value in earnings in the period in which the changes occur.

4. At its initial adoption, permits a one-time reclassification of available-for-sale securities to trading securities by entities with recognized servicing rights, without calling into question the treatment of other available-for-sale securities under Statement 115, provided that the available-for-sale securities are identified in some manner as offsetting the entity's exposure to changes in fair value of servicing assets or servicing liabilities that a servicer elects to subsequently measure at fair value.

5. Requires separate presentation of servicing assets and servicing liabilities subsequently measured at fair value in the statement of financial position and additional disclosures for all separately recognized servicing assets and servicing liabilities.[26]

"The election shall be made separately for each class of servicing assets and servicing liabilities. An entity shall apply the same subsequent measurement method to each servicing asset and servicing liability in a class. Classes of servicing assets and servicing liabilities shall be identified based on (a) the availability of market inputs used in determining the fair value of servicing assets or servicing liabilities, (b) an entity's method for managing the risks of its servicing assets or servicing liabilities, or (c) both. Once an entity elects the fair value measurement method for a class of servicing assets and servicing liabilities, that election shall not be reversed."[27]

(a) EXAMPLE OF A FINANCIAL ASSET TRANSFER RECORDED AS A SALE WITH A SERVICING RIGHT   The following example illustrates the accounting for a financial asset transfer recorded as a sale that includes cash proceeds and a servicing asset.

(i) Facts[28]   Company C originates $1,000 of loans that yield 10 percent interest income for their estimated lives of 9 years. Company C sells the $1,000 principal plus the right to receive interest income of 8 percent to another entity for $1,000. Company C will continue to service the loans, and the contract stipulates that its compensation for performing the servicing is the right to receive half of the interest income not sold. The remaining half of the interest income not sold is considered an interest-only strip receivable that Company C classifies as an available-for-sale

26. FASB Statement No. 156, *Accounting for Servicing of Financial Assets—An Amendment of FASB Statement No. 140*, March 2006 (from Summary page).

27. Statement 140 (paragraph 13A).

28. Example taken from Statement 140 (paragraph 65).

security. At the date of the transfer, the fair value of the loans is $1,100. The fair values of the servicing asset and the interest-only strip receivable are $40 and $60, respectively.

Fair Values

Cash proceeds	$1,000
Servicing asset	40
Interest-only strip receivable	60

Net Proceeds

Cash received	$1,000
Plus: Servicing asset	40
Net proceeds	$1,040

Carrying Amount Based on Relative Fair Values

	Fair Value	Percentage of Total Fair Value	Allocated Carrying Amount
Loans sold	$1,040.00	$ 94.55	$ 945.50
Interest-only strip receivable	60.00	5.45	54.50
Total	$1,100.00	$100.00	$1,000.00

Gain on Sale

Net proceeds	$1,040.00
Less: Carrying amount of loans sold	(945.50)
Gain on sale	$ 94.50

Journal Entry to Record Transfer and Recognize Interest-Only Strip Receivable and Servicing Asset

Cash	$1,000.00	
Interest-only strip receivable	$ 54.50	
Servicing asset	$ 40.00	
Loans		$1,000.00
Gain on sale		$ 94.50

Journal Entry to Begin to Subsequently Measure Interest-Only Strip Receivable Like an Available-for-Sale Security

Interest-only strip receivable	$5.50	
Other comprehensive income		$5.50

18A.14   WHEN SHOULD A TRANSFER OF FINANCIAL ASSETS BE RECORDED AS A SECURED BORROWING?

A transfer should be accounted for as a secured borrowing if the transfer does not meet the sale criteria specified by paragraph 9 of Statement 140.

An agreement that both entitles and obligates the transferor to repurchase or redeem transferred assets from the transferee maintains the transferor's effective control over those assets under paragraph 9(c)(1), and the transfer is therefore to be accounted for as a secured borrowing, if and only if all of the following conditions are met:

- The assets to be repurchased or redeemed are the same or substantially the same as those transferred.
- The transferor is able to repurchase or redeem them on substantially the agreed terms, even in the event of default by the transferee.
- The agreement is to repurchase or redeem them before maturity, at a fixed or determinable price.
- The agreement is entered into concurrently with the transfer.[29]

Generally, secured borrowings result in the transferor recognizing cash from the borrowing and a liability to return the cash to the transferee.

(a) THE ASSETS TO BE REPURCHASED OR REDEEMED ARE THE SAME OR SUBSTANTIALLY THE SAME AS THOSE TRANSFERRED[30]   Assets to be repurchased or redeemed are considered the same or substantially the same as those transferred if they have the same primary obligator, identical form and type, the same maturity, identical contractual interest rates, similar assets as collateral, and the same aggregate unpaid principal amount.

(b) THE TRANSFEROR IS ABLE TO REPURCHASE OR REDEEM THEM ON SUBSTANTIALLY THE AGREED TERMS, EVEN IN THE EVENT OF DEFAULT BY THE TRANSFEREE[31]   To be able to repurchase or redeem assets on substantially the agreed terms, even in the event of default by the transferee, a transferor must at all times during the contract term have obtained cash or other collateral sufficient to fund substantially all of the cost of purchasing replacement assets from others.

(c) THE AGREEMENT IS TO REPURCHASE OR REDEEM THEM BEFORE MATURITY, AT A FIXED OR DETERMINABLE PRICE   The agreement must require the transferor to repurchase or redeem the transferred assets before the maturity of the transferred assets at a fixed or determinable price. If the term of the repurchase agreement extends to the maturity date of the transferred asset, this condition would not be met.

---

29.   Statement 140 (paragraph 47).
30.   Section taken from Statement 140 (paragraph 48).
31.   Section taken from Statement 140 (paragraph 49).

(d) THE AGREEMENT IS ENTERED INTO CONCURRENTLY WITH THE TRANSFER

The agreement to repurchase or redeem the transferred assets must be entered into at the same time that the transferor transfers the financial assets. If the right or obligation to repurchase the transferred assets is not entered into concurrently with the initial transfer, the transferor would not effectively maintain control over the transferred assets at the time of transfer.

18A.15   HOW SHOULD COLLATERAL BE ACCOUNTED FOR WITHIN A SECURED BORROWING?[32]

A debtor may grant a security interest in certain assets to a lender (the secured party) to serve as collateral for its obligation under a borrowing, with or without recourse to other assets of the debtor. If collateral is transferred to the secured party, the custodial arrangement is commonly referred to as a pledge. Secured parties sometimes are permitted to sell or repledge (or otherwise transfer) collateral held under a pledge. The accounting for noncash collateral by the debtor (or obligor) and the secured party depends on whether the secured party has the right to sell or repledge the collateral and on whether the debtor has defaulted.

- If the secured party (transferee) has the right by contract or custom to sell or repledge the collateral, then the debtor (transferor) shall reclassify that asset and report that asset in its statement of financial position separately (e.g., as security pledged to creditors) from other assets not so encumbered.
- If the secured party (transferee) sells collateral pledged to it, it shall recognize the proceeds from the sale and its obligation to return the collateral. The sale of the collateral is a transfer subject to the provisions of Statement 140.
- If the debtor (transferor) defaults under the terms of the secured contract and is no longer entitled to redeem the pledged asset, it shall derecognize the pledged asset, and the security party (transferee) shall recognize the collateral as its asset initially measured at fair value or, if it has already sold the collateral, derecognize its obligation to return the collateral.
- Except as provided in paragraph 15(c), the debtor (transferor) shall continue to carry the collateral as its asset, and the secured party (transferee) shall not recognize the pledged asset.

18A.16   WHAT ARE SECURITIES LENDING TRANSACTIONS?[33]

"Securities lending transactions are initiated by broker-dealers and other financial institutions that need specific securities to cover a short sale or a customer's failure to deliver securities sold. Transferees ('borrowers') of securities generally are required to provide collateral to the transferor ('lender') of securities, commonly cash but sometimes other securities or standby letters of credit, with a value slightly higher than that of the securities borrowed. If the collateral is cash, the transferor typically earns a return by investing that cash at rates higher than the rate paid or rebated to the transferee. [. . .] If the 'collateral' is other than cash, the transferor typically receives a fee. Securities custodians or other agents commonly carry out securities lending activities on behalf of clients."

---

32.   Statement 140 (paragraph 15).
33.   Statement 140 (paragraph 91).

The accounting for a securities lending transaction is based on whether the transaction meets the criteria for sale accounting in paragraph 9 of Statement 140.

(a) EXAMPLE OF A SECURITIES LENDING TRANSACTION ACCOUNTED FOR AS A SECURED BORROWING   The following example illustrates the accounting for a securities lending transaction treated as a secured borrowing, in which the securities borrower (transferee) sells the securities upon receipt and later buys similar securities to return to the securities lender (transferor).

Facts[34]

Transferor's carrying amount and fair value of security loaned	$1,000
Cash collateral	$1,020
Transferor's return from investing cash collateral at a 5 percent annual rate	$ 5
Transferor's rebate to the securities borrower at a 4 percent annual rate	$ 4

For simplicity, the fair value of the security is assumed not to change during the 35-day term of the transaction.

Journal Entries for the Transferor

At inception:

Journal entry to record the receipt
of cash collateral

Cash	$1,020	
Payable under securities loan agreements		$1,020

Journal entry to reclassify loaned
securities that the secured party has the
right to sell or repledge

Securities pledged to creditors	$1,000	
Securities		$1,000

Journal entry to record investment of
cash collateral

Money market instrument	$1,020	
Cash		$1,020

(Continued)

---

34.   Example taken from Statement 140 (paragraph 95).

Journal Entries for the Transferor *(Continued)*

At conclusion:

Journal entry to record results of
investment

Cash		$1,025	
	Interest		$5
	Money market instrument		$1,020

Journal entry to record return of
security

Securities		$1,000	
	Securities pledged to creditors		$1,000

Journal entry to record repayment of
cash collateral plus interest

Payable under securities loan agreements		$1,020	
Interest		$4	
	Cash		$1,024

Journal Entries for the Transferee

At inception:

Journal entry to record transfer of cash
collateral

Receivable under securities loan agreements		$1,020	
	Cash		$1,020

Journal entry to record sale of borrowed
securities to a third party and the resulting obligation to return securities that it
no longer holds

Cash		$1,000	
	Obligation to return borrowed securities		$1,000

At conclusion:

Journal entry to record the repurchase
of securities borrowed

Obligation to return borrowed securities		$1,000	
	Cash		$1,000

Journal Entries for the Transferee

Journal entry to record the receipt of cash
collateral and rebate interest

Cash	$1,024	
Receivable under securities loan agreements	$1,200	
Interest revenue		$4

18A.17   WHAT ARE REPURCHASE AGREEMENTS AND "WASH SALES"?

Government securities dealers, banks, other financial institutions, and corporate investors commonly use repurchase agreements to obtain or use short-term funds. Under those agreements, the transferor ("repo party") transfers a security to a transferee ("repo counterparty" or "reverse party") in exchange for cash and concurrently agrees to reacquire that security at a future date for an amount equal to the cash exchanged plus a stipulated "interest" factor.[35]

"Repurchase agreements can be effected in a variety of ways. Some repurchase agreements are similar to securities lending transactions in that the transferee has the right to sell or repledge the securities to a third party during the term of the repurchase agreement. In other repurchase agreements, the transferee does not have the right to sell or repledge the securities during the term of the repurchase agreement."[36]

"If the criteria in paragraph 9 of Statement 140 are met, including the criterion in paragraph 9(c)(1), the transferor shall account for the repurchase agreement as a sale of financial assets and a forward repurchase commitment, and the transferee shall account for the agreement as a purchase of financial assets and a forward resale commitment. Other transfers that are accompanied by an agreement to repurchase the transferred assets that shall be accounted for as sales include transfers with agreements to repurchase at maturity and transfers with repurchase agreements in which the transferee has not obtained collateral sufficient to fund substantially all of the cost of purchasing replacement assets."[37]

"As with securities lending transactions, under many agreements to repurchase transferred assets before their maturity the transferor maintains effective control over those assets. Repurchase agreements that do not meet all the criteria in paragraph 9 shall be treated as secured borrowings."[38]

A *wash sale* transaction is one in which a transferor both sells and repurchases the same or similar securities over a short period of time (generally less than 30 days). If the wash sale transaction did not involve a concurrent contract to repurchase or redeem the transferred financial assets from the transferee, then the transfer of financial assets should be recorded as a sale, provided all other criteria within paragraph 9 are met.

---

35.   Statement 140 (paragraph 96).
36.   Statement 140 (paragraph 97).
37.   Statement 140 (paragraph 98).
38.   Statement 140 (paragraph 100).

18A.18   WHAT ARE LOAN SYNDICATIONS AND LOAN PARTICIPATIONS?[39]

Borrowers often borrow amounts greater than any one lender is willing to lend. Therefore, it is common for groups of lenders to jointly fund those loans. That may be accomplished by a syndication under which several lenders share in lending to a single borrower, but each lender loans a specific amount to the borrower and has the right to repayment from the borrower.

A loan syndication is not a transfer of financial assets. Each lender in the syndication shall account for the amounts it is owed by the borrower. Repayments by the borrower may be made to a lead lender that then distributes the collections to the other lenders of the syndicate. In those circumstances, the lead lender is simply functioning as a servicer and, therefore, shall not recognize the aggregate loan as an asset.

Groups of banks or other entities also may jointly fund large borrowings through loan participations in which a single lender makes a large loan to a borrower and subsequently transfers undivided interests in the loan to other entities.

Transfers by the originating lender may take the legal form of either assignments or participations. The transfers are usually on a nonrecourse basis, and the transferor ("originating lender") continues to service the loan. The transferee ("participating entity") may or may not have the right to sell or transfer its participation during the term of the loan, depending on the terms of the participation agreement.

If the loan participation agreement gives the transferee the right to pledge or exchange those participations and the other criteria in paragraph 9 are met, the transfers to the transferee shall be accounted for by the transferor as sales of financial assets. A transferor's right of first refusal on a bona fide offer from a third party, a requirement to obtain the transferor's permission that shall not be unreasonably withheld, or a prohibition on sale to the transferor's competitor if other potential willing buyers exist is a limitation on the transferee's rights but presumptively does not constrain a transferee from exercising its right to pledge or exchange. However, if the loan participation agreement constrains the transferees from pledging or exchanging their participations, the transferor presumptively receives a more than trivial benefit, has not relinquished control over the loan, and shall account for the transfers as secured borrowings.

18A.19   WHAT ARE BANKER'S ACCEPTANCES AND RISK PARTICIPATIONS IN THEM?[40]

Banker's acceptances provide a way for a bank to finance a customer's purchase of goods from a vendor for periods usually not exceeding six months. Under an agreement between the bank, the customer, and the vendor, the bank agrees to pay the customer's liability to the vendor upon presentation of specified documents that provide evidence of delivery and acceptance of the purchased goods. The principal document is a draft or bill of exchange drawn by the customer that the bank stamps to signify its "acceptance" of the liability to make payment on the draft on its due date.

Once the bank accepts a draft, the customer is liable to repay the bank at the time the draft matures. The bank recognizes a receivable from the customer and a liability for the acceptance it has issued to the vendor. The accepted draft becomes a negotiable financial instrument. The

---

39.   Statement 140 (paragraphs 102–106).
40.   Section taken from Statement 140 (paragraphs 107–110).

vendor typically sells the accepted draft at a discount either to the accepting bank or in the marketplace.

A risk participation is a contract between the accepting bank and a participating bank in which the participating bank agrees, in exchange for a fee, to reimburse the accepting bank in the event that the accepting bank's customer fails to honor its liability to the accepting bank in connection with the banker's acceptance. The participating bank becomes a guarantor of the credit of the accepting bank's customer.

An accepting bank that obtains a risk participation shall not derecognize the liability for the banker's acceptance, because the accepting bank is still primarily liable to the holder of the banker's acceptance even though it benefits from a guarantee of reimbursement by a participating bank. The accepting bank shall not derecognize the receivable from the customer because it has not transferred the receivable: It controls the benefits inherent in that receivable and it is still entitled to receive payment from the customer. The accepting bank shall, however, record the guarantee purchased, and the participating bank shall record a liability for the guarantee issued.

(a) EXAMPLE OF A BANKER'S ACCEPTANCE WITH A RISK PARTICIPATION TRANS-ACTION ACCOUNTED FOR AS A SECURED BORROWING   The following example illustrates the accounting for a transaction in which an accepting bank assumes a liability to pay a customer's vendor and obtains a participation from another bank. The details of the banker's acceptance are provided below:

Facts[41]

Face value of the draft provided to vendor	$1,000
Term of the draft provided to vendor	90 days
Commission with an annual rate of 10 percent	$ 25
Fee paid for risk participation	$ 10

The following journal entries show the accounting treatment for this arrangement:

Journal Entries for Accepting Bank

At issuance of acceptance:

Receivable from customer	$1,000	
Cash	$ 25	
Time draft payable to vendor		$1,000
Deferred acceptance commission revenue		$ 25

(Continued)

---

41.   Example taken from Statement 140 (paragraph 111).

At purchase of risk participation from a participating bank: *(Continued)*

Guarantee purchased	$10	
Cash		$10

Upon presentation of the accepted time draft:

Time draft payable to vendor	$1,000	
Deferred acceptance commission revenue	$ 25	
Cash		$1,000
Acceptance commission revenue		$ 25

Upon collection from the customer (or the participating bank, if the customer defaults):

Cash	$1,000	
Guarantee expense	$ 10	
Receivable from customer		$1,000
Guarantee purchased		$ 10

Journal Entries for Participating Bank

Upon issuing the risk participation:

Cash	$10	
Guarantee liability		$10

Upon payment by the customer to the accepting bank:

Guarantee liability	$10	
Guarantee revenue		$10

OR:

In the event of total default by the customer:

Guarantee loss	$990	
Guarantee liability	$ 10	
Cash (paid to accepting bank)		$1,000

18A.20   WHAT ARE FACTORING ARRANGEMENTS AND TRANSFERS OF RECEIVABLES WITH RECOURSE?[42]

Factoring arrangements are a means of discounting accounts receivable on a nonrecourse, notification basis. Accounts receivable are sold outright, usually to a transferee (the factor) that assumes the full risk of collection, without recourse to the transferor in the event of a loss. Debtors are directed to send payments to the transferee. Factoring arrangements that meet the criteria in paragraph 9 of Statement 140 shall be accounted for as sales of financial assets because the transferor surrenders control over the receivables to the factor.

In a transfer of receivables with recourse, the transferor provides the transferee with full or limited recourse. The transferor is obligated under the terms of the recourse provision to make payments to the transferee or to repurchase receivables sold under certain circumstances, typically for defaults up to a specified percentage. The effect of a recourse provision on the application of paragraph 9 of Statement 140 may vary by jurisdiction. In some jurisdictions, transfers with full recourse may not place transferred assets beyond the reach of the transferor and its creditors, but transfers with limited recourse may. A transfer of receivables with recourse shall be accounted for as a sale, with the proceeds of the sale reduced by the fair value of the recourse obligation, if the criteria in paragraph 9 of Statement 140 are met. Otherwise, a transfer of receivables with recourse shall be accounted for as a secured borrowing.

18A.21   HOW SHOULD TRANSFERS OF FINANCIAL ASSETS BE MEASURED AT FAIR VALUE UNDER STATEMENT 157?

Statement 157 was issued in September 2006 and defines fair value, establishes a framework for measuring fair value in generally accepted accounting principles, and expands disclosures about fair value measurements. As noted above, Statement 157 is effective for financial statements issued for fiscal years beginning after November 15, 2007, and interim periods within those fiscal years.

(a) MEASUREMENT[43]   *Fair value* is the price that would be received to sell an asset or paid to transfer a liability in an orderly transaction between market participants at the measurement date.

A fair value measurement is for a particular asset or liability. Therefore, the measurement should consider attributes specific to the asset or liability, for example, the condition and/or location of the asset or liability and restrictions, if any, on the sale or use of the asset at the measurement date. The asset or liability might be a standalone asset or liability (for example, a financial instrument or an operating asset) or a group of assets and/or liabilities (for example, an asset group, a reporting unit, or a business). Whether the asset or liability is a standalone asset or liability or a group of assets and/or liabilities depends on its unit of account. The unit of account determines what is being measured by reference to the level at which the asset or liability is aggregated (or disaggregated) for purposes of applying other accounting pronouncements. The unit of account for the asset or liability should be determined in accordance with the provisions of other accounting pronouncements, except as provided in paragraph 27 of Statement 157.

---

42.   Section taken from Statement 140 (paragraphs 112–113).
43.   Section taken from FASB Statement No. 157, *Fair Value Measurements*, September 2007 (paragraphs 5–7).

A fair value measurement assumes that the asset or liability is exchanged in an orderly transaction between market participants to sell the asset or transfer the liability at the measurement date. An orderly transaction is a transaction that assumes exposure to the market for a period prior to the measurement date to allow for marketing activities that are usual and customary for transactions involving such assets or liabilities; it is not a forced transaction (for example, a forced liquidation or distress sale). The transaction to sell the asset or transfer the liability is a hypothetical transaction at the measurement date, considered from the perspective of a market participant that holds the asset or owes the liability. Therefore, the objective of a fair value measurement is to determine the price that would be received to sell the asset or paid to transfer the liability at the measurement date (an exit price).

A fair value measurement assumes that the transaction to sell the asset or transfer the liability occurs in the principal market for the asset or liability or, in the absence of a principal market, the most advantageous market for the asset or liability. The principal market is the market in which the reporting entity would sell the asset or transfer the liability with the greatest volume and level of activity for the asset or liability. The most advantageous market is the market in which the reporting entity would sell the asset or transfer the liability with the price that maximizes the amount that would be received for the asset or minimizes the amount that would be paid to transfer the liability, considering transaction costs in the respective market(s). In either case, the principal (or most advantageous) market (and thus, market participants) should be considered from the perspective of the reporting entity, thereby allowing for differences between and among entities with different activities. If there is a principal market for the asset or liability, the fair value measurement shall represent the price in that market (whether that price is directly observable or otherwise determined using a valuation technique), even if the price in a different market is potentially more advantageous at the measurement date.

The price in the principal (or most advantageous) market used to measure the fair value of the asset or liability shall not be adjusted for transaction costs. Transaction costs represent the incremental direct costs to sell the asset or transfer the liability in the principal (or most advantageous) market for the asset or liability. Transaction costs are not an attribute of the asset or liability; rather, they are specific to the transaction and will differ depending on how the reporting entity transacts. However, transaction costs do not include the costs that would be incurred to transport the asset or liability to (or from) its principal (or most advantageous) market. If location is an attribute of the asset or liability (as might be the case for a commodity), the price in the principal (or most advantageous) market used to measure the fair value of the asset or liability shall be adjusted for the costs, if any, that would be incurred to transport the asset or liability to (or from) its principal (or most advantageous) market.

(b) STATEMENT 157 APPLICATION TO ASSETS[44]   A fair value measurement for an asset assumes the highest and best use of the asset by market participants, considering the use of the asset that is physically possible, legally permissible, and financially feasible at the measurement date. In broad terms, *highest and best use* refers to the use of an asset by market participants that would maximize the value of the asset or the group of assets within which

---

44.   Section taken from Statement 157 (paragraph 12).

the asset would be used. Highest and best use is determined based on the use of the asset by market participants, even if the intended use of the asset by the reporting entity is different.

(c) STATEMENT 157 APPLICATION TO LIABILITIES[45]   A fair value measurement for a liability assumes that the liability is transferred to a market participant at the measurement date (the liability to the counterparty continues; it is not settled) and that the nonperformance risk relating to that liability is the same before and after its transfer. Nonperformance risk refers to the risk that the obligation will not be fulfilled and affects the value at which the liability is transferred. Therefore, the fair value of the liability shall reflect the nonperformance risk relating to that liability. Nonperformance risk includes but may not be limited to the reporting entity's own credit risk. The reporting entity shall consider the effect of its credit risk (credit standing) on the fair value of the liability in all periods in which the liability is measured at fair value. That effect may differ depending on the liability, for example, whether the liability is an obligation to deliver cash (a financial liability) or an obligation to deliver goods or services (a nonfinancial liability), and the terms of credit enhancements related to the liability, if any.

18A.22   WHAT ARE APPROPRIATE VALUATION TECHNIQUES UNDER STATEMENT 157?[46]

Valuation techniques consistent with the market approach, income approach, and/or cost approach shall be used to measure fair value. Key aspects of those approaches are summarized below:

- *Market approach.* The market approach uses prices and other relevant information generated by market transactions involving identical or comparable assets or liabilities (including a business). For example, valuation techniques consistent with the market approach often use market multiples derived from a set of comparables. Multiples might lie in ranges with a different multiple for each comparable. The selection of where within the range the appropriate multiple falls requires judgment, considering factors specific to the measurement (qualitative and quantitative). Valuation techniques consistent with the market approach include matrix pricing. Matrix pricing is a mathematical technique used principally to value debt securities without relying exclusively on quoted prices for the specific securities, but rather relying on the securities' relationship to other benchmark quoted securities.
- *Income approach.* The income approach uses valuation techniques to convert future amounts (for example, cash flows or earnings) to a single present amount (discounted). The measurement is based on the value indicated by current market expectations about those future amounts. Those valuation techniques include present value techniques; option-pricing models, such as the Black-Scholes-Merton formula (a closed-form model) and a binomial model (a lattice model), which incorporate present value techniques; and the multiperiod excess earnings method, which is used to measure the fair value of certain intangible assets.

---

45.   Section taken from Statement 157 (paragraph 15).
46.   Section taken from Statement 157 (paragraph 18).

• *Cost approach.* The cost approach is based on the amount that currently would be required to replace the service capacity of an asset (often referred to as *current replacement cost*). From the perspective of a market participant (seller), the price that would be received for the asset is determined based on the cost to a market participant (buyer) to acquire or construct a substitute asset of comparable utility, adjusted for obsolescence. Obsolescence encompasses physical deterioration, functional (technological) obsolescence, and economic (external) obsolescence and is broader than depreciation for financial reporting purposes (an allocation of historical cost) or tax purposes (based on specified service lives).

18A.23   WHAT ARE VALUATION INPUTS, AND HOW ARE THEY PRIORITIZED?

Valuation inputs are the assumptions that market participants use to price assets and liabilities. Valuation inputs maybe observable or unobservable. *Observable* inputs are inputs that reflect the assumptions that market participants would use in pricing the asset or liability developed based on market data obtained from sources independent of the reporting entity. *Unobservable* inputs are inputs that reflect the reporting entity's own assumptions about the assumptions market participants would use in pricing the asset or liability developed based on the best information available in the circumstances. Valuation techniques used to measure fair value should attempt to maximize the use of observable inputs and minimize the use of unobservable inputs.[47]

Statement 157 establishes a fair value hierarchy that gives the highest priority to quoted prices in active markets for identical assets or liabilities and the lowest priority to unobservable inputs. The levels of valuation inputs in the fair-value hierarchy are as follows:

Level 1 inputs are quoted prices (unadjusted) in active markets for identical assets or liabilities that the reporting entity has the ability to access at the measurement date. An active market for the asset or liability is a market in which transactions for the asset or liability occur with sufficient frequency and volume to provide pricing information on an ongoing basis.

Level 2 inputs are inputs other than quoted prices included within Level 1 that are observable for the asset or liability, either directly or indirectly. If the asset or liability has a specified (contractual) term, a Level 2 input must be observable for substantially the full term of the asset or liability. Level 2 inputs include the following:

a. Quoted prices for similar assets or liabilities in active markets
b. Quoted prices for identical or similar assets or liabilities in markets that are not active, that is, markets in which there are few transactions for the asset or liability, the prices are not current, or price quotations vary substantially either over time or among market makers (for example, some brokered markets), or in which little information is released publicly (for example, a principal-to-principal market)

---

47.   Statement 157 (paragraph 21).

   c. Inputs other than quoted prices that are observable for the asset or liability (for example, interest rates and yield curves observable at commonly quoted intervals, volatilities, prepayment speeds, loss severities, credit risks, and default rates)

   d. Inputs that are derived principally from or corroborated by observable market data by correlation or other means (market-corroborated inputs)

     Level 3 inputs are unobservable inputs for the asset or liability. Unobservable inputs shall be used to measure fair value to the extent that observable inputs are not available, thereby allowing for situations in which there is little, if any, market activity for the asset or liability at the measurement date.[48]

18A.24   WHAT ARE THE FINANCIAL STATEMENT DISCLOSURE REQUIREMENTS OF STATEMENT 140, AS AMENDED?[49]

Paragraph 17 of Statement 140, as amended by Statement 156, lists the disclosures that companies are required to make in their financial statements. These disclosures are as follows:

   a. For collateral:

     (1) If the entity has entered into repurchase agreements or securities lending transactions, its policy for requiring collateral or other security.

     (2) If the entity has pledged any of its assets as collateral that are not reclassified and separately reported in the statement of financial position pursuant to paragraph 15(a), the carrying amount and classification of those assets as of the date of the latest statement of financial position presented.

     (3) If the entity has accepted collateral that it is permitted by contract or custom to sell or repledge, the fair value as of the date of each statement of financial position presented of that collateral and of the portion of that collateral that it has sold or repledged, and information about the sources and uses of that collateral.

   b. If debt was considered to be extinguished by in-substance defeasance under the provisions of FASB Statement No. 76, *Extinguishment of Debt,* prior to the effective date of Statement 125, a general description of the transaction and the amount of debt that is considered extinguished at the end of the period so long as that debt remains outstanding.

   c. If assets are set aside after the effective date of Statement 125 solely for satisfying scheduled payments of a specific obligation, a description of the nature of restrictions placed on those assets.

   d. If it is not practicable to estimate the fair value of certain assets obtained or liabilities incurred in transfers of financial assets during the period, a description of those items and the reasons why it is not practicable to estimate their fair value.

   e. For all servicing assets and servicing liabilities:

---

48.   Statement 157 (summarized from paragraphs 22–30).

49.   Statement 140 (paragraph 17).

(1) Management's basis for determining its classes of servicing assets and servicing liabilities (paragraph 13A).

(2) A description of the risks inherent in servicing assets and servicing liabilities and, if applicable, the instruments used to mitigate the income statement effect of changes in fair value of the servicing assets and servicing liabilities. (Disclosure of quantitative information about the instruments used to manage the risks inherent in servicing assets and servicing liabilities, including the fair value of those instruments at the beginning and end of the period, is encouraged but not required.)

(3) The amount of contractually specified servicing fees (as defined in the glossary), late fees, and ancillary fees earned for each period for which results of operations are presented, including a description of where each amount is reported in the statement of income.

f. For servicing assets and servicing liabilities subsequently measured at fair value:

(1) For each class of servicing assets and servicing liabilities, the activity in the balance of servicing assets and the activity in the balance of servicing liabilities (including a description of where changes in fair value are reported in the statement of income for each period for which results of operations are presented), including, but not limited to, the following:

(a) The beginning and ending balances.

(b) Additions (through purchases of servicing assets, assumptions of servicing obligations, and servicing obligations that result from transfers of financial assets).

(c) Disposals.

(d) Changes in fair value during the period resulting from:

(i) Changes in valuation inputs or assumptions used in the valuation model.

(ii) Other changes in fair value and a description of those changes.

(e) Other changes that affect the balance and a description of those changes.

(2) A description of the valuation techniques or other methods used to estimate the fair value of servicing assets and servicing liabilities. If a valuation model is used, the description shall include the methodology and model validation procedures, as well as quantitative and qualitative information about the assumptions used in the valuation model (e.g., discount rates and prepayment speeds). (An entity that provides quantitative information about the instruments used to manage the risks inherent in the servicing assets and servicing liabilities, as encouraged by paragraph 17(e)(2), is also encouraged, but not required, to disclose a description of the valuation techniques, as well as quantitative and qualitative information about the assumptions used to estimate the fair value of those instruments.)

g. For servicing assets and servicing liabilities subsequently amortized in proportion to and over the period of estimated net servicing income or loss and assessed for impairment or increased obligation:

(1) For each class of servicing assets and servicing liabilities, the activity in the balance of servicing assets and the activity in the balance of servicing liabilities (including a description of where changes in the carrying amount are reported in the statement of income for each period for which results of operations are presented), including, but not limited to, the following:

    (a) The beginning and ending balances.

    (b) Additions (through purchases of servicing assets, assumption of servicing obligations, and servicing obligations that result from transfers of financial assets).

    (c) Disposals.

    (d) Amortization.

    (e) Application of valuation allowance to adjust carrying value of servicing assets.

    (f) Other-than-temporary impairments.

    (g) Other changes that affect the balance and a description of those changes.

(2) For each class of servicing assets and servicing liabilities, the fair value of recognized servicing assets and servicing liabilities at the beginning and end of the period if it is practicable to estimate the value.

(3) A description of the valuation techniques or other methods used to estimate fair value of the servicing assets and servicing liabilities. If a valuation model is used, the description shall include the methodology and model validation procedures, as well as quantitative and qualitative information about the assumptions used in the valuation model (e.g., discount rates and prepayment speeds). (An entity that provides quantitative information about the instruments used to manage the risks inherent in the servicing assets and servicing liabilities, as encouraged by paragraph 17(e)(2), is also encouraged, but not required, to disclose a description of the valuation techniques as well as quantitative and qualitative information about the assumptions used to estimate the fair value of those instruments.)

(4) The risk characteristics of the underlying financial assets used to stratify recognized servicing assets for purposes of measuring impairment in accordance with paragraph 63.

(5) The activity by class in any valuation allowance for impairment of recognized servicing assets—including beginning and ending balances, aggregate additions charged and recoveries credited to operations, and aggregate write-downs charged against the allowance—for each period for which results of operations are presented.

h. If the entity has securitized financial assets during any period presented and accounts for that transfer as a sale, for each major asset type (e.g., mortgage loans, credit card receivables, and automobile loans):

    (1) Its accounting policies for initially measuring the interests that continue to be held by the transferor, if any, and servicing assets and servicing liabilities, if any, including the methodology (whether quoted market price, prices based on sales of similar assets and liabilities, or prices based on valuation techniques) used in determining their fair value.

(2) The characteristics of securitizations (a description of the transferor's continuing involvement with the transferred assets, including, but not limited to, servicing, recourse, and restrictions on interests that continue to be held by the transferor) and the gain or loss from sale of financial assets in securitizations.

(3) The key assumptions used in measuring the fair value of interests that continue to be held by the transferor and servicing assets or servicing liabilities, if any, at the time of securitization (including, at a minimum, quantitative information about discount rates, expected prepayments including the expected weighted-average life of prepayable financial assets, and anticipated credit losses, if applicable).

(4) Cash flows between the securitization SPE and the transferor, unless reported separately elsewhere in the financial statements or notes (including proceeds from new securitizations, proceeds from collections reinvested in revolving-period securitizations, purchases of delinquent or foreclosed loans, servicing fees, and cash flows received on interests that continue to be held by the transferor).

i. If the entity has interests that continue to be held by the transferor in financial assets that it has securitized or servicing assets or servicing liabilities relating to assets that it has securitized, at the date of the latest statement of financial position presented, for each major asset type (e.g., mortgage loans, credit card receivables, and automobile loans):

(1) Its accounting policies for subsequently measuring those interests, including the methodology (whether quoted market price, prices based on sales of similar assets and liabilities, or prices based on valuation techniques) used in determining their fair value.

(2) The key assumptions used in subsequently measuring the fair value of those interests (including, at a minimum, quantitative information about discount rates, expected prepayments including the expected weighted-average life of prepayable financial assets, and anticipated credit losses, including expected static pool losses, if applicable).

(3) A sensitivity analysis or stress test showing the hypothetical effect on the fair value of those interests (including any servicing assets or servicing liabilities) of two or more unfavorable variations from the expected levels for each key assumption that is reported under (2) above independently from any change in another key assumption, and a description of the objectives, methodology, and limitations of the sensitivity analysis or stress test.

(4) For the securitized assets and any other financial assets that it manages together with them:

(a) The total principal amount outstanding, the portion that has been derecognized, and the portion that continues to be recognized in each category reported in the statement of financial position, at the end of the period.

(b) Delinquencies at the end of the period.

(c) Credit losses, net of recoveries, during the period.

18A.25 WHAT ARE THE FASB'S PROPOSED AMENDMENTS TO STATEMENT 140?[50]

(a) SUMMARY OF DECISIONS REACHED TO DATE   The FASB staff has redeliberated topics related to Statement 140 several times in recent years. On June 18, 2008, the FASB staff prepared a summary of Board decisions for informational purposes only. The following six Board decisions are tentative and do not change current accounting:

1. *Redeliberations of 2005 Exposure Draft and Project Plan.* Recently, the Board deliberated several topics, including the unit of account for derecognition, the isolation criterion, and permitted activities of a qualifying SPE. The remaining issues for the Board to deliberate on are a proposal for a linked presentation model, disclosure requirements, the measurement of transferor-held beneficial interests, servicing, and the effective date and transition provisions for all proposed amendments.

2. *Qualifying SPE.* The Board decided to remove the concept of a qualifying SPE from Statement 140 and to remove the scope exception for QSPEs from Interpretation 46(R). This will require that variable-interest entities, previously accounted for as qualifying SPEs in Statement 140, will need to be analyzed for consolidation according to Interpretation 46(R). It will eliminate the provision in paragraph 9(b) that allowed entities to "look-through" to the rights of beneficial interest holders when analyzing control.

3. *Derecognition.*

   (a) Participating Interest Definition—The Board decided that only an entire financial asset or a portion of a financial asset that meets the definition of a participating interest will be eligible for derecognition. The participating interest may not be an interest in an equity instrument, a derivative financial instrument, or a hybrid financial instrument with an embedded derivative not clearly and closely related to the original financial asset. Additionally, a participating interest requires that (1) the cash flows received from the assets are divided among the interests in proportion to the share of ownership represented by each, (2) the participating interest holders have no recourse, other than standard representations and warranties, to the transferor or to each other, (3) no interest holder is subordinated to another, and (4) neither the transferor nor any participating interest holder has the right to pledge or exchange the entire financial asset in which it owns a participating interest.

   (b) Paragraph 9 Requirements—The Board also decided to amend the derecognition criteria in Statement 140 to improve financial reporting in the short term. Specifically, the Board voted to amend paragraphs 9(a) and 9(c) and to remove paragraph 9(b). Paragraph 9(a) will be clarified to require that the transferred financial assets must be beyond the reach of the transferor or any of its consolidated

---

50. Section derived from www.fasb.org/project/transfers_of_financial_assets.shtml.

affiliates. Additionally, the isolation analysis must consider all arrangements made in connection with the transfer. Paragraph 9(c) will be amended to (1) state that the transferor and its consolidated affiliates cannot maintain effective control over the financial assets and (2) include an additional criterion that states that if the transferor or its consolidated affiliates constrain the transferee and benefit from that constraint, the transferor maintains effective control over the transferred assets. This change incorporates similar requirements currently in paragraph 9(b).

(c)   Minimum Threshold—The Board decided not to add a specific minimum requirement for the amount of beneficial interests that must be held by parties other than the transferor and its consolidated affiliates for a transferor to meet the sale accounting conditions for transfers of financial assets.

4.   *Initial and Subsequent Measurement.* The Board decided that beneficial interests received by a transferor, in connection with a sale of an entire financial asset to an entity that is not consolidated by the transferor, should be considered proceeds of the sale and initially measured at fair value. Additionally, the Board decided that a participating interest in a financial asset that continues to be held by a transferor should be initially measured at its allocated carrying amount in accordance with the existing measurement guidance in paragraph 10 of Statement 140.

5.   *Guaranteed Mortgage Securitization (GMS).* The Board decided to delete the exception that requires a transferor to reclassify interests received in a GMS securitization to securities under Statement 115 if the transfer does not qualify as a sale. The Board also decided to remove the exception for GMS transactions that requires a transferor to recognize a servicing asset or liability if the transfer does not qualify as a sale.

6.   *Disclosures.* Subject to drafting changes, the Board decided on the following disclosure amendments in Statement 140:

(a)   To provide an overall objective for the disclosure requirements.

(b)   To include aggregation guidance for similar transfers.

(c)   To require additional information about a transferor's calculation of gains and losses when that transfer involves an SPE, a transferor's continuing involvement in transferred financial assets, and liquidity, guarantee, and other commitments provide by third parties, and other amendments.

(d)   To provide a definition of continuing involvement in the glossary.

(e)   To require that paragraph 17(c) disclosure apply to all transfers within the scope of Statement 140.

(f)   To eliminate explicit references to the methodology used in determining fair value as described in paragraphs 17(h)(1) and 17(i)(1).

(g)   To eliminate footnote 10, which provides an exception for the disclosures required by paragraph 17(i)(4) if the transferor's only continuing involvement is servicing.

(b) PROPOSED EFFECTIVE DATE   The Board decided that the proposed amendments to Statement 140 should be applied in fiscal years beginning after November 15, 2008 (effective date), on a prospective basis (e.g., a calendar year-end entity would apply the proposed amendments to Statement 140 for new transactions completed after January 1, 2009).

However, qualifying SPEs that existed prior to the effective date would be subject to the consolidation guidance in fiscal years beginning after November 15, 2009. Transition disclosures would be provided for existing QSPEs during the one-year deferral period.

(c) **NEXT STEPS**   The Board authorized the staff to proceed to draft the proposed amendments to Interpretation 46(R) and Statement 140 for vote by written ballot. The Board expects to issue a proposed Exposure Draft in the third quarter of 2008.

GOODWILL AND OTHER INTANGIBLE ASSETS: AN UPDATE[1] (NEW)

Barry Jay Epstein, PhD, CPA
Russell Novak & Company LLP
Christopher J. Leisner, CPA, CMC
Creative IP Solutions LLC

---

1. Portions of this chapter originally appeared in Chapter 20, "Goodwill and Other Intangible Assets," written by Lailani Moody, CPA, MBA, of Grant Thornton LLP. This entire chapter also appeared in the 2006 Cumulative Supplement to the *Accountants' Handbook*, Tenth Edition.

20A.1 CHARACTERIZATION OF INTANGIBLE ASSETS

Intangible assets are assets—other than financial assets—that lack physical substance yet do have utility and value in the hands of the reporting entity. Examples include patents, copyrights, trade names, customer lists, royalty agreements, databases, and computer software. They also include the assets called leasehold improvements, which are frequently but mistakenly viewed as being tangible assets.

The range of intangibles is quite broad, and this fact is perhaps more clearly understood now than during earlier years, since changing business and economic conditions have brought intellectual property and certain other intangible assets to much greater prominence than had formerly been the case. While for many mostly traditional (e.g., manufacturing) businesses the value of intangibles may still be underappreciated, for high-technology and other so-called knowledge-based companies, the primary assets may be intangible ones such as patents and copyrights. Even for professional services firms, the key assets may be "soft" resources such as knowledge bases and client relationships.

There are several possible taxonomies of intangible assets. First, intangible assets can be classified either as *identifiable*—for example, trademarks and most other intangibles—or as *unidentifiable*, which generally implies goodwill. A second way to classify intangible assets is based on how they are acquired. They can be internally developed or acquired from external sources, which include both simple purchases of one or more intangibles (e.g., groups of related patents) or those that are part of business combinations. Intangible assets acquired in a business combination may be recognized as assets separate from goodwill or as part of goodwill, depending on whether the intangible assets satisfy certain criteria. As discussed in this chapter, the applicable accounting pronouncements and accounting requirements differ significantly, depending on whether the intangible asset is identifiable, whether it is internally developed or acquired externally, and, if acquired externally, whether it was acquired in a business combination.

Yet other classification schemes for intangible assets were first offered by the now superseded Accounting Principles Board (APB) Opinion No. 17, which indicated that intangible assets could also be categorized based on either

1. Expected period of benefit—whether limited by law or contract, related to human or economic factors, or indefinite or indeterminate duration; or
2. Separability from an entire enterprise—rights transferable without title, salable, or inseparable from the enterprise or a substantial part of it.

While all of the foregoing taxonomies assist one in thinking about intangibles and are to a greater or lesser extent incorporated into current generally accepted accounting principles (GAAP) (primarily SFAS No. 142), perhaps the most important distinctions are between intangibles acquired in business combinations accounted for under SFAS No. 141 or otherwise; between those having finite lives and those having indefinite lives; and between those that are severable from the reporting entity and those that are not. All of these matters are addressed in this chapter.

20A.2   ACCOUNTING AND FINANCIAL MANAGEMENT OVERVIEW

Numerous pronouncements provide guidance on the accounting for intangibles. This section provides an overview of those pronouncements.

(a) INTANGIBLE ASSETS INCLUDING GOODWILL ACQUIRED IN A BUSINESS COMBINATION   Under SFAS No. 141, "Business Combinations," all business combinations must now be accounted for as purchases; pooling accounting is no longer permitted. This necessitates purchase-price allocation. It provides initial measurement and recognition guidance for intangible assets and goodwill acquired in a business combination, including mandates as to the recognition of intangible assets apart from goodwill.

Subsequent accounting for intangible assets, including goodwill, is provided in SFAS No. 142, "Goodwill and Other Intangible Assets." SFAS No. 142 provides that goodwill should not be amortized; it mandates that impairment tests of goodwill be conducted annually or, in some circumstances, more frequently; and it provides guidance on recognizing impairments. In contrast with earlier GAAP, which required amortization of all intangibles, SFAS No. 142 addresses whether intangible assets other than goodwill have *indefinite* useful lives and therefore should not be amortized but instead tested at least annually for impairment, or *finite* useful lives and therefore should be amortized over their estimated useful lives.

Intangible assets with finite useful lives are tested for impairment under SFAS No. 144, "Accounting for the Impairment or Disposal of Long-Lived Assets." Intangibles that have finite lives and thus are amortized must also be reviewed for recoverability of carrying amounts in a process similar to that under SFAS No. 144, and useful lives must be reassessed and altered when warranted by circumstances (e.g., technological obsolescence making the useful life of a patent much shorter than the legal term).

(b) INTANGIBLE ASSETS ACQUIRED SEPARATELY OR WITH OTHER ASSETS   SFAS No. 142 provides initial recognition and measurement guidance for intangible assets acquired other than in a business combination—that is, intangible assets acquired individually or together with a group of other assets that do not constitute a business. SFAS No. 142 also provides guidance to the subsequent accounting for intangible assets, including determining whether they have finite or indeterminate useful lives and therefore whether they should be amortized or not. Finally, it addresses accounting for impairments of intangible assets with indeterminate lives. A separate standard, SFAS No. 144, provides guidance on impairment of intangible assets with finite useful lives.

(c) INTERNALLY DEVELOPED INTANGIBLE ASSETS   SFAS No. 142 addresses the initial and subsequent accounting for internally developed intangible assets. It carries forward the requirement set forth by the predecessor standard, APB No. 17, that the costs of internally developing, maintaining, or restoring intangibles that cannot be identified specifically, have indeterminate lives, or are inherent in an ongoing business and pertain to the entity as a whole cannot be capitalized. Such costs must be expensed currently as incurred.

(d) INTANGIBLE ASSETS RECOGNIZED ON ACQUISITION OF A NONCONTROL-LING INTEREST IN A SUBSIDIARY   SFAS No. 142 provides guidance on the initial and subsequent accounting for goodwill and other intangible assets recognized on acquisition of noncontrolling interests in a subsidiary. Under current GAAP, goodwill associated with minority (i.e., noncontrolling) interests is not recognized. Note, however, that the Financial Accounting Standards Board (FASB) is currently considering a major change in purchase-business combination accounting that will, if adopted, result in the recognition of goodwill associated with minority interests.

(e) GOODWILL RECOGNIZED WHEN APPLYING THE EQUITY METHOD   SFAS No. 142 provides that amounts recognized as corresponding to goodwill in applying the equity method accounting to investments should not be amortized. Equity method goodwill is tested for impairment under APB Opinion No. 18, "The Equity Method of Accounting for Investments in Common Stock."

(f) SPECIFIC GUIDANCE ON CERTAIN INTANGIBLES   Accounting pronouncements, such as Statements of Position issued by the Accounting Standards Executive Committee of the American Institute of Certified Public Accountants (AICPA), provide guidance on the accounting for specific intangible assets, such as start-up costs, internally developed software, and advertising. These matters are addressed subsequently.

(g) INTANGIBLE ASSETS IN SPECIALIZED INDUSTRIES   Certain FASB Statements and Interpretations provide guidance on accounting for certain intangibles of specialized industries, such as airlines and computer software development. Impairment testing for intangible assets in many specialized industries is performed under the general requirements (SFAS No. 144), but for certain industries or assets, such as broadcasters' program rights, guidance under particular AICPA Industry Audit and Accounting Guides must be followed instead.

(h) THE NEW EMPHASIS ON MANAGEMENT OF INTANGIBLE ASSETS
(i) Sarbanes-Oxley Act of 2002—Implications for the Financial Reporting of Intangible Assets   Sound financial and operating management of reporting entities has always been a critical concern, of course, but developments in the early 2000s have caused renewed emphasis on managements' and directors' fiduciary duties, including the duty to maximize the value of all assets under management. The widely reported corporate management and financial

reporting scandals of the late 1990s, in particular, created a groundswell of demand for reforms in corporate governance practices. Among other things, this led to the hurried passage by Congress of the Sarbanes-Oxley Act of 2002 ("Sarbanes" or "the Act"), the ramifications of which are still being comprehended.

Sarbanes has generated a considerable amount of interest in, and focus on, the quality of financial reporting and the reliability of internal control systems. The widely publicized and sometimes controversial Section 404 requirements for reporting on the effectiveness of internal controls, certified by both management and the entity's independent accountants, has been a costly and demanding undertaking for many companies, including some whose quality of controls and financial management were previously unquestioned by investors.

Sarbanes has also highlighted the historically troublesome disparity between corporate managers and shareholders regarding many entities' true financial condition, which is sometimes referred to as the "transparency" issue. GAAP-basis financial reporting is based on a "mixed-attribute" model that combines historical costs and current fair values, with some costs subject to amortization and others only sporadically tested for impairment, making financial statements often unsuited for directly assessing the reporting entity's value. Because intangible assets now account for the majority of many publicly traded companies' stock values (by some estimates, as much as two-thirds), and because accounting for intangibles has been largely overlooked in the accounting pronouncements and literature, this area is now overdue for much greater attention. The demand for greater transparency has increased the pressure on accountants to develop the means to more fully report the value of intangible assets of the companies they manage, report, and/or opine on.

When the 2002 Sarbanes requirements are evaluated in conjunction with the 2001 FASB pronouncements regarding goodwill, intangibles, and business combinations (SFAS Nos. 141 and 142), it is clear that today's accountants (both internal staff and outside auditors) must increase their awareness of the intangible assets a company possesses and the value those assets bring to the company, which may in part be driven by the potential value those assets may hold for other entities. Even the SEC now recognizes that the way in which intangible assets are accounted for, as well as which valuation method is employed, can have a material effect on investors' decisions (see discussion by SEC staff on "market participation" valuation requirements in Section 20A.3(a)(ii)).

For example, when the accountant considers how off-balance-sheet transactions may impact (either negatively or positively) the financial condition of a company, intangible assets will be, in many instances, a likely asset class to inspect and analyze. Section 401(a) of the Act directed the SEC to enact rules so that

> [E]ach annual and quarterly report required to be filed with the Commission shall disclose all material off-balance-sheet transactions, arrangements, obligations (including contingent obligations), and other relationships of the issuer with unconsolidated entities or other persons, that may have a material current or future effect on financial condition, changes in financial condition, results of operations, liquidity, capital expenditures, capital resources, or significant components of revenues or expenses.

In its rules (Final Rule: Disclosure in Management's Discussion and Analysis about Off-Balance-Sheet Arrangements and Aggregate Contractual Obligations, effective April 7, 2003), the SEC mandated that registrants provide explanations of off-balance-sheet arrangements in separately captioned subsections of the so-called Management Discussion and Analysis (MD&A)

section of their periodic filings with the Commission. While certain of these disclosures were already required under MD&A rules, the new requirements are somewhat more comprehensive. These rules do not, however, alter underlying accounting for or disclosures about owned intangible assets, nor do they alter the accounting, under GAAP, for transfers or sales of such assets.

The SEC rule does require that executory contracts, such as purchase obligations for goods or services, be included in a new tabular presentation of off-balance-sheet obligations, which is at variance with GAAP requirements but deemed to be important because of liquidity implications. In the case of a license arrangement (e.g., for patent rights previously sold), disclosure in the MD&A under this rule would be appropriate, even though the obligation is not a liability under GAAP definitions.

(ii) Improved Internal Controls over Intangible Assets under Sarbanes   In Section 404(a), the Act addresses a new requirement for management to prepare an internal control report that shall

(1)   state the responsibility of management for establishing and maintaining an adequate internal control structure and procedures for financial reporting and

(2)   contain an assessment, as of the end of the most recent fiscal year of the issuer, of the effectiveness of the internal control structure and procedures of the issuer for financial reporting.

As discussed previously, SFAS Nos. 141 and 142 require revised accounting for intangibles and goodwill arising from business combinations. Similarly, as a company generates new intellectual property through innovation, invention, or operational insights, it may be necessary to establish new accounting procedures to measure the carrying value and fair value of an acquired reporting unit (and perhaps existing reporting units), including the value of intangibles.

Both the cost to create and the cost to protect intangibles are measured and reported in the financial statements, either as an expense (if properly considered research and development costs under GAAP) or as capital assets. In general, due to SFAS No. 2's strict requirements, most of the cost of patent or other intellectual property development, if internally accomplished, will be expensed—one reason that GAAP-compliant financial reporting sometimes underserves entities that rely on intellectual property for their operations and valuation.

An important concern, then, is that if these assets are largely missing from the financial statements, how can these entities ensure that fiduciary responsibilities relative to these hidden assets are properly discharged? There are at least two aspects to this concern: first, developing and implementing internal controls over these assets such that the requirements of Sarbanes will be met; and second, that the value of these assets is recognized for the benefit of the shareholders.

An axiom in management is that what is not measured is not managed; a corollary to that is that what is not in plain sight is also likely not to be well managed. The relatively trivial carrying values of intellectual property often can result in undermanagement, meaning a failure to manage these assets for the benefit of shareholders, whether by using them more effectively internally or by seeking external sources of income from these intangible assets.

As part of a comprehensive effort to establish meaningful controls over their intangible assets, entities should consider developing metrics that would raise the profile of both the holdings of intangibles and of the productivity derived therefrom. Productivity measures would address (as appropriate) both internal usage and external revenue generation. When such internal control procedures are devised and monitored, compliance with this section of Sarbanes would seem to have been accomplished.

(iii) Practical Approaches to Internal Control Structures for Intangible Assets   The authors propose the following approach to the fabrication of an internal control structure used to capture, measure, and report the presence and value of intangible assets. This can be accomplished by assisting personnel in the legal, research, and/or technology transfer departments to establish the appropriate record-keeping and asset-control procedures. Those procedures would relate to documenting the creation, acquisition, and disposal of intellectual assets. Such documentation could include data about the specific identity of the asset; correspondence with appropriate patent, trademark, or copyright offices; ownership and/or assignments; estimated useful lives; associated costs to acquire or create; and, when appropriate, market values.

It is potentially the case that in-house and/or outside counsel may be aware of existing third-party claims that could be asserted against the company, as well as claims the company may be able to assert against third parties. Such analyses may already be in process by the tech-transfer and/or legal staff as part of their normal process of selecting what technologies to outlicense or protect through an infringement action. They may also be in possession of demand letters from other entities that are asserting claims based on their intellectual assets.

Accounting for such claims may also suggest that a review of the company's various insurance policies, vendor and customer contracts, and licensing agreements might be warranted. Because the accountant is typically required under SFAS No. 5 to assess the likelihood that a loss event will occur and whether the estimated loss amounts can be reasonably determined, this should be a routine procedure. Under SFAS No. 5, however, indemnification and insurance provisions may give rise to a recovery claim, but this cannot be offset.

As part of an assessment of the company's disclosure controls, it may be helpful to prepare documentation procedures throughout the life cycle of the intangible asset. If the company is International Organization for Standardization (ISO) compliant, much of the key information regarding intangibles may already be documented relating to

1. Creation and acquisition identification of the intangible asset
2. Applicable filings and prosecution of applications to obtain a formal or registered intellectual property right for the intangible asset
3. Encumbrances to ownership rights, including licensing and assignments that may narrow or eliminate rights for the intangible asset
4. Maintenance of the asset, such as repair and upkeep or the payment of appropriate registration fees
5. Outlicensing and/or cross-licensing agreements
6. Infringement claims against and/or by third parties regarding the intangible asset
7. Disposal, retirement, or expiration of the asset

An additional reference to assist accountants to structure internal control procedures is the guidance presented in the AICPA toolkit, "The Fair Value Measurement Valuation Toolkit for Financial Accounting Standards Board Statements of Financial Accounting Standards No. 141, Business Combinations, and No. 142, Goodwill and Other Intangible Assets."

Much of the foregoing is directed toward maintaining a current record of the existence of intangible assets and various agreements, such as licensing arrangements. Another aspect, and one vital to the goal of maximizing shareholder wealth, is to address those actions that are not currently being taken but that could be valuable for the enterprise and its various stakeholders. Doing this requires that external data sources be incorporated into the entity's information system. Without external references, poor performance may be misread as good simply because of an improvement over prior periods.

One cited statistic, for example, is that each patent in existence (circa 2000) was producing an average of $60,000 in licensing revenues per year, or about $1,000,000 over its economic life. Information about the average licensing revenue per patent is an external metric that can be used to evaluate the entity's own licensing portfolio. Over time, such analyses can be used to gauge portfolio trends, to show whether the licensing revenue of the patent portfolio is acceptable versus expected licensing revenues, based on statistical averages. If not, an investigation can be focused to determine why not. This control mechanism is fully consistent with the explicit requirements and implicit objectives of Sarbanes.

This type of information also sets out a framework for an internal metric. The licensing revenue per patent can be determined for a company patent portfolio. An average licensing revenue can be determined and tracked over time. Patents that are underperforming can be reviewed to ascertain whether these should be preserved for commercial purposes other than licensing, or whether they should be sold or abandoned. Trend data can be accumulated over time to report on whether the portfolio is underperforming based on internally set expectations.

Some examples of metrics that can be used to evaluate an intellectual property (IP) program include the number of patents or patent applications owned by type (utility or design), by country, by the royalty income received from each patent, and by an average royalty for each type of patent or type of technology. Patents owned should include all patents to which the company has unimpaired title. (Title would be deemed impaired if the reporting entity is not the sole assignee.) The dollar value of sales for products covered by the patents is another metric that permits such evaluations of a patent portfolio or IP program.

20A.3 INITIAL RECOGNITION AND MEASUREMENT OF INTANGIBLE ASSETS

(a) ACQUIRED INTANGIBLE ASSETS SFAS No. 142, "Goodwill and Other Intangible Assets," issued in June 2001, superseded the former standard, APB Opinion No. 17, "Intangible Assets." It uses the term *intangible assets* to refer to intangible assets other than goodwill. While amortization is no longer universally required, as it had been for more than 30 years under APB No. 17, SFAS No. 142 did carry forward certain of the requirements of that former standard.

(i) Cost Allocation and Other Valuation Issues An intangible asset acquired either individually or with a group of other assets—other than as part of a business combination—is initially recognized and measured based on its fair value. The cost of a group of assets acquired in a transaction other than a business combination is allocated to the individual assets acquired based on their relative fair values and cannot result in the recognition of goodwill.

Intangible assets acquired in a business combination are initially recognized and measured in conformity with SFAS No. 141—that is, via the purchase price allocation process, which is based on fair values or—for goodwill only—represents the residual cost of the acquisition. Goodwill can arise only in connection with purchase accounting for business combinations. So-called *negative goodwill* is not included in the definition of goodwill as discussed in this chapter. (Under SFAS No. 141, any excess of fair value of net assets acquired over the cost of a business combination is recognized in earnings immediately.)

(ii) SEC/PCAOB Valuation Issues for Intangible Assets—More Changes, Greater Confusion on the Horizon   In unofficial remarks before the December 2004 AICPA National Conference on Current SEC and PCAOB Developments, a staff member of the SEC's Office of the Chief Accountant explained why fair value, determined by using the actual amounts negotiated by the buyer and seller (referred to below as "entity specific") would be superseded by an "estimated" · fair value based on an analysis from a "marketplace participant" perspective. In these remarks, it was stated that

> An underpinning to the determination of fair value of an acquired intangible asset under SFAS No. 141 is that it is determined from the perspective of a marketplace participant.

This is clear in SFAS No. 141, paragraph B174, which indicates that the fair value estimate

> should incorporate assumptions that marketplace participants would use in making estimates of fair value, such as assumptions about future contract renewals and other benefits such as those that might result from acquisition-related synergies. . . .

In contrast, the useful life concept in SFAS No. 142 is not necessarily viewed from that of a marketplace participant. Rather the useful life of an intangible asset is inherently related to the expectations of the particular entity and therefore would incorporate entity-specific assumptions.

In this context, the entity may believe that the fair value determination should therefore be entirely consistent with the useful life then assigned to the intangible asset as in this case, both were developed based on entity-specific assumptions.

I would point out, however, that the utilization of entity-specific assumptions to determine fair value in this case is just a proxy for those assumptions that may be developed by a marketplace participant.

Subsequent to these remarks, the FASB issued an Exposure Draft of SFAS No. 141(R) (June 2005), which in many particulars is based on an analysis of international accounting standards. At paragraph 20, proposed SFAS No. 141(R) seeks to clarify the definition of fair value for a business combination when it states:

> Business combinations are usually arm's-length exchange transactions in which knowledgeable, unrelated willing parties exchange equal values. Therefore, in the absence of evidence to the contrary, the exchange price (referred to as the consideration transferred in this Statement) paid by the acquirer on the acquisition date is presumed to be the best evidence of the acquisition date fair value of the acquirer's interest in the acquiree.

The SEC remarks and the FASB exposure draft provisions are indicative of a changing landscape of the acceptable valuation methodologies and technical experts to whom the accountant can turn for support when computing an intangible's fair value.

FASB Concept Statement No. 7 was identified in SFAS No. 142, issued in 2002, as guidance for valuation methodologies, principally citing the comparables and income method approaches. However, intangible asset values measured in actual business transactions are often based more on expected and potential benefits rather than on historical and/or actual revenues. Therefore, the application of the income approach requires a stacking or layering of assumptions. As the number of those assumptions increases, compliance with Rule 201 of the AICPA *Code of Professional Conduct* (specifically concerning the reliance on sufficient relevant data in support of any professional opinion) becomes more and more difficult.

There are real-world situations in which technical experts from other disciplines have addressed the situation of determining the fair value of intangibles where historical cash flows do not exist. One of those situations arises during the dispute resolution process, and a second is seen in the technology-transfer industry.

(iii) Valuation Approaches Supported by Court Opinions   In the federal courts, a jury is frequently asked to estimate the damages attributable to a violation of intellectual property rights. Several cases, including *Georgia Pacific v. United States Plywood Corp.* and *Panduit Corp. v. Stahlin Bros. Fibre Works, Inc.*, have compiled a technical body of knowledge regarding methodologies to determine the fair value of intangible assets. For example, *Panduit* sets forth these four tests:

1. Is there demand for the patented product?
2. Are there acceptable noninfringing alternatives to the infringing product?
3. Does the patent holder have the manufacturing and marketing capacity to make and sell more of the product?
4. Can the damages consultant quantify the lost profits to a reasonable degree of certainty?

In the earlier *Georgia-Pacific* case, the court considered 15 factors as a means to compute damages arising from a dispute over intangible assets:

1. The royalties received by Georgia-Pacific for licensing the patent, proving or tending to prove an established royalty
2. The rates paid by the licensee for the use of other similar patents
3. The nature and scope of the license, such as whether it is exclusive or nonexclusive, restricted or nonrestricted in terms of territory or customers
4. Georgia-Pacific's policy of maintaining its patent monopoly by licensing the use of the invention only under special conditions designed to preserve the monopoly
5. The commercial relationship between Georgia-Pacific and licensees, such as whether they are competitors in the same territory in the same line of business or whether they are inventor and promoter
6. The effect of selling the patented specialty in promoting sales of other Georgia-Pacific products; the existing value of the invention to Georgia-Pacific as a generator of sales of nonpatented items; and the extent of such derivative or "convoyed" sales
7. The duration of the patent and the term of the license
8. The established profitability of the patented product, its commercial success, and its current popularity
9. The utility and advantages of the patent property over any old modes or devices that had been used
10. The nature of the patented invention, its character in the commercial embodiment owned and produced by the licensor, and the benefits to those who have used it

11. The extent to which the infringer used the invention and any evidence probative of the value of that use
12. The portion of the profit or selling price that is customary in the particular business or in comparable businesses
13. The portion of the realizable profit that should be credited to the invention as distinguished from any nonpatented elements, manufacturing process, business risks, or significant features or improvements added by the infringer
14. The opinion testimony of qualified experts
15. The amount that Georgia-Pacific and a licensee would have agreed upon at the time the infringement began if they had reasonably and voluntarily tried to reach an agreement

In a subsequent case based in part on the *Panduit* findings, the courts have held that damages based on a loss of market share can be used to compute damages (*State Industries, Inc. v. Mor-Flo Industries, Inc.*). In *State Industries,* the Federal Circuit accepted evidence of the patentee's market share to prove that the patentee would have made at least a percentage of the infringer's sales had there been no infringement. Quantifying market share allows the patentee to measure lost profits in the ratio of their original market share to their diluted market share after the infringement.

In these cases and several others, the courts have held that intellectual property owners may be entitled to lost profits that can never be realized (hence the claim for "lost" profits), but were nonetheless measured to "a reasonable degree of accounting certainty."

(iv) Valuation Approaches Used by Tech-Transfer Practitioners   Taking a page from the dispute resolution practitioners, several technology-transfer specialists (also referred to as licensing professionals) have adopted market-based measures of value. Here, however, rather than measure the amount of damages, the computation is made for the purpose of measuring the amount of benefits that would be recognized by the adoption of the licensor's technology by the licensee. In 2002 Ted Hagelin analyzed different concepts and methods of valuation, including the cost, market, and income methods.[2] Other valuation methods developed especially for intellectual property law were also examined, including the "25 percent" rule, industry standards, ranking, surrogate measures, disaggregation, Monte Carlo, and option methods. In his article, Professor Hagelin presents a newly devised tech-transfer valuation model labeled "Competitive Advantage Valuation" and suggests that

> The . . . premise of the CAV [Competitive Advantage Valuation] method is that the value of a given intellectual property asset can best be measured by the competitive advantage which that asset contributes.

When one incorporates this tech-transfer CAV approach with the previously cited assertion by SEC staff that "market-participant" value drivers must be considered under SFAS Nos. 141 and 142, it becomes obvious that there are multiple, well-established, fully vetted intangible

---

2.   Ted Hagelin, "A New Method to Value Intellectual Property," *American Intellectual Property Law Association Quarterly Journal,* Vol. 30 (2000), p. 33.

asset valuation approaches that accounting practitioners can employ when answering the question, "What are the values of these intangible assets?"

(v) Valuation Approaches Seen in Wall Street Transactions An additional market validation of the alignment of these various intangible asset valuation approaches is found in the emergence of numerous intellectual asset-based transactions on Wall Street. One of the most familiar transactions seen in the entertainment and garment industries is the securitization of anticipated intangible asset-based revenues, as reflected in the Bowie Bond (David Bowie) and Bill Blass securitizations.

Another example is the adaptation of the traditional lending structure known as a sale lease-back (used for tangible assets) that has been deployed using intangible assets and has been referred to as a sale/license-back. In a presentation to the National Knowledge and Intellectual Property Management Taskforce's annual executive briefing in September 2002, Mitchell Fillet, of Riderwood Group, Inc., stated that

> We are in the midst of a paradigm shift that is so economically powerful that it ranks with the other two that have defined our economic history. . . .
>
> I am suggesting that intellectual property, primarily patents and derivative products from those patents, as well as licenses to use that intellectual property, is emerging as an important asset class both on corporate balance sheets and off them, as collateral for loans and legally separate securitizations.

As a result of the sale/license-back structure, intangible assets are now being acquired by large investment banking firms, much as mortgage portfolios were acquired starting in the 1970s, thus giving birth to a highly liquid market for what had previously been difficult-to-trade assets. As such, the value drivers associated with intangible assets now reflect several of the financial modeling aspects found in commercial paper and various asset-backed securitizations.

As evidence of the importance such intangible assets have, and the market-based impact they can make, we can review the Federal Reserve Chairman's October 2005 comments on this market built on intangibles, citing the significant economic benefits to the U.S. economy of the secondary market launched in the mid-1970s:

> These increasingly complex financial instruments have contributed to the development of a far more flexible, efficient, and hence resilient financial system than the one that existed just a quarter-century ago. After the bursting of the stock market bubble in 2000, unlike previous periods following large financial shocks, no major financial institution defaulted, and the economy held up far better than many had anticipated.[3]

To gain an understanding about how intangible assets account for such significant market values, the accounting of a sale/license-back transaction can be reviewed; both the buyer and the seller in this transaction recognize distinct benefits.

---

3. Alan Greenspan, speech on economic flexibility, presented before the National Italian American Foundation, Washington, DC, October 12, 2005.

From the seller's position, the closing would generate significant pretax earnings, as the only significant offset to sales price paid for internally generated intangibles would be the transaction fees (attorneys, financial consultants, valuation experts) and any unamortized capitalized cost of the underlying assets. In the sale/license-back structure, the attributes of the intangible assets permit the transaction to unleash earnings (unlike the sale/lease-back that was treated as a financing), principally because title to the intangible asset is transferred to the buyer.

Additionally, any license-back provision would qualify as a fully deductible expense for tax purposes. Unlike the sale/lease-back of a tangible asset, which is governed by SFAS No. 13, the "license" in a sale/license-back is a period expense and not debt; the license is consumed in the period in which the expense is incurred. Such accounting treatment suggests that the seller's cost of capital would be reduced to the extent that the proceeds from the sale are used to reduce bank or other outstanding debt, thereby deleveraging the balance sheet.

From the buyer's perspective, intangible assets with measurable, market-based value (presumably from outlicensing potential) can be selectively acquired, without incurring all of the fixed and sunk costs attributed to a research and development facility. Generally speaking, the licensing activity of a large corporation enjoys a greater contribution margin than the company taken as a whole. Additionally, the operating costs would be partially offset by the license granted to the seller, and the intangible assets acquired would be treated as an amortizable asset.

(vi) Identifiable Intangibles Distinguishable from Goodwill   SFAS No. 141 provides that intangible assets acquired in a business combination are to be recognized as an asset *apart from goodwill*, but only if they meet the asset recognition criteria in the FASB's Statement of Financial Accounting Concept No. 5 (CON 5), *and* if either (1) control over the future economic benefits of the assets results from contractual or other legal rights (the "legal/contractual" criterion) or (2) the intangible assets are capable of being separated or divided and sold, transferred, licensed, rented, or exchanged (referred to as the separability criterion). Even if the intangible assets cannot be sold, transferred, licensed, rented, or exchanged individually, the assets would still meet the separability criterion if they could be sold, transferred, licensed, rented, or exchanged along with a related contract, asset, or liability.

Examples of intangible assets that meet the "legal/contractual" criterion include trademarks, newspaper mastheads, Internet domain names, order backlog, books, magazines, musical works, license agreements, construction permits, broadcast rights, mortgage servicing contracts, patented technology, and computer software. Examples of assets that meet the separability criterion include customer lists, noncontractual customer relationships, unpatented technology, and databases such as title plants. Note that it is not necessary for the acquiring entity to actually intend to dispose of, sell, or rent the separable intangible in order to satisfy this criterion.

SFAS No. 141 presents a lengthy listing of intangibles that are to be separately recognized, along with the useful lives relevant for amortization purposes. Certain exceptions are identified, such as for those intangibles having indefinite lives, as is the case for perpetually renewable broadcast licenses, which are maintained at cost (subject to potential impairment write-downs) until a finite life can be ascertained, if ever. These intangibles generally can be categorized as being (1) customer- or market-based assets (e.g., customer lists, newspaper mastheads, and trademarked brand names); (2) contract-based assets (e.g., covenants not to compete, broadcast rights); (3) artistic-based assets (e.g., plays, other literary works, musical compositions); and (4) technology-based assets (e.g., title plant, databases, computer software). With the exception of indefinite-life intangibles, all identifiable intangibles are to be amortized over their estimated useful lives, defined as the period over which the intangible asset is expected to directly or indirectly generate cash flows for the entity. Appendix A to SFAS No. 141 identifies intangible assets that have characteristics that meet one of the two criteria (legal/contractual or separability). However, depending on the facts and circumstances, a specific acquired intangible asset might not meet the criteria. A good approach would be to first consider whether the acquired intangibles are among those specifically described by the FASB, and then to consider whether other intangibles also meeting the two criteria for separate capitalization might also be present.

Identified intangibles can be aggregated into permits, intellectual property, technology tools, procurement rights, competitor arrangements, and customer arrangements. *Permits* include:

- *Broadcast rights:* a license to transmit over certain bandwidths in the radio frequency spectrum, granted by the operation of communication laws
- *Certification marks:* the right to be able to assert that a product or service meets certain standards of quality or origin, such as "ISO 14000 Certified"
- *Collective marks:* rights to signify membership in an association
- *Construction permits:* rights to build a specified structure at a specified location
- *Franchise rights:* permits to engage in a trade-named business, to sell a trademarked good, or to sell a service-marked service in a particular geographic area
- *Internet domain names:* domain names using alphabetical characters such as www. samplecompany.com in lieu of using numeric addresses provide more memorable internet addresses
- *Operating rights:* permits to operate in a certain manner, such as that granted to a carrier to transport specified commodities
- *Use rights:* permits to use specified land, property, or air space in a particular manner, such as the right to cut timber, expel emissions, or land airplanes

Intellectual property includes, inter alia, the following:

- *Copyrights:* the rights to reproduce, distribute, and so on an original work of literature, music, art, photography, or film
- *Newspaper mastheads:* the rights to use the information that is displayed on the top of the first pages of newspapers
- *Patents:* the rights to make, use, or sell an invention for a specified period
- *Service marks:* the rights to use the name or symbol that distinguishes a service
- *Trade dress:* access to the overall appearance and image (unique color, shape, or package design) of a product
- *Trademarks:* rights to use the word, logo, or symbol that distinguishes a product
- *Trade names:* the right to use the name or symbol that distinguishes a business
- *Trade secrets:* information, such as a formula, process, or recipe, that is kept confidential
- *Unpatented technology:* access to the knowledge about the manner of accomplishing a task

Technology tools may consist of computer software, including programs, procedures, and documentation associated with computer hardware, as well as databases, which are collections of a particular type of information, such as scientific data or credit information.

Procurement rights include the following:

- *Construction contracts:* rights to acquire the subject of the contract in exchange for taking over the remaining obligations (including any payments)
- *Employment contracts:* rights to take the seller's place as the employer under the contract and thus obtain the employee's services in exchange for fulfilling the employer's remaining duties, such as payment of salaries and benefits, under the contract
- *Lease agreements:* if assignable, rights to step into the shoes of the lessee and thus obtain the rights to use assets that are the subject of the agreement, in exchange for making the remaining lease payments
- *License agreements:* rights to access or use properties that are the subjects of licenses in exchange for making any remaining license payments and adhering to other responsibilities as licensee
- *Royalty agreements:* rights to take the place of payors and thus assume the payors' remaining rights and duties under the agreements
- *Service or supply contracts:* rights to become the customer of particular contracts and thus purchase the specified products or services for the prices specified in those contracts

Competitor arrangements may include

- *Noncompete agreements:* rights to assurances that companies or individuals will refrain from conducting similar businesses or selling to specific customers for an agreed-upon period
- *Standstill agreements,* which convey rights to assurances that companies or individuals will refrain from engaging in certain activities for specified periods

Customer arrangements are items such as

- *Customer lists:* information about companies' customers, including names, contact information, and order histories that a third party, such as a competitor or a telemarketing firm, would want to use in its own business
- *Customer relationships:* the relationships between entities and their customers for which
  - The entities have information about the customers and have regular contacts with the customers and
  - The customers have the ability to make direct contact with the entity
- *Contracts and related customer relationships:* relationships that arise through contracts and are of value to buyers who can "step into the shoes" of the sellers and assume their remaining rights and duties under the contracts, and that hold the promise that the customers will place future orders with the entity
- *Noncontractual customer relationships:* relationships that arise through means such as regular contacts by sales or service representatives, the value of which are derived from the prospect of the customers placing future orders with the entities
- *Order or production backlogs:* providing buyers rights to step into the shoes of sellers on unfilled sales orders for services and for goods in amounts that exceed the quantity of finished goods and work-in-process on hand for filling the orders

(b) INTERNALLY DEVELOPED INTANGIBLE ASSETS   Costs of internally developing, maintaining, or restoring intangible assets including goodwill that are not specifically identifiable, that have indeterminate lives, or that are inherent in a continuing business and related to a reporting entity as a whole are recognized as an expense when incurred. This rule was grounded, in part, on the traditional aversion to recognition of self-developed goodwill, which is a prohibition nominally still in effect (although the prescribed procedures for the impairment testing of goodwill under SFAS No. 142 implicitly allow for recognition of self-created goodwill, to the extent that it replaces acquired goodwill).

As a practical matter, capitalization of internally developed intangibles is generally obviated by the requirements of SFAS No. 2, which requires that all research and development costs be expensed as incurred. This rule, which is controversial (e.g., the corresponding international financial reporting standard requires expensing of research costs but capitalization of development expenditures) and likely to become more so (as general awareness of the importance of intangibles increases and as the move toward the "knowledge-based economy" continues and even accelerates), would probably preclude most costs incurred in connection with internal generation of intangibles from being recognized as assets in any event.

20A.4 ACCOUNTING FOR INTANGIBLE ASSETS

(a) DETERMINING THE USEFUL LIFE OF AN INTANGIBLE ASSET The accounting for recognized intangible assets is based on their useful lives *to the reporting entity*. Note that these may well differ from the legal or contractual lives, and could also easily diverge from the useful lives in the hands of *other* reporting entities holding similar or even identical assets. The amounts of intangible assets with finite useful lives are amortized, whereas the amounts assigned to intangible assets with indefinite useful lives are not amortized. The useful lives of intangible assets to a reporting entity are the respective periods over which the assets are expected to contribute directly or indirectly to the future cash flows of the reporting entity. The estimates of the useful lives of intangible assets to the reporting entity are based on analyses of all pertinent factors. Particular attention is to be given to the following:

- Expected use of the assets by the reporting entity
- Expected useful lives of other assets or groups of assets to which the useful lives of the intangible assets may relate, such as mineral rights to depleting assets
- Any legal, regulatory, or contractual provisions that may limit the useful lives
- Any legal, regulatory, or contractual provisions that enable renewals or extensions of the assets' legal or contractual lives without substantial cost, provided that there is evidence to support renewals or extensions, and renewals or extensions can be accomplished without material modifications of the respective existing terms and conditions
- Effects of obsolescence, demand, competition, and other economic factors, such as the stability of the industry, known technological advances, legislative action that results in an uncertain or changing regulatory environment, and expected changes in distribution channels
- Levels of maintenance expenditures required to obtain the expected future cash flows from the assets—for example, a material level of required maintenance in relation to the carrying amount of an asset may suggest a very limited useful life

If no legal, regulatory, contractual, competitive, economic, or other factors limit the useful lives of the intangible assets to the reporting entity, those useful lives are considered to be indefinite, which does not mean *infinite*.

(b) INTANGIBLE ASSETS SUBJECT TO AMORTIZATION   The amounts of recognized intangible assets are to be amortized over the useful lives of the respective assets to the reporting entity, unless those lives are determined to be indefinite. SFAS No. 142 requires that the recorded amounts of intangible assets with finite lives, but without precisely known lives, be amortized over the best estimates of the useful lives. The methods of amortization should reflect the patterns by which the economic benefits of the intangible assets are consumed or otherwise used up. If the patterns cannot be reliably determined, the straight-line amortization method is to be used. Intangible assets are not written down or off in the period of acquisition unless impairments occur during that initial period, which is unlikely but not impossible.

Under SFAS No. 142, the amount of an intangible asset subject to amortization is the value initially assigned to the asset less any residual value. However, the residual value of an intangible asset must be presumed to be zero unless at the end of the useful life to the reporting entity the asset is expected to continue to have a useful life to another entity *and* either (a) the reporting entity has a commitment from a third party to purchase the asset at the end of its useful life to the reporting entity or (b) the residual value can be determined by reference to an exchange transaction in an existing market for that asset and that market is expected to exist at the end of the asset's useful life. In practice, residual values are rarely justified for intangibles subject to amortization.

Reporting entities must evaluate the remaining useful lives of intangible assets that are being amortized each reporting period to determine whether events and circumstances warrant a revision to the remaining periods of amortization. If estimates of intangible assets' useful lives are changed, the remaining carrying amounts of the intangible assets are to be amortized prospectively over their revised remaining useful lives.

If any of the intangible assets being amortized are subsequently determined to have indefinite useful lives, these assets are to be tested for impairment, as is discussed subsequently. These intangible assets are then no longer amortized and are instead accounted for the same way as other intangible assets not subject to amortization.

Intangible assets subject to amortization are to be reviewed for impairments in conformity with SFAS No. 144. After an impairment loss is recognized, the adjusted carrying amount of that intangible asset is its new accounting basis. A previously recognized impairment loss is not subsequently reversed, despite evidence of value recovery.

(c) INTANGIBLE ASSETS NOT SUBJECT TO AMORTIZATION   Intangible assets that were determined to have indefinite useful lives are not amortized until their respective useful lives are determined no longer to be indefinite. The reporting entity is required to evaluate the remaining useful lives of intangible assets not being amortized each reporting period, in order to determine whether events and circumstances continue to support indefinite useful lives. Intangible assets not being amortized, but subsequently determined to have finite useful lives, are tested for impairment, as discussed next. The assets are then amortized prospectively over their estimated remaining useful lives and accounted for the same way as other intangible assets subject to amortization.

Intangible assets not subject to amortization are to be tested for impairments annually, or more frequently if events or changes in circumstances indicate that the assets might have become impaired. The impairment tests consist of making comparisons of the fair values of the assets with their respective carrying amounts. If the carrying amount for a given intangible asset exceeds its fair value, an impairment loss is recognized in an amount equal to the excess. After an impairment loss is recognized, the asset's adjusted carrying amount is the intangible asset's new accounting basis. A previously recognized impairment loss cannot be reversed.

In EITF Issue No. 02-7, "Unit of Accounting for Testing Impairment of Indefinite-Lived Intangible Assets," there was a consensus that separately recorded indefinite-lived intangible assets should be combined into a single unit of accounting for impairment testing purposes if they are operated as a single asset and are therefore essentially inseparable. EITF Issue No. 02-7 includes indicators and illustrations of when intangible assets should be—and when they should not be—combined.

Indicators that suggest that indefinite-lived intangibles should be combined as a single unit of accounting include the following:

1. The intangibles will be used together to construct or enhance a single asset.
2. If the intangibles had been part of the same acquisition, they would have been recorded as a single asset.
3. The intangibles, as a group, represent "the highest and best use of the assets" (e.g., they could probably realize a higher sales price if sold together than if they were sold separately). Indicators pointing to this situation are
    a. The degree to which it is unlikely that a substantial portion of the assets would be sold separately, or
    b. The fact that should a substantial portion of the intangibles be sold individually, there would be a significant reduction in the fair value of the remaining assets in the group.
4. The marketing or branding strategy of the entity treats the assets as being complementary (e.g., a trademark and its related trade name, formulas, recipes, and patented or unpatented technology can all be complementary to an entity's brand name).

Indicators that imply that indefinite-lived intangibles should not be combined as a single unit of accounting include the following:

1. Each separate intangible generates independent cash flows.
2. In a sale, it would be likely that the intangibles would be sold separately. If the entity had previously sold similar assets separately, this would constitute evidence that combining the assets would not be appropriate.
3. The entity is either considering or has already adopted a plan to dispose of one or more of the intangibles separately.
4. The intangibles are used exclusively by different asset groups (as defined in SFAS No. 144).
5. The assets have different useful economic lives.

EITF 02-7 provided additional guidance regarding the "unit of accounting" determination that must be made for impairment testing purposes.

1. Goodwill and finite-lived intangibles may not be combined in the "unit of accounting" since they are subject to different impairment testing rules (set forth by SFAS Nos. 142 and 144, respectively).
2. If the intangibles collectively constitute a business, they may not be combined into a unit of accounting.

3. If the unit of accounting includes intangibles recorded in the separate financial statements of consolidated subsidiaries, it is possible that the sum of impairment losses recognized in the separate financial statements of the subsidiaries will not equal the consolidated impairment loss.

4. Should a unit of accounting be included in a single reporting unit, that same unit of accounting and associated fair value are to be used in computing the implied fair value of goodwill for measuring any goodwill impairment loss.

Identifiable intangible assets, such as franchise rights, customer lists, trademarks, patents and copyrights, and licenses, are to be amortized over their expected useful economic lives, even if they exceed the former 40-year ceiling. However, if longer amortization periods (useful lives) are elected, impairment reviews of the assets' recoverability are required when necessitated by changes in facts and circumstances in the same manner as set forth in SFAS No. 144 for tangible long-lived assets. SFAS No. 144 also requires consideration of the intangible assets' residual values (which are analogous to salvage values for tangible assets) in determining the amounts of the intangibles to amortize. Residual value is defined as the value of the intangible to the entity at the end of its (entity-specific) useful life reduced by any estimated disposition costs. The residual value of an amortizable intangible is assumed to be zero unless the intangible will continue to have a useful life to another party after the end of its useful life to its current holder, and one or both of the following criteria are met:

1. The current holder has received a third-party commitment to purchase the intangible at the end of its useful life, *or*

2. A market for the intangible exists and is expected to continue to exist at the end of the asset's useful life as a means of determining the residual value of the intangible by reference to marketplace transactions.

A broadcast license is nominally subject to expiration in five years, but might be indefinitely renewable at little additional cost to the broadcaster. If cash flows can be projected indefinitely, and assuming a market exists for the license, no amortization is to be recorded until such time as a finite life is predicted. However, it is required that the asset be tested for impairment at least annually, to ensure that it is carried at no greater than its fair value.

20A.5   CERTAIN IDENTIFIABLE INTANGIBLE ASSETS

(a) PATENTS   Accounting for patents is affected by the laws governing the legal rights of a patent holder. A U.S. patent is a nonrenewable right granted by the federal government that enables the recipient to exclude others from the manufacture, sale, or other use of an invention for a period of 17 years from the date of grant. Enforceability of a patent begins only on its grant, and the exclusive right of use is not retroactive. However, the filing of a patent application provides protection from the claims of a later inventor for the same item so that the period of partial protection may be considered to extend from the date of the original application. While the legal term of the patent is 17 years, the effective period of competitive advantage may extend beyond the original 17-year patent term if additional patents are obtained as improvements are made. Many patent holders do endeavor to create various modifications and improvements that can be patented in their own right, to accomplish this de facto extension of protection for many years. The rights to a patent may be assigned in whole or in part, as can the right to use the patent (i.e., licenses under the patent) on a royalty or other basis.

(i) Capitalizable Amounts for Patents   Patents may be purchased from others or developed internally as a result of research and development activities. The cost of a purchased patent includes the purchase price and any related expenditures, such as attorneys' fees. If a patent is developed internally, its cost includes legal fees in connection with patent applications, patent fees, litigation fees, litigation costs, costs of sale or licensing, and filing fees. Any related research, experimental, and developmental expenditures, including the cost of models and drawings not specifically required for a patent application, are research and development (R&D) costs and should be expensed as incurred in accordance with SFAS No. 2.

The grant of a patent through the U.S. Patent Office is no guarantee of protection. It is often necessary to defend the patent's validity in court tests and also to refute allegations of infringement of other patents and to prosecute infringement of the patent by others. The costs of successful court tests may be capitalized as additional costs of the patent, and then amortized over the remaining useful life of the underlying patent. However, if the litigation is unsuccessful, the costs of the litigation should be written off immediately, as should any carrying value of the patent that has been stripped of its economic value.

(ii) Amortization of Patents   A U.S. patent has a specified legal life. It provides protection for 17 years, and that is the maximum amortization period. The period used in practice is often less because of technological or market obsolescence factors, such as the issuance of new patents to competitors, improved models, substitutes, or general technological progress. These factors must be taken into account in determining the original useful life and during the subsequent reviews of remaining economic life. The amortization period should not extend beyond the market life of the product with which the patent is associated, unless it is demonstrable that the patent can also be used in other applications. However, if it is possible to extend a patent's economic life by obtaining additional patents, it is permissible to amortize the remaining balance of the costs of the old patent over the estimated economic lives of the new ones. (For example, if a patent is half amortized when a successor patent is issued and the estimated life of the successor is ten years, the unamortized carrying value of the original patent should be added to the cost of the new one, with the entire sum then amortized over ten years.)

The impairment accounting guidance in SFAS No. 144 is applicable to patents. Once it is determined that the monopolistic advantage offered by use and ownership of the patent no longer exists, the remaining unamortized balance should be written off. Also, any increases in separately identified deferred costs, due to such factors as an additional lawsuit establishing the validity of the patent, should be written off over the remaining estimated economic life of the patent.

(b) COPYRIGHTS   A copyright is the exclusive right to reproduce, publish, and sell a literary product or artistic work. The term of the copyright in the United States is now the life of the author plus 50 years (formerly 28 years with a single renewal option). As in the case of a patent, the rights to a copyright may be assigned, licensed, or sold.

(i) Capitalizable Amounts for Copyrights   The costs of developing copyrights and the costs of purchased copyrights may be substantial and should be deferred. For a copyright developed internally, costs include expenditures for government filing fees and attorneys' fees and expenses, along with outlays for wages and materials in the preparation of the material to be copyrighted and expenditures incurred to establish the right. If a copyright is purchased, the initial valuation includes the acquisition price plus any costs incurred in establishing the right.

(ii) Amortization of Copyrights   Copyrighted materials, for various reasons, often do not have an active market past the first few years after the issuance of the copyright. It is rare that copyrighted materials will have lengthy economic lives, although there are exceptions. The capitalized amounts are to be amortized over the number of years in which sales or royalties related to the copyright can be expected to occur.

SFAS No. 144, "Accounting for the Impairment or Disposal of Long-Lived Assets," provides guidance on the impairment of intangible assets with finite lives, such as copyrights. Continuing review of the status of copyrights is essential to determine whether they have continuing value. If the copyrighted material will no longer be used, it should be written off.

(c) CUSTOMER AND SUPPLIER LISTS   Customer and supplier lists can be particularly valuable to a business, as they represent groups of customers or suppliers with whom business relations have been established. The value of such lists is based on the assumption of continuing business relationships, as well as possibly reducing the marketing costs that would otherwise be necessary (e.g., to develop customer lists).

(i) Capitalizable Amounts for Customer and Supplier Lists   Customer or supplier lists often are developed internally, and the cost specifically identified with development generally is impossible to determine. These costs are often analogous to research and development expenditures; accordingly, such costs are not deferred. However, when lists are purchased from others, the acquisition cost should be deferred. While generally these are identifiable assets and thus separately recognizable, a customer or supplier list acquired in a business combination would not meet the criteria for recognition apart from goodwill if there are terms of confidentiality or other agreements that prohibit the selling, leasing, or otherwise exchanging of the acquired customer or supplier information.

(ii) Amortization of Customer and Supplier Lists   The value of customer or supplier lists decreases as customers or suppliers are lost or cease to exist. Ideally, the cost of a list should be written off based on these factors—that is, on a units-lost basis. However, since it is often difficult to track lost customers or suppliers precisely, straight-line amortization over a reasonable average customer or supplier retention period is commonly used. The estimate of the useful life should consider all available information and should be reevaluated each reporting period. To the extent that there is a rapid turnover of customers or suppliers, this suggests that little or even no value should have been attributed to the acquired lists.

(d) FRANCHISES   Franchises may be granted by governmental units, individuals, or corporate entities. Public utilities are granted franchises by the communities they serve. These franchises establish the right to operate and specify the conditions under which utilities must function. Such franchises may place certain restrictions on the enterprise concerning rates and operating conditions, but they also confer certain privileges, ranging from minor ones to the granting of a full monopoly.

Private franchises are contracts for the exclusive right to perform certain functions or to sell certain (usually branded) products or services. Such agreements involve the use by the franchisee of a trademark, trade name, patent, process, or know-how of the franchisor for the term of the franchise. For example, a manufacturer may grant a dealer a franchise to market a product within a given territory and agree not to allow other dealers to market the same product in that area.

Costs of obtaining a franchise include any fees paid to the franchisor along with legal and other expenditures incurred in obtaining the franchise. If a franchise agreement covers a specified period of time, the cost of the franchise should be written off over that period unless the economic life is anticipated to be less. If the franchise is perpetual, the franchisee should evaluate the expected useful life of the franchise, considering the effect of obsolescence, demand, competition, and other relevant economic factors. Additional periodic payments based on revenues or other factors may be required in addition to initial fees. These period costs should be expensed as incurred, because they pertain to only the current period and represent no future benefit. The franchise agreement may also require certain property improvements that should be capitalized and included in property, plant, and equipment.

(e) LEASES AND LEASEHOLD RIGHTS   A favorable lease is one in which the property rights obtained under the lease could presently be obtained only at a higher rental. This concept is not to be mistaken for the issue of capitalized leases or capital additions classified as leasehold improvements. Favorable leases may be recognized when a business is purchased or when a payment is made to an existing lessee for the right to sublease, if indeed there is sufficient evidence to demonstrate a below-market rate of rental payments.

(i) Capitalizable Amounts for Favorable Leases and Leasehold Rights   The favorable lease usually is measured by the present value of the cost differential between the terms of the lease and the amount that could be obtained currently in an arm's-length transaction. This corresponds to the economic or fair value of the favorable terms.

(ii) Amortization of Favorable Leases   The cost assigned to a favorable lease is amortized over the lease term. A lump-sum payment at the inception of the lease should be amortized to rent expense over the life of the lease.

(f) ORGANIZATION COSTS   Organization costs are expenditures made to promote and organize a concern, including costs (i.e., legal and state filing fees) of establishing the entity's existence. Under Statement of Position (SOP) 98-5, "Reporting on the Costs of Start-Up Activities," start-up activities include organization costs. This SOP concludes that costs of start-up activities, including organization costs, should be expensed as incurred.

(g) REGISTRATION COSTS   The Securities and Exchange Commission staff in Staff Accounting Bulletin (SAB) Topic 5A stated that specific incremental costs directly attributable to a proposed or actual offering of securities may properly be deferred and charged against the gross proceeds of the offering. Management salaries or other general and administrative expenses may not be allocated as costs of the offering. Costs of an aborted offering may not be deferred and charged against a subsequent offering. According to SEC staff, a short postponement of up to 90 days does not represent an aborted offering.

(h) RESEARCH AND DEVELOPMENT COSTS   So-called R&D expenses have long been a controversial accounting topic. Prior to the imposition of current GAAP, it had been common to defer such costs, and investors often were dismayed at sporadic "big baths" when the hoped-for developments failed to be consummated or proved to have less economic value than expected. In reaction to the formerly liberal practices of deferring R&D costs, therefore, one of the FASB's first acts was to impose SFAS No. 2, "Accounting for Research and Development Costs," which requires that all R&D costs be charged to expense as incurred.

SFAS No. 142 did not change the stringent accounting requirements of SFAS No. 2. It includes the following definitions of research and development:

Research is planned search or critical investigation aimed at discovery of new knowledge with the hope that such knowledge will be useful in developing a new product or service . . . or a new process or technique . . . or in bringing about a significant improvement to an existing product or process.

Development is the translation of research findings or other knowledge into a plan or design for a new product or process or for a significant improvement to an existing product or process whether intended for sale or use. It includes the conceptual formulation, design, and testing of product alternatives, construction of prototypes, and operation of pilot plants. It does not include routine or periodic alterations to existing products, production lines, manufacturing processes, and other on-going operations even though those alterations may represent improvements, and it does not include market research or market testing activities. (SFAS No. 2, para. 8.)

The distinction between "research" and "development" is more than semantic. For example, under International Financial Reporting Standards (IFRS), while research costs must be expensed at once, as under U.S. GAAP, development costs are to be deferred and amortized over the economic lives of the resultant products or processes. Even under U.S. GAAP the distinction between "research" and "development" is germane, albeit not as a general principle. However, for certain categories of software development costs, costs incurred before technological feasibility has been demonstrated (i.e., those that are analogous to research costs) are expensed, whereas those incurred after feasibility has been demonstrated (which are, arguably, more suggestive of development costs) are capitalized and amortized.

Given the huge economic significance of R&D expenditures and the growing recognition that substantial amounts of assets are being omitted from many reporting entities' balance sheets (with an equivalent understatement of net stockholders' equity), this is likely to receive renewed attention. Particularly given the FASB's commitment to "converge" U.S. GAAP and International Financial Reporting Standards there would appear to be some possibility that future GAAP will permit or require deferral of development-type expenses, subject to amortization and, perhaps, impairment assessments.

Research and development costs, according to SFAS No. 2, include the following elements:

Materials, Equipment and Facilities. The cost of materials . . . and equipment or facilities that are acquired or constructed for research and development activities and that have alternative future uses . . . shall be capitalized as tangible assets when acquired or constructed. The cost of such materials consumed in research and development activities and the depreciation of such equipment or facilities used in those activities are research and development costs. However, the costs of materials, equipment, or facilities that are acquired or constructed for a particular research and development project and that have no alternative future uses . . . are research and development costs at the time the costs are incurred.

Personnel. Salaries, wages, and other related costs of personnel engaged in research and development activities shall be included in research and development costs.

Intangibles Purchased from Others. The costs of intangibles that are purchased from others for use in research and development activities and that have alternative future uses . . . shall be accounted for in accordance with FASB Statement No. 142, "Goodwill and Other Intangible Assets." . . . The amortization of those intangible assets used in research and development activities is a research and development cost. However, the costs of intangibles that are purchased from others for a particular research and development project and that have no alternative future uses . . . are research and development costs at the time the costs are incurred.

Contract Services. The costs of services performed by others in connection with the research and development activities of an enterprise, including research and development conducted by others in behalf of the enterprise, shall be included in research and development costs.

Indirect Costs. Research and development costs shall include a reasonable allocation of indirect costs. However, general and administrative costs that are not clearly related to research and development activities shall not be included as research and development costs. SFAS No. 2 requires that all costs of activities identified as R&D be charged to expense as incurred. The only exception is that government-regulated enterprises may be required to defer certain costs for rate-making purposes. This occurs when the rate regulator reasonably assures the recovery of R&D costs by permitting the inclusion of the costs in allowable costs for rate-making purposes. SFAS No. 2 also requires disclosure of total R&D costs charged to expense in each period. (SFAS No. 2, paras. 11–13)

There are three ways in which R&D costs may be incurred by a reporting entity:

1. Conducting R&D activities for the benefit of the reporting entity itself
2. Conducting R&D for others under a contractual arrangement
3. Purchasing R&D from other entities

As noted, under SFAS No. 2 all research and development expenditures must be expensed as incurred. Examples of such R&D costs include

1. Laboratory research to discover new knowledge
2. Formulation and design of product alternatives:
   a. Testing for product alternatives
   b. Modification of products or processes
3. Preproduction prototypes and models:
   a. Tools, dies, and so on, for new technology
   b. Pilot plants not capable of commercial production
4. Engineering activity performed until the product is ready for manufacture

Not all costs that appear related to research and development are to be accounted for as such, however. Examples of costs that are *not* considered R&D include

1. Engineering during an early phase of commercial production
2. Quality control for commercial production
3. Troubleshooting during a commercial production breakdown
4. Routine, ongoing efforts to improve products
5. Adaptation of existing capacity for a specific customer or other requirements

6. Seasonal design changes to products
7. Routine design of tools, dies, and so on
8. Design, construction, start-up, and so on, of equipment except that used solely for R&D

In many cases, entities will pay other parties to perform R&D activities on their behalf. In some instances, these are simply rational business decisions and are not undertaken with any financial reporting motive ("earnings management") in mind. In some instances, however, the intent of "outsourcing" certain R&D activities is to try to avoid the immediate expensing requirement of SFAS No. 2, and to instead disguise these expenditures as capital asset purchases.

In applying substance over form in evaluating these arrangements, a financial reporting result cannot be obtained indirectly if it would not have been permitted if accomplished directly. Thus, if costs incurred to engage others to perform R&D activities that, in substance, could have been performed by the reporting entity itself, those costs must be expensed as incurred. On the other hand, if the payment is to acquire intangibles for use in R&D activities, and these assets have other uses, then the expenditure is capitalized and accounted for in accordance with SFAS No. 142.

When R&D costs are incurred as a result of contractual arrangements, the nature of the agreement dictates the accounting treatment of the costs involved. The key determinant is the transfer of the risk associated with the R&D expenditures. If the business receives funds from another party to perform R&D and is obligated to repay those funds regardless of the outcome, a liability must be recorded and the R&D costs must be expensed as incurred. In order to conclude that a liability does not exist, the transfer of the financial risk must be substantive and genuine.

The SEC staff has stated that if a significant portion of the purchase price in a business combination is expensed as purchased R&D, the SEC staff may raise issues such as the following:

- Purchased R&D must be valued based on appropriate assumptions and valuation techniques; it may not be determined as a residual amount similar to goodwill.
- Allocation of purchase price to purchased R&D will be questioned if it differs significantly from the estimated replacement cost for the acquiring enterprise.
- Policies used for internally developed products should be used to determine whether R&D is in process or complete and whether alternative future uses exist.
- If substantially all of the purchase price is allocated to purchase R&D, the staff will challenge whether some should be allocated to other identifiable intangible assets and goodwill and would object to useful lives of those intangible assets and goodwill exceeding five to seven years.

The AICPA has issued the following Practice Aid on accounting for R&D projects acquired in a business combination: "Assets Acquired in a Business Combination to Be Used in Research and Development Activities: A Focus on Software, Electronic Devices, and Pharmaceutical Industries."

(i) RESEARCH AND DEVELOPMENT ARRANGEMENTS   Research and development arrangements may take a variety of forms, but a central feature of each of these is to conduct R&D that is to be financed by another entity. According to SFAS No. 68, certain of these arrangements are actually financing transactions, and funds to be repaid, irrespective of the outcome of the research, must be reported as liabilities, with actual research or development costs expensed as incurred by the reporting entity. Only if there is a substantive risk transfer to the entity providing financing will it be appropriate not to record such a liability.

The actual obligation can take various forms, including an outright unconditional commitment to repay the funds advanced; an option giving the other entity the right to require that the reporting entity purchase the other party's interest in the outcome of the R&D efforts; and a firm obligation to issue debt or equity instruments to the funding party at completion. In all such instances, the payment for R&D is actually a loan, not a purchase of R&D services. Accordingly, the reporting entity (the party conducting R&D) must currently expense all R&D expenditures.

On the other hand, to the extent that the financial risk associated with the research and development has been transferred because repayment of any of the funds provided is conditioned on the results of the R&D having future economic benefit, the reporting entity is to account for its obligation as a contract to perform research and development for others, not as debt.

(j) ACQUIRED IN-PROCESS RESEARCH AND DEVELOPMENT So-called in-process research and development (IPRD) has long been a difficult financial reporting issue. On one hand, purchase business combination accounting suggests that the purchase cost be allocated to the fair value of all assets acquired; on the other hand, to allow capitalization of IPRD would result in deferral of costs that would have to be immediately expensed under SFAS No. 2 if incurred directly by the reporting entity.

In many business combinations, a part of the premium (i.e., the amounts in excess of the fair value of tangible net assets) paid is in recognition of the value of the acquiree's previously expensed research and development efforts. Since what is banned under GAAP (e.g., capitalization of R&D costs) if accomplished directly cannot be attained indirectly (e.g., via a business combination), it was logical to prohibit the creation of an intangible asset in purchase business combinations to reflect the value of research and development already completed by the acquiree entity.

IPRD is virtually the only asset acquired in a purchase business combination transaction that is expensed rather than being capitalized. This includes not only the amount paid for actual in-process work (which was, per SFAS No. 2, already expensed as incurred by the acquiree entity), but also certain tangible assets used in research and development. As stated in FASB Interpretation No. 4, "Applicability of FASB Statement No. 2 to Business Combinations Accounted for by the Purchase Method," any identifiable assets of the acquiree to be used in research and development (R&D) projects that do not also have an alternative future use should be first valued as part of the purchase price allocation, and then charged to expense of the combined companies simultaneous with consummation of acquisition. This matter was considered by the EITF (in Issue 86-14, "Purchased Research and Development Projects in a Business Combination"), but no changes to the requirement were made.

In the mid- to late 1990s, overly aggressive use of the mandate that "in-process research and development" costs be immediately expensed upon consummation of a purchase business combination became something of a concern. In many acquisitions a disproportionately large part of the premium paid was assigned to in-process R&D, on the assumption that immediate charge-offs as part of purchase accounting were less of a concern to stockholders and other stakeholding parties than would be regular periodic charges against earnings lasting many years. There were even some instances, in fact, where more than 99 percent of the entire purchase cost was allocated to in-process R&D cost, and then immediately written off. This phenomenon drew the attention of the SEC as well as of accounting standard setters.

The elimination of goodwill amortization by SFAS No. 142 reduced the motivation for exaggerated allocations to IPRD, but this remains a concern. In response to this perceived problem, the FASB at first indicated an intent to develop a new requirement that, it was widely presumed, would have imposed a requirement that purchased in-process R&D costs be capitalized and amortized. However, upon further reflection, it became clear that to have a diametrically opposite rule for in-process R&D costs, as distinguished from internally generated R&D, would be neither logical nor defensible. Consequently, no action was taken by the FASB, and the requirement that purchased in-process R&D be immediately expensed, after purchase cost is first allocated to it, remained.

Clearly, the last chapter has not yet been written regarding proper accounting for research and/or development costs in general, or regarding in-process R&D acquired in purchase transactions in particular.

(k) ROYALTY AND LICENSE AGREEMENTS   Royalty and license agreements are contracts allowing the use of patented, copyrighted, or proprietary (trade secrets) material in return for royalty payments. An example is the licensing of a patented chemical process for use in a customer's operating system.

The costs to be assigned to royalty and license agreements include any initial payments required plus legal costs incurred in establishing the agreements. Royalty or usage fees are expensed as incurred, because they relate to services of products and not to future benefits.

The capitalized costs of royalty and license agreements should be amortized over the lesser of the life of the agreement or the expected economic life, with the useful life reassessed each reporting period. Unamortized costs of royalty and license agreements should be written off when it is determined that they have become worthless.

(l) SECRET FORMULAS AND PROCESSES   A formula or process known only to a particular producer may be a valuable asset, even if not patented. As in the case of a patent, the value of a trade secret is derived from the exclusive control that it gives. Trade secrets, like patents and copyrights, are recognized legal property and are transferable. Costs that can be directly identified with secret formulas and processes are properly capitalized, except that costs of activities constituting R&D as defined by SFAS No. 2 must be expensed. Costs are normally assigned only to acquired secret formulas and processes. Because secret formulas and secret processes have unlimited lives in a legal sense, costs capitalized are amortized over the useful life of the secret formula or are not amortized if the secret formula is determined to have an indefinite useful life. Whether the value of the formula or process is impaired because of lack of demand for the related product, development of a substitute product or process, loss of exclusivity, or other factors should be determined as discussed in Section 20A.4(b) or 4(c), as appropriate.

(m) START-UP ACTIVITIES   Under SOP 98-5, "Reporting on the Costs of Start-Up Activities," costs of start-up activities, including organization costs, should be expensed as incurred. For purposes of the SOP, start-up activities are defined broadly as those one-time activities related to opening a new facility, introducing a new product or service, conducting business in a new territory, conducting business with a new class of customer or beneficiary, initiating a new process in an existing facility, or commencing some new operation. Start-up activities include activities related to organizing a new entity (commonly referred to as organization costs). The SOP applies to all nongovernmental entities and would apply to development-stage entities as well as established operating entities.

(n) TOOLING COSTS   Initial tooling costs are sometimes treated as an intangible asset, but they are more often considered an element of property, plant, and equipment or, in the case of certain long-term contracts, inventory. SFAS No. 2 states that the design of tools, jigs, molds, and dies involving new technology is a R&D cost, which must be expensed as incurred. However, routine design of those items is not R&D, and the cost may be deferred and amortized over the periods expected to benefit. Deferred tooling may be written off over a period of time (generally less than five years, with shorter periods used when tooling relates to products with frequent style or design obsolescence) or anticipated production (using the unit-of-production method). Replacements of parts of tooling for reasons other than changes in the product are usually expensed.

If deferred initial tooling costs are material, the accounting policy regarding those costs should be disclosed. SEC registrants are required to state, if practicable, the amount of unamortized deferred tooling costs applicable to long-term contracts or programs (Regulation S-X, Rule 5.02-6(d)(i)).

EITF Issue No. 99-5, "Accounting for Pre-Production Costs Related to Long-Term Supply Arrangements," provides guidance on design and development and tooling costs related to new long-term supply arrangements. The Task Force concluded that

- Design and development costs for products to be sold under long-term supply arrangements should be expensed as incurred.
- Design and development costs for molds, dies, and other tools that a supplier will own and that will be used in producing the products under the long-term supply arrangements should, in general, be capitalized as part of the cost of the molds, dies, and other tools. However, if the molds, dies, and tools involve new technology, their costs should be expensed as incurred.
- If the supplier will not own the molds, dies, and other tools, the design and development costs should be capitalized only if the supply arrangement provides the supplier the noncancelable right to use them during the supply arrangement. Otherwise, the design and development costs should be expensed as incurred, including costs incurred before the supplier receives a noncancelable right to use the molds, dies, and other tools during the supply arrangement.
- Design and development costs that would otherwise be expensed should be capitalized if the supplier has a contractual guarantee for reimbursement of those costs. A contractual guarantee means a legally enforceable agreement under which the amount of the reimbursement can be objectively measured and verified.

SEC registrants are expected to disclose their accounting policy for preproduction design and development costs and the aggregate amount of the following:

- Assets recognized pursuant to agreements that provide for contractual reimbursement of preproduction design and development costs
- Assets recognized for molds, dies, and other tools that the supplier owns
- Assets recognized for molds, dies, and other tools that the supplier does not own

Design and development costs for molds, dies, and other tools that are capitalized are subject to impairment assessment under SFAS No. 144.

(o) TRADEMARKS AND TRADE NAMES   Broadly defined, a trademark is any distinguishing label, symbol, or design used by a concern in connection with a product or service. A trade name identifies the entity.

Trademarks can be registered with the U.S. Patent Office to provide access to the federal courts for litigation and to serve as notice of ownership. Proof of prior and continuing use of the trademark is required to obtain and retain the right to use the registered item. Protection of trademarks and trade names that cannot be registered or are not registered can also be sought through common law. These assets have an unlimited life as long as they are used continuously, although technically the term of registration at the U.S. Patent Office is 20 years with indefinite renewal for additional 20-year periods.

They may also be registered under the laws of most states. It is customary to consider trademarks and trade names as being of value only as long as they are used. The value of a trademark or trade name consists of the product differentiation and identification that it provides, which theoretically contributes to revenue by enabling a business to sell such products at a higher price than unbranded products. Although closely related to goodwill, trademarks and trade names are property rights that are separately identifiable and, as such, can be assigned or sold.

(i) Capitalizable Amounts for Trademarks and Trade Names Costs   The cost of a trademark or trade name developed internally consists of legal fees associated with successful litigation involving the trademark or trade name, registration fees, and all developmental expenditures that can be reasonably associated with trademarks, such as payments to design firms. The cost of a purchased trademark or trade name is its purchase price, along with any other costs required to maintain exclusive use of the mark or name. Obviously, much of the value of a trademark or trade name is established by continuing operations that create a reputation with customers. Some of that reputation, however, may have been gained through the use of advertising and other marketing techniques.

The costs should be amortized over the trademark's or trade name's useful life to the entity, unless the trademark or trade name is determined to have an indefinite useful life, in which case it is not amortized, as discussed in Section 20A.4(c). The expected useful life should be reassessed each reporting period. These expenditures should be accounted for under SOP 93-7, which is discussed next.

(ii) Amortization of Trademarks and Trade Names   Because of the legal status of trademarks and trade names, established trademarks and trade names have unlimited legal lives as long as they are used. There is no specified statutory life that restricts the amortization period.

(p) ADVERTISING   While many, if not most, businesses engage in some forms of advertising, it has long been held that demonstrating the actual effectiveness of such efforts is too speculative to warrant deferral of costs to future periods. Put another way, advertising has been held to be a "sunk cost," and thus must be expensed as incurred. However, SOP 93-7, "Reporting on Advertising Costs," did provide a limited exception to this general principle.

Under this SOP, the costs of advertising should be expensed either as incurred or the first time the advertising takes place, unless the advertising is direct-response advertising that meets specific, rather rigorous criteria, in which case deferral and amortization is prescribed. Examples of first-time advertising include the first public showing of a television commercial for its intended purpose or the first appearance of a magazine advertisement for its intended purpose. The cost of direct-response advertising is deferred and reported as an asset, subject to amortization, if the primary purpose of the advertising is to elicit sales to customers who can be shown to have responded specifically to the advertising, *and* if the advertising results in *probable* future benefits. Showing that a customer responded to specifically identifiable direct-response advertising requires documentation, including a record that can identify the name of the customer and the advertising that elicited the direct response. Such documentation could include, for example, files listing the customer names and the related direct-response advertisement, a coded order form, coupon, or response card included with the advertisement that would indicate the customer's name, or a log of customers who made phone calls responding to a number appearing in an advertisement.

Probable future benefits are highly likely future primary revenues resulting from the direct-response advertising, net of future costs to realize the revenues. Probable future primary revenues are limited to revenues from sales to customers receiving and responding to the direct-response advertising. To demonstrate that direct-response advertising will result in probable future benefits, an entity is required to provide persuasive evidence that the results of the advertising will be similar to the results of its past direct-response advertising activities that had future benefits. The evidence should include verifiable historical patterns of results specific to the entity. To determine if results will be similar, attributes to consider include the demographics of the audience, the method of advertising, the product, and economic conditions. Industry statistics would not provide objective evidence of probable future benefits in the absence of the entity's own operating history.

Other requirements of the SOP include the following:

- Costs of direct-response advertising should include only incremental direct costs incurred in transactions with independent third parties plus payroll and payroll-related costs for the activities of employees that are directly associated with the direct-response advertising project. Allocated administrative costs, rent, depreciation, and other occupancy costs are not costs of direct-response advertising activities.
- The costs of the direct-response advertising directed to all prospective customers, not just the cost related to the portion of the potential customers that is expected to respond to the advertising, should be deferred.
- Deferred direct-response advertising costs should be amortized using a cost-pool method over the period during which the future benefits are expected to be received. The amortization should be the ratio that current period revenues for a cost pool bear to the total current and estimated future period revenues for that cost pool. The amount of estimated future revenues should not be discounted, but it may be adjusted in subsequent periods. The ratio should be recalculated at each reporting date.
- The realizability of the deferred advertising should be evaluated, at each balance sheet date, by comparing, on a cost-pool by cost-pool basis, the carrying amount of the deferred advertising with the probable remaining future net revenues expected to result directly from such advertising. Only probable future primary revenues should be used to determine the probable remaining future net revenues.
- There are certain disclosures required, such as the accounting policy selected for advertising, the total amount charged to advertising, a description of the direct-response advertising reported as assets (if any), the accounting policy and amortization period of direct-response advertising, the total amount of advertising reported as assets, and the amounts, if any, written down to net realizable income.

The SEC staff considers the requirements for deferral of direct-response advertising costs to be met only if the advertising results in a direct revenue-generating response—for example, if the respondent orders the product when placing the call to the advertised number. The staff believes capitalization is not appropriate for advertising that results not in sales but only in sales opportunities, even if these are likely to produce results. For example, an advertisement for aluminum siding that includes a phone number to call to schedule a visit from a sales representative would not qualify for capitalization as direct-response advertising because the advertisement leads only indirectly to the revenue-generating transaction. The SEC staff also would object to the classification of deferred advertising costs as current assets, because such costs do not meet the definition of a current asset in ARB No. 43.

(q) WEB SITE DEVELOPMENT COSTS   With the rapid growth in so-called e-commerce in the late 1990s, many reporting entities incurred costs to develop and maintain Web sites. EITF Issue No. 00-2 provided the following guidance for accounting for Web site development costs:

- During the planning phase, an entity develops a project plan, determines the desired functionalities of the Web site, identifies the needed hardware and software applications, and determines whether suitable technology exists. All costs incurred in the planning stage should be expensed as incurred.
- During the Web site development phase, the entity acquires or develops hardware and software to operate its Web site and develops appropriate graphics. Costs related to software and graphics should be accounted for under SOP 98-1 as software for internal use unless the entity has or is developing a plan to market the software. Software, including graphics, to be marketed should be accounted for under SFAS No. 86, "Accounting for the Costs of Computer Software to Be Sold, Leased, or Otherwise Marketed." See Section 20A.6(f) for a discussion of SOP 98-1 and SFAS No. 86. Costs incurred for Web site hosting should generally be expensed over the period of benefit.

20A.6   INTANGIBLE ASSETS IN SPECIALIZED INDUSTRIES

Intangible assets are particularly significant or receive unique accounting treatment in certain industries. These requirements are generally to be found in AICPA Industry Audit and Accounting Guides or in Statements of Position.

(a) AIRLINES   Under the AICPA Industry Audit Guide, *Audits of Airlines*, as amended by SOP 88-1, "Accounting for Developmental and Preoperating Costs, Purchases and Exchanges of Take-off and Landing Slots, and Airframe Modifications," and SOP 98-5, "Reporting on the Costs of Start-Up Activities," the capitalization of preoperating costs related only to the integration of new types of aircraft. The costs of acquiring take-off and landing slots, whether by exchange of stock or through purchase, are identifiable intangible assets. Developmental costs related to preparation of new routes should not be capitalized.

(b) BANKING AND THRIFTS   During the thrift and banking crises of the late 1980s and early 1990s, precipitated in part by the high interest rate environment and negative interest rate spreads of those years, many insured financial institutions, when evaluated on a fair value basis, were threatened with insolvency or already were insolvent. The federal insurers (FDIC and FSLIC) were themselves facing insolvency, and would likely have been unable to repay all depositors of closed institutions from available reserves. It was hoped that, with an anticipated return to a normal interest rate environment, many of these banks and thrifts would regain solvency and survive, sparing the insurers (and ultimately the taxpayers) these losses.

Given this situation, there was a concerted political effort to postpone bank and thrift closings, and one perhaps ill-conceived solution was to encourage the takeovers of failing banks and thrifts by offering the acquirers the ability to treat the net liabilities acquired (measured at fair value) as so-called supervisory goodwill. Although this did not comport with the traditional GAAP concept of goodwill, the profession accommodated this regulatory mandate. Under SFAS No. 72, "Accounting for Certain Acquisitions of Banking or Thrift Institutions," this goodwill was to be amortized over the terms set forth in the assisted, supervisory mergers (often 20 or more years), even though the so-called core deposit intangible (related to the expected holding term of deposits acquired) would have a much shorter expected life.

The elimination of goodwill amortization by SFAS No. 142 necessitated a change to many of the SFAS No. 72 provisions. SFAS No. 147, "Acquisitions of Certain Financial Institutions," eliminates the special accounting imposed by SFAS No. 72, with the exception that mergers between mutual enterprises continue to be governed by that standard. Thus, as amended, SFAS No. 72 applies only to acquisitions of financial institutions that are mutual enterprises by other financial institutions that are also mutual enterprises. For those acquisitions, goodwill that is created by an excess of the fair value of liabilities assumed over the fair value of tangible and identified intangible assets acquired is to be amortized by the interest method over a period no greater than the estimated remaining life of the long-term, interest-bearing assets acquired. If the assets acquired do not include a significant amount of long-term, interest-bearing assets, such goodwill is to be amortized over a period not exceeding the estimated average life of the existing customer (deposit) base acquired.

At the effective date of SFAS No. 147, any remaining unidentified intangible other than that arising from a business combination continued to be amortized, while that arising from business combinations (the assisted supervisory mergers, for example) was to be reclassified as goodwill and thereafter tested for impairment per SFAS No. 142. Transitional impairment testing procedures were also specified.

(c) MORTGAGE BANKING   Under SFAS No. 140, "Accounting for Transfers and Servicing of Financial Assets and Extinguishments of Liabilities—A Replacement of FASB Statement No. 125," servicing of mortgage loans becomes a distinct asset or liability only when contractually separated from the underlying amounts by sale or securitization of the assets with servicing retained, or through the separate purchase or assumption of the servicing rights.

An entity that undertakes a contract to service financial assets shall recognize either a servicing asset or a servicing liability, unless the transferor transfers the assets in a guaranteed mortgage securitization, retains all of the resulting securities, and classifies them as debt securities held to maturity in accordance with SFAS No. 115, in which case the servicing asset or liability may be reported together with the asset being serviced. Each sale or securitization with servicing retained or separate purchase or assumption of servicing results in a servicing contract. Each servicing contract results in a servicing asset (when the benefits of servicing are expected to be more than adequate compensation to the servicer for performing the servicing) or a servicing liability (when the benefits of servicing are not expected to compensate the servicer adequately for performing the servicing). If the servicer is more than adequately compensated and if the servicing was retained in a sale or securitization, the servicer shall account for the contracts to service the mortgage loans separately from the loans by initially measuring the servicing assets at their allocated previous carrying amounts based on relative fair value at the date of sale or securitization. If the servicing asset is purchased or servicing liability assumed, it is measured at fair value. If the servicer is not adequately compensated, a servicing liability undertaken in a sale or securitization is measured at fair value.

Servicing assets are amortized in proportion to and over the period of estimated net servicing income—the excess of service revenues over servicing costs. Servicing liabilities are amortized in proportion to and over the period of estimated net servicing loss—the excess of servicing costs over servicing revenues, if practicable.

Impairment of servicing assets should be measured as follows:

1. Stratify servicing assets based on one or more of the predominant risk characteristics of the underlying assets.

2. Recognize impairment through a valuation allowance for an individual stratum for the amount by which the carrying amount of the servicing assets for the stratum exceeds their fair value.

3. Adjust the valuation allowance to reflect changes in the measurement of impairment subsequent to the initial measurement of impairment.

Rights for future income from the serviced assets that exceed contractually specified servicing fees should be accounted for separately. Those rights are not servicing assets; they are financial assets, effectively interest-only strips to be accounted for in accordance with paragraph 14 of SFAS No. 140.

In EITF No. 95-5, "Determination of What Risks and Rewards, If Any, Can Be Retained and Whether Any Unresolved Contingencies May Exist in a Sale of Mortgage Loan Servicing Rights," the issue addressed was whether the inclusion of any provision that results in the seller's retention of specified risk (1) precludes recognition of a sale at the date title passes or (2) allows recognition of the sale at that date if (a) the seller can reasonably estimate, and record a liability for, the costs related to protection provisions, or (b) the sale agreement provides for substantially all risks and rewards to irrevocably pass to the buyer, and the seller can reasonably estimate, and record a liability for, the minor protection provisions.

The EITF consensus was that sales of rights to service mortgage loans should be recognized when the following conditions are met: (1) title has passed, (2) substantially all risks and rewards of ownership have irrevocably passed to the buyer, and (3) any protection provisions retained by the seller are minor and can be reasonably estimated. If a sale is recognized and minor protection provisions exist, a liability should be accrued for the estimated obligation associated with those provisions. The seller retains only minor protection provisions if (a) the obligation associated with those provisions is estimated to be no more than 10 percent of the sales price and (b) risk of prepayment is retained for no longer than 120 days. Mortgage banking is covered in more detail in Chapter 29.

(d) BROADCASTING INDUSTRY   The principal intangible assets in the broadcasting industry are Federal Communications Commission (FCC) licenses, broadcast rights (license agreement to program material), and network affiliation agreements. Television and radio stations may not operate without a FCC license, which specifies, for example, the frequency to be used. A broadcasting license is granted for a 10-year period and is renewable for additional 10-year periods if the entity provides at least an average level of service to its customers and complies with applicable FCC rules and policies. Licenses thus may be renewed indefinitely at little cost.

If the entity intends to renew the license indefinitely and has the ability to do so, a broadcast license would be deemed to have an indefinite useful life. It would not be amortized until its useful life was no longer deemed to be indefinite. Impairment would be tested as provided in Section 20A.4(c). On the other hand, if the entity does not intend to renew a broadcast license indefinitely, if would amortize the license over its remaining useful life and follow the impairment guidance in SFAS No. 144.

(i) Broadcast Rights   SFAS No. 63, "Financial Reporting by Broadcasters," contains industry-specific GAAP. Its primary mandate is that broadcasters must account for license agreements for program materials as purchases of rights, thus necessitating the presentation of assets and liabilities on the entities' balance sheets. Broadcast rights result from a contract or license to exhibit films, programs, or other works and permit one or more exhibitions during a specified license period. Compensation is ordinarily payable in installments over a period shorter than the period of the licensing contract, but it may also take the form of a lump-sum payment at the beginning of the period. The license expires at the end of the contract period.

Amounts recorded for broadcasting rights are to be segregated on the balance sheet as current and noncurrent assets based on estimated usage within one year. Rights should be amortized based on the estimated number of future showings. Items that may be used on an unlimited basis, rather than a limited number of showings, may be amortized over the period covered by the agreement. An accelerated method of amortization is required when the first showing is more valuable than reruns, as is usually the case. Straight-line amortization is allowable only when each telecast or broadcast is expected to generate approximately the same revenue.

Feature programs are to be amortized on a program-by-program basis; however, amortization as a package may be appropriate if it approximates the amortization that would have been provided on a program-by-program basis. The capitalized costs of rights to program material should be reported in the balance sheet at the lower of unamortized cost or estimated net realizable value on a program-by-program, series, package, or "daypart" basis, as appropriate. If management's expectations of the programming usefulness of a program, series, package, or daypart are revised downward, it may be necessary to write down unamortized cost to estimated net realizable value. *Daypart* is defined in SFAS No. 63 as an aggregation of programs broadcast during a particular time of day (e.g., daytime, evening, late night) or programs of a similar type (e.g., sports, news, children's shows). A write-down from unamortized cost to a lower estimated net realizable value establishes a new cost basis.

(ii) Revoked or Nonrenewed Broadcast Licenses   When broadcasting licenses are not renewed or are revoked, unamortized balances should be written off. If a network affiliation is terminated and is not immediately replaced or under agreement to be replaced, the unamortized balance of the amount originally allocated to the network affiliation agreement should be charged to expense. If a network affiliation is terminated and immediately replaced or is under agreement to be replaced, a loss is recognized to the extent that the unamortized cost of the terminated affiliation exceeds the fair value of the new affiliation. Gain is not to be recognized if the fair value of the new network affiliation exceeds the unamortized cost of the terminated affiliation.

(e) CABLE TELEVISION   Cable television companies experience a long preoperating and development period. SFAS No. 51, "Financial Reporting by Cable Television Companies," defines the "pre-maturity period" as that during which a cable television system is partially under construction and partially in service. Costs incurred during this period that relate to both current and future operations are partially expensed and partially capitalized. In a cable system, portions or segments that are in the pre-maturity period and can be clearly distinguished from the remainder of the system should be accounted for separately. Costs incurred to obtain and retain subscribers and general and administrative expenses incurred during the pre-maturity period are to be expensed as period costs. Programming costs and other system costs that will not vary significantly regardless of the number of subscribers are allocated between current and future operations. The amount currently expensed is based on a relationship of subscribers during the current month (as prescribed in the SFAS) and the total number of subscribers expected at the end of the pre-maturity period. The capitalized portions decrease each month as the cable company progresses toward the end of the pre-maturity period. Prior to the pre-maturity period, system-related costs are capitalized; subsequent thereto, none of these costs is deferred. Capitalized costs should be amortized over the same period used to depreciate the main cable television plant. Costs of successful franchise applications are capitalized and amortized in accordance with SFAS No. 142. Costs of unsuccessful applications and abandoned franchises are charged to expense.

(f) COMPUTER SOFTWARE   SFAS No. 86, "Accounting for the Costs of Computer Software to Be Sold, Leased, or Otherwise Marketed," prescribes the accounting for the costs of computer software purchased or internally developed as a marketable product by itself. Costs incurred to establish the technological feasibility are charged to expense when incurred. Technological feasibility is established on completion of all planning design, coding, and testing activities necessary to establish that the product can be produced. The completion of a detailed program design or completion of a working model provides evidence of the establishment of technological feasibility.

Costs incurred subsequent to the establishment of technological feasibility are capitalized. Software used as an integral part of product or process is not capitalized until both technological feasibility has been established and all R&D activities for the other components have been completed. When the product is available for release to customers, capitalization ceases. Costs of maintenance and customer support are expensed when the related revenue is recognized or when the costs are incurred, whichever occurs first. Purchased software that has alternative future uses should be capitalized but subsequently accounted for according to its use.

Amortization of capitalized software costs is based on the ratio that current gross revenues bear to the total current and anticipated revenues with a minimum amortization equivalent to straight-line over the remaining estimated economic life of the product. The excess of unamortized capitalized costs over a product's net realizable value is written off (and not subsequently restored).

The unamortized computer costs included in the balance sheet, the total amortization charged to expense in each income statement presented, and amounts written down to net realizable value should be disclosed.

FIN (FASB Interpretations) No. 6 (par. 4) states that to the extent the acquisition, development, or improvement of a process for use in selling and administrative activities includes costs for computer software, these costs are not R&D costs. Examples given of excluded costs are the development by an airline of a computerized reservation system or the development of a general management information system. SFAS No. 86 does not cover accounting for costs of software used internally. For that subject, see the discussion of SOP 98-1 in this subsection.

In Issue No. 96-6, "Accounting for the Film and Software Costs Associated with Developing Entertainment and Educational Software Products," the EITF considered the issue of how companies should account for the film and software costs associated with developing entertainment and educational software (EE) products such as computer games, interactive videos, and other multimedia products. The SEC staff announced that EE products that are sold, leased, or otherwise marketed are subject to the accounting requirements of SFAS No. 86. The SEC staff believes that the film costs incurred in development of an EE product should be accounted for under the provisions of SFAS No. 86. In addition, exploitation costs should be expensed as incurred unless those costs include advertising costs that qualify for capitalization in accordance with SOP 93-7. Because of the SEC staff's position, the EITF was not asked to reach a consensus on this issue.

In EITF No. 97-13, "Accounting for Costs Incurred in Connection with a Consulting Contract or an Internal Project That Combines Business Process Reengineering and Information Technology Transformation," the EITF addressed the accounting for business process reengineering costs. These costs may be included in a contract that combines business process reengineering and a project to acquire, develop, or implement internal-use software. The issue does not address the accounting for internal-use software development costs (which was, however, dealt with subsequently by SOP 98-1). The EITF reached a consensus that costs of business process reengineering, whether done internally or by third parties, should be expensed as incurred. If the project is carried out by a third party and some of the costs are capitalizable, such as fixed asset costs, the EITF concluded that the total contract cost should be allocated to various activities based on the relative fair value of the separate activities. The allocation should be based on the objective evidence of the fair value of the elements in the contract, not separate prices stated within the contract. The consensus opinion identified the following as third-party or internally generated costs typically associated with business process reengineering activities that should be expensed as incurred:

- Preparation of request for proposal
- Current state assessment
- Process reengineering
- Restructuring the workforce

The cost of software used internally is accounted for under SOP 98-1, "Accounting for the Costs of Computer Software Developed of Obtained for Internal Use." The SOP divides the process of computer software development into three stages: (1) preliminary project stage (conceptual formulation and evaluation of alternatives, determination of existence of needed technology, and final selection of alternatives); (2) application development stage (design of chosen path, coding, installation to hardware, and testing); and (3) postimplementation/operation stage (training and application maintenance). Computer software costs that are incurred in the preliminary project stage should be expensed as incurred.

Once the capitalization criteria of the SOP have been met, external direct costs of materials and services consumed in developing or obtaining internal-use computer software, payroll costs for employees who are directly associated with and who devote time to the project, and interest costs incurred in developing the software should be capitalized. Capitalization should cease no later than the point at which a computer software project is substantially complete and ready for its intended use.

Internal and external training costs and maintenance costs incurred in the postimplementation/ operation stage should be expensed as incurred. General and administrative costs and overhead costs should not be capitalized as costs of internal-use software.

(g) EXTRACTIVE INDUSTRIES   Intangible assets in the extractive industries include leased or purchased rights to exploit mineral and other natural resources based on lump-sum, periodic, or production-based payments. The rights are usually included in the property section of the balance sheet.

A comprehensive discussion of the accounting for these and other assets in the extractive industries is given in Chapter 27.

(h) PRODUCERS OR DISTRIBUTORS OF FILMS   SOP 00-2, "Accounting by Producers or Distributors of Films," provides guidance on the accounting for costs related to all types of films and is applicable to both producers and distributors of films. The costs of producing a film include film costs, participation costs, exploitation costs, and manufacturing costs. Marketing and other exploitation costs, other than advertising, should be expensed as incurred. Advertising costs should be accounted for under SOP 93-7, "Reporting on Advertising Costs." Entities are required to amortize film costs using the individual-film-forecast-computation method. That method provides for amortization of costs in the same ratio that current-period actual revenue bears to estimated remaining unrecognized ultimate revenue as of the beginning of the current fiscal year. Amortization begins when a film is released and the entity begins to recognize revenue from the film.

Certain events or changes in circumstances, such as an adverse change in the expected performance of a film or a substantial delay in completion of the film, indicate that the fair value of the film may be less than the related unamortized film costs. If such an event occurs, an entity should assess whether the fair value of the film is less than its unamortized film costs. If the unamortized capitalized film costs exceed the film's fair value, the excess should be written off and may not be subsequently restored. See Chapter 30 for more on this topic.

(i) PUBLIC UTILITIES   The general provisions of accounting for intangible assets of various types apply to public utilities. However, since public utilities are required by regulatory agencies to maintain their accounts in accordance with accounting practices that may vary from GAAP, certain differences in treatment may result. An example is R&D costs, which certain regulatory agencies allow to be deferred.

The rate regulator may reasonably assure the existence of an asset by permitting the inclusion of a cost in allowable costs for rate-making purposes. SFAS No. 71, "Accounting for the Effects of Certain Types of Regulation," sets forth two criteria that must both be met in order for a utility to capitalize a cost that would otherwise be required, under GAAP, to be expensed currently:

1.   It is probable that future revenue in an amount at least equal to the capitalized cost will result from inclusion of that cost in allowable costs for rate-making purposes.
2.   Based on available evidence, the future revenue will be provided to permit recovery of the previously incurred cost rather than to provide for expected levels of similar future costs. If the revenue will be provided through an automatic rate-adjustment clause, this criterion requires that the regulator's intent clearly be to permit recovery of the previously incurred cost.

If at any time the capitalized cost no longer meets those two criteria, it is to be expensed. The value of an asset may be impaired by a regulator's rate actions. If a rate regulator excludes all or part of a capitalized cost from allowable costs and the cost was capitalized based on the foregoing criteria, the asset should be reduced to the extent of the excluded cost. Whether other assets have been impaired is determined under the general rules for impairment, which are described in Sections 20A.4(b) and 20A.4(c).

If an enterprise discontinues application of SFAS No. 71 because, for example, its operations have been deregulated, it would eliminate from its GAAP balance sheet assets consisting of costs capitalized that would not have been capitalized by unregulated entities. Numerous state legislatures and/or regulatory commissions have approved or are considering deregulating utilities' generation (production) cost of electricity, although the portion of the kilowatt charge attributable to transmission of the electricity to the local area and the distribution cost to the customer are not being deregulated. If some, but not all, of a utility's operations are regulated, SFAS No. 71 should be applied to the portion of the operations that continue to meet the requirements of SFAS No. 71 for regulatory accounting. SFAS No. 101, "Regulated Enterprises—Accounting for the Discontinuation of Application of FASB Statement No. 71," addresses how an entity that ceases to meet the criteria for application of SFAS No. 71 to all or part of its operations should report that event in its financial statements.

An issue related to the current deregulation environment is when an entity should cease to apply the regulated enterprise accounting model prescribed by SFAS No. 71 to the generation portion of its operations if deregulation is under consideration. In Issue No. 97-4, "Deregulation of the Price of Electricity—Issues Related to the Application of FASB Statements No. 71 and 101," the EITF reached a consensus that when deregulatory legislation or a rate order is issued that contains sufficient detail to determine how the deregulatory plan will affect the portion of the business being deregulated, the entity should stop applying SFAS No. 71 to that separable portion of its business. The Task Force considered the following fact situation: If legislation is passed requiring deregulation of generation charges at the end of five years, the date the legislation is passed is the latest date that the entity can discontinue application of the SFAS No. 71 accounting model to the generation portion of its operations. The consensus does not address whether an entity should stop applying SFAS No. 71 at an earlier time. The Task Force also observed that the financial statements should segregate, either on their face or in the notes, the amounts that pertain to the separable portion.

With regard to goodwill, a regulator may permit a utility to amortize purchased goodwill over a specified period, may direct a utility not to amortize goodwill, or may direct the utility to write off goodwill. SFAS No. 71 requires the goodwill to be amortized for financial reporting purposes over the period during which it will be allowed for rate-making purposes. If the regulator either excludes amortization from allowable costs for rate-making purposes or directs the utility to write off goodwill, goodwill should not be amortized, and it should be accounted for under SFAS No. 142.

(j) RECORD AND MUSIC INDUSTRY   Significant intangible assets in the record and music industry include record masters, recording artist contracts, and copyrights. Accounting for copyrights generally follows that used in other industries, but the accounting for record masters and recording artist contracts is unique.

SFAS No. 50, "Financial Reporting in the Record and Music Industry," is the primary source of accounting principles in this area. Costs of producing a record master include the costs of musical talent; technical talent for engineering, directing, and mixing; equipment to record and produce the master; and studio facility charges. When past performance of an artist provides a reasonable basis for estimating that the cost of a record master borne by the record company will be recovered from future sales, that cost should be recorded as an asset and, when material, should be separately disclosed. The cost of record masters should be amortized by a method that reasonably relates the cost to the net revenue expected to be realized. Ordinarily, amortization occurs over a very short period. Unamortized amounts should be written off when it becomes apparent that they will not be recovered through future sales. The cost of the record master recoverable from the artist's royalties is to be accounted for as an advance royalty.

A recording artist contract is an agreement for personal services. A major portion of the artist's compensation consists of participation in earnings (measured by sales and license fee income, commonly referred to as a "royalty") or of a nonrefundable advance against royalties. Advances should be recorded as an asset (as a prepaid royalty, classified as current or noncurrent depending on when amounts are expected to be realized) if it is anticipated that they will be recovered against royalties otherwise payable to the artist. When it is determined that a prepayment will not be recovered, the balance should be written off.

(k) TIMBER INDUSTRY   Companies in the forest products industry may make lump-sum payments for timber-cutting rights, which allow them to remove trees for a specified period or in specified quantities. Lump-sum payments made at the inception of an agreement are properly deferred and amortized over the period of the agreement or on the basis of estimates of recoverable timber. Periodic or production-based payments are expensed as they do not represent future benefits. Cutting rights are ordinarily included in the Property section of the balance sheet and are stated at cost less amortization. The amortization policy should be disclosed.

20A.7   ACCOUNTING FOR GOODWILL

(a) INITIAL VALUATION   SFAS Nos. 141, "Business Combinations," and 142, "Goodwill and Other Intangible Assets," were both issued in June 2001 and replaced Accounting Principles Board (APB) Opinions Nos. 16 and 17. In these standards, goodwill is defined as

> The excess of the cost of an acquired entity over the net of the amounts assigned to assets acquired and liabilities assumed. The amount recognized as goodwill includes acquired intangible assets that do not meet the criteria in SFAS No. 141, "Business Combinations," for recognition as an asset apart from goodwill.

The previously referenced criteria for separate recognition of intangibles are discussed in Section 20A.3(a). For accounting purposes, the cost of purchased goodwill is the residual cost remaining after all other identifiable assets and liabilities have been valued.

(b) SUBSEQUENT ACCOUNTING   Goodwill is not amortized. It is tested for impairment at a level of reporting referred to as a reporting unit (see Section 20A.7(b)(iv) for a definition of a reporting unit). Impairment is the condition that exists when the carrying amount of goodwill is greater than its implied fair value. A two-step impairment test, discussed next, is used to identify potential goodwill impairment and measure the amount of a goodwill impairment loss to be recognized, if any.

(i) Recognition and Measurement of an Impairment Loss   The first step of a goodwill impairment test compares the fair value of a reporting unit with its carrying amount, including goodwill, applying the guidance provided in Section 20A.7(b)(ii). If the fair value of the

reporting unit is more than its carrying amount, goodwill of the reporting unit is considered not impaired, and the second step of the impairment test is not performed. If the carrying amount of the reporting unit is more than its fair value, the second step of the goodwill impairment test, discussed next, is performed to measure the amount of impairment, if any.

The second step of the goodwill impairment test compares the implied fair value of reporting unit goodwill (explained in the next paragraph) with the carrying amount of the goodwill. If the carrying amount of reporting unit goodwill is more than the implied fair value of the goodwill, an impairment loss is recognized in an amount equal to the excess. The loss recognized cannot exceed the carrying amount of goodwill. When a goodwill impairment loss is recognized, the adjusted carrying amount of goodwill is its new accounting basis. Subsequent to the measurement and recognition of the goodwill impairment loss, a later recovery in value cannot be recognized. Thus, goodwill impairments cannot be reversed.

The implied fair value of goodwill is determined in the same way as is the amount of goodwill to be recognized in a business combination. The reporting entity allocates the fair value of the reporting unit to all of the assets and liabilities of the unit, including any unrecognized intangible assets, the same way it would be allocated had the reporting unit been acquired in a business combination and had the fair value of the reporting unit been the price paid to acquire the reporting unit. The excess of the fair value of the reporting unit over the amounts assigned to its assets and liabilities is the *implied fair value of goodwill.*

The allocation process just described is performed only for the purpose of testing goodwill for impairment. A reporting entity does not write up or down a recognized asset or liability, and it does not recognize a previously unrecognized intangible asset as a result of the allocation process exercise.

If the second step of the goodwill impairment test is not complete before the financial statements are issued and a goodwill impairment loss is probable and can be reasonably estimated, the best estimate of the loss is recognized in those financial statements. Any adjustment to the estimated loss based on completion of the measurement of the impairment loss is recognized in the next reporting period.

(ii) Fair Value Measurements   SFAS No. 142 defines *fair value* the same way FASB Statement of Concepts No. 7 does:

> The amount at which that asset (or liability) could be bought (or incurred) or sold (settled) in a current transaction between willing parties, that is, other than in a forced or liquidation sale.

According to that definition, the fair value of a reporting unit is the amount at which the unit as a whole could be bought or sold in a current transaction between willing parties. Quoted market prices in active markets are the best evidence of fair value and are used as the basis for measurement, if available. However, the market price of an individual equity security and thus the market capitalization of a reporting unit with publicly traded equity securities may not be representative of the fair value of the reporting unit as a whole, because of a control premium. The quoted market price of an individual equity security, therefore, need not be the sole measurement basis of the fair value of a reporting unit. SEC registrants should be aware that the SEC staff has sometimes questioned valuations not based on the market price of the equity security.

If quoted market prices are not available, the estimate of fair value is based on the best information available, including prices for similar assets and liabilities and the results of using other valuation techniques. A present value technique is often the best available technique with which to estimate the fair value of a group of net assets (i.e., a reporting unit). If a present value technique is used to measure fair value, estimates of future cash flows used in the technique are to be consistent with the objective of measuring fair value. The cash flow estimates should incorporate assumptions that marketplace participants would use in their estimates of fair value. If that information is not available without undue cost and effort, a reporting entity may use its own assumptions.

An entity should base the cash flow estimates on reasonable and supportable assumptions after consideration of all available evidence. The weight given to the evidence should be commensurate with the extent to which the evidence can be verified objectively. If the entity estimates a range for the amount or timing of possible cash flows, it should consider the likelihood of possible outcomes. FASB Concepts Statement No. 7 gives guidance. It states that an "expected present value technique" which uses the sum of probability-weighted present values in a range of estimated cash flows adjusted for risk, all discounted using the same interest rate convention, is the preferred—but not required—approach. The FASB has indicated that such a technique is a more effective measurement tool than was the traditional present value approach, especially in situations in which the timing or the amount of estimated cash flows is uncertain, as is the case in measuring nonfinancial assets and liabilities.

In estimating the fair value of a reporting unit, a valuation technique based on multiples of earnings or revenue or a similar performance measure may be used if that technique is consistent with the objective of measuring fair value. Use of such multiples may be appropriate, for example, when the fair value of an entity that has comparable operations and economic characteristics is observable and the relevant multiples of the comparable entity are known. Conversely, such multiples are not used in situations in which the operations or activities of an entity whose multiples are known are not of a comparable nature, scope, or size as the reporting unit for which fair value is being estimated.

(iii) When to Test Goodwill for Impairment   Goodwill of a reporting unit is tested for impairment annually and between annual tests in certain circumstances, as discussed subsequently. The annual goodwill impairment test may be performed any time during the fiscal year provided the timing of the test is consistent from year to year. Different reporting units may be tested for impairment at different times.

A detailed determination of the fair value of a reporting unit may be carried forward from one year to the next if all of the following criteria have been met:

- The assets and liabilities that make up the reporting unit have not changed significantly since the most recent fair value determination.
- The most recent fair value determination resulted in an amount that exceeded the carrying amount of the reporting unit by a substantial margin.
- Based on an analysis of events that have occurred and circumstances that have changed since the most recent fair value determination, the likelihood that a current fair value determination would be less than the current carrying amount of the reporting unit is remote.

Goodwill of a reporting unit is tested for impairment between annual tests if an event occurs or circumstances change that would more likely than not reduce the fair value of a reporting unit below its carrying amount.

Examples of such events or circumstances include the following:

- A significant adverse change in legal factors or in the business climate
- An adverse action or assessment by a regulator
- Unanticipated competition
- A loss of key personnel
- A more-likely-than-not expectation that a reporting unit or a significant portion of a reporting unit will be sold or otherwise disposed of
- Testing for recoverability under SFAS No. 144 of a significant asset group within a reporting unit
- Recognition of a goodwill impairment loss in the financial statements of a subsidiary that is a component of a reporting unit

Also see Section 20A.7(b)(vii) for the need to test goodwill for impairment after a portion of goodwill has been allocated to a business to be disposed of.

If goodwill and another asset or asset group of a reporting unit are tested for impairment at the same time, the other asset or asset group is tested before goodwill. If the asset or asset group is found to be impaired, the impairment loss is recognized before goodwill is tested for impairment.

(iv) Reporting Unit   A reporting unit is an operating segment or one level below an operating segment, referred to as a component. An operating segment is defined by SFAS No. 131, "Disclosures about Segments of an Enterprise and Related Information." A component of an operating segment is a reporting unit if the component constitutes a business, as discussed in EITF Issue No. 98-3, for which discrete financial information is available and segment management, as defined by SFAS No. 131, regularly reviews the operating results of that component.

Segment management may consist of one or more segment managers. Two or more components of an operating segment are aggregated and deemed a single reporting unit if the components have similar economic characteristics, as discussed in SFAS No. 131. An operating segment is deemed a reporting unit if all of its components are similar, if none of its components is a reporting unit, or if it comprises only a single component.

Because considerable judgment is required for entities to determine their reporting units and the guidance in SFAS No. 142 is quite limited, the FASB staff provided further clarification of that guidance in EITF Topic No. D-101. The basic guidance is that a component of an operating segment is a reporting unit if (1) it constitutes a business, (2) discrete financial information on the component is available, and (3) segment management regularly reviews the results of the reporting unit. A fourth requirement provides that components with similar economic characteristics should be combined into one reporting unit. Topic No. D-101 provides that the first three factors are required for a component to be a reporting unit, but no one factor is individually determinative.

The determinative factors are how an entity manages its operations and how an acquired entity is integrated with the acquiring entity. Topic No. D-101 provides the following clarification of each factor:

- *Component constitutes a business.* Judgment is required to determine whether a component constitutes a business, and entities are required to consider the guidance in EITF Issue No. 98-3 in determining that. To be a business under the guidance in EITF Issue No. 98-3, the activities and assets should include "all the inputs and processes necessary" to conduct normal operations. The fact that operating information may be available does not mean the operations constitute a business. They may be just a part of a business, such as one product line.

- *Discrete financial information.* For purposes of both SFAS No. 131 and SFAS No. 142, discrete financial information can consist of just operating information, with no balance sheet information prepared for the component. However, if the component is a reporting unit, the entity would be required to identify and allocate assets and liabilities applicable to the component to test goodwill for impairment.
- *Reviewed by segment management.* Under SFAS No. 131, segment management may be one level below the chief operating decision maker, and there may be one or more segment managers. The focus of SFAS No. 142 is on how operating segments are managed rather than on how the entity as a whole is managed.
- *Similar economic characteristics.* The evaluation of whether two components have similar economic characteristics requires consideration of the factors in paragraph 17 of SFAS No. 131: similar economic characteristics, such as similar long-term average gross margins; the nature of the products and/or services; the nature of production processes; the type or class of customers; the methods used to distribute products and provide services; and the nature of any regulatory environment. Topic No. D-101 provides that not all factors have to be met for economic similarity to exist, and the evaluation should be more qualitative than quantitative.

Topic No. D-101 also provides additional factors to consider when evaluating whether components should be combined in a reporting unit because they are economically similar:

- How an entity operates its business and the nature of the operations
- Whether goodwill is recoverable from the separate operations of each component business or from the components working together because, for example, the components are economically interdependent
- The extent to which the component businesses share assets and other resources
- Whether the components provide support and receive benefits from the same R&D projects

Components of different operating segments for purposes of SFAS No. 131 cannot be combined into the same reporting unit, even if they have similar economic characteristics. This might occur, for example, if the entity organized its operating segments on a geographic basis.

Questions have arisen about whether one or more components of operating units aggregated into one reporting unit under SFAS No. 131 could be economically dissimilar and therefore be in separate reporting units under SFAS No. 142. Topic No. D-101 provides two explanations of why that could happen:

1. The determination of reportable segments under SFAS No. 131 requires identification of operating segments and subsequent determination of whether economically similar operating segments should be aggregated. However, the determination of reporting units under SFAS No. 142 begins with operating segments and then requires an analysis of whether economically dissimilar components of an operating segment should be disaggregated.

2. For a component of an operating segment to be an operating segment under SFAS No. 131, its operating performance must be regularly reviewed by the chief operating decision maker. That same component, however, could be a reporting unit if a segment manager regularly reviews its operating performance.

For the purpose of testing goodwill for impairment, acquired assets and assumed liabilities are assigned to a reporting unit as of the acquisition date if both of the following criteria are met:

1. The asset will be employed in or the liability relates to the operations of a reporting unit.
2. The asset or liability will be considered in determining the fair value of the reporting unit.

Assets or liabilities that an entity considers part of its corporate assets or liabilities are also assigned to a reporting unit if both of the preceding criteria are met. Examples are environmental liabilities that relate to an existing operating facility of the reporting unit and a pension obligation that would be included in the determination of the fair value of the reporting unit. Some assets or liabilities may be employed in or relate to the operations of multiple reporting units. The methodology used to determine the amount of those assets or liabilities to assign to a reporting unit is on a reasonable and supportable basis and applied in a consistent manner. For example, this would include assets and liabilities not directly related to a specific reporting unit but from which the reporting unit benefits could be allocated according to the benefit received by the different reporting units or based on the relative fair values of the different reporting units. A pro rata allocation based on payroll expense might be used for pension items.

For the purpose of testing goodwill for impairment, all goodwill acquired in a business combination is assigned to one or more reporting units as of the acquisition date. Goodwill is assigned to reporting units of the acquiring entity expected to benefit from the synergies of the combination even though other assets or liabilities of the acquired entity may not be assigned to that reporting unit. The total amount of acquired goodwill may be divided among a number of reporting units. The methodology used to determine the amount of goodwill to assign to a reporting unit should be reasonable and supportable and applied in a consistent manner. Also, the methodology has to be consistent with the objectives of the process of assigning goodwill to reporting units, described next. In concept, the amount of goodwill assigned to a reporting unit would be determined in a manner similar to how the amount of goodwill recognized in a business combination is determined.

The fair value of the acquired business or portion of the acquired business that will be included in a particular reporting unit is, in essence, the purchase price of that business. The entity allocates that purchase price to the assets acquired and liabilities incurred related to (the portion of) the acquired business assigned to the reporting unit. Any excess purchase price is the amount of goodwill assigned to that reporting unit. However, if the goodwill is to be assigned to a reporting unit that has not been assigned any of the assets acquired or liabilities assumed in that acquisition, the amount of goodwill to be assigned to that unit might be determined by applying a "with and without" computation. That is, the difference between the fair value of that reporting unit before the acquisition and its fair value after the acquisition represents the amount of goodwill to be assigned to that reporting unit.

When an entity reorganizes its reporting structure in a manner that changes the composition of one or more of its reporting units, the guidance given earlier in this section for assigning acquired assets and assumed liabilities to reporting units is used to reassign assets and liabilities to the reporting units affected. However, goodwill is reassigned to the reporting units affected using a relative fair value allocation approach similar to that used when a portion of a reporting unit is to be disposed of, which is discussed in Section 20A.7(b)(vii). For example, if existing reporting unit A is to be integrated with reporting units B, C, and D, goodwill of reporting unit A would be assigned to units B, C, and D based on the relative fair values of the three portions of reporting unit A before those portions are integrated with reporting units B, C, and D.

(v) Goodwill Impairment Testing by a Subsidiary   All goodwill recognized by a public or nonpublic subsidiary in its separate financial statements prepared in conformity with GAAP, known as subsidiary goodwill, is accounted for in conformity with SFAS No. 142. It is tested for impairment at the subsidiary level using the subsidiary's reporting units. If a goodwill impairment loss is recognized at the subsidiary level, goodwill of the reporting unit or units at the consolidated level in which the subsidiary's reporting unit with impaired goodwill resides is tested for impairment if the event that gave rise to the loss at the subsidiary level more likely than not would reduce the fair value of the reporting unit at the consolidated level below its carrying amount. A goodwill impairment loss is recognized at the consolidated level only if goodwill at the consolidated level is impaired.

(vi) Goodwill Impairment Testing When a Noncontrolling Interest Exists   Goodwill from a business combination with a continuing noncontrolling (minority) interest is tested for impairment using an approach consistent with the approach used to measure the noncontrolling interest at the acquisition date. For example, if goodwill is first recognized based on only the controlling interest of the parent, the fair value of the reporting unit used in the impairment test is based on the controlling interest and does not reflect the portion of fair value attributable to the noncontrolling interest. Similarly, the implied fair value of goodwill determined in the second step of the impairment test used to measure the impairment loss reflects only the parent's interest in the goodwill.

(vii) Disposal of All or a Portion of a Reporting Unit   When a reporting unit is to be disposed of in its entirety, the carrying amount of goodwill of the reporting unit is included in the carrying amount of the reporting unit in determining the gain or loss on disposal. When a portion of a reporting unit that constitutes a business is to be disposed of, the carrying amount of goodwill associated with the business is included in the carrying amount of the business in determining the gain or loss on disposal. The portion of the carrying amount of goodwill to be included in that carrying amount is based on the relative fair values of the business to be disposed of and the portion of the reporting unit to be retained. However, if the business to be disposed of was never integrated into the reporting unit after its acquisition and thus the benefits of the acquired goodwill were never realized by the rest of the reporting unit, the current carrying amount of the acquired goodwill is included in the carrying amount of business to be disposed of. When only a portion of goodwill is allocated to a business to be disposed of, the goodwill remaining in the portion of the reporting unit to be retained is tested for impairment.

(viii) Equity Method Investments   The portion of the difference between the cost of an investment and the amount of underlying equity in net assets of an equity method investee recognized as goodwill in conformity with paragraph 19(b) of APB Opinion No. 18, "The Equity Method of Accounting for Investments in Common Stock," known as equity method goodwill, is not amortized. However, equity method goodwill is not tested for impairment in conformity with SFAS No. 142.

Equity method investments continue to be reviewed for impairment in conformity with paragraph 19(h) of APB Opinion No. 18.

(ix) Entities Emerging from Bankruptcy   SOP 90-7, "Financial Reporting by Entities in Reorganization Under the Bankruptcy Code," provides that when an entity applies fresh-start accounting on emerging from bankruptcy, the reorganization value should be allocated to all tangible and intangible assets following the procedures in APB Opinion No. 16, "Business

Combinations." SFAS No. 142 stipulates that entities should report the excess reorganization value as goodwill and account for it in the same manner as other elements of goodwill.

20A.8 DEFERRED INCOME TAXES

SFAS No. 142 does not change the requirements in SFAS No. 109, "Accounting for Income Taxes," paragraphs 30, 261, and 262, for recognition of deferred income taxes related to goodwill and intangible assets.

20A.9 FINANCIAL STATEMENT PRESENTATION

(a) INTANGIBLE ASSETS   All intangible assets are aggregated and presented as a separate line item in the statement of financial position. In addition, individual intangible assets or classes of intangible assets may be presented as separate line items. Amortization expense and impairment losses for intangible assets are presented in income statement line items within continuing operations as deemed appropriate for each entity. An impairment loss resulting from such an impairment test should not be recognized as a change in accounting principle.

(b) GOODWILL   The aggregate amount of goodwill is presented as a separate line item in the statement of financial position. The aggregate amount of goodwill impairment losses are presented as a separate line item in the income statement before the subtotal *income from continuing operations,* or a similar caption, unless a goodwill impairment loss is associated with a discontinued operation. A goodwill impairment loss associated with a discontinued operation is included net of tax within the results of discontinued operations.

20A.10 DISCLOSURES

The following information is disclosed in the notes to the financial statements in the period of acquisition of intangible assets acquired either individually or with a group of assets:

A. For intangible assets subject to amortization:
   1. The total amount assigned and the amount assigned to any major intangible asset class
   2. The amount of any significant residual value, in total and by major intangible asset class
   3. The weighted-average amortization period, in total and by major intangible asset class
B. For intangible assets not subject to amortization, the total amount assigned and the amount assigned to any major intangible asset class
C. The amount of R&D assets acquired and written off in the period and the line item in the income statement in which the amounts written off are aggregated

The following information is disclosed in the financial statements or the notes to the financial statements for each period for which a statement of financial position is presented:

A. For intangible assets subject to amortization:
   1. The gross carrying amount and accumulated amortization, in total and by major intangible asset class
   2. The aggregate amortization expense for the period

3. The estimated aggregate amortization expense for each of the five succeeding fiscal years

B. For intangible assets not subject to amortization, the total carrying amount and the carrying amount for each major intangible asset class

C. The changes in the carrying amount of goodwill during the period, including:
   1. The aggregate amount of goodwill acquired
   2. The aggregate amount of impairment losses recognized on goodwill
   3. The amount of goodwill included in the gain or loss on disposal of all or a portion of a reporting unit

Reporting entities that report segment information in conformity with SFAS No. 131 should provide the preceding information about goodwill in total and for each reportable segment and should disclose any significant changes in the allocation of goodwill by reportable segment. If any portion of goodwill has not yet been allocated to a reporting unit at the date the financial statements are issued, that unallocated amount and the reasons for not allocating the amount are disclosed. For each impairment loss recognized related to an intangible asset, the following information is disclosed in the notes to the financial statements that include the period in which the impairment loss is recognized:

- Description of the impaired intangible asset and the facts and circumstances leading to the impairment
- Amount of the impairment loss and the method for determining fair value
- Caption in the income statement or the statement of activities in which the impairment loss is aggregated
- If applicable, the segment in which the impaired intangible asset is reported under SFAS No. 131

For each goodwill impairment loss recognized, the following information is disclosed in the notes to the financial statements that include the period in which the impairment loss is recognized:

- A description of the facts and circumstances leading to the impairment
- The amount of the impairment loss and the method of determining the fair value of the associated reporting unit
- If a recognized impairment loss is an estimate that has not yet been finalized, that fact and the reasons for it and, in subsequent periods, the nature and amount of any significant adjustments made to the initial estimate of the impairment loss

20A.11   EFFECTIVE DATE AND TRANSITION PROVISIONS OF SFAS NO. 142

The provisions of SFAS No. 142 were initially applied in fiscal years beginning after December 15, 2001, to all goodwill and other intangible assets recognized in a reporting entity's statement of financial position at the beginning of that fiscal year, regardless of when those previously recognized assets were first recognized. Early application was permitted for entities with fiscal years beginning after March 15, 2001, provided that the first interim financial statements had not been issued previously. The provisions of the statement were to be first applied at the beginning of a fiscal year. They were not to be applied retroactively.

SFAS No. 142's provisions are not to be applied to previously recognized goodwill and intangible assets acquired in a combination between two or more mutual enterprises, acquired in a combination between not-for-profit organizations, or from the acquisition of a for-profit business entity by a not-for-profit organization until interpretive guidance related to the application of the purchase method to those transactions is issued. As of late 2005, this guidance has yet to be promulgated, although this is anticipated to occur in the near future.

See Section 10.3(o) for transition provisions related to goodwill and intangible assets acquired in business combination for which the acquisition date was before July 1, 2001, that were accounted for by the purchase method.

(a) GOODWILL AND INTANGIBLE ASSETS ACQUIRED AFTER JUNE 30, 2001 Goodwill acquired in a business combination for which the acquisition date is after June 30, 2001 is not amortized. Intangible assets other than goodwill acquired in a business combination or other transaction for which the date of acquisition is after June 30, 2001 are amortized or not amortized in conformity with the discussion in Sections 20A.4(b) and 20A.4(c). Goodwill and intangible assets acquired in a transaction for which the acquisition date is after June 30, 2001 but before the date that SFAS No. 142 was first applied in its entirety were to be reviewed for impairment in conformity with APB Opinion No. 17 or SFAS No. 121 (as appropriate) until the date SFAS No. 142 was applied in its entirety. The financial statement presentation and disclosure provisions of SFAS No. 142 were not to be applied to those assets until SFAS No. 142 was applied in its entirety.

Goodwill and intangible assets acquired in a combination between two or more mutual enterprises, acquired in a combination between not-for-profit organizations, or from the acquisition of a for-profit business entity by a not-for-profit organization for which the acquisition date is after June 30, 2001, continue to be accounted for in conformity with APB Opinion No. 17 until the FASB provides guidance on issues related to the application of the purchase method to such transactions.

(b) PREVIOUSLY RECOGNIZED INTANGIBLE ASSETS   To apply SFAS No. 142 to previously recognized intangible assets (those acquired in a transaction for which the acquisition date is on or before June 30, 2001), the useful lives of those assets are reassessed using the guidance in Section 20A.4(a) and the remaining amortization periods are adjusted accordingly. For example, the amortization period for a previously recognized intangible asset might be increased if its original useful life was estimated to be longer than the 40-year maximum amortization period allowed by APB Opinion No. 17. The reassessment was to be completed before the end of the first interim period of the fiscal year in which SFAS No. 142 was first applied.

Previously recognized intangible assets deemed to have indefinite useful lives were to be tested for impairment as of the beginning of the fiscal year in which SFAS No. 142 was first applied. The transitional intangible asset impairment test was to be completed in the first interim period in which SFAS No. 142 was first applied, and any resulting impairment loss was to be recognized as the effect of a change in accounting principle. The effect of the accounting change and related income tax effects were to be presented in the income statement between the captions extraordinary items and net income. The per-share information presented in the income statement included the per-share effect of the accounting change.

(c) PREVIOUSLY RECOGNIZED GOODWILL   At the date SFAS No. 142 was first applied, the reporting entity was required to establish its reporting units based on its reporting structure at that date and the guidance described in Section 20A.7(b)(iv). Recognized net assets and liabilities that did not relate to a reporting unit, such as an environmental liability for an operation previously disposed of, did not need to be assigned to a reporting unit. All goodwill recognized in a reporting entity's statement of financial position at the date that SFAS No. 142 was first applied was to be assigned to one or more reporting units. Goodwill was to be assigned in a reasonable and supportable manner. The sources of previously recognized goodwill were to be considered in making that initial assignment as well as the reporting units to which the related acquired net assets were assigned. Section 20A.7(b)(iv) provides guidance on assigning goodwill to reporting units on initial application of SFAS No. 142.

Goodwill in each reporting unit was tested for impairment as of the beginning of the fiscal year in which SFAS No. 142 was first applied in its entirety. The first step of the test was to be completed within six months from the date the reporting entity first applied SFAS No. 142. The amounts used in the transitional goodwill impairment test were measured as of the beginning of the year of first application. If the carrying amount of the net assets of a reporting unit (including goodwill) exceeded the fair value of the reporting unit, the second step of the transitional goodwill impairment test was completed as soon as possible, but no later than the end of the year of first application.

An impairment loss as a result of a transitional goodwill impairment test was recognized as the effect of a change in accounting principle. The effect of the accounting change and related income tax effects were to be presented in the income statement between the captions extraordinary items and net income. The per-share information presented in the income statement included the per-share effect of the accounting change. Though a transitional impairment loss for goodwill could be measured in other than the first interim reporting period, it was to be recognized in the first interim period regardless of the period in which it was measured, consistent with paragraph 10 of SFAS No. 3, "Reporting Accounting Changes in Interim Financial Statements."

The financial information for the interim periods of the fiscal year that preceded the period in which the transitional goodwill impairment loss was measured was to be restated to reflect the accounting change in those periods. The aggregate amount of the accounting change is included in restated net income of the first interim period of the year of first application (and in any year-to-date or last-12-months-to-date financial reports that included the first interim period). Whenever financial information is presented that includes the periods that precede the period in which the transitional goodwill impairment loss was measured, that financial information should be presented on the restated basis.

A reporting entity was required to perform the required annual goodwill impairment test in the year that SFAS No. 142 was first applied in its entirety, in addition to the transitional goodwill impairment test, unless the reporting entity designated the beginning of its fiscal year as the date for its annual goodwill impairment test.

(d) EQUITY METHOD GOODWILL   When SFAS No. 142 was first applied, the portion of the excess of cost over the underlying equity in net assets of an investee accounted for using the equity method that had been recognized as goodwill was no longer to be amortized. However, equity method goodwill is not to be tested for impairment under SFAS No. 142.

Rather, the guidance under APB No. 18 continues to be applicable in assessing impairment of equity method investments.

(e) TRANSITIONAL DISCLOSURES   Expanded disclosures were mandated during the initial implementation period for SFAS No. 142. Since all entities have now fully adopted this standard, and since comparative disclosures including preimplementation periods are now unlikely to be encountered in practice, this will not be described in detail.

20A.12   SOURCES AND SUGGESTED REFERENCES

Accounting Principles Board, "Restatement of Revision of Accounting Research Bulletins," Accounting Research Bulletin No. 43. New York: AICPA, 1968.

Accounting Principles Board, "Disclosure of Accounting Policies," APB Opinion No. 22. New York: AICPA, 1973.

Accounting Principles Board, "Reporting the Results of Operations," APB Opinion No. 30. New York: AICPA, 1973.

American Accounting Association Financial Accounting Standards Committee, "Equity Valuation Models and Measuring Goodwill Impairment," *Accounting Horizons,* June 2001.

American Institute of Certified Public Accountants, "Push Down Accounting," Issues Paper. New York: AICPA, 1979.

American Institute of Certified Public Accountants, "Accounting for Developmental and Preoperating Costs, Purchases and Exchanges of Take-off and Landing Slots, and Airframe Modifications," Statement of Position 88-1. New York: AICPA, 1988.

American Institute of Certified Public Accountants, "Financial Reporting by Entities in Reorganization Under the Bankruptcy Code," Statement of Position 90-7. New York: AICPA, November 19, 1990.

American Institute of Certified Public Accountants, "Reporting on Advertising Costs," Statement of Position 93-7. New York: AICPA, December 29, 1993.

American Institute of Certified Public Accountants, "Accounting for the Costs of Computer Software Developed or Obtained for Internal Use," Statement of Position 98-1. New York: AICPA, 1998.

American Institute of Certified Public Accountants, "Reporting on the Costs of Start-Up Activities," Statement of Position 98-5. New York: AICPA, 1998.

American Institute of Certified Public Accountants, "Accounting by Producers or Distributors of Films," Statement of Position 00-2. New York: AICPA, 2000.

American Institute of Certified Public Accountants, "Assets Acquired in a Business Combination to Be Used in Research and Development Activities: A Focus on Software, Electronic Devices, and Pharmaceutical Industries," AICPA Practice Aid Series. New York: AICPA, 2001.

American Institute of Certified Public Accountants, "The Fair Value Measurement Valuation Toolkit for Financial Accounting Standards Board Statements of Financial Accounting Standards No. 141, Business Combinations, and No. 142, Goodwill and Other Intangible Assets." New York: AICPA, 2002.

Financial Accounting Standards Board, "Accounting for Research and Development Costs," Statement of Financial Accounting Standards No. 2. Norwalk, CT: FASB, 1974.

Financial Accounting Standards Board, "Applicability of FASB Statement No. 2 to Computer Software (An Interpretation of FASB Statement No. 2)," FASB Interpretation No. 6. Norwalk, CT: FASB, 1975.

Financial Accounting Standards Board, "Accounting for Franchise Fee Revenue," Statement of Financial Accounting Standards No. 45. Norwalk, CT: FASB, 1981.

Financial Accounting Standards Board, "Financial Reporting in the Record and Music Industry," Statement of Financial Accounting Standards No. 50. Norwalk, CT: FASB, 1981.

Financial Accounting Standards Board, "Financial Reporting by Cable Television Companies," Statement of Financial Accounting Standards No. 51. Norwalk, CT: FASB, 1981.

Financial Accounting Standards Board, "Financial Reporting by Broadcasters," Statement of Financial Accounting Standards No. 63. Norwalk, CT: FASB, 1982.

Financial Accounting Standards Board, "Accounting for the Effects of Certain Types of Regulation," Statement of Financial Accounting Standards No. 71. Norwalk, CT: FASB, 1982.

Financial Accounting Standards Board, "Accounting for Certain Acquisitions of Banking or Thrift Institutions," Statement of Financial Accounting Standards No. 72. Norwalk, CT: FASB, 1983.

Financial Accounting Standards Board, "Accounting for the Costs of Computer Software to Be Sold, Leased, or Otherwise Marketed," Statement of Financial Accounting Standards No. 86. Norwalk, CT: FASB, 1985.

Financial Accounting Standards Board, "Statement of Cash Flows," Statement of Financial Accounting Standards No. 95. Norwalk, CT: FASB, 1987.

Financial Accounting Standards Board, "Issues Relating to Accounting for Leases," FASB Technical Bulletin No. 88-1. Norwalk, CT: FASB, 1988.

Financial Accounting Standards Board, "Accounting for Income Taxes," Statement of Financial Accounting Standards No. 109. Norwalk, CT: FASB, February, 1992.

Financial Accounting Standards Board, "Recognition of Liabilities in Connection with a Purchase Business Combination," EITF Issue No. 95-3. Norwalk, CT: FASB, 1995.

Financial Accounting Standards Board, "Determination of What Risks and Rewards, If Any, Can Be Retained and Whether Any Unresolved Contingencies May Exist in a Sale of Mortgage Loan Servicing Rights," EITF Issue No. 95-5. Norwalk, CT: FASB, 1995.

Financial Accounting Standards Board, "Accounting for Contingent Consideration Paid to the Shareholders of an Acquired Enterprise in a Purchase Business Combination," EITF Issue No. 95-8. Norwalk, CT: FASB, 1995.

Financial Accounting Standards Board, "Accounting for the Film and Software Costs Associated with Developing Entertainment and Educational Software Products," EITF Issue No. 96-6. Norwalk, CT: FASB, 1996.

Financial Accounting Standards Board, "Disclosures about Segments of an Enterprise and Related Information," Statement of Financial Accounting Standards No. 131. Norwalk, CT: FASB, 1997.

Financial Accounting Standards Board, "Deregulation of the Price of Electricity—Issues Related to the Application of FASB Statements 71 and 101," EITF Issue No. 97-4. Norwalk, CT: FASB, 1997.

Financial Accounting Standards Board, "Accounting for Contingent Consideration Issued in a Purchase Business Combination," EITF Issue No. 97-8. Norwalk, CT: FASB, 1997.

Financial Accounting Standards Board, "Accounting for Costs Incurred in Connection with a Consulting Contract or an Internal Project That Combines Business Process Reengineering and Information Technology Transformation," EITF Issue No. 97-13. Norwalk, CT: FASB, 1997.

Financial Accounting Standards Board, "Accounting for Transfers and Servicing of Financial Assets and Extinguishments of Liabilities—A Replacement of FASB Statement No. 125," Statement of Financial Accounting Standards No. 140. Norwalk, CT: FASB, 2000.

Financial Accounting Standards Board, "Business Combinations," Statement of Financial Accounting Standards No. 141. Norwalk, CT: FASB, June 2001.

Financial Accounting Standards Board, "Goodwill and Other Intangible Assets," Statement of Financial Accounting Standards No. 142. Norwalk, CT: FASB, June 2001.

Financial Accounting Standards Board, "Accounting for the Impairment or Disposal of Long-Lived Assets," Statement of Financial Accounting Standards No. 144. Norwalk, CT: FASB, June 2001.

Financial Accounting Standards Board, "Accounting for Costs Associated with Exit or Disposal Activities," Statement of Financial Accounting Standards No. 146. Norwalk, CT: FASB, June 2002.

Financial Accounting Standards Board, "Acquisitions of Certain Financial Institutions," Statement of Financial Accounting Standards No. 147. Norwalk, CT: FASB, October 2002.

Financial Accounting Standards Board, "Unit of Accounting for Testing Impairment of Indefinite-Lived Assets," EITF Issue No. 02-7. Norwalk, CT: FASB, 2002.

Financial Accounting Standards Board, "Deferred Income Tax Considerations in Applying the Goodwill Impairment Test in FASB Statement No. 142," EITF Issue No. 02-13. Norwalk, CT: FASB, 2002.

Financial Accounting Standards Board, "Recognition of Customer Relationship Intangible Assets Acquired in a Business Combination," EITF Issue No. 02-17. Norwalk, CT: FASB, 2002.

Financial Accounting Standards Board, "Interaction of Paragraphs 11 and 12 of FASB Statement No. 142 Regarding Determination of the Useful Life and Amortization of Intangible Assets," EITF Issue No. 03-9. Norwalk, CT: FASB, 2003.

Financial Accounting Standards Board, "Interaction of FASB Statements No. 141, *Business Combinations,* and No. 142, *Goodwill and Other Intangible Assets,* and EITF Issue No. 04-2, *Whether Mineral Rights Are Tangible or Intangible Assets,*" FASB Staff Positions 141-1 and 142-1. Norwalk, CT: FASB, 2003.

Financial Accounting Standards Board, "Accounting for Pre-Existing Contractual Relationships Between the Parties to a Business Combination," EITF Issue No. 04-1. Norwalk, CT: FASB, 2004.

Financial Accounting Standards Board, "Whether Mineral Rights Are Tangible or Intangible Assets and Related Issues," EITF Issue No. 04-2. Norwalk, CT: FASB, 2004.

Financial Accounting Standards Board, "Fair Value Measurements," Exposure Draft. Norwalk, CT: FASB, June 2004.

Financial Accounting Standards Board, "Business Combinations (a Replacement of FASB Statement No. 141," Exposure Draft SFAS No. 141(R). Norwalk, CT: FASB, June 2005.

Financial Accounting Standards Board, "Selected Issues Relating to Assets and Liabilities with Uncertainties," Invitation to Comment. Norwalk, CT: FASB, September 2005.

Securities and Exchange Commission, "Expenses of Offering," Staff Accounting Bulletin Topic 5A. Washington, DC: SEC: 1975.

Securities and Exchange Commission, "Acquisitions Involving Financial Institutions," Staff Accounting Bulletin Topic 2-A3. Washington, DC: SEC: 1981.

Securities and Exchange Commission, "Push Down Basic of Accounting Required in Certain Limited Circumstances," Staff Accounting Bulletin Topic 5J. Washington, DC: SEC: 1983.

CHAPTER 21

PROPERTY, PLANT, EQUIPMENT, AND DEPRECIATION (REVISED)

GEORGE I. VICTOR, CPA
Giambalvo, Giammarese & Stalzer, CPAs, P.C.[†]

[†] The information contained in this chapter does not necessarily represent the views of Giambalvo, Giammarese & Stalzer, CPAs, P.C.

21.1 NATURE OF PROPERTY, PLANT, AND EQUIPMENT

(a) DEFINITION   Property, plant, and equipment (PP&E) are presented as noncurrent assets in a classified balance sheet. The category includes such items as land, buildings, equipment, furniture, fixtures, tools, machinery, and leasehold improvements. It excludes intangibles and investments in affiliated companies.

(b) CHARACTERISTICS   Property, plant, and equipment have several important characteristics:

- A relatively long life
- The production of income or services over its life
- Tangibility—having physical substance

(c) AUTHORITATIVE LITERATURE   Generally accepted accounting principles (GAAP) for property, plant, and equipment have evolved without the promulgation of any Level A or B GAAP rule making on a comprehensive basis. Because of this lack of authoritative literature, many believe that diversity in practice has developed with respect to both the type of costs capitalized and the amounts.

In 2001, the Accounting Standards Executive Committee (AcSEC) of the American Institute of Certified Public Accountants (AICPA) issued an exposure draft (ED) of a Statement of Position (SOP) titled *Accounting for Certain Costs and Activities Related to Property, Plant; and Equipment.* The proposal was not adopted, since the Financial Accounting Standards Board (FASB) indicated that it addressed significant issues that should be addressed by the FASB. Nevertheless, in the absence of subsequent action by the FASB, this document reflects the "best thinking" of the AcSEC at the time.

The proposal addresses accounting for costs related to initial acquisition, construction, improvements, betterments, additions, repairs and maintenance, planned major maintenance, turnaround, overhauls and other similar costs related to property, plant, and equipment. The ED proposed a project stage framework consisting of the following:

1. *Preliminary stage*
This stage occurs before the acquisition of any specific PP&E asset and before it is probable that a specific PP&E asset will be acquired or constructed. All costs, with the exception of costs related for payment of an option to acquire PP&E, should be charged to expense during the preliminary stage.

2. *Preacquisition stage*
This stage is similar to the preliminary stage as no PP&E asset has yet been acquired. However, acquisition or construction of a specific PP&E asset is considered probable. All costs related to PP&E incurred during this stage should be charged to expense unless the costs are directly identifiable with the specific PP&E. Directly identifiable costs include only (a) incremental direct costs incurred in transactions with independent third parties and (b) payroll and payroll-benefit-related costs for employees who devote time to the PP&E activity. All general and administrative and overhead costs should be charged to expense and not capitalized as a cost of PP&E.

3. *Acquisition-or-construction stage*
This stage begins when the entity obtains ownership of the PP&E. Only directly identifiable costs as outlined in the previous paragraph are capitalizable along with depreciation of machinery and equipment used directly in the construction of PP&E and inventory

used directly in the construction or installation of PP&E. All general and administrative and overhead costs should also be charged to expense and not capitalized as a cost of PP&E.

4. *In-service stage*

This stage begins when a PP&E asset is substantially complete and ready for its intended use. All costs incurred in this stage are charged to expense except for costs relating to replacement of existing components of a PP&E asset or acquisition of additional components. The principles outlined under the acquisition-or-construction stage are used to determine what costs of the replacements or additional components are capitalizable. Accordingly, all costs of repairs and maintenance are charged to expense, because they cannot be considered replacements or additional components. In conjunction with the replacement of a component of PP&E, an estimate of the remaining net book value of that replaced component should be charged to expense in the period of replacement.

5. *Planned major maintenance activities*

The ED prohibited the following accounting methods for planned major maintenance activities:

- Accrual of a liability before incurring the costs for a planned major maintenance activity
- Deferral and amortization of the cost of a planned major maintenance activity
- Current recognition of additional depreciation to cover future costs of a planned major maintenance activity

6. *Component accounting*

A *component* of a PP&E asset is defined as a tangible part or portion that can be separately identified as an asset, and it is expected to provide economic benefit for more than one year. The ED provided that if a component has an expected useful life that differs from the expected useful life of the PP&E asset to which it relates, the cost of the component should be accounted for separately and depreciated over its separate expected useful life.

7. *Current practice*

Over 400 comment letters were received by AcSEC in response to this proposed SOP. The ED would have made the following major changes in existing practice:

- The capitalization criteria would have prohibited capitalization of indirect costs, overhead, and general and administrative costs, which many entities capitalize currently as a part of their PP&E cost.
- Many entities currently use the methods prohibited under the section titled "Planned Major Maintenance Activities" to account for plant turnarounds and other major maintenance activities.
- Requirements to use component accounting would have effectively prohibited entities from using group and composite methods of accounting for depreciation.

Since the withdrawal of this ED, the FASB has not taken action in providing guidance on these issues.

21.2 COST

Property, plant, and equipment usually are recorded at *cost,* defined as the amount of consideration paid or incurred to acquire or construct an asset. Cost consists of several elements. Welsch and Zlatkovich explain:

The capitalizable costs include the invoice price (less discounts), plus other costs such as sales tax, insurance during transit, freight, duties, ownership searching, ownership registration, installation, and break-in costs.[1]

(a) DETERMINING COST   Generally, three principles are followed for determining the cost of an asset:

1. An asset acquired by exchanging cash or other assets is recorded at cost—that is, at the amount of cash disbursed or the fair value of other assets distributed.
2. An asset acquired by incurring liabilities is recorded at cost—that is, at the present value of the future amounts to be paid.
3. An asset acquired by issuing shares of stock of the acquiring corporation is recorded at the fair value of the asset—that is, shares of stock issued are recorded at the fair value of the consideration received for the stock. That fair value is considered cost.

(i) Acquisition by Exchange   Property, plant, and equipment may be acquired by exchange, as well as by purchase. In that case, the applicable accounting requirements are set forth in Accounting Principles Board (APB) Opinion No. 29, *Accounting for Nonmonetary Transactions*, which defines an exchange (par. 3c) as "a reciprocal transfer between an enterprise and another entity that results in the enterprise's acquiring assets or services or satisfying liabilities by surrendering other assets or services or incurring other obligations."

After defining nonmonetary assets (par. 3b) to include property, plant, and equipment, Opinion No. 29 further provides (par. 18) the general rule:

Accounting for nonmonetary transactions should be based on the fair values of the assets (or services) involved. . . . Thus, the cost of a nonmonetary asset acquired in exchange for another nonmonetary asset is the fair value of the asset surrendered to obtain it, and a gain or loss should be recognized on the exchange. The fair value of the asset received should be used to measure the cost if it is more clearly evident than the fair value of the asset surrendered.

However, the Opinion recognizes (par. 21) an exception to its general rule if an exchange of nonmonetary assets "is not essentially the culmination of an earning process." In that case, the accounting "should be based on the recorded amount (after reduction, if appropriate, for an indicated impairment of value) of the nonmonetary asset relinquished."

Among the exchanges of nonmonetary assets that do not culminate the earning process, the Opinion includes (par. 21b) "an exchange of a productive asset [defined to include property, plant, and equipment] not held for sale in the ordinary course of business for a similar productive asset or an equivalent interest in the same or similar productive asset."

However, the rule about basing exchanges of productive (nonmonetary) assets on recorded amounts has its own exception if the exchange includes monetary consideration. In that case, the Opinion (par. 22) states:

The Board believes that the recipient of the monetary consideration has realized gain on the exchange to the extent that the amount of the monetary receipt exceeds a proportionate share of the recorded amount of the asset surrendered.

---

1.   Glenn A. Welsch and Charles T. Zlatkovich, *Intermediate Accounting, Eighth Edition* (Homewood, IL: Irwin, 1989).

The portion of the cost applicable to the realized amount should be based on the ratio of the monetary consideration to the total consideration received (monetary consideration plus the estimated fair value of the nonmonetary asset received) or, if more clearly evident, the fair value of the nonmonetary asset transferred. The Board further believes that the entity paying the monetary consideration should not recognize any gain on [an exchange not culminating the earning process] but should record the asset received at the amount of the monetary consideration paid plus the recorded amount of the nonmonetary asset surrendered. If a loss is indicated by the terms of [an exchange not culminating the earning process], the entire indicated loss on the exchange should be recognized.

The Financial Accounting Standards Board (FASB)'s Emerging Issues Task Force (EITF) later reached a consensus (EITF Issue No. 86-29) that an exchange of nonmonetary assets should be considered a monetary (rather than nonmonetary) transaction if monetary consideration is significant, and agreed that *significant* should be defined as at least 25 percent of the fair value of the exchange.

(ii) Acquisition by Issuing Debt   If property, plant, and equipment are acquired in exchange for payables or other contractual obligations to pay money (referred to collectively as *notes*), APB Opinion No. 21, *Interest on Receivables and Payables* (par. 12), states:

There should be a general presumption that the rate of interest stipulated by the parties to the transaction represents fair and adequate compensation to the supplier for the use of the related funds.

However, the Opinion continues:

That presumption . . . must not permit the form of the transaction to prevail over its economic substance and thus would not apply if (1) interest is not stated, or (2) the stated interest rate is unreasonable . . . or (3) the stated face amount of the note is materially different from the current cash sales price for the same or similar items or from the market value of the note at the date of the transaction.

In any of these circumstances, both the assets acquired and the note should be recorded at the fair value of the assets or at the market value of the note, whichever can be more clearly determined. If the amount recorded is not the same as the face value of the note, the difference is a discount or premium, which should be accounted for as interest over the life of the note. If there is no established price for the assets acquired and no evidence of the market value of the note, the amount recorded should be determined by discounting all future payments on the note using an imputed rate of interest.

In selecting the imputed rate of interest to be used, APB Opinion No. 21 (par. 14) states that consideration should be given to:

(a) An approximation of the prevailing market rates for the source of credit that would provide a market for sale or assignment of the note; (b) the prime or higher rate for notes which are discounted with banks, giving due weight to the credit standing of the maker; (c) published market rates for similar quality bonds; (d) current rates for debentures with substantially identical terms and risks that are traded in open markets; and (e) the current rate charged by investors for first or second mortgage loans on similar property.

(iii) Acquisition by Issuing Stock   Assets acquired by issuing shares of stock should be recorded at either the fair value of the shares issued or the fair value of the property acquired, whichever is more clearly evident.

Smith and Skousen further explain:

> When securities do not have an established market value, appraisal of the acquired assets by an independent authority may be required to arrive at an objective determination of their fair market value. If satisfactory market values cannot be obtained for either securities issued or the assets acquired, values may have to be established by the board of directors for accounting purposes. The source of the valuation should be disclosed on the balance sheet.[2]

(iv) Mixed Acquisition for Lump Sum   Several assets may be acquired for a lump-sum payment. This type of acquisition is often called a *basket purchase*. It is essential to allocate the joint cost carefully, because the assets may include both depreciable and nondepreciable assets, or the depreciable assets may be depreciated at different rates.

Welsch and Zlatkovich discuss the methods of allocating joint costs:

> The allocation of the purchase price should be based on some realistic indicator of the relative values of the several assets involved, such as current appraised values, tax assessment, cost savings, or the present value of estimated future earnings.[3]

(v) Donated Assets   Property, plant, and equipment may be donated to an entity. The accounting for such donations is addressed by Statement of Financial Accounting Standards (SFAS) No. 116, *Accounting for Contributions Received and Contributions Made*. Paragraph 8 of SFAS No. 116 concludes that donated property, plant, and equipment should be measured at fair value.

Paragraph 19 provides guidance for determining the fair value of donated assets and indicates that quoted market prices, if available, are the best evidence of the fair value. It further indicates that if quoted market prices are not available, fair value may be estimated based on quoted market prices for similar assets, independent appraisals, or valuation techniques, such as the present value of estimated cash flows.

(b) OVERHEAD ON SELF-CONSTRUCTED ASSETS   Companies often construct their own buildings and equipment. Materials and labor directly identifiable with the construction are part of its cost.

As to whether overhead should be included in the cost of construction, Lamden, Gerboth, and McRae suggest:

> In the absence of compelling evidence to the contrary, overhead costs considered to have "discernible future benefits" for the purpose of determining the cost of inventory should be presumed to have "discernible future benefits" for the purpose of determining the cost of a self-constructed depreciable asset.[4]

---

2.   Jay M. Smith and K. Fred Skousen, *Intermediate Accounting, Comprehensive Volume, Ninth Edition* (Cincinnati: South-Western Publishing, 1987).
3.   Welsch and Zlatkovich.
4.   Charles Lamden, Dale L. Gerboth, and Thomas McRae, "Accounting for Depreciable Assets," *Accounting Research Monograph*, No. 1 (New York: AICPA, 1975).

Mosich and Larsen agree and go on to discuss two alternative views as to what overhead should be included:

Allocate Only Incremental Overhead Costs to the Self-Constructed Asset. This approach may be defended on the grounds that incremental overhead costs represent the relevant cost that management considered in making the decision to construct the asset. Fixed overhead costs, it is argued, are period costs. Because they would have been incurred in any case, there is no relationship between the fixed overhead costs and the self-constructed project. This approach has been widely used in practice because it does not distort the cost of normal operations.

Allocate a Portion of All Overhead Costs to the Self-Constructed Asset. The argument for this approach is that the proper function of cost allocation is to relate all costs incurred in an accounting period to the output of that period. If an enterprise is able to construct an asset and still carry on its regular activities, it has benefited by putting to use some of its idle capacity, and this fact should be reflected in larger income. To charge the entire overhead to only a portion of the productive activity is to disregard facts and to understate the cost of the self-constructed asset. This line of reasoning has considerable merit.[5]

(c) INTEREST CAPITALIZATION   SFAS No. 34, *Capitalization of Interest Cost* (par. 6), states:

The historical cost of acquiring an asset includes the costs necessarily incurred to bring it to the condition and location necessary for its intended use. If an asset requires a period of time in which to carry out the activities necessary to bring it to that condition and location, the interest cost incurred during that period as a result of expenditures for the asset is a part of the historical cost of acquiring the asset.

Paragraph 9 describes the assets that qualify for interest capitalization:

- Assets that are constructed or otherwise produced for an enterprise's own use (including assets constructed or produced for the enterprise by others for which deposits or progress payments have been made)
- Assets intended for sale or lease that are constructed or otherwise produced as discrete projects (e.g., ships or real estate developments)

The amount of interest capitalized is computed by applying an interest rate to the average amount of accumulated expenditures for the asset during the period. To the extent that specific borrowings are associated with the asset, the interest rate on those borrowings may be used. Otherwise, the interest rate should be the weighted average rate applicable to other borrowings outstanding during the period. In no event should the total interest capitalized exceed total interest costs incurred for the period. Imputing interest costs on equity is not permitted.

---

5.   A. N. Mosich and John E. Larsen, *Intermediate Accounting, Sixth Edition* (New York: McGraw-Hill, 1986).

Descriptions of capitalized interest are often seen in footnotes, such as the following example from 1989 financial statements:

Delta Air Lines, Inc.

Notes to Consolidated Financial Statements

Note 1. Summary of Significant Accounting Policies

Interest Capitalized—Interest attributable to funds used to finance the acquisition of new aircraft and construction of major ground facilities is capitalized as an additional cost of the related asset. Interest is capitalized at the Company's average interest rate on long-term debt or, where applicable, the interest rate related to specific borrowings. Capitalization of interest ceases when the property or equipment is placed in service.

(d) COST OF LAND   Determining the cost of land presents particular problems, as described by Pyle and Larson:

When land is purchased for a building site, its cost includes the amount paid for the land plus real estate commissions. It also includes escrow and legal fees, fees for examining and insuring the title, and any accrued property taxes paid by the purchaser, as well as expenditures for surveying, clearing, grading, draining, and landscaping. All are part of the cost of the land. Furthermore, any assessments incurred at the time of purchase or later for such things as the installation of streets, sewers, and sidewalks should be debited to the Land account because they add a more or less permanent value to the land.[6]

Excavation of land for building purposes, however, is chargeable to buildings rather than to land.

See Chapter 30 for a discussion of the accounting for land acquired as part of a real estate operation.

(i) Purchase Options   If a company acquires an option to purchase land and later exercises that option, the cost of the option generally becomes part of the cost of the land. Even if an option lapses without being exercised, its cost can be capitalized if the option is one of a series of options acquired as part of an integrated plan to acquire a site. In that case, if any one of the options is exercised, the cost of all may be capitalized as part of the cost of the site.

(ii) Interest   SFAS No. 34 (par. 11) describes the proper accounting for interest cost related to land:

Land that is not undergoing activities necessary to get it ready for its intended use is not [an asset qualifying for interest capitalization]. If activities are undertaken for the purpose of developing land for a particular use, the expenditures to acquire the land qualify for interest capitalization while those activities are in progress. The interest cost capitalized on those expenditures is a cost of acquiring the asset that results from those activities. If the resulting asset is a structure,

---

6.   William W. Pyle and Kermit D. Larson, *Fundamental Accounting Principles, Tenth Edition* (Homewood, IL: Irwin, 1984).

such as a plant or a shopping center, interest capitalized on the land expenditures is part of the acquisition cost of the structure. If the resulting asset is developed land, such as land that is to be sold as developed lots, interest capitalized on the land expenditures is part of the acquisition cost of the developed land.

(iii) Other Carrying Charges   SFAS No. 67, *Accounting for Costs and Initial Rental Operations of Real Estate Projects* (par. 6), states:

> Costs incurred on real estate for property taxes and insurance shall be capitalized as property cost only during periods in which activities necessary to get the property ready for its intended use are in progress. Costs incurred for such items after the property is substantially complete and ready for its intended use shall be charged to expense as incurred.

Even though the scope of the Statement excludes "real estate developed by an enterprise for use in its own operations, other than for sale or rental," this guidance is followed in capitalizing carrying charges generally.

(e) COST OF ASSETS HELD FOR RESEARCH AND DEVELOPMENT ACTIVITIES
Although SFAS No. 2, *Accounting for Research and Development Costs* (par. 12), generally requires that research and development costs be charged to expense when incurred, it makes an exception (par. 11a) for "the costs of materials (whether from the enterprise's normal inventory or acquired specially for research and development activities) and equipment or facilities that are acquired or constructed for research and development activities and that have alternate future uses (in research and development projects or otherwise)." These costs, the Statement says, "shall be capitalized as tangible assets when acquired or constructed."

21.3   IMPAIRMENT OF VALUE

(a) AUTHORITATIVE PRONOUNCEMENTS   SFAS No. 144, *Accounting for the Impairment or Disposal of Long-Lived Assets*, prescribes the accounting for the impairment of long-lived assets, including property, plant, and equipment. The SFAS applies to property, plant, and equipment that is "held and used" and to property, plant, and equipment that is held for disposal (referred to in the Statement as *assets to be disposed of*).

(b) ASSETS TO BE HELD AND USED   SFAS No. 144 requires the following three-step approach for recognizing and measuring the impairment of assets to be held and used:

1. Consider whether indicators of impairment of property, plant, and equipment are present.
2. If indicators of impairment are present, determine whether the sum of the estimated undiscounted future cash flows attributable to the assets in question is less than their carrying amounts.
3. If less, recognize an impairment loss based on the excess of the carrying amount of the assets over their fair values.

(i) Recognition   SFAS No. 144 requires that property, plant, and equipment that are used in operations be reviewed for impairment whenever events or changes in circumstances indicate that the carrying amount of the assets might not be recoverable—that is, information indicates that an impairment might exist. Accordingly, companies do not need to perform a periodic assessment of assets for impairment in the absence of such information. Instead, companies would assess the need for an impairment write-down only if an indicator of impairment is present. The SFAS lists the following examples of events or changes in circumstances that may indicate to management that an impairment exists:

- A significant decrease in the market value of an asset
- A significant adverse change in the extent or manner in which an asset is used or in its physical condition
- A significant adverse change in legal factors or in the business climate that affects the value of an asset or an adverse action or assessment by a regulator
- An accumulation of costs significantly in excess of the amount originally expected to acquire or construct an asset
- A current period operating or cash flow loss combined with a history of operating or cash flow losses or a projection or forecast that demonstrates continuing losses associated with an income-producing asset
- A current expectation that an asset will be sold before the end of its previously estimated useful life

The preceding list is not all-inclusive, and there may be other events or changes in circumstances, including circumstances that are peculiar to a company's business or industry, indicating that the carrying amount of a group of assets might not be recoverable and thus impaired. If indicators of impairment are present, companies must then disaggregate the assets by grouping them at the lowest level for which there are identifiable cash flows that are largely independent of the cash flows of other groups of assets. Then future cash flows expected to be generated from the use of those assets and their eventual disposal must be estimated. That estimate is comprised of the future cash inflows expected to be generated by the assets less the future cash outflows expected to be necessary to obtain those inflows. If the estimated undiscounted cash flows are less than the carrying amount of the assets, an impairment exists and an impairment loss must be calculated and recognized.

The FASB recognized that certain long-lived assets could not be readily identified with specific cash flows (e.g., a corporate headquarters building and certain property and equipment of not-for-profit organizations). In those situations, the assets should be evaluated for impairment at an entity-wide level. If management estimates that the entity as a whole will generate cash flows sufficient to recover the carrying amount of all assets used in its operations, including its corporate headquarters building, no impairment loss would be recognized.

The SFAS No. 144 provides little guidance for estimating future cash flows, even though the accounting consequences of small changes in those estimates could be significant. Accordingly, estimating future undiscounted cash flows requires a great deal of judgment. Companies must make their best estimate based on reasonable and supportable assumptions and projections that are applied on a consistent basis. SFAS No. 144 indicates that all available evidence should be considered in developing the cash flow estimates, and the weight given that evidence should be commensurate with the extent to which the evidence can be verified objectively.

(ii) Measurement Once it is determined that an impairment exists, an impairment loss is calculated based on the excess of the carrying amount of the asset over the asset's *fair value*.

In September 2006, the FASB issued FASB Statement of Financial Accounting Standards (SFAS) No. 157, *Fair Value Measurements*. FAS 157 defines fair value, establishes a framework for measuring fair value in generally accepted accounting principles (GAAP), and expands disclosure about fair value measurements. The effective date of SFAS No. 157 is for financial statements of fiscal years beginning after November 15, 2007. FAS 157 defines *fair value* as "the price that would be received to sell an asset or paid to transfer a liability in an orderly transaction between market participants at the measurement date." FAS 157 changes to current practice related to the definition of fair value, the methods used to measure fair value, and expands the disclosures about fair value measurements.

FAS 157 clarifies that the exchange price is the price in an orderly transaction between market participants to sell the asset or transfer the liability in the market in which the reporting entity would transact for the asset or liability, that is, the principal or most advantageous market for the asset or liability. The transaction to sell the asset or transfer the liability is a hypothetical transaction at the measurement date, considered from the perspective of a market participant that holds the asset or owes the liability. Therefore, the definition focuses on the price that would be received to sell the asset or paid to transfer the liability (an exit price), not the price that would be paid to acquire the asset or received to assume the liability (an entry price).

Once management determines that an asset (or a group of assets) is impaired and the asset is written down to fair value, the reduced carrying amount represents the new cost basis of the asset. As a result, subsequent depreciation of the asset is based on the revised carrying amount, and companies are prohibited from reversing the impairment loss should facts and circumstances change or conditions improve in the future.

(c) ASSETS TO BE DISPOSED OF   SFAS No. 144 indicates that assets to be disposed of other than by sale (e.g., abandonment, exchange for another long-lived asset) shall continue to be classified as held and used until they are disposed of. An asset or asset group to be disposed of by sale should be classified as held for sale during the period in which all of the following criteria are met:

- Management commits to a plan of disposal.
- The asset is available for immediate sale.
- An active program to locate a buyer has been initiated.
- Sale of the asset within one year is probable.
- The asset is being actively marketed for sale at a reasonable price.
- Actions required to complete the plan indicate that it is unlikely the plan will be significantly modified or withdrawn.

If at any time while an asset is classified as held for sale any of the above criteria are no longer met or the entity's plans change, the asset should be reclassified to the held and used category. The asset should be reclassified at the lower of the original carrying amount immediately before the asset is transferred to held for sale (adjusted for any depreciation expense that would have been recognized had the asset been continuously classified as held and used) or fair value at the date of the change in status. An asset classified as held for sale should be measured at the lower of its carrying amount or fair value less incremental direct costs of sale. An asset classified as held for sale should not be depreciated. SFAS No. 144 requires subsequent revisions to the carrying amount of assets classified as held for sale if the estimate of fair value less cost to sale changes during the holding period. After an initial write-down of an asset to fair value less cost to sell, the carrying amount can be increased or decreased depending on changes in the fair value less cost to sell of the asset. However, an increase in carrying value cannot exceed the carrying amount of the asset immediately before its classification into the held for sale category.

SFAS No. 144 also supersedes APB Opinion No. 30 with respect to discontinued operations. The Statement indicates that the results of operations relating to assets to be disposed of comprising a component of an entity should be classified as discontinued operations if both of the following conditions are met:

1. The operations and cash flows of the component have been eliminated or will be eliminated from the ongoing operations of the entity as a result of the disposal.
2. The entity will not have any continuing involvement in the operations of the component after the disposal.

A *component* of an entity is defined as operations and cash flows that can be clearly distinguished from the rest of the entity both operationally and for financial reporting purposes. The definition of component of an entity under SFAS No. 144 is much broader than the APB Opinion No. 30 definition of a segment of a business. Accordingly, many more discontinued operations will be reported under SFAS No. 144 than previously. For example, if a real estate entity disposes of an individual property, that property would likely qualify as a component of an entity under SFAS No. 144 but would generally not have qualified as a disposal of a segment of a business under APB Opinion No. 30.

21.4 EXPENDITURES DURING OWNERSHIP

(a) DISTINGUISHING CAPITAL EXPENDITURES FROM OPERATING EXPENDITURES

After property, plant, and equipment have been acquired, additional expenditures are incurred to keep the assets in satisfactory operating condition. Certain of these expenditures—capital expenditures—are added to the asset's cost. The remainder—operating expenditures (sometimes called *revenue expenditures*)—are charged to expense.

Kohler defines a *capital expenditure* in the following two ways:

1. An expenditure intended to benefit future periods, in contrast to a revenue expenditure, which benefits a current period; an addition to a capital asset. The term is generally restricted to expenditures that add fixed-asset units or that have the effect of increasing the capacity, efficiency, life span, or economy of operation of an existing fixed asset.
2. Hence, any expenditure benefiting a future period.[7]

Although the distinction is important, immaterial capital expenditures can be charged to expense.

Expenditures during ownership fall into four categories: (1) maintenance and repairs; (2) replacements, improvements, and additions; (3) rehabilitation; (4) rearrangement and reinstallation.

---

7.   Eric Louis Kohler, *Kohler's Dictionary for Accountants, Sixth Edition* (Englewood Cliffs, NJ: Prentice-Hall, 1983).

(b) MAINTENANCE AND REPAIRS   The terms *maintenance* and *repairs* generally are used interchangeably. However, Kohler defines them separately, and his definitions are useful in identifying expenditures that should be accounted for as maintenance and repairs. He defines *maintenance* as follows:

> The keeping of property in operable condition; also, the expense involved. Maintenance costs include outlays for (a) labor and supplies; (b) the replacement of any part that constitutes less than a retirement unit; and (c) major overhauls the items of which may involve elements of the first two classes. Items falling under (a) and (b) are always regarded as operating costs, chargeable to current expense directly or through the medium of a maintenance reserve. . . . Costs under (c) are similarly treated unless they include the replacement of a retirement unit the outlay for which is normally capitalized.[8]

He defines *repairs* (p. 428) as follows:

> The restoration of a capital asset to its full productive capacity, or a contribution thereto, after damage, accident, or prolonged use, without increase in the asset's previously estimated service life or productive capacity. The term includes maintenance primarily "preventive" in character, and capitalizable extraordinary repairs.

(i) Accounting Alternatives   As Kohler states, except for extraordinary repairs (or major overhauls), discussed below, maintenance and repairs expenditures are accounted for in two ways:

1. Charge to expense when the cost is incurred
2. Charge to a maintenance allowance account[9]

Charge to Expense When the Cost Is Incurred. Since ordinary maintenance and repairs expenditures are regarded as operating costs, they are usually charged directly to expense when incurred.

Charge to a Maintenance Allowance Account. The charge to expense may be accomplished through an allowance account. In some cases, the purpose of an allowance account is to equalize monthly repair costs within a year. Total repair costs are estimated at the beginning of the year, and the total is spread evenly throughout the year. The difference between the estimated and actual amounts at the end of the year is usually spread retroactively over all months of the year rather than being absorbed entirely by the last month. In the balance sheet, this allowance account may be treated as a reduction of the related asset account.

This latter approach is supported by APB Opinion No. 28, *Interim Financial Reporting* (par. 16a):

> When a cost that is expensed for annual reporting purposes clearly benefits two or more interim periods (e.g., annual major repairs), each interim period should be charged for an appropriate portion of the annual cost by the use of accruals or deferrals.

In other cases, the purpose of a maintenance allowance account is to charge the costs of major repairs over the entire period benefited, which may be longer than one year. When

---

8.   Id., p. 315.
9.   Id., p. 428.

airlines acquire new aircraft, for example, they begin immediately to accrue the cost of the first engine overhaul, which usually is scheduled for more than one year hence. As illustrated by the following example from 1987 financial statements, the accrual charges are credited to a maintenance allowance account, which is then charged for cost of the overhaul.

Stateswest Airlines, Inc. and Subsidiaries

Notes to Consolidated Financial Statements

Summary of Significant Accounting Policies

Engine Overhaul Reserve. For all the leased aircraft, the Company accrues maintenance expense, on the basis of hours flown, for the estimated cost of engine overhauls.

(ii) Extraordinary Repairs   Welsch, Anthony, and Short define *extraordinary repairs* as repairs that

> . . . occur infrequently, involve relatively large amounts of money, and tend to increase the economic usefulness of the asset in the future because of either greater efficiency or longer life, or both. They are represented by major overhauls, complete reconditioning, and major replacements and betterments.[10]

Because expenditures for extraordinary repairs increase the future economic usefulness of an asset, they benefit future periods and are therefore capital expenditures. Ordinarily, they are added to the related asset account, as illustrated in the following example from 1987 financial statements.

Air Midwest, Inc. and Subsidiaries

Notes to Consolidated Financial Statements

Note 1. Summary of Significant Accounting Policies

d. Maintenance and Repairs

Major renewals and betterments are capitalized and depreciated over the remaining useful life of the asset.

Some authorities recommend that the expenditures for extraordinary repairs be charged against the accumulated depreciation account. The rationale for charging accumulated depreciation is provided by Smith and Skousen:

> Often it is not possible to identify the cost related to a specific part of an asset. In these instances, by debiting accumulated depreciation, the undepreciated book value is increased without creating a build-up of the gross asset values.[11]

Other authorities argue against debiting accumulated depreciation for extraordinary repairs because the accumulated depreciation on the asset may be less than the cost of the repairs and because the practice allows the original cost of any parts replaced to remain in the asset account.

---

10.   Glenn A. Welsch, Robert N. Anthony, and Daniel G. Short, *Fundamentals of Financial Accounting* (Homewood, IL: Irwin, 1984).
11.   Smith and Skousen.

(c) REPLACEMENTS, IMPROVEMENTS, AND ADDITIONS   Replacements, improvements, and additions are related concepts. Kohler defines a *replacement* as "the substitution of one fixed asset for another, particularly of a new asset for an old, or of a new part for an old part." He defines an *improvement* (which he calls a *betterment*) as "an expenditure having the effect of extending the useful life of an existing fixed asset, increasing its normal rate of output, lowering its operating cost, increasing rather than merely maintaining efficiency or otherwise adding to the worth of benefits it can yield."[12] Improvements ordinarily do not increase the physical size of the productive facility. Such an increase is an *addition*.

The distinctions among *replacement, improvement,* and *addition* notwithstanding, the accounting for all three is substantially the same. Expenditures for them are capital expenditures, that is, additions to property, plant, and equipment. (In practice, immaterial amounts are often charged to expense.) The cost of existing assets that are replaced, together with their related accumulated depreciation accounts, is eliminated from the accounts.

(d) REHABILITATION   Expenditures to rehabilitate buildings or equipment purchased in a rundown condition with the intention of rehabilitating them should be capitalized. Normally the acquisition price of a rundown asset is less than that of a comparable new asset, and the rehabilitation expenditures benefit future periods. Capitalization of the expenditures is therefore appropriate. However, the total capitalized cost of the asset should not exceed the amount recoverable through operations.

When rehabilitation takes place over an extended period, care should be taken to distinguish between the cost of rehabilitation and the cost of maintenance.

(e) REARRANGEMENT AND REINSTALLATION   Kieso and Weygandt describe *rearrangement and reinstallation costs* and the accounting for them:

> Rearrangement and reinstallation costs, which are expenditures intended to benefit future periods, are different from additions, replacements, and improvements. An example is the rearrangement and reinstallation of a group of machines to facilitate future production. If the original installation cost and the accumulated depreciation taken to date can be determined or estimated, the rearrangement and reinstallation cost can be handled as a replacement. If not, which is generally the case, the new costs of material in amount should be capitalized as an asset to be amortized over those future periods expected to benefit. If these costs are not material, if they cannot be separated from other operating expenses, or if their future benefit is questionable, they instead should be expensed in the period in which they are incurred.[13]

(f) ASBESTOS REMOVAL OR CONTAINMENT   Removal or containment of asbestos is regulated and required by various federal, state, and local laws. The diversity of practice in capitalizing or expensing the cost of asbestos removal or containment resulted in asbestos removal being considered by the EITF. Issue No. 89-13 asked "whether the costs incurred to treat asbestos when a property with a known asbestos problem is acquired should be

---

12.   Kohler.
13.   Donald E. Kieso and Jerry J. Weygandt, *Intermediate Accounting, Fifth Edition* (New York: John Wiley & Sons, 1986).

capitalized or charged to expense" and "whether the costs incurred to treat asbestos in an existing property should be capitalized or charged to expense."

The EITF reached a conclusion that the costs incurred to treat asbestos within a reasonable time period after a property with a known asbestos problem is acquired should be capitalized as part of the cost of the acquired property subject to an impairment test for that property. The consensus on existing property was not as conclusive and stated the costs "may be capitalized as a betterment subject to an impairment test for that property."

The EITF also reached a consensus that when costs are incurred in anticipation of a sale of property, they should be deferred and recognized in the period of the sale to the extent that those costs can be recovered from the estimated sales price.

The Standards Executive Committee (SEC) observer at the EITF meeting noted that regardless of whether asbestos treatment costs are capitalized or charged to expense, SEC registrants should disclose significant exposure for asbestos treatment costs in "Management's Discussion and Analysis."

The EITF in Issue No. 90-8 affirmed the Issue No. 89-13 consensus but did not provide further guidance on capitalizing or charging to expense the costs incurred on existing properties. In practice, there continues to be wide diversity of the types of costs capitalized, if any, and the accrual of costs to remove or contain asbestos in existing properties.

(g) COSTS TO TREAT ENVIRONMENTAL CONTAMINATION   Costs to remove, contain, neutralize, or prevent existing or future environmental contamination may be incurred voluntarily or as required by federal, state, and local laws. In Issue No. 90-8, the EITF considered whether environmental contamination treatment costs should be capitalized or charged to expense.

The EITF reached a consensus that, in general, environmental contamination treatment costs should be charged to expense unless the costs are recoverable and meet one of the following three criteria:

1. The costs extend the life, increase the capacity, or improve the safety or efficiency of property owned by the company. For purposes of this criterion, the condition of that property after the costs are incurred must be improved as compared with the condition of that property when originally constructed or acquired, if later.
2. The costs mitigate or prevent environmental contamination that has yet to occur and that otherwise may result from future operations or activities. In addition, the costs improve the property compared with its condition when constructed or acquired, if later.
3. The costs are incurred in preparing for sale property currently held for sale.

Costs to remediate environmental contamination that do not meet one of the criteria above should be expensed under the provisions of the AICPA's SOP 96-1, *Environmental Remediation Liabilities*. SOP 96-1 provides authoritative guidance on the recognition, measurement, display, and disclosure of environmental remediation liabilities. The AICPA issued SOP 96-1 to improve and narrow the manner in which existing authoritative accounting literature, principally SFAS No. 5, *Accounting for Contingencies*, is applied in recognizing, measuring, and disclosing environmental liabilities.

SFAS No. 5 generally requires loss contingencies to be accrued when they are both probable and estimable. According to SOP 96-1, the probability criterion of SFAS No. 5 is met for environmental liabilities if both of the following conditions have occurred on or before the date the financial statements are issued:

- Litigation, a claim, or an assessment has been asserted, or is probable of being asserted.
- It is probable that the outcome of such litigation, claim, or assessment will be unfavorable.

The AICPA concluded that there is a presumption that the outcome will be unfavorable if litigation, a claim, or an assessment has been asserted, or is probable of assertion, and if the entity is associated with the site. Assuming that both of the above conditions are met, a company would need to accrue at least the minimum amount that can reasonably be estimated as an environmental remediation liability.

Once a company has determined that it is probable that a liability has been incurred, the entity should estimate the remediation liability based on available information. In estimating its allocable share of costs, a company should include incremental direct costs of the remediation effort and postremediation monitoring costs that are expected to be incurred after the remediation is complete. An entity also should include in its estimate costs of compensation and related benefit costs for employees who are expected to devote a significant amount of their time directly to the remediation effort. The accrual of expected legal defense costs related to remediation is not required.

In cases in which joint and several liability exists and the company is one of several parties responsible for remediation, which often will be the case, the entity is required to estimate the percentage of the liability that will be allocated. The entity also must assess the likelihood that each of the other parties will pay their allocable share of the remediation liability. An entity would accrue its estimated share of amounts related to the site that will not be paid by other parties or the government.

SOP 96-1 provides that discounting environmental liabilities is permitted, but not required, only if the aggregate amount of the obligation and the amount and timing of the cash payments are fixed or reliably determinable. Because of the nature of the remediation process and the inherent subjectivity involved in estimating remediation liabilities, most companies will find it difficult to meet the criteria for discounting.

An asset relating to recoveries can be recognized only when realization of the claim for recovery is deemed probable. If a claim for recovery is the subject of litigation, a rebuttable presumption exists that realization of the claim is not probable. An environmental liability should be evaluated independently from any potential claim for recovery. SOP 96-1 requires that probable recoveries be recorded at fair value. However, discounting a recovery claim is not required in determining the value of the recovery when the related liability is not discounted and the timing of the recovery is dependent on the timing of the payment of the liability.

The EITF provided examples of applying the consensus in Issue No. 90-8.

21.5   DISPOSALS

Asset disposals may be voluntary, through retirement, sale, or trade-in, or involuntary, from fire, storm, flood, or other casualty. In general, these terms have the same meaning for accounting purposes as they do in ordinary discourse. The one exception is *retirement*, which for accounting purposes means the removal of an asset from service, whether or not the asset is removed physically. This is clear from Kohler's (1983) definition of *retirement* as "the removal of a fixed asset from service, following its sale or the end of its productive life, accompanied by the necessary adjustment of fixed asset and depreciation-reserve accounts."

(a) **RETIREMENTS, SALES, AND TRADE-INS**   Davidson, Stickney, and Weil describe the accounting for retirements, which applies also to assets that are sold or traded in:

> When an asset is retired from service, the cost of the asset and the related amount of accumulated depreciation must be removed from the books. As part of this entry, the amount received from the sale or trade-in and any difference between that amount and book value must be recorded. The difference between the proceeds received on retirement and book value is a gain (if positive) or a loss (if negative).[14]

As discussed in the following, when composite or group rate depreciation is used, no gain or loss on disposal is recognized.

When an asset is traded in, the amount that should in theory be recorded as received from the trade-in is the asset's fair market value (which is not necessarily the amount by which the cash purchase price of the replacement asset is reduced). However, in practice, a reliable market value for the old asset may not be available. In that case, the usual practice is to recognize no gain or loss on the exchange, but to record as the acquisition cost of the replacement asset the net book value of the old asset plus the cash or other consideration paid.

(b) **CASUALTIES**   Casualties, the accidental loss or destruction of assets, can give rise to gain or loss, even when the assets are replaced. The FASB Interpretation No. (FIN) No. 30, *Accounting for Involuntary Conversions of Nonmonetary Assets to Monetary Assets* (par. 2), makes this clear:

> Involuntary conversions of nonmonetary assets to monetary assets are monetary transactions for which gain or loss shall be recognized even though an enterprise reinvests or is obligated to reinvest the monetary assets in replacement nonmonetary assets.

21.6 ASSET RETIREMENT OBLIGATIONS

SFAS No. 143, *Accounting for Asset Retirement Obligations*, was issued in June 2001. This project was undertaken by the FASB because diversity in practice had developed in accounting for the obligations associated with the retirement of long-lived assets. Some entities were accruing the obligations over the life of the related asset either as a liability or a reduction of the carrying amount of the asset while others did not recognize the liability until the asset was retired. The Statement requires that a liability be recorded for legal obligations resulting from the acquisition, construction, or development and normal operations of a long-lived asset.

(a) **INITIAL RECOGNITION AND MEASUREMENT**   If a reasonable estimate of an asset retirement obligation can be made, an entity shall recognize the fair value of the liability in the period in which it is incurred. Fair value is usually defined as the amount at which the liability could be settled in a current transaction between willing parties. (That definition is ambiguous. See Section 1.3(b)(v).) Quoted market prices in active markets are the best evidence of fair value. However, when such prices are not available, fair value should be based on the best available information, including prices for similar liabilities and the results of present value techniques. SFAS No. 143 indicates that if present value techniques are used to estimate

---

14.   Sidney Davidson, Clyde P. Stickney, and Roman L. Weil, *Financial Accounting: An Introduction to Concepts, Methods and Uses, Fifth Edition* (Hinsdale, IL: Dryden Press, 1988).

fair value, estimates of future cash flows should be consistent with the expected cash flow approach outlined in Concepts Statement No. 7.

When an asset retirement obligation is initially recognized, the entity should capitalize an asset retirement cost by increasing the carrying amount of the related long-lived asset by the same amount. This cost should be charged to expense over the estimated useful life of the asset. When the asset is tested for impairment under SFAS No. 144, the asset retirement cost should be included in the carrying value tested for impairment.

(b) SUBSEQUENT RECOGNITION AND MEASUREMENT　Subsequent to initial recognition, an entity should recognize period-to-period changes in the asset retirement liability for the passage of time and revisions to either the timing or amount of the original estimate of undiscounted cash flows. Adjustments for the passage of time should use an interest method based on the credit-adjusted risk-free rate at the time of initial recognition of the liability. The adjustment should increase the amount of the liability and be charged to accretion expense. Adjustments relating to revisions in the timing or amounts of cash flows will increase or decrease the asset retirement liability and the related asset.

21.7　DEPRECIATION

Property, plant, and equipment used by a business in the production of goods and services is a depreciable asset. That is, its cost is systematically amortized by charges to goods produced or to operations over the asset's estimated useful service life. That meaning is captured by International Accounting Standards (IAS) No. 4, *Depreciation Accounting*, which defines depreciable assets as "assets that (a) are expected to be used during more than one accounting period, and (b) have a limited useful life, and (c) are held by an enterprise for use in the production or supply of goods and services, for rental to others, or for administrative purposes."

(a) *DEPRECIATION* DEFINED　Despite its widespread use, *depreciation* has no single, universal definition. Economists, engineers, the courts, accountants, and others have definitions that meet their particular needs. Seldom are the definitions identical.

The generally accepted accounting definition is set forth in Accounting Terminology Bulletin No. 1:

> Depreciation accounting is a system of accounting which aims to distribute the cost or other basic value of tangible capital assets, less salvage (if any), over the estimated useful life of the unit (which may be a group of assets) in a systematic and rational manner. It is a process of allocation, not of valuation. Depreciation for the year is the portion of the total charge under such a system that is allocated to the year.

As the definition says, the depreciation accounting is "a process of allocation, not of valuation." That is, its purpose is to allocate the net cost (cost less salvage) of an asset over time, not to state the asset at its current or long-term value.

Depreciation, as accountants use the term, applies only to buildings, machinery, and equipment. It is thus distinguished first from *depletion*, which is a process of allocating the cost of wasting resources, such as mineral deposits, and second from *amortization*, which is a process of allocating the cost of intangible assets.

(b) BASIC FACTORS IN THE COMPUTATION OF DEPRECIATION   Three basic factors enter into the computation of depreciation:

1. The estimate of the service life (sometimes called the *useful life*) of the asset
2. The determination of the depreciation base
3. The choice of a depreciation method

21.8   SERVICE LIFE

(a) SERVICE LIFE AS DISTINGUISHED FROM PHYSICAL LIFE   Depreciation allocates the net cost of an asset over its service life, not its physical life. The *service* life of an asset represents the period of usefulness to its present owner. The *physical* life of an asset represents its total period of usefulness, perhaps to more than one owner. For any given asset, and any given owner, physical and service life may be identical, or service life may be shorter. For example, a company that supplies automobiles to its sales force may replace its automobiles every 50,000 miles. An automobile's physical life is usually longer than 50,000 miles. But to this particular company, the service life of an automobile in their fleet is 50,000 miles, and the company's depreciation policies would allocate the net cost of its automobiles over 50,000 miles.

(b) FACTORS AFFECTING SERVICE LIFE   Service life may be affected by two factors—*physical* or *functional*—as follows:

1. Physical factors:
   a. Wear and tear
   b. Deterioration and decay
   c. Damage or destruction
2. Functional factors:
   a. Inadequacy
   b. Obsolescence

(i) Physical Factors   Mosich and Larsen discuss physical factors:

> Physical deterioration results largely from wear and tear from use and the forces of nature. These physical forces terminate the usefulness of plant assets by rendering them incapable of performing the services for which they were intended and thus set the maximum limit on economic life.[15]

Wear and tear and deterioration and decay act gradually and are reasonably predictable. They are ordinarily taken into consideration in estimating service life. Damage or destruction, however, usually occurs suddenly, irregularly, infrequently, and unpredictably. Either one is ordinarily not taken into consideration in estimating service life. Its effects are therefore usually not recognized in the depreciation charge but as a charge to expense when the damage or destruction occurs.

(ii) Functional Factors   Asset inadequacy may result from business growth, requiring the company to replace existing assets with larger or more efficient assets. Or assets may become inadequate because of changes in the market, in plant location, in the nature or variety of products manufactured, or in the ownership of the business. For example, a warehouse may be in

---

15.   Mosich and Larsen.

good structural condition, but if more space is needed and cannot be economically provided by adding a wing or a separate building, the warehouse has become inadequate, and its remaining service life to its present owner is ended.

Obsolescence usually arises from events that are more clearly external, such as progress, invention, technological advances, and improvements. For example, the Boeing 707 and the Douglas DC-8 jet aircraft made many propeller-driven airplanes obsolete, at least as to major airlines, because propeller-driven planes were no longer economical in long-range service, compared to more modern and efficient jets.

A distinction should be made between ordinary obsolescence and extraordinary obsolescence. Ordinary obsolescence is due to normal, reasonably predictable technical progress; extraordinary obsolescence arises from unforeseen events that result in an asset being abandoned earlier than expected. For example, computers and related software generally have a short service life span in anticipation of more advanced computers and software releases in the market within a few years.

The American Accounting Association (AAA) publication, "A Statement of Basic Accounting Theory" (1966), states: "Obsolescence, to the extent it can be quantified by equipment replacement studies or similar means, should be recognized explicitly and regularly." Thus ordinary obsolescence, like wear and tear, should be considered in estimating useful life so that it can be recognized in the annual depreciation charge. But extraordinary obsolescence, like damage or destruction, is recognized outside depreciation accounting as a charge when it occurs.

(c) THE EFFECT OF MAINTENANCE   As Welsch and Zlatkovich note, "The useful life of operational assets also is influenced by the repair and maintenance policies of the company."[16] The expected effect of a company's maintenance policy is therefore considered in estimating service lives.

(d) STATISTICAL METHODS OF ESTIMATING SERVICE LIVES   In several industries, notably utilities, estimates of service lives have been based on historical analyses of retirement rates for specific groups of assets, such as telephone or electric wire poles. These analyses have resulted in the development of statistical techniques for predicting retirement rates and service lives. Utilities have used such techniques in defending depreciation practices, replacement needs and policies, and investment valuations for rate-making purposes. Statistical techniques are appropriate for any group of homogeneous assets where estimating individual service lives is not possible or practical (e.g., mattresses and linens in a hotel, overhead and underground cables of telephone companies, and rails and ties for railroads).

Grant and Norton mention two other statistical approaches to determining service lives:

1.   *Actuarial methods*, which aim at determining survivor curves and frequency curves for annual retirements, as well as giving estimates of average life. These methods are generally similar to the methods developed by life insurance actuaries for the study of human mortality. They require plant records in sufficient detail so that the age of each unit of plant is known at all times.

2.   *Turnover methods*, which aim only at estimating average life. Since turnover methods require only information about additions and retirements, they require less detail in the plant records than do actuarial methods.[17]

---

16.   Welsch and Zlatkovich.

17.   E. Grant and P. Norton, *Depreciation* (New York: Ronald Press, 1955).

(e) SERVICE LIVES OF LEASEHOLD IMPROVEMENTS   Leasehold improvements are depreciated over the shorter of the remaining term of the lease or the expected life of the asset. Lease renewal terms are usually not considered unless renewal is probable.

In February 2005, almost concurrent with the filing of the first wave of SOX Section 404 filings, the SEC clarified that certain accounting principles for leasehold improvements, rent holidays, and landlord/tenant incentives should be followed, despite "industry practice" that had arisen where these principles were not always being adhered to. This clarification forced a spate of restatements and material weakness determinations by some larger retail establishments. The timing of this announcement made it difficult for some companies to remediate the control deficiency in time to avoid reporting a material weakness in internal controls. At the time of this edition, the letter from the SEC Chief Accountant Don Nicolaison could be found at www.sec.gov/info/accountants/staffletters/cpcaf020705.htm.

(f) REVISIONS OF ESTIMATED SERVICE LIVES   Service life estimates should be reviewed periodically and revised as appropriate. The National Association of Accountants (NAA) Statement on Management Accounting Practices No. 7, *Fixed Asset Accounting: The Allocation of Costs*, suggests that reviews of estimates involve operations, management, engineering, and accounting personnel.

A change in the estimated useful lives of depreciable assets should be accounted for as a change in an accounting estimate. As prescribed by APB Opinion No. 20, *Accounting Changes*, the change is recognized in the period of change and in future periods affected. If future periods are affected, the Opinion also requires disclosure of the effect on income before extraordinary items, on net income, and on related per-share amounts of the current period. The following is an example of this disclosure from 2007 financial statements:

EXAMPLE

TANGER PROPERTIES LTD PARTNERSHIP FORM 10-K (PERIOD END 12/31/07)

CHANGE IN ACCOUNTING ESTIMATE
During the first quarter of 2007, the general partner's Board of Trustees formally approved a plan to reconfigure our center in Foley, Alabama. As a part of this plan, approximately 42,000 square feet was relocated within the property by September 2007. The depreciable useful lives of the buildings demolished were shortened to coincide with their demolition dates throughout the first three quarters of 2007 and the change in estimated useful life was accounted for as a change in accounting estimate. Approximately 28,000 relocated square feet had opened as of December 31, 2007 with the remaining 14,000 square feet expected to open in the next two quarters. Accelerated depreciation recognized related to the reconfiguration reduced income from continuing operations and net income by approximately $6.0 million for the year ended December 31, 2007. The effect on income from continuing operations per diluted unit and net income per diluted unit was a decrease of $.32 per unit for the year ended December 31, 2007.

21.9 DEPRECIATION BASE

The cost to be depreciated, otherwise known as the *depreciation base*, is the total cost of an asset less its estimated net salvage value. When immaterial, net salvage value is commonly ignored.

(a) NET SALVAGE VALUE   *Kohler's Dictionary for Accountants* defines *salvage* as: "Value remaining from a fire, wreck, or other accident or from the retirement or scrapping of an asset."[18] Salvage value may be determined by reference to quoted market prices for similar items or to estimated reproduction costs, reduced by an allowance for usage. Salvage value reduced by the cost to remove the asset is net salvage value.

Net salvage value can be taken into account in either of two ways: directly, by reducing the depreciation base; or indirectly, by adjusting the depreciation rate.

To illustrate the latter, assume an asset with a total cost of $1,000, a service life of 10 years, and an estimated net salvage value of $250. A 7.5 percent rate applied to the cost will yield the same annual depreciation charge as a 10 percent rate applied to cost less estimated net salvage value. This point should be borne in mind in interpreting stated rates of depreciation; the rates may be applied to the asset cost or to cost less net salvage value.

(b) PROPERTY UNDER CONSTRUCTION   Assets are generally not depreciated during construction, which includes any necessary pilot testing or breaking in. Such assets are not yet placed in service, and the purpose of depreciation accounting is to allocate the cost of an asset over its service life.

An exception to the general rule arises when an asset under construction is partially used in an income-producing activity. In that case, the part in use should be depreciated. An example is a building that is partially rented while still under construction.

(c) IDLE AND AUXILIARY EQUIPMENT   NAA Statement on Management Accounting Practices No. 7 recommends that depreciation be continued on idle, reserve, or standby assets. When the period of idleness is expected to be long, the assets should be separately disclosed in the balance sheet; however, depreciation should continue.

EITF Issue No. 84-28 raises the question of how idle facilities or facilities operating significantly below normal operating levels should be depreciated. Some EITF members stated that they were aware of a limited number of cases in which the depreciation method for such assets was changed to one of the usage methods (see below), but none expressed knowledge of cases in which depreciation of the assets was totally suspended. The EITF reached no consensus.

(d) ASSETS TO BE DISPOSED OF   SFAS No. 144 prohibits depreciation from being recorded during the period in which the asset is being held for disposal, even if the asset is still generating revenue.

(e) USED ASSETS   The depreciation base of a used asset is the same as for a new asset, that is, cost less net salvage value. The carrying value of a used asset in the accounts of the previous owner should not be carried over to the accounts of the new owner. See, however, Chapter 22 for the accounting for assets acquired in a business combination.

21.10 DEPRECIATION METHODS

Assets are depreciated by a variety of methods, including the following five:

1. Straight-line method
2. Usage methods:

---

18.   Kohler.

    a. Service-hours method
    b. Productive-output method
3. Decreasing-charge methods:
    a. Sum-of-digits method
    b. Fixed-percentage-of-declining-balance method
    c. Double-declining-balance method
4. Interest methods:
    a. Annuity method
    b. Sinking-fund method
5. Other methods:
    a. Appraisal method
    b. Retirement method
    c. Replacement method
    d. Arbitrary assignment

(a) STRAIGHT-LINE METHOD   This method recognizes equal periodic depreciation charges over the service life of an asset, thereby making depreciation a function solely of time without regard to asset productivity, efficiency, or usage. The periodic depreciation charge is computed by dividing the cost of the asset, less net salvage value, by the service life expressed in months or years:

$$\frac{\text{Cost} - \text{Net salvage value}}{\text{Service life}} = \text{Depreciation charge per period}$$

Assuming an asset cost $15,000 and had an estimated net salvage value of $750 (5 percent of cost) and a service life of 10 years, the annual depreciation charge would be $1,425, calculated as follows:

$$\frac{\$15,000 - \$750}{10 \text{ years}} = \$1,425$$

When the use or productivity of an asset differs significantly over its life, the straight-line method produces what some believe is a distorted allocation of costs. For example, if an asset is more productive during its early life than later, some view an equal amount of depreciation in each year as distorted. Nevertheless, the method is widely used because of its simplicity.

    A survey reported by Lamden, Gerboth, and McRae showed that the straight-line method is most frequently used for financial statement purposes by companies with the following five characteristics:

1. Relatively large investments in depreciable assets
2. Relatively high depreciation charges
3. Stock traded on one of the major stock exchanges or in the over-the-counter market
4. Managements with a high level of concern for (a) matching costs with revenues and (b) maintaining comparability with other firms in the industry
5. Managements with a low level of concern for conforming depreciation for financial statement to depreciation for tax purposes[19]

---

19.   Lamden, Gerboth, and McRae.

(b) USAGE METHODS   Two other methods, the service-hours method and the productive-output method, vary the periodic depreciation charge to recognize differences in asset use or productivity.

(i) Service-Hours Method   This method assumes that if an asset is used twice as much in period 1 as in period 2, the depreciation charge should differ accordingly. The depreciation rate is calculated as it is for the straight-line method, except that service life is expressed in terms of hours of use:

$$\frac{\text{Cost} - \text{Net salvage value}}{\text{Service life}} = \text{Rate per hour of use}$$

If an asset cost $15,000 and had an estimated net salvage value of $750 and an estimated service life of 38,000 hours, the calculation would be as follows:

$$\frac{\$15,000 - \$750}{38,00 \text{ hours}} = \$0.375 \text{ per hour of use}$$

If the asset is used 4,000 hours in the first year, the annual depreciation charge would be $1,500 (4,000 hours × $0.375 per hour).

Welsch and Zlatkovich state, "The service hours method usually is appropriate when obsolescence is not a primary factor in depreciation and the economic service potential of the asset is used up primarily by running time."[20]

(ii) Productive-Output Method   This method is essentially the same as the service-hours method, except that service life is expressed in terms of units of production rather than hours of use. If the asset described above had a service life of 95,000 units of production rather than 38,000 hours of use, the depreciation rate would be calculated as follows:

$$\frac{\$15,000 - \$750}{95,00 \text{ units}} = \$0.15 \text{ per unit of product}$$

Depreciation by the productive-output method is illustrated by the following example from 1987 financial statements:

McDermott International, Inc.

Notes to Consolidated Financial Statements

Note 3. Change in Depreciation Method

Effective April 1, 1986, McDermott International changed the method of depreciation for major marine vessels from the straight-line method to a units-of-production method based on the utilization of each vessel. Depreciation expense calculated under the units-of-production method may be less than, equal to, or greater than depreciation expense calculated under the straight-line method in any period. McDermott International employs utilization factors as a key element in the management of marine construction operations and believes the units-of-production method, which recognizes both time and utilization factors, accomplishes a better matching of costs and revenues than the straight-line method. The cumulative effect of the change on prior years at March 31, 1986, of $25,711,000,

---

20.   Welsch and Zlatkovich.

net of income taxes of $17,362,000 ($0.70 per share), is included in the accompanying Consolidated Statement of Income (Loss) and Retained Earnings for the fiscal year ended March 31, 1987. The effect of the change on the fiscal year ended March 31, 1987, was to increase Income from Continuing Operations before Extraordinary Items and Cumulative Effect of Accounting Change and decrease Net Loss $6,556,000 ($0.18 per share). Pro forma amounts showing the effect of applying the units-of-production method of depreciation retroactively, net of related income taxes, are presented in the Consolidated Statement of Income (Loss) and Retained Earnings.

The productive-output method is sometimes used to adjust depreciation calculated by the straight-line method, when asset usage varies from normal. The adjustment may be limited to a specified range, as illustrated in the following example drawn from 1986 financial statements:

Wheeling-Pittsburgh Steel Corporation

Notes to Financial Statements

Note G. Property, Plant, and Equipment

The Corporation utilizes the modified units-of-production method of depreciation which recognizes that the depreciation of steelmaking machinery is related to the physical wear of the equipment as well as a time factor. The modified units-of-production method provides for straight-line depreciation charges modified (adjusted) by the level of production activity. On an annual basis, adjustments may not exceed a range of 60% (minimum) to 110% (maximum) of related straight-line depreciation. The adjustments are based on the ratio of actual production to a predetermined norm. Eighty-five percent of capacity is considered the norm for the Corporation's primary steelmaking facilities; 80% of capacity is considered the norm for finishing facilities. No adjustment is made when the production level is equal to norm. In 1986 depreciation under the modified units of production method exceeded straight-line depreciation by $1.5 million or 3.2%. For 1985 and 1984 aggregate straight-line depreciation exceeded that recorded under the modified units-of-production method by $10.1 million or 18.3%, $7.0 million or 12.6%, respectively.

The productive-output method recognizes that not all hours of use are equally productive. Therefore, the theory underlying the preference for a usage method would point to the productive-output method as the better of the two.

(c) DECREASING-CHARGE METHODS Decreasing-charge methods allocate a higher depreciation charge to the early years of an asset's service life. These methods are justified on the following grounds:

- Most equipment is more efficient (hence more productive) in its early life. Therefore, the early years of service life should bear more of the asset's cost.
- Repairs and maintenance charges generally increase as an asset gets older. Therefore, depreciation charges should decrease as the asset gets older so as to produce a more stable total charge (repairs and maintenance plus depreciation) for the use of the asset during its service life.

(i) Sum-of-Digits Method   This method applies a decreasing rate to a constant depreciation base (cost less net salvage value). The rate is a fraction. The denominator is the sum of the digits representing periods (years or months) of asset life. The numerator, which changes each period, is the digit assigned to the particular period. Digits are assigned in reverse order. For example, if an asset has an estimated service life of five years, the denominator would be 15, calculated as follows:

$$1 + 2 + 3 + 4 + 5 = 15$$

In the first year the rate fraction would be 5/15, in the second year 4/15, in the third year 3/15, and so on. The denominator may be calculated by means of the following formula, where n is the service life in years or months:

$$\frac{n+1}{2} \times n = \text{Denominator}$$

For example, if the service life is estimated to be 25 years:

$$\frac{25+1}{2} \times 25 = 325$$

(ii) Fixed-Percentage-of-Declining-Balance Method   This method produces results similar to the sum-of-digits method. However, whereas the sum-of-digits method multiplies a declining rate times a fixed balance, the fixed-percentage-of-declining-balance method multiplies a fixed rate times a declining balance. The rate is calculated by means of the following formula, where n equals the service life in years:

$$\text{Depreciation rate} = 1 - \sqrt[n]{\frac{\text{Net salvage value}}{\text{Cost}}}$$

The rate thus determined is then applied to the cost of the asset, without regard to salvage value, reduced by depreciation previously recognized. The result is to reduce the cost of the asset to its estimated net salvage value at the end of the asset's service life. (Some salvage value must be assigned to the asset, since it is not possible to reduce an amount to zero by applying a constant rate to a successively smaller remainder. In the absence of an expected salvage value, a nominal value of $1 can be assumed.)

To illustrate, assume an asset with a cost of $10,000, an estimated salvage value of $1,296, and an estimated service life of four years:

$$\text{Depreciation rate} = 1 - \sqrt[4]{\frac{\$1,296}{\$10,000}} = 1 - \frac{6}{10} = 40\%$$

The first year's depreciation will be $4,000 ($10,000 × 40%), the second year's $2,400 [($10,000 − $4,000) × 40%], and so on, leaving at the end of the fourth year a net asset of $1,296.

(iii) Double-Declining-Balance Method   The double-declining-balance method was introduced into the income tax laws in 1954. Since then, it has gained increased acceptability for financial reporting as well. This method differs from the fixed-percentage-of-declining-balance method by specifying that the fixed rate should be twice the straight-line rate. Otherwise, the two methods are identical: The fixed rate is applied to the undepreciated book value of the asset—a declining balance.

To illustrate, assume an asset with a cost of $15,000, an estimated net salvage value of $750, and an estimated service life of 10 years. Twice the straight-line rate would be 20 percent. Exhibit 21.1 shows the calculation for the first four years.

Year	Book Value Beginning of Period	Rate (%)	Annual Depreciation Charge	Book Value End of Period
1	$15,000	20	$3,000	$12,000
2	12,000	20	2,400	9,600
3	9,600	20	1,920	7,680
4	7,680	20	1,536	6,144

Exhibit 21.1   Depreciation Using the Double-Declining-Balance Method

Note that, as with the fixed-percentage-of-declining-balance method, the rate is applied to the cost of the asset without regard to net salvage value. This means that by the end of the asset's estimated service life, some amount of undepreciated book value will be left in the asset account. But since the depreciation rate is determined without regard to estimated net salvage value, the undepreciated amount left in the account will likely differ from net salvage value. For example, at the end of the 10-year service life of the asset illustrated in Exhibit 21.1, the asset's book value would be $1,611, which is $861 greater than estimated net salvage value. To avoid such differences, companies usually switch from the double-declining-balance method to the straight-line method sometime during an asset's service life.

To calculate the straight-line depreciation charge at the time of the switch, the net book value (cost less accumulated depreciation), less estimated net salvage value, is divided by the estimated remaining service life. For example, if an asset has a remaining depreciation base (cost less estimated net salvage value) of $4,620 and seven years of remaining service life, a straight-line charge of $660 for the next seven years will depreciate the asset to its net salvage value.

The optimal time to make a switch is when the year's depreciation computed using the straight-line method exceeds depreciation computed using the double-declining-balance method. That is usually sometime after the midpoint of the asset's life.

Exhibit 21.2 compares the annual depreciation charges computed by the straight-line method, the sum-of-digits method, and the double-declining-balance method with switch to straight-line.

Year	Straight-Line	Sum-of-Digits	Double-Declining-Balance, Switch to Straight-Line
1	$14,250	$ 2,591	$ 3,000
2	1,425	2,322	2,400
3	1,425	2,073	1,920
4	1,425	1,814	1,536
5	1,425	1,555	1,229
6	1,425	1,295	983
7	1,425	1,036	796
8	1,425	777	796
9	1,425	518	795
10	1,425	259	795
	$14,250	$14,250	$14,250

Exhibit 21.2   Comparison of Annual Depreciation Charges: Straight-Line, Sum-of-Digits, and Double-Declining-Balance with Switch to Straight Line

Note that although all three methods charge the same total amount to expense over the same service life, the amounts charged at the midpoint of the asset's service life differ:

1. Straight-line has charged 50 percent of the total.
2. Sum-of-digits has charged nearly 73 percent.
3. Double-declining-balance with switch to straight-line has charged about 71 percent.

(d) INTEREST METHODS   Two methods, the annuity method and the sinking-fund method, compute depreciation using compound interest factors. Both methods produce an increasing annual depreciation charge. Neither method is used much in practice.

(i) Annuity Method   The annuity method equalizes each year's sum of depreciation and an imputed interest charge calculated at a constant rate on the asset's undepreciated book value. Each year's sum of depreciation and imputed interest is calculated by the following formula, where n is the estimated service life of the asset in years and i is the imputed rate of interest:

$$\frac{\text{Cost of asset less present value of net salvage value}}{\text{Present value of an ordinary of annuity of } n \text{ payments of 1 at } i}$$

Assume, for example, that an asset with an economic life of five years and a net salvage value of $67,388 is acquired at a cost of $800,000. Using an imputed rate of interest of 10 percent, each year's sum of depreciation and imputed interest would be computed as follows:

$$\frac{\$800,000 - (\$67,388 \times 0.620921^*)}{3.790787}$$

$$\frac{\$800,000 - \$41,843}{3.790787}$$

$$= \$200,000$$

*Present value of $1 for five periods at 10%.

The result is presented in Exhibit 21.3.

Imputed interest is computed only for purposes of computing depreciation; it is not charged to expense.

(ii) Sinking-Fund Method   The sinking-fund method produces a depreciation pattern that is identical to that of the annuity method but by means of a different rationale and a different formula. Under the sinking-fund method, the amount of annual depreciation is equal to the increase in a hypothetical interest-earning asset-replacement fund. The increase in the fund consists of assumed equal periodic deposits to the fund plus interest at the assumed rate on the fund balance.

Each year's depreciation charge is calculated by the following formula, where n is the remaining service life of the asset in years and i is the assumed rate of interest:

$$\text{Depreciation} = \frac{\text{Cost of asset less net residual value}}{\text{Ordinary annuity of } n \text{ payments of 1 at } i}$$

Year	Combined Depreciation and Imputed Interest	Imputed Interest (10% of Carrying Amount)	Depreciation	Accumulated Depreciation	Carrying Amount of Asset
0					$800,000
1	$ 200,000	$ 80,000	$120,000	$120,000	680,000
2	200,000	68,000	132,000	252,000	548,000
3	200,000	54,800	145,200	397,200	402,800
4	200,000	40,280	159,720	556,920	243,080
5	200,000	24,308	175,692	732,612	67,388
	$1,100,000	$267,388	$732,612		

Exhibit 21.3 Depreciation Using the Annuity Method
Source: Mosich and Larsen, Intermediate Accounting, McGraw-Hill, 1986, p. 627 [adapted].

Using the same facts as in Exhibit 21.3 (an asset cost of $800,000, a 5-year life, a net salvage value of $67,388, and a 10 percent interest rate), the first year's depreciation would be computed as follows:

$$\text{Depreciation} = \frac{\text{Cost of asset less net residual value}}{\text{Ordinary annuity of 5 payments of 1 at 10\%}}$$

$$\frac{\$800,000 - \$67,388}{6.1051}$$

$$= \$120,000$$

(e) DEPRECIATION FOR PARTIAL PERIODS   Since assets are often acquired and disposed of throughout the year, companies must compute depreciation for partial periods. Five computation alternatives are found in practice:

1. Depreciation is recognized to the nearest whole month. Assets acquired on or before the 15th of the month or sold after the 15th are reduced by a full month's depreciation; assets acquired after the 15th or sold on or before the 15th are excluded from the month's depreciation computation.
2. Depreciation is recognized to the nearest whole year. Assets acquired during the first six months or sold during the last six months are reduced by a full year's depreciation; assets acquired during the last six months or sold during the first six months are excluded from the year's depreciation computation.
3. One-half year's depreciation only is recognized on all assets purchased or sold during the year.
4. No depreciation is recognized on all assets purchased or sold during the year.
5. A full year's depreciation is recognized on assets acquired during the year; none is recognized on assets retired during the year.

(f) CHANGE IN DEPRECIATION METHOD   A change in depreciation method is a change in an accounting principle. In accordance with APB Opinion No. 20 (par. 18), the cumulative effect of the change is recognized in net income of the period of change. Accounting changes are discussed more fully in Chapter 9.

21.11   DEPRECIATION RATES

(a) SOURCES OF DEPRECIATION RATES   Information concerning depreciation rates for various classes of business property is available from several sources. Depreciation rates have been given attention by authors of manuals on accounting, engineering, management, rate making, and other aspects of the business process. They have been the subject of special investigation by industry through individual studies and studies conducted under the auspices of manufacturing and other trade associations.

The choice of depreciation rates has also been influenced by the requirements of tax law and regulation, discussed later in this chapter.

(b) GROUP AND COMPOSITE RATES   A group of assets may be depreciated at a single rate. Assets of electrical utilities and hotels are sometimes depreciated in this manner. The two most common methods of depreciating asset groups are the group depreciation method and the collective depreciation method.

(i) Group Depreciation   Mosich and Larsen define *group depreciation* as the "process of averaging the economic lives of a number of plant assets and computing depreciation on the entire class of assets as if it were an operating unit."[21] Smith and Skousen elaborate:

> Because the accumulated depreciation account under the group procedure applies to the entire group of assets, it is not related to any specific asset. Thus, no book value can be calculated for any specific asset and there are no fully depreciated assets. To arrive at the periodic depreciation charge, the depreciation rate is applied to the recorded cost of all assets remaining in service, regardless of age.[22]

To illustrate, assume that a company purchased a group of 100 similar machines having an average expected service life of five years at a total cost of $200,000. Of this group, 30 machines are expected to be retired at the end of four years, 40 at the end of five years, and the remaining 30 at the end of six years. Under the group depreciation method, depreciation is based on the average expected service life of five years, which converts to an annual depreciation rate of 20 percent. This rate is applied to those assets in service each year. Assuming the machines are retired as expected, the charges for depreciation and the changes in the group asset and accumulated depreciation accounts are summarized in Exhibit 21.4.

---

21.   Mosich and Larsen.
22.   Smith and Skousen.

END OF YEAR	DEPRECIATION (20% OF COST)	ASSET			ACCUMULATED DEPRECIATION			ASSET BOOK VALUE
		DEBIT	CREDIT	BALANCE	DEBIT	CREDIT	BALANCE	
		$200		$200				$200
1	$40			200		$40	$ 40	160
2	40			200		40	80	120
3	40			200		40	120	80
4	40		$60	140	$60	40	100	40
5	28			80	60	80	28	48	12

EXHIBIT 21.4   GROUP DEPRECIATION (ALL AMOUNTS IN THOUSANDS)

It should be noted that the depreciation charge per machine-year is $400—one-fifth of the unit price of $2,000. In each of the first four years, 100 machines are in use, and the annual depreciation charge is $40,000. In the fifth year, when the number of machines in use drops to 70, the charge is $28,000. In the sixth year, when only 30 units are in use, the charge is $12,000.

When an asset in the group is disposed of, no gain or loss is recognized. The asset's cost is removed from the group asset account, and the difference between the cost and the asset's actual net salvage value is removed from the accumulated depreciation account.

The advantage of group depreciation, according to Smith and Skousen, is "an annual charge that is more closely related to the quantity of productive facilities being used. Gains and losses due solely to normal variations in asset lives are not recognized, and operating results are more meaningfully stated."[23]

But what Smith and Skousen see as an advantage, Geiger sees as a weakness:

> Since, for all practical purposes, the actual depreciation rate of an item is unknown and is not used, the true gain or loss at time of its sale or disposal cannot be computed. Accordingly, gain or loss on disposal of fixed assets is not recognized in the income accounts.[24]

But Smith and Skousen counter: "With normal variations in asset lives, the losses not recognized on early retirements are offset by the continued depreciation charges on those assets still in service after the average life has elapsed."[25]

(ii) Composite Depreciation   Composite depreciation applies group depreciation procedures to groups of dissimilar assets with varying service lives.

---

23.   Smith and Skousen.
24.   H. Dwight Geiger, "Composite Depreciation under Depreciation Guidelines," *AAA Bulletin*, Vol. 44, No. 11, July 1963.
25.   Smith and Skousen.

Asset Item	Cost	New Salvage Value	Depreciation Base	Annual Rate	Depreciation
A	$ 2,000	$ —	$ 2,000	20.0%	$ 400
B	5,000	500	4,500	12.0	540
C	8,000	1,000	7,000	10.0	700
D	15,000	1,000	14,000	8.0	1,120
Group	$30,000	$2,500	$27,500		$2,760

Composite life: $27,500 ÷ $2,760 = 9.96 years.
Composite rate: $2,760 ÷ $30,000 = 9.2%.

EXHIBIT 21.5   COMPOSITE DEPRECIATION

Exhibit 21.5 illustrates the calculation of composite rates. The composite life of the assets is 9.96 years; the resulting composite depreciation rate is 9.2 percent. To determine the annual depreciation, the composite rate of 9.2 percent is applied to the asset account balance at the beginning of the year. The total acquisition cost of $30,000 is thus reduced to the estimated salvage value of $2,500 in 9.96 years.

As in group depreciation, when an asset is disposed of, no gain or loss is recognized. The asset's cost is removed from the group asset account, and the difference between cost and actual net salvage value is removed from the accumulated depreciation account.

Once a composite rate has been established, it is usually continued until a significant event indicates the need for a new rate. Such an event may be a material change in the service lives of the assets included in the group, a major asset addition, or a major asset retirement. Composite depreciation is based on the assumptions that assets are regularly retired near the end of their service lives and that the retired assets are replaced with similar assets. If replacements do not take place according to the assumptions, if the service lives of replacement assets differ substantially from the service lives of the assets replaced, or if the cost of replacement assets differs materially from the cost of the assets replaced, continued use of the same composite rate is inappropriate.

Mosich and Larsen discuss the advantages and disadvantages of composite depreciation:

> The primary disadvantage . . . is that the averaging procedure may obscure significant variations from average. The accuracy of the . . . composite depreciation rate may be verified by recomputing depreciation on the straight-line basis for individual plant assets. Any significant discrepancies between the two results require a change in the composite depreciation rate.
>
> The advantages . . . are simplicity, convenience, and a reduction in the amount of detail involved in plant asset records and depreciation computations. The availability of computers has reduced the force of this argument.[26]

(c) THE EFFECTS OF REPLACEMENTS, IMPROVEMENTS, AND ADDITIONS   As stated in Subsection 21.4(c), major expenditures that extend the service lives of assets or otherwise benefit future years are capitalized. Such expenditures require new depreciation computations.

---

26.   Mosich and Larsen.

The new periodic depreciation charge is determined by dividing the asset's new book value by the new remaining service life, illustrated for straight-line depreciation, as follows:

Original asset cost (original estimated life, 10 years)	$8,000
Six years' depreciation	–4,800
Net book value before capital expenditure	3,200
Net increase in book value resulting from capital expenditure	2,400
New book value (new estimated life, 8 years)	$5,600
New annual depreciation charge ($5,600 ÷ 8)	$ 700

Retroactive adjustment of previous years' depreciation is not appropriate, since the expenditures benefit future years only.

(d) TOOLS AND RELATED ASSETS   Tools are sometimes divided into two classes: *semidurable* (lives of five years or more) and *perishable*. The cost of semidurable tools is capitalized and depreciated, usually at a group or composite rate. The rate is usually high because tools are hard to control.

Perishable tools may be handled in a variety of ways. Their cost may be charged directly to the appropriate expense or production cost account. Or the cost may be capitalized, often at some arbitrarily reduced amount, and written down when periodic inventories reveal shrinkage and deterioration. A third method is to capitalize the original cost and charge all subsequent expenditures for replacements to expense.

21.12   DEPRECIATION FOR TAX PURPOSES

Tax regulations contain their own depreciation requirements. Before 1954, the Internal Revenue Service generally allowed only the straight-line method of depreciation. Subsequently, the tax laws and regulations have been amended several times to permit accelerated depreciation methods and arbitrarily short asset lives. As a result, depreciation for financial reporting purposes and depreciation for tax purposes commonly differ. The difference between an asset's tax and accounting basis is a temporary difference that requires interperiod tax allocation under SFAS No. 109, *Accounting for Income Taxes* (see Chapter 24).

(a) CURRENT REQUIREMENTS   Depreciation for tax purposes is currently determined under the *accelerated cost recovery system* (ACRS), enacted in the Economic Recovery Act of 1981, and the *modified accelerated cost recovery system* (MACRS), enacted in the Tax Reform Act of 1986. ACRS and MACRS provide for accelerated write-offs. In many cases, the asset service lives allowable for tax purposes under ACRS and MACRS are shorter than the realistic economic service lives used for financial reporting purposes.

(b) MODIFIED ACCELERATED COST RECOVERY SYSTEM   MACRS is mandatory for most tangible depreciable property placed in service after December 31, 1986, but not if the taxpayer uses a depreciation method, such as the service-hours method, based on a service life expressed other than in years.

Under MACRS, property other than real estate is depreciated over 3, 5, 7, 10, 15, or 20 years, depending on its classification. Real estate is classified as residential rental property, which is depreciated over 27.5 years, or nonresidential real property, which is depreciated over 39 years, for purchases made after May 13, 1993. Prior to that date, nonresidential real property will be depreciated over 31.5 years.

Most property can be depreciated using an alternative method, which computes depreciation using the straight-line method with no salvage value over the applicable MACRS class life.

(c) ADDITIONAL FIRST-YEAR DEPRECIATION   The Internal Revenue Code also allows, with certain limitations, up to $17,500 of qualified tangible personal property to be deducted as an expense in the year acquired. The additional expense must be deducted from cost to determine the asset's depreciable base for tax purposes.

21.13   FINANCIAL STATEMENT PRESENTATION AND DISCLOSURE

(a) GENERAL REQUIREMENTS   APB Opinion No. 12, *Omnibus Opinion—1967* (par. 5), requires the following four disclosures in the financial statements or notes:

1. Depreciation expense for the period
2. Balances of major classes of depreciable assets, by nature or function, at the balance sheet date
3. Accumulated depreciation, either by major asset classes or in total, at the balance sheet date
4. A general description of the method or methods used in computing depreciation for major classes of depreciable assets

Special disclosures may also include the method of accounting for fully depreciated assets, liens against property, impairments, and property held for sale. Ordinarily, the basis of valuation is also disclosed.

(b) CONSTRUCTION IN PROGRESS   Payments to contractors for construction in progress are usually recorded as advances, since the payor does not acquire ownership until completion of the construction. Self-constructed assets are normally classified separately as construction in progress until construction is complete.

(c) GAIN OR LOSS ON RETIREMENT   Under APB Opinion No. 30, *Reporting the Results of Operations* (par. 23), gains or losses from the sale or abandonment of property, plant, or equipment used in the business are usually not reported as extraordinary items. They are expected to recur as a consequence of customary and continuing business activities. Exceptions are recognized for gains and losses that are "a direct result of a major casualty (such as an earthquake), an expropriation, or a prohibition under a newly enacted law or regulation" and that clearly meet both criteria of unusual nature and infrequency of occurrence.

(d) FULLY DEPRECIATED AND IDLE ASSETS   Many authorities recommend that the cost and accumulated depreciation of fully depreciated assets still in use be kept in the accounts until the assets are sold or retired. Stettler recommends disclosure not only of fully depreciated assets in use, but also of idle assets:

> Disclosure should also be made if there are material amounts of fully depreciated assets still in use or material amounts of assets still subject to depreciation that are not currently in productive use.[27]

---

27.   Howard F. Stettler, *Auditing Principles, Fifth Edition* (Englewood Cliffs, NJ: Prentice-Hall, 1982).

(e) IMPAIRMENT OF ASSETS

(i) Presentation   The SFAS No. 144 requires that impairment losses related to assets to be held and used in operations and that impairment losses from initial adjustments (and gains and losses from subsequent adjustments) of the carrying amount of assets to be disposed of be reported as a component of income from continuing operations, before income taxes. However, it provides the following options as to how such losses may be presented within the financial statements:

- As a separate line item in the income statement
- Aggregated in an appropriate line item in the income statement (e.g., as part of "other expenses") with the amount of the loss noted parenthetically on the face of the income statement
- Aggregated in an appropriate line item in the income statement supplemented by disclosure in the notes to the financial statements of the amount of impairment loss and the income statement caption in which the loss is included

If a company presents a subtotal in its income statement (e.g., income from operations, or operating income), the impairment loss must be included in such subtotal.

(ii) Disclosures for Assets to Be Held and Used   The SFAS No. 144 requires the following disclosures in the notes to the financial statements when an impairment loss is reported:

- A description of the assets that are impaired and the facts and circumstances leading to the impairment
- The amount of the impairment loss and how the fair value of the impaired assets was determined
- The caption in the income statement (or statement of activities for a not-for-profit organization) in which impairment gains or losses are aggregated if those gains or losses have not been presented in a separate caption or reported parenthetically on the face of the statement
- If applicable, the business segment(s) affected

(iii) Disclosures for Assets to Be Disposed Of   The SFAS No. 144 requires that an entity that holds assets to be disposed of should disclose the following in financial statements that include a period during which those assets are held:

- A description of the assets to be disposed of, the facts and circumstances leading to the expected disposal, the expected disposal date, and the carrying amount of those assets, if not separately presented on the face of the balance sheet
- If applicable, the business segment(s) in which assets to be disposed of are being held
- In the period in which an initial impairment loss is recorded, the amount of the impairment loss, and in years after the initial impairment is recorded, the gain or loss, if any, resulting from subsequent changes in the carrying amounts of the assets
- The caption in the income statement (or statement of activities for a not-for-profit organization) in which impairment gains or losses are aggregated if those gains or losses have not been presented in a separate caption or reported parenthetically on the face of the statement
- If applicable, amounts of revenue and pretax profit or loss reported in discontinued operations

(f) SEGMENT INFORMATION   The SFAS No. 131, *Disclosures about Segments of an Enterprise and Related Information*, requires disclosure of two items of information about property, plant, and equipment for each reportable segment:

1. Total assets, for each reportable segment
2. The aggregate amount of depreciation, depletion, and amortization expense and the amount of capital expenditures for each reportable segment

21.14 SOURCES AND SUGGESTED REFERENCES

Accounting Principles Board, "Omnibus Opinion—1967," APB Opinion No. 12, AICPA, New York, 1967.

Accounting Principles Board, "Accounting Changes," APB Opinion No. 20, AICPA, New York, 1971.

Accounting Principles Board, "Interest on Receivables and Payables," APB Opinion No. 21, AICPA, New York, 1971.

Accounting Principles Board, "Interim Financial Reporting," APB Opinion No. 28, AICPA, New York, 1973.

Accounting Principles Board, "Accounting for Nonmonetary Transactions," APB Opinion No. 29, AICPA, New York, 1973.

Accounting Principles Board, "Reporting the Results of Operations," APB Opinion No. 30, AICPA, New York, 1973.

American Accounting Association, "A Statement of Basic Accounting Theory," AAA, Sarasota, FL, 1966.

American Institute of Certified Public Accountants, "Accounting Research and Terminology Bulletins—Final Edition," AICPA, New York, 1961.

American Institute of Certified Public Accountants, "Accounting for the Inability to Fully Recover the Carrying Amount of Long-Lived Assets," Issues Paper, AICPA, New York, July 15, 1980.

American Institute of Certified Public Accountants, "Illustrations of Accounting for the Inability to Fully Recover the Carrying Amounts of Long-Lived Assets," AICPA, New York, April 1987.

American Institute of Certified Public Accountants, "Environmental Remediation Liabilities," Statement of Position 96-1, AICPA, New York, October 1996.

American Institute of Certified Public Accountants, "Accounting for Certain Costs and Activities Related to Property, Plant, and Equipment," Proposed Statement of Position, AICPA, New York, 2001.

Bendel, C. W., "Streamlining the Property Accounting Procedures," *NACA Bulletin*, Vol. 31, No. 11, 1950.

Davidson, Sidney, Stickney, Clyde P., and Weil, Roman L., *Financial Accounting, An Introduction to Concepts, Methods and Uses, Fifth Edition*, Dryden Press, Hinsdale, IL, 1988.

Financial Accounting Standards Board, "Fair Value Measurements," Statement of Financial Accounting Standards No. 157, FASB, Norwalk, CT, 2006.

Financial Accounting Standards Board, "Impairment of Long-Lived Assets and Depreciation of Idle Facilities," EITF Issue No. 84-28, FASB, Stamford, CT, October 18, 1984, December 19, 1985, and February 6, 1986.

Financial Accounting Standards Board, "Nonmonetary Transactions: Magnitude of Boot and the Exceptions to the Use of Fair Value," EITF Issue No. 86-29, FASB, Stamford, CT, December 3–4, 1986, January 15, 1987, and February 26, 1987.

Financial Accounting Standards Board, "Applicability of FASB Statement No. 2 to Business Combinations Accounted for by the Purchase Method," FASB Interpretation No. 4, FASB, Stamford, CT, 1975.

Financial Accounting Standards Board, "Accounting for the Cost of Asbestos Removal," EITF Issue No. 89-13, FASB, Norwalk, CT, October 26, 1989.

Financial Accounting Standards Board, "Capitalization of Costs to Treat Environmental Contamination," EITF Issue No. 90-8, FASB, Norwalk, CT, May 31, 1990, and July 12, 1990.

Financial Accounting Standards Board, "Accounting for Involuntary Conversions of Nonmonetary Assets to Monetary Assets," FASB Interpretation No. 30, FASB, Stamford, CT, 1979.

Financial Accounting Standards Board, "Accounting for Research and Development Costs," Statement of Financial Accounting Standards No. 2, FASB, Stamford, CT, 1974.

Financial Accounting Standards Board, "Financial Reporting for Segments of a Business Enterprise," Statement of Financial Accounting Standards No. 14, FASB, Stamford, CT, 1976.

Financial Accounting Standards Board, "Capitalization of Interest Cost," Statement of Financial Accounting Standards No. 34, FASB, Stamford, CT, 1979.

Financial Accounting Standards Board, "Accounting for Costs and Initial Rental Operations of Real Estate Projects," Statement of Financial Accounting Standards No. 67, FASB, Stamford, CT, 1982.

Financial Accounting Standards Board, "Accounting for Income Taxes," Statement of Financial Accounting Standards No. 109, FASB, Norwalk, CT, 1992.

Financial Accounting Standards Board, "Disclosures about Segments of an Enterprise and Related Information," Statement of Financial Accounting Standards No. 131, FASB, Norwalk, CT, 1997.

Financial Accounting Standards Board, "Accounting for Asset Retirement Obligations," Statement of Financial Accounting Standards No. 143, FASB, Norwalk, CT, 2001.

Financial Accounting Standards Board, "Accounting for the Impairment or Disposal of Long-Lived Assets," Statement of Financial Accounting Standards No. 144, FASB, Norwalk, CT, 2001.

Financial Accounting Standards Board, "Using Cash Flow Information and Present Value in Accounting Measurements," Statement of Financial Accounting Concepts No. 7, FASB, Norwalk, CT, 2000.

Financial Executives Institute, "Survey of Unusual Charges," Morristown, NJ, September 26, 1986.

Geiger, H. Dwight, "Composite Depreciation under Depreciation Guidelines," *AAA Bulletin*, Vol. 44, No. 11, July 1963.

Grant, E., and Norton, P., *Depreciation*. Ronald Press, New York, 1955.

International Accounting Standards Committee, "Depreciation Accounting," International Accounting Standards No. 4, IASC, London, 1977.

Kieso, Donald E., and Weygandt, Jerry J., *Intermediate Accounting, Fifth Edition*, John Wiley & Sons, New York, 1986.

Kohler, Eric Louis, *Kohler's Dictionary for Accountants, Sixth Edition*, Prentice-Hall, Englewood Cliffs, NJ, 1983.

Lambert, S. J., III, and Lambert, Joyce C., "Concepts and Applications in APB Opinion No. 29," *Journal of Accountancy*, March 1977, pp. 60–68.

Lamden, Charles, Gerboth, Dale L., and McRae, Thomas, "Accounting for Depreciable Assets," *Accounting Research Monograph*, No. 1, AICPA, New York, 1975.

Mosich, A. N., and Larsen, John E., *Intermediate Accounting, Sixth Edition*, McGraw-Hill, New York, 1986.

National Association of Accountants, Management Accounting Practices Committee, "Fixed Asset Accounting: The Capitalization of Costs," Statement on Management Accounting Practices No. 4, NAA, New York, 1973.

National Association of Accountants, Management Accounting Practices Committee, "Fixed Asset Accounting: The Allocation of Costs," Statement on Management Accounting Practices No. 7, NAA, New York, 1974.

Pyle, William W., and Larson, Kermit D., *Fundamental Accounting Principles, Tenth Edition*, Irwin, Homewood, IL, 1984.

Smith, Jay M., and Skousen, K. Fred, *Intermediate Accounting, Comprehensive Volume, Ninth Edition*, South-Western Publishing, Cincinnati, OH, 1987.

Stettler, Howard F., *Auditing Principles, Fifth Edition*, Prentice-Hall, Englewood Cliffs, NJ, 1982.

Welsch, Glenn A., Anthony, Robert N., and Short, Daniel G., *Fundamentals of Financial Accounting*, Irwin, Homewood, IL, 1984.

Welsch, Glenn A., and Zlatkovich, Charles T., *Intermediate Accounting, Eighth Edition*, Irwin, Homewood, IL, 1989.

ACCOUNTANTS' HANDBOOK

ELEVENTH EDITION

SPECIAL INDUSTRIES AND SPECIAL TOPICS

CHAPTER 30

REAL ESTATE AND CONSTRUCTION (REVISED)

BENEDETTO BONGIORNO, CPA, CRE
Natural Decision Systems, Inc.

30.1 THE REAL ESTATE INDUSTRY

(a) OVERVIEW Real estate encompasses a variety of interests (developers, investors, lenders, tenants, homeowners, corporations, conduits, etc.) with a divergence of objectives (tax benefits, security, long-term appreciation, etc.). The industry is also a tool of the federal government's income tax policies (evidenced by the rules on mortgage interest deductions and restrictions on "passive" investment deductions). The real estate industry consists primarily of private developers and builders.

Other important forces in the industry include pension funds and insurance companies, as well as large public corporations, whose occupancy (real estate) costs generally are the second largest costs after personnel costs.

After a period of growth spurred by increasing demand for all types of real estate in an expanding economy, the new millennium brought in its wake a series of traumatic events that highlighted the uncertainties inherent in the real estate industry:

- *Collapse of the stock market.* The sudden rise and dramatic collapse of the stock market delivered the first shock to real estate markets since the financial collapse of the 1930s. The refinancing market was turned on end as rapid retrenchment left behind a source of capital for real estate.
- *The dramatic rise in tenant closures and bankruptcies.* The reduction of tenant demand dealt a hard blow to an already declining economy and real estate market. It was preceded by a sharp rise in unemployment and severe weakness in financial markets that also curtailed demand for existing and new real estate.

Weak markets will continue to plague the recovery of many real estate markets. The sources and extent of available capital for financings, refinancings, and construction will continue to be a concern.

This concern will be centered on the ability and willingness of financing institutions, especially the Wall Street firms, to continue lending in an uncertain and changed market, and lenders will increasingly require creditworthiness or enhancements to reduce their exposure to real estate risk.

(b) FASB ACCOUNTING STANDARDS CODIFICATION   The Financial Accounting Standards Board (FASB) has completed the Accounting Standards Codification Project. On July 1, 2009, the *FASB Accounting Standards Codification™* has officially become the single source of authoritative nongovernmental U.S. generally accepted accounting principles (GAAP), superseding existing FASB, American Institute of Certified Public Accountants (AICPA), Emerging Issues Task Force (EITF), and related literature. After that date, only one level of authoritative GAAP will exist. All other literature will be considered nonauthoritative. All public companies' SEC filings after September 30, 2009, when referencing GAAP, must refer to the new segmented topics referred below.

FASB has segmented the authoritative literature into various topics, subtopics, sections, and subsections. The following topic references apply to real estate that incorporate the direct authoritative literature referenced in this chapter.

30.2   SALES OF REAL ESTATE

(a) ANALYSIS OF TRANSACTIONS   Real estate sales transactions are generally material to the entity's financial statements. "Is the earnings process complete?" is the primary question that must be answered regarding such sales. In other words, assuming all the conditions precedent to closing have occurred, have the risks and rewards of ownership been transferred to the buyer?

(b) ACCOUNTING BACKGROUND   Prior to 1982, guidance related to real estate sales transactions was contained in two AICPA Accounting Guides: "Accounting for Retail Land Sales" and "Accounting for Profit Recognition on Sales of Real Estate." These guides had been supplemented by several AICPA Statements of Position (SOPs) that provide interpretations.

In October 1982, Statement of Financial Accounting Standards (SFAS) No. 66, "Accounting for Sales of Real Estate," was issued as part of the FASB project to incorporate, where appropriate, AICPA Accounting Guides into FASB Statements. This Statement adopted the specialized profit recognition principles of the aforementioned guides.

The FASB formed the EITF in 1984 for the early identification of emerging issues. The EITF has dealt with many issues affecting the real estate industry, including issues that clarify or address SFAS No. 66.

Regardless of the seller's business, SFAS No. 66 covers all sales of real estate, determines the timing of the sale and resultant profit recognition, and deals with seller accounting only. This Statement does not discuss nonmonetary exchanges, cost accounting, and most lease transactions or disclosures.

The two primary concerns under SFAS No. 66 are:

1. Has a sale occurred?
2. Under what method and when should profit be recognized?

The concerns are answered by determining the buyer's initial and continuing investment and the nature and extent of the seller's continuing involvement. The guidelines used in determining these criteria are complex and, within certain provisions, arbitrary. Companies dealing with these types of transactions are often faced with the difficult task of analyzing the exact nature of a transaction in order to determine the appropriate accounting approach. Only with a thorough understanding of the substance and details of a transaction can the accountant perform the analysis required to decide on the appropriate accounting method.

(c) CRITERIA FOR SALES RECOGNITION SFAS No. 66 (pars. 44–50) discusses separate rules for retail land sales (see Subsection 30.2(h)). The following information is for all real estate sales other than retail land sales. To determine whether profit recognition is appropriate, a test must first be made to determine whether a sale has occurred. Then additional tests are made related to the buyer's investment and the seller's continued involvement.

Generally, real estate sales should not be recorded prior to closing. Since an exchange is generally required to recognize profit, a sale must be consummated. A sale is consummated when all the following conditions have been met:

- The parties are bound by the terms of a contract.
- All consideration has been exchanged.
- Any permanent financing for which the seller is responsible has been arranged.
- All conditions precedent to closing have been performed.

Usually all those conditions are met at the time of closing. They are not usually met at the time of a contract to sell or a preclosing.

Exceptions to the "conditions precedent to closing" have been specifically provided for in SFAS No. 66. They are applicable where a sale of property includes a requirement for the seller to perform future construction or development. Under certain conditions, partial sale recognition is permitted during the construction process because the construction period is extended. This exception usually is not applicable to single-family detached housing because of the shorter construction period.

Transactions that should not be treated as sales for accounting purposes because of continuing seller's involvement include the following:

- The seller has an option or obligation to repurchase the property.
- The seller guarantees return of the buyer's investment.
- The seller retains an interest as a general partner in a limited partnership and has a significant receivable.
- The seller is required to initiate or support operations or continue to operate the property at its own risk for a specified period or until a specified level of operations has been obtained.

If the criteria for recording a sale are not met, the deposit, financing, lease, or profit-sharing (co-venture) methods should be used, depending on the substance of the transaction.

(d) ADEQUACY OF DOWN PAYMENT Once it has been determined that a sale can be recorded, the next test relates to the buyer's investment. For the seller to record full profit recognition, the buyer's down payment must be adequate in size and in composition.

(i) Size of Down Payment The minimum down payment requirement is one of the most important provisions in SFAS No. 66. Appendix A of this pronouncement, reproduced here as Exhibit 30.1, lists minimum down payments ranging from 5 percent to 25 percent of sales

	MINIMUM INITIAL INVESTMENT PAYMENT EXPRESSED AS A PERCENTAGE OF SALES VALUE
Land:	
Held for commercial, industrial, or residential development to commence within two years after sale	20%
Held for commercial, industrial, or residential development after two years	25%
Commercial and industrial property:	
Office and industrial buildings, shopping centers, and so forth:	
Properties subject to lease on a long-term lease basis to parties having satisfactory credit rating; cash flow currently sufficient to service all indebtedness	10%
Single-tenancy properties sold to a user having a satisfactory credit rating	15%
All other	20%
Other income-producing properties (hotels, motels, marinas, mobile home parks, and so forth):	
Cash flow currently sufficient to service all indebtedness	15%
Start-up situations or current deficiencies in cash flow	25%
Multifamily residential property:	
Primary residence:	
Cash flow currently sufficient to service all indebtedness	10%
Start-up situations or current deficiencies in cash flow	15%
Secondary or recreational residence:	
Cash flow currently sufficient to service all indebtedness	10%
Start-up situations or current deficiencies in cash flow	25%
Single-family residential property (including condominium or cooperative housing)	
Primary residence of buyer	5%[a]
Secondary or recreational residence	10%[a]

[a] As set forth in Appendix A of SFAS No. 66, if collectability of the remaining portion of the sales price cannot be supported by reliable evidence of collection experience, the minimum initial investment shall be at least 60% of the difference between the sales value and the financing available from loans guaranteed by regulatory bodies, such as the FHA or the VA, or from independent financial institutions.

This 60% test applies when independent first mortgage financing is not utilized and the seller takes a receivable from the buyer for the difference between the sales value and the initial investment. If independent first mortgage financing is utilized, the adequacy of the initial investment on sales of single-family residential property should be determined as described in Subsection 30.2(d)(i).

(*Source:* SFAS No. 66, "Accounting for Sales of Real Estate" (Appendix A), FASB, 1982. Reprinted with permission of FASB.)

EXHIBIT 30.1   MINIMUM INITIAL INVESTMENT REQUIREMENTS

value based on usual loan limits for various types of properties. These percentages should be considered as specific requirements because it was not intended that exceptions be made. Additionally, EITF Consensus No. 88-24, "Effect of Various Forms of Financing under FASB Statement No. 66," discusses the impact of the source and nature of the buyer's down payment on profit recognition. Exhibit A to EITF No. 88-24 has been reproduced here as Exhibit 30.2.

Situation	Cash Received by Seller at Closing	Components of Cash Received by Seller at Closing		
		Buyer's Initial Investment	Buyer's Independent First Mortgage	Assumption of Seller's Nonrecourse Mortgage
1.	100	20	80	
2.	100	0	100	
3.	20	20		80
4.	0	0		100
5.	20	20		
6.	20	20		
7.	80	20	60	
8.	20	20		60
9.	20	20		
10.	0	0		
11.	0	0		
12.	0	0		
13.	80	0	80	
14.	10	10		
15.	10	10		
16.	90	10	80	
17.	10	10		80
18.	10	10		

Assumptions:
Sales price: $100.
Seller's basis in property sold: $70.
Initial investment requirement: 20%.
All mortgage obligations meet the continuing investment requirements of Statement 66.

Source: EITF Issue No. 88-24, "Effect of Various Forms of Financing under FASB Statement No. 66" (Exhibit 88-24A), FASB, 1988. (Reprinted with permission of FASB.)

Seller Financing[1]	Assumption of Seller's Recourse Mortgage[2]	Recognition Under Consensus Paragraph	Profit Recognized at Date of Sale[3]		
			Full Accrual	Installment	Cost Recovery
		#1	30		
		#1	30		
		#1	30		
		#1	30		
80(1)		#2	30		
	80	#2	30		
20(2)		#2	30		
20(2)		#2	30		
20(2)	60	#2	30		
	100	#3		0	0
100(1)		#3		0	0
20(2)	80	#3		0	0
20(2)		#3		10	10
90(1)		#3		3	0
	90	#3		3	0
10(2)		#3		20	20
10(2)		#3		20	20
10(2)	80	#3		3	0

(Continued)

[1] First or second mortgage indicated in parentheses.

[2] Seller remains contingently liable.

[3] The profit recognized under the reduced profit method is dependent on various interest rates and payment terms. An example is not presented due to the complexity of those factors and the belief that this method is not frequently used in practice. Under this method, the profit recognized at the consummation of the sale would be less than under the full accrual method, but normally more than the amount under the installment method.

EXHIBIT 30.2   EXAMPLES OF THE APPLICATION OF THE EITF CONSENSUS ON ISSUE NO. 88-24

If a newly placed permanent loan or firm permanent loan commitment for maximum financing exists, the minimum down payment must be the higher of (1) the amount derived from Appendix A or (2) the excess of sales value over 115 percent of the new financing. However, regardless of this test, a down payment of 25 percent of the sales value of the property is usually considered sufficient to justify the recognition of profit at the time of sale.

An example of the down payment test—Appendix A compared to the newly placed permanent loan test—is given in the following:

ASSUMPTIONS

Initial payment made by the buyer to the seller on sale of an apartment building	$200,000
First mortgage recently issued and assumed by the buyer	1,000,000
Second mortgage given by the seller at prevailing interest rate	200,000
Stated sales price and sales value	1,400,000
115% of first mortgage (1.15 × $1,000,000)	1,150,000
Down payment necessary	250,000

RESULT

Although the down payment required under Appendix A is only $140,000 (10% of $1,400,000), the $200,000 actual down payment is inadequate because the test relating to the newly placed first mortgage requires $250,000.

The down payment requirements must be related to sales value, as described in SFAS No. 66 (par. 7). Sales value is the stated sales price increased or decreased for other consideration that clearly constitutes additional proceeds on the sale, services without compensation, imputed interest, and so forth.

Consideration payable for development work or improvements that are the responsibility of the seller should be included in the computation of sales value.

(ii) Composition of Down Payment   The primary acceptable down payment is cash, but additional acceptable forms of down payment are:

- Notes from the buyer (only when supported by irrevocable letters of credit from an independent established lending institution)
- Cash payments by the buyer to reduce previously existing indebtedness
- Cash payments that are in substance additional sales proceeds, such as prepaid interest that by the terms of the contract is applied to amounts due the seller

Examples of other forms of down payment, which are not acceptable, are:

- Other noncash consideration received by the seller, such as notes from the buyer without letters of credit or marketable securities. Noncash consideration constitutes down payment only at the time it is converted into cash.
- Funds that have been or will be lent to the buyer builder/developer for acquisition, construction, or development purposes or otherwise provided directly or indirectly by the seller. Such amounts must first be deducted from the down payment in determining whether the down payment test has been met. An exemption from this requirement was provided in paragraph 115 of SFAS No. 66, which states that if a future loan on normal terms from a seller who is also an established lending institution bears a fair market interest rate and the proceeds of the loan are conditional on use for specific development of or construction on the property, the loan need not be subtracted in determining the buyer's investment.
- Funds received from the buyer from proceeds of priority loans on the property. Such funds have not come from the buyer and therefore do not provide assurance of collectability of the remaining receivable; such amounts should be excluded in determining the adequacy of the down payment. In addition, EITF Consensus No. 88-24 provides guidelines on the impact that the source and nature of the buyer's initial investment can have on profit recognition.
- Marketable securities or other assets received as down payment will constitute down payment only at the time they are converted to cash.
- Cash payments for prepaid interest that are not in substance additional sales proceeds.
- Cash payments by the buyer to others for development or construction of improvements to the property.

(iii) Inadequate Down Payment   If the buyer's down payment is inadequate, the full accrual method of accounting is not appropriate, and the deposit, installment, or cost recovery method of accounting should be used.

When the sole consideration (in addition to cash) received by the seller is the buyer's assumption of existing nonrecourse indebtedness, a sale could be recorded and profit recognized if all other conditions for recognizing a sale were met. If, however, the buyer assumes recourse debt and the seller remains liable on the debt, he has a risk of loss comparable to the risk involved in holding a receivable from the buyer, and the full accrual method would not be appropriate.

EITF Consensus No. 88-24 states that the initial and continuing investment requirements for the full accrual method of profit recognition of SFAS No. 66 are applicable unless the seller receives one of the following as the full sales value of the property:

- Cash, without any seller contingent liability on any debt on the property incurred or assumed by the buyer
- The buyer's assumption of the seller's existing nonrecourse debt on the property
- The buyer's assumption of all recourse debt on the property with the complete release of the seller from those obligations
- Any combination of such cash and debt assumption

(e) RECEIVABLE FROM THE BUYER   Even if the required down payment is made, a number of factors must be considered by the seller in connection with a receivable from the buyer. They include:

- Collectability of the receivable
- Buyer's continuing investment—amortization of receivable

- Future subordination
- Release provisions
- Imputation of interest

(i) Assessment of Collectability of Receivable Collectability of the receivable must be reasonably assured and should be assessed in light of factors such as the credit standing of the buyer (if recourse), cash flow from the property, and the property's size and geographical location. This requirement may be particularly important when the receivable is relatively short-term and collectability is questionable because the buyer will be required to obtain financing. Furthermore, a basic principle of real estate sales on credit is that the receivable must be adequately secured by the property sold.

(ii) Amortization of Receivable Continuing investment requirements for full profit recognition require that the buyer's payments on its total debt for the purchase price must be at least equal to level annual payments (including principal and interest) based on amortization of the full amount over a maximum term of 20 years for land and over the *customary term of a first mortgage* by an independent established lending institution for other property. The annual payments must begin within one year of recording the sale and, to be acceptable, must meet the same composition test as used in determining adequacy of down payments. The customary term of a first mortgage loan is usually considered to be the term of a new loan (or the term of an existing loan placed in recent years) from an independent financial lending institution. In today's lending environment, the terms of the loan have been tightened in the areas of both loan-to-value ratios and shortened amortization periods.

All indebtedness on the property need not be reduced proportionately. However, if the seller's receivable is not being amortized, realization may be in question and the collectability must be more carefully assessed. Lump-sum (balloon) payments do not affect the amortization requirement as long as the scheduled amortization is within the maximum period and the minimum annual amortization tests are met.

For example, if the customary term of the mortgage by an independent lender required amortizing payments over a period of 15 years, then the continuing investment requirement would be based on such an amortization schedule. If the terms of the receivable required principal and interest payments on such a schedule only for the first five years with a balloon payment at the end of year 5, the continuing investment requirements are met. In such cases, however, the collectability of the balloon payment should be carefully assessed.

If the amortization requirements for full profit recognition as set forth in the preceding paragraphs are not met, a reduced profit may be recognized by the seller if the annual payments are at least equal to the total of:

- Annual level payments of principal and interest on a maximum available first mortgage
- Interest at an appropriate rate on the remaining amount payable by the buyer

The reduced profit is determined by discounting the receivable from the buyer to the present value of the lowest level of annual payments required by the sales contract, excluding requirements to pay lump sums. The present value is calculated using an appropriate interest rate, but not less than the rate stated in the sales contract.

The amount calculated would be used as the value of the receivable for the purpose of determining the reduced profit. The calculation of reduced profit is illustrated in Exhibit 30.3.

Assumptions:		
Down payment (meets applicable tests)		$ 150,000
First mortgage note from independent lender at market rate of interest (new, 20 years—meets required amortization)		750,000
Second mortgage notes payable to seller, interest at a market rate is due annually, with principal due at the end of the 25th year (the term exceeds the maximum permitted)		100,000
Stated selling price		$1,000,000
Adjustment required in valuation of receivable from buyer:		
Second mortgage payable to seller	$100,000	
Less: present value of 20 years annual interest payments on second mortgage (lowest level of annual payments over customary term of first mortgage—thus 20 years not 25)	70,000	30,000
Adjusted sales value for profit recognition		$ 970,000
The sales value as well as profit is reduced by $30,000. In some situations profit will be entirely eliminated by this calculation.		

Exhibit 30.3 Calculation of Reduced Profit

The requirements for amortization of the receivable are applied cumulatively at the closing date (date of recording the sale for accounting purposes) and annually thereafter. Any excess of down payment received over the minimum required is applied toward the amortization requirements.

(iii) Receivable Subject to Future Subordination   If the receivable is subject to future subordination to a future loan available to the buyer, profit recognition cannot exceed the amount determined under the cost recovery method (see Subsection 30.2(j)(iii)) unless proceeds of the loan are first used to reduce the seller's receivable. Although this accounting treatment is controversial, the cost recovery method is required because collectability of the sales price is not reasonably assured. The future subordination would permit the primary lender to obtain a prior lien on the property, leaving only a secondary residual value for the seller, and future loans could indirectly finance the buyer's initial cash investment. Future loans would include funds received by the buyer arising from a permanent loan commitment existing at the time of the transaction unless such funds were first applied to reduce the seller's receivable as provided for in the terms of the sale.

The cost recovery method is not required if the receivable is subordinate to a previous mortgage on the property existing at the time of sale.

(iv) Release Provisions   Some sales transactions have provisions releasing portions of the property from the liens securing the debt as partial payments are made. In this situation, full profit recognition is acceptable only if the buyer must make, at the time of each release, cumulative payments that are adequate in relation to the sales value of property not released.

(v) Imputation of Interest   Careful attention should be given to the necessity for imputation of interest under Accounting Principles Board (APB) Opinion No. 21, "Interest on Receivables and Payables," since it could have a significant effect on the amount of profit or loss recognition. As stated in the first paragraph of APB Opinion No. 21: "The use of an interest rate that varies from prevailing interest rates warrants evaluation of whether the face amount and the stated interest rate of a note or obligation provide reliable evidence for properly recording the exchange and subsequent related interest."

If imputation of interest is necessary, the mortgage note receivable should be adjusted to its present value by discounting all future payments on the notes using an imputed rate of interest at the prevailing rates available for similar financing with independent financial institutions. A distinction must be made between first and second mortgage loans, because the appropriate imputed rate for a second mortgage would normally be significantly higher than the rate for a first mortgage loan. It may be necessary to obtain independent valuations to assist in the determination of the proper rate.

(vi) Inadequate Continuing Investment   If the criteria for recording a sale have been met but the tests related to the collectability of the receivable as set forth herein are not met, the full accrual method of accounting is not appropriate and either the installment method or the cost recovery method of accounting should be used. These methods are discussed in Subsection 30.2(j) of this chapter.

(f) SELLER'S CONTINUED INVOLVEMENT   A seller sometimes continues to be involved over long periods of time with property legally sold. This involvement may take many forms, such as participation in future profits, financing, management services, development, construction, guarantees, and options to repurchase. With respect to profit recognition when a seller has continued involvement, the two key principles are as follows:

1. A sales contract should not be accounted for as a sale if the seller's continued involvement with the property includes the same kinds of risk as does ownership of property.
2. Profit recognition should follow performance and in some cases should be postponed completely until a later date.

(i) Participation Solely in Future Profits   A sale of real estate may include or be accompanied by an agreement that provides for the seller to participate in future operating profits or residual values. As long as the seller has no further obligations or risk of loss, profit recognition on the sale need not be deferred. A receivable from the buyer is permitted if the other tests for profit recognition are met, but no costs can be deferred.

(ii) Option or Obligation to Repurchase the Property   If the seller has an option or obligation to repurchase property (including a buyer's option to compel the seller to repurchase), a sale cannot be recognized (SFAS No. 66, par. 26). However, neither a commitment by the seller to assist or use his or her best efforts (with appropriate compensation) on a resale nor a right of first refusal based on a bona fide offer by a third party would preclude sale recognition. The accounting to be followed depends on the repurchase terms. EITF Consensus No. 86-6 discusses accounting for a sale transaction when antispeculation clauses exist. A consensus was reached that the contingent option would not preclude sale recognition if the probability of buyer noncompliance is remote.

When the seller has an obligation or an option that is reasonably expected to be exercised to repurchase the property at a price higher than the total amount of the payments received and to be received, the transaction is a financing arrangement and should be accounted for under the financing method. If the option is not reasonably expected to be exercised, the deposit method is appropriate.

In the case of a repurchase obligation or option at a lower price, the transaction usually is, in substance, a lease or is part lease, part financing, and should be accounted for under the lease method. Where an option to repurchase is at a market price to be determined in the future, the transaction should be accounted for under the deposit method or the profit-sharing method.

(iii) General Partner in a Limited Partnership with a Significant Receivable When the seller is a general partner in a limited partnership and has a significant receivable related to the property, the transaction would not qualify as a sale. It should usually be accounted for as a profit-sharing arrangement. As a guide, a significant receivable is one that is in excess of 15 percent of the maximum first lien financing that could be obtained from an established lending institution for the property sold.

(iv) Lack of Permanent Financing The buyer's leveraged investment in the property cannot be evaluated until adequate permanent financing at an acceptable cost is available to the buyer. If the seller must obtain or provide this financing, obtaining the financing is a prerequisite to a sale for accounting purposes. Even if not required to do so, the seller may be presumed to have such an obligation if the buyer does not have financing and the collectability of the receivable is questionable. The deposit method is appropriate if lack of financing is the only impediment to recording a sale.

(v) Guaranteed Return of Buyer's Investment SFAS No. 66 (par. 28) states: "If the seller guarantees return of the buyer's investment, ... the transaction shall be accounted for as a financing, leasing, or profit-sharing arrangement."

Accordingly, if the terms of a transaction are such that the buyer may expect to recover the initial investment through assured cash returns, subsidies, and net tax benefits, even if the buyer were to default on debt to the seller, or expect to liquidate the debt to the seller from property operations or sale, the transaction is probably not in substance a sale.

(vi) Other Guaranteed Returns on Investment—Other Than Sale-Leaseback When the seller guarantees cash returns on the buyer's investment, the accounting method to be followed depends on whether the guarantee is for an extended or a limited period and whether the seller's expected cost of the guarantee is determinable.

EXTENDED PERIOD
SFAS No. 66 states that when the seller contractually guarantees cash returns on investments to the buyer for an extended period, the transaction should be accounted for as a financing, leasing, or profit-sharing arrangement. An *extended period* was not defined but should at least include periods that are not limited in time or specified lengthy periods, such as more than five years. Specified lengthy periods may be impacted by the buyer's traditional holding period and the terms of the financing, if any.

LIMITED PERIOD
If the guarantee of a return on the buyer's investment is for a limited period, SFAS No. 66 indicates that the deposit method of accounting should be used until such time as operation of the property covers all operating expenses, debt service, and contractual payments. At that time, profit should be recognized based on performance (see Subsection 30.2(j)). A *limited period* was not defined but is believed to relate to specified shorter periods, such as five years or less.

Irrespective of the preceding, if the guarantee is determinable or limited, it may be appropriate if the sales price is reduced by the maximum exposure to loss as described next.

GUARANTEE AMOUNT DETERMINABLE
If the amount can be reasonably estimated, the seller should record the guarantee as a cost at the time of sale, thus either reducing the profit or increasing the loss on the transaction.

GUARANTEE AMOUNT NOT DETERMINABLE
If the amount cannot be reasonably estimated, the transaction is probably in substance a profit-sharing or co-venture arrangement.

GUARANTEE AMOUNT NOT DETERMINABLE BUT LIMITED
If the amount cannot be reasonably estimated but a maximum cost of the guarantee is determinable, the seller may record the maximum cost of the guarantee as a cost at the time of sale, thus either reducing the profit or increasing the loss on the transaction. Alternatively, the seller may account for the transaction as if the guarantee amount is not determinable. Implications of a seller's guarantee of cash flow on an operating property that is not considered a sale-leaseback arrangement are discussed in Subsection 30.2(f)(x).

(vii) Guaranteed Return on Investment—Sale-Leaseback   A guarantee of cash flow to the buyer sometimes takes the form of a leaseback arrangement. Since the earnings process in this situation has not usually been completed, profits on the sale should generally be deferred and amortized.

Accounting for a sale-leaseback of real estate is governed by SFAS No. 13, "Accounting for Leases," as amended by SFAS No. 28, "Accounting for Sales with Leasebacks"; SFAS No. 98, "Accounting for Leases: Sale-Leaseback Transactions Involving Real Estate"; and SFAS No. 66. SFAS No. 98 specifies the accounting by a seller-lessee for a sale-leaseback transaction involving real estate, including real estate with equipment. SFAS No. 98 provides that:

• A sale-leaseback transaction involving real estate, including real estate with equipment, must qualify as a sale under the provisions of SFAS No. 66 as amended by SFAS No. 98, before it is appropriate for the seller-lessee to account for the transaction as a sale. If the transaction does not qualify as a sale under SFAS No. 66, it should be accounted for by the deposit method or as a financing transaction (see Subsection 30.2(j)(v)).

• A sale-leaseback transaction involving real estate, including real estate with equipment, that includes any continuing involvement other than a normal leaseback in which the seller-lessee intends to actively use the property during the lease should be accounted for by the deposit method or as a financing transaction.

• A lease involving real estate may not be classified as a sales-type lease unless the lease agreement provides for the transfer of title to the lessee at or shortly after the end of the lease term. Sales-type leases involving real estate should be accounted for under the provisions of SFAS No. 66.

PROFIT RECOGNITION
Profits should be deferred and amortized in a manner consistent with the classification of the leaseback:

• If the leaseback is an operating lease, deferred profit should be amortized in proportion to the related gross rental charges to expense over the lease term.

- If the leaseback is a capital lease, deferred profit should be amortized in proportion to the amortization of the leased asset. Effectively, the sale is treated as a financing transaction. The deferred profit can be presented gross, but normally is offset against the capitalized asset for balance sheet classification purposes.

In situations where the leaseback covers only a minor portion of the property sold or the period is relatively minor compared to the remaining useful life of the property, it may be appropriate to recognize all or a portion of the gain as income. Sales with minor leasebacks should be accounted for based on the separate terms of the sale and the leaseback unless the rentals called for by the leaseback are unreasonable in relation to current market conditions. If rentals are considered to be unreasonable, they must be adjusted to a reasonable amount in computing the profit on the sale.

The leaseback is considered to be minor when the present value of the leaseback based on reasonable rentals is 10 percent or less of the fair value of the asset sold. If the leaseback is not considered to be minor (but less than substantially all of the use of the asset is retained through a leaseback) profit may be recognized to the extent it exceeds the present value of the minimum lease payments (net of executory costs) in the case of an operating lease or the recorded amount of the leased asset in the case of a capital lease.

Loss Recognition

Losses should be recognized immediately to the extent that the remaining cost (net carrying value) exceeds the fair value of the property under the provisions of SFAS No. 157 and FSP FAS 157. Fair value is frequently determined by the selling price from which the loss on the sale is measured. Many sale-leasebacks are entered into as a means of financing or for tax reasons, or both. The terms of the leaseback are negotiated as a package. Because of the interdependence of the sale and concurrent leaseback, the selling price in some cases is not representative of fair value. It would not be appropriate to recognize a loss on the sale that would be offset by future cost reductions as a result of either reduced rental costs under an operating lease or depreciation and interest charges under a capital lease. Therefore, to the extent that the fair value is greater than the sales price, losses should be deferred and amortized in the same manner as profits.

(viii) Services without Adequate Compensation   A sales contract may be accompanied by an agreement for the seller to provide management or other services without adequate compensation. Compensation for the value of the services should be imputed, deducted from the sales price, and recognized over the term of the contract. See discussion of implied support of operations in Subsection 30.2(f)(x) if the contract is noncancelable and the compensation is unusual for the services to be rendered.

(ix) Development and Construction   A sale of undeveloped or partially developed land may include or be accompanied by an agreement requiring future seller performance of development or construction. In such cases, all or a portion of the profit should be deferred. If there is a lapse of time between the sale agreement and the future performance agreement, deferral provisions usually apply if definitive development plans existed at the time of sale and a development contract was anticipated by the parties at the time of entering into the sales contract.

In addition, SFAS No. 66 (par. 41) provides that "The seller is involved with future development or construction work if the buyer is unable to pay amounts due for that work or has the right under the terms of the arrangement to defer payment until the work is done."

If the property sold and being developed is an operating property (such as an apartment complex, a shopping center, or an office building) as opposed to a nonoperating property (such as a land lot, a condominium unit, or a single-family detached home), Subsection 30.2(f)(x) may also apply.

COMPLETED CONTRACT METHOD

If a seller is obligated to develop the property or construct facilities and total costs and profit cannot be reliably estimated (e.g., because of lack of seller experience or definitive plans), all profit, including profit on the sale of land, should be deferred until the contract is completed or until the total costs and profit can be reliably estimated. Under the completed contract method, all profit, including profit on the sale of land, is deferred until the seller's obligations are fulfilled.

PERCENTAGE OF COMPLETION METHOD (COST-INCURRED METHOD)

If the costs and profit can be reliably estimated, profit recognition over the improvement period on the basis of costs incurred (including land) as a percentage of total costs to be incurred is required. Thus, if the land was a principal part of the sale and its market value greatly exceeded cost, part of the profit that can be said to be related to the land sale is deferred and recognized during the development or construction period.

The same rate of profit is used for all seller costs connected with the transaction. For this purpose, the cost of development work, improvements, and all fees and expenses that are the responsibility of the seller should be included. The buyer's initial and continuing investment tests, of course, must be met with respect to the total sales value. Exhibit 30.4 illustrates the cost-incurred method.

(x) Initiation and Support of Operations   If the property sold is an operating property, as opposed to a nonoperating property, deferral of all or a portion of the profit may be required under SFAS No. 66 (pars. 28–30). These paragraphs establish guidelines not only for stated support but also for implied support.

Although the implied support provisions do not usually apply to undeveloped or partially developed land, they do apply if the buyer has commitments to construct operating properties and there is stated or implied support.

Assuming that the criteria for recording a sale and the test of buyer's investment are met, the following sets forth guidelines for profit recognition where there is stated or implied support.

STATED SUPPORT

A seller may be required to support operations by means of a guaranteed return to the buyer. Alternatively, a guarantee may be made to the buyer that there will be no negative cash flow from the project, but may not guarantee a positive return on the buyer's investment. For example, EITF Consensus No. 85-27, "Recognition of Receipts from Made-Up Rental Shortfalls," considers the impact of a master lease guarantee. The broad exposure that such a guarantee creates has a negative impact on profit recognition.

IMPLIED SUPPORT

The seller may be presumed to be obligated to initiate and support operations of the property sold, even in the absence of specified requirements in the sale contract or related document.

ASSUMPTIONS

1. Sale of land for commercial development—$475,000
2. Development contract—$525,000
3. Down payment and other buyer investment requirements met
4. Land costs—$200,000
5. Development costs $500,000 (reliably estimated)—$325,000 incurred in initial year

CALCULATION OF PROFIT TO BE RECOGNIZED IN INITIAL YEAR

Sale of land	$475,000
Development contract price	525,000
Total sales price	1,000,000
Costs:	
Land	200,000
Development	500,000
Total costs	700,000
Total profit anticipated	$300,000
Cost incurred through end of initial year:	
Land	200,000
Development	325,000
Total	$525,000
Profit to be recognized in initial year—($525,000/$700,000) × $300,000	$225,000

EXHIBIT 30.4 PERCENTAGE OF COMPLETION, OR COST-INCURRED, METHOD

The following conditions under which support is implied are described in footnote 10 of SFAS No. 66:

- A seller obtains an interest as general partner in a limited partnership that acquires an interest in the property sold.
- A seller retains an equity interest in the property, such as an undivided interest or an equity interest in a joint venture that holds an interest in the property.
- A seller holds a receivable from a buyer for a significant part of the sales price, and collection of the receivable is dependent on the operation of the property.
- A seller agrees to manage the property for the buyer on terms not usual for the services to be rendered and that are not terminable by either seller or buyer.

STATED OR IMPLIED SUPPORT

When profit recognition is appropriate in the case of either stated or implied support, the following general rules apply:

- Profit is recognized on the ratio of costs incurred to total costs to be incurred. Revenues for gross profit purposes include rent from operations during the rent-up period; costs include land and operating expenses during the rent-up period as well as other costs.

- As set forth in SFAS No. 66 (par. 30):

  [S]upport shall be presumed for at least two years from the time of initial rental unless actual rental operations cover operating expenses, debt service, and other contractual commitments before that time. If the seller is contractually obligated for a longer time, profit recognition shall continue on the basis of performance until the obligation expires.

- Estimated rental income should be adjusted by reducing estimated future rent receipts by a safety factor of $33\frac{1}{3}$ percent unless signed lease agreements have been obtained to support a projection higher than the rental level thus computed. As set forth in SFAS No. 66 (par. 29), when signed leases amount to more than $66\frac{2}{3}$ percent of estimated rents, no additional safety factor is required but only amounts under signed lease agreements can be included.

(xi) Partial Sales   A partial sale includes the following:

- A sale of an interest in real estate
- A sale of real estate where the seller has an equity interest in the buyer (e.g., a joint venture or partnership)
- A sale of a condominium unit

SALE OF AN INTEREST IN REAL ESTATE
Profit recognition is appropriate in a sale of a partial interest if the transaction is in fact a partial sale of real estate and all the following conditions exist:

- Sale is to an independent buyer.
- Collection of sales price is reasonably assured.
- The seller will not be required to support the property, its operations, or related obligations to an extent greater than its proportionate interest.
- Buyer does not have preferences as to profits or cash flow. (If the buyer has such preferences, the cost recovery method is required.)

In the case of a sale of a partial interest in real estate, if the conditions set forth in the preceding paragraph are met, profit recognition must reflect an adjustment for the implied presumption that the seller is obligated to support the operations.

SELLER HAS EQUITY INTEREST IN BUYER
No profit may be recognized if the seller controls the buyer. If seller does not control the buyer, profit recognition (to the extent of the other investors' proportionate interests) is appropriate if all other necessary requirements for profit recognition are satisfied. The portion of the profit applicable to the equity interest of the seller/investor should be deferred until such costs are charged to operations by the venture. Again, with respect to a sale of real estate, a portion of the profit relating to other investors' interests may have to be spread as described in Subsection 30.2(f)(x), because there is an implied presumption that the seller is obligated to support the operations.

(g) SALES OF CONDOMINIUMS   Although the definition of *condominium* varies by state, the term generally is defined as a multiunit structure in which there is fee simple title to individual units combined with an undivided interest in the common elements associated with the structure. The common elements are all areas exclusive of the individual units, such as hallways, lobbies, and elevators.

A cooperative is contrasted to a condominium in that ownership of the building is generally vested in the entity, with the respective stockholders of the entity having a right to occupy specific units. Operation, maintenance, and control of the building are exercised by a governing board elected by the owners. This section covers only sales of condominium units.

(i) Criteria for Profit Recognition   The general principles of accounting for profit on sales of condominiums are essentially those previously discussed for sales of real estate in general. The following criteria must be met prior to recognition of any profit on the sale of a dwelling unit in a condominium project:

- All parties must be bound by the terms of the contract. For the buyer to be bound, the buyer must be unable to require a refund. Certain state and federal laws require appropriate filings by the developer before the sales contract is binding; otherwise, the sale may be voidable at the option of the buyer.
- All conditions precedent to closing, except completion of the project, must be performed.
- An adequate cash down payment must be received by the seller. The minimum down payment requirements are 5 percent for a primary residence and 10 percent for a secondary or recreational residence.
- The buyer must be required to adequately increase the investment in the property annually; the buyer's commitment must be adequately secured. Typically, a condominium buyer pays the remaining balance from the proceeds of a permanent loan at the time of closing. If, however, the seller provides financing, the same considerations as other sales of real estate apply concerning amortization of the buyer's receivable.
- The developer must not have an option or obligation to repurchase the property.

(ii) Methods of Accounting   Sales of condominium units are accounted for by using the closing (completed contract) method or the percentage of completion method. Most developers use the closing method.

Additional criteria must be met for the use of the percentage of completion method:

- The developer must have the ability to estimate costs not yet incurred.
- Construction must be beyond a preliminary stage of completion. This generally means at least beyond the foundation stage.
- Sufficient units must be sold to assure that the property will not revert to rental property.
- The developer must be able to reasonably estimate aggregate sales proceeds.

CLOSING METHOD

This method involves recording the sale and related profit at the time a unit closes. Since the unit is completed, actual costs are used in determining profit to be recognized.

All payments or deposits received prior to closing are accounted for as a liability. Direct selling costs may be deferred until the sale is recorded. Where the seller is obligated to complete construction of common areas or has made guarantees to the condominium association, profit should be recognized based on the relationship of costs already incurred to total estimated costs, with a portion deferred until the future performance is completed.

Percentage of Completion Method

This method generally involves recording sales at the date a unit is sold and recognizing profit on units sold as construction proceeds. As a result, this method allows some profit recognition during the construction period. Although dependent on estimates, this method may be considered preferable for some long-term projects. A lack of reliable estimates, however, would preclude the use of this method.

Profit recognition is based on the percentage of completion of the project multiplied by the gross profit arising from the units sold. Percentage of completion may be determined by using either of the following alternatives:

- The ratio of costs incurred to date to total estimated costs to be incurred. These costs could include land and common costs or could be limited to construction costs. The costs selected for inclusion should be those that most clearly reflect the earnings process.
- The percentage of completed construction based on architectural plans or engineering studies.

Under either method of accounting, if the total estimated costs exceed the estimated proceeds, the total anticipated loss should be charged against income in the period in which the loss becomes evident so that no anticipated losses are deferred to future periods. See further discussion of this method in Section 30.6, "Construction Revenue Recognition."

(iii) Estimated Future Costs   As previously mentioned, future costs to complete must be estimated under either the closing method or the percentage of completion method. Estimates of future costs to complete are necessary to determine net realizable value of unsold units. Estimated future costs should be based on adequate plans and detail studies and should include reasonable provisions for:

- Unforeseen costs in accordance with sound cost estimation practices
- Anticipated cost inflation in the construction industry
- Costs of off-site improvements, utility facilities, and amenities (to the extent that they will not be recovered from outside third parties)
- Operating losses of utility operations and recreational facilities (Such losses would be expected to be incurred for a relatively limited period of time—usually prior to sale of facilities or transfer to some public authority.)
- Other guaranteed support arrangements or activities to the extent that they will not be recovered from outside parties or be the responsibility of a future purchaser

Estimates of amounts to be recovered from any sources should be discounted to present value as of the date the related costs are expected to be incurred.

Estimated costs to complete and the allocation of such costs should be reviewed at the end of each financial reporting period, with costs revised and reallocated as necessary on the basis of current estimates, as recommended in SFAS No. 67, "Accounting for Costs and Initial

Rental Operations of Real Estate Projects." How to record the effects of changes in estimates depends on whether full revenues have been recorded or reporting of the revenue has been deferred due to an obligation for future performance or otherwise.

When sales of condominiums are recorded in full, it may be necessary to accrue certain estimated costs not yet incurred and also related profit thereon. Adjustments of accruals for costs applicable to such previously recognized sales, where deferral for future performance was not required, must be recognized and charged to costs of sales in the period in which they become known. See Subsection 30.2(g)(ii) for further discussion.

In many cases, sales are not recorded in full (such as when the seller has deferred revenue because of an obligation for future performance to complete improvements and amenities of a project). In these situations, the adjustments should not affect previously recorded deferred revenues applicable to future improvements but should be recorded prospectively in the current and future periods. An increase in the estimate of costs applicable to deferred revenues will thus result in profit margins lower than those recorded on previous revenues from the project. Consistency in the result of gross profit percentages (relative sales value) from period to period is an indicator of adequate development performance and sales.

An exception exists, however, when the revised total estimated costs exceed the applicable deferred revenue. If that occurs, the total anticipated loss should be charged against income in the period in which the need for adjustment becomes evident.

In addition, an increase in estimated costs to complete without comparable increases in market value could raise questions as to whether the estimated total costs of the remaining property exceed the project's net realizable value.

APB Opinion No. 20, "Accounting Changes," has been interpreted to permit both the cumulative catch-up method and the prospective method of accounting for changes in accounting estimates. It should be noted that SFAS No. 67 (pars. 42–43) requires the prospective method.

(h) RETAIL LAND SALES Retail land sales, a unique segment of the real estate industry, is the retail marketing of numerous lots subdivided from a larger parcel of land. The relevant accounting guidance originally covered by the AICPA Industry Accounting Guide, "Accounting for Retail Land Sales," and now included in SFAS No. 66, applies to retail lot sales on a volume basis with down payments that are less than those required to evaluate the collectability of casual sales of real estate. Wholesale or bulk sales of land and retail sales from projects comprising a small number of lots, however, are subject to the general principles for profit recognition on real estate sales.

(i) Criteria for Recording a Sale   Sales should not be recorded until:

- The customer has made all required payments and the period of cancellation with refund has expired.
- Aggregate payments (including interest) equal or exceed 10 percent of contract sales price.
- The selling company is clearly capable of providing land improvements and off-site facilities promised as well as meeting all other representations it has made.

If these conditions are met, either the full accrual or the installment method can be used. If the conditions are not met, the deposit method of accounting should be used.

(ii) Criteria for Full Accrual Method　　The following tests for the use of full accrual method should be applied on a project-by-project basis:

- The seller has fulfilled the obligation to complete improvements and to construct amenities or other facilities applicable to the lots sold.
- The receivable is not subject to subordination to new loans on the property, except subordination for home construction purposes under certain conditions.
- The collection experience for the project indicates that collectability of receivable balances is reasonably predictable and that 90 percent of the contracts in force six months after sales are recorded will be collected in full. A down payment of at least 20 percent shall be an acceptable indication of collectability.

To predict collection results of current sales, there must be satisfactory experience on prior sales of the type of land being currently sold in the project. In addition, the collection period must be sufficiently long to allow reasonable estimates of the percentage of sales that will be fully collected. In a new project, the developers' experience on prior projects may be used if they have demonstrated an ability to successfully develop other projects with the same characteristics (environment, clientele, contract terms, and sales methods) as the new project.

Collection and cancellation experience within a project may differ with varying sales methods (such as telephone, broker, and site visitation sales). Accordingly, historical data should be maintained with respect to each type of sales method used.

Unless all conditions for use of the full accrual method are met for the entire project, the installment method of accounting should be applied to all recorded sales of the project.

(iii) Full Accrual Method　　Revenues and costs should be accounted for under the full accrual method as follows:

- The contract price should be recorded as gross sales.
- Receivables should be discounted to reflect an appropriate interest rate using the criteria established in APB Opinion No. 21.
- An allowance for contract cancellation should be recorded and deducted from gross sales to derive net sales.
- Cost of sales should be calculated based on net sales after reductions for sales reasonably expected to cancel.

(iv) Percentage of Completion Method　　Frequently, the conditions for use of the full accrual method are met, except the seller has not yet completed the improvements, amenities, or other facilities required by the sales contract. In this situation the percentage of completion method should be applied provided both of the following conditions are met:

- There is a reasonable expectation that the land can be developed for the purposes represented.
- The project's improvements have progressed beyond preliminary stages, and there are indications that the work will be completed according to plan. Indications that the project has progressed beyond the preliminary stage include the following:
  - Funds for the proposed improvements have been expended.
  - Work on the improvements has been initiated.

○ Engineering plans and work commitments exist relating to the lots sold.
○ Access roads and amenities such as golf courses, clubhouses, and swimming pools have been completed.

In addition, there shall be no indication of significant delaying factors such as the inability to obtain permits, contractors, personnel, or equipment, and estimates of costs to complete and extent of progress toward completion shall be reasonably dependable.

The following general procedures should be used to account for revenues and costs under the percentage of completion method of accounting:

• The amount of revenue recognized (discounted where appropriate pursuant to APB Opinion No. 21) is based on the relationship of costs already incurred to the total estimated costs to be incurred.
• Costs incurred and to be incurred should include land, interest, and project carrying costs incurred prior to sale, selling costs, and an estimate for future improvement costs.

Estimates of future improvement costs should be reviewed at least annually. Changes in those estimates do not lead to adjustment of deferred revenue applicable to future improvements that has been previously recorded unless the adjusted total estimated costs exceed the applicable revenue. When cost estimates are revised, the relationship of the two elements included in the revenue not yet recognized—cost and profit—should be recalculated on a cumulative basis to determine future income recognition as performance takes place. If the adjusted total estimated cost exceeds the applicable deferred revenue, the total anticipated loss should be charged to income. When anticipated losses on lots sold are recognized, the enterprise should also consider recognizing a loss on land and improvements not yet sold.

Future performance costs such as roads, utilities, and amenities may represent a significant obligation for a retail land developer. Estimates of such costs should be based on detail estimates, appropriately adjusted for anticipated inflation in the local construction industry, and should include reasonable estimates for unforeseen costs.

(v) Installment and Deposit Methods   If the criteria for the full accrual or percentage of completion methods are not satisfied, the installment or deposit method may be used. See Subsection 30.2(j) for a general discussion of these methods.

When the conditions required for use of the percentage of completion method are met on a project originally recorded under the installment method, the percentage of completion method of accounting should be adopted for the entire project (current and prior sales). The effect should be accounted for as a change in accounting estimate due to different circumstances and revised estimates. See Subsection 30.2(g)(iii) for further discussion of methodology.

(i) ACCOUNTING FOR SYNDICATION FEES   On February 6, 1992, the AICPA issued Statement of Position (SOP) 92-1, which provides guidance on accounting for real estate syndication income.

Syndicators expect to earn fees and commissions from a variety of sources: up-front fees such as lease-up fees, construction supervision fees, and financing fees; fees serving as an incentive; property management; participation in future profit or appreciation. At the time of the syndication, partnerships usually pay cash to the syndicator for portions of their up-front fees. These fees are usually paid from investor contributions or the proceeds of borrowings. Subsequent fees are expected to be paid from operations, refinancings, sales of property, or remaining investor payments.

The SOP states that SFAS No. 66 applies to the recognition of profit on the sales of real estate by syndicators to partnerships. It concludes that profit on real estate syndication transactions be accounted for in accordance with SFAS No. 66, even if the syndicator never had ownership interests in the properties acquired by the real estate partnerships.

The SOP states that fees charged by syndicators (except for syndication fees and fees for future services) should be included in the determination of "sales value" in conformity with SFAS No. 66. It further states that SFAS No. 66 does not apply to the fees excluded from sales value. Fees for future services should be recognized when the earning process is complete and collection of the fee is reasonably assured.

This SOP requires that income recognition on syndication fees and fees for future services be deferred if the syndicator is exposed to future losses or costs from material involvement with the properties, partnerships or partners, or uncertainties regarding the collectability of partnership notes. The income should be deferred until the losses or costs can be reasonably estimated.

The SOP requires that for the purpose of determining whether buyers' initial and continuing investments satisfy the requirements for recognizing full profit in accordance with SFAS No. 66, cash received by syndicators should be allocated to unpaid syndication fees before being allocated to the initial and continuing investment. After the syndication fee is fully paid, additional cash received should first be allocated to unpaid fees for future services, to the extent those services have been performed by the time the cash is received, before being allocated to the initial and continuing investment.

(j) ALTERNATE METHODS OF ACCOUNTING FOR SALES   As previously discussed, in some circumstances the full accrual method is not appropriate and other methods must be used. It is not always clear which method should be used or how it should be applied. Consequently, it is often difficult to determine the appropriate method and whether alternative ones are acceptable.

The methods of profit recognition prescribed where the buyer's initial or continuing investment is inadequate are the deposit, installment, cost recovery, and reduced profit methods.

The methods prescribed for a transaction that cannot be considered a sale because of the seller's continuing involvement are the financing, lease, and profit-sharing (or co-venture) methods.

(i) Deposit Method   When the substance of a real estate transaction indicates that as a result of the buyer's inadequate investment a sale has not occurred, recognition of the sale should be deferred and the deposit method used even if it was a legal sale. This method should be continued until the conditions have changed to indicate a sale. For example, when the down payment is so small that the substance of the transaction is an option arrangement, the sale should not be recorded.

All cash received under the deposit method (including down payment and principal and interest payments by the buyer to the seller) should be reported as a deposit (liability). An exception is interest received that is not subject to refund, which may appropriately offset carrying charges (property taxes and interest on existing debt) on the property. Note also the following related matters:

- Notes receivable arising from the transaction should not be recorded.
- The property and any related mortgage debt assumed by the buyer should continue to be reflected on the seller's balance sheet, with appropriate disclosure that such properties and debt are subject to a sales contract. Even nonrecourse debt assumed by the buyer should not be offset against the related property.
- Subsequent payments on the debt assumed by the buyer become additional deposits and thereby reduce the seller's mortgage debt payable and increase the deposit liability account until a sale is recorded for accounting purposes.
- Depreciation should be continued.

. Under the deposit method, a sale is not recorded for accounting purposes until the conditions in SFAS No. 66 are met. Therefore, for purposes of the down payment tests, interest received and credited to the deposit account can be included in the down payment and sales value at the time a sale is recorded.

If a buyer defaults and forfeits his or her nonrefundable deposit, the deposit liability is no longer required and may be credited to income. The circumstances underlying the default should be carefully reviewed since such circumstances may indicate deteriorating value of the property. In such a case it may be appropriate to treat the credit as a valuation reserve. These circumstances may require a provision for additional loss. See Section 30.5 for further discussion.

(ii) Installment Method When the substance of a real estate transaction indicates that a sale has occurred for accounting purposes, but that collectability of the total sales price cannot be reasonably estimated (e.g., inadequate buyer's investment), the installment method may be appropriate. However, circumstances may indicate that the cost recovery method is required or is otherwise more appropriate. For example, when the deferred gross profit exceeds the net carrying value of the related receivable, profit may have been earned to the extent of such excess.

Profit should be recognized on cash payments, including principal payments by the buyer on any debt assumed (either recourse or nonrecourse), and should be based on the ratio of total profit to total sales value (including a first mortgage debt assumed by the buyer, if applicable). Interest received on the related receivable is properly recorded as income when received.

The total sales value (from which the deferred gross profit should be deducted) and the cost of sales should be presented in the income statement. Deferred gross profit should be shown as a deduction from the related receivable, with subsequent income recognition presented separately in the income statement.

(iii) Cost Recovery Method The cost recovery method must be used when the substance of a real estate transaction indicates that a sale has occurred but major uncertainties exist. This may occur when (1) the receivable is subject to future subordination, (2) the seller retains an interest in the property sold and the buyer has preferences, (3) uncertainty exists as to whether all or a portion of the cost will be recovered, or (4) there is uncertainty as to the amount of proceeds. As a practical matter, the cost recovery method can always be used as an alternative to the installment method.

Under the cost recovery method, no profit is recognized until cash collections (including principal and interest payments) and existing debt assumed by the buyer exceed the cost of the property sold. Cash collections in excess of cost should be recorded as revenue in the period of collection.

Financial statement presentation under the cost recovery method is similar to that for the installment method.

(iv) Reduced Profit Method   When the substance of a real estate transaction indicates that a sale has occurred for accounting purposes, but the continuing investment criteria for full profit recognition are not met by the buyer, the seller may sometimes recognize a reduced profit at the time of sale (see additional discussion in Subsection 30.2(e)(ii)). This alternative is usually used when the portion of the seller's receivable that is contingent upon some indicator is applied as a reduction of the sales price, thereby reducing the full profit, if any, until collection is assured.

(v) Financing Method   A real estate transaction may be, in substance, a financing arrangement rather than a sale. This is frequently the case when the seller has an obligation to repurchase the property or can be compelled by the buyer to repurchase the property. In such a case the financing method of accounting must be used.

Accounting procedures under the financing method should be similar to the accounting procedures under the deposit method, with one exception. Under the financing method, the difference between (1) the total amount of all payments received and to be received and (2) the repurchase price is presumed to be interest expense. As such, it should be accrued on the interest method over the period from the receipt of cash to the date of repurchase. As in the deposit method, cash received is reflected as a liability in the balance sheet. Thus, at the date of repurchase, the full amount of the repurchase obligation should be recorded as a liability.

In the case of a repurchase option, if the facts and circumstances at the time of the sale indicate a presumption or a likelihood that the seller will repurchase the property, interest should be accrued as if there were an obligation to repurchase. This presumption could result from the value of the property, the property being an integral part of development, or from management's intention. If such a presumption does not exist at the time of the sale transaction, interest should not be accrued and the deposit method is appropriate.

(vi) Lease Method   A real estate transaction may be, in substance, a lease rather than a sale. Accounting procedures under the lease method should be similar to the deposit method, except as follows:

- Payments received and to be received that are in substance deferred rental income received in advance should be deferred and amortized to income over the presumed lease period. Such amortization to income should not exceed cash paid to the seller.
- Cash paid out by the seller as a guarantee of support of operations should be expensed as paid.

The seller may agree to make *loans* to the *buyer* in support of operations, for example, when cash flow does not equal a predetermined amount or is negative. In such a situation, deferred rental income to be amortized to income should be reduced by all the loans made or reasonably anticipated to be made to the buyer, thus reducing the periodic income to be recognized. Where the loans made or anticipated exceed deferred rental income, a loss provision may be required if the collectability of the loan is questionable.

(vii) Profit-Sharing or Co-Venture Method   A real estate transaction may be, in substance, a profit-sharing arrangement rather than a sale. For example, a sale of real estate to a limited partnership in which the seller is a general partner or has similar characteristics is often a profit-sharing arrangement. If such a transaction does not meet the tests for recording a sale, it usually would be accounted for under the profit-sharing method. This accounting method should also be followed when it is clear that the buyer and seller are acting in consort for future profits.

Under the profit-sharing method, giving consideration to the seller's continued involvement, the seller would be required to account for its share of the operations of the property through the venture's income statement on an equity or consolidated basis.

30.3 CAPITALIZED COST OF REAL ESTATE

(a) CAPITALIZATION OF COSTS   In October 1982, the FASB issued SFAS No. 67. This statement incorporates the specialized accounting principles and practices from the AICPA SOP No. 80-3, "Accounting for Real Estate Acquisition, Development, and Construction Costs," and SOP No. 78-3, "Accounting for Costs to Sell and Rent, and Initial Rental Operations of Real Estate Projects," and those in the AICPA Industry Accounting Guide, "Accounting for Retail Land Sales," that address costs of real estate projects. SFAS No. 67 establishes whether costs associated with acquiring, developing, constructing, selling, and renting real estate projects should be capitalized. Guidance is also provided on the appropriate methods of allocating capitalized costs to individual components of the project.

SFAS No. 67 also established that a rental project changes from nonoperating to operating when it is substantially completed and held available for occupancy, but not later than one year from cessation of major construction activities.

Costs incurred in real estate operations range from bricks-and-mortar costs that clearly should be capitalized to general administrative costs that clearly should not be capitalized. Between these two extremes lies a broad range of costs that are difficult to classify. Therefore, judgmental decisions must be made as to whether such costs should be capitalized.

(b) PREACQUISITION COSTS   These costs include payments to obtain options to acquire real property and other costs incurred prior to acquisition such as legal, architectural, and other professional fees, salaries, environmental studies, appraisals, marketing and feasibility studies, and soil tests. Capitalization of costs related to a property that are incurred before the enterprise acquires the property, or before the enterprise obtains an option to acquire it, is appropriate provided all of the following conditions are met:

- The costs are directly identifiable with the specific property.
- The costs would be capitalized if the property had already been acquired.
- Acquisition of the property or of an option to acquire the property is probable (i.e., likely to occur). This condition requires that the prospective purchaser is actively seeking acquisition of the property and has the ability to finance or obtain financing for the acquisition. In addition, there should be no indication that the property is not available for sale.

Capitalized preacquisition costs should be included as project costs on acquisition of the property or should be written off to expense when it is probable that the property will not be acquired. The charge to expense should be reduced by the amount recoverable by the recapturing of the preacquistion costs.

(c) LAND ACQUISITION COSTS   Costs directly related to the acquisition of land should be capitalized. These costs include option fees, purchase cost, transfer costs, title insurance, legal and other professional fees, surveys, appraisals, and real estate commissions. The purchase cost may have to be increased or decreased for market adjustment imputation of interest on mortgage notes payable assumed or issued in connection with the purchase, as required under APB Opinion No. 21.

(d) LAND IMPROVEMENT, DEVELOPMENT, AND CONSTRUCTION COSTS   Costs directly related to improvements of the land should be capitalized by the developer. They usually include:

- Land planning costs, including marketing and feasibility studies, direct salaries, legal and other professional fees, zoning costs, soil tests, architectural and engineering studies, appraisals, environmental studies, and other costs directly related to site preparation and the overall design and development of the project
- On-site and off-site improvements, including demolition costs, streets, traffic controls, sidewalks, street lighting, sewer and water facilities, utilities, parking lots, landscaping, and related costs such as permits and inspection fees
- Construction costs, including onsite material and labor, direct supervision, engineering and architectural fees, permits, and inspection fees
- Project overhead and supervision, such as field office costs
- Recreation facilities, such as golf courses, clubhouses, swimming pools, and tennis courts
- Sales center and models, including furnishings

General and administrative costs not directly identified with the project should be accounted for as period costs and expensed as incurred.

Construction activity on a project may be suspended before a project is completed for reasons such as insufficient funding, sales, or rental demand. These conditions may indicate an impairment of the value of a project that is other than temporary, which suggests valuation issues (see Section 30.5).

(e) ENVIRONMENTAL ISSUES   In EITF Issue No. 90-8, "Capitalization of Costs to Treat Environmental Contamination," the EITF reached a consensus that, in general, costs incurred as a result of environmental contamination should be charged to expense. Such costs include costs to remove contamination, such as that caused by leakage from underground tanks; costs to acquire tangible property, such as air pollution control equipment; costs of environmental studies; and costs of fines levied under environmental laws. Nevertheless, those costs may be capitalized if recoverable but only if any one of the following criteria is met:

- The costs extend the life, increase the capacity, or improve the safety or efficiency of property owned by the company, provided that the condition of the property after the costs are incurred must be improved as compared with the condition of the property when originally constructed or acquired, if later.
- The costs mitigate or prevent environmental contamination that has yet to occur and that otherwise may result from future operations or activities. In addition, the costs

improve the property compared with its condition when constructed or acquired, if later.

- The costs are incurred in preparing for sale that property currently held for sale.

In EITF Issue No. 93-5, "Accounting for Environmental Liabilities," the EITF reached a consensus that an environmental liability should be evaluated independently from any potential claim for recovery (a two-event approach) and that the loss arising from the recognition of an environmental liability should be reduced only when it is probable that a claim for recovery will be realized.

The EITF also reached a consensus that discounting environmental liabilities for a specific clean-up site to reflect the time value of money is allowed, but not required, only if the aggregate amount of the obligation and the amount and timing of the cash payments for that site are fixed or reliably determinable.

The EITF discussed alternative rates to be used in discounting environmental liabilities but did not reach a consensus on the rate to be used. However, the Securities and Exchange Commission (SEC) observer stated that SEC registrants should use a discount rate that will produce an amount at which the environmental liability theoretically could be settled in an arm's-length transaction with a third party. That discount rate should not exceed the interest rate on monetary assets that are essentially risk-free (e.g., U.S. Treasury notes) and have maturities comparable to that of the environmental liability. In addition, SEC Staff Accounting Bulletin (SAB) 92 requires registrants to separately present the gross liability and related claim recovery in the balance sheet. SAB 92 also requires other accounting and disclosure requirements relating to product or environmental liabilities.

In October 1996, the AICPA issued SOP 96-1, "Environmental Remediation Liabilities." The SOP has three parts. Part I provides an overview of environmental laws and regulations. Part II provides authoritative guidance on the recognition, measurement, display, and disclosure of environmental liabilities. And Part III (labeled as an appendix) provides guidance for auditors. A major objective of the SOP is to articulate a framework for the recognition, measurement, and disclosure of environmental liabilities. That framework is derived from SFAS No. 5, "Accounting for Contingencies."

The accounting guidance in the SOP is generally applicable when an entity is mandated to remediate a contaminated site by a governmental agency. However, the SOP does not address the following:

- Accounting for pollution control costs with respect to current operations, which is addressed in EITF Issue No. 90-8, "Capitalization of Costs to Treat Environmental Contamination"
- Accounting for costs with respect to asbestos removal, which is addressed in EITF Issue No. 89-13, "Accounting for the Costs of Asbestos Removal"
- Accounting for costs of future site restoration or closure that are required upon the cessation of operations or sale of facilities, which is the subject of the FASB's project, "Obligations Associated with Disposal Activities"
- Accounting for environmental remediation actions that are undertaken at the sole discretion of management and that are not undertaken by the threat of assertion of litigation, a claim, or an assessment
- Recognizing liabilities of insurance companies for unpaid claims, which is addressed in SFAS No. 60, "Accounting and Reporting by Insurance Enterprises"

- Asset impairment issues discussed in SFAS No. 144, "Accounting for the Impairment or Disposal of Long-Lived Assets," and EITF Issue No. 95-23, "The Treatment of Certain Site Restoration/Environmental Exit Costs When Testing a Long-Lived Asset for Impairment"

(f) INTEREST COSTS   Prior to 1979, many developers capitalized interest costs as a necessary cost of the asset in the same way as bricks-and-mortar costs. Others followed an accounting policy of charging off interest cost as a period cost on the basis that it was solely a financing cost that varied directly with the capability of a company to finance development and construction through equity funds. This long-standing debate on capitalization of interest costs was resolved in October 1979 when the FASB published SFAS No. 34, "Capitalization of Interest Cost," which provides specific guidelines for accounting for interest costs.

SFAS No. 34 requires capitalization of interest costs as part of the historical cost of acquiring assets that need a period of time in which to bring them to that condition and location necessary for their intended use. The objectives of capitalizing interest are to obtain a measure of acquisition cost that more closely reflects the enterprise's total investment in the asset and to charge a cost that relates to the acquisition of a resource that will benefit future periods against the revenues of the periods benefited. Interest capitalization is not required if its effect is not material.

(i) Assets Qualifying for Interest Capitalization   Assets qualifying for interest capitalization in conformity with SFAS No. 34 include real estate constructed for an enterprise's own use or real estate intended for sale or lease. Qualifying assets also include investments accounted for by the equity method while the investee has activities in progress necessary to commence its planned principal operations, but only if the investee's activities include the use of such to acquire qualifying assets for its operations.

Capitalization is not permitted for assets in use or ready for their intended use, assets not undergoing the activities necessary to prepare them for use, assets that are not included in the consolidated balance sheet, or investments accounted for by the equity method after the planned principal operations of the investee begin. Thus, land that is not undergoing activities necessary for development is not a qualifying asset for purposes of interest capitalization. If activities are undertaken for developing the land, the expenditures to acquire the land qualify for interest capitalization while those activities are in progress.

(ii) Capitalization Period   The capitalization period commences when:

- Costs for the asset have been incurred.
- Activities that are necessary to get the asset ready for its intended use are in progress.
- Interest cost is being incurred.

Activities are to be construed in a broad sense and encompass more than just physical construction. All steps necessary to prepare an asset for its intended use are included. This broad interpretation includes administrative and technical activities during the preconstruction stage (such as developing plans or obtaining required permits).

Interest capitalization must end when the asset is substantially complete and ready for its intended use. A real estate project should be considered substantially complete and held available for occupancy upon completion of major construction activity, as distinguished from activities such as routine maintenance and cleanup. In some cases, such as in an office building, tenant improvements are a major construction activity and are frequently not completed until a lease contract is arranged. If such improvements are the responsibility of the developer, SFAS No. 67 indicates that the project is not considered substantially complete until the earlier of (1) completion of improvements or (2) one year from cessation of major construction activity without regard to tenant improvements. In other words, a one-year grace period has been provided to complete tenant improvements.

If substantially all activities related to acquisition of the asset are suspended, interest capitalization should stop and be expensed until such activities are resumed. However, brief interruptions in activities, interruptions caused by external factors, and inherent delays in the development process do not necessarily require suspension of interest capitalization.

Under SFAS No. 34, interest capitalization must end when the asset is substantially complete and ready for its intended use. For projects completed in parts, where each part is capable of being used independently while work continues on other parts, interest capitalization should stop and be expensed on each part that is substantially complete and ready for use. Examples include individual buildings in a multiphase or condominium project. For projects that must be completed before any part can be used, interest capitalization should continue until the entire project is substantially complete and ready for use. Where an asset cannot be used effectively until a particular portion has been completed, interest capitalization continues until that portion is substantially complete and ready for use. An example would be an island resort complex with sole access being a permanent bridge to the project. Completion of the bridge is necessary for the asset to be used effectively.

Interest capitalization should not stop when the capitalized costs exceed net realizable value. In such instances, a valuation reserve should be recorded or appropriately increased to reduce the carrying value to net realizable value.

(iii) Methods of Interest Capitalization The basic principle is that the amount of interest cost to be capitalized should be the amount that theoretically could have been avoided during the development and construction period if expenditures for the qualifying asset had not been made. These interest costs might have been avoided either by forgoing additional borrowing or by using the funds expended for the asset to repay existing borrowings in the case where no new borrowings were obtained.

The amount capitalized is determined by applying an interest rate to the average amount of accumulated capitalized expenditures for the asset during the period. Such expenditures include cash payments, transfer of other assets, or incurrence of liabilities on which interest has been recognized, and they should be net of progress payments received against such capitalized costs. Liabilities such as trade payables, accruals, and retainages on which interest is not recognized, are not expenditures. Reasonable approximations of net capitalized expenditures may be used.

In general, the interest rate should be based on the weighted average of the rates applicable to borrowings outstanding during the period. If a specific new borrowing is associated with an asset, the rate on that borrowing may be used. If the average amount of accumulated expenditures for the asset exceeds the amounts of specific new borrowings associated with the asset, a weighted average interest rate of all other borrowings must be applied to the excess. Under this alternative, judgment will be required to select the borrowings to be included in the weighted average rate so that a reasonable measure will be obtained of the interest cost incurred that could otherwise have been avoided. It should be remembered that the principle is not one of capitalizing interest costs incurred for a specific asset, but one of capitalizing interest costs that could have been avoided if it were not for the acquisition, development, and construction of the asset.

The amount of interest cost capitalized in an accounting period is limited to the total amount of interest cost incurred in the period. However, interest cost should include amortization of premium or discount resulting from imputation of interest on certain types of payables in accordance with APB Opinion No. 21 and that portion of minimum lease payments under a capital lease treated as interest in accordance with SFAS No. 13.

(iv) Accounting for Amount Capitalized   Interest cost capitalized is an integral part of the cost of acquiring a qualifying asset, and therefore its disposition should be the same as any other cost of that asset. For example, if a building is subsequently depreciated, capitalized interest should be included in the depreciable base the same as bricks and mortar.

In the case of interest capitalized on an investment accounted for by the equity method, its disposition should be made as if the investee were consolidated. In other words, if the assets of the investee were being depreciated, the capitalized interest cost should be depreciated in the same manner and over the same lives. If the assets of the investee were developed lots being sold, the capitalized interest cost should be written off as the lots are sold.

(g) TAXES AND INSURANCE   Costs incurred on real estate for property taxes and insurance should be treated similarly to interest costs. They should be capitalized only during periods in which activities necessary to get the property ready for its intended use are in progress. Costs incurred for such items after the property is substantially complete and ready for its intended use should be charged to expense as incurred.

(h) INDIRECT PROJECT COSTS   Indirect project costs that relate to a specific project, such as costs associated with a project field office, should be capitalized as a cost of that project. Other indirect project costs that relate to several projects, such as the costs associated with a construction administration department, should be capitalized and allocated to the projects to which the cost relates. Indirect costs that do not clearly relate to projects under development or construction should be charged to expense as incurred. The principal problem is defining and identifying the cost to be capitalized. It is necessary to consider all of the following points:

- Specific information should be available (such as time cards) to support the basis of allocation to specific projects.
- The costs incurred should be incremental costs; that is, in the absence of the project or projects under development or construction, these costs would not be incurred.
- The impact of capitalization of such costs on the results of operations should be consistent with the pervasive principle of matching costs with related revenue.
- The principle of conservatism should be considered.

Indirect costs related to a specific project that should be considered for capitalization include direct and indirect salaries of a field office and insurance costs. Costs that are not directly related to the project should be charged to expense as incurred. An appropriate test for the capitalization of indirect costs is to question the existence of these costs if no project were being developed. If the answer is yes then they should be expensed as incurred.

(i) GENERAL AND ADMINISTRATIVE EXPENSES   Real estate developers incur various types of general and administrative expenses, including officers' salaries, accounting and legal fees, and various office supplies and expenses. Some of these expenses may be closely associated with individual projects, whereas others are of a more general nature. For example, a developer may open a field office on a project site and staff it with administrative personnel, such as a field accountant. The expenses associated with the field office are directly associated with the project and are therefore considered to be overhead. By contrast, the developer may have a number of expenses associated with general office operations that benefit numerous projects and for which specifically identifiable allocations are not reasonable or practicable. Those administrative costs that cannot be clearly related to projects under development or construction should be charged to current operations.

(j) AMENITIES   Real estate developments often include amenities such as golf courses, utilities, clubhouses, swimming pools, and tennis courts. The accounting for the costs of these amenities should be based on management's intended disposition as follows:

- *Amenity to be sold or transferred with sales units.* All costs in excess of anticipated proceeds should be allocated as common costs because the amenity is clearly associated with the development and sale of the project. Common costs should include estimated net operating costs to be borne by the developer until they are assumed by buyers of units in the project.
- *Amenity to be sold separately or retained by developer.* Capitalizable costs of the amenity in excess of its estimated fair value on the expected date of its substantial physical completion should be allocated as common costs. The costs capitalized and allocated to the amenity should not be revised after the amenity is substantially completed and available for use. A later sale of the amenity at more or less than the determined fair value as of the date of substantial physical completion, less any accumulated depreciation, should result in a gain or loss in the period in which the sale occurs.

(k) ABANDONMENTS AND CHANGES IN USE   Real estate, including rights to real estate, may be abandoned, for example, by allowing a mortgage to be foreclosed or by allowing a purchase option to lapse. Capitalized costs, including allocated common costs, of real estate abandoned should be written off as current expenses or, if appropriate, to allowances previously established for that purpose. They should not be allocated to other components of the project or to other projects, even if other components or other projects are capable of absorbing the losses.

Donation of real estate to municipalities or other governmental agencies for uses that will benefit the project are not abandonment. The cost of real estate donated should be allocated as a common cost of the project.

Changes in the intended use of a real estate project may arise after significant development and construction costs have been incurred. If the change in use is made pursuant to a formal plan that is expected to produce a higher economic yield (as compared to its yield based on use before change), the project costs should be charged to expense to the extent the capitalized costs incurred and to be incurred exceed the estimated fair value less cost to sell of the revised project when it is substantially completed and ready for its intended use.

(l) SELLING COSTS   Costs incurred to sell real estate projects should be accounted for in the same manner as, and classified with, construction costs of the project when they meet both of the following criteria:

- The costs incurred are for tangible assets that are used throughout the selling period or for services performed to obtain regulatory approval for sales.
- The costs are reasonably expected to be recovered from sales of the project or incidental operations.

Examples of costs incurred to sell real estate projects that ordinarily meet the criteria for capitalization are costs of model units and their furnishings, sales facilities, legal fees for the preparation of prospectuses, and semipermanent signs.

SFAS No. 67 states that other costs incurred to sell real estate projects should be capitalized as prepaid costs if they are directly associated with and their recovery is reasonably expected from sales that are being accounted for under a method of accounting other than full accrual. Costs that do not meet the criteria for capitalization should be expensed as incurred.

Capitalized selling costs should be charged to expense in the period in which the related revenue is recognized as earned. When a sales contract is canceled (with or without refund) or the related receivable is written off as uncollectible, the related unrecoverable capitalized selling costs are charged to expense or to an allowance previously established for that purpose.

(m) ACCOUNTING FOR FORECLOSED ASSETS   AICPA SOP 92-3, "Accounting for Foreclosed Assets," provides guidance on determining the balance sheet treatment of foreclosed assets after foreclosure.

The SOP contains a rebuttable presumption that foreclosed assets are held for sale, rather than for the production of income. That presumption may be overcome if (1) management intends to hold a foreclosed asset, (2) laws and regulations as applied permit management to hold the asset, and (3) management's intent is supported by a preponderance of the evidence.

(i) Foreclosed Assets Held for Sale   After foreclosure, foreclosed assets held for sale should be carried at the lower of (1) fair value less estimated costs to sell or (2) net book value. The SOP states that, if the fair value of the asset less the estimated cost to sell is less than the asset's net book value, the deficiency should be recognized as an impairment expense. However, that provision has been superseded by SFAS No. 121 and SFAS No. 144, which prohibit the subsequent restoration of previously recognized impairment losses.

The amount of any senior debt (principal and accrued interest) to which the asset is subject should be reported as a liability at the time of foreclosure and should not be deducted from the carrying amount of the asset.

(ii) Foreclosed Assets Held for Production of Income   After foreclosure, assets determined to be held for the production of income (and not held for sale) should be accounted for in the same way that they would have been had the asset been acquired other than through foreclosure.

30.4   ALLOCATION OF COSTS

After it has been determined what costs are capitalized, it becomes important to determine how the costs should be allocated, because those costs will enter into the calculation of cost of sales of individual units and depreciation. Although a number of methods of allocation can be used in different circumstances, judgment often must be used to make sure that appropriate results are obtained.

(a) METHODS OF ALLOCATION   Capitalized costs of real estate projects should first be assigned to individual components of the project based on specific identification. If specific identification on an overall basis is not practicable, capitalized costs should be allocated as follows:

* Land costs and all other common costs should be allocated to each land parcel benefited. Allocation should be based on the relative fair value before construction.
* Construction costs should be assigned to buildings on a specific identification basis and allocated to individual units on the basis of relative value of each unit.

In the usual situation, individual sales prices or rental units are available to compute relative values. In rare situations, however, where relative value is impracticable, capitalized costs may be allocated based on the area method/or the relative cost method as appropriate under the circumstances.

The following sections describe the specific identification, value, and area methods of cost allocation.

(i) Specific Identification Method   The specific identification method of cost allocation is based on determining actual costs applicable to each component of real estate. It rarely is used for land costs because such costs usually encompass more than one parcel. However, it frequently is used for direct construction costs because these costs are directly related to the property being sold or held for use. This method should be used wherever practicable.

(ii) Value Method   The relative value method is the method usually used after direct costs have been assigned on a specific identification basis. Under this method, the allocation of common costs should be based on relative fair value (before value added by on-site development and construction activities) of each land parcel benefited. In multiproject developments, common costs are normally allocated based on estimated sales prices net of direct improvements and selling costs. This approach is usually the most appropriate because it is less likely to result in deferral of losses.

With respect to condominium sales, certain units will usually have a higher price because of location. With respect to time-sharing sales, holiday periods such as Easter, Fourth of July, and Christmas traditionally sell at a premium. Depending on the resort location, the summer or winter season will also sell at a premium compared with the rest of the year. Caution should be exercised to ensure that the relative sales values utilized in cost allocation are reasonable.

(iii) Area Method   This method of cost allocation is based on square footage, acreage, or frontage. The use of this method will not always result in a logical allocation of costs. When negotiating the purchase price for a large tract of land, the purchaser considers the overall utility of the tract, recognizing that various parcels in the tract are more valuable than others. For example, parcels on a lakefront are usually more valuable than those set back from the lake. In this situation, if a simple average based on square footage or acreage is used to allocate costs to individual parcels, certain parcels could be assigned costs in excess of their net realizable value.

Generally, the area method should be limited to situations where each individual parcel is estimated to have approximately the same relative value. Under such circumstances, the cost allocations as determined by either the area method or the value method would be approximately the same.

30.5 VALUATION ISSUES

Currently there are two major pronouncements issued by FASB that have a dramatic impact on real estate accounting. FASB issued SFAS No. 144, "Accounting for the Impairment or Disposal of Long-Lived Assets," and SFAS 157, "Fair Value Measurements."

(a) ACCOUNTING FOR THE IMPAIRMENT OR DISPOSAL OF LONG-LIVED ASSETS

FASB issued SFAS No. 144, "Accounting for the Impairment or Disposal of Long-Lived Assets," which supersedes SFAS No. 121, "Accounting for the Impairment of Long-Lived Assets and for Long-Lived Assets to Be Disposed Of." SFAS No. 144 retains many of the fundamental provisions of SFAS No. 121, particularly that long-lived assets be measured at the lower of carrying amount or fair value less cost to sell.

A major change to previous practice is that the accounting model for long-lived assets to be disposed of by sale applies to all long-lived assets, including discontinued operations, thus superseding provisions of APB Opinion No. 30, "Reporting Results of Operations—Reporting the Effects of Disposal of a Segment of a Business." Discontinued operations no longer are measured at net realizable value, nor do they include amounts for operating losses that have not yet occurred. However, SFAS No. 144 retains the requirement in APB Opinion No. 30 to report separately discontinued operations and extends the reporting of discontinued operations to include all components of an entity with operations that can be distinguished from the rest of the entity and that will be eliminated from the ongoing operations of the entity in a disposal transaction. The new reporting requirements are intended to more clearly communicate in the financial statements a change in its business that results from a decision to dispose of operations and, thus, provide users with information needed to better focus on the ongoing activities of the entity.

In another major change from SFAS No. 121, the scope of SFAS No. 144 does not encompass goodwill. That is, goodwill will not be written down as a result of applying the statement, but goodwill may be included in the carrying amount of an asset group for purposes of applying the statement's provisions if that group is a reporting unit or includes a reporting unit. SFAS No. 144 also does not address impairment of other intangible assets that are not amortized; SFAS No. 142, "Goodwill and Other Intangible Assets," issued in July 2001, addresses impairment of goodwill and intangible assets that are not amortized.

(i) Real Estate to Be Held and Used   SFAS No. 144 establishes the following three steps for recognizing and measuring impairment on long-lived assets and certain identifiable intangibles to be held and used:

1. *Indicators.* The statement provides a list of indicators that serve as a warning light when the value of an asset to be held and used may have been impaired. The presence of any of the following indicators evidence a need for additional investigation:

   ○ A significant decrease in the market value of an asset
   ○ A significant change in the extent or manner in which an asset is used or a significant change in an asset
   ○ A significant adverse change in legal factors or in business climate that could affect the value of an asset or an adverse action or assessment by a regulator

  o An accumulation of costs significantly in excess of the amount originally expected to acquire or construct an asset

  o A current period operating or cash flow loss combined with a history of operating or cash flow losses or a projection or forecast that demonstrates continuing losses associated with an asset used for the purpose of producing revenue

  o A current expectation that it is more likely than not (greater than 50 percent likelihood) that an asset will be sold or otherwise disposed of significantly before the end of its previously estimated useful life

  The list of indicators is not intended to be all-inclusive. Other events or changes in circumstances may indicate that the carrying amount of an asset that an entity expects to hold and use may not be recoverable.

2. *Gross cash flow analysis.* An entity that detects one or more of the aforementioned indicators should evaluate whether the sum of the expected future net cash flows (undiscounted and without interest charges) associated with an asset to be held and used is at least equal to the asset's carrying amount. The FASB imposed a high threshold for triggering the impairment analysis. The selection of a cash flow test based on undiscounted amounts will trigger the recognition of an impairment loss less frequently than would a test based on fair value.

3. *Measurement.* For assets to be held and used, SFAS No. 144 requires an impairment loss to be measured as the amount by which the carrying amount of the impaired asset exceeds its fair value. The distinction between the recognition process, which uses undiscounted cash flows, and the measurement process, which uses fair value or discounted cash flows, is significant. As a result of a relatively minor change in undiscounted cash flows, the impairment measurement process might kick in, thus causing the balance sheet amount to drop off suddenly in any period in which undiscounted cash flows fall below a long-lived asset's carrying amount. Once assets to be held and used are written down, the statement does not permit them to be written back up.

  Thus, a new depreciable cost basis is established after a write-down, and subsequent increases in the value or recoverable cost of the asset may not be recognized until its sale or disposal. In addition, an asset that is assessed for impairment should be evaluated to determine whether a change to the useful life or salvage value estimate is warranted under APB Opinion No. 20, "Accounting Changes." SFAS No. 144 thus forces entities to immediately record a loss on an impaired asset instead of shortening the depreciable life or decreasing the salvage value of the asset.

(ii) Real Estate to Be Disposed Of SFAS No. 144 requires long-lived assets held for sale to be reported at the lower of carrying amount or fair value less cost to sell regardless of whether the assets previously were held for use or recently acquired with the intent to sell. The cost to sell generally includes the incremental direct costs to transact the sale, such as broker commissions, legal and title transfer fees, and closing costs. Costs generally excluded from cost to sell include insurance, security services, utility expenses, and other costs of protecting or maintaining the asset. Subsequent upward adjustments to the carrying amount of an asset to be disposed of may not exceed the carrying amount of the asset before an adjustment was made to reflect the decision to dispose of it. A long-lived asset that is classified as held for sale is not depreciated during the holding period.

  While SFAS No. 121 required an entity's management to be committed to a disposal plan before it could classify that asset as held for sale, it did not specify other factors that an entity should consider before reclassifying the asset. SFAS No. 144 lists six criteria that must be met in order to classify an asset as held for sale:

1. Management with the authority to do so commits to a plan to sell the asset (disposal group).
2. The asset (disposal group) is available for immediate sale in its present condition subject only to terms that are usual and customary for sales of such assets (disposal groups). This criterion does not preclude an entity from using an asset while it is classified as held for sale, nor does it require a binding agreement for future sale as a condition of reporting an asset as held for sale.
3. The entity initiates an active program to locate a buyer and other actions that are required to complete the plan to sell the asset (disposal group).
4. The entity believes that the sale of the asset (disposal group) is probable (i.e., likely to occur), and, in general, it expects to record the transfer of the asset (disposal group) as a completed sale within one year.
5. The entity actively is marketing the asset (disposal group) for sale at a price that is reasonable in relation to its current fair value.
6. Actions required to complete the plan indicate that it is unlikely that significant changes to the plan will be made or that the plan will be withdrawn.

SFAS No. 144 requires an asset or group that will be disposed of other than by sale to continue to be classified as held for use until the disposal transaction occurs. As a result, the asset continues to be depreciated until the date of disposal. Dispositions other than by sale include abandonment or a transaction that will be accounted for at the asset's carrying amount, such as an exchange for a similar productive long-lived asset or a distribution to owners in a spin-off.

(iii) Real Estate under Development   For home builders and other real estate developers, SFAS No. 144 classifies land to be developed and projects under development as assets to be held and used until the six criteria for reclassification as held for sale are met (see previous subsection). As a result, unlike assets to be disposed of, such assets are analyzed in light of the impairment indicator list and gross cash flows generated before any consideration is given to measuring an impairment loss. In the absence of such a provision, nearly all long-term projects, regardless of their overall profitability, would be subject to write-downs in their early stages of development, only to be reversed later in the life of the project. Upon completion of development, the project is reclassified as an asset to be disposed of.

(b) FAIR VALUE MEASUREMENTS   Statement 157, "Fair Value Measurements," defines fair value, and it is used in the determination of the impairment of real estate. There are more than 14 accounting standards that permit or require fair value, and this standard establishes a framework for measuring fair value and expands disclosures about how fair value measurements are used.

Real estate fair value is based on an exchange price principle. It no longer assumes that the transaction price, entry price, or purchase price represents fair value. Fair value is defined as an exit price or sales price in an orderly transaction between market participants. Entry and exit prices are often different. In all cases the transaction price will be equal to an exit price and therefore represents a fair value of the asset.

Real estate fair value measurements assume the highest and best use of the property by independent market participants. The highest and best use of the real estate is measured by market participants that would maximize value and use of the property, which may not be the same intended use by the reporting company.

(i) Fair Value Hierarchy Statement 157 requires valuation techniques consistent with what are used by the real estate market participants. Inputs to valuation techniques are assumptions that market participants would use in pricing the real estate.

The statement defines three distinct approaches or levels, of which two are based on observable inputs.

Level 1—quoted prices in active markets for identical assets. Generally, real estate does not fall into this category because of its distinct nature and operating unit.

Level 2—inputs other than quoted prices that are observable in a market either directly or indirectly. Many observable inputs for real estate fall in this category, such as cap rates, market rents, discount rates, risk-free rates, and sales price per square foot. Generally, the projection of real estate operations using observable inputs to determine fair value would fall under level 3.

Level 3—inputs that are unobservable in a market either directly or indirectly. Even though real estate valuations are based on observable inputs, the fair value hierarchy within which the fair value is measured falls to the lowest-level input, which is the projected operations.

(ii) Fair Value Techniques Real estate valuation techniques are numerous and should be based on observable inputs for the assumptions. The most common technique is the discounted net operating income approach. Current and future operations are projected and discounted back to the valuation date using current and future market rents and rates of return.

30.6 CONSTRUCTION REVENUE RECOGNITION

Although most real estate developers acquire land in order to develop and construct improvements for their own use or for sale to others, some develop and construct improvements solely for others. There are also many general contractors whose principal business is developing and constructing improvements for others and rarely, if ever, do they own the land.

This section covers guidelines for accounting for development and construction contracts where the contractor does not own the land but is providing such services for others. The principal issue in accounting for construction contracts is when to record income. Construction contracts are generally of two types: fixed-price and cost-plus. Under fixed-price contracts, a contractor agrees to perform services for a fixed amount. Although the contract price is fixed, it may frequently be revised as a result of change orders as construction proceeds. If the contract is longer than a few months, the contractor usually receives advances from the customer as construction progresses.

Cost-plus contracts are employed in a variety of forms, such as cost plus a percentage of cost or cost plus a fixed fee. Sometimes defined costs may be limited and penalties provided in situations where stated maximum costs are exceeded. Under cost-plus agreements, the contractor is usually reimbursed for its costs as costs are incurred and, in addition, is paid a specified fee. In most cases, a portion of the fee is retained until the construction is completed and accepted. The method of recording income under cost-plus contracts generally is the same as for fixed-price contracts and is described shortly.

(a) AUTHORITATIVE LITERATURE   In 1955, the AICPA Committee on Accounting Procedures issued Accounting Research Bulletin (ARB) No. 45, "Long-Term Construction-Type Contracts." This document describes the generally accepted methods of accounting for long-term construction-type contracts for financial reporting purposes and the circumstances in which each method is preferable.

In 1981, the AICPA issued SOP 81-1, "Accounting for Performance of Construction-Type and Certain Production-Type Contracts." This statement culminated extensive reconsideration by the AICPA of construction-type contracts. The recommendations set forth therein provide guidance on the application of ARB No. 45 but do not amend that bulletin. In 1982, the FASB issued SFAS No. 56, "Contractor Accounting," which states that the specialized accounting and reporting principles and practices contained in SOP 81-1 are preferable accounting principles for purposes of justifying a change in accounting principles.

Prior to the issuance of SOP 81-1, authoritative accounting literature used the terms *long term* and *short term* in identifying types of contracts. SOP 81-1 chose not to use those terms as identifying characteristics because other characteristics were considered more relevant for identifying the types of contracts covered. The guidelines set forth next are based largely on SOP 81-1.

(b) METHODS OF ACCOUNTING   The determination of the point or points at which revenue should be recognized as earned and costs should be recognized as expenses is a major accounting issue common to all business enterprises engaged in the performance of construction contracting. Accounting for such contracts is essentially a process of measuring the results of relatively long-term events and allocating those results to relatively short-term accounting periods. This involves considerable use of estimates in determining revenues, costs, and profits and in assigning the amounts to accounting periods. The process is complicated by the need to continually evaluate the uncertainties that are inherent in the performance of contracts and by the need to rely on estimates of revenues, costs, and the extent of progress toward completion.

There are two generally accepted methods of accounting for construction contracts: the percentage of completion method and the completed contract method. The determination of the preferable method should be based on an evaluation of the particular circumstances, as the two methods are not acceptable alternatives for the same set of circumstances. The method used and circumstances describing when it is used should be disclosed in the accounting policy footnote to the financial statements.

(i) Percentage of Completion Method   The use of this approach depends on the ability of the contractor to make reasonably dependable estimates. The percentage of completion method should be used in circumstances in which reasonably dependable estimates can be made and in which all the following conditions exist:

- The contract is clear about goods or services to be provided, the consideration to be exchanged, and the manner and terms of settlement.
- The buyer can be expected to pay for the services performed.
- The contractor can be expected to be able to perform its contractual obligations.

The percentage of completion method presents the economic substance of activity more clearly and in a more timely manner than does the completed contract method. It should be noted that estimates of revenues, costs, and measurements of performance are the primary criteria for income recognition. Billings alone may have no real relationship to performance and generally are not a suitable basis for income recognition.

(ii) Completed Contract Method   This method is usually used in circumstances in which an entity's financial position and results of operations would not vary materially from those resulting from the percentage of completion method. The completed contract method should be used when reasonably dependable estimates cannot be made or when there are inherent hazards that cause forecasts to be doubtful.

(iii) Consistency of Application   It is possible that a contractor may use one method for some contracts and the other for additional contracts. There is no inconsistency, since consistency in application lies in using the same accounting treatment for the same set of conditions of a contract from one accounting period to another. The method used, and circumstances when it is used, should be disclosed in the accounting policy footnote to the financial statements.

(c) PERCENTAGE OF COMPLETION METHOD   The percentage of completion method recognizes economic results of contract performance on a timely basis. Financial statements based on the percentage of completion method present the economic substance of a company's transactions and events more clearly and in a more timely manner than financial statements based on the completed contract method, and they present more accurately the relationships between gross profit from contracts and related period costs. The percentage of completion method informs the users of the general-purpose financial statements concerning the volume of a company's economic activity.

In practice, several methods are used to measure the extent of progress toward completion. These methods include the cost-to-cost method, the efforts-expended method, the units-of-delivery method, and the units-of-work-performed method. These methods are intended to conform to the recommendations of ARB 45 (par. 4), which states:

CHECK ORIGINAL

... that the recognized income be that percentage of estimated total income, either:

- that incurred costs to date bear to estimated total costs after giving effect to estimates of costs to complete based upon most recent information, or
- that may be indicated by such other measure of progress toward completion as may be appropriate having due regard to work performed.

One generally accepted method of measuring such progress is the stage of construction, as determined through engineering or architectural studies.

When using the cost-incurred approach, there may be certain costs that should be excluded from the calculation. For example, substantial quantities of standard materials not unique to the project may have been delivered to the job site but not yet utilized. Or engineering and architectural fees incurred may represent 20 percent of total estimated costs whereas only 10 percent of the construction has been performed.

The principal disadvantage of the percentage of completion method is that it is necessarily dependent on estimates of ultimate costs that are subject to the uncertainties frequently inherent in long-term contracts.

The estimation of total revenues and costs is necessary to determine estimated total income. Frequently a contractor can estimate total contract revenue and total contract cost in single amounts. However, on some contracts a contractor may be able to estimate only total contract revenue and total contract cost in ranges of amounts. In such situations, the most likely amounts within the range should be used, if determinable. If not, the least favorable amounts should be used until the results can be estimated more precisely.

(i) Revenue Determination   Estimating revenue on a contract is an involved process. The major factors that must be considered in determining total estimated revenue include the basic contract price, contract options, change orders, claims, and contract provisions for incentive payments and penalties. All these factors and other special contract provisions must be evaluated throughout the life of a contract in estimating total contract revenue.

(ii) Cost Determination   At any time during the life of a contract, total estimated contract cost consists of two components: costs incurred to date and estimated cost to complete the contract. A company should be able to determine costs incurred on a contract with a relatively high degree of precision. The other component, estimated cost to complete, is a significant variable in the process of determining income earned and is thus a significant factor in accounting for contracts. SOP 81-1 states that the following five practices should be followed in estimating costs to complete:

1. Systematic and consistent procedures that are correlated with the cost accounting system should be used to provide a basis for periodically comparing actual and estimated costs.
2. In estimating total contract costs, the quantities and prices of all significant elements of cost should be identified.
3. The estimating procedures should provide that estimated cost to complete includes the same elements of cost that are included in actual accumulated costs; also, those elements should reflect expected price increases.
4. The effects of future wage and price escalations should be taken into account in cost estimates, especially when the contract performance will be carried out over a significant period of time. Escalation provisions should not be blanket, overall provisions but should cover labor, materials, and indirect costs based on percentages or amounts that take into consideration experience and other pertinent data.
5. Estimates of cost to complete should be reviewed periodically and revised as appropriate to reflect new information.

(iii) Revision of Estimates   Adjustments to the original estimates of the total contract revenue, cost, or extent of progress toward completion are often required as work progresses under the contract, even though the scope of the work required under the contract has not changed. Such adjustments are changes in accounting estimates as defined in APB Opinion No. 20. Under this opinion, the cumulative catch-up method is the only acceptable method. This method requires the difference between cumulative income and income previously recorded to be recorded in the current year's income.

Exhibit 30.5 illustrates the percentage of completion method.

	To Date	Recognized Prior Year (Thousands of Dollars)	Current Year
Year 1 (25% completed)			
Earned revenue ($9,000,000 × 0.25)	$2,250.0		$2,250.0
Cost of earned revenue			
($8,050,000 × 0.25)	2,012.5		2,012.5
Gross profit	$237.5		$237.5
Gross profit rate	10.5%		10.5%
Year 2 (75% completed)			
Earned revenue ($9,100,000 × 0.75)	$6,825.0	$2,250.0	$4,575.0
Cost of earned revenue			
($8,100,000 × 0.75)	6,075.0	2,012.5	4,062.5
Gross profit	$750.0	$237.5	$512.5
Gross profit rate	11.0%	10.5%	11.2%
Year 3 (100% completed)			
Earned revenue	$9,200.0	$6,825.0	$2,375.0
Cost of earned revenue	8,200.0	6,075.0	2,125.0
Gross profit	$1,000.0	$0,750.0	$0,250.0
Gross profit rate	10.9%	11.0%	10.5%

(*Source:* AICPA.)

Exhibit 30.5 Percentage of Completion, Three-Year Contract

The amount of revenue, costs, and income recognized in the three periods would be as follows:

A contracting company has a lump-sum contract for $9 million to build a bridge at a total estimated cost of $8 million. The construction period covers three years. Financial data during the construction period (in thousands of dollars) are:

(d) COMPLETED CONTRACT METHOD   This method recognizes income only when a contract is completed or substantially completed, such as when the remaining costs to be incurred are not significant. Under this method, costs and billings are reflected in the balance sheet, but there are no charges or credits to the income statement.

	Year 1	Year 2	Year 3
Total estimated revenue	$9,000	$9,100	$9,200
Cost incurred to date	2,050	6,100	8,200
Estimated cost to complete	6,000	2,000	—
Total estimated cost	8,050	8,100	8,200
Estimated gross profit	$950	$1,000	$1,000
Billings to date	$1,800	$5,500	$9,200
Collections to date	$1,500	$5,000	$9,200
Measure of progress	25%	75%	100%

As a general rule, a contract may be regarded as substantially completed if remaining costs and potential risks are insignificant in amount. The overriding objectives are to maintain consistency in determining when contracts are substantially completed and to avoid arbitrary acceleration or deferral of income. The specific criteria used to determine when a contract is substantially completed should be followed consistently. Circumstances to be considered in determining when a project is substantially completed include acceptance by the customer, departure from the site, and compliance with performance specifications.

The completed contract method may be used in circumstances in which financial position and results of operations would not vary materially from those resulting from use of the percentage of completion method (e.g., in circumstances in which an entity has primarily short-term contracts). In accounting for such contracts, income ordinarily is recognized when performance is substantially completed and accepted. For example, the completed contract method, as opposed to the percentage of completion method, would not usually produce a material difference in net income or financial position for a small contractor that primarily performs relatively short-term contracts during an accounting period.

If there is a reasonable assurance that no loss will be incurred on a contract (e.g., when the scope of the contract is ill-defined but the contractor is protected by a cost-plus contract or other contractual terms), the percentage of completion method based on a zero profit margin, rather than the completed contract method, should be used until more precise estimates can be made.

The significant difference between the percentage of completion method applied on the basis of a zero profit margin and the completed contract method relates to the effects on the income statement. Under the zero profit margin approach to applying the percentage of completion method, equal amounts of revenue and cost, measured on the basis of performance during the period, are presented in the income statement and no gross profit amount is presented in the income statement until the contract is completed. The zero profit margin approach to applying the percentage of completion method gives the users of general-purpose financial statements an indication of the volume of a company's business and of the application of its economic resources.

The principal advantage of the completed contract method is that it is based on results as finally determined, rather than on estimates for unperformed work that may involve unforeseen costs and possible losses. The principal disadvantage is that it does not reflect current performance when the period of the contract extends into more than one accounting period. Under these circumstances, it may result in irregular recognition of income.

(e) PROVISION FOR LOSSES   Under either of these methods, provision should be made for the entire loss on the contract in the period when current estimates of total contract costs indicate a loss. The provision for loss should represent the best judgment that can be made in the circumstances.

Other factors that should be considered in arriving at the projected loss on a contract include target penalties for late completion and rewards for early completion, nonreimbursable costs on cost-plus contracts, and the effect of change orders. When using the completed contract method and allocating general and administrative expenses to contract costs, total general and administrative expenses that are expected to be allocated to the contract are to be considered together with other estimated contract costs.

(f) CONTRACT CLAIMS   Claims are amounts in excess of the agreed contract price that a contractor seeks to collect from customers or others for customer-caused delays, errors in specifications and designs, unapproved change orders, or other causes of unanticipated additional costs. Recognition of amounts of additional contract revenue relating to claims is appropriate only if it is probable that the claim will result in additional contract revenue and if the amount can be reliably estimated. These requirements are satisfied by the existence of all the following conditions:

- The contract or other evidence provides a legal basis for the claim.
- Additional costs are caused by circumstances that were unforeseen at the contract date and are not the result of deficiencies in the contractor's performance.
- Costs associated with the claim are identifiable and are reasonable in view of the work performed.
- The evidence supporting the claim is objective and verifiable.

If the foregoing requirements are met, revenue from a claim should be recorded only to the extent that contract costs relating to the claim have been incurred. The amounts recorded, if material, should be disclosed in the notes to the financial statements.

Change orders are modifications of an original contract that effectively change the provisions of the contract without adding new provisions. They may be initiated by either the contractor or the customer. Many change orders are unpriced; that is, the work to be performed is defined, but the adjustment to the contract price is to be negotiated later. For some change orders, both scope and price may be unapproved or in dispute. Accounting for change orders depends on the underlying circumstances and contract conditions, which may differ for each change order depending on the customer, the type of contract, and the nature of the change. Priced change orders represent an adjustment to the contract price and contract revenue, and costs should be adjusted to reflect these change orders.

Accounting for unpriced change orders depends on their characteristics and the circumstances in which they occur. Under the completed contract method, costs attributable to unpriced change orders should be deferred as contract costs if it is probable that aggregate contract costs, including costs attributable to change orders, will be recovered from contract revenues. For all unpriced change orders, recovery should be deemed probable if the future event or events necessary for recovery are likely to occur. Some factors to consider in evaluating whether recovery is probable are the customer's written approval of the scope of the change order, separate documentation for change order costs that are identifiable and reasonable, and the entity's favorable experience in getting change orders (especially as it relates to the specific type of contract and change order being evaluated). The following guidelines should be used in accounting for unpriced change orders under the percentage of completion method:

- Costs attributable to unpriced change orders should be treated as costs of contract performance in the period in which the costs are incurred if it is not probable that the costs will be recovered through a change in the contract price.
- If it is probable that the costs will be recovered through a change in the contract price, the costs should be deferred (excluded from the cost of contract performance) until the parties have agreed on the change in contract price, or, alternatively, they should be treated as costs of contract performance in the period in which they are incurred, and contract revenue should be recognized to the extent of the costs incurred.
- If it is probable that the contract price will be adjusted by an amount that exceeds the costs attributable to the change order and the amount of the excess can be reliably

estimated, the original contract price should also be adjusted for that amount when the costs are recognized as costs of contract performance if its realization is probable. However, since the substantiation of the amount of future revenue is difficult, revenue in excess of the costs attributable to unpriced change orders should be recorded only in circumstances in which realization is assured beyond a reasonable doubt, such as circumstances in which an entity's historical experience provides assurance or in which an entity has received a bona fide pricing offer from the customer and records only the amount of the offer as revenue.

If change orders are in dispute or are unapproved in regard to both scope and price, they should be evaluated as claims.

30.7 OPERATIONS OF PROPERTIES IN USE

(a) RENTAL OPERATIONS   Operations of properties in use represent a distinct segment of the real estate industry. Owners are often referred to as *real estate operators*. Properties in use include office buildings, shopping centers, apartments, industrial buildings, and similar properties rented to others. A lease agreement is entered into between the owner/operator and the tenant for periods ranging from one month to many years, depending on the type of property. Sometimes an investor will acquire an existing property or alternatively will have the builder or developer construct the property. Some developers, frequently referred to as *investment builders*, develop and construct income properties for their own use as investment properties.

Currently, SFAS No. 13 is the principal source of standards of financial accounting and reporting for leases, although FASB and the International Financial Reporting Standards (IFRS) organization have it on their agendas to issue new guidelines based on the principle of recognizing lease intangibles. Under SFAS No. 13, a distinction is made between a capital lease and an operating lease. The lessor is required to account for a capital lease as a sale or a financing transaction. The lessee accounts for a capital lease as a purchase. An operating lease, in contrast, requires the lessor to reflect rent income, operating expenses, and depreciation of the property over the lease term; the lessee must record rent expense.

Accounting for leases is discussed in Chapter 23 and therefore is not covered in depth here. Certain unique aspects of accounting for leases of real estate classified as operating leases, however, are covered in this chapter.

(b) RENTAL INCOME   Rental income from an operating lease should be recorded by a lessor as it becomes earned in accordance with the provisions of the lease agreement.

FTB No. 85-3 provides that the effects of scheduled rent increases, which are included in minimum lease payments under SFAS No. 13, should be recognized by lessors and lessees on a straight-line basis over the lease term unless another systematic and rational allocation basis is more representative of the time pattern in which the leased property is physically employed. Using factors such as the time value of money, anticipated inflation, or expected future revenues to allocate scheduled rent increases is inappropriate because these factors do not relate to the time pattern of the physical usage of the leased property. However, such factors may affect the periodic reported rental income or expense if the lease agreement involves rentals based on contingent events occurring during the lease period, which are excluded from minimum lease payments and accounted for separately under SFAS No. 13, as amended by SFAS No. 29.

A lease agreement may provide for scheduled rent increases designed to accommodate the lessee's projected physical use of the property. In these circumstances, FTB No. 88-1 provides for the lessee and the lessor to recognize the lease payments as follows:

- If rents escalate in contemplation of the lessee's physical use of the leased property, including equipment, but the lessee takes possession of or controls the physical use of the property at the beginning of the lease term, all rental payments, including the escalated rents, should be recognized as rental expenses or rental revenue on a straight-line basis in accordance with paragraph 15 of Statement No. 13 and Technical Bulletin 85-3 starting with the beginning of the lease term.
- If rents escalate under a master lease agreement because the lessee gains access to and control over additional leased property at the time of the escalation, the escalated rents should be considered rental expense or rental revenue attributable to the leased property and recognized in proportion to the additional leased property in the years that the lessee has control over the use of the additional leased property. The amount of rental expense or rental revenue attributed to the additional leased property should be proportionate to the relative fair value of the additional property, as determined at the inception of the lease, in the applicable time periods during which the lessee controls its use.

(i) Cost Escalation   Many lessors require that the lessee pay operating costs of the leased property such as utilities, real estate taxes, and common area maintenance. Some lessors require the lessee to pay for such costs when they escalate and exceed a specified rate or amount. In some cases, the lessee pays these costs directly. More commonly, however, the lessor pays the costs and is reimbursed by the lessee. In this situation, the lessor should generally record these reimbursement costs as receivables at the time the costs are accrued, even though they may not be billed until a later date. Since these costs are sometimes billed at a later date, collectability from the lessee should, of course, be considered.

(ii) Percentage Rents   Many retail leases, such as those on shopping centers, enable the lessor to collect additional rents, based on the excess of a stated percentage of the tenant's gross sales over the specified minimum rent. While the minimum rent is usually payable in periodic level amounts, percentage rents (sometimes called *overrides*) are usually based on annual sales, often with a requirement for periodic payments toward the annual amount.

SFAS No. 29, "Determining Contingent Rentals," states (par. 13): "Contingent rentals shall be includable in the determination of net income as accruable."

(c) RENTAL COSTS   The following considerations help determine the appropriate accounting for rental costs.

(i) Chargeable to Future Periods   All costs, direct or indirect, incurred to rent real estate should be deferred and charged to future periods when they are related to and their recovery is reasonably expected from future operations. Examples include initial direct costs such as commissions, legal fees, costs of credit investigations, costs of preparing and processing documents for new leases acquired, and that portion of compensation applicable to the time spent on consummated leases. Other examples include costs of model units and related furnishings, rental facilities, semipermanent signs, grand openings, and unused rental brochures, but not rental overhead, such as rental salaries (see "Period Costs," next).

For leases accounted for as operating leases, deferred rental costs that can be directly related to revenue from a specific operating lease should be amortized over the term of the related lease in proportion to the recognition of rental income. Deferred rental costs that cannot be directly related to revenue from a specific operating lease should be amortized to expense over the period of expected benefit. The amortization period begins when the project is substantially completed and held available for occupancy. Estimated unrecoverable deferred rental costs associated with a lease or group of leases should be charged to expense when it becomes probable that the lease(s) will be terminated.

For leases accounted for as sales-type leases, deferred rental costs must be charged against income at the time the sale is recognized.

(ii) Period Costs   Costs that are incurred to rent real estate projects that do not meet the aforementioned criteria should be charged to expense as incurred. SFAS No. 67 specifically indicates that rental overhead, which is defined in its glossary to include rental salaries, is an example of such period costs. Other examples of expenditures that are period costs are initial indirect costs, such as that portion of salaries and other compensation and fees applicable to time spent in negotiating leases that are not consummated; supervisory and administrative expenses; and other indirect costs.

(d) DEPRECIATION   Under GAAP, the costs of income-producing properties must be depreciated. Depreciation, as defined by GAAP, is the systematic and rational allocation of the historical cost of depreciable assets (tangible assets, other than inventory, with limited lives of more than one year) over their useful lives.

In accounting for real estate operations, the most frequently used methods of depreciation are straight-line and decreasing charge methods. The most common decreasing charge methods are the declining balance and sum of the years' digits methods. Increasing charge methods, such as the sinking fund method, are not generally used in the real estate industry in the United States.

The major components of a building, such as the plumbing and heating systems, may be identified and depreciated separately over their respective lives. This method, which is frequently used for tax purposes, usually results in a more rapid write-off.

(e) INITIAL RENTAL OPERATIONS

(i) Held in Use   When a real estate project is substantially complete and held available for occupancy (held in use), the procedures listed here should be followed:

- Rental revenue should be recorded in income as earned.
- Operating costs should be charged to expense currently.
- Amortization of deferred rental costs should begin.
- Full depreciation of rental property should begin.
- Carrying costs, such as interest and property taxes, should be charged to expense as accrued.

If portions of a rental project are substantially completed and occupied by tenants or held available for occupancy and other portions have not yet reached that stage, the substantially completed portions should be accounted for as a separate project. Costs incurred should be allocated between the portions under construction and the portions substantially completed and held available for occupancy.

(ii) Held for Sale   When a real estate project is substantially complete and available for occupancy but held for sale, the procedures listed here should be used:

- Positive rental operations should be recorded as a reduction of the net cost basis.
- Full depreciation of the rental property should be suspended.

(f) RENTAL EXPENSE   Rental expense under an operating lease normally should be charged to operations by a lessee over the lease term on a basis consistent with the lessor's recording of income, with the exception of periodic accounting for percentage rent expense, which should be based on the estimated annual percentage rent.

30.8 ACCOUNTING FOR INVESTMENTS IN REAL ESTATE VENTURES

(a) ORGANIZATION OF VENTURES   The joint venture vehicle—the sharing of risk—has been widely utilized for many years in the construction, mining, and oil and gas industries as well as for real estate developments. Real estate joint ventures are typically entered into in recognition of the need for external assistance—for example, financing or market expertise. The most common of these needs is capital formation.

Real estate ventures are organized either as corporate entities or, more frequently, as partnerships. Limited partnerships are often used because of the advantages of limited liability. The venture is typically formed by a small group, with each investor actively contributing to the success of the venture and participating in overall management, and with no one individual or corporation controlling its operations. The venture is usually operated separately from other activities of the investors. Regardless of the legal form of the real estate venture, the accounting principles for recognition of profits and losses should be the same.

(b) ACCOUNTING

(i) Background   Accounting practices in the real estate industry in general and, more specifically, accounting for investments in real estate ventures have varied. The result was lack of comparability and, in some cases, a lack of comprehension. Therefore, the following relevant pronouncements were issued:

- *APB Opinion No. 18.* In response to the wide variation in accounting for investments, the APB, in March 1971, issued Opinion No. 18, "The Equity Method of Accounting for Investments in Common Stock." This opinion became applicable to investments in unincorporated ventures, including partnerships, because of an interpretation promulgated in November 1971.
- *AICPA Statement of Position (SOP) No. 78-9.* The AICPA recognized the continuing diversity of practice and in December 1978 issued SOP 78-9, "Accounting for Investments in Real Estate Ventures." This statement was issued to narrow the range of alternative practices used in accounting for investments in real estate ventures and to establish industry uniformity. The AICPA currently is reconsidering the guidance in SOP 78-9 as part of a broader project, "Equity Method Investments."
- *SFAS No. 94.* In response to the perceived problem of off-balance-sheet financing, of which unconsolidated majority-owned subsidiaries were deemed to be the most significant aspect, the FASB issued SFAS No. 94, "Consolidation of All Majority-Owned Subsidiaries," in October 1987. SFAS No. 94 eliminates the concept of not

consolidating nonhomogeneous operations and replaces it with the concept that the predominant factor in determining whether an investment requires consolidation should primarily be control rather than ownership of a majority voting interest. This statement is also applicable to investments in unincorporated ventures, including partnerships.

• *AICPA Notice to Practitioners on ADC [Acquisition, Development, and Construction] Arrangements, February 1986.* Recognizing that financial institutions needed guidance on accounting for real estate acquisition, development, and construction (ADC) arrangements, the AICPA issued this notice (also known as the *Third Notice*). The notice provides accounting guidance on ADC arrangements that have virtually the same risks and potential rewards as those of joint ventures. It determined that accounting for such arrangements as loans would not be appropriate and provides guidance on the appropriate accounting.

The SEC incorporated the notice into SAB No. 71, "Views Regarding Financial Statements of Properties Securing Mortgage Loans." SAB No. 71, and its amendment, SAB No. 71A, provide guidance to registrants on the required reporting under this notice. Also, EITF Issue Nos. 84-4 and 86-21, as well as SAB No. 71, extend the provisions of this notice to all entities, not just financial institutions.

• *Proposed FASB Interpretation, Consolidation of Certain Special-Purpose Entities (SPEs).* The FASB has approved for issuance an exposure draft of a proposed interpretation that establishes accounting guidance for consolidation of SPEs. The proposed interpretation, "Consolidation of Certain Special-Purpose Entities," would apply to any business enterprise—both public and private companies—that has an ownership interest, contractual relationship, or other business relationship with an SPE. Under current practice, two enterprises generally have been included in consolidated financial statements because one enterprise controls the other through voting ownership interests.

The proposed interpretation would explain how to identify an SPE that is not subject to control through voting ownership interests and would require each enterprise involved with such an SPE to determine whether it provides financial support to the SPE through a variable interest. Variable interests may arise from financial instruments, service contracts, nonvoting ownership interests, or other arrangements. If an enterprise holds (1) a majority of the variable interests in the SPE or (2) a significant variable interest that is significantly more than any other party's variable interest, that enterprise would be the primary beneficiary. The primary beneficiary would be required to include the assets, liabilities, and results of the activities of the SPE in its consolidated financial statements.

(ii) Current Status FAS 141(R), "Business Combinations, FIN 46(R)," and FAS 160, "Noncontrolling Interests in Consolidated Statements," address financial accounting and reporting for business combinations and supersede APB Opinion No. 16, "Business Combinations," and FASB Statement No. 38, "Accounting for Preacquisition Contingencies of Purchased Enterprises." All business combinations in the scope of this statement are to be accounted for using one method, the purchase method. The standard is now effective for all companies. Although some of the provisions seem straightforward, the impacts are pervasive. The concept of fair value derives important changes to the model, including changes in the accounting for partial business combination and step acquisitions. The traditional concepts mentioned earlier have also undergone fundamental change. Examples are:

- Expands the definition of a business and business combination
- Requires the recognition of a contingent consideration of fair value on the acquisition and requires an acquisition-related transaction course to be expensed as incurred
- Changes the way certain assets are valued
- Requires a retrospective application of measurement, with period adjustments

Importantly, this new standard may dramatically impact the accounting of real estate ventures. The new standard could increase the number of companies reporting units, change the calculation of goodwill impairment, and cause tax adjustments to the recorded in earnings.

(c) **INVESTOR ACCOUNTING ISSUES** The accounting literature mentioned earlier covers many of the special issues investors encounter in practice. The major areas are:

- Investor accounting for results of operations of ventures
- Special accounting issues related to venture losses
- Investor accounting for transactions with a real estate venture, including capital contributions
- Financial statement presentation and disclosures

Initially, one should determine the status of the venture in relation to each joint venture. The following criteria should be evaluated to determine controlling interests as measured by the contractual interest in the venture.

- Is the interest at risk and not sufficient to permit the entity to finance its activities without additional subordinated financial support provided by any parties, including the equity holders?
- Do the investors lack one or more of the following essential characteristics of a controlling financial interest?
  - The direct or indirect ability to make decisions about the entity's activities through voting rights or similar rights
  - The obligation to absorb the expected losses of the entity
  - The right to receive the expected residual returns of the entity
- Do the investors have voting rights that are not proportionate to their economic interests? Do the activities of the entity involve or are they conducted on behalf of an investor with a disproportionately small voting interest?

A controlling investor should account for its income and losses from real estate ventures under the principles that apply to investments in subsidiaries, which usually require consolidation of the venture's operations. The consolidated net income is to be reported at amounts that include the amounts attributable to both the parent and the noncontrolling interest. It also requires disclosure, on the face of the consolidated statement of income, of the amounts of consolidated net income attributable to the parent and to the noncontrolling interest. Previously, net income attributable to the noncontrolling interest generally was reported as an expense or other deduction in arriving at consolidated net income. It also was often presented in combination with other financial statement amounts. A noncontrolling investor should account for its share of income and losses in real estate ventures by using the equity method. Under the equity method, the initial investment is recorded by the investor at cost; thereafter, the carrying amount is increased by the investor's share of current earnings and decreased by the investor's share of current losses or distributions.

In accounting for transactions with a real estate venture, a controlling investor must eliminate all intercompany profit. When the investor does not control the venture, some situations require that all intercompany profit be eliminated, whereas in others intercompany profit is eliminated by the investor only to the extent of its ownership interest in the venture. For example, as set forth in AICPA SOP 78-9, even a noncontrolling investor is precluded from recognizing any profit on a contribution of real estate or services to the venture. Accounting for other transactions covered by SOP 78-9 includes sales of real estate and services to the venture, interest income on loans and advances to the venture, and venture sales of real estate or services to an investor.

With regard to financial statement presentation, a controlling investor is usually required to consolidate venture operations. A noncontrolling investor should use the equity method, with the carrying value of the investment presented as a single amount in the balance sheet and the investor's share of venture earnings or losses as a single amount in the income statement. The proportionate share approach, which records the investor's share of each item of income, expense, asset, and liability, is not considered acceptable except for legal undivided interests.

The preceding material is only a very brief summary of the literature, and there are exceptions to some of those guidelines. In accounting for real estate venture operations and transactions, judgment must be exercised in applying the principles to ensure that economic substance is fairly reflected no matter how complex the venture arrangements.

(d) ACCOUNTING FOR TAX BENEFITS RESULTING FROM INVESTMENTS IN AFFORDABLE HOUSING PROJECTS   The Revenue Reconciliation Act of 1993 provides tax benefits to investors in entities operating qualified affordable housing projects. The benefits take the form of tax deductions from operating losses and tax credits. In EITF Issue No. 94-1, "Accounting for Tax Benefits Resulting from Investments in Affordable Housing Projects," the EITF reached a consensus that a limited partner in a qualified low-income housing project may elect to use the effective yield method (described in the next section) if the following three conditions are met:

1. The availability of the limited partner's share of the tax credits is guaranteed by a creditworthy entity through a letter of credit, tax indemnity agreement, or other arrangement.
2. The limited partner's projected yield based solely on the cash flows from the guaranteed tax credits is positive.
3. The limited partner's liability for both legal and tax purposes is limited to its capital investment.

Under the effective yield method, the investor recognizes tax credits as they are allocated and amortizes the initial cost of the investment to provide a constant effective yield over the period that tax credits are allocated to the investor. The effective yield is the internal rate of return on the investment, based on the cost of the investment and the guaranteed tax credits allocated to the investor. Any expected residual value of the investment should be excluded from the effective yield calculation. Cash received from operations of the limited partnership or sale of the property, if any, should be included when realized or realizable.

Under the effective yield method, the tax credit allocated, net of the amortization of the investment in the limited partnership, is recognized in the income statement as a component (usually a reduction) of income taxes attributable to continuing operations. Any other tax benefits received should be accounted for pursuant to FASB Statement No. 109, "Accounting for Income Taxes."

An investment that does not qualify for accounting under the effective yield method should be accounted for under SOP 78-9, which requires use of the equity method unless the limited partner's interest is so minor as to have virtually no influence over partnership operating and financial policies. The EITF did not establish a so-called bright line as to what percentage ownership threshold is required under SOP 78-9 for selecting between the cost and equity methods. The AICPA is currently reconsidering the guidance in SOP 78-9 in its project titled "Equity Method Investments."

If the cost method is used, the excess of the carrying amount of the investment over its residual value should be amortized over the period in which the tax credits are allocated to the investor. Annual amortization should be based on the proportion of tax credits received in the current year to total estimated tax credits to be allocated to the investor. The residual value should not reflect anticipated inflation.

During the deliberations of EITF Issue No. 94-1, the staff of the SEC announced that they had revised their position on accounting for investments in limited partnerships. Previously, the SEC had not objected to the use of the cost method for limited partnership investments of up to 20 percent, provided the investor did not have significant influence as defined in APB Opinion No. 18, "The Equity Method of Accounting for Investments in Common Stock." However, the revised position is that the equity method should be used to account for limited partnership investments, unless the investment is "so minor that the limited partner may have virtually no influence over partnership operating and financial policies." In practice, investments of more than 3 to 5 percent would be considered more than minor. For public companies, this guidance is to be applied to any limited partnership investment made after May 18, 1995. This would include not only the investments in low-income housing projects, but all real estate partnerships and any other types of limited partnership investments (such as oil and gas).

30.9 FINANCIAL REPORTING

(a) FINANCIAL STATEMENT PRESENTATION   There are matters of financial statement presentation—as opposed to footnote disclosures—that are unique to the real estate industry. The financial reporting guidelines in this section are based on the principles set forth in authoritative literature and reporting practice.

(i) Balance Sheet   Real estate companies frequently present nonclassified balance sheets; that is, they do not distinguish between current and noncurrent assets or liabilities. This is because the operating cycle of most real estate companies exceeds one year.

Real estate companies sometimes list their assets on the balance sheet in the order of liquidity, in the same manner as other companies. A more popular method, however, is to list the real estate assets first, to demonstrate their importance to the companies. In either case, real estate assets should be disclosed in the manner that is most demonstrative of the company's operations. These assets are often grouped broadly according to the type of investment or operation as follows:

- Real Estate under Development
- Real Estate Held for Sale
- Real Estate Held for Use
  - Commercial
  - Residential
  - Retail
  - Industrial

(ii) Statement of Income   Operations are generally classified in a manner consistent with that described for real estate investments. In 1976, the FASB issued SFAS No. 14, "Financial Reporting for Segments of a Business Enterprise," which states that the financial statements of an enterprise should include certain information about the industry segments of the enterprise. An industry segment is defined in paragraph 10(a) as "a component of an enterprise engaged in providing a product or service or a group of related products and services primarily to unaffiliated customers (i.e., customers outside the enterprise) for profit." Some developers, however, have traditionally considered themselves to be in only one line of business.

In June 1997, the FASB issued SFAS No. 131, "Disclosures about Segments of an Enterprise and Related Information." SFAS No. 131 supersedes SFAS No. 14, although it retains the requirement to report information about major customers. SFAS No. 131 adopts a "management approach" to identifying segments and permits entities to aggregate operating segments if certain attributes are present.

(b) ACCOUNTING POLICIES   Because of the alternatives currently available in accounting for real estate developments, it is especially important to follow the guidelines of APB Opinion No. 22, "Disclosure of Accounting Policies." The opinion states (par. 12) that disclosures should include the accounting principles and methods that involve any of the following:

A selection from existing acceptable alternatives.
Principles and methods peculiar to the industry in which the reporting entity operates, even if such principles and methods are predominantly followed in that industry.
Unusual or innovative applications of GAAP (and, as applicable, of principles and methods peculiar to the industry in which the reporting entity operates).

The following lists four accounting policy disclosures that are appropriate in the financial statements of a real estate company, as opposed to a manufacturing or service enterprise.

1. *Profit recognition.* The accounting method used to determine income should be disclosed. Where different methods are used, the circumstances surrounding the application of each should also be disclosed. Similarly, a comment should be included indicating the timing of sales and related profit recognition.

2. *Cost accounting.* The method of allocating cost to unit sales should be disclosed (e.g., relative market values, area, unit, specific identification). Financial statement disclosure should include, where applicable, capitalization policies for property taxes and other carrying costs, and policies with respect to capitalization or deferral of start-up or preoperating costs (selling costs, rental costs, initial operations).

3. *Impairment of long-lived assets.* Real estate held for development and sale, including property to be developed in the future as well as that currently under development, should follow the recognition and measurement principles set forth in SFAS No. 121 for assets to be held and used. A real estate project, or parts thereof, that is substantially complete and ready for its intended use shall be accounted for at the lower of carrying amount or fair value less cost to sell.

4. *Investment in real estate ventures.* Disclosures of the following accounting policies should be made:

   o   Method of inclusion in investor's accounts (e.g., equity or consolidation)
   o   Method of income recognition (e.g., equity or cost)
   o   Accounting principles of significant ventures
   o   Profit recognition practices on transactions between the investor and the venture

(c) **NOTE DISCLOSURES**   The following list describes other financial statement disclosures that are appropriate in the notes to the financial statements of a real estate developer.

- *Real estate assets.* If a breakdown is not reflected on the balance sheet, it should be included in the footnotes. Disclosure should also be made of inventory subject to sales contracts that have not been recorded as sales and the portion of inventory serving as collateral for debts.
- *Impairment of long-lived assets.* The footnotes should provide a detailed description of the methodology of when and how impairments of real estate are determined.
- *Inventory write-downs.* Summarized information or explanations with respect to significant inventory write-downs should be disclosed in the footnotes, because write-downs are generally important and unusual items.
- *Nonrecourse debt.* Although it is not appropriate to offset nonrecourse debt against the related asset, a note to the financial statements should disclose the amount and interrelationship of the nonrecourse debt with the cost of the related property.
- *Capitalization of interest.* SFAS No. 34 requires the disclosure of the amount of interest expensed and the amount capitalized.
- *Deferral of profit recognition.* When transactions qualify as sales for accounting purposes but do not meet the tests for full profit recognition and, as a result, the installment or cost recovery methods are used, disclosure should be made of significant amounts of profit deferred, the nature of the transaction, and any other information deemed necessary for complete disclosure.
- *Investments in real estate ventures.* Typical disclosures with respect to significant real estate ventures include name of venture; percentage of ownership interest; accounting and tax policies of the venture; the difference, if any, between the carrying amount of the investment and the investor's share of equity in net assets and the accounting policy regarding amortization of the difference; summarized information as to assets, liabilities, and results of operations or separate financial statements; and investor commitments with respect to joint ventures.
- *Construction contractors.* The principal reporting considerations for construction contractors relate to the two methods of income recognition: the percentage of completion method and the completed contract method.

    When the completed contract method is used, an excess of accumulated costs over related billings should be shown in a classified balance sheet as a current asset, and an excess of accumulated billings over related costs should be shown as a current liability. If costs exceed billings on some contracts and billings exceed costs on others, the contracts should ordinarily be segregated so that the asset side includes only those contracts on which costs exceed billings, and the liability side includes only those on which billings exceed costs.

Under the percentage of completion method, assets may include costs and related income not yet billed, with respect to certain contracts. Liabilities may include billings in excess of costs and related income with respect to other contracts.

The following disclosures, which are required for SEC reporting companies, should generally be made by a nonpublic company whose principal activity is long-term contracting:

○ Amounts billed but not paid by customers under retainage provisions in contracts, and indication of amounts expected to be collected in various years

○ Amounts included in receivables representing the recognized sales value of performance under long-term contracts where such amounts had not been billed and were not billable at the balance sheet date, along with a general description of the prerequisites for billing and an estimate of the amount expected to be collected in one year

○ Amounts included in receivables or inventories representing claims or other similar items subject to uncertainty concerning their determination or ultimate realization, together with a description of the nature and status of principal items, and amounts expected to be collected in one year

○ Amount of progress payments (billings) netted against inventory at the balance sheet date

(d) CURRENT VALUE   The traditional accounting model does not permit the recognition of appreciation of real estate assets. This most affects depreciable income properties, but it also affects land. Using the historical cost model, appreciation of good investments cannot be used to offset losses on unsuccessful projects. Real estate companies have thus been among the strongest proponents of fair value and current value reporting, particularly during periods of rapid appreciation in property values.

(i) Current Value   The AICPA had a project on current value reporting by real estate companies that was shelved after issuance of an October 10, 1994, exposure draft of a proposed SOP, "Reporting by Real Estate Companies of Supplemental Current-Value Information." As described in the exposure draft, the measurement of current value would consider the entity's intent and ability to realize asset values and settle liabilities. In addition, the reported amounts would represent the values of specific balance sheet elements—not the value of the entity as a whole. The AICPA attempted to ensure that the guidance would serve solely as the basis for optional supplemental disclosure and not as the framework for an "other comprehensive basis of accounting" (OCBOA).

The exposure draft was developed from the AICPA Real Estate Committee's 1984 "Guidance for an Experiment on Reporting Current Value Information for Real Estate," which provided for a comprehensive approach and a piecemeal approach to the presentation of current value information. Although the piecemeal approach is not discouraged, the current value project focuses primarily on the comprehensive approach, in which all assets and liabilities are reported at their current amounts in balance sheet form.

Both the guidance for an experiment and the exposure draft recommend presentation of current value information side by side with the corresponding GAAP information in comparative form. Although the experiment discussed the idea of including current value statements of operating performance and changes in equity, those statements are not addressed in the exposure draft. Instead, the exposure draft focuses on the disclosure of interperiod changes in revaluation equity—the difference between (1) the net current value of assets and liabilities and (2) the corresponding net carrying amount determined in conformity with GAAP.

(ii) Deferred Taxes on Current Value   The reporting of the deferred income tax liability in the current value balance sheet has been controversial. The exposure draft would permit either of the following two methods to be used in determining the deferred income tax liability to be reported in the current value balance sheet:

- *Method 1*—The reported deferred income tax liability is equal to the discounted amount of the estimated future tax payments, adjusted for the use of existing net operating loss carryforwards or other carryforwards. The determination of the deferred income tax liability is based on the enacted income tax rates and regulations at the balance sheet date (even if not in effect at that date). The exposure draft contains a deemed sale provision at the end of the fifteenth year, with the discounted amount of the tax that would be paid on such a sale included in the reported liability.
- *Method 2*—The reported deferred income tax liability is based on enacted rates and regulations at the balance sheet date (even if not in effect at that date). The enacted rate is multiplied by the difference between the current value of total net assets and liabilities and their tax bases, adjusted for the use of existing net operating loss carryforwards or other carryforwards. Although this method of determining the anticipated tax liability is conceptually inconsistent with the principle of determining current value based on the discounted amount of estimated future cash flows, the method was included in the exposure draft because it is easy to apply as a result of the fact that it reflects the effect of an immediate and complete liquidation of the reporting entity's portfolio.

(e) ACCOUNTING BY PARTICIPATING MORTGAGE LOAN BORROWERS   In May 1997, the AICPA issued SOP 97-1, "Accounting by Participating Mortgage Loan Borrowers." The SOP establishes the borrower's accounting when a mortgage lender participates in either or both of the following:

- Increases in the market value of the mortgaged real estate project
- The project's results of operations

If a lender participates in the market appreciation of the mortgaged property, the borrower must determine the fair value of the appreciation feature at the inception of the loan. A liability equal to the appreciation feature is recognized with a corresponding charge to a debt discount account. The debt discount should be amortized using the interest method.

Interest expense in participating mortgage loans consists of the following items:

- Amounts designated in the mortgage agreement as interest
- Amounts related to the lender's participation in operations
- Amounts representing amortization of the debt discount related to the lender's participation in the project's appreciation

The borrower remeasures the participation liability each period. Any revisions to the participation liability resulting from the remeasurement results in an adjustment to the participation liability via a debit or credit to the related debt discount. The revised debt discount should be amortized prospectively using the effective interest rate.

(f) REAL ESTATE INVESTMENT TRUSTS   Real estate investment trusts generally are formed as trusts, associations, or corporations. They employ equity capital, coupled with substantial amounts of debt financing, in making real estate loans and investments. Real estate investment trusts must distribute substantially all of their taxable income to their shareholders annually in order to retain their favorable tax status (that is, dividends paid are treated as deductions in arriving at taxable income).

30.10 SOURCES AND SUGGESTED REFERENCES

(a) SOURCES BY CURRENT CODIFICATION   The Codification is a major restructuring of accounting and reporting standards. While the content may reside in new locations within the Codification, the FASB's intent in creating the Codification is that the content accurately represents existing standards.

Their goal in developing the Codification is to simplify user access to all authoritative U.S. GAAP by providing all the authoritative literature related to a particular topic in one place.

The term *authoritative* includes all nongovernmental level A–D GAAP that has been issued by a standard setter. The Codification does not include practice, textbooks, articles, and other similar content. The Codification also includes relevant authoritative content issued by the SEC, as well as selected SEC staff interpretations and administrative guidance.

As of July 1, 2009, the Codification is the single source of authoritative U.S. accounting and reporting standards, other than guidance issued by the SEC. The Codification supersedes all then-existing non-SEC accounting and reporting standards. All other nongrandfathered, non-SEC accounting literature not included in the Codification becomes nonauthoritative. All the literature stated earlier, changes, and current updates can be cross-referenced to the listed topics.

The following is the listing of the applicable real estate topics with the applicable cross-referenced other topics.

(i) 970 Real Estate—General
   10 Overall
   230 Statement of Cash Flows
   323 Investments—Equity Method and Joint Ventures
   340 Other Assets and Deferred Costs
   360 Property, Plant, and Equipment
   470 Debt
   605 Revenue Recognition
   720 Other Expenses
   810 Consolidation
   835 Interest

(ii) 972 Real Estate—Common Interest Associations
10 Overall
205 Presentation of Financial Statements
235 Notes to Financial Statements
360 Property, Plant, and Equipment
430 Deferred Revenue
605 Revenue Recognition
720 Other Expenses
7408 Income Taxes
850 Related Party Disclosure

(iii) 974 Real Estate—Real Estate Investment Trusts
10 Overall
323 Investments—Equity Method and Joint Ventures
605 Revenue Recognition
810 Consolidation
835 Interest
840 Leases

(iv) 976 Real Estate—Retail Land
10 Overall
310 Receivables
330 Inventory
605 Revenue Recognition
705 Cost of Sales and Service

(v) 978 Real Estate—Time-Sharing Activities
10 Overall
230 Statement of Cash Flow
250 Accounting Changes and Error Correction
310 Receivables
330 Inventory
340 Other Assets and Deferred Costs
605 Revenue Recognition
720 Other expenses
810 Consolidation
840 Leases

(b) SUGGESTED REFERENCES PRIOR TO CODIFICATION
Accounting Principles Board, "Accounting Changes," APB Opinion No. 20. AICPA, New York, 1971.

_____. "The Equity Method of Accounting for Investments in Common Stock," APB Opinion No. 18. AICPA, New York, March 1971.

_____. "Interest on Receivables and Payables," APB Opinion No. 21. AICPA, New York, August 1971.

_____. "The Equity Method of Accounting for Investments in Common Stock," APB Opinion No. 18, Interpretation No. 18-2. AICPA, New York, November 1971.

_____. "Disclosure of Accounting Policies," APB Opinion No. 22. AICPA, New York, April 1972.

FAS 141(R), "Business Combinations, FIN 46(R)."

FAS 144, "Accounting for the Impairment or Disposal of Long-Lived Assets."

FAS 157, "Fair Value Measurements."

FAS 160, "Noncontrolling Interests in Consolidated Statements."

American Institute of Certified Public Accountants, "Inventory Pricing," "Restatement and Revision of Accounting Research Bulletins," Accounting Research Bulletin No. 43. AICPA, New York, June 1953.

_____. "Long-Term Construction-Type Contracts," Accounting Research Bulletin No. 45. AICPA, New York, October 1955.

_____. "Accounting Practices of Real Estate Investment Trusts," Statement of Position No. 75-2. AICPA, New York, June 27, 1975.

_____. "Accounting for Costs to Sell and Rent, and Initial Real Estate Operations of Real Estate Projects," Statement of Position No. 78-3. AICPA, New York, 1978.

_____. "Accounting for Investments in Real Estate Ventures," Statement of Position No. 78-9. AICPA, New York, December 29, 1978.

_____. Issues Paper, "Accounting for Allowances for Losses on Certain Real Estate and Loans and Receivables Collateralized by Real Estate." AICPA, New York, June 1979.

_____. "Accounting for Real Estate Acquisition, Development, and Construction Costs," Statement of Position No. 80-3. AICPA, New York, 1980.

_____. "Audit and Accounting Guide for Construction Contractors," Accounting Guide. AICPA, New York, 1981.

_____. "Accounting for Performance of Construction-Type and Certain Production-Type Contracts," Statement of Position 81-1. AICPA, New York, July 15, 1981.

_____. Third Notice to Practitioners, "Accounting for Real Estate Acquisition, Development, and Construction Arrangements." AICPA, New York, February 10, 1986.

_____. "Guide for the Use of Real Estate Appraisal Information," Accounting Guide. AICPA, New York, 1987.

_____. "Accounting for Real Estate Syndication Income," Statement of Position No. 92-1. AICPA, New York, 1992.

_____. "Accounting for Foreclosed Assets," Statement of Position 92-3. AICPA, New York, 1992.

_____. "Accounting by Participating Mortgage Loan Borrowers," Statement of Position 97-1. AICPA, New York, 1997.

_____. "Proposed Statement of Position: Accounting for Certain Costs and Activities Related to Property, Plant, and Equipment." AICPA, New York, June 29, 2001.

Financial Accounting Standards Board, "Financial Reporting for Segments of a Business Enterprise," Statement of Financial Accounting Standards No. 14. FASB, Stamford, CT, 1976.

_____. "Accounting for Leases," Statement of Financial Accounting Standards No. 13. FASB, Stamford, CT, November 1976.

_____. "Accounting for Sales with Leasebacks (an amendment of FASB Statement No. 13)," Statement of Financial Accounting Standards No. 28. FASB, Stamford, CT, 1979.

_____. "Determining Contingent Rentals (an amendment of FASB Statement No. 13)," Statement of Financial Accounting Standards No. 29. FASB, Stamford, CT, 1979.

_____. "Capitalization of Interest Cost," Statement of Financial Accounting Standards No. 34. FASB, Stamford, CT, October 1979.

_____. "Designation of AICPA Guide and Statement of Position (SOP) 81-1 on Contractor Accounting and SOP 81-2 Concerning Hospital-Related Organizations as Preferable for Purposes of Applying APB Opinion 20," Statement of Financial Accounting Standards No. 56. FASB, Stamford, CT, February 1982.

_____. "Accounting for Sales of Real Estate," Statement of Financial Accounting Standards No. 66. FASB, Stamford, CT, October 1982.

_____. "Accounting for Costs and Initial Rental Operations of Real Estate Projects," Statement of Financial Accounting Standards No. 67. FASB, Stamford, CT, October 1982.

_____. "Acquisition, Development, and Construction Loans," EITF Issue No. 84-4. FASB, Stamford, CT, 1984.

_____. "Recognition of Receipts from Made-Up Rental Shortfalls," EITF Issue No. 85-27. FASB, Stamford, CT, 1985.

_____. "Accounting for Operating Leases with Scheduled Rent Increases," FASB Technical Bulletin No. 85-3. FASB, Stamford, CT, November 1985.

_____. "Antispeculation Clauses in Real Estate Sales Contracts," EITF Issue No. 86-6. FASB, Stamford, CT, 1986.

_____. "Application of the AICPA Notice to Practitioners Regarding Acquisition, Development, and Construction Arrangements to the Acquisition of an Operating Property," EITF Issue No. 86-21. FASB, Stamford, CT, 1986.

_____. "Consolidation of All Majority-Owned Subsidiaries," Statement of Financial Accounting Standards No. 94. FASB, Stamford, CT, October 1987.

_____. "Statement of Cash Flows," Statement of Financial Accounting Standards No. 95. FASB, Stamford, CT, November 1987.

_____. EITF Abstracts: A Summary of Proceedings of the FASB Emerging Issues Task Force, "Profit Recognition on Sale of Real Estate with Insurance Mortgages on Surety Bonds," EITF Issue No. 87-9. FASB, Norwalk, CT, 1988.

_____. "Effect of Various Forms of Financing under Statement of Financial Accounting Standards No. 66," EITF Issue No. 88-24. FASB, Norwalk, CT, 1988.

————. "Accounting for Leases," Statement of Financial Accounting Standards No. 98. FASB, Norwalk, CT, May 1988.

————. "Issues Relating to Accounting for Leases," FASB Technical Bulletin No. 88-1. FASB, Norwalk, CT, December 1988.

————. "Accounting for Tax Benefits Resulting from Investments in Affordable Housing Projects," EITF Issue No. 94-1. FASB, Norwalk, CT, 1994.

————. "Accounting for the Impairment of Long-Lived Assets and for Long-Lived Assets to Be Disposed Of," Statement of Financial Accounting Standards No. 121. FASB, Norwalk, CT, March 1995.

————. "Disclosures about Segments of an Enterprise and Related Information," Statement of Financial Accounting Standards No. 131. FASB, Norwalk, CT, 1997.

————. "Goodwill and Other Intangible Assets," Statement of Financial Accounting Standards No. 142. FASB, Norwalk, CT, 2001.

————. "Accounting for the Impairment or Disposal of Long-Lived Assets," Statement of Financial Accounting Standards No. 144. FASB, Norwalk, CT, 2001.

————.

Securities and Exchange Commission:

————. "Consolidation of Financial Statements of the Registrant and Its Subsidiaries," Regulation S-X, Article 3A, Rule 3A-02. SEC, Washington, DC.

————. "Offsetting Assets and Liabilities," Staff Accounting Bulletin Topic No. 11D. SEC, Washington, DC.

————. "Preparation of Registration Statements Relating to Interests in Real Estate Limited Partnerships," Guide 5. SEC, Washington, DC.

————. "Reporting Cash Flow and Other Related Data," Financial Reporting Policy 202. SEC, Washington, DC.

————. "Requirement for Financial Statements of Special Purpose Limited Partnerships," Financial Reporting Policy 405. SEC, Washington, DC.

————. "Special Instructions for Real Estate Operations to Be Acquired," Regulation S-X, Article 3, Rule 3–14. SEC, Washington, DC.

————. "Views Regarding Financial Statements of Properties Securing Mortgage Loans," Staff Accounting Bulletin 71-71A (Topic No. 1I). SEC, Washington, DC.

*CHAPTER **31**

FINANCIAL INSTITUTIONS (REVISED)

Zabihollah "Zabi" Rezaee, PhD, CPA, CMA, CIA, CGFM, CFE, CSOXP, CGRCP, CGOVP
The University of Memphis

31.1 OVERVIEW

(a) CHANGING THE ENVIRONMENT   The financial institutions industry has changed significantly in the last two decades. The conventional model of providing and receiving financial services disappeared in the post–Gramm–Leach–Bliley (GLB) Financial Services Modernization Act of 1999. The continuous wave of consolidations in the financial services industry has resulted in fewer but bigger financial institutions, and they are now often perceived as "too big to fail." Financial services and products of banks, insurance companies, mutual funds, and brokerage firms that once were distinguishable, with separate roles, are now consolidated and converged. Regulatory changes and increased global competition have further blurred the lines among depository institutions, mortgage banking activities, investment companies, credit unions, investment banks, insurance companies, finance companies, and securities brokers and dealers.

Global competition has increased as all types of financial services firms conduct business directly with potential depositors and borrowers. Transactions traditionally executed through depository institutions are now handled by all types of financial institutions. Increased global competition has heightened the depository institutions' desire for innovative approaches to attracting depositors and borrowers worldwide. Financial institutions are seeking higher levels of noninterest income, restructuring banking operations to reduce costs, and continuing consolidation within the industry. Consolidation, convergence, and competition derived primarily from deregulation and technological advances have reshaped the financial services industry. The passage of the Gramm–Leach–Bliley Act has accelerated the pace of consolidation and convergence in the financial services industry and has raised some concerns that its implementation has created concentration of economic power in the financial services industry that would have made it more difficult for government to effectively oversee the industry's activities and strategies in managing risk. Some overriding reasons for the current financial crises are ineffective regulation, greed, and incompetency of executives of troubled financial institutions, nature of bank lending and investment, inadequate risk assessment, and conflicts of interest financial services activities. This chapter presents an overview of the financial services industry, its role in the economy, types and nature of financial firms and their regulatory framework, and financial activities and related risks.

(b) ROLE IN THE ECONOMY   Financial services firms play an important role in our economy by financing individual and business projects, lending to individuals and businesses and investing in capital markets. Financial institutions can promote economic growth and prosperity for the nation, but their inefficiency can cause significant threats and the uncertainty and volatility in the markets, which adversely affects investor confidence worldwide. This lack of public trust and investor confidence has caused either disappearance or reorganization of once-prominent Wall Street firms: Bear Stearns that merged with JPMorgan Chase; Lehman Brothers that went bankrupt; Merrill Lynch that was acquired by Bank of America; and Morgan Stanley and Goldman Sachs that changed their corporate structures, becoming bank holding companies. The U.S. government appeared to facilitate the establishment of giant companies (e.g., AIG, Fannie Mae, Freddie Mac) to promote its social, economic, and political policies. Such companies' executives continuously make high-risk decisions and receive outrageous compensation to make these decisions, while lawmakers and regulators allow market mechanisms to rectify the problems that result from unsound business decisions via deregulation. Having become too big to fail—that is, so large that their failure could bring about systemic financial crisis—they are thus protected from implosion; in efforts to prevent their demise, the government steps in to bail them out at the taxpayers' expense. Financial institutions worldwide have lost more than $1.5 trillion on mortgage-related losses. The failed financial institutions of Bear Stearns, Lehman Brothers, AIG, and Merrill Lynch all played a vital role in the recent economic meltdown, as they all engaged in risky mortgage-lending practices, credit derivatives, hedge funds, and corporate loans.

Financial institutions are essential financial intermediaries in the economy in the sense that they provide liquidity transformation and monitoring mechanisms. Financial institutions in their basic role provide a medium of exchange; however, they may also serve as a tool to regulate the economy. In a complex financial and economic environment, the regulation of financial institutions—directly and indirectly—is used to impact economic activity. The Dodd–Frank Wall Street Reform and Consumer Protection Act of 2010 was passed to minimize the probability of future financial crisis and systemic distress by empowering regulators to require higher capital requirements and establish a new regulatory regime for large financial firms, by developing regulatory and market structures for financial derivatives, and by creating systemic risk assessment and monitoring. Dodd–Frank created the Financial Services Oversight Council (FSOC) to identify and monitor systematic risk in the financial system. The FSOC recommends appropriate leverage, liquidity, capital, and risk management rules to the Federal Reserve. The FSOC can practically take control of and liquidate troubled financial services firms if their failure would pose significant threat to the nation's financial stability. Ineffective functioning of financial institutions can be detrimental to the real economy, as evidenced in the recent financial crisis. Many banks in the United States and Europe went bankrupt, had to be rescued by government, or were taken over by other financial institutions—which then made them "too big to fail"—or perhaps, "too big to save."

(c) TYPES OF FINANCIAL INSTITUTIONS Financial services institutions include banks and savings institutions, mortgage institutions, investment companies, credit unions, investment banks, insurance companies, finance companies, securities brokers and dealers, real estate investment trusts, as well as less common financial institutions such as sovereign wealth firms. The more common types of financial institutions are described in this section. In view of the range and diversity within financial institutions, this chapter will focus on three major types of entities/activities: banks and savings institutions, mortgage institutions, and investment companies.

(i) Banks and Savings Institutions Banks and savings institutions (including thrifts) continue in their traditional role as financial intermediaries. They provide a link between entities that have capital and entities that need capital, while also providing an efficient means for payment and transfer of funds between these entities. Banks also provide a wide range of services to their customers, including cash management and fiduciary services, accepting demand and time deposits, making loans to individuals and organizations, and providing other financial services of documentary collections, international banking and trade financing.

Financial modernization and financial reform legislation (Dodd–Frank Act of 2010) continues to change the way banks and savings institutions conduct business. Banks and savings institutions have developed sophisticated products to meet customer needs and technological advances to support such complex and specialized transactions. Continued financial reform may change the types and nature of permissible banking activities and affiliations.

(ii) Mortgage Institutions Mortgage banking activities include the origination, sale, and servicing of mortgage loans. Mortgage loan origination activities are performed by entities such as mortgage banks, mortgage brokers, credit unions, and commercial banks and savings institutions. Mortgages are purchased by government-sponsored entities, sponsors of mortgage-backed security (MBS) programs, and private companies such as insurance companies, other mortgage banking entities, and pension funds. These financial institutions typically provide long-term loans to businesses and individuals.

(iii) Investment Companies Investment companies pool shareholders' funds to provide the shareholders with professional investment management. Typically, an investment company sells its capital shares to the public, invests the proceeds to achieve its investment objectives, and distributes to its shareholders the net income and net gains realized on the sale of its investments. The types of investment companies include management investment companies, unit investment trusts, collective trust funds, investment partnerships, certain separate accounts of insurance companies, and offshore funds. Investment companies grew significantly in recent years, primarily due to growth in mutual funds.

(iv) Credit Unions Credit unions are member-owned, not-for-profit cooperative financial institutions, organized around a defined membership. The members pool their savings, borrow funds, and obtain other related financial services. A credit union relies on volunteers who represent the members. Its primary objective is to provide services to its members, rather than to generate earnings for its owners. More recently, many credit unions have made arrangements to share branch offices with other credit unions and depository institutions to reduce operating costs.

(v) Investment Banks   Investment banks or merchant banks deal with the financing requirements of corporations and institutions. They may be organized as corporations or partnerships. Investment banks are financial institutions that assist corporations and governments in raising capital by underwriting and acting as the agent in the issuance of *securities*. An investment bank also assists companies involved in *mergers and acquisitions, derivatives*, and provides ancillary services such as *market making* and the trading of *derivatives, fixed-income* instruments, *foreign exchange, commodity*, and *equity securities*.

(vi) Insurance Companies   The primary purpose of insurance is the spreading of risks. The two major types of insurance are life, and property and casualty. The primary purpose of life insurance is to provide financial assistance at the time of death. It typically has a long period of coverage. Property and casualty insurance companies provide policies to individuals (personal lines) and to business enterprises (commercial lines). Examples of personal lines include homeowners' and individual automobile policies. Examples of commercial lines include general liability and workers' compensation. Banks, mutual funds, and health maintenance organizations are aggressively trying to expand into products traditionally sold by insurance companies. During the 1990s and early 2000s, the insurance industry benefited from the strong stock and bond markets; however, recent slow premium growth and the increased competition and economic meltdown continued to pressure insurers to reduce costs and improve profitability. Many companies in the insurance sector have been adversely affected by the financial crisis, particularly; insurance companies that were involved in activities traditionally associated with investment banks, valuation, and rating pressures have been deeply impacted by the recent crisis.

Implementation of provisions of Dodd–Frank Act will significantly affect insurance companies by impacting their business transactions. The newly established Federal Insurance Office (FIO) is intended to play an important role in overseeing and coordinating insurance activities between the international insurance market and the U.S. insurance market. Nonetheless, the FIO will not be in charge of state regulation of insurance companies. Dodd–Frank Act directed the SEC to establish rules and standards for broker-dealers and investment advisors that would have a substantial impact on insurance companies. The FIO will oversee all aspects of the insurance industry, including systemic risk, capital standards, consumer protection, and international coordination of insurance regulation.

(vii) Finance Companies   Finance companies provide lending and financing services to consumers (consumer financing) and to business enterprises (commercial financing). The more common types of consumer financing include mortgage loans, retail sales contracts, and insurance service. The more common types of commercial financing include factoring, revolving loans, installment, term and floor plan loans, portfolio purchase agreements, and lease financing. Captive finance entities represent manufacturers, retailers, wholesalers, and other business enterprises who provide financing to encourage customers to buy their products and services. Many captive finance companies also finance third-party products. More recently, mortgage finance companies and diversified finance companies have increased their presence by increasing the number of loans made to higher risk niches at higher yields.

(viii) Securities Brokers and Dealers   Securities brokers and dealers serve in various roles within the securities industry. Brokers, acting in an agency capacity, buy and sell securities, commodities, and related financial instruments for their customers and charge a commission. Dealers or traders, acting in a principal capacity, buy and sell for their own account and trade with customers and other dealers. Broker-dealers perform a wide range of both types of activities, such as assisting with private placements, underwriting public securities, developing new products, facilitating international investment activity, serving as a depository for customers' securities, extending credit, and providing research and advisory services.

(ix) Real Estate Investment Trusts   The new class of Real Estate Investment Trusts (REITs), formed since 1991, are basically self-contained real estate companies. They are designed to align the interests of active management and passive investors, generate cash flow growth, and create long-term value. Traditionally, REITs relied on mortgage debt to finance their development and acquisition activities. Recently, many REITs have taken advantage of their large market capitalization and strong balance sheets to raise cash by issuing debt on an unsecured basis.

31.2 BANKS AND SAVINGS INSTITUTIONS

(a) PRIMARY RISKS OF BANKS AND SAVINGS INSTITUTIONS   General business and economic risk factors exist for many industries; however, increased competition and consolidation among banks and savings institutions has resulted in the industry's aggressive pursuit of profitable activities. Techniques for managing assets and liabilities and financial risks have been enhanced in order to maximize income levels. Technological advances have accommodated increasingly complex transactions such as the sale of securities backed by cash flows from other financial assets. Regulatory policy has radically changed the business environment for banks, savings, and other financial institutions. Additionally, there are other risk factors common to most banks and savings institutions, based on their business activities. Dodd–Frank Act establishes stricter disclosure requirements and restricts risk-taking appetite of banks by encouraging them to redesign their business lines and services. The other primary risk factors are described next.

(i) Interest-Rate Risk   Interest-rate risk is the risk that adverse movements in interest rates may result in loss of profits since banks and savings institutions routinely earn on assets at one rate and pay on liabilities at another rate. Techniques used to minimize interest-rate risk are a part of asset/liability management.

(ii) Liquidity Risk   Liquidity risk is the risk that an institution may be unable to meet its obligations as they become due. An institution may acquire funds short term and lend funds long term to obtain favorable interest rate spreads, thus creating liquidity risk if depositors or creditors demand repayment. The primary function of banks in transforming short-term deposits into long-term loans makes them vulnerable to liquidity risk. Effective liquidity risk management is essential to banks to ensure their ability to meet cash flow obligations. The Basel Committee has established guidance on managing liquidity risk that provides details on eight functions:

1. "The importance of establishing a liquidity risk tolerance;
2. The maintenance of an adequate level of liquidity, including through a cushion of liquid assets;

3. The necessity of allocating liquidity costs, benefits and risks to all significant business activities;
4. The identification and measurement of the full range of liquidity risks, including contingent liquidity risks;
5. The design and use of severe stress test scenarios;
6. The need for a robust and operational contingency funding plan;
7. The management of intraday liquidity risk and collateral; and
8. Public disclosure in promoting market discipline"

(iii) Asset-Quality Risk   Asset-quality risk is the risk that the loss of expected cash flows due to, for example, loan defaults and inadequate collateral will result in significant losses. Examples include credit losses from loans and declines in the economic value of mortgage servicing rights, resulting from prepayments of principal during periods of falling interest rates.

(iv) Fiduciary Risk   Fiduciary risk is the risk of loss arising from failure to properly process transactions or handle the custody, management, or both, of financially related assets on behalf of third parties. Examples include administering trusts, managing mutual funds, and servicing the collateral behind asset-backed securities.

(v) Processing Risk   Processing risk is the risk that transactions will not be processed accurately or timely, due to large volumes, short periods of time, unauthorized access of computerized records, or the demands placed on both computerized and manual systems. Examples include electronic funds transfers, loan servicing, and check processing.

(vi) Operating Risk   Operating risk is the risk that losses can occur from internal failures and external events aside from financial risk. Operating risk is the risk of loss resulting from inadequate or failed internal processes, people, and systems, or from adverse effects of external events. This risk imposes a new capital charge to cover losses associated with operational risk.

(vii) Market Risk   Market risk is the risk associated with earning volatility that is caused by adverse price movements in the bank's principal trading positions. Market risk can be measured in terms of value-at-risk (VAR).

(b) REGULATION AND SUPERVISION OF BANKS AND SAVINGS INSTITUTIONS
The legal system that governed the financial services industry in the United States was created in response to the stock market crash of 1929 and the resulting Great Depression. Thousands of banks went out of business and, in response, Congress passed the Glass–Steagall Act in 1933. Glass–Steagall prohibited commingling the businesses of commercial and investment banking. Its intent was to restrict banks from engaging in business activities that allegedly contributed to and accelerated the stock market crash. In the view of legislators, the way to do this was to confine banks to certain strictly defined activities.

In 1945, Congress enacted the McCarran–Ferguson Act as comprehensive legislation governing the insurance industry. McCarran–Ferguson effectively delegated the responsibility for regulating the business of insurance to the states. Since then, the states have maintained autonomy in their regulatory role with relatively minor, but increasing, exceptions. With the Bank Holding Company Act of 1956 and amendments in 1970, Congress limited affiliations between bank and nonbank businesses.

Section 20 of the Glass–Steagall Act took on a life of its own. Section 20 limited banks' ability to own subsidiaries "principally engaged" in securities underwriting. Over time, that section evolved from being considered a prohibition against any securities underwriting to permitting banks to do so through a subsidiary, as long as underwriting revenues did not exceed 25 percent of total revenues of that subsidiary—thus allowing them to meet the "not principally engaged" test. Over the years, the effective relaxation of those restrictions enabled numerous acquisitions of securities firms by U.S. bank-holding companies and by foreign banks.

These barriers also eroded over time through a combination of changes in customer demands and market activities, the increasing use of more sophisticated financial management techniques, advances in technology, regulatory interpretations, and legal decisions. Product innovation played a role, as the industry learned how to rapidly bundle and unbundle risk, creating new securitization products and accessing the capital markets in ways that had not been contemplated under the then-existing regulatory framework.

As banks assumed a larger role in insurance sales, brokerage, and securities underwriting activities, products began to converge in the marketplace, and the perceived benefits from the convergence of these and related activities instilled a new urgency in the effort to modernize and clarify the regulatory framework governing financial services companies.

The Gramm–Leach–Bliley Act of 1999 (GLB Act) amended the Bank Holding Company Act to allow a bank holding company or foreign bank that qualifies as a financial holding company to engage in a broad range of activities that are defined by the GLB Act to be financial in nature or incidental to a financial activity, or that the Federal Reserve Board (FRB), in consultation with the secretary of the treasury, determines to be financial in nature or incidental to a financial activity. The GLB Act also allows a financial holding company to seek board approval to engage in any activity that the FRB determines both to be complementary to a financial activity and not to pose a substantial risk to the safety and soundness of depository institutions or the financial system generally. Bank holding companies that do not qualify as financial holding companies are limited to engaging in those nonbanking activities that were permissible for bank holding companies before the GLB Act was enacted.

On July 21, 2010, President Barack Obama signed into law the Dodd–Frank Wall Street Reform and Consumer Protection Act of 2010 (Dodd–Frank), which is cited as the most sweeping financial reform since the Great Depression. The Act is named after Senate Banking Committee Chairman Christopher Dodd (D-CT) and House Financial Services Committee Chairman Barney Frank (D-MA). Its provisions pertain to banks, hedge funds, credit-rating agencies, and the derivatives market. Dodd–Frank is about 2,300 pages, and more than 200 regulations that will arise from Dodd–Frank have not yet been written. It authorizes the establishment of an oversight council to monitor systemic risk of financial institutions and the creation of a consumer protection bureau within the Federal Reserve. Dodd–Frank requires the development of more than 240 new rules by the Securities and Exchange Commission (SEC), the Government Accountability Office (GAO), and the Federal Reserve to implement its provisions over a five-year period. Dodd–Frank Act will impact many aspects of the financial services industry:

- Foreign banking organizations and foreign nonbank financial companies
- SEC examination and enforcement
- Systemic risk/prudential supervision
- Banks/bank holding companies

- Credit-rating agencies
- Non-U.S. asset managers
- Derivatives
- Consumer and mortgage banking
- Alternatives (hedge funds/private equity)
- Large asset managers
- Brokers/dealers
- Insurance companies

Some provisions of the Dodd–Frank Act of 2010 are summarized as follows:

1. Broaden the supervisory and oversight role of the Federal Reserve Board (Fed) to include all entities that own an insured depository institution and other large and nonbank financial services firms that could threaten the nation's financial system.
2. Establish a new Financial Services Oversight Council to indentify and address existing and emerging systematic risks threatening the health of financial services firms.
3. Develop new processes to liquidate failed financial services firms.
4. Establish an independent Consumer Financial Protection Bureau to oversee consumer and investor financial regulations and their enforcement.
5. Create rules to regulate over-the-counter (OTC) derivatives.
6. Coordinate and harmonize the supervision, setting, and regulatory authorities of the SEC and the Commodities Futures Trading Commission (CFTC).
7. Mandate registration of advisers of private funds and disclosures of certain information of those funds.
8. Empower shareholders with a say on pay of nonbonding votes on executive compensation.
9. Increase accountability and transparency for credit-rating agencies.
10. Create a Federal Insurance Office within the Treasury Department.
11. Restrict and limit some activities of financial firms, including limiting bank proprietary investing and trading in hedge funds and private equity funds as well as limiting bank swaps activities.
12. Provide cooperation and consistency with international financial and banking standards.
13. Make permanent the exemption from its section 404(b) requirement for nonaccelerated filers (those with less than $75 million in market capitalization).
14. Require auditors of all broker-dealers to register with the Public Company Accounting Oversight Board (PCAOB) and give the PCAOB rule-making power to require a program of inspection for those auditors.
15. Empower the Financial Stability Oversight Council to monitor domestic and international financial regulatory proposals and developments, to strengthen the integrity, efficiency, competitiveness, and stability of the U.S. financial markets.
16. Make it easier for the SEC to prosecute aiders and abettors of those who commit securities fraud under the Securities Act of 1933, the Securities Exchange Act of 1934, and the Investment Advisers Act of 1940 by lowering the legal standard from "knowing" to "knowing or reckless."
17. Direct the SEC to issue rules requiring companies to disclose in the proxy statement why they have separated, or combined, the positions of chairman and CEO.

In August 2010, the Basel Committee on Banking Supervision issued its guidance on "Microfinance Activities and the Core Principles for Effective Banking Supervision." This supervisory guidance highlights the application of the Basel Core Principles for Effective Banking Supervision (BCP) to microfinance activities in order to improve practices on regulating and supervising microfinance activities. The guidance is intended to assist global banking organizations to develop a coherent and comprehensive approach to microfinance supervision that address three key elements:

1. Adequate and specialized knowledge of supervisors to effectively identify and assess risks that are specific to microfinance and microlending
2. Proper and effective allocation of supervisory resources to microfinance activities
3. Establishment of regulatory and supervisory framework that is cost-effective and efficient

(c) REGULATORY BACKGROUND Banks and savings institutions have special privileges and protections granted by government. These incentives, such as credit through the Federal Reserve System and federal insurance of deposits, have not been similarly extended to commercial enterprises. Accordingly, the benefits and responsibilities associated with their public role as financial intermediaries have brought banks and savings institutions under significant governmental oversight. For example, to stabilize the financial system during the financial crisis caused by subprime mortgage in the late 2007 and 2008, several bailouts were implemented by the governments in the United States, the United Kingdom, and some Western European countries. In September 2008, after the government brokered sale of investment banks such as Bear Stearns and Lehman Brothers, U.S. Treasury Secretary Henry Paulson and Federal Reserve Chairman Ben S. Bernanke proposed a $700 billion bailout for the stabilization of the financial institutions.

This was the greatest government intervention in financial markets in more than half a century. As a result of the financial repercussions of the Great Depression in the 1930s, the government took certain measures to maintain the stability of the country's financial system. Several new regulatory and supervisory agencies were created to promote economic stability, particularly in the banking industry, and to strengthen the regulatory and supervisory agencies that were in existence at the time. Among the agencies created were the Federal Deposit Insurance Corporation (FDIC), the Securities and Exchange Commission (SEC), the Federal Home Loan Bank Board (FHLBB), and the Federal Savings and Loan Insurance Corporation (FSLIC). The agencies that were strengthened included the Office of the Comptroller of the Currency (OCC) and the FRB. These entities were responsible for designing and establishing policies and procedures for the regulation and supervision of national and state banks, foreign banks doing business in the United States, and other depository institutions. This regulatory and supervisory structure, created during the 1930s, was in place for almost 60 years. In 1989, Congress enacted the Financial Institutions Reform, Recovery and Enforcement Act (FIRREA), which changed the regulatory and supervisory structure of thrift institutions. The FIRREA eliminated the FHLBB and the FSLIC. In their place, it created the Office of Thrift Supervision (OTS) as the primary regulator of the thrift industry and the Savings Association Insurance Fund (SAIF) as the thrift institutions' insurer to be administered by the FDIC.

Even though several of the aforementioned federal agencies have overlapping regulatory and supervisory responsibilities over depository institutions, in general terms, the OCC has primary responsibility for national banks; the FRB has primary responsibility over state banks that are members of the FRB, all financial holding companies and bank holding companies

Bank Classifications*	OTS	OCC	State Banking Department	Federal Reserve	FDIC
National banks		X			
State banks and trust companies					
Federal Reserve members			X	X	
Nonmembers					
FDIC insured			X		X
Noninsured			X		
Bank holding companies				X	
Thrift holding companies	X				
Savings banks	X			X	X
Savings and loan	X				
Associations					

*All national banks are members of the Federal Reserve Board. All national banks and state chartered member banks are insured by the FDIC.

EXHIBIT 31.1 SUPERVISOR AND REGULATOR

and their nonbank subsidiaries, and most U.S. operations of foreign banks; the FDIC has primary responsibility for all state-insured banks that are not members of the FRB (nonmember banks); and the OTS has primary responsibility for thrift institutions. Exhibit 31.1 lists these regulatory responsibilities.

(i) Office of the Comptroller of the Currency   The Office of the Comptroller of the Currency (OCC) charters, regulates, and supervises all national banks. It also supervises the federal branches and agencies of foreign banks. Headquartered in Washington, D.C., the OCC has six district offices plus an office in London to supervise the international activities of national banks.

The OCC was established in 1863 as a bureau of the U.S. Department of the Treasury. The OCC is headed by the comptroller, who is appointed by the president, with the advice and consent of the Senate, for a five-year term. The comptroller also serves as a director of the FDIC and a director of the Neighborhood Reinvestment Corporation.

The OCC's nationwide staff of examiners conducts on-site reviews of national banks and provides sustained supervision of bank operations. The agency issues rules, legal interpretations, and corporate decisions concerning banking, bank investments, bank community development activities, and other aspects of bank operations.

National bank examiners supervise domestic and international activities of national banks and perform corporate analyses. Examiners analyze a bank's loan and investment portfolios, funds management, capital, earnings, liquidity, sensitivity to market risk, and compliance with consumer banking laws, including the Community Reinvestment Act. They review the bank's internal controls, internal and external audits, and compliance with law. They also evaluate bank management's ability to identify and control risk.

In regulating national banks, the OCC has the power to do the following:

- Examine the banks.
- Approve or deny applications for new charters, branches, capital, or other changes in corporate or banking structure.
- Take supervisory actions against banks that do not comply with laws and regulations or that otherwise engage in unsound banking practices. The agency can remove

officers and directors, negotiate agreements to change banking practices, and issue cease-and-desist orders as well as civil money penalties.

• Issue rules and regulations governing bank investments, lending, and other practices.

(ii) Federal Reserve Board The Federal Reserve Board (FRB) was created by Congress in 1913 by the Federal Reserve Act. The primary role of the FRB as the nation's central bank is to establish and conduct monetary policy, as well as to regulate and supervise a wide range of financial activities. The structure of the FRB includes a board of governors, 12 Federal Reserve banks, and the member banks. The board of governors consists of seven members appointed by the president, subject to Senate confirmation. National banks must be members of the FRB. State banks are not required to, but may elect to, become members. Member banks and other depository institutions are required to keep reserves with the FRB, and member banks must subscribe to the capital stock of the reserve bank in the district to which they belong.

Since all national banks are supervised by the OCC, the FRB primarily regulates and supervises member state banks, including administering the registration and reporting requirements of the 1934 Act.

The regulatory and supervisory functions and other services provided by the FRB include the following:

• Examining the Federal Reserve banks, state member banks, bank holding companies and their nonbank subsidiaries, and state-licensed U.S. branches of foreign banks
• Requiring reports of member and other banks
• Setting the discount rate
• Providing credit facilities to members and other depository institutions for liquidity and other purposes
• Monitoring compliance with the money-laundering provisions contained in the Bank Secrecy Act
• Regulating transactions between banking affiliates
• Approving or denying applications by state banks to become members and to branch or merge with nonmember banks
• Approving or denying applications to become bank holding companies and for bank holding companies to acquire bank or nonbank subsidiaries
• Approving or denying applications by foreign banks to establish representative offices, branches, agencies, or bank subsidiaries in the United States
• Supplying currency when needed
• Regulating the establishment of foreign operations of national and state member banks and the operations of foreign banks doing business in the United States
• Enforcing legislation and issuing rules and regulations dealing with consumer protection
• Operating the nation's payment system

The Federal Reserve recently undertook five initiatives to mitigate the negative impacts of the financial crisis:

1. Extending credit facilities to financial institutions and thus improving market liquidity
2. Lowering interest rates to zero by the end of 2008

3. Taking several quantitative measures to reduce long-term interest rates and purchasing treasury bonds and Fannie Mae and Freddie Mac mortgage-backed securities (MBS)
4. Increasing deposit insurance limits and guaranteeing bank debt
5. Ordering the 19 largest banks holding companies to conduct compensation stress tests to ensure that they had sufficient capital to withstand financial difficulties and they could raise needed capital

(iii) Federal Deposit Insurance Corporation   The Federal Deposit Insurance Corporation (FDIC) was created under the Banking Act of 1933. The main purpose for its creation was to insure bank deposits in order to maintain economic stability in the event of bank failures. FIRREA restructured the FDIC during 1989 to carry out broadened functions by insuring thrift institutions as well as banks. The FDIC now insures all depository institutions except credit unions.

The FDIC is an independent agency of the U.S. government, managed by a five-member board of directors, consisting of the Comptroller of the Currency, the Director of the OTS, and three other members, including a chairman, appointed by the president, subject to Senate confirmation.

The FDIC insures deposits under two separate funds: the Bank Insurance Fund (BIF) and the SAIF. From its BIF, the FDIC insures national and state banks that are members of the FRB. These institutions are required to be insured. Also insured from this fund are state non-member banks and a limited number of insured branches of foreign banks (after 1991 foreign bank branches could no longer apply for FDIC insurance).

From its SAIF, the FDIC insures all federal savings and loan associations and federal savings banks. These institutions are required to be insured. State thrift institutions are also insured from this fund.

Currently, each account, subject to certain FDIC rules, in an insured depository institution is insured to a maximum of $100,000. Other responsibilities of the FDIC include the following:

*   Supervising the liquidation of insolvent insured depository institutions
*   Providing financial support and additional measures to prevent insured depository institution failures
*   Supervising state nonmember insured banks by conducting bank examinations, regulating bank mergers, consolidations and establishment of branches, and establishing other regulatory controls
*   Administering the registration and reporting requirements of the 1934 Act as applied to state nonmember banks

(iv) Office of Thrift Supervision   In 1989, FIRREA created the Office of Thrift Supervision (OTS) under the Department of the Treasury. The OTS regulates federal and state thrift institutions and thrift holding companies. As a principal rule maker, examiner, and enforcement agency, OTS exercises primary regulatory authority to grant federal thrift institution charters, approve branching applications, and allow mutual-to-thrift charter conversions. OTS is headed by a presidentially appointed director. The 12 district Federal Home Loan Banks (FHLBs) continue to be the primary source of credit for thrift institutions.

(d) REGULATORY ENVIRONMENT   The early 1980s were marked by the removal of interest-rate ceilings, the applications of reserve requirements to all depository institutions, expanded thrift powers, and related deregulatory actions. However, the failures of a large number of thrift institutions and commercial banks caused legislators in 1989 and 1991 to increase regulatory oversight. Both FIRREA and the Federal Deposit Insurance Corporation Improvement Act of 1991 (FDICIA) were directed toward protection of federal deposit insurance funds through early detection of an intervention in problem institutions with an emphasis on capital adequacy. FIRREA also established the Resolution Trust Corporation (RTC), which took over the conservatorship and liquidation of a large number of failed thrift institutions due to the bankruptcy of the FSLIC. The RTC completed its mission in 1996 at a net cost of approximately $150 billion to the federal government.

In addition to safety and soundness considerations, current banking regulations recognize economic issues, such as the desire for banks and savings institutions to successfully compete with other, less regulated financial services providers, as well as to address social issues, such as community reinvestment, nondiscrimination, and fair treatment in consumer credit, including residential lending. Costs and benefits of regulations are weighed as the approach to regulation of the industry is redefined.

Many provisions of Dodd–Frank Act are considered to be positive and useful in protecting consumers and investors, including the establishment of a consumer protection bureau and a systemic risk regulator, as well as provisions requiring derivatives to be put on clearinghouses/exchanges. The new Consumer Financial Products Commission (CFPC) will make rules for most retail products offered by banks such as certificates of deposit and consumer loans. The Dodd–Frank Act requires managers of hedge funds (but not the funds themselves) with more than $150 million in assets to register with the SEC. Some provisions are subject to study and further regulatory actions by regulators, including the one so-called Volcker rule to be implemented. Dodd–Frank fails to address this misconception of "too-big-to-fail" financial institutions, the main cause of the financial crisis—Fannie Mae, Freddie Mac, and the housing agencies and the excessive use of market-based short-term funding by financial services firms.

Worldwide, the Basel Committee on Banking Supervision reached an agreement on July 26, 2010, to strengthen global capital and liquidity requirements to promote a more resilient banking sector with proper ability to absorb shocks arising from financial and economic stress, to improve risk management, governance, transparency, and disclosures. The Basel Committee addresses the market failures caused by the recent financial crisis and establish measures to strengthen bank-level and microprudential regulation.

(e) FEDERAL DEPOSIT INSURANCE CORPORATION IMPROVEMENT ACT SECTION 112

Regulations implementing Section 36 of the Federal Deposit Insurance Act (FDI Act), as added by Section 112 of FDICIA, became effective July 2, 1993. These regulations imposed additional audit, reporting, and attestation responsibilities on management, directors (especially the audit committee), internal auditors, and independent accountants of banks and savings institutions with $500 million or more in total assets. The reporting requirements were effective for fiscal years ending on or after December 31, 1993. Congress amended the law in 1996 to eliminate attestation reports concerning compliance with certain banking laws; however, management is still required to report on compliance with such laws.

(i) The Regulation and Guidelines   The Dodd–Frank Wall Street Reform and Consumer Protection Act of 2010 is aimed at minimizing the probability of future financial crisis and systemic distress by empowering regulators to require higher capital requirements and establish

new regulatory regime large financial firms. Dodd–Frank is intended to provide more cost-effective and efficient regulatory guidelines for financial service firms and other impacted organizations. These regulatory guidelines are presented in Appendix A. The guidelines often leave discretion with an institution or its board, while simultaneously providing guidance that, if followed, would provide a safe harbor from examiner criticism.

(ii) Basic Requirements   Each FDIC-insured depository institution with assets in excess of $500 million at the beginning of its fiscal year ("covered institutions") is subject to the following requirements:

ANNUAL REPORT

Covered institutions must file an annual report, within 90 days of its fiscal year end, with the FDIC and its other appropriate state or federal bank regulator. The annual report must include:

    a. Audited financial statements prepared in accordance with generally accepted accounting principles (GAAP) and audited by an independent public accountant (IPA) meeting the qualifications.

    b. A management report signed by its chief executive and chief financial officer or chief accounting officer containing:

       ○ A statement of management's responsibilities for:

          ◇ Preparing the annual financial statements.

          ◇ Establishing and maintaining an adequate internal control structure and procedures for financial reporting.

          ◇ Complying with particular laws designated by the FDIC as affecting the safety and soundness of insured depositories.

       ○ Assessment by management of:

          ◇ The effectiveness of the institution's internal control structure and procedures for financial reporting as of the end of the fiscal year.

          ◇ The institution's compliance, during the fiscal year, with the designated safety and soundness laws. The FDIC designated only two kinds of safety and soundness laws to be addressed in the compliance report: (1) federal statutes and regulations concerning transactions with insiders and (2) federal and state statutes and regulations restricting the payment of dividends.

    c. An attestation report, by an IPA, on internal control structure and procedures for financial reporting. The institution's IPA must examine, attest to, and report separately on management's assertions about internal controls and about compliance. The attestations are to be made in accordance with generally accepted standards for attestation engagements.

In FIL No. 86-94, the FDIC indicated that financial reporting, at a minimum, includes financial statements prepared under GAAP and the schedules equivalent to the basic financial statements that are included in the institution's appropriate regulatory report (e.g., Schedules RC, RI, and RI-A in the Call Report).

On February 6, 1996, the Board of the FDIC amended the procedures that IPAs follow in testing compliance to streamline the procedures and to reduce regulatory burden. Financial services firms must also comply with Sections 302, 906, and 404 of the Sarbanes–Oxley

Act (SOX) to include executive certifications of both financial statements and internal control over financial reporting in their annual reports files with regulators and submitted to shareholders.

CORPORATE GOVERNANCE

The globalization of capital markets and financial institutions demands convergence in regulatory reforms and corporate governance measures and practices. Corporate governance measures are state and federal statutes, judicial deliberations, listing standards, and best practices. In the United States, the Sarbanes–Oxley Act of 2002 (SOX) and financial reform legislation signed into law in July 2010 through the Dodd–Frank Wall Street Reform and Consumer Protection Act have influenced regulatory reforms for financial institutions. The U.K. corporate governance reforms are specified in the 2003 Combined Code on Corporate Governance.

In October 2010, the Basel Committee issued its principles for enhancing corporate governance to promote effective corporate governance of financial institutions and banking organizations worldwide. These corporate governance principles address six areas:

1. The role of the board
2. The qualifications and composition of the board
3. The importance of an independent risk management function, including a chief risk officer or equivalent
4. The importance of monitoring risks on an ongoing firmwide and individual entity basis
5. The board's oversight of the compensation systems
6. The board and senior management's understanding of the bank's operational structure and risks

On October 12, 2010, the International Federation of Accountants (IFAC) and the United Nations Conference on Trade and Development (UNCTAD) hosted the Accountancy Summit on Corporate Governance Reform Looks Beyond the Global Financial Crisis. Participants from more than 50 countries collectively supported the following points relevance to convergence in global corporate governance:

- "The accountancy profession has a key role to play in strengthening corporate governance and facilitating the integration of governance and sustainability into the strategy, operations, and reporting of an organization.
- Boards should be focused on the long-term sustainability of their businesses. As such, corporate governance reform must include strengthening board oversight of management, positioning risk management as a key board responsibility, and encouraging remuneration practices that balance risk and long-term (social, environmental, and economic) performance criteria.
- Governance is more than having the right structures, regulation and principles in place—it is about ensuring that the right behaviors and processes are in place.
- Governance mechanisms need to be strengthened at banks and other companies to ensure better oversight of risk management and executive compensation.
- More dialogue is needed between policy makers, the accounting profession, and other financial industries to consider how we can work together effectively on a global level."

AUDIT COMMITTEE

Covered institutions must establish an independent audit committee composed of directors who are independent of management. The entire board of directors annually is required to adopt a resolution documenting its determination that the audit committee has met all FDIC-imposed requirements.

The audit committee of any "large" Insured Depository Institute (i.e., total assets of more than $3 billion, measured as of the beginning of each fiscal year) shall include members with banking or related financial management expertise, have access to its own outside counsel, and not include any large customers of the institution. If a large institution is a subsidiary of a holding company and relies on the audit committee of the holding company to comply with this rule, the holding company audit committee shall not include any members who are large customers of the subsidiary institution. Appendix A to Part 363 provides guidelines in determining whether the audit committee meets these criteria.

The audit committee is required to review with management and the IPA the basis for the reports required by the FDIC's regulation. FDIC suggests, but does not mandate, additional audit committee duties, including overseeing internal audit, selecting the IPA, and reviewing significant accounting policies.

Each subject institution must provide its independent accountant with copies of the institution's most recent reports of condition and examination; any supervisory memorandum of understanding or written agreement with any federal or state regulatory agency; and a report of any action initiated or taken by federal or state banking regulators.

Recent global financial crises and related economic meltdowns underscore the importance of board committees, particularly the audit committee in overseeing managerial function of troubled banks and other financial institutions. Audit committees in the post–Sarbanes–Oxley Act of 2002 are required to protect investor interests by assuming more effective oversight responsibilities in the areas of internal controls, financial reporting, risk assessment, audit activities, and compliance with applicable laws and regulations. In the post–Sarbanes–Oxley (SOX) period, the audit committee selects the bank's external auditor and reviews the company's annual audited financial statements and internal control over financial reporting.

Lawmakers (SOX), regulators (SEC rules), and listing standards of national stock exchanges (NYSE, Nasdaq, AMEX) generally require public committees to have an audit committee, which must be composed of independent directors with no personal, financial, or family ties to management. Rezaee (2007) describes four elements of audit committees:

1. Audit committee members must be independent.
2. Audit committee members must select and oversee the issuer's independent account.
3. There must be a procedural process for handling complaints regarding the issuer's accounting practice.
4. The audit committee must have authority to engage advisors.

Audit committee oversight responsibilities can be grouped into the following categories:

*   *Corporate governance.* The audit committee should protect investor interests by overseeing managerial functions in planning, coordinating and monitoring banks financial activities.
*   *Internal controls.* The audit committee should review management and external auditor reports on the effectiveness of internal control over financial reporting (ICFR).

- *Financial reporting.* The audit committee should review and oversee executive certifications on the completeness and accuracy of financial statements.
- *Audit activities.* The audit committee should be in charge of hiring, firing, compensating, and overseeing audit activities, as well as reviewing external auditors' reports on financial statements and ICFR.
- *Code of ethics conduct.* The audit committee should review and oversee the design, implementation and enforcement of banks' codes of ethical conduct.
- *Whistleblower program.* The audit committee should oversee the design and implementation of banks' whistleblower policies and programs to ensure that employees, customers, and others can come forward in reporting bank irregularities, violations of laws and other concerns without being retaliated.
- *Enterprise risk management.* The audit committee should oversee the proper development and functioning of bank risk management in addressing liquidity, interest-rate, operating, credit, and other risks presented in the previous sections.
- *Financial statement fraud.* The audit committee should oversee bank antifraud policies and procedures designed to prevent and detect financial reporting fraud.

(iii) Holding Company Exception   The requirements of the FDIC's regulation, in some instances, may be satisfied by a bank's or savings association's parent holding company. The requirement for audited financial statements always may be satisfied by providing audited financial statements of the consolidated holding company. The requirements for other reports, as well as for an independent audit committee, may be satisfied by the holding company if:

- The holding company's services and functions are comparable to those required of the depository institution.
- The depository institution has total assets as of the beginning of the fiscal year either of less than $5 billion or equal to or greater than $5 billion and a CAMELS composite rating of 1 or 2. Section 314(a) of the Riegle Community Development and Regulatory Improvement Act of 1994 amended Section 36(i) of the FDI Act to expand the holding company exception to be equal to or greater than $5 billion. The requirement that the institution must have a CAMELS composite rating of 1 or 2 remained unchanged.

The appropriate federal banking agency may revoke the exception for any institution with total assets in excess of $9 billion for any period of time during which the appropriate federal banking agency determines that the institution's exception would create a significant risk to the affected deposit insurance fund.

(iv) Availability of Reports   All of management's reports are made publicly available. The independent accountant's report on the financial statements and attestation report on financial reporting controls is also made publicly available. The Sarbanes–Oxley Act of 2002 requires public reporting on the following:

- The audit committee review of both financial statements and internal control over financial reporting
- Management certifications of accuracy and completeness of financial statements and the effectiveness of internal control over financial reporting
- External auditor report on fair presentation of financial statements and the effectiveness of internal control over financial reporting

(f) CAPITAL ADEQUACY GUIDELINES   Capital is one of the primary tools used by regulators to monitor the financial health of insured banks and savings institutions. Statutorily mandated supervisory intervention is focused primarily on an institution's capital levels relative to regulatory standards. The federal banking agencies detail these requirements in their respective regulations under capital adequacy guidelines. The capital adequacy requirements are implemented through quarterly regulatory financial reporting ("Call Reports" and "Thrift Financial Reports [TFRs]").

On September 12, 2010, global bank regulators agreed to require banks to significantly increase their amount of top-quality capital in an attempt to prevent further international financial crisis. The Basel III reforms developed by the Basel Committee on Banking Supervision will require banks to maintain top-quality capital totaling 7 percent of their risk-bearing assets compared to currently required 2 percent. Effective compliance with Basel III rules would require banks to raise substantial new capital over the next several years; the rules become effective in January 2019. The primary objective of Basel III rules is to strengthen global capital standards to ensure sustainable financial stability and growth for banks worldwide. There rules are intended to encourage banks to engage in appropriate risk business strategies to ensure their financial health and their ability to withstand financial shocks without government bailout supports. Specifically, Basel III will require banks to: (1) maintain top-quality capital (Tier 1 capital, consisting or equity and retained earnings) up to 4.5 percent of their assets; (2) hold a new separate "capital conservation buffer" of common equity worth at least 2.5 percent of their assets; and (3) build a separate "countercyclical buffer" of up to 2.5 percent when their credit markets are booming. The Tier 1 rule will take effect January 2015, and the requirements for the capital conversation buffer will be phased in between January 2016 and January 2019.

(i) Risk-Based and Leverage Ratios   Capital adequacy is measured mainly through two risk-based capital ratios and a leverage ratio, with thrifts subject to an additional tangible capital ratio.

(ii) Tier 1, Tier 2, and Tier 3 Components   Regulatory capital may be composed of three components: core capital or Tier 1, supplementary capital or Tier 2, and for those institutions meeting market risk capital requirements, Tier 3. Tier 1 capital includes elements such as common stock, surplus, retained earnings, minority interest in consolidated subsidiaries and qualifying preferred stock, adjustments for foreign exchange translation, and unrealized losses on equity securities available for sale with readily determinable market values. Tier 2 capital includes, with certain limitations, elements such as general loan loss reserves, certain forms of preferred stock, long-term preferred stock, qualifying intermediate-term preferred stock and term subordinated debt, perpetual debt, and other hybrid debt/equity instruments. Tier 3 capital consists of short-term subordinated debt that meets certain conditions and may be used only by institutions subject to market-risk capital requirements to the extent that Tier 1 and Tier 2 capital elements do not provide adequate Tier 1 and total risk-based capital ratio levels.

Specifically, Tier 3 capital must have an original maturity of at least two years; it must be unsecured and fully paid up; it must be subject to a lock-in clause that prevents the issuer from repaying the debt even at maturity if the issuer's capital ratio is, or with repayment would become, less than the minimum 8 percent risk-based capital ratio; it must not be redeemable before maturity without the prior approval of the institution's supervisor; and it must not contain or be covered by any covenants, terms, or restrictions that may be inconsistent with safe and sound banking practices. Tier 2 capital elements individually and together are variously restricted in proportion to Tier 1 capital, which is intended to be the dominant capital component.

Certain deductions are made to determine regulatory capital, including goodwill and other disallowed intangibles, excess portions of qualifying intangibles and deferred tax assets, investments in unconsolidated subsidiaries, and reciprocal holdings of other bank's capital instruments. Certain adjustments made to equity under GAAP for unrealized gains and losses on debt and equity securities available for sale under Financial Accounting Standards Board (FASB) Statement No. 115, mainly unrealized gains, are excluded from Tier 1 and Total Capital. Portions of qualifying, subordinated debt, and limited-life preferred stock exceeding 50 percent of a bank's Tier 1 capital are also deducted. Any regulatory capital deduction is also made to average total assets for ratio computation purposes. The new market-risk capital guidelines discussed below also contained further capital constraints, by stating that the sum of Tier 2 and Tier 3 capital allocated for market risk may not exceed 250 percent of Tier 1 capital allocated for market risk. Thrift's tangible capital is generally defined as Tier 1 capital less intangibles.

(iii) Risk-Weighted Assets   The capital ratios are calculated using the applicable regulatory capital component in the numerator and either risk-weighted assets or total adjusted on-balance-sheet assets as the denominator, as appropriate. Risk-weighted assets are ascertained pursuant to the regulatory guidelines that allocate gross average assets among four categories of risk weights (0%, 20%, 50%, and 100%). The allocations are based mainly on type of asset, type of obligor, and nature of collateral, if any. Gross assets include on-balance sheet assets, credit equivalents of certain off-balance-sheet exposures, and credit equivalents of certain assets sold with recourse, limited recourse, or that are treated as financings for regulatory reporting purposes.

Credit equivalents of off-balance-sheet exposures are determined by the nature of the exposure. For example, direct credit substitutes (e.g., standby letters of credit) are credit converted at 100 percent of the face amount. Other off-balance-sheet activities are subject to the current exposure method, which is composed of the positive mark-to-market value (if any) and an estimate of the potential increase in credit exposure over the remaining life of the contract. These "add-ons" are estimated by applying defined credit conversion factors, differentiated by type of instrument and remaining maturity, to the contract's notional value. The nature and extent of recourse impacts the calculation of credit equivalents amounts of assets sold or securitized. In December 2001, the banking agencies issued a final rule amending the agencies' regulatory capital standards to align more closely the risk-based capital treatment of recourse obligations and direct credit substitutes. The rule also varies the capital requirements for position in securitized transactions and certain other exposures according to their relative credit risk and requires capital commensurate with the risks associated with residual interests.

(iv) Capital Calculations and Minimum Requirements   The capital ratios, calculations, and minimum requirements are presented in Exhibit 31.2.

In summary, Basel rules set forth tougher capital requirements by providing more restrictive capital definitions, requiring higher risk-weighted assets (RWA), capital buffers, and higher minimum capital ratios. These new Basel standards are expected to affect profitability and transformation of the business models of many banks, as well as other bank activities relevant to stress testing, counterparty risk, and capital management infrastructure. Implementation of provisions of Basel III is expected to require more standardized risk-adjusted capital requirements, which will enable investors to better analyze and compare risk-adjusted performance.

In the United States, the Supervisory Capital Assessment Program (SCAP) has increased capital levels by:

Capital Ratio	Calculation	Minimum Requirement
Total risk-based ratio:	Tier 1 + Tier 2/Risk-weighted assets	≥ 8.0%
Unadjusted	Tier 1 + Tier 2 + Tier 3/Risk-weighted	≥ 8.0%
Adjusted for marked risk	assets plus market-risk equivalent assets	
Tier 1 risk-based ratio	Tier 1/Risk-weighted assets	≥ 4.0%
Tier 1 leverage capital ratio	Tier 1/Average on-balance sheet assets	≥ 4.0%*
Tangible ratio (Thrifts)	Tangible capital/on-balance sheet assets	≥ 1.5%

*3.0% for institutions CAMELS/MACRO rated "1" (overall).

Basel III Accord will require banks to: (1) maintain top-quality capital (tier 1 capital, consisting or equity and retained earnings) up to 4.5 percent of their assets; and (2) hold a new separate "capital conservation buffer" of common equity worth at least 2.5 percent of their assets; and (3) build a separate" countercyclical buffer" of up to 2.5 percent when their credit markets are booming. The Tier 1 rule will take effect from January 2015 and the requirement for the capital conversation buffer will be phased in between January 2016 and January 2019. Exhibit 31.3 summarizes the Basel III capital requirements.

Calibration of the Capital Framework Capital requirements and buffers (all number in percent)			
	Common Equity (after deductions)	Tier 1 Capital	Total Capital
Minimum	4.5	6.0	8.0
Conservation buffer	2.5		
Minimum plus Conservation buffer	7.0	8.5	10.5
Countercyclical buffer Range*	0–2.5		

According to Basel III Accord:
Tier 1 capital ratio = 6%
Core Tier 1 capital ratio (common equity after deductions) = 4.5%
Core Tier 1 capital ratio (common equity after deductions) before 2013 = 2%, 1st January 2013 = 3.5%, 1st January 2014 = 4%, 1st January 2015 = 4.5%. The transition periods in meeting capital requirements are presented in Exhibit 31.4.

Annex 2: Phase-in arrangements (shading indicates transition periods) (all dates are as on 1 January)

	2011	2012	2013	2014	2015	2016	2017	2018	As of 1 January 2019
Leverage ratio	Supervisory monitoring		Parallel run 1 Jan 2012–1 Jan 2017 Disclosures starts 1 Jan 2015					Migration to Pillar 1	
Minimum common equity capital ratio			3.5%	4.0%	4.5%	4.5%	4.5%	4.5%	4.5%
Capital Conservation Buffer						0.625%	1.25%	1.875%	2.50%
Minimum common equity plus capital conservation buffer			3.5%	4.0%	4.5%	5.125%	5.75%	6.375%	7.0%
Phase-in of deductions from CET1 (including amounts exceeding the limit for DTAs, MSRs and financials)				20%	40%	60%	80%	100%	100%
Minimum Tier 1 capital			4.5%	5.5%	6.0%	6.0%	6.0%	6.0%	6.0%
Minimum total capital			8.0%	8.0%	8.0%	8.0%	8.0%	8.0%	8.0%
Minimum total capital plus conservation buffer			8.0%	8.0%	8.0%	8.625%	9.125%	9.875%	10.5%
Capital instruments that no longer qualify as noncore Tier 1 capital or Tier 2 capital			Phased out over 10-year horizon beginning 2013						
Liquidity coverage ratio	Observation period begins				Introduce minimum standard				
Net stable funding ratio		Observation period begins						Introduce minimum standard	

Source: Basel III Accord: The new Basel III framework From: http://www.basel-iii-accord.com/

EXHIBIT 31.2 Capital Ratio Calculations and Minimum Requirements

- Requiring many U.S. banks to increase their capital levels. The current Tier 1 common median for U.S. banks is at 9 percent.
- Providing adequate transition period of eight years to generate further capital buffers through earnings generation.

(v) Interest Rate Risk and Capital Adequacy   OTS capital rules require that certain savings associations with excessive interest rate risk exposure (as defined) must deduct 50 percent of the estimated decline in its net portfolio value resulting from a 200 basis point change in market interest rates in excess of 2 percent of the estimated economic value of portfolio assets. In August 1995, the banking agencies amended their minimum capital requirements explicitly to include consideration of interest rate risk, but established no means for quantifying that risk to a specific amount of additional capital. During 1996, the federal bank regulatory agencies approved a policy statement on sound practices for managing interest rate risk in commercial banks, but did not include a standardized framework for measuring interest rate risk. The agencies elected not to pursue a standardized measure and explicit capital charge for interest rate risk, due to concerns about the burden, accuracy, and complexity of a standardized measure and recognition that industry techniques for measuring interest rate risk are continuing to evolve.

(vi) Capital Allocated for Market Risk   In September 1996, the federal bank regulatory agencies (OCC, FDIC, FRB) amended their respective risk-based capital standards to address market risk. Specifically, an institution subject to the market risk capital requirement must adjust its risk-based capital ratio to take into account the general market risk of all positions located in its trading account and foreign exchange and commodity positions, wherever located and for the specific risk of debt and equity positions located in its trading account. Market risk capital requirements generally apply to any bank or bank holding company whose trading activities equal 10 percent or more of its total assets, or whose trading activity equals $1 billion or more. In addition, on a case-by-case basis, an agency may require an institution that does not meet the applicability criteria to comply with the market risk guidelines, if the agency deems it necessary for safety and soundness purposes, or may exclude an institution that meets the applicability criteria.

No later than January 1, 1998, institutions with significant market risk were required to:

- Maintain regulatory capital on a daily basis at an overall minimum of eight percent ratio of total qualifying capital to risk-weighted assets, adjusted for market risk.
- Include a supplemental market-risk capital charge in their risk-based capital calculations and quarterly regulatory reports.
- Maintain appropriate internal measurement, reporting, and risk management systems to generate and monitor the basis for the value-at-risk (VAR) and the associated capital charge.

The institution's risk-based capital ratio adjusted for market risk is its risk-based capital ratio for purposes of prompt corrective action and other statutory and regulatory purposes.

Institutions are permitted to use different assumptions and modeling techniques reflecting distinct business strategies and approaches to risk management. The agencies do not specify VAR modeling parameters for internal risk management purposes; however, they do specify minimum qualitative requirements for internal risk management processes, as well as certain quantitative requirements for the parameters and assumptions for internal models used to measure market risk exposure for regulatory capital purposes.

There are several models of risk assessment and management, including most widely used model of VAR developed through statistical ideas and probability theories VAR utilizes a group of related models that share a mathematical framework by measuring the boundaries of risk in a portfolio over short durations. The portfolio can consist of equities, bonds, derivatives, or other financial instruments, and risks can be measured in terms of diversification, leverage, and volatility as a proxy for market risk. VAR takes into consideration both individual risks and firmwide risks.

Financial institutions use VAR to quantify their risk positions for both internal and external purposes. The extensive use of derivatives by many firms in the late 1990s and the early 2000s encouraged regulators such as the SEC and the Basel Committee on Banking Supervision to establish rules and guidance to require public quantitative disclosures of market risks in their financial statements. VAR then became the primary model of assessing and managing risks. The Basel Committee even allowed banks to rely on their own internal VAR measures in determining their capital requirements.

BACKTESTING

Institutions must perform backtests of their VAR measures as calculated for internal risk management purposes. The backtests must compare daily VAR measures calibrated to a one-day movement in rates and prices and a 99 percent (one-tailed) confidence level against the institution's actual daily net trading profit or loss (trading outcome) for each of the preceding 250 business days. The backtests must be performed once each quarter. An institution's obligation to backtest for regulatory capital purposes does not arise until the institution has been subject to the final rule for 250 business days (approximately one year) and, thus, has accumulated the requisite number of observations to be used in backtesting. Institutions that are found not to have appropriate models and backtesting programs or if backtesting results reflect insufficient accuracy likely will be required to incorporate more conservative calculation factors that would result in a higher capital charge for market risk. It has been argued that too much reliance on VAR and its widespread use in determining capital requirement did not consider the important risk of potential financial meltdown.

Basel rules require that bank stress tests consist of four elements:

1. The stressed VAR (SVAR), which is computed on a 10-day 99% confidence level; three times the 10-day 99% stressed VAR should be maintained.
2. Model inputs are calibrated to historical data from a continuous 12-month period of significant financial stress.
3. Maintenance is required on a daily basis. The capital requirement is determined based on the higher of its latest stress VAR number and an average of SVAR numbers calculated over the preceding 60 business days multiplied by the multiplication factor.
4. Risk factors considered in pricing models should also be included in VAR calculations.

(g) PROMPT CORRECTIVE ACTION The federal banking agencies are statutorily mandated to assign each FDIC insured depository institution to one of five capital categories, quantitatively defined by the risk-based and leverage capital ratios:

1. *Well capitalized.* If capital level significantly *exceeds* the required minimum level for each relevant capital category.
2. *Adequately capitalized.* If capital level *meets* the minimum level.

Capital Category	Total Risk-Based Ratio		Tier 1 Risk-Based Ratio		Tier 1 Leverage Capital Ratio
Well capitalized	≥ 10%	and	≥ 6%	and	≥ 5%
Adequately capitalized	≥ 8%	and	≥ 4%	and	≥ 4%*
Undercapitalized	< 8%	or	< 4%	or	< 4%*
Significantly undercapitalized	< 6%	or	< 3%	or	< 3%
Critically undercapitalized	If the ratio of tangible equity (as statutorily defined) to total assets is 2% or less				

*3% for institutions that have a rating of "1" under the regulatory CAMELS, MACRO, or related rating system; that are not anticipating or experiencing significant growth; and that have well-diversified risk.

EXHIBIT 31.3   Regulatory Capital Categories

3. *Undercapitalized.* If capital level *fails to meet one or more* of the minimum levels.
4. *Significantly undercapitalized.* If capital level is *significantly below one or more* of the minimum levels.
5. *Critically undercapitalized.* If the ratio of tangible equity (as statutorily defined) to total assets *is 2 percent or less.*

Institutions falling into the last three categories are subject to a variety of "prompt corrective actions," such as limitations on dividends, prohibitions on acquisitions and branching, restrictions on asset growth, and removal of officers and directors. Irrespective of the ratios reported, the agencies may downgrade an institution's capital category based on adverse examination findings.

The regulatory capital ratio ranges defining the "prompt corrective action" capital categories are summarized in Exhibit 31.3.

(h) REGULATORY EXAMINATIONS   Federally insured banks and savings institutions are required to have periodic full-scope, on-site examinations by the appropriate agency. In certain cases, an examination by a state regulatory agency is accepted. Full-scope and other examinations are intended primarily to provide early identification of problems at insured institutions rather than as a basis for expressing an opinion on the fair presentation of the institution's financial statements. Dodd–Frank Act has substantially increased the enforcement oversight function of the SEC and the Federal Reserve Board and their examination programs to effectively regulate the financial services industry.

The Basel Committee is intended to strengthen global capital and liquidity regulations to promote a more resilient banking sector with proper ability to absorb shocks arising from financial and economic stress, to improve risk management, governance, transparency, and disclosures. The Basel Committee addresses the market failures caused by the recent financial crisis and establishes measures to strengthen bank-level and microprudential regulation.

(i) Scope   The scope of an examination is generally unique to each institution based on risk factors assessed by the examiner, and some examinations are targeted to a specific area of operations, such as real estate lending or trust operations. Separate compliance examination programs also exist to address institutions' compliance with laws and regulations in areas such as consumer protection, insider transactions, and reporting under the Bank Secrecy Act.

ENTITY	ASSIGNS RATING	RATING SCALE	RATING COMPONENTS
Banks and Thrifts	OCC, FDIC, OTS, and FRB	**CAMELS** Ratings 1-5	Capital adequacy Asset quality Management's performance Earnings Liquidity Sensitivity to Market Risk
Bank holding companies	FRB	**BOPEC** Ratings 1-5	Bank's CAMELS rating Operation of nonbanking subs Parent's strength Earnings Capital adequacy
Parents of foreign banks with U.S. branches or agencies	FRB	**SOSA*** (Strength of Support Assessment) Ratings A–E	Effectiveness of home country supervision and other country factors Institution-specific issues Ability of parent to maintain adequate internal controls and compliance with procedures in United States
U.S. branches and agencies of foreign banking organizations	FRB, OCC, and FDIC	**ROCA** Ratings 1-5	Risk management Operational controls Compliance Asset quality

*SOSA ratings will not be disclosed to the bank, branch, or home supervisor. Ratings are for U.S. internal supervisory use only.

EXHIBIT 31.4 REGULATORY RATING SYSTEMS

(ii) Regulatory Rating Systems   Regulators use regulatory rating systems to assign ratings to banks, thrifts, holding companies, parents of foreign banks, and U.S. branches and agencies of foreign banking organizations. The rating scales vary, although each is based on a five-point system, with "1" (or "A") being the highest rating. The rating systems are presented in Exhibit 31.4. Additionally, in November 1995, the FRB issued SR No. 95-51, "Rating the Adequacy of Risk Management Processes and Internal Controls at State Member Banks and Bank Holding Companies," stating that Federal Reserve System examiners, beginning in 1996, are instructed to assign a formal supervisory rating to the adequacy of an institution's risk management processes, including its internal controls.

Dodd–Frank Act addresses activities, practices, and structure of the nationally recognized statistical rating organizations (NRSROs), better known as credit-rating agencies. Specifically, seven provisions of Dodd–Frank pertain to NRSROs:

1. Mandate internal control requirements for NRSROs.
2. Improve governance practices of NRSROs.
3. Address potential conflicts of interest of NRSROs.
4. Impose new liability exposure on NRSROs.
5. Require new methodology and procedures to be used in the credit-ratings process.
6. Require more transparent disclosures on the credit-ratings process.
7. Increase SEC oversight of NRSROs.

(iii) Risk-Focused Examinations   Over the last two decades, the banking agencies have been developing and implementing a risk-focused examination/supervisory program that focuses on the business activities that pose the greatest risks to the institutions and an assessment of an organization's management systems to identify, measure, monitor, and control its risks. Bank examiners should learn from factors that caused the global financial crisis and pay attention to all types of bank risks and the importance of risk-focused examination and supervision in preventing further financial crisis. It is evidenced by the extend, nature, and complexity of international financial transactions substantially in many years preceding the start of financial crisis in 2007 while bank supervisors and examiners failed to develop adequate and effective risk-focused techniques to properly deal with the complex situations.

(i) ENFORCEMENT ACTIONS   Regulatory enforcement is carried out through a variety of informal and formal mechanisms. Informal enforcement measures are consensual between the bank and its regulator but not legally enforceable. Formal measures carry the force of law and are issued subject to certain legal procedures, requirements, and penalties. Examples of formal enforcement measures include ordering an institution to cease and desist from certain practices of violations, removing an officer, prohibiting an officer from participating in the affairs of the institution or the industry, assessing civil money penalties, and terminating insurance of an institution's deposits. As previously discussed, other mandatory and discretionary actions may be taken by regulators under "prompt corrective action" provisions of the Federal Deposit Insurance Act. The Dodd–Frank Act of 2010 has provided resources and mechanisms for U.S. regulators such as the SEC and the Federal Reserve to more effectively enforce irregularities and violations of securities laws that cause threat to the health and financial stability of the nation.

(j) DISCLOSURE OF CAPITAL MATTERS   Beginning in 1996, the American Institute of Certified Public Accountants (AICPA)'s *Audit Guide for Banks and Savings Institutions* required that the GAAP financial statements of banks and savings associations include footnote disclosures of regulatory capital adequacy/prompt corrective action categories. The following describes the five minimum disclosures:

1. A description of the regulatory capital requirements (a) for capital adequacy purposes and (b) established by the prompt corrective action provisions
2. The actual or possible material effects of noncompliance with such requirements
3. Whether the institution is in compliance with the regulatory capital requirements, including, as of each balance sheet date presented: (a) the institution's required and actual ratios and amounts of Tier 1 leverage, Tier 1 risk-based, total risk-based capital, and, for savings institutions, tangible capital, and (for certain banks and bank holding companies) Tier 3 capital for market risk and (b) factors that may significantly affect capital adequacy such as potentially volatile components of capital, qualitative factors, and regulatory mandates
4. The prompt corrective action category in which the institution was classified as of its most recent notification, as of each balance sheet date presented
5. Whether management believes any conditions or events since notification have changed the institution's category, as of the most recent balance sheet date

If, as of the most recent balance sheet date presented, the institution is (1) not in compliance with capital adequacy requirements, (2) considered less than adequately capitalized under the prompt corrective action provisions, or (3) both, the possible material effects of such conditions and events on amounts and disclosures in the financial statements should be disclosed. Additional disclosures may be required where there is substantial doubt about the institution's ability to continue as a going concern.

The disclosures described here should be presented for all significant subsidiaries of a holding company. Bank holding companies should also present the disclosures as they apply to the holding company, except for the prompt corrective disclosure required by item 4.

As with all footnotes to the financial statements, any management representations included in the footnotes, such as with respect to capital matters, would be subject to review by the independent accountant. Provisions of Dodd–Frank Act of 2010 and Basel III rules have significantly increased disclosures of capital requirements for many banks and other financial institutions.

(k) SECURITIES AND EXCHANGE COMMISSION

(i) Background   The Securities and Exchange Commission (SEC) was created by Congress in 1934 to administer the Securities Act of 1933 (1933 Act) and the Securities Exchange Act of 1934 (1934 Act). The SEC is an independent agency of the U.S. government, consisting of five commissioners appointed by the president, subject to Senate confirmation.

The 1933 Act requires companies to register securities with the SEC before they may be sold, unless the security or the transaction is exempt. Banks are exempt from the registration requirements of the 1933 Act; however, bank holding companies and their nonbank subsidiaries are not.

(ii) Reporting Requirements   SEC registrants are required to comply with certain industry-specific financial statement requirements, set forth in Article 9 for Bank Holding Companies of SEC Regulation S-X. In addition, they must comply with other nonfinancial disclosures required by Guide 3 for Bank Holding Companies of Regulation S-K.

In 1997, the SEC amended rules and forms for domestic and foreign issuers to clarify and expand existing disclosure requirements for market risk-sensitive instruments. Refer to Financial Reporting Release No. 48, "Disclosure of Accounting Policies for Derivative Financial Instruments and Derivative Commodity Instruments and Disclosure of Quantitative and Qualitative Information about Market Risk Inherent in Derivative Financial Instruments, Other Financial Instruments," for further discussion. Other SEC guidance is listed in "Sources and Suggested References." Additionally, the SEC is undertaking a review of Guide 3 to evaluate potential changes to improve the usefulness of financial institution disclosures.

On December 12, 2001, the SEC issued a financial reporting release, FR-60, "Cautionary Advice Regarding Disclosure about Critical Policies" (FR-60). The SEC's Cautionary Advice alerts public companies to the need for improved disclosures about critical accounting policies. FR-60 defines "critical accounting policies" as those most important to the financial statement presentation and that require the most difficult, subjective, complex judgments.

Perhaps because FR-60 was released late in the year, the Management's Discussion and Analysis (MD&A) disclosures made by registrants in response to FR-60 did not meet the SEC's expectations. As a result, on May 10, 2002, the SEC published a proposed rule, "Disclosure in Management's Discussion and Analysis about the Application of Critical Accounting Policies." The proposed rule would mandate the MD&A disclosure about critical accounting estimates that was encouraged in FR-60, but it is much more specific than FR-60 as to the nature of the disclosures and the basis for the sensitivity analysis. Readers should be alert for any final rules.

On January 22, 2002, the SEC issued a financial reporting release, FR-61, which provides specific considerations for MD&A disclosures. The SEC issued FR-61 to remind public companies of existing MD&A disclosure requirements and to suggest steps for meeting those requirements in 2001 annual reports. The SEC action responds to a December 31 petition from the Big Five firms, which was endorsed by the AICPA. FR-61 is largely consistent with the MD&A interpretive guidance suggested by the Big Five petition.

FR-61 focuses on MD&A disclosure about liquidity and off-balance-sheet arrangements (including special purpose entities (SPE)), trading activities that include nonexchange traded commodity contracts accounted for at fair value, and the effects of transactions with related and certain other parties. Following the collapse of Enron in 2001, these areas began receiving particular public and regulatory scrutiny. The SEC believes that the quality of information provided by public companies in these areas should be improved. The SEC expects registrants to consider FR-61 when preparing year-end and interim financial reports, effective immediately.

Dodd–Frank Act enhances the SEC's oversight function on the financial services industry in several ways by: (1) providing incentives and protection for witnesses to come forward in reporting violations of the security laws; (2) expanding the types of charges that the SEC can bring against those who help others violate the securities laws with "aiding and abetting" or secondary liability; (3) giving the SEC additional resources and means to sanction wrongdoers; (4) encouraging cooperation among regulators such as the PCAOB and foreign securities regulators; and (5) requiring disclosure of additional information to the SEC, including foreign auditors to produce work papers upon request and institutional investors report on data on their short sales activities on at least a monthly basis.

(l) FINANCIAL STATEMENT PRESENTATION

(i) Income Statements   Banks and savings institutions place heavy emphasis on the interest margin, that is, the difference between interest earned and the cost of funds. Accordingly, a specialized income statement format has evolved that focuses on net interest income. Supplemental income statement information may be provided separately to show the impact of investing in certain tax-exempt securities. Such "taxable equivalent" data purport to illustrate income statement data as if such tax-exempt securities were fully taxable.

(ii) Balance Sheets   The balance sheets of banks and savings institutions are not classified into short-term and long-term categories for assets and liabilities, but are generally presented in descending order of maturity. Supplemental information is also presented by many banking institutions showing average balances of assets and liabilities and the associated income or expense and average rates paid or earned.

(iii) Statements of Cash Flow   The statements of cash flow are presented in accordance with Statement of Financial Accounting Standards (SFAS) No. 95, "Statement of Cash Flows," amended by SFAS No. 102, "Statement of Cash Flows—Exemption of Certain Enterprises and Classification of Cash Flows from Certain Securities Acquired for Resale (an Amendment of FASB Statement No. 95)," and SFAS No. 104, "Statement of Cash Flows—Net Reporting of Certain Cash Receipts and Cash Payments and Classification of Cash Flows for Hedging Transactions (an amendment of FASB Statement No. 95)." The amendments permit certain financial institutions, such as banks and savings institutions, to net the cash flows for selected activities such as trading, deposit taking, and loan activities. The Financial Accounting Standard

Board (FASB), in December 2004, issued revised Statement of Financial Accounting Standard (SFAS), 123R, "Share-Based Payment." SFAS 123R replaces SFAS 123, "Accounting for Stock-Based Compensation." Among other provisions, SFAS 123R amends SFAS 95, "Statement of Cash Flows," requiring firms to report excess tax benefits arising from expensing employee stock options as a financial cash flow rather than an operating cash flow.

(iv) Commitments and Off-Balance-Sheet Risk   Banks and savings institutions offer a variety of financial services, and, accordingly, they enter into a wide range of financial transactions and issue a variety of financial instruments. Depending on the nature of these transactions, they may not appear on the balance sheet and are only disclosed in the footnotes to the financial statements. Statement of Financial Accounting Standard No. 105 (SFAS 105) footnote disclosures of off-balance-sheet financial instruments and derivatives provide additional risk-relevant information above and beyond that provided by the balance sheet.

(v) Disclosures of Certain Significant Risks and Uncertainties   AICPA Statement of Position (SOP) 94-6, "Disclosure of Certain Significant Risks and Uncertainties," requires institutions to include in their financial statements disclosures about the nature of their operations and the use of estimates in the preparation of their financial statements.

SOP 94-6 also requires disclosure regarding:

Certain Significant Estimates. Estimates used in the determination of the carrying amounts of assets or liabilities or in gain or loss contingencies is required to be disclosed when information available prior to issuance of the financial statements indicates that (a) it is at least reasonably possible that the estimate of the effect on the financial statements of a condition, situation or set of circumstances that existed at the date of the financial statements will change in the near term due to one or more future confirming events, and (b) the effect of the change would be material to the financial statements.

SOP 94-6 further states that (a) the disclosure should indicate the nature of the uncertainty and include an indication that it is at least reasonably possible that a change in the estimate will occur in the near term and (b) if the estimate involves a loss contingency covered by SFAS No. 5, "Accounting for Contingencies," the disclosure should also include an estimate of the possible loss or range of loss, or state that such an estimate cannot be made.

Current Vulnerability Due to Certain Concentrations. Institutions are required to disclose concentrations, as defined in the Statement, if, based on information known to management prior to issuance of the financial statements, (a) the concentration exists at the date of the financial statements, (b) the concentration makes the institution vulnerable to the risk of a near-term severe impact, and (c) it is at least reasonably possible that the events that could cause the severe impact will occur in the near term.

Provisions of Dodd–Frank Act and Basel III rules are considered as macroprudential reforms intended to focus on systemic risks. The systemic risk is the risk that banks and other financial institutions may pose on the global financial system. Financial institutions should provide proper disclosure of their systemic risk.

(m) ACCOUNTING GUIDANCE   In addition to the main body of professional accounting literature that composes generally accepted accounting principles (GAAP), more specific industry guidance is provided in the industry-specific audit and accounting guides published by the AICPA, specifically "Banks and Savings Institutions" issued in 2000. Additionally, the Emerging Issues Task Force (EITF) of the FASB addresses current issues.

(n) GENERALLY ACCEPTED ACCOUNTING PRINCIPLES VERSUS REGULATORY ACCOUNTING PRINCIPLES   Under the Federal Financial Institutions Examination Council (FFIEC), the three federal banking agencies have developed uniform reporting standards for commercial banks that are used in the preparation of the Reports of Condition and Income (Call Report). The FDIC has also applied these uniform Call Report standards to savings banks under its supervision. Effective with the March 31, 1997, reports, the reporting standards set forth for the Call Report are based on GAAP for banks, and, as a matter of law, many deviate to a more stringent requirement than GAAP only in those instances where statutory requirements or overriding supervisory concerns warrant a departure from GAAP. The OTS maintains its own separate reporting forms for the savings institutions under its supervision. The reporting form used by savings institutions, known as the *TFR*, is based on GAAP as applied by savings institutions, which differs in some respects from GAAP for banks.

Certain differences between GAAP and regulatory accounting principles (RAP) remain after the amendments to the March 1997 Call Report Instructions. Many of these differences remain because the agencies generally default to SEC reporting principles for registrants. The more significant remaining differences between Call Report Instructions and GAAP are related to the following areas: impaired collateral-dependent loans; pushdown accounting; credit losses on off-balance-sheet commitments and contingencies; related party transactions; and the application of accounting changes.

(o) LOANS AND COMMITMENTS   Loans generate the largest proportion of most bank and saving institutions' revenues. Institutions originate, purchase and sell (in whole or in part), and securitize loans. The parameters used to create the loan portfolio include many of the institution's key strategies, such as credit risk strategy, diversification strategy, liquidity, and interest rate margin strategy. Accordingly, the composition of the loan portfolio varies by institution. The loan portfolio is critical to the institutions' overall asset/liability management strategy.

(i) Types of Loans   Loans are offered on a variety of terms to meet the needs of the borrower and of the institution. The following are the types of loan arrangements normally issued.

COMMERCIAL LOANS

Institutions have developed different types of credit facilities to address the needs of commercial customers. Some of the characteristics that distinguish these facilities are: security (whether the loan is collateralized or unsecured); term (whether the loan matures in the short term, long term, on demand, or on a revolving credit arrangement); variable or fixed interest rates; and currency (whether the loan is repayable in the local currency or in a foreign currency).

Loan facilities can be tailored to match the needs of commercial borrowers and may include many combinations of specific loan terms. Some of the common general types are described next.

SECURED LOANS

Collateral (security) to a loan is usually viewed as a characteristic of any type of loan rather than as a loan category itself. Nevertheless, it is not uncommon for institutions to analyze their loan portfolios in part by looking at the proportion of secured credits and the entire balance.

A significant portion of bank lending is not supported by specific security. The less creditworthy a potential borrower, however, the more likely it becomes that an institution will require some form of collateral in order to minimize its risk of loss.

Loan security is normally not taken with the intention of liquidating it in order to obtain repayment. Maintenance and liquidation of collateral is, in fact, often time consuming and unprofitable for the foreclosing bank. Most loan security takes the form of some kind of fixed or floating claim over specified assets or a mortgage interest in property.

LINES OF CREDIT

Lines of credit, including facilities that are referred to as *revolving lines of credit*, originate with an institution extending credit to a borrower with a specified maximum amount and a stated maturity. The borrower then draws and repays funds through the facility in accordance with its requirements. Lines of credit are useful for short-term financing of working capital or seasonal borrowings. A commitment fee is usually charged on the unused portion of the facility.

DEMAND LOANS

Demand loans are short-term loans that may be "called" by the institution at any time, hence the term *demand*. Demand loans are often unsecured and are normally made to cover short-term funding requirements. There is usually no principal reduction during the loan term, the entire balance coming due at maturity.

TERM LOANS

Term loans are often used to finance the acquisition of capital assets such as plant and equipment. Due to their longer term, they involve greater credit risk than short-term advances (all other things being equal). To reduce the credit risk, these loans typically are secured and require amortization of principal over the loan term. Loan agreements often contain restrictive covenants that require the borrower to maintain specified financial ratios and to refrain from defined types of transactions for as long as the loan is outstanding.

ASSET-BASED LENDING

Asset-based lending is a form of revolving line of credit that is related directly to the value of specific underlying assets (typically accounts receivable or inventory). The primary difference between asset-based lending and a simple line of credit is the direct correlation, upon which the institution insists, between the funds advanced and the underlying security. While funds may be advanced on a line of credit up to the approved maximum amount, they may be drawn under an asset-based lending arrangement only to the extent allowed by predetermined formulas related to collateral value. Requests for funds are normally monitored closely, and repayments may be demanded where collateral values fall.

SYNDICATIONS

A syndicated loan is one where a number of institutions, in a form of joint venture, provide funds they would individually be unwilling or unable to provide. Syndications are used for customers requiring large-scale financing, too great for any single institution to accommodate without distorting its loan portfolio. In addition, consortium banks group together banks from different countries to specialize in and centralize large-scale finance for specific projects.

The members of a syndicate appoint one or more of themselves as the managing bank for the syndicate. In certain cases, the borrower might appoint the managing bank, in which case the other members would commonly appoint an agent bank to act on their behalf. The managing bank is responsible for negotiating with the borrower, preparing the appropriate documentation, collecting the loan funds from the syndicate and disbursing them to the borrower, and collecting amounts due from the borrower and distributing them to the syndicate members.

Apart from the managing bank, the syndicate members will not necessarily have any direct dealings with the borrower, although the borrower is aware of the existence of the syndicate. Credit risk rests with each syndicate member to the extent of its participation.

PARTICIPATIONS

Banks sell loans, or part shares in loans, to other financial institutions for a number of reasons: to serve large customers whose financing needs exceed their lending ability; to diversify their loan portfolios; to alter the maturity structure of their loan portfolios; or to increase their liquidity. Participation agreements usually specify such matters as the method of payment of proceeds from the borrower, responsibilities in the event of default, and interest in collateral. Loans may be sold with or without recourse and on terms that may or may not agree with those of the underlying loan.

Loans that are "participated out" (i.e., sold) are normally reported on the seller's balance sheet net of the sold portion (which is reported with other loan assets by the buyer). The fact that another institution has researched and agreed to extend the loan does not reduce the risk of the purchasing bank.

LOANS HELD FOR RESALE

Loans may be originated by an institution that intends to resell them to other parties. They may be purchased with the intention to resell. The reasons for such transactions vary. Some institutions wish to provide a type of loan service to their customers, which they do not wish to retain in their portfolio. Some institutions use loan origination as a source of fee income. Some purchase debt to use as securitization for other instruments that they package and sell to specialized markets.

REAL ESTATE LOANS

Real estate loans may be made for commercial or personal purposes, and most banks differentiate their portfolios between the two uses. The rationale for this segregation lies in the fact that while both are classified as real estate lending, the portfolios are subject to different types of risk and/or different degrees of risk. Also, the type and level of expertise required to successfully manage residential and commercial real estate loan portfolios differs, just like the type of financing provided to the homeowner is typically not the same as to an owner or developer of commercial real estate.

Incremental knowledge with respect to the particular financing provided must be obtained and constantly updated to successfully manage commercial real estate property lending. For example, construction loan monitoring, appraisal methods, comparable properties in the area, the status of the economy, use of the property, future property developments, occupancy rates, and projected operating cash flows are all important factors in reaching lending decisions.

MORTGAGE LOANS

Real estate mortgage loans are term loans collateralized by real estate. The loans are generally fairly long term, though some are short term with a large principal (balloon) payment due at maturity. The loan commitments usually involve a fee to be paid by the borrower upon approval or upon closing.

Some institutions originate residential mortgage loans for sale to investors. Under these arrangements, the bank usually continues to service the loans on a fee basis. The sale allows the bank to provide mortgage financing services for its customers without funding a large volume of loans.

CONSTRUCTION LOANS

Construction loans are used to finance the construction of particular projects and normally mature at the scheduled completion date. They are generally secured by a first mortgage on the property and are backed by a purchase (or "takeout") agreement from a financially responsible permanent lender. They may include the financing of loan interest through the construction period.

Construction loans are vulnerable to a number of risks related to the uncertainties that are characteristic of building projects. Examples of risks associated with construction loans include construction delays, nonpayment of material bills or subcontractors, and the financial collapse of the project contractor prior to project completion.

Construction loan funds are generally disbursed on a standard payment plan (for relatively small, predictable projects) or a progress payment plan (for more complex projects). Extent of completion may be verified by an architect's certification or by evidence of labor and material costs.

In certain construction loans, consideration should be given to accounting for the loan as an investment in real estate if the lender is subject to virtually the same risks and rewards as the owner.

DIRECT LEASE FINANCING

Leasing is a form of debt financing for fixed assets that, although differing in legal form, is similar in substance to term lending. Like a more conventional loan, the institution's credit concerns in extending lease financing are ones of cash flow, credit history, management, and projections of future operations. The type of property to be leased and its marketability in the event of default or termination of the lease are concerns quite parallel to the bank's evaluation of collateral. In a leasing arrangement, the bank formally owns the property rather than having a lien on it.

Lease financing arrangements may be accounted for either as financings (i.e., as loans) or as operating leases, depending on the precise terms of the transaction and on the applicable accounting principles.

CONSUMER LOANS

Consumer loans—personal loans to individual borrowers—can originate through a bank's own customers (direct loans) or through merchants with whom the borrowers deal (indirect loans). They may relate specifically to the purchase of items that can serve as collateral for the borrowing (e.g., vehicles, mobile homes, boats, furniture) or to other needs that provide no basis for a security interest (e.g., vacations, income tax payments, medical expenses, educational costs). Consumer loans may be made on an installment, single payment, or demand basis. They are often broken down into classifications that describe the purpose of the financing (student loans or home equity loans) or the terms of disbursement and repayment (installment loans, credit card loans, check credit).

INSTALLMENT LOANS

Installment loans are the most common type of consumer credit. Their terms normally include repayment over a specified period of time with fixed minimum periodic (usually monthly) payments. Interest rates are generally fixed on origination but may be variable over the term of the loan. The term is generally determined by the type of purchase being financed and is usually relatively short—10 years or less.

STANDBY LETTERS OF CREDIT

A standby letter of credit is a promise made by an institution to provide compensation to a third party on behalf of its customer in the event that the customer fails to perform in accordance with the terms specified by an underlying contract. Standby letters of credit may be available under a credit facility or may be issued for a specified amount with an expiration date. Normally, payment under such agreements depends on performance or lack of performance of some act required by the underlying contract.

Standby letters of credit are typically recorded as contingent liabilities in memorandum records and are offset by customer liability memorandum accounts. In the event that funds are disbursed under a standby letter of credit agreement, the drawing would be recorded as a loan.

SOVEREIGN RISK

Sovereign risk lending involves the granting of credit facilities to foreign governments or to companies based in foreign countries. The facilities are normally denominated in a currency other than the domestic currency of the borrower and are typically used to finance imports or to refinance existing foreign currency debt.

In addition to all of the customary considerations surrounding credit risk, sovereign risk lending involves economic, social, and political considerations that bear on the ability of the borrower to repay foreign currency obligations.

TRADE FINANCE

- *Letters of credit.* Letters of credit are instruments used to facilitate trade (most commonly international trade) by substituting an institution's credit for that of a commercial importing company. A letter of credit provides assurance to a seller that it will be paid for goods shipped. At the same time, it provides assurance to the buyer that payment will not be made until conditions specified in the sales contract have been met.

  Letter of credit transactions can vary in any number of ways. The issuing and advising institutions may deal with each other through their own local correspondent banks. Some of the documents may flow in different patterns. The requirements for payment and security will certainly vary from transaction to transaction. One of the attractive features of letter of credit financing from the customer's point of view is its flexibility. Facilities can be tailored to individual transactions or groups of transactions.

- *Bankers' acceptances.* A bankers' acceptance is like a letter of credit in that it provides a seller of goods with a guarantee of payment, thus facilitating trade. The institution's customer is the buyer who, having established an acceptance facility with the bank, notifies the seller to draw up a bill of exchange. The bank "accepts" that bill (by physically stamping "accepted" on its face and having an authorized bank officer sign it) and, in so doing, commits itself to disburse funds on the bill's due date.

  A banker's acceptance represents both an asset and a liability to the accepting bank. The asset is a receivable from the bank's customer, the buyer in the transaction. The liability is a payable to the holder of the acceptance. The bank's accounting for open acceptances varies from country to country. In some countries, the asset and liability are both reflected on the bank's balance sheet. In others, they are netted against each other and thus become, in effect, off-balance-sheet items. In European Union (EU) countries, they appear as memorandum items on the face of the balance sheet.

By substituting its own credit for that of the buying company, the accepting bank creates a financial instrument that is readily marketable. Bankers' acceptances trade as bearer paper on active secondary markets.

MORTGAGE-BACKED ASSETS

Mortgage-backed assets (MBSs) are asset-backed securities having cash flows backed by the principal and interest payments of a pool of mortgage loans which are made periodically over the lifetime of the underlying loans. Collateralized mortgage obligations (CMOs) are more complex than MBSs, consist of pools of home mortgages backed by government-insured agencies such as Freddie Mac and Fannie Mae. MBSs and CMOs received significant popularity with investors in the late 1990s and the early 2000s. During the subprime mortgage crisis period in late 2006 and 2007, many investors holding MBSs or CMOs suffered substantial losses because the values of the underlying assets sharply declined.

(ii) Accounting for Loans

PRINCIPAL

Loans expected to be held until maturity should be reported as outstanding principal, net of charge-offs, specific valuation accounts and any deferred fees or costs, or unamortized premiums or discounts on purchased loans. Total loans should be reduced by the allowance for credit losses.

Loans held for sale should be reported at the lower of cost or fair value determined as of the balance sheet. Mortgage loans held for sale should be reported at the lower of cost or market value in conformity with SFAS No. 65, "Accounting for Certain Mortgage Banking Activities." Mortgage-backed securities held for sale in conjunction with mortgage banking activities shall be classified as trading securities and reported at fair value in conformity with SFAS No. 115, "Accounting for Certain Investments in Debt and Equity Securities."

The amount by which the cost exceeds the fair value may be accounted as a valuation allowance. Any change in the valuation allowance may be included for determining the net income. This may be accounted for the period for which the change is occurring. The fair value of mortgage loans and mortgage-backed securities held for sale is essentially determined by the type of loan. The loans are further determined by following classes:

- *Committed loans.* The investor commitment will form the base for fair values of loans.
- *Uncommitted loans.* The fair value for these loans is based on the market where the mortgage banking entity functions.
- *Uncommitted mortgage-backed securities.* The fair value for such loans collateralized by a mortgage banking entity's own loans shall be based on the fair value of the securities.

INTEREST

Interest income on all loans should be accrued and credited to interest income as it is earned using the interest method. Interest income on certain impaired loans should be recognized in accordance with SFAS No. 114, "Accounting by Creditors for Impairment of a Loan," as amended by SFAS No. 118, "Accounting by Creditors for Impairment of a Loan-Income Recognition and Disclosures."

The accrual of interest is usually suspended on loans that are in excess of 90 days past due, unless the loan is both well secured and in the process of collection. When a loan is placed on such nonaccrual status, interest that has been accrued but not collected is reversed, and interest subsequently received is recorded on a cash basis or applied to reduce the principal balance depending on the bank's assessment of ultimate collectability of the loan. An exception to this rule is that many banks do not place certain types of consumer loans on nonaccrual since they automatically charge off such loans within a relatively short period of becoming delinquent— generally within 120 days.

Loan Fees

Various types of fees are collected by banks in connection with lending activities. SFAS No. 91, "Accounting for Nonrefundable Fees and Costs Associated with Originating or Acquiring Loans and Initial Direct Costs of Leases (an Amendment of FASB Statements No. 13, 60, and 65 and a Rescission of FASB Statement No. 17)," requires that the majority of such fees and associated direct origination costs be offset. The net amount must be deferred as part of the loan (and reported as a component of loans in the balance sheet) and recognized in interest income over the life of the loan and/or loan commitment period as an adjustment of the yield on the loan. The requirements for cost deferral under this standard are quite restrictive and require direct linkage to the loan origination process. Activities for which costs may be deferred include: (1) evaluating the borrower, guarantees, collateral, and other security; (2) preparation and processing of loan documentation for loan origination; and (3) negotiating and closing the loan. Certain costs are specifically precluded from deferral, for example, advertising and solicitation, credit supervision and administration, costs of unsuccessful loan originations, and other activities not directly related to the extension of a loan.

Loan fees and costs for loans originated or purchased for resale are deferred and are recognized when the related loan is sold.

Commitment fees to purchase or originate loans, net of direct origination costs, are generally deferred and amortized over the life of the loan when it is extended. If the commitment expires, then the fees are recognized in other income on expiration of the commitment. There are two main exceptions to this general treatment:

1. If past experience indicates that the extension of a loan is unlikely, then the fee is recognized over the commitment period.
2. Nominal fees, which are determined retroactively, on a commitment to extend funds at a market rate may be recognized in income at the determination date.

Certain fees may be recognized when received, primarily loan syndication fees. Generally, the yield on the portion of the loan retained by the syndicating bank must at least equal the yield received by the other members of the syndicate. If this is not the case, a portion of the fees designated as a syndication fee must be deferred and amortized to income to achieve a yield equal to the average yield of the other banks in the syndicate. EITF Issue No. 97-3, "Accounting for Fees and Costs Associated with Loan Syndication's and Loan Participation's after the Issuance of FASB Statement No. 125," states that loan participation should be accounted for in accordance with the provision of SFAS No. 140, and loan syndication's should be accounted for in accordance with the provision of SFAS No. 91.

Purchased loans are recorded at cost net of fees paid/received. The difference between this recorded amount and the principal amount of the loan is amortized to income over the life of the loan to produce a level yield. Acquisition costs are not deferred, but are expensed as incurred. The AICPA's Accounting Standards Executive Committee has a project underway that is expected to result in a new SOP titled "Accounting for Certain Purchased Loans." Readers should be alert for a final pronouncement. Additional EITFs have been issued to address purchases of credit card portfolios.

ACQUISITION, DEVELOPMENT, AND CONSTRUCTION ARRANGEMENTS
Certain transactions that appear to be loans are considered effectively to be investments in the real estate property financed. These transactions are required to be presented separately from loans and accounted for as real estate investments using the guidance set forth in the AICPA Notice to Practitioners dated February 1986. This notice was reprinted without any change in November 1987 issues as Exhibit I in the Appendix of AICPA Practice Bulletin. Factors indicating such treatment include six arrangements whereby the financial institution:

1. Provides substantially all financing to acquire, develop, and construct the property, that is, borrower has little or no equity in the property
2. Funds the origination or commitment fees through the loan
3. Funds substantially all interest and fees through the loan
4. Has security only in the project with no recourse to other assets or guarantee of the borrower
5. Can recover its investment only through sale to third parties, refinancing, or cash flow of the project
6. Is unlikely to foreclose on the project during development since no payments are due during this period and therefore the loan cannot normally become delinquent

TROUBLED DEBT RESTRUCTURINGS AND IMPAIRED LOANS
Banks may routinely restructure loans to meet a borrower's changing circumstances. The new loan terms are reflected in the financial statements essentially as if a new loan has been made. However, if "a creditor for economic or legal reasons related to the debtor's financial difficulties grants a concession . . . that it would not otherwise consider," then SFAS No. 15, "Accounting by Debtors and Creditors for Troubled Debt Restructurings," as amended by FASB Statements No. 114, No. 121, "Accounting for Impairment of Long-Lived Assets and Long-Lived Assets to Be Disposed Of," and No. 144, "Accounting for the Impairment or Disposal of Long-Lived Assets," applies.

The guidance in the impairment or disposal of Long-Lived Assets Subsections is applicable to the following activities:

A. The transactions relating to the long lived assets to be held and used or to be disposed of, including:
   ○ Capital leases of lessees
   ○ Long-lived assets of lessors subject to operating leases
   ○ Proved oil and gas properties that are being accounted for using the successful-efforts method of accounting
   ○ Long-term prepaid assets
B. The following relates to assets and liabilities, which are further considered part of an asset group or a disposal group:
   ○ In case a long-lived asset belongs to a group that further includes other assets and liabilities not covered, the guidance will apply to such group. In such scenarios, the unit of accounting is its group. If the long-lived asset has to be held

and used, it is classified as an asset group. In case the long-lived asset is to be disposed of by sale or otherwise, it is then classified as a disposal group.

○   The guidance does not affect the GAAP applicable to those other individual assets and liabilities not covered by the Impairment or Disposal of Long-Lived Assets Subsections that are included in such groups.

The guidance in the impairment or disposal of Long-Lived Assets Subsections is not applicable to certain transactions. They include but are not limited to the following activities:

* Goodwill
* Intangible assets not being amortized that are to be held and used
* Servicing assets
* Financial instruments, including investments in equity securities accounted for under the cost or equity method
* Deferred policy acquisition costs
* Deferred tax assets

Troubled Debt Restructurings

Troubled debt restructurings may include one or both of the following:

* Transfers of assets of the debtor or an equity interest in the debtor to partially or fully satisfy a debt
* Modification of debt terms, including reduction of one or more of the following: (1) interest rates with or without extensions of maturity date(s), (2) face or maturity amounts, and (3) accrued interest

Prior to the release of SFAS No. 114, under a SFAS No. 15 restructuring involving a modification of terms, the creditor accumulated the undiscounted total future cash receipts and compared them to the recorded investment in the loan. If these cash receipts exceeded the recorded investment in the loan, no loss or impairment was deemed to exist; however, if the total cash receipts did not exceed the recorded investment, the recorded investment was adjusted to reflect the total undiscounted future cash receipts. For restructurings involving a modification of terms that occurred before the effective date of SFAS No. 114, this accounting still applies as long as the loan does not become impaired relative to the restructured terms. Restructurings involving a modification of terms after the effective date of SFAS No. 114 must be accounted for in accordance with SFAS No. 114.

Impaired Loans

In May 1993, SFAS No. 114, "Accounting by Creditors for Impairment of a Loan (an Amendment of FASB Statements No. 5 and 15)," was issued primarily to provide more consistent guidance on the application of SFAS No. 5 loss criteria and to provide additional direction on the recognition and measurement of loan impairment in determining credit reserve levels. The application of this statement was required beginning in 1995.

SFAS No. 114 applies to all impaired loans, uncollateralized as well as collateralized, except: large groups of smaller balance homogeneous loans that are collectively evaluated for impairment such as credit card, residential mortgage, and consumer installment loans; loans that are measured at fair value or at the lower of cost or fair value; leases; and debt securities, as defined in SFAS No. 115, "Accounting for Certain Investments in Debt and Equity Securities."

A loan is impaired when, based on current information and events, it is probable (consistent with its use in SFAS No. 5—an area within a range of the likelihood that a future event or events will occur confirming the fact of the loss) that a creditor will be unable to collect all amounts due according to the contractual terms of the loan agreement. As used in SFAS No. 114 and in SFAS No. 5, as amended, all amounts due according to the contractual terms means that both the contractual interest payments and the contractual principal payments of a loan will be collected as scheduled in the loan agreement.

It is important to note that an insignificant delay or insignificant shortfall in the amount of payments does not require application of SFAS No. 114. A loan is not impaired during a period of delay in payment if the creditor expects to collect all amounts due including interest accrued at the contractual interest rate for the period of delay.

SFAS No. 114 provides that the measurement of impaired value should be based on one of the following methods:

- Present value of expected cash flows discounted at the loan's effective interest rate
- The observable value of the loan's market price
- The fair value of the collateral if the loan is collateral dependent

The effective rate of a loan is the contractual interest rate adjusted for any net deferred loan fees or costs, premium, or discount existing at the origination or acquisition of the loan. For variable rate loans, the loan's effective interest rate may be calculated based on the factor as it changes over the life of the loan, or it may be fixed at the rate in effect at the date the loan meets the SFAS No. 114 impairment criterion. However, that choice should be applied consistently for all variable rate loans.

All impaired loans do not have to be measured using the same method; the method selected may vary based on the availability of information and other factors. However, the ultimate valuation should be critically evaluated in determining whether it represents a reasonable estimate of impairment.

If the measure of the impaired loan is less than the recorded investment in the loan (including accrued interest, net deferred loan fees or costs, and unamortized premium or discount), a creditor should recognize an impairment by creating a valuation allowance with a corresponding charge to bad-debt expense.

Subsequent to the initial measurement of impairment, if there is a significant change (increase or decrease) in the amount or timing of an impaired loan's expected future cash flows, observable market price, or fair value of the collateral, a creditor should recalculate the impairment by applying the procedures described above and by adjusting the valuation allowance. However, the net carrying amount of the loan should at no time exceed the recorded investment in the loan.

Any restructurings performed under the provisions of SFAS No. 15 need not be reevaluated unless the borrower is not performing in accordance with the contractual terms of the restructuring.

EITF Issue No. 96-22, "Applicability of the Disclosures Required by FASB Statement No. 114 When a Loan Is Restructured in a Troubled Debt Restructuring into Two (or More) Loans," states that when a loan is restructured in a troubled debt restructuring into two (or more) loan agreements, the restructured loans should be considered separately when assessing the applicability of the disclosures in years after the restructuring because they are legally distinct from the original loan. However, the creditor would continue to base its measure of loan impairment on the contractual terms specified by the original loan agreements.

IN-SUBSTANCE FORECLOSURES
SFAS No. 114 clarified the definition of in-substance foreclosures as used in SFAS No. 15, "Accounting by Debtors and Creditors for Troubled Debt Restructurings," by stating that the phrase "foreclosure by the creditor" in paragraph 34 should be read to mean "*physical* possession of debtor's assets regardless of whether formal foreclosure proceedings take place." Further, until foreclosure occurs, these assets should remain as loans in the financial statements.

(p) CREDIT LOSSES   Credit loss estimates are subjective and, accordingly, require careful judgments in assessing loan collectability and in estimating losses.

(i) Accounting Guidance   SFAS No. 114, "Accounting by Creditors for Impairment of a Loan (an Amendment of FASB Statements No. 5 and 15)" and SFAS No. 5, "Accounting for Contingencies (as amended by SFAS No. 118, 'Accounting by Creditors for Impairment of Loan-Income Recognition and Disclosures')" are the primary sources of guidance on accounting for the allowance for loan losses. Also, the update released by the Financial Accounting Standards Board called "Accounting Standards Update 2010-20" mentions the "Disclosures about the Credit Quality of Financing Receivables and the Allowance for Credit Losses." In summary, this update offers greater transparency about an entity's allowance for credit losses and the credit quality of its financing receivables. SFAS No. 5 requires that an estimated loss from a contingency should be accrued by a charge to income if both of the following conditions are met:

- Information available prior to issuance of the financial statements indicates that it is probable that an asset had been impaired or a liability had been incurred at the date of the financial statements. It is implicit in this condition that it must be probable that one or more future events will occur confirming the fact of the loss.
- The amount of loss can be reasonably estimated.

SFAS No. 5 states that when a loss contingency exists, the likelihood that the future event or events will confirm the loss or impairment of an asset (whether related to contractual principal or interest) can range from remote to probable. Probable means the future event or events are likely to occur; however, the conditions for accrual are not intended to be so rigid that they require virtual certainty before a loss is accrued.

The allowance for loan losses should be adequate to cover probable credit losses related to specifically identified loans, as well as probable credit losses inherent in the remainder of the loan portfolio that have been incurred as of the balance sheet date. Credit losses related to off-balance-sheet instruments should also be accrued if the conditions of SFAS No. 5 are met.

Actual credit losses should be deducted from the allowance, and the related balance should be charged off in the period in which they are deemed uncollectible. Recoveries of loans previously charged off should be added to the allowance when received.

SFAS No. 114 addresses the accounting by creditors for impairment of certain loans, as discussed in Subsection 31.2(o)(ii).

(ii) Regulatory Guidance   The regulatory agencies issued the "Interagency Policy on the Allowance for Loan and Lease Losses (ALLL)" in December 1993. The policy statement provides guidance with respect to the nature and purpose of the allowance; the related responsibilities of the board of directors, management, and the bank examiners; adequacy of

loan review systems; and issues related to international transfer risk. The policy statement also includes an analytical tool to be used by bank examiners for assessing the reasonableness of the allowance; however, the policy statement cautions the bank examiners against placing too much emphasis on the analytical tool, rather than performing a full and thorough analysis.

The OCC also provides guidance in its "Comptrollers' Handbook, Allowance for Loan and Lease Losses," issued in June 1996.

In separate releases on July 6, 2001, the SEC and the FFIEC issued guidance on methodologies and documentation related to the allowance for loan losses. In Staff Accounting Bulletin (SAB) No. 102, "Selected Loan Loss Allowance Methodology and Documentation Issues," the SEC staff expressed certain of their views on the development, documentation, and application of a systematic methodology as required by Financial Reporting Release No. 28 for determining allowances for loan and lease losses in accordance with GAAP. In particular, the guidance focuses on the documentation the staff normally would expect registrants to prepare and maintain in support of their allowances for loan losses. Concurrent with the release of SAB No. 102, the federal banking agencies issued related guidance through the FFIEC titled "Policy Statement on Allowance for Loan and Lease Losses (ALLL) Methodologies and Documentation for Banks and Savings Institutions." The Policy Statement, developed in consultation with the SEC staff, provides guidance on the design and implementation of ALLL methodologies and supporting documentation practices. Both SAB No. 102 and the Policy Statement reaffirm the applicability of existing accounting guidance; neither attempts to overtly change GAAP as they relate to the ALLL.

(iii) Allowance Methodologies   An institution's method of estimating credit losses is influenced by many factors, including the institution's size, organization structure, business environment and strategy, management style, loan portfolio characteristics, loan administration procedures, and management information systems.

COMMON FACTORS TO CONSIDER

Although allowance methodologies may vary between institutions, the factors to consider in estimating credit losses are often similar. Both SAB No. 102 and the Policy Statement require that when developing loss measurements, banks consider the effect of current environmental factors and then document which factors were used in the analysis and how those factors affected the loss measurements. The following are examples of factors that should be considered:

- Levels of and trends in delinquencies and impaired loans
- Levels of and trends in charge-offs and recoveries
- Trends in volume and terms of loans
- Effects of any changes in risk selection and underwriting standards, and other changes in lending policies, procedures, and practices
- Experience, ability, and depth of lending management and other relevant staff
- National and local economic trends and conditions
- Industry conditions
- Effects of changes in credit concentrations

Supplemental data, such as historical loss rates or peer group analyses, can be helpful; however, they are not, by themselves, sufficient basis for an allowance methodology.

PORTFOLIO SEGMENTS

Another common practice is dividing the loan portfolio into different segments. Each segment typically includes similar characteristics, such as risk classification and type of loan. Segments typically include large problem loans by industry or collateral type and homogeneous pools of smaller loans, such as credit cards, automobile loans, and residential mortgages.

CREDIT CLASSIFICATION PROCESS

A credit classification process involves categorizing loans into risk categories and is often applied to large loans that are evaluated individually. The categorization is based on conditions that may affect the ability of borrowers to service their debt, such as current financial information, historical payment experience, credit documentation, public information, and current trends. Many institutions classify loans using a rating system that incorporates the regulatory classification system. These definitions are as follows:

- *Special mention.* Some loans are considered criticized but not classified. Such loans have potential weaknesses that deserve management's close attention. If left uncorrected, these potential weaknesses may result in deterioration of the repayment prospects for the assets or of the institution's credit position at some future date. Special mention loans are not adversely classified and do not expose an institution to sufficient risk to warrant adverse classification.

- *Substandard.* Loans classified as substandard are inadequately protected by the current sound worth and paying capacity of the obligor or of the collateral pledged, if any. Loans so classified must have a well-defined weakness or weaknesses that jeopardize the liquidation of the debt. They are characterized by the distinct possibility that the institution will sustain some loss if the deficiencies are not corrected.

- *Doubtful.* Loans classified as doubtful have all the weaknesses inherent in those classified as substandard, with the added characteristic that the weaknesses make collection or liquidation in full, on the basis of currently existing facts, conditions, and values, highly questionable and improbable.

- *Loss.* Loans classified as loss are considered uncollectible and of such little value that their continuance as bankable assets is not warranted. This classification does not mean that the loan has absolutely no recovery or salvage value, but rather that it is not practical or desirable to defer writing off this basically worthless asset even though partial recovery may be effected in the future.

- *Pools of smaller-balance homogeneous loans.* Loans not evaluated individually are included in pools and loss rates are derived for each pool. The loss rates to be applied to the pools of loans are typically derived from the combination of a variety of factors. Examples of the factors include: historical experience, expected future performance, trends in bankruptcies and troubled collection accounts, and changes in the customer's performance patterns.

- *Foreign loans.* The Interagency Country Exposure Risk Committee (ICERC) requires certain loans to have allocated transfer risk reserves (ATRRs). ATRRs are minimum specific reserves related to loans in particular countries and, therefore, must be reviewed by each institution. The ICERC's supervisory role is pursuant to the International Supervision Act of 1983. The collectability of foreign loans that do not have ATRRs should be assessed in the same way as domestic loans.

Documentation, Completeness, and Frequency
The institution's allowance methodology should be based on a comprehensive, adequately documented, and consistently applied analysis. The analysis should consider all significant factors that affect collectability of the portfolio and should be based on an effective loan review and credit grading (classification) system. Additionally, the evaluation of the adequacy of the allowance should be performed as of the end of each quarter, and appropriate provisions should be made to maintain the allowance at an adequate level.

SAB No. 102 and the 2001 Policy Statement specifically require, for any adjustments of loss measurements for environmental factors, that banks maintain sufficient *objective* evidence (1) to support the amount of the adjustment and (2) to explain why the adjustment is necessary to reflect current information, events, circumstances, and conditions in the loss measurements.

SAB No. 102 requires that bank methodology in determining Allowance for Loan and Lease Losses (ALLL) should:

1. Provide a detailed analysis of the loan portfolio performed on a regular basis.
2. Consider all loans (whether on an individual or group basis).
3. Identify loans to be assessed for impairment on an individual basis under SFAS No. 114 and segment the remainder of the portfolio into groups of loans with similar risk characteristics for evaluation and analysis under SFAS No. 5.
4. Consider all known relevant internal and external factors that may affect loan collectability.
5. Be applied consistently but, when appropriate, be modified for new factors affecting ALLL.

(q) LOAN SALES AND MORTGAGE BANKING ACTIVITIES   Banks may originate and sell loans for a variety of reasons, such as generating income streams from servicing and other fees, increasing liquidity, minimizing interest rate exposure, enhancing asset/liability management, and maximizing their use of capital.

(i) Underwriting Standards   When loans are originated for resale, the origination process includes not only finding an investor but also preparing the loan documents to fit the investor's requirements. Loans originated for resale must normally comply with specific underwriting standards regarding items such as borrower qualifications, loan documentation, appraisals, mortgage insurance, and loan terms. Individual loans that do not meet the underwriting standards are typically eliminated from the pool of loans eligible for sale. Generally, the originating institutions may be subject to recourse by the investor for underwriting exceptions identified subsequent to the sale of the loans and any related defaults by borrowers.

(ii) Securitizations   Securitization is simply a method of financing a pool of assets intended to generate cash where sellers of assets can transfer part of ownership's risk and benefit to a third party who is willing or has the ability to take the risks. A common method of transforming real estate assets into liquid marketable securities is through securitization. Securitization is where loans are sold to a separate entity that finances the purchase through the issuance of debt securities or undivided interest in the loans. The real estate securities are backed by the cash flows of the loans.

Securitization of residential mortgages has expanded to include commercial and multi-family mortgages, auto and home equity loans, credit cards, and leases. The securitization of mortgage loans is a complex process affected by many players with different incentives that are often conflicting and thus create frictions among players. Ashcraft and Schuermann (2008) identified seven frictions among securitization players:

1. Frictions between the mortgagor and the originator: Predatory lending
2. Frictions between the originator and the arranger: Predatory borrowing and lending
3. Frictions between the arranger and third-parties: Adverse selection
4. Frictions between the servicer and the mortgagor: Moral hazard
5. Frictions between the servicer and third-parties: Moral hazard
6. Frictions between the asset manager and investor: Principal-agent
7. Frictions between the investor and the credit-rating agencies: Model error

The accounting guidance for sales of loans through securitizations is discussed in Section 31.3, "Mortgage Banking Activities."

(iii) Loan Servicing   When loans are sold, the selling institution sometimes retains the right to service the loans for a servicing fee, which is collected over the life of the loans as payments are received. The servicing fee is often based on a percentage of the principal balance of the outstanding loans. A typical servicing agreement requires the servicer to perform the billing, collection, and remittance functions, as well as maintain custodial bank accounts. The servicer may also be responsible for certain credit losses.

(iv) Regulatory Guidance   Regulatory guidance with respect to loan sales and mortgage banking activities continues to evolve with the increased activity by institutions. In December 1997, the OCC issued regulatory guidance for national banks in its *Comptroller's Handbook: Asset Securitization*. Federal Deposit Insurance Corporation (FDIC); Board of Governors of the Federal Reserve System (Board), Office of the Comptroller of the Currency, Treasury (OCC); and Office of Thrift Supervision, Treasury (OTS) agencies collectively issued guidance regarding correspondent concentration risks for financial institutions. These financial institutions include all banks and their subsidiaries, bank holding companies and their nonbank subsidiaries, savings associations and their subsidiaries, and savings and loan holding companies and their subsidiaries. These guidelines mention the expectations from all banks and their subsidiaries, bank holding companies and their nonbank subsidiaries, savings associations and their subsidiaries, and savings and loan holding companies and their subsidiaries to other institutions. It lays down the guidance to conduct relevant and appropriate due diligence for credit exposures with other financial institutions. The FRB issued a Supervision and Regulation Letter, "Risk Management and Capital Adequacy of Exposures Arising from Secondary Market Credit Activities." In August 2010, The Basel Committee on Banking Supervision issued its "Microfinance Activities and Core Principles for Effective Banking Supervision" that addresses:

1. Efficient allocation of supervisory resources
2. Effective evaluation of the risks of microfinance activities through development of specialized knowledge within the supervisory team
3. Establishment of proven control and managerial practices relevant to microfinance activities
4. Achievement of clarity in the regulations pertaining to microfinance activities

(v) Accounting Guidance   The accounting guidance for purchasing, acquiring, and selling mortgage servicing rights is discussed in Section 31.3.

(vi) Valuation   The accounting guidance addressing the valuation of loans held for sale is discussed in Section 31.3.

(r) REAL ESTATE INVESTMENTS, REAL ESTATE OWNED, AND OTHER FORECLOSED ASSETS   The type and nature of assets included in real estate investments, former bank premises, and other foreclosed assets can vary significantly. Such assets are described next.

(i) Real Estate Investments   Certain institutions make direct equity investments in real estate projects, and other institutions may grant real estate loans that have virtually the same risks and rewards as those of joint venture participants. Both types of transactions are considered to be real estate investments, and such arrangements are treated as if the institution has an ownership interest in the property.

Specifically, GAAP for real estate investments is established in the following authoritative literature:

- AICPA SOP 78-9, "Accounting for Investments in Real Estate Ventures"
- SFAS No. 34, "Capitalization of Interest Cost"
- SFAS No. 58, "Capitalization of Interest Cost in Financial Statements That Include Investments Accounted for by the Equity Method"
- SFAS No. 66, "Accounting for Sales of Real Estate"
- SFAS No. 67, "Accounting for Costs and Initial Rental Operations of Real Estate Projects"
- SFAS No. 144, "Accounting for the Impairment or Disposal of Long-Lived Assets"
- SFAS 140, "Accounting for Transfer and Servicing of Financial Assets and Extinguishments of Liabilities"
- IAS 39, "Financial Instruments: Recognition and Measurement" issued by IASB in 2003

(ii) Former Bank Premises   Many institutions have former premises that are no longer used in operations. Such former bank premises may be included in real estate owned.

(iii) Foreclosed Assets   Foreclosed assets include all assets received in full or partial satisfaction of a receivable and include real and personal property; equity interests in corporations, partnerships, and joint ventures; and beneficial interests in trusts. However, the largest component of real estate owned by banks and savings institutions comprises foreclosed real estate assets. Subprime loans account for the majority of loans in foreclosure. In 2008, about 11 percent of subprime loans were in foreclosure, and this rate is expected to rise in the coming years.

Guidance on accounting for and reporting of foreclosed assets is established in the following authoritative literature:

- SFAS No. 15, "Accounting by Debtors and Creditors for Troubled Debt Restructurings"
- SFAS No. 144, "Accounting for the Impairment or Disposal of Long-Lived Assets"
- SOP 92-3, "Accounting for Foreclosed Assets"

In October 2001, the FASB issued SFAS No. 144, "Accounting for the Impairment or Disposal of Long-Lived Asset" (SFAS No. 144, or the Statement). The Statement supersedes FASB Statement No. 121, "Accounting for the Impairment of Long-Lived Assets and for Long-Lived Assets to Be Disposed Of"; however, it retains the fundamental provisions of that

Statement related to the recognition and measurement of the impairment of long-lived assets to be "held and used." In addition, the Statement provides more guidance on estimating cash flows when performing a recoverability test, requires that a long-lived asset (group) to be disposed of other than by sale (e.g., abandoned) be classified as "held and used" until it is disposed of, and establishes more restrictive criteria to classify as asset (group) as "held for sale."

The Statement is effective for year ends beginning after December 15, 2001 (e.g., January 1, 2002, for a calendar year entity) and interim periods within those fiscal years. Earlier application was encouraged. Transition is prospective for committed disposal activities that are initiated after the effective date of the Statement or an entity's initial application of the Statement. The Statement also provides transition provisions for assets "held for sale" that were initially recorded under previous models (Accounting Principles Board (APB) No. 30 or FAS No. 121) and do not meet the new "held for sale" criteria within one year of the initial application of the Statement (e.g., December 31, 2002, for a calendar year-end entity that adopts the Statement effective January 1, 2002).

(s) INVESTMENTS IN DEBT AND EQUITY SECURITIES   Banks use a variety of financial instruments for various purposes, primarily to provide a source of income through investment or resale and to manage interest-rate and liquidity risk as part of an overall asset/liability management strategy.

Institutions purchase U.S. government obligations, such as U.S. Treasury bills, notes, and bonds, in addition to the debt of U.S. government agencies and government-sponsored enterprises, such as the U.S. Government National Mortgage Association (Finnie Mae) and Federal Home Loan Mortgage Corporation (Freddie Mac). Institutions also purchase municipal obligations, such as municipal bonds and tax anticipation notes.

Another common form of investments, which can be tailored to a wide variety of needs, is called *asset-backed securities* (ABSs). ABS values are based on the values of specific assets that back, or get pooled into, the securities. Those assets can include mortgage loans, student loans, credit card payments, auto loans, and nearly any other kind of asset that provides a steady flow of payments. Securitization helps expand the availability and lowers the cost of credit for homeowners, consumers, and businesses because as lenders pool the assets into securities and sell them to investors, the lenders then get more money to turn into loans.

For the purpose of categorizing asset-backed securities, each individual asset-backed security should be included in the item that most closely describes the predominant type of asset that collateralizes the security and this categorization should be used consistently over time. In 2010, the SEC voted to issue new regulatory proposals covering $2 trillion plus of the ABS market. The securitization had fostered poor lending practices by encouraging lenders to shift their risk of loss to investors, resulting in investors largely withdrawing from the market when those securities went bad after the U.S. housing bust. Because of the role played by the mortgage-backed securities (MBSs) in the current financial crisis, the securitized U.S. subprime mortgages are observed to serve as the crisis's immediate trigger. During the financial crisis, ABS holders suffered significant losses, revealing the fact that many investors are not fully aware of the risk in the underlying mortgages within the pools of securitized assets and overrely on credit ratings assigned by rating agencies. The proposed rules seek to address the problems highlighted by the crisis and to head off the next one by giving investors the tools they need to accurately assess risk and by better aligning the interests of the issuer with those of the investor.

Banks can hold ABSs as securities, or they can be the issuer of ABSs along with both governmental and private issuers. The ABSs are repaid from the underlying cash flow generated from other financial instruments, such as mortgage loans, credit card receivables, and mobile home loans. ABSs secured by real estate mortgages are often called *mortgage-backed securities* (MBSs). The level of risk related to ABSs is often related to the level of risk in the collateral. For example, securitized subprime auto loans experiencing a decline in credit quality might also cause a reduction in the value of the ABS if receipt of the underlying cash flow becomes questionable.

ABSs often include a credit enhancement designed to reduce the degree of credit risk to the holder of the ABS security. Examples of credit enhancement include guarantees, letters of credit, overcollateralization, private insurance, and senior/subordinate structures. The degree of protection provided by the credit enhancement depends on the nature of the collateral and the type and extent of the credit enhancement.

ABSs are structured into a variety of products, many of which are complex. Risk variables, such as prepayment risk, changes in prevailing interest rates, and delayed changes in indexed interest rates, make the forecasting of future cash flows more difficult. ABSs with several investment classes may have varying terms such as maturity dates, interest rates, payment schedules, and residual rights, which further complicates an analysis of the investment. Collateralized mortgage obligations (CMOs) and real estate mortgage investment conduits (REMICs) are two examples of multiclass mortgage securities. The underlying objective of all types of ABSs and mortgage securities is to redistribute the cash flows generated from the collateral to all security holders, consistent with their contractual rights, without a shortfall or an overage.

Banks are generally restricted in the types of financial instruments they may deal in, underwrite, purchase, or sell. Essentially, banks may only deal in U.S. government and U.S. government agency securities, municipal bonds, and certain other bonds, notes, and debentures. These restrictions are also limited based on capitalization. The FFIEC policy statement issued in February 1992 addresses the selection of securities dealers, policies and strategies for securities portfolios, unsuitable investment practices, and mortgage derivations. FFIEC in Sept 2010 has announced the availability of data on mortgage lending transactions at 8,124 U.S. financial institutions covered by the Home Mortgage Disclosure Act (HMDA). Covered institutions include banks, savings associations, credit unions, and mortgage companies. The HMDA data made available today cover 2009 lending activity—applications, originations, denials (and other actions such as incomplete or withdrawn applications), and purchases of loans.

(i) Accounting for Investments in Debt and Equity Securities   SFAS No. 115, "Accounting for Certain Investments in Debt and Equity Securities," issued in May 1993 addresses the accounting and reporting for investments in equity securities that have readily determinable fair values and for all investments in debt securities superseding SFAS No.12, "Accounting for certain marketable securities," and related interpretations and amends FASB Statement No. 65, *Accounting for Certain Mortgage Banking Activities,* to eliminate mortgage-backed securities from its scope. This Statement does not apply to unsecuritized loans. However, after mortgage loans are converted to mortgage-backed securities, they are subject to its provisions. This Statement is effective for fiscal years beginning after December 15, 1993. It is to be initially applied as of the beginning of an enterprise's fiscal year and cannot be applied retroactively to prior years' financial statements. However, an enterprise may elect to initially apply this Statement as of the end of an earlier fiscal year for which annual financial statements have not previously been issued. Investment securities are classified in three categories: held-to-maturity, trading, and available-for-sale.

HELD-TO-MATURITY

Debt securities for which an institution has both the ability and positive intent to hold to maturity are classified as held-to-maturity and are carried at amortized cost. (Any difference between cost and fair value is recorded as a premium or discount, which is amortized to income using the level yield method over the life of the security.)

TRADING

Securities that are purchased and held principally for the purpose of selling them in the near term are carried at fair value with unrealized gains and losses included in earnings.

AVAILABLE-FOR-SALE

All other securities are classified as available-for-sale and carried at fair value with unrealized gains and losses included as a separate component of shareholders' equity.

SFAS No. 115 addresses changes in circumstances that may cause an enterprise to change its intent to hold a certain security to maturity without calling into question its intent to hold other debt securities to maturity in the future.

For individual securities classified as either available-for-sale or held-to-maturity, entities are required to determine whether a decline in fair value below the amortized cost basis is other than temporary. If such a decline is judged to be other than temporary, the cost basis of the individual security should be written down to fair value as the new cost basis. The amount of the write-down should be treated as a realized loss and recorded in earnings. The new cost basis shall not be changed for subsequent recoveries.

Investment securities are required to be recorded on a trade date basis. Interest income on investment securities is recorded separately as a component of interest income. Realized gains and losses on available-for-sale securities and realized and unrealized gains and losses on trading securities are recorded as a separate component of noninterest income or loss. Upon the sale of an available-for-sale security, any unrealized gain or loss previously recorded in the separate component of equity is reversed and recorded as a separate component of noninterest income or loss.

Discounts and premiums should be accreted or amortized using the interest method in accordance with SFAS No. 91, "Accounting for Nonrefundable Fees and Costs Associated with Originating or Acquiring Loans and Initial Direct Costs of Leases." The interest method provides for a periodic interest income at a constant effective yield on the net investment. The amortization or accretion period should be from the purchase date to the maturity date rather than an earlier call date, except for large numbers of similar loans where prepayments are expected and can be reasonably estimated, such as with certain ABSs.

Transfers among the three categories are performed at fair value. Transfers out of held-to-maturity should be rare.

(ii) Wash Sales   If the same financial asset is purchased shortly before or after the sale of a security, it is called a *wash sale*. SFAS No. 140 addresses wash sales, stating that unless there is a concurrent contract to repurchase or redeem the transferred financial assets from the purchaser, the seller does not maintain effective control over the transferred assets, and, therefore, the sale should be recorded. SFAS No. 140 provides the accounting guidance for recognizing gains and losses from wash sales, as more fully discussed in Section 31.3.

(iii) Short Sales   An institution may sell a security it does not own with the intention of buying or borrowing securities at an agreed-on future date to cover the sale. Given the nature of these transactions, such sales should be within the trading portfolio. Obligations incurred in these short sales should be reported as liabilities and recorded at fair value at each reporting date with change in fair value recorded through income. The Dodd–Frank Act of 2010 directs the SEC to issue rules requiring financial institutions to publically report on their short sales activities on at least a monthly basis.

(iv) Securities Borrowing and Lending An institution may borrow securities from a counterparty to fulfill its obligations and may advance cash, pledge other securities, or issue letters of credit as collateral for borrowed securities. If cash is pledged as collateral, the institution that loans the securities typically earns a return by investing that cash at rates higher than the rate paid or "rebated" back to the institution that borrows the securities. If the collateral is other than cash, the institution that loans the collateral typically receives a fee. Because most securities lending transactions are short term, the value of the pledged collateral is usually required to be higher than the value of the securities borrowed, and collateral is usually valued daily and adjusted frequently for changes in the market price, most securities lending transactions by themselves do not represent significant credit risks. However, other risks exist in securities lending transactions, such as market and credit risks, relative to the maintenance and safeguarding of the collateral. For example, the manner in which cash collateral is invested could present market and credit risk.

SFAS No. 140 addresses the accounting for securities lending transactions (i.e., for transfers and servicing of financial assets and extinguishments of liabilities a replacement of FASB Statement 125). Those standards are based on consistent application of a *financial-components approach* that focuses on control. It provides that if the transferor (institution loaning the securities) surrenders control over those securities, the transfer shall be accounted for as a sale, to the extent that consideration (other than beneficial interest) is received in exchange. SFAS No. 140 states that the transferor has surrendered control over the transferred asset only if *all* three of the following conditions have been met:

1. The transferred assets have been isolated from the transferor—put presumptively beyond the reach of the transferor and its creditors, even in bankruptcy or other receivership (pars. 27 and 28).
2. Each transferee (or, if the transferee is a qualifying SPE (par. 35), each holder of its beneficial interests) has the right to pledge or exchange the assets (or beneficial interests) it received, and no condition both constrains the transferee (or holder) from taking advantage of its right to pledge or exchange and provides more than a trivial benefit to the transferor (pars. 29–34).
3. The transferor does not maintain effective control over the transferred assets through either (1) an agreement that both entitles and obligates the transferor to repurchase or redeem them before their maturity (pars. 47–49) or (2) the ability to unilaterally cause the holder to return specific assets, other than through a cleanup call (pars. 50–54).

If all three conditions are met, the securities lending transaction shall be accounted for as a sale, in the following manner:

- *Institution loaning the securities.* Recognizes the sale of the loaned securities, proceeds consisting of the collateral. Also recognizes the forward repurchase commitment.
- *Institution borrowing the securities.* Recognizes the purchase of the borrowed securities, consideration representing the collateral. Also recognizes the forward resale commitment.

Lending securities transactions accompanied by an agreement that entitles and obligates the institution loaning the securities to repurchase or redeem them before their maturity should be accounted for as secured borrowings. The cash (or securities) received as collateral is considered the amount borrowed, and the securities loaned are considered pledged as collateral against the cash borrowed. Any rebate paid to the institution borrowing the securities is treated as interest on the cash borrowed.

When the transfer is recorded as a sale, the cash (or securities) received in conjunction with loaning securities should be recognized as an asset and a corresponding liability established, recording the obligation to return the cash (or securities).

However, most securities lending transactions are accompanied by an agreement that entitles and obligates the securities lender to repurchase or redeem the transferred assets before their maturity. Such transactions will not typically be reported as sales under SFAS No. 140 because of the obligation of the transferor to repurchase the transferred assets. However, the provisions of SFAS No. 140 relating to the recognition of collateral could require that the transfer of securities and related collateral be recorded. The principal criterion to determine whether the collateral will be required to be recorded is whether the parties to the arrangement have the right to sell or repledge it. If such a right is present, the securities lender records the cash or noncash collateral received as its own asset as well as a corresponding obligation to return it. If the securities lender sells the collateral, it would recognize the proceeds and derecognize the collateral. The securities borrower will typically not record the securities received or an obligation to return them unless they are sold. Additionally, the securities borrower will not typically be required to reclassify the collateral provided, if such collateral is in the form of securities.

Additional guidance on accounting for and reporting of investments in debt and equity securities is established in the following:

- FASB Technical Bulletin (TB) No. 94-1, "Application of SFAS No. 115 to Debt Securities Restructured in a Troubled Debt Restructuring." This clarifies that any loan that was restructured in a troubled debt restructuring involving a modification of terms would be subject to SFAS No. 115 if the debt instrument meets the definition of a security.
- SFAS No. 91, "Accounting for Nonrefundable Fees and Costs Associated with Originating or Acquiring Loans and Initial Direct Costs of Leases." SFAS 91 specifies that discounts or premiums associated with the purchase of debt securities should be accreted or amortized using the interest method.
- SFAS No. 15, "Accounting by Debtors and Creditors for Troubled Debt Restructurings," applies to troubled debt restructurings involving debt securities.
- SFAS No. 114, "Accounting by Creditors for Impairment of a Loan (an Amendment, FASB No. 5 and 15)," addresses troubled debt restructurings involving a modification of terms of a receivables. That is, the creditor should evaluate the collectability of both contractual interest and contractual principal of all receivables when assessing the need for a loss accrual. This Statement applies to financial statements for fiscal years beginning after December 15, 1994.

(t) DEPOSITS   Generally, the most significant source of a bank's funding is customer deposits. Institutions now offer a wide range of deposit products having a variety of interest rates, terms, and conditions. The more common types of deposits are described in the following:

(i) Demand Deposits   Customer deposit accounts from which funds may be withdrawn on demand. Checking and negotiable order of withdrawal (NOW) accounts are the most common form of demand deposits. Deposits and withdrawals are typically made through a combination of deposits, check writing, automatic teller machines (ATMs), point-of-sale terminals, electronic funds transfers (EFTs), and preauthorized deposits and payment transactions, such as payroll deposits and loan payments.

(ii) Savings Deposits   Interest-bearing deposit accounts that normally carry with them certain access restrictions or minimum balance requirements. Passbook and statement savings accounts and money market accounts are the most common form of savings accounts. Deposits and withdrawals are typically made at teller windows, ATMs, by electronic funds transfers, or by preauthorized payment. Money market accounts often permit the customer to write checks, although the number of checks that may be written is limited.

(iii) Time Deposits   Interest-bearing deposit accounts that are subject to withdrawal only after a fixed term. Certificates of deposit (CDs), individual retirement accounts (IRAs), and open accounts are the most common form of time deposits.

CDs may be issued in bearer form or registered form and may be negotiable and nonnegotiable. Negotiable CDs, for which there is an active secondary market, are generally short term and are most commonly sold to corporations, pension funds, and government bodies in large denominations, such as $100,000 to $1 million. Nonnegotiable CDs are generally in smaller denominations, and depositors are subject to a penalty fee if they elect to withdraw their funds prior to the stated maturity.

Individual retirement accounts, Keogh accounts, and self-employed-person accounts (SEPs) are generally maintained as CDs; however, due to the tax benefits to depositors, they typically have longer terms than most CDs.

Brokered deposits are third-party time deposits placed by or through the assistance of a deposit broker. Deposit brokers sometimes sell interests in placed deposits to third parties. Federal law restricts the acceptance and renewal of brokered deposits by an institution based on its capitalization.

(u) FEDERAL FUNDS AND REPURCHASE AGREEMENTS   Federal funds and repurchase agreements are often used as a source of liquidity and as a cost-effective source of funds.

(i) Federal Funds   Generally, federal funds are short-term funds maturing overnight bought between banks that are members of the Federal Reserve System. Federal funds transactions can be secured or unsecured. If the funds are secured, U.S. government securities are placed in a custody account for the seller.

(ii) Repurchase Agreements   Repurchase agreements, or repos, occur when an institution sells securities and agrees to repurchase the identical (or substantially the same) securities at a specified date for a specified price. The institution may be a seller or a buyer. Most repo transactions occur with other depository institutions, dealers in securities, state and local governments, and customers (retail repurchase agreements), and involve obligations of the federal government or its agencies, commercial paper, bankers' acceptances, and negotiable CDs. The difference between the sale and repurchase price represents interest for the use of the funds. There are also several types of repurchase agreements, such as collar repurchase agreements, fixed-coupon agreements, and yield-maintenance agreements. The terms of the agreements are

often structured to reflect the substance of the transaction, such as a borrowing and lending of funds versus a sale and purchase of securities. Some repurchase agreements are similar to securities lending transactions, whereby the seller may (or may not) have the right to sell or repledge the securities to a third party during the term of the repurchase agreement.

SFAS No. 140 provides the accounting guidance for repurchase agreements. In addition to replacing Statement 125 and rescinding FASB Statement No. 127, *Deferral of the Effective Date of Certain Provisions of FASB Statement No. 125,* this Statement carries forward the actions taken by Statement 125. In general, SFAS No. 140 uses the three conditions discussed previously in Subsection 31.2(s)(iv), "Securities Borrowing and Lending," when accounting for repurchase agreements. If all three conditions specified in SFAS No. 140 are met, the seller shall account for the repurchase agreement as a sale of financial assets and a forward repurchase commitment, and the buyer shall account for the agreement as a purchase of financial assets and a forward resale commitment. This Statement was made effective for transfers and servicing of financial assets and extinguishments of liabilities occurring after March 31, 2001, and for the recognition and reclassification of collateral and for disclosures relating to securitization transactions and collateral for fiscal years ending after December 15, 2000.

Government securities dealers, banks, other financial institutions, and corporate investors commonly use repurchase agreements to obtain or use short-term funds. Under those agreements, the transferor ("repo party") transfers a security to a transferee ("repo counterparty" or "reverse party") in exchange for cash and concurrently agrees to reacquire that security at a future date for an amount equal to the cash exchanged plus a stipulated "interest" factor. Repurchase agreements can be effective in a variety of ways. Some repurchase agreements are similar to securities lending transactions in that the transferee has the right to sell the securities to a third party during the term of the repurchase agreement. In other repurchase agreements, the transferee does not have the right to sell the securities during the term of the repurchase agreement.

Two reasons advanced in support of the treatment of repurchase agreements and securities lending transactions as secured borrowings are that (1) those transactions are difficult to characterize because they have attributes of both borrowings and sales and (2) supporting arguments can be found for accounting for those transactions as borrowings or sales. The only supporting arguments cited for the treatment of repurchase agreements and securities lending transactions as secured borrowings that are not equally applicable to certain securitizations are that (1) forward contracts that are fully secured should be treated differently than those that are unsecured and (2) making a change in existing accounting practice would have a substantial impact on the reported financial position of certain entities and on the markets in which they participate.

Also similar to the treatment for securities lending transactions, repurchase agreements where the institution selling the securities maintains effective control over the securities (and thereby not meeting the three sale conditions, described previously, provided by SFAS No. 140) should be accounted for as secured borrowings.

(v) DEBT   Banks and savings institutions use long- and short-term borrowings as a source of funds.

(i) Long-Term Debt   Debentures and notes are the most common form of long-term debt; however, institutions also use long-term mortgages, obligations, commitments under capital leases, and mandatorily redeemable preferred stock to provide long-term funding. Funds are

also borrowed through Eurodollar certificates, CMOs, and REMICs; mortgage-backed bond (MBBs), mortgage-revenue bonds, and FHLB advances. The terms of long-term debt vary; they may be secured or unsecured, and they may be convertible.

(ii) Short-Term Debt   Repurchase agreements and federal funds purchased are the most common form of the short-term debt described earlier. Commercial paper is another common source of short-term funding. Commercial paper is an unsecured short-term promissory note typically issued by bank or savings institution holding companies.

MBBs are any borrowings (other than those from an FHLB) collateralized in whole or in part by one or more real estate loans.

Member institutions may borrow from their regional Federal Reserve Bank in the form of discounts and advances, which are primarily used to cover shortages in the required reserve account and also in times of liquidity problems.

(iii) Accounting Guidance   In general, the accounting for debt is the same for banks and savings institutions as for other enterprises, although banks and savings institutions have unclassified balance sheets. SFAS Statement No. 140 provides guidance for transfers of financial assets and extinguishments of liabilities. While few respondents support the reasoning of Statement 125, others argue that existing accounting guidance found in AICPA Statement (American Institute of CPAs), *Definition of the Term Substantially the Same for Holders of Debt Instruments, as Used in Certain Audit Guides and a Statement of Position*, has proven adequate to constrain the characteristics of assets that are to be reacquired.

(w) TAXATION   Taxation of financial institutions is extremely complex; specific discussion is therefore beyond the scope of this book. However, certain significant factors affecting bank and thrift taxation are discussed next.

(i) Loan Loss Reserves
BANKS
Prior to the Tax Reform Act of 1986 (1986 Act), banks were permitted to deduct loan loss provisions based on either the experience method or on a percentage of eligible loans method. Since the mid-1980s, provision for loan losses has been one of the most important factors affecting bank profitability. The federal banking regulators (Federal Deposit Insurance Corporation, Office of the Controller of the Currency, and Federal Reserve) require that all banks include in their financial statements an account named as *allowance for loan losses* (also known as reserves for *loan losses*). When loan losses are recognized (i.e., when a bank decides that some portion of a loan will not be collected and therefore must be *charged off* or *written down*), the amount of the loss is deducted from the asset category loans and also from reserves for loan losses.

The 1986 Act passed by Congress simplified the tax code and eliminated some deductions quoting its significance in the tax structure of the United States and it modified the Internal Revenue Code Section 585, which now allows only a "small" bank with $500 million or less in average assets (calculated by taking into account the average assets of all other members of an institution's controlled group, if applicable) to calculate an addition to the bad debt reserve using the experience method.

A "large" bank with over $500 million in assets may not use the reserve method. It is limited to the specific charge-off method under IRC Section 166. If a bank becomes a large bank, it is required to recapture its reserve, usually over a four-year period. A deduction under Section 166 is generally allowed for wholly or partially worthless debt for the year in which the worthlessness occurs. The total or partial worthlessness of a debt is a facts-and-circumstance, loan-by-loan determination. Larger banks may claim losses only when loans are written off. A bank may make a conformity election, however, which provides a presumptive conclusion of worthlessness for charge-offs made for regulatory purposes.

In comparison to GAAP, the specific charge-off method generally results in an unfavorable temporary difference (i.e., the book expense is recognized prior to the tax deduction being allowed) because the actual charge-off of a loan usually occurs later than the time the reserve is established for it. The act also eliminated the deductibility of nonmortgage consumer interest payments such as interest on credit card balances, automobile loans, and life insurance loans.

THRIFTS

Effective for tax years beginning after December 31, 1995, thrift institutions are subject to the same loan loss rules as banks. Thrifts that qualify as "small" banks (average assets of $500 million or less) can use the experience-based reserve method already described. Thrifts that are treated as "large" banks must use the specific charge-off method.

A thrift that is treated as either a large or small bank is required to recapture or recognize as income its "applicable excess reserves." Such income is generally recognized ratably over a six-year period beginning with the first tax year beginning after 1995.

If a thrift becomes a large bank, the amount of the thrift's applicable excess reserves is generally the excess of (1) the balance of its reserves as of the close of its last taxable year beginning before January 1, 1996, over (2) the balance of its reserves as of the close of its last taxable year beginning before January 1, 1988 (its "pre-1988" or "base year" reserve). Thus, a thrift treated as a large bank generally is required to recapture all post-1987 additions to it bad debt reserves.

In the case of a thrift becoming a small bank, the thrift's applicable excess reserves is the excess of (1) the balance of its reserves as of the close of its last taxable year beginning before January 1, 1996, over (2) the greater of the balance of (a) its pre-1988 reserves, or (b) what the thrift's reserves would have been at the close of its last taxable year beginning before January 1, 1996, had the thrift always used the experience method. Thus, a thrift treated as a small bank may not have any applicable excess reserves (and therefore no recapture) if it had always used the experience method.

A special rule, the "residential loan requirement," may allow the six-year recapture period to be delayed for one or two years, that is, recapture could actually start as late as the first taxable year beginning after 1997. An institution meets the requirement for a taxable year if the principal amount of residential loans made by the institution during the year is not less than its "base amount," defined generally as the average of the principal amounts of residential loans made by the institution during the six most recent tax years beginning before January 1, 1996.

A "residential loan" is generally defined as a loan secured by residential real property, but only to the extent the loan is made to the property owner to acquire, construct, or improve the property. Thus, mortgage refinancing and home equity loans are not considered to be residential loans, except to the extent the proceeds of the loan are used to acquire, construct, or improve qualified real property. Other rules govern the calculation of the base amount for purposes of the requirement.

The residential loan requirement is applicable only for taxable years beginning after December 31, 1995, and before January 1, 1998, and must be applied separately with respect to each such year. Thus, all institutions are required to recapture their applicable excess reserves within the first six, seven, or eight taxable years beginning after December 31, 1995.

(ii) Mark-to-Market   Contrary to normal realization-based tax accounting principles, IRC Section 475 requires "dealers in securities" to recognize gain or loss through "marking-to-market" their securities holdings, unless such securities are validly identified by the taxpayer as excepted from the provisions.

As used in this context, the terms *dealer* and *securities* have very broad application. Virtually all financial institutions are considered dealers in securities for mark-to-market purposes though regulations provide exceptions for certain institutions not engaging in more than de minimus dealer activities. Securities required to be marked (unless validly identified as excepted) include notes, bonds, and other evidences of indebtedness; stock; notional principal contracts; or any evidence of an interest in or a derivative of such security (other than Section 1256(a) contracts); and any clearly identified hedge of such security.

Securities that may be identified as exempted from the mark-to-market provisions are:

- Securities "held for investment," and property identified as such for tax purposes.
- Notes and other evidences of indebtedness (and obligations to acquire such) that are acquired or originated by the taxpayer in the ordinary course of a trade or business that are "not held for sale."
- Hedges of positions or liabilities that are not securities in the hands of the taxpayer, and hedges of positions or liabilities that are exempt from mark-to-market under the two foregoing provisions. This does not apply for hedges held as a dealer.

To be exempted from mark-to-market, the security must be identified by the taxpayer on a contemporaneous basis (generally, day of acquisition) as meeting one of the exceptions.

Whether or not a security is required to be marked-to-market for financial accounting purposes is *not* dispositive for purposes of determining whether such security is treated as "held for investment" or "not held for sale."

Some financial institutions identify all or a significant portion of their loans to customers as exempted from the mark-to-market provisions because they intend to hold those loans to maturity. A possible exception are mortgages that are originated for sale (pipeline or warehoused loans), which do not meet the exception criteria and must be marked-to-market.

(iii) Tax-Exempt Securities   For tax purposes, gross income does not include interest on any obligation of a state or political subdivision thereof (e.g., county, city). Interest on certain nonqualified private activity bonds, unregistered bonds, and arbitrage bonds does not qualify for this exemption.

A deduction is not allowed for interest expense on indebtedness incurred to purchase or carry tax-exempt obligations. Deposit-taking financial institutions (banks and thrifts) are subject to a special two-part formula to determine how much of the total interest expense of an institution is disallowed interest expense.

Interest expense related to tax-exempt obligations acquired after August 1986 is disallowed and is calculated by multiplying total interest expense by the ratio of the tax basis of such obligations to the tax basis of all assets.

Interest expense related to tax-exempt obligations acquired between January 1983 and August 1986 is 20 percent disallowed and is calculated in a manner similar to that just described.

Certain qualified tax-exempt obligations (generally, obligations issued by an entity that will not issue more than $10 million of tax-exempt obligations during the year and that are not private activity bonds) issued after August 1986 are treated as if issued prior to that date (i.e., subject to the 20 percent disallowance rule rather than the 100 percent disallowance rule).

(iv) Nonaccrual Loans   Generally, interest on a loan must be accrued as income unless the taxpayer can demonstrate that the interest is uncollectible at the time of accrual. The tax rule is dependent on the facts and circumstances for the nonaccrual loans at issue. The FAS No. 114 uses a "probable" test in determining when a loan is impaired. When it is probable that a creditor will be unable to collect all amounts due according to the contractual terms of the loan agreement, the loan is considered impaired. Use of this analysis may now provide substantiation of the tax treatment for impairment of loans.

(v) Hedging   Financial institutions that are involved in hedging transactions treat the gain or loss from these transactions as ordinary for tax purposes. A hedging transaction must be entered into primarily to manage a taxpayer's risk of interest rate changes, price changes, or currency fluctuations. A taxpayer must also have risk on an overall (or macro) basis. A hedge of a single ordinary asset or liability will be respected if it is reasonably expected to manage the taxpayer's overall risk. Hedges entered into as part of an overall risk reduction program also will qualify.

"Fixed to floating" hedges (e.g., hedges that convert a fixed-rate liability into a floating-rate liability) may satisfy the risk management requirement if, for example, a taxpayer's income varies with interest rates. In addition, hedges entered into to reverse or counteract another hedging transaction may qualify for ordinary gain or loss treatment. Because tax hedges are permissible only with ordinary property, hedges of mortgage servicing rights generally do not qualify as tax hedges, since mortgage servicing rights are generally capital assets.

Hedges of ordinary liabilities qualify as "hedging transactions" regardless of the use of the proceeds from the borrowing. Consequently, gain or loss from a hedge of a liability used to fund the purchase of a capital asset will be ordinary. However, recent guidance in the form of final Treasury regulations provide that the purchase or sale of a debt instrument, an equity security, or an annuity contract is not hedging a transaction even if the transaction limits or reduces the taxpayer's risk.

The timing of the gain or loss from a hedging transaction must reasonably be "matched" with the gain or loss of the item being hedged. This applies to global hedges and other hedges of aggregate risk.

If a taxpayer disposes of a hedged item but retains the hedge, the taxpayer may redesignate the hedge. The taxpayer generally must mark-to-market the hedge on the date that the taxpayer disposes of the hedged item.

There are detailed contemporaneous identification and record-keeping requirements with which an institution must comply to support its treatment of hedging transactions. Failure to comply could lead to characterization of losses from these transactions as capital losses (which may only be used to offset capital gains).

(vi) Loan Origination Fees and Costs   Loan origination fees shall be deferred and recognized over the life of the loan as an adjustment of yield (interest income). Loan origination fees and related direct loan origination costs for a given loan shall be offset, and only the net amount shall be deferred and amortized. The practice of recognizing a portion of loan origination fees as revenue in a period to offset all or part of the costs of origination shall no longer be acceptable.

For financial accounting purposes, SFAS No. 91 requires that all loan origination fees (including loan commitment fees and points) be deferred and generally recognized over the life of the related loan or commitment period as an adjustment of yield. This statement establishes the accounting for nonrefundable fees and costs associated with originating or acquiring loans and initial direct costs of leases (i.e., association with lending, committing to lend, or purchasing a loan or group of loans). The statement specifies that loan origination fees shall be recognized over the life of the related loan as an adjustment of yield. All loan commitment fees shall be deferred except for certain retrospectively determined fees; commitment fees meeting specified criteria shall be recognized over the loan commitment period; all other commitment fees shall be recognized as an adjustment of yield over the related loan's life or, if the commitment expires unexercised, recognized in income upon expiration of the commitment. Overall, it changes the practice of recognizing loan origination and commitment fees at or prior to inception of the loan.

For tax accounting purposes, loan fees received as cash payments incident to a lending transaction (e.g., points) that represent an amount charged for the use of forbearance of money (rather than payment for services) are deferred. Points received in connection with a lending transaction are applied as a reduction to the issue price of the loan and generally create original issue discounts (OIDs) to be recognized over the life of the loan on a constant yield method. In instances where the OID on a loan is de minimus (as defined in regulations), the de minimus OID is recognized in proportion to principal payments received.

For book purposes, the costs associated with origination of a loan are deferred and recognized over the life of the loan, together with the origination fees. For tax purposes, institutions generally deduct these costs currently because to date there has been no published guidance requiring capitalization. However, in January 2002, the Treasury issued an Advance Notice of Proposed Rule Making (ANPRM), providing notice that it plans to issue future guidance for loan origination costs. The Notice suggests further guidance will permit a current deduction for de minimis internal costs (e.g., employee salaries) in connection with the origination of intangible assets (e.g., loans).

(vii) Foreclosed Property

BANKS

Generally, a bank recognizes gain or loss on foreclosure of property securing a loan, but is not permitted to deduct any further decrease in or impairment of value. Any decrease in value occurring after foreclosure is recognized when the property is disposed of by the institution. If real property acquired through foreclosure is operated in a trade or business after foreclosure (e.g., as rental property), the institution may deduct depreciation (and other operating expenses) computed in accordance with general tax depreciation provisions.

THRIFTS

Effective for taxable years beginning after December 31, 1995, thrift institutions are subject to the same rules as banks.

Under prior law, a special rule treated the acquisition of property by a thrift as a nontaxable event, with no gain or loss recognized at time of foreclosure and no depreciation allowed on the property. A subsequent write-down charge to the bad debt reserve was allowed if the fair market value of the property was less than the tax basis of the loan. Upon final disposition, the gain or loss was credited or charged to the bad debt reserve.

(viii) Leasing Activities
Direct financing activities may qualify as financings for tax purposes. As a result, a bank will be considered the owner of the leased property for tax purposes. Accordingly, rental income and depreciation deductions on the leased asset will be recognized for tax purposes but not for financial reporting purposes. This will result in a difference between book and tax accounting under SFAS No. 109.

(ix) FHLB Dividends
Banks and savings institutions may become members of the FHLB by purchasing stock in individual FHLB member banks. Banks generally become a member of the FHLB for access to additional funding for borrowed funds. The FHLB member banks, of which there are 12, generally pay cash or stock dividends to shareholders, depending on the member bank. Cash dividends paid on FHLB stock that was issued prior to March 28, 1942, are exempt from federal income taxes. This exemption applied even for such stock that was subsequently acquired through merger or otherwise. Cash dividends on FHLB stock issued on or after March 28, 1942, are not exempt from taxation. Stock dividends on FHLB stock are generally not taxable when distributed. These stock dividends create a book/tax difference that is recognized on the sales or redemption of the FHLB shares.

(x) Bank-Owned Life Insurance
Bank-owned life insurance (BOLI) is commonly used by financial institutions for its financial benefits to help fund benefit programs and to offset certain costs typically incurred when losing key employees of the bank. BOLI is life insurance purchased by a financial institution on the lives of specific employees. The economically beneficial aspects of BOLI are tax-free growth in the cash surrender value of the policy and a tax-free treatment of the death proceeds, which are both realized by the bank as the owner of a given policy. Insurance premiums on life insurance policies are not tax deductible.

(xi) Original Issue Discount
Original issue discount (OID) rules apply to all debt instruments after July 1, 1982, with certain exceptions. Generally, OID is the excess of what a borrower is obligated to repay when the loan comes due over the amount borrowed. More technically, OID is the excess of the stated redemption price at maturity over its issue price. Under OID rules, the holder of the debt must accrue stated interest under the constant yield method.

(xii) Market Discount
The primary difference between OIDs and market discounts is that purchase of a security at its original purchase versus the secondary market, respectively. Generally, if a debt instrument has declined in value from the time when it was originally issued (other than as a result of principal payments), a purchaser of the bond will acquire it with market discount.

A holder of a market discount may choose between two methods of recognizing accrued market discount. Market discount accrues under a ratable method, in proportion to the payment of principal, unless a constant interest method is elected. The primary difference between a market discount and an OID is that the borrower is not required to include accrued market discount in taxable income currently, but may elect to do so. Instead, the market discount rules require borrowers to recognize accrued market discount only on receipt of the proceeds of a disposition or a principal payment is made.

(x) FUTURES, FORWARDS, OPTIONS, SWAPS, AND SIMILAR FINANCIAL INSTRU-MENTS Futures, forwards, swaps, and options, and other financial instruments with similar characteristics (collectively, derivatives) have become important financial management tools for banks. The complexity and volume of derivatives and derivatives trading has increased significantly in recent years. Institutions continue to enhance risk management systems to enable them to monitor the risks involved. Bank regulatory agencies continue to encourage institutions to upgrade policies and procedures, risk measurement and reporting systems, and independent oversight and internal control processes. Senior management has increased its knowledge of the derivative products and how risks are monitored.

Derivatives are receiving considerable attention primarily due to the underlying volatility in the markets, relatively large size of the transactions, and the potential for significant earnings fluctuations. Derivatives have many similar risk characteristics as other credit products, such as credit risk, market risk, legal risk, and control risk. The specific risks in a derivatives portfolio are often difficult to identify due to the complexity of the transactions. For example, two or more basic risks are often used in combination, which may be further complicated by the fact that economic interaction between various positions within an institution (on- and off-balance-sheet) may be difficult to assess.

Underlying cash flows for derivatives are often referenced to such items as rates, indexes (which measure changes in specific markets), value of underlying positions in financial instruments, in equity instruments, in foreign currencies, commodities, or other derivatives.

Derivatives can generally be described as either forward-based or option-based, or combinations of the two. A forward-based contract (futures, forwards, and swap contracts) obligates one party to buy and a counterparty to sell an underlying financial instrument, foreign currency, or commodity at a future date at an agreed-upon price. An option-based derivative (options, interest-rate caps, and interest-rate floors) are one-sided in that if the right is exercised, only the holder can have a favorable outcome and the writer can have only an unfavorable outcome. Most derivatives are generally combinations of these two types of contracts.

Derivatives traded through an organized exchange typically have standardized contracts, such as futures and certain options, and the risk characteristics are more related to market risk than to credit risk. Alternatively, derivatives traded over-the-counter are customized to meet certain objectives or needs and often vary in structure, such as swaps and forward contracts. Customized derivative products traded privately typically present a greater degree of credit risk and liquidity risk, depending on the counterparty's financial strength, value of the collateral, if any, and the liquidity of the specific instrument.

The complexity of derivative instruments is largely the result of the pricing mechanisms, flexibility and options features, and value calculation formulas. In addition, derivatives can be structured to be more sensitive to general price movements than the cash market instruments from which their value is derived. The types of derivatives products available varies considerably; however, the following is a brief description of the basic types of contracts.

(i) Futures A futures contract is an agreement to make or take delivery of a financial instrument (interest rate instrument, currency, and certain stock indices) at a future date. Most futures contracts are closed out prior to the delivery date by entering into an offsetting contract.

The type of financial instrument delivered depends on the type of futures contract. For example: Investment-grade financial instruments, such as U.S. Treasury securities or mortgage-backed securities are delivered under interest rate futures; foreign currency (in the currency specified) is delivered under foreign currency futures contracts; and commodities such as oil, gold bullion, or coffee are delivered under commodities futures contracts.

Buyers and sellers are required to deposit assets (such as cash, government securities, or letters of credit) with a broker. The assets are called a *margin* and are subject to increases and decreases, if losses or gains are incurred on the open position.

(ii) Forwards   A forward contract is a contract between two parties to purchase and sell a specified quantity of a financial instrument, foreign currency, or commodity at a specified price, with delivery and settlement at a specified future date. Such contracts are not traded on exchanges and therefore may have a high degree of credit and liquidity risk. Forward rate agreements are forward contracts used to manage interest-rate risk.

(iii) Options   Option contracts provide the purchaser of the option with the right, but not the obligation, to buy (or sell) a specified instrument, such as currencies, interest rate products, or futures. They also put the seller under the obligation to deliver (or take delivery of) the instrument to the buyer of the option but only at the buyer's option.

A premium is typically paid to the seller of the option, representing both the time value of money and any intrinsic value. Intrinsic value, which cannot be less than zero, is derived from the excess of market price for the underlying item in the contract over the price specified in the contract (strike price).

Holders of option contracts can minimize downside price risks because the loss on a purchased option contracts is limited to the amount paid for the option. On the other hand, while the profit on written option contracts is limited to the premium received, the loss potential is unlimited because the writer is obligated to settle at the strike price if the option is exercised. Options are often processed through a clearinghouse, which guarantees the writer's performance and minimizes credit risk.

Option-based derivative contracts, such as caps, floors, collars, and swaptions, can be combined to transfer risks form one entity to another. The following describes each type of contract:

* *Interest rate caps.* These are contracts in which a cap writer, in return for a premium, agrees to make cash payments to the cap holder equal to the excess of the market rate over the strike price multiplied by the notional principal amount if rates go above specified interest rate (strike price). The cap holder has the right, not the obligation, to exercise the option, and if rates move down, the cap holder will lose only the premium paid. The cap writer has virtually unlimited risk resulting from increases in interest rates above the cap rate.
* *Interest rate floors.* These are contracts in which a floor writer, in return for a premium, agrees to limit the risk of declining interest rates based on a notional amount such that if rates go below a specified interest rate (strike price), the floor holder will receive cash payments equal to the difference between the market rate and the strike price multiplied by the notional principal amount. As with interest rate caps, the floor holder has the right, not the obligation, to exercise the option, and if rates move up, the floor holder will lose only the premium paid. The floor writer has risk resulting from decreases in interest rates below the floor rate.

- *Interest rate collars.* These are combinations of interest rate caps and interest rate floors, that is, one held and one written. Such contracts are often used by institutions to lock a floating-rate contract into a predetermined interest rate range.
- *Swaptions.* These are option contracts to enter into an interest rate swap contract at some future date or to cancel an existing swap in the future.

(iv) Swaps   Swaps are contracts between parties to exchange sets of cash flows based on a predetermined notional principal; only the cash flows are exchanged (usually on a net basis) with no principal exchanged. Swaps are used to change the nature or cost of existing transactions, for example, exchanging fixed-rate debt cash flows for floating rate cash flows. Swap contracts are not exchange-traded; therefore, they are not as liquid as futures contracts. The principal types of swaps are interest rate swaps and currency swaps. However, there are also basis swaps, equity swaps, commodity swaps, and mortgage swaps. A brief description of seven swaps follows:

1. *Interest rate swaps.* Interest rate swaps are used to manage interest rate risks, such as from floating to fixed or fixed to floating. Periodic fixed payments are made by one party, while another counterparty is obligated to make variable payments, depending on a market interest rate. Master netting agreements are used to permit entities to legally set off related payable and receivable swap contract positions for settlement purposes.
2. *Foreign currency swaps.* Foreign currency swaps are used to fix the value of foreign currency exchange transactions that will occur in the future. Typically, principal is exchanged at inception, interest is paid in accordance with the agreed-on rate and term, and principal is reexchanged at maturity.
3. *Fixed-rate currency swaps.* Fixed-rate currency swaps occur when two counterparties exchange fixed-rate interest in one currency for fixed-rate interest in another currency.
4. *Basis swaps.* Basis swaps represent a variation on interest-rate swap contracts where both rates are variable but tied to different index rates.
5. *Equity swaps.* Equity swaps occur when counterparties exchange cash flow streams tied to an equity index with a fixed or floating interest.
6. *Commodity swaps.* Commodity swaps occur when counterparties exchange cash flow streams tied to the difference between a commodity's agreed-on price and its variable price, applied to an agreed-on price of the commodity.
7. *Mortgage swaps.* Typical mortgage swaps occur when an investor exchanges interest payments tied to a short-term floating rate, for cash flows based an a generic class of mortgage-backed securities over a specified period. The cash flows received by the investor include the fixed coupon on the generic class or mortgage-backed securities and any discount or premium. The notional amount of the mortgage swap is adjusted monthly, based on amortization and prepayment experience of the generic class of mortgage-backed securities. When the contract expires, the investor may either have to take physical delivery of the mortgages (at a predetermined price) or settle in cash for the difference between the predetermined price and the current market value for the mortgages. Collateral may be posted to reduce counterparty credit risk.

(v) Foreign Exchange Contracts   These contracts are used both to provide a service to customers and as a part of the institution's trading or hedging activities. The bank profits by

maintaining a margin between the purchase price and sale price. Contracts may be for current trades (spot contract), future dates (forward contract), or swap contracts. The bank may also enter into these contracts to hedge a foreign currency exposure.

(vi) Other Variations   Other types of derivative products are discussed in Chapter 26, "Derivatives and Hedge Accounting."

(vii) Accounting Guidance   The FASB issued Statement No. 133, "Accounting for Derivative Instruments and Hedging Activities," in June 1998. Statement No. 133 provides a comprehensive and consistent standard for the recognition and measurement of derivatives and hedging activities. The first step in considering whether the benefits of a new accounting standard will justify the related costs is to identify the problems in the existing accounting guidance that a new standard seeks to resolve. Hence, this statement resolves the inconsistencies that existed with respect to accounting for derivatives and changes considerably the way many derivatives transactions and hedged items are reported.

This Statement mitigates several issues. It increases the visibility, comparability, and understandability of the risks associated with derivatives by requiring that all derivatives be reported as assets or liabilities and measured at fair value. It reduces the inconsistency, incompleteness, and difficulty of applying previous accounting guidance and practice by providing comprehensive guidance for all derivatives and hedging activities. The comprehensive guidance in this statement also eliminates some accounting practices, such as "synthetic instrument accounting," that had evolved beyond the authoritative literature. This Statement accommodates a range of hedge accounting practices by (a) permitting hedge accounting for most derivative instruments, (b) permitting hedge accounting for cash flow hedges of forecasted transactions for specified risks, and (c) eliminating the requirement in Statement 80 that an entity demonstrate risk reduction on an entity-wide basis to qualify for hedge accounting. The combination of accommodating a range of hedge accounting practices and removing the uncertainty about the accounting requirements for certain strategies should facilitate, and may actually increase, entities' use of derivatives to manage risks.

SFAS No. 133 requires all derivatives to be recorded on the balance sheet at fair value and establishes "special accounting" for the following three different types of hedges: hedges of changes in the fair value of assets, liabilities, or firm commitments (referred to as *fair value hedges*); hedges of the variable cash flows of forecasted transactions (cash flow hedges); and hedges of foreign currency exposures of net investments in foreign operations. The accounting treatment and criteria for each of the three types of hedges are unique. Changes in fair value of derivatives that do not meet the criteria of one of these three categories of hedges are included in income.

There are four basic underlying premises of the new approach:

1. Derivatives represent rights or obligations that meet the definitions of assets (future cash inflows due from another party) or liabilities (future cash outflows owed to another party) and should be reported in the financial statements.
2. Fair value is the most relevant measure for financial instruments and the only relevant measure for derivatives. Derivatives should be measured at fair value, and adjustments to the carrying amount of hedged items should reflect changes in their fair value (i.e., gains and losses) attributable to the risk being hedged arising while the hedge is in effect.

3. Only items that are assets or liabilities should be reported as such in the financial statements. (The Board believes gains and losses from hedging activities are not assets or liabilities and, therefore, should not be deferred.)

4. Special accounting for items designated as being hedged should be provided only for qualifying transactions, and one aspect of qualification should be an assessment of the expectation of the effectiveness of the hedge (i.e., offsetting changes in fair values or cash flows).

See Chapter 26 for further guidance on SFAS No. 133.

(y) FIDUCIARY SERVICES AND OTHER FEE INCOME

(i) Fiduciary Services In their fiduciary capacity, banks must serve their clients' interests and must act in good faith at a level absent in most other banking activities. In view of this high degree of fiduciary responsibility, banks usually segregate the responsibilities of the trust department from that of the rest of the bank. This segregation is designed to maintain a highly objective viewpoint in the fiduciary area. Fiduciary services range from the simple safekeeping of valuables to the investment management of large pension funds.

Custodial, safekeeping, and safe deposit activities involve the receipt, storage, and issuance of receipts for a range of valuable assets. This may involve the holding of bonds, stocks, and currency in escrow pending the performance under a contract, or merely the maintenance of a secure depository for valuables or title deeds. As custodian, the bank may receive interest and dividends on securities for the account of customers.

Investment management may be discretionary, whereby the bank has certain defined powers to make investments, or nondiscretionary, whereby the bank may only execute investment transactions based on customers' instructions. The former obviously involves a higher degree of risk to the institution and creates an obligation to make prudent investment decisions.

Other fiduciary services include trust administration, stock and bond registrar, and bank trustee. Trust administration involves holding or management of property, such as pension funds and estates for the benefit of others. Stock and bond registrar and bank trustee functions include the maintenance of records and execution of securities transactions, including changes in ownership and payment of dividends and interest.

Since the assets and liabilities of the trust department of the bank are held in an agency capacity, they are not recorded on the balance sheet of the bank. These activities can, however, generate significant fee income, which is recorded when earned in the statement of income.

(ii) Other Fee Income Emphasis on fee income-generating activities has increased in response to both the risk-based capital guidelines, which created more pressure to reduce the size of the balance sheet, and a general increase in competition in the financial services industry.

Some of the principal forms of fee-generating activity include the following:

- *Annuities.* Banks sell fixed and variable annuities.
- *Brokerage.* Banks may arrange for the purchase and sale of securities on behalf of customers in return for a commission.
- *Corporate and advisory services.* These activities involve advice on mergers and acquisitions, capital raising, and Treasury management in return for a fee.
- *Private banking.* This activity involves investment planning, tax assistance, and credit extensions to wealthy individuals.

- *Private placements.* This activity normally involves the placement of securities on a *best efforts* basis as opposed to an underwriting commitment.
- *Underwriting.* Banks may guarantee to purchase certain allowable securities if they are not fully subscribed to in an offering.
- *401(k) plans and mutual funds.* Banks may distribute mutual funds in a 401(k) plan.

Many of the activities, particularly underwriting, are subject to restriction by regulation as to the type of securities that may be transacted, and separately capitalized subsidiaries may be required. These restrictions are subject to change at the current time and may be significantly relaxed in the near future.

These activities generate fee income that is recorded when earned. Certain activities are conducted in conjunction with credit extension activities, and therefore particular attention is required to ensure that fees generated are appropriately recorded. It is essential to distinguish between fees that may be recorded immediately and fees that are essentially loan origination fees to be accounted for over the life of the loan (SFAS No. 91).

(z) ELECTRONIC BANKING AND TECHNOLOGY RISKS   Conducting banking by personal computer is a growing area for many institutions. The types of transactions customers can perform online has also increased. For example, customers can transfer funds, pay bills, and apply for loans by using electronic banking. The start-up costs of an e-bank are high. Establishing a trusted brand is very costly as it requires significant advertising expenditure in addition to the purchase of expensive technology (as security and privacy is key to gaining customer approval). E-banking services are designed to support the true integration of trade documentation with financing products and cash management on consistent platforms linking banks with corporate customers via multiple channels, from Web-based to fully integrated using Web services or EDI-related technologies. An advantage should be taken of the current technology as it can help manage fair lending, pricing, fraud detection, and other aspects of compliance and risk.

Transaction/operations risk arises from fraud, processing errors, system disruptions, or other unanticipated events resulting in the institution's inability to deliver products or services. This risk exists in each product and service offered. The level of transaction risk is affected by the structure of the institution's processing environment, including the types of services offered and the complexity of the processes and supporting technology. In most instances, e-banking activities will increase the complexity of the institution's activities and the quantity of its transaction/operations risk. E-banking has unique characteristics that may increase an institution's overall risk profile and the level of risks associated with traditional financial services, particularly strategic, operational, legal, and reputation risks. These unique e-banking characteristics include speed of technological change, changing customer expectations, increased visibility of publicly accessible networks (e.g., the Internet), less face-to-face interaction with financial institution customers, need to integrate e-banking with the institution's legacy computer systems, dependence on third parties for necessary technical expertise, and proliferation of threats and vulnerabilities in publicly accessible networks.

The rules and regulation should be defined by the central authority and share it with all the banking organization in order to reduce the level of risk. The risk can be measure on both quantities and qualitative way. Information security is essential to a financial institution's ability to deliver e-banking services, protect the confidentiality and integrity of customer information, and ensure that accountability exists for changes to the information and the processing and communications systems. Depending on the extent of in-house technology, a financial institution's e-banking systems can make information security complex with numerous networking and control issues. Financial institutions should have processes to identify, monitor, and address training needs. Each financial institution should train their personnel in the technologies they use and the institution's rules governing the use of that technology. Technical training is particularly important for those who oversee the key technology controls such as firewalls, intrusion detection, and device configuration. Security awareness training is important for all users, including the institution's e-banking customers.

Additionally, many institutions are using client/server systems and personal computers, rather than mainframe computers, to process customer transactions and maintain bank records. Accordingly, security and database management controls surrounding these client/servers and personal computers becomes very important.

The information technology (IT) has significantly impacted the financial services industry. Information technology has enabled the transfer between different accounts is at the tip of the fingers through the use of mobile and online banking. There has some innovation with the mobile banking applications in the industry to the point that banks can offer a variety of capabilities with their mobile applications. For example, financial services firms of Citi, Wells Fargo, State Farm's Bank, and JPMorgan Chase provide remote deposits, initiate or approve wire transfers and outgoing payments for corporate customers, online view transaction details and other online banking services. Regulatory agencies have issued guidance addressing the safety and soundness aspects of electronic banking and personal computer banking and the security risks associated with the Internet and phone banking.

31.3 MORTGAGE BANKING ACTIVITIES

(a) OVERVIEW   Mortgage banking activities primarily include the origination or purchase, sale, and subsequent long-term servicing of mortgage loans. Mortgage loans are originated or purchased from a variety of sources including applications received directly from borrowers (retail originations) and loans acquired from mortgage brokers or other mortgage lenders (wholesale or correspondent purchases). These loans are then generally sold through the secondary mortgage market to permanent investors or retained by the lender in its own loan portfolio. Typically, loans are sold to permanent investors through conduits, although mortgage loans can also be sold through whole loan sales directly to investors or through public or private securitizations completed by the mortgage banker. Secondary market conduits include government-sponsored entities such as GNMA, FNMA, and FHLMC, and other private companies involved in the acquisition and securitization of mortgage loans. Loan servicing includes the collection, recording, and remittance to investors of monthly mortgage payments, the maintenance of records relating to the loans, and the management of escrows for taxes and insurance. In return for performing these servicing activities, mortgage servicers earn a fee, which is usually a percentage of the loan's unpaid principal balance. Profits are earned from loan-servicing activities if the mortgage banker's cost of performing the servicing of the loans is less than the fee received. The major risks associated with mortgage banking are interest rate risk associated with the loans in the pipeline and warehouse, credit risk associated with loans held for sale or held in portfolio, operational risk associated with performing servicing functions improperly, and prepayment risk associated with mortgage servicing rights.

(b) ACCOUNTING GUIDANCE   The principal accounting guidance for the mortgage banking industry is found in SFAS No. 65, "Accounting for Certain Mortgage Banking

Activities," SFAS No. 91, "Accounting for Nonrefundable Fees and Costs Associated with Originating or Acquiring Loans and Initial Direct Costs of Leases," and SFAS No. 140, "Accounting for Transfers and Servicing of Financial Assets and Extinguishments of Liabilities." SFAS No. 140 supersedes SFAS No. 125. SFAS No. 140 is effective for transfers and servicing of financial assets and extinguishments of liabilities occurring after March 31, 2001, and is to be applied prospectively. Earlier or retroactive application is not permitted. There are also several issues related to the accounting for mortgage banking activities that have been addressed by the EITF. EITF (Emerging Issues Task Force) that was formed in response to the recommendations of FASB's task force on timely financial reporting guidance through timely identification, discussion, and resolution of financial accounting issues within the framework of the *FASB Accounting Standards Codification* (Accounting Standards Codification), which represents the source of authoritative standards of accounting and reporting, other than those issued by the SEC, to be applied by nongovernmental entities.

An *EITF Update* summarizes issues discussed at meetings held by the Emerging Issues Task Force, including an overview of both consensuses and consensuses-for-exposure. Because consensuses and consensuses-for-exposure are subject to ratification by the FASB, and because some details of the conclusions reached at an EITF meeting are determined during the process of developing the meeting minutes, the contents of the EITF Update are preliminary.

(c) MORTGAGE LOANS HELD FOR SALE   Mortgage loans held for sale represent a mortgage banker's "inventory" of loans that have been originated or purchased and are awaiting sale to permanent investors. SFAS No. 65 requires that mortgage loans held for sale be reported at the lower of their cost or market value, determined as of the balance sheet date determined on an individual loan or aggregate basis. The excess of cost over market value is required to be accounted for as a valuation allowance with changes in the valuation allowance included in net income of the period in which the change occurs. SFAS No. 91 requires that loan origination fees and direct loan origination costs be deferred until the related loan is sold. Therefore, any net deferred fees or costs should be included in the cost basis of the loan and considered in determining the required valuation allowance at any balance sheet date. Capitalized costs of acquiring the rights to service mortgage loans associated with the purchase or origination of these assets should be excluded from the cost of the mortgage loans for the purposes of determining lower of cost or market. Likewise, the fair value of the servicing rights associated with the loans included in a mortgage banker's loans held for sale classification should be excluded from the determination of lower of cost or market.

The market value of mortgage loans held for sale shall be determined by type of loan. At a minimum, separate determinations of market value for residential and commercial mortgage loans shall be made. Either the aggregate or individual loan basis may be used in determining the lower of cost or market value for each type of loan under SFAS No. 65. The market value for loans subject to investor purchase commitments shall be based on those commitment prices. The market value for uncommitted loans held on a speculative basis shall be based on the market in which the mortgage banker normally operates.

At any balance sheet date, a mortgage banker will also have outstanding rate commitments, which represent commitments made to loan applicants to fund a loan at a locked-in interest rate provided that loan application eventually closes. These rate commitments make up a mortgage banker's "pipeline." SFAS No. 65 does not specifically address a mortgage banker's pipeline as being subject to a lower of cost or market determination. However, the pipeline should be evaluated for the impact of any adverse commitments. This may be done in conjunction with the lower of cost or market analysis on loans held for sale. The analysis of the pipeline typically would only be done on those commitments expected to become loans (i.e., close) and not on those loans expected to "fall out" (i.e., not close). The existence of losses inherent in the pipeline after adjustment for fallout can often be determined by comparing commitment prices to investor delivery prices for similar loans. If any losses are determined to exist in the mortgage banker's pipeline, the loss should be accrued pursuant to SFAS No. 5.

(d) MORTGAGE LOANS HELD FOR INVESTMENT   Mortgage loans can be originated or purchased by a mortgage banker with the intention of holding the loan to maturity, or the loans can be transferred into a mortgage banker's "loans held for investment" category from a "loans held for sale" category after it is determined that the loan is unsalable or the mortgage banker decides to retain the loan for investment purposes. SFAS No. 65 requires that mortgage loans held for investment be reported at cost. For mortgage loans transferred into mortgage loans held for investment from loans held for sale, their initial cost basis shall be determined as the lower of the loan's cost or market value on the date of the transfer. A mortgage loan shall not be classified as held for investment unless the mortgage banker has both the intent and the ability to hold the loan for the foreseeable future or until maturity.

If the ultimate recovery of the carrying amount of a mortgage loan held as a long-term investment is doubtful, and the impairment is considered to be other than temporary, the carrying amount of the loan shall be reduced to its expected collectible amount, which then becomes its new cost basis. The amount of the reduction shall be recorded as a loss. A recovery from the new cost basis shall be reported as a gain only at the sale, maturity, or disposition of the loan.

As already noted, SFAS No. 91 requires that loan origination fees and direct loan origination costs be deferred. For mortgage loans held for investment, any net deferred fees or costs should be included in the cost basis of the loan and amortized into interest income on a level yield method. Under level-yield method, unamortized premiums and discounts are taken into income so as to recognize accounting income—coupon interest plus amortized premium or discount—at a constant yield over the life of an investment. It calculates income for each period by multiplying the beginning of period carrying value by the internal rate of return of the investment. The carrying value is then increased by income and reduced by cash flow to get the next period's carrying value.

(e) SALES OF MORTGAGE LOANS AND SECURITIES   Mortgage bankers typically sell the majority of the loans they originate or purchase to third-party investors in order to remove these loans from their balance sheet and provide funds for the continued origination and purchase of future loans. The sale of mortgage loans results in a gain or loss that should be recognized when the mortgage banker has surrendered control over the assets to a purchaser in a manner such that the transfer of the loans can be accounted for as a sale. SFAS No. 140, which provides guidance concerning the transfers and servicing of financial assets and extinguishments of liabilities, states that a transfer of financial assets in which the transferor surrenders control over those financial assets shall be accounted for as a sale to the extent that consideration other than beneficial interests in the transferred assets have been received in exchange.

The control over financial assets is deemed to have been surrendered under SFAS No. 140 to the extent that all of the following three conditions have been met:

1. The transferred assets have been isolated from the transferor, that is, put presumptively beyond the reach of the transferor and its creditors even in bankruptcy.
2. Each transferee has the right to pledge or exchange the transferred assets, and no condition both constrains the transferee from taking advantage of its right to pledge or exchange and provides more than a trivial benefit to the transferor.
3. The transferor does not maintain effective control over the transferred assets through either: (a) an agreement that both entitles and obligates the transferor to repurchase or redeem them before their maturity, or (b) the ability to unilaterally cause the holder to return specified assets, other than through a clean-up call.

The sale of mortgage loans can occur primarily through one of three methods. Loans can be sold (1) through whole loan or bulk transactions to third-party investors where individual loans or groups of loans are transferred; (2) through government sponsored mortgage-backed securities programs of investors such as FNMA, FHLMC, or GNMA; and (3) through private securitizations where the originator or loan purchaser will securitize and sell directly to third-party investors interests in an underlying pool of mortgage loans.

The most common type of sale utilized by mortgage bankers is the sale of mortgage-backed securities through programs sponsored by FNMA, FHLMC, and GNMA. These sales are relatively straightforward and generally do not have the complex kinds of terms that could call into question sale treatment for the transfer under SFAS No. 140. Whole loan sales are also generally straightforward and do not present complex SFAS No. 140 sales issues; however, in instances where mortgage-backed securities or whole loans are sold through private securitizations or on a recourse basis, surrender of control issues under SFAS No. 140 may be encountered.

Depending on the type of structure utilized in a private mortgage loan securitization, including those with terms where significant interests in securitized pools are retained, those with significant continued involvement of the seller in the securitized pool, and those with unusual legal structures, the attainment of sale accounting under SFAS No. 140 may also not be straightforward and may be difficult to assess. Careful consideration should be given to the requirements of SFAS No. 140 to ensure that a sale of the mortgage loans has occurred before a gain or loss on the transaction can be realized.

(i) Gain or Loss on Sale of Mortgage Loans   Upon completion of a transfer of mortgage loans that satisfies the conditions of SFAS No. 140 to qualify as a sale, the mortgage banker shall allocate the previous cost basis of the loans, including all deferred SFAS No. 91 costs and fees, between interests sold (i.e., the underlying loans) and interests retained (i.e., the loans' servicing rights, or other retained portions of a securitization such as residual spreads, subordinate bonds, and IO or PO strips) based on the relative fair value of those components on the date of the sale. The allocated basis assigned to interests in the mortgage loans that are sold should then be derecognized, and a gain or loss should be calculated as the difference between this allocated basis and proceeds received on the sale, net of any assets or liabilities created in the transaction that should be recorded. Newly created assets and liabilities from the sale should be initially recorded at their fair value and accounted for in accordance with current GAAP for similar assets and liabilities. Interests retained in the sale of mortgage loans are initially recorded at their allocated cost basis and subsequently accounted for in accordance with current GAAP for similar assets and liabilities.

(ii) Financial Assets Subject to Prepayment Interest-only strips, loans, and other receivables and retained interests from sales or securitizations of mortgage loans that can be contractually prepaid or otherwise settled in a way such that the holder would not recover substantially all of its recorded investment shall be subsequently measured like investments in debt securities and classified as available-for-sale or trading assets under SFAS No. 115.

(f) MORTGAGE SERVICING RIGHTS A mortgage banking entity may purchase mortgage servicing rights separately, or it may acquire mortgage servicing rights by purchasing or originating mortgage loans and selling or securitizing those mortgage loans with the servicing rights retained. When a mortgage banker purchases or originates mortgage loans, the cost of acquiring those loans includes the cost of the related servicing rights. These servicing rights become separate and distinct assets only when their respective mortgage loans are sold with the servicing rights retained.

SFAS No. 140 provides the primary accounting guidance for mortgage servicing rights and requires that servicing assets and other retained interests in the mortgage loans sold be measured by allocating the previous carrying amount of the mortgage loans (as previously discussed) between the mortgage loans sold and the servicing rights retained, based on their relative fair values at the date of the sale. Statement 125 amends and extends to all servicing assets and liabilities the accounting standards for mortgage servicing rights now in FASB Statement No. 65, "Accounting for Certain Mortgage Banking Activities," and supersedes FASB Statement No. 122, "Accounting for Mortgage Servicing Rights."

Previously, net *mortgage servicing rights* were recognized as assets, and the amount recognized as net mortgage servicing rights was based on the fair value of certain expected cash inflows, net of expected cash outflows. The expected cash inflow, future servicing revenues, includes a normal servicing fee, expected late charges, and other ancillary revenues. The expected cash outflow, future servicing costs, includes various costs of performing the servicing.

SFAS No. 140 also requires that servicing assets and liabilities be subsequently (a) amortized in proportion to and over the period of estimated net servicing income or loss and (b) assessed for asset impairment or increased obligation based on their fair values.

SFAS No. 140 requires that a mortgage banking enterprise assess its capitalized mortgage servicing rights for impairment based on the fair value of those rights. A mortgage banking enterprise should stratify its mortgage servicing rights based on one or more of the predominant risk characteristics of the underlying loans. Impairment should be recognized through a valuation allowance for each impaired stratum. Each stratum should be recorded at the lower of cost or market value.

(i) Initial Capitalization of Mortgage Servicing Rights Under SFAS No. 140, each time an entity undertakes an obligation to service mortgage loans, the entity shall recognize either a servicing asset or a servicing liability for that servicing contract, unless it retains the underlying mortgage loans as an investment on its balance sheet. If a servicing asset was purchased or assumed rather than undertaken in a sale or securitization of the mortgage loans being serviced, the servicing asset shall be measured initially at its fair value—presumptively, the price paid for the right to service the underlying loans.

Under SFAS No. 140, servicing rights retained in a sale of mortgage loans shall be initially recorded on the balance sheet at their allocated portion of the total cost of the mortgage loans purchased or originated. The allocation of the total cost basis of the mortgage loans shall be based on the relative fair values of the mortgage loans and their respective servicing rights.

(ii) Amortization of Mortgage Servicing Rights   SFAS No. 140 requires that amounts capitalized as servicing assets (net of any recorded valuation allowances) be amortized in proportion to, and over the period of, estimated net servicing income. For this purpose, estimates of future servicing revenue shall include expected late charges and other ancillary revenue, including float. Estimates of expected future servicing costs shall include direct costs associated with performing the servicing function and appropriate allocations of other costs. Estimated future servicing costs may be determined on an incremental cost basis.

(iii) Impairment of Mortgage Servicing Rights   For the purpose of evaluating and measuring impairment of servicing assets, SFAS No. 140 requires that servicing assets be stratified based on one or more of the predominant risk characteristics of the underlying loans. Those characteristics may include loan type, size, note rate, date of origination, term, and geographic location. Historically, note or interest rate has been the predominant prepayment risk characteristic considered by most mortgage bankers because in declining interest rate environments, loans have tended to prepay more rapidly with corresponding impairment to the servicing asset.

Impairment shall be recognized through a valuation allowance for an individual stratum. The amount of impairment recognized shall be the amount by which the carrying value of the servicing assets in a stratum exceeds their fair value. The fair value of servicing assets that have not been recognized through a sale or securitization shall not be used in the evaluation of impairment.

Subsequent to the initial measurement of impairment, the mortgage banking enterprise shall adjust the valuation allowance to reflect changes in the measurement of impairment. Fair value in excess of the amount capitalized as servicing assets (net of amortization), however, shall not be recognized. SFAS No. 140 does not address when a mortgage banking enterprise should record a direct write-down of servicing assets.

(iv) Fair Value of Mortgage Servicing Rights   A nonpublic entity shall make a policy decision of whether to measure all of its liabilities incurred under share-based payment arrangements at fair value or to measure all such liabilities at intrinsic value. Regardless of the method selected, a nonpublic entity shall remeasure its liabilities under share-based payment arrangements at each reporting date until the date of settlement. The fair-value-based method is preferable for purposes of justifying a change in accounting principle under FASB Statement No. 154, "Accounting Changes and Error Corrections." Assumptions used to estimate the fair value of equity and liability equipments granted to employees should be determined in a consistent manner from period to period.

The subprime scandals of 2008 can be attributed to many factors, including the improper application of fair value estimates by the real estate appraising industry. The conflicting interest between real estate appraisal firms and real estate brokerage firms provided incentives and opportunities for the appraisers to provide fair value estimates above and beyond reasonable and realistic fair value to get financing needs to close the deal. Banks had all the incentives and opportunities to get the highest fair value estimates to provide subprime loans to customers and then sell the mortgages to mortgage buyers such as Freddie Mac and Fannie Mae, quasi-government corporations established to buy up mortgages from banks. The other factor is banks' securitization vehicles of variable interest entities (VIEs) or special purpose entities (SPEs). The tone that management sets regarding the corporate culture within which financial reports are produced is vital to the integrity of financial reporting process. When the tone set at the top is lax, fraudulent financial reporting is more likely to occur and not be prevented.

SFAS No. 140 defines the fair value of an asset or a liability as the amount at which that asset or liability could be bought or sold in a current transaction between willing parties, that is, other than in a forced or liquidation sale. Quoted market prices in active markets are the best evidence of fair value, and under SFAS No. 140, they shall be used as the basis for the measurement, if available. The Financial Accounting Standards Board (FASB) and the International Accounting Standards Board (IASB) both agree fair value should be set as an exit price. Both standard setters are trying to converge their accounting standards by 2012. Fair value, or mark-to-market, accounting has been controversial and blamed for helping exacerbate the financial crisis.

Standard setters have shown some flexibility to allow financial institutions more discretion in valuing assets such as mortgage-backed securities in recent years. If a quoted market price is available, the fair value is the product of the number of trading units times that market price. If quoted market prices are not available, the estimate of fair value shall be based on the best information available in the circumstances. The estimate of fair value shall consider prices for similar assets or liabilities and the results of valuation techniques to the extent available in the circumstances. Examples of valuation techniques include the present value of estimated expected future cash flows using a discount rate commensurate with the risks involved, option-pricing models, matrix pricing, option-adjusted spread models, and fundamental analysis. Valuation techniques for measuring financial assets and liabilities and servicing assets and liabilities shall be consistent with the objective of measuring fair value. Those techniques shall incorporate assumptions that market participants would use in their estimates of values, future revenues, and future expenses, including assumptions about interest rates, default, prepayment, and volatility. In measuring financial liabilities and servicing liabilities at fair value by discounting estimated future cash flows, an objective is to use discount rates at which those liabilities could be settled in an arm's-length transaction.

Estimates of expected future cash flows, if used to estimate fair value, shall be the best estimate based on reasonable and supportable assumptions and projections. All available evidence shall be considered in developing estimates of expected future cash flows. The weight given to the evidence shall be commensurate with the extent to which the evidence can be verified objectively. If a range is estimated for either the amount or timing of possible cash flows, the likelihood of possible outcomes shall be considered in determining the best estimate of future cash flows.

If it is not practicable to estimate the fair values of assets, the transferor shall record those assets at zero. If it is not practicable to estimate the fair values of liabilities, the transferor shall recognize no gain on the transaction and shall record those liabilities at the greater of:

- The excess, if any, of (1) the fair values of assets obtained, less the fair values of other liabilities incurred, over (2) the sum of the carrying values of the assets transferred
- The amount that would be recognized in accordance with SFAS No. 5, "Accounting for Contingencies," as interpreted by FASB Interpretation No. 14, "Reasonable Estimation of the Amount of a Loss"

Statement of Financial Accounting Standards No. 157 (SFAS 157), *"Fair Value Measurements," sets the category* the source of information used in fair value measurements into three levels: (1) Level 1, where there are observable inputs from quoted prices in active markets; (2) Level 2, where there are indirectly observable inputs from quoted prices of comparable items in active markets, identical items in inactive markets, or other market-related information; and (3) Level 3, where there are unobservable, firm-generated inputs in determining fair value.

(v) Sales of Mortgage Servicing Rights   EITF No. 95-5 provides the primary accounting guidance for sales of mortgage servicing rights. It determines of what risks and rewards, if any, can be retained and whether any unresolved contingencies may exist in a sale of mortgage loan servicing rights. The consensus reached in EITF No. 95-5 states that a sale of mortgage servicing rights should be recognized at the date title passes if substantially all risks and rewards of ownership have irrevocably passed to the buyer and any protection provisions retained by the seller are minor and can be reasonably estimated. If a sale is recognized and minor protection provisions exist, a liability should be accrued for the estimated obligation associated with those provisions. The seller retains only minor protection provisions if (1) the obligation associated with those provisions is estimated to be no more than 10 percent of the sales price and (2) the risk of prepayment is retained by the seller for no more than 120 days. The consensus additionally noted that a temporary subservicing agreement in which the seller would subservice the loans for a short period of time after the sale would not necessarily preclude recognizing a sale at the closing date.

(vi) Retained Interests   In certain asset sale or securitizations transactions, the mortgage banker may retain an interest in the transferred assets. Examples of retained interests include servicing assets, interest-only strips, and retained (or residual) interests in securitizations. Historically, excess servicing resulted from the sale of loans where the contractual service fee (the difference between the mortgage rate and the pass-through rate to the investor in the loans, after deducting any guarantee fees) was greater than a "normal servicing fee rate." This excess servicing asset was then capitalized separately and subsequently accounted for distinctly from the normal servicing asset recorded. Under SFAS No. 140, the accounting distinction for excess servicing fees was eliminated. In general, under agency servicing contracts, past excess servicing fees represent contractually specified servicing fees, as defined under SFAS No. 140, and are combined with servicing rights as a servicing asset. The combined servicing asset will then be subject to the stratified impairment test that was described in Subsection 31.3(f)(iii).

Generally, a servicing fee in excess of a contractually stated servicing fee would only be encountered in an instance where an entity securitizes and sells mortgage loans and creates an interest-only strip above and beyond the compensation allocated to the loan's servicer in the pooling and servicing agreements. If it is determined that an entity's "excess servicing fees" exceed contractually specified amounts, those amounts would be required to be classified as interest-only strips under SFAS No. 140.

Interest-only strips are rights to future interest income from the serviced assets that exceed contractually specified servicing fees. Interest-only strips are not servicing assets; they are financial assets. These assets should be originally recorded at allocated cost and subsequently recorded as an available-for-sale or trading asset in accordance with FAS No. 115.

Retained or residual interests in securitizations represents the mortgage banker's right to receive cash flows from the mortgage assets that are not required to: (1) pay certificate holders their contractual amounts of principal and interest; (2) fund reserve accounts stipulated in the securitization structure; (3) pay expenses of the securitization; and (4) make any other payments stipulated in the securitization. Such retained interests must be evaluated for impairment pursuant to EITF No. 99-20, "Recognition of Interest Income and Impairment on Purchased and Retained Beneficial Interests in Securitized Financial Assets."

(g) TAXATION Mortgage banks are subject to federal income taxes and certain state and local taxes. The British government now requires all U.K banks to sign tax avoidance code to ensure that they pay their share of tax at a time of tight budgetary process and public spending. The taxation of mortgage banks is extremely complex; therefore, a discussion in depth is beyond the scope of this book. However, the following sections discuss certain significant factors of mortgage banking taxation.

(i) MORTGAGE SERVICING RIGHTS The tax treatment of servicing rights changed substantially in 1991 for both mortgage loan originators and subsequent purchasers of mortgage loans. Under Rev. Rule 91-46, a lender selling mortgages while retaining the right to service the loans for an amount in excess of reasonable compensation is deemed to have two types of income resulting from a servicing contract: "normal" (i.e., reasonable) or "excess" servicing compensation.

Generally, taxable income for normal servicing is recognized as received (i.e., as asset is not created at the time of loan sale as it is for book purposes); thus, a book-to-tax difference will exist upon sale of the underlying loan to a third party. Income deemed received for excess servicing is included in income on a yield-to-maturity basis.

The Treasury has provided safe-harbor amounts providing guidance as to what is deemed normal or reasonable compensation. Normal compensation is for the performance of general mortgage services, including a contract requiring the servicer to collect the periodic mortgage payments from the mortgagors and remit these payments to the owner of the mortgages.

The safe harbors establish that compensation for the performance of all services under the mortgage servicing contracts should generally be between 25 and 44 basis points, annually, determined more specifically on the type of residential loans. Guidance as to reasonable compensation on commercial mortgages has not been provided; it is the taxpayer's responsibility to establish and support what is reasonable compensation for the services it performs.

Excess servicing is those funds received in excess of reasonable compensation; thus, the term *excess servicing rights*. Excess servicing rights have been determined to represent a stripped coupon, while the underlying mortgage that was sold represents a stripped bond. The fair value of the stripped coupon (i.e., servicing right) is determined based on the relevant facts and circumstances.

The mortgage servicing business is fueled by volume; thus, it is common for a mortgage bank to be an originator of mortgage loans, a purchaser of mortgage loans, and a purchaser of servicing. If both the loan and the servicing right are purchased, and the loan is subsequently sold with servicing retained, tax treatment will generally follow the same treatment as if the seller originated the mortgage loan.

This treatment is significantly different compared to the purchase of only mortgage servicing rights. Purchased mortgage servicing rights (PMSRs) are amortized over 15 years when acquired in connection with a trade or business, or over 108 months when a servicing portfolio is separately acquired. Certain restrictions prevent the recognition of loss in value of a servicing portfolio unless the entire portfolio or individually identified loans within a pool of serviced loans are disposed of. Thus, taxpayers may have difficulty realizing the loss in value of a servicing portfolio that has significant prepayments until all the underlying mortgages have been paid down.

(ii) Mark-to-Market   Contrary to normal realization-based tax accounting principles, IRC Section 475 requires "dealers in securities" to recognize gain or loss through "marking-to-market" their securities holdings, unless such securities are validly identified by the taxpayer as excepted from the provisions.

As used in this context, the terms *dealer* and *securities* have very broad application. Virtually all financial institutions are considered dealers in securities for mark-to-market purposes, though regulations provide exceptions for certain institutions not engaging in more than de minimus dealer activities. Securities required to be marked (unless validly identified as excepted) include notes, bonds, and other evidences of indebtedness; stock, notional principal contracts; or any evidence of an interest in or a derivative of such security (other than Section 1256(a) contracts); and any clearly identified hedge of such security.

Securities that may be identified as excepted from the mark-to-market provisions are as follows:

- Securities "held for investment" and property identified as such for tax purposes.
- Notes and other evidences of indebtedness (and obligations to acquire such) that are acquired or originated by the taxpayer in the ordinary course of a trade or business that are "not held for sale."
- Hedges of positions or liabilities that are not securities in the hands of the taxpayer, and hedges of position or liabilities that are exempt from mark-to-market under the two foregoing provisions. This does not apply for hedges held as a dealer.

To be excepted from mark-to-market, the securities must be identified by the taxpayer on a contemporaneous basis (generally day of acquisition) as meeting one of these exceptions.

Whether a security is required to be marked-to-market for financial accounting purposes is *not* dispositive for purposes of determining whether such security is treated as "held for investment" or "not held for sale."

Some financial institutions identify all or a significant portion of their loans to customers as exempted from mark-to-market provisions because they intend to hold these loans to maturity. Possible exceptions are mortgages that are originated for sale (pipeline or warehoused loans) that do not meet the exception criteria and must be marked-to-market.

31.4 INVESTMENT COMPANIES

(a) BACKGROUND   An investment company (referred to as a *fund* or a *mutual fund*) generally pools investors' funds to provides them with professional investment management and diversification of ownership in the securities markets. Typically, an investment company sells its capital shares to the public and invests the net proceeds in stock, bonds, government obligations, or other securities, intended to meet the fund's stated investment objectives. A brief history of investment companies is included in paragraphs 1.07 and 1.08 of the *AICPA Audit and Accounting Guide,* "Investment Companies." One of the more notable distinctions between investment companies and companies in other industries is the extremely high degree of compliance to which registered investment companies must adhere. The *Audit and Accounting Guide* family of publications summarizes applicable practices and delivers how-to advice for handling almost every type of financial statement. It describes relevant matters, conditions, and procedures unique to the investment industry, and illustrates treatments of financial statements and reports to caution auditors and accountants about unusual problems. As a financial statement preparer or auditor, it is essential to understand the unique operational, regulatory, accounting, reporting, and auditing aspects of investment companies. AICPA publications provide background on the industry as well as interpretive guidance for both new and existing rules.

(i) Securities and Exchange Commission Statutes   The SEC is responsible for the administration and enforcement of the following statutes governing investment companies:

- *The Investment Company Act of 1940 (the "1940 Act")*. Regulates registered investment companies and provides extensive rules and regulations that govern record keeping, reporting, fiduciary duties, and other responsibilities of an investment company's management.
- *The Investment Advisers Act of 1940*. Requires persons who are paid to render investment advice to individuals or institutions, including investment companies, to register with the SEC and regulates their conduct and contracts.
- *The Securities Act of 1933*. Governs the content of prospectuses and addresses the public offering and distribution of securities (including debt securities and the capital shares of investment companies).
- *The Securities Exchange Act of 1934*. Regulates the trading of securities in secondary markets after the initial public offering and distribution of the securities under the 1933 Act. Periodic SEC financial reporting requirements pursuant to Section 13 or Section 15(d) of the 1934 Act are satisfied by the semiannual filing of Form N-SAR pursuant to Section 30 of the 1940 Act.

(ii) Types of Investment Companies   Three common methods of classification are (1) by securities law definition, (2) by investment objectives, and (3) by form of organization.

CLASSIFICATION BY SECURITIES LAW DEFINITION
Securities law divides investment companies into three types: management companies, face amount certificate companies, and unit investment trusts. The most common classification is the management company. The term *mutual fund* refers to an open-end management company as described under Section 5 of the 1940 Act. Such a fund stands ready to redeem its shares at net asset value whenever requested to do so and usually continuously offers its shares for sale, although it is not required to do so. A closed-end management company does not stand ready to redeem its shares when requested (although it may occasionally make tender offers for its shares) and generally does not issue additional shares, except perhaps in connection with a dividend reinvestment program. Its outstanding shares are usually traded on an exchange, often at a premium or discount from the fund's underlying net asset value. In addition to open-end and closed-end management companies, there are also management companies that offer the ability for shareholders to periodically redeem their shares on specified dates or intervals.

Other management investment companies include Small Business Investment Companies and Business Development Companies (SBICs and BDCs, respectively). Management companies, at their own election, are further divided into diversified companies and nondiversified companies. A fund that elects to be a diversified company must meet the 75 percent test required under Section 5(b)(1) of the 1940 Act. Nondiversified companies are management companies that have elected to be nondiversified and do not have to meet the requirements of Section 5(b)(1).

The 1940 Act also provides for face amount certificate companies, which are rather rare, and unit investment trusts. Unit investment trusts normally are established under a trust indenture by a sponsoring organization that acquires a portfolio (often tax-exempt or taxable bonds that are generally held to maturity) and then sells undivided interests in the trust. Units of the trust may be offered continuously, such as for a trust purchasing treasury securities, but normally do not make any additional portfolio acquisitions. Units remain outstanding until they are tendered for redemption or the trust is terminated.

Separate accounts of an insurance company that underlie variable annuity and variable life insurance products are also subject to the requirements of the 1940 Act. They may be established as management companies or as unit investment trusts. Variable annuities and variable life products are considered to be both securities subject to the 1933 Act and insurance products subject to regulation by state insurance departments.

CLASSIFICATION BY INVESTMENT OBJECTIVES
Investment companies can also be classified by their investment objectives or types of investments, for example, growth funds, income funds, tax-exempt funds, global funds, money market funds, and equity funds.

CLASSIFICATION BY FORM OF ORGANIZATION
Investment companies can also be classified by their form of organization. Funds may be organized as corporations or trusts (and, to a lesser extent, as partnerships).

Incorporation offers the advantages of detailed state statutory and interpretive judicial decisions governing operations and limited liability of shareholders, and, in normal cases, it requires no exemptions to comply with the 1940 Act.

The business trust, or Massachusetts Trust, is an unincorporated business association established by a declaration or deed of trust and governed largely by the law of trusts. In general, a business trust has the advantages of unlimited authorized shares, no annual meeting requirement, and long duration. However, Massachusetts Trusts have a potential disadvantage in that there is unlimited liability to the business trust shareholders in the event of litigation or other negative factors. Generally, however, the Trust undertakes to indemnify the shareholders against loss.

(b) FUND OPERATIONS   When a new fund is established, it enters into a contract with an investment adviser (often the sponsoring organization) to manage the fund and, within the terms of the fund's stated investment objectives, to determine what securities should be purchased, sold, or exchanged. The investment adviser places orders for the purchase or sale of portfolio securities for the fund with brokers or dealers selected by it. The officers of the fund, who generally are also officers of the investment adviser or fund administrator, give instructions to the custodian of the fund holdings as to delivery of securities and payments of cash for the account of the fund. The investment adviser normally furnishes, at its own expense, all necessary advisory services, facilities, and personnel in connection with these responsibilities. The investment adviser may also act as administrator; administrative duties include preparation of regulatory filings and managing relationships with other service providers. The investment adviser and administrator are usually paid for these services through a fee based on the value of net assets.

The distributor or underwriter for an investment company markets the shares of the fund—either directly to the public ("no-load" funds) or through a sales force. The sales force may be compensated for their services through a direct sales commission included in (deducted from) the price at which the fund's shares are offered (redeemed), through a distribution fee (also referred to as a *12b-1 plan fee*) paid by the fund as part of its recurring expenses, or in both ways. Rule 12b-1 under the 1940 Act permits an investment company to pay for distribution expenses, which otherwise are paid for by the distributor and not the fund.

A fund has officers and directors (and in some cases, trustees) but generally has no employees, the services it requires being provided under contract by others. Primary servicing organizations are summarized below.

(i) Fund Accounting Agent   The fund accounting agent maintains the fund's general ledger and portfolio accounting records and computes the net asset value per share, usually on a daily basis. In some instances, this service is provided by the investment adviser or an affiliate of the adviser, or a nonaffiliated entity may perform this service. The fund accounting agent, or in some cases a separate administrative agent, may also be responsible for preparation of the fund's financial statements, tax returns, semiannual and annual filings with the SEC on Form N-SAR, and the annual registration statement filing.

(ii) Custodian   The custodian maintains custody of the fund's assets, collects income, pays expenses, and settles investment transactions. The 1940 Act provides for three alternatives in selecting a custodian. The most commonly used is a commercial bank or trust company that meets the requirements of Sections 17 and 26 of the 1940 Act. The second alternative is a member firm of a national securities exchange; the third alternative is for the fund to act as its own custodian and utilize the safekeeping facilities of a bank or trust company. Section 17(f) and Rules 17f-1 and 17f-2 of the 1940 Act provide for specific audit procedures to be performed by the fund's independent accountant when either alternative two or three is used.

(iii) Transfer Agent   The fund's transfer agent maintains the shareholder records and processes the sales and redemptions of the fund's capital shares. The transfer agent processes the capital share transactions at a price per share equal to the net asset value per share of the fund next determined by the fund accounting agent (forward pricing). In certain instances, shareholder servicing—the direct contact with shareholders, usually by telephone—is combined with the transfer agent processing.

(c) ACCOUNTING   The *AICPA Audit and Accounting Guide*, "Audits of Investment Companies" (May 1, 2001) (the "Audit Guide") provides specific guidance on accounting issues relevant to investment companies. The SEC has set forth in Financial Reporting Policies, Section 404.03, "Accounting, Valuation, and Disclosure of Investment Securities," its views on accounting for securities by registered investment companies.

Because for federal income tax purposes the fund is a conduit for the shareholders, the operations of an investment company are normally influenced by federal income tax to the shareholder. Accordingly, conformity between book and tax accounting is usually maintained whenever practicable under GAAP. In general, investment companies carry securities, which are their most significant asset, at current value, not at historical cost. In such a "mark-to-market" environment, the deviation between book and tax accounting has no effect on net asset value.

Uniquely, most mutual funds close their books daily and calculate a net asset value per share, which forms the pricing basis for shareholders who are purchasing or redeeming fund shares. SEC Rules 2a-4 and 22c-1 set forth certain accounting requirements, including a one cent per share pricing criterion. Because of this daily closing of the books, mutual funds and their agents must maintain well-controlled and current accounting systems to provide proper records for their highly compliance-oriented industry.

The SEC has promulgated extensive rules under each of the statutes that it administers, including the following:

- *Article 6 of Regulation S-X (Article 3-18 and Article 12-12).* Sets forth requirements as to the form and content of, and requirements for, financial statements filed with the SEC, including what financial statements must be presented and for what periods.
- *Financial reporting policies.* Section 404 relates specifically to registered investment companies.

(d) FINANCIAL REPORTING

(i) New Registrants   Any company registered under the 1940 Act that has not previously had an effective registration statement under the 1933 Act must include, in its initial registration statement, financial statements and financial highlights of a date within 90 days prior to the date of filing. For a company that did not have any prior operations, this would be limited to a seed capital statement of assets and liabilities and related notes.

Section 14 of the 1940 Act requires that an investment company have a net worth of at least $100,000. Accordingly, a new investment company is usually incorporated by its sponsor with seed capital of that amount.

(ii) General Reporting Requirements   The SEC reporting requirements are outlined in Section 30 of the 1940 Act and the related rules and regulations thereunder, which supersede any requirements under Section 13 or Section 15(d) of the 1934 Act to which an investment company would otherwise be subject. A registered management investment company is deemed by the SEC to have satisfied its requirement under the 1934 Act to file an annual report by the filing of semiannual reports on Form N-SAR.

The SEC requires that every registered management company send to its shareholders, at least semiannually, a report containing financial statements and financial highlights. Only the financial statements and financial highlights in the annual report are required to be audited.

Some funds prepare quarterly reports to shareholders, although they are not required to do so. They generally include a portfolio listing, and in relatively few cases, they include full financial statements. Closed-end funds listed on an exchange have certain quarterly reporting requirements under their listing agreements with the exchange.

(iii) Financial Statements   Article 6 of Regulation S-X deals specifically with investment companies and requires the following statements:

- A statement of assets and liabilities (supported by a separate listing of portfolio securities) or a statement of net assets, which includes a detailed list of portfolio securities at the reporting date
- A statement of operations for the year
- A statement of changes in net assets for the latest two years

SFAS No. 95 provides that a statement of cash flows should be included with financial statements prepared in accordance with GAAP. This Statement requires that a statement of cash flows classify cash receipts and payments according to whether they stem from operating, investing, or financing activities and provides definitions of each category. It requires that information about investing and financing activities not resulting in cash receipts or payments in the period be provided separately. A business enterprise that provides a set of financial statements that reports both financial position and results of operations shall also provide a statement of cash flows for each period for which results of operations are provided. The information provided in a statement of cash flows, if used with related disclosures and information in the other financial statements, should help investors, creditors, and others to (1) assess the enterprise's ability to generate positive future net cash flows; (2) assess the enterprise's ability to meet its obligations, its ability to pay dividends, and its needs for external financing; (3) assess the reasons for differences between net income and associated cash receipts and payments; and (4) assess the effects on an enterprise's financial position of both its cash and noncash investing and financing transactions during the period. Financial statements that show only cash receipts and payments during a short period, such as a year, cannot adequately indicate whether an enterprise's performance is successful. Important uses of information about an entity's financial position include helping users to assess factors such as the entity's liquidity, financial flexibility, profitability, and risk.

SFAS No. 102 exempts investment companies from providing a statement of cash flows, provided certain conditions are met. A statement of changes in net assets should be presented even if the statement of cash flows is presented because a statement of changes in net assets presents the changes in shareholders' equity required by GAAP and by Article 6 of Regulation S-X.

(e) TAXATION   Investment companies are subject to federal income taxes and certain state and local taxes. However, investment companies registered under the 1940 Act may qualify for special federal income tax treatment as regulated investment companies (RICs) under the IRC and may deduct dividends paid to shareholders. If a fund fails to qualify as a RIC, it will be taxed as a regular corporation, and the deduction for dividends paid by the fund is disallowed. Subchapter M (§§851–855) of the IRC applies to RICs. Chapter 6 of the Audit Guide discusses the tax considerations related to RICs.

To qualify as an RIC, the fund must:

- Be a domestic entity registered under the 1940 Act
- Derive 90 percent of its total income from dividends, interest, and gross gains on sales of securities
- Have 50 percent of its assets composed of cash, U.S. government securities, securities of other funds, and "other issues," as defined
- Have not more than 25 percent of the value of its total assets invested in the securities (other than U.S. government securities or the securities of other regulated investment companies) of any one issuer or of two or more issuers controlled by the fund that are determined to be engaged in the same or similar trades or businesses

In order for a RIC to use its distributions to offset taxable income, it must distribute at least 90 percent of its net investment company taxable income and net tax-exempt interest income to its shareholders. Also, to avoid a 4 percent nondeductible excise tax, a fund must distribute, by December 31 of each year, 98 percent of its ordinary income measured on a calendar year basis and 98 percent of its net capital gains measured on a fiscal year basis ending October 31. Actual payment of the distribution must be before February 1 of the following year.

(f) FILINGS   SEC registration forms applicable to investment companies include the following:

- *Form N-8A.* The notification of registration under the 1940 Act.
- *Form N-1A.* The registration statement of open-end management investment companies under the 1940 and the 1933 Acts. (It is not to be used by SBICs, BDCs, or insurance company separate accounts.) Form N-1A describes in detail the company's objectives, policies, management, investment restrictions, and similar matters. It consists of the prospectus, the statement of additional information (SAI), and a third section of other information, including detailed information on the SEC-required yield calculations. Post-effective amendments on Form N-1A, including updated audited financial statements, must be filed and become effective under the 1933 and 1940 Acts within 16 months after the end of the period covered by the previous audited financial statements if the fund is to continue offering its shares.
- *Form N-SAR.* A reporting form used for semiannual and annual reports by all registered investment companies that have filed a registration statement that has become effective pursuant to the 1933 Act, with the exception of face amount certificate companies and BDCs. BDCs file periodic reports pursuant to Section 13 of the 1934 Act. Management investment companies file the form semiannually; unit investment trusts are only required to file annually. There is no requirement that the form or any of the items be audited. The annual report filed by a management investment company must be accompanied by a report on the company's system of internal accounting controls from its independent accountant. The requirement for an accountant's report on internal accounting controls does not apply to SBICs or to management investment companies not required by either the 1940 Act or any other federal or state law or rule or regulation thereunder to have an audit of their financial statements.
- *Form N-2.* A registration statement for closed-end funds comparable to Form N-1A for open-end funds. Under Rule 8b-16 of the 1940 Act, if certain criteria are met in the Annual Report of a closed-end fund, the fund may not need to annually update its Form N-2 filing with the SEC.
- *Forms N-1, N-3, N-4, and N-6.* The registration statements for various types of insurance-related products, including variable annuities and variable life insurance.
- *Form N-5.* The registration statement for SBICs, which are also licensed under the Small Business Investment Act of 1958, is used to register the SBIC under both the 1933 Act and the 1940 Act.
- *Form N-14.* The statement for registration of securities issued by investment companies in business combination transactions under the 1933 Act. It contains information about the companies involved in the transaction, including historical and pro forma financial statements.

(g) INVESTMENT PARTNERSHIPS—SPECIAL CONSIDERATIONS   Investment partnerships may be described generally as limited partnerships organized under state law to trade and/or invest in securities. They are sometimes also referred to as *hedge funds*, which has become a generic industry term for an investment partnership (or another nonpublic investment company), although this may be a misnomer, depending on the partnership's investment strategy. Investment partnerships, if certain conditions are met, are generally not required to register under the 1940 Act and are also generally not subject to the Internal Revenue Code rules and regulations that apply to RICs.

An investment partnership is governed by its partnership agreement. This is the basis for legal, structural, operational, and accounting guidelines. The majority of the capital in an investment partnership is owned by its limited partners. The general partner usually has a minimal investment in the partnership, if any at all. Limited partners may be a variety of entities, including private and public pension plans, foreign investors, insurance companies, bank holding companies, and individuals. There are legal, regulatory, and accounting and tax considerations associated with each of these types of investors. For example, investment in an investment partnership by pension plans may subject the investment partnership to the rules and regulations of the Employee Retirement Income Security Act of 1974 (ERISA) (generally, investment partnerships will not be subject to ERISA if less than 25 percent of the partnership's capital is derived from pension or other employee benefit plan assets); foreign investors may be subject to foreign withholding taxes; and the number of partners in an investment partnership may subject the investment partnership to registration under the 1940 Act (generally, an investment partnership must have fewer than 100 partners [or must have partners who are all "qualified purchasers"] to avoid registration under the 1940 Act).

The limited partners are generally liable for the repayment and discharge of all debts and obligations of the investment partnership, but only to the extent of their respective interest in the partnership. They usually have no part in the management of the partnership and have no authority to act on behalf of the partnership in connection with any matter. The general partner can be an individual, a corporation, or other entity. The general partner usually has little or no investment in the investment partnership (often 1% of total contributed capital) and is responsible for the day-to-day administration of the investment partnership. The general partner, however, usually has unlimited liability for the repayment and discharge of all debts and obligations of the partnership irrespective of its interest in the partnership. The general partner may also be the investment adviser or an affiliate of the adviser.

Although investment partnerships are generally not *investment companies* as defined in federal securities laws, they do meet the definition of investment companies as contained in the *Audit Guide*. Accordingly, the *Audit Guide* is generally applicable to investment partnerships. There are, however, certain disclosure requirements in the *Audit Guide* to which most partnerships have historically taken exception and have not followed. The AICPA clarified the appropriate disclosure for partnerships in its issuance of SOP 95-2, "Financial Reporting for Nonpublic Investment Partnerships," as amended by SOP 01-1, "Amendment to Scope of Statement of Position 95-2," which is applicable for fiscal years beginning after December 15, 1994.

A partnership is classified as a pass-through entity for tax purposes, meaning that the partners, not the partnership, are taxed on the income, expenses, gains, and losses incurred by the partnership. The partners recognize the tax effects of the partnership's operations regardless of whether any distribution is made to such partners. This differs from a corporation, which incurs an entity level tax on its earnings and whose owners (stockholders) incur a second level of tax when the corporation's profits are distributed to them.

(h) OFFSHORE FUNDS—SPECIAL CONSIDERATIONS Offshore funds may be described generally as investment funds set up to permit international investments with minimum tax burden on the fund shareholders. This is achieved by setting up the funds in countries with favorable tax laws, as well as in countries with nonburdensome administrative regulations. Popular offshore locations include Bermuda, the Cayman Islands, and the Netherlands Antilles.

An offshore fund's shares are offered to investors (generally non-U.S.) residing outside the country in which the fund is domiciled. Assuming the offshore fund is not publicly sold in the United States and does not have more than 100 U.S. shareholders (or only "qualified purchasers"), the offshore fund will not be subject to SEC registration or reporting requirements. Similar to hedge funds, because of the lack of regulatory restrictions, offshore funds often have higher risk investment strategies than U.S. regulated funds.

A major U.S. tax advantage to non-U.S. shareholders of investing in U.S. securities through an offshore fund as opposed to a U.S. domiciled fund is the avoidance of certain U.S. withholding taxes. By investing through the offshore fund, the shareholder avoids withholding taxes on most U.S.-sourced interest income and short-term capital gains, which would be subject to withholding taxes if the amounts were paid to the non-U.S. shareholder through a U.S. domiciled fund. Offshore funds also avoid the U.S. Internal Revenue Code distribution requirements imposed on U.S. funds. This allows for the potential "roll-up" of income in the fund (i.e., the deferral of income recognition for the shareholder for tax purposes, depending on the tax residence of the shareholder).

Under new tax legislation, a fund's U.S. administrative and other activities, which were previously required to be performed offshore to comply with IRC Reg. Sec. 1.864–2(c)2 (the "Ten Commandments"), generally will not create tax nexus for U.S. federal income tax purposes. However, depending on the laws of the particular jurisdiction in which its U.S. activities are conducted, those same U.S. activities might, under some circumstances, create tax nexus in certain state or local jurisdictions. Careful consideration should be given to the potential state and local tax consequences of onshore activities before any activities that were previously recommended to be conducted outside the United States are brought onshore.

Fund managers and advisers should consider several nontax factors before bringing certain functions onshore. These include the following:

- Whether the performance of more operations onshore will make it more likely that the fund, manager, and/or advisers can be subject to the jurisdiction of U.S. courts and/or applicable U.S., state, or local laws and regulations
- The regulatory requirements of the fund's domicile (e.g., Luxembourg, Dublin, and Bermuda require administration and certain other functions to be performed locally)
- The investor's desire for confidentiality
- The potential applicability of federal, state, and local tax or other filing requirements
- The potential effect on prospectus disclosure

31.5 SOURCES AND SUGGESTED REFERENCES

American Institute of Certified Public Accountants Audit and Accounting Guide. "Banks and Savings Institutions." New York: AICPA, 1997.

———. "Audits of Investment Companies." New York: AICPA, 2001.

———. AICPA Practice Bulletin No. 1, "Purpose and Scope of AcSEC Practice Bulletins and Procedures for Their Issuance (1987), including the following: Exhibit I—ADC

Arrangements (1986)—provides guidance in accounting for Acquisition, Development and Construction (ADC) arrangements in which the leader participates in an expected residual profit, such as an equity kicker." AICPA, New York, 1987.

―――. AICPA Practice Bulletin No. 4, "Accounting for Foreign Debt/Equity Swaps." AICPA, New York, 1988.

―――. AICPA Practice Bulletin No. 5, "Income Recognition on Loans to Financially Troubled Countries." AICPA, New York, 1998.

―――. AICPA Practice Bulletin No. 6, "Amortization of Discounts on Certain Acquired Loans." AICPA, New York, 1989.

―――. Accounting Standards Codification. "360 Property, Plant, and Equipment, Overall, Scope and Scope Exceptions." Also available at asc.fasb.org/link&sourceid=SL2163854-110220&objid=6390208.

―――. Accounting Standards Division, Statement of Position 78-9, "Accounting for Investments in Real Estate Ventures." New York: AICPA, 1978.

Accounting Principles Board Opinion 30. "Reporting the Results of Operations—Reporting the Effects of Disposal of a Segment of a Business and Extraordinary, Unusual and Infrequently Occurring Events and Transactions." New York: AICPA, 1973.

Ashcraft, Adam B., and Schuermann, Til. 2008. *Understanding the Securitization of Subprime Mortgage Credit.* Federal Reserve Bank of New York. Staff Reports.

Basel Committee on Bank Supervision. "Principles for Sound Liquidity Risk Management and Supervision." June 2008. Available at www.bis.org/publ/bcbs138.htm.

Basel Committee on Banking Supervision. "Microfinance Activities and the Core Principles for Effective Banking Supervision—Consultative Document." August 2010. Available at www.bis.org/publ/bcbs175.htm.

Cammarano, Nicholas, and James J. Klink Jr. *Real Estate Accounting and Reporting: A Guide for Developers, Investors, and Lenders*, 3rd ed. New York: John Wiley & Sons, 1995.

Dodd–Frank Wall Street Reform and Consumer Protection Act of 2010, Pub. L. 111-203 (2010). "John R. Walter." Loan Loss Reserve, *American Banker* (1991).

Financial Accounting Standards Board. EITF Abstracts: A Summary of Proceedings of the FASB Emerging Issues Task Force, EITF Issue No. 84-14, "Deferred Interest Rate Setting." Norwalk, CT: FASB, 1984.

―――. EITF Abstracts: A Summary of Proceedings of the FASB Emerging Issues Task Force, EITF Issue No. 84-36, "Interest Rate Swap Transactions." Norwalk, CT: FASB, 1984.

―――. EITF Abstracts: A Summary of Proceedings of the FASB Emerging Issues Task Force, EITF Issue No. 85-6, "Futures Implementation Question." Norwalk, CT: FASB, 1985.

―――. EITF Abstracts: A Summary of Proceedings of the FASB Emerging Issues Task Force, EITF Issue No. 86-25, "Offsetting Foreign Currency Swaps." Norwalk, CT: FASB, 1986.

―――. EITF Abstracts: A Summary of Proceedings of the FASB Emerging Issues Task Force, EITF Issue No. 86-28, "Accounting Implications of Indexed Debt Instruments." Norwalk, CT: FASB, 1986.

————. EITF Abstracts: A Summary of Proceedings of the FASB Emerging Issues Task Force, EITF Issue No. 87-1, "Deferral Accounting for Cash Securities That Are Used to Hedge Rate or Price Risk." Norwalk, CT: FASB, 1987.

————. EITF Abstracts: A Summary of Proceedings of the FASB Emerging Issues Task Force, EITF Issue No. 87-26, "Hedging of Foreign Currency Exposure with a Tandem Currency." Norwalk, CT: FASB, 1987.

————. EITF Abstracts: A Summary of Proceedings of the FASB Emerging Issues Task Force, EITF Issue No. 88-8, "Mortgage Swaps." Norwalk, CT: FASB, 1988.

————. EITF Abstracts: A Summary of Proceedings of the FASB Emerging Issues Task Force, EITF Issue No. 88-11, "Allocation of Recorded Investment When a Loan or Part of a Loan Is Sold." Norwalk, CT: FASB, 1995.

————. EITF Abstracts: A Summary of Proceedings of the FASB Emerging Issues Task Force, EITF Issue No. 90-17, "Hedging Foreign Currency Risk with Purchased Options." Norwalk, CT: FASB, 1990.

————. EITF Abstracts: A Summary of Proceedings of the FASB Emerging Issues Task Force, EITF Issue No. 91-1, "Hedging Intercompany Foreign Currency Risks." Norwalk, CT: FASB, 1991.

————. EITF Abstracts: A Summary of Proceedings of the FASB Emerging Issues Task Force, EITF Issue No. 91-4, "Hedging Foreign Currency Risk with Complex Options and Similar Transactions." Norwalk, CT: FASB, 1991.

————. EITF Abstracts: A Summary of Proceedings of the FASB Emerging Issues Task Force, EITF Issue No. 93-10, "Accounting for Dual Currency Bonds." Norwalk, CT: FASB, 1993.

————. EITF Abstracts: A Summary of Proceedings of the FASB Emerging Issues Task Force, EITF Issue No. 94-7, "Accounting for Financial Instruments Indexed to, and Potentially Settled in, a Company's Own Stock." Norwalk, CT: FASB, 1994.

————. EITF Abstracts: A Summary of Proceedings of the FASB Emerging Issues Task Force, EITF Issue No. 94-8, "Accounting for Conversion of a Loan into a Debt Security in a Debt Restructuring." Norwalk, CT: FASB, 1994.

————. EITF Abstracts: A Summary of Proceedings of the FASB Emerging Issues Task Force, EITF Issue No. 94-9, "Determining a Normal Servicing Fee Rate for the Sale of an SBA Loan." Norwalk, CT: FASB, 1994.

————. EITF Abstracts: A Summary of Proceedings of the FASB Emerging Issues Task Force, EITF Issue No. 95-2, "Determination of What Constitutes a Firm Commitment for Foreign Currency Transactions Not Involving a Third Party." Norwalk, CT: FASB, 1995.

————. EITF Abstracts: A Summary of Proceedings of the FASB Emerging Issues Task Force, EITF Issue No. 95-5, "Determination of What Risks and Rewards, If Any, Can Be Retained and Whether Any Unresolved Contingencies May Exist in a Sale of Mortgage Loan Servicing Rights." Norwalk, CT: FASB, 1995.

————. EITF Abstracts: A Summary of Proceedings of the FASB Emerging Issues Task Force, EITF Issue No. 95-11, "Accounting for Derivative Instruments Containing Both a Written Option-Based Component and a Forward-Based Component." Norwalk, CT: FASB, 1995.

————. EITF Abstracts: A Summary of Proceedings of the FASB Emerging Issues Task Force, EITF Issue No. 96-1, "Sale of Put Options on Issuer's Stock that Require or Permit Cash Settlement." Norwalk, CT: FASB, 1996.

————. EITF Abstracts: A Summary of Proceedings of the FASB Emerging Issues Task Force, EITF Issue No. 96-2, "Impairment Recognition When a Nonmonetary Asset Is Exchanged or Is Distributed to Owners and Is Accounted the Asset's Recorded Amount." Norwalk, CT: FASB, 1996.

————. EITF Abstracts: A Summary of Proceedings of the FASB Emerging Issues Task Force, EITF Issue No. 96-10, "Impact of Certain Transactions on the Held-to-Maturity Classification under FASB Statement No. 115." Norwalk, CT: FASB, 1996.

————. EITF Abstracts: A Summary of Proceedings of the FASB Emerging Issues Task Force, EITF Issue No. 96-11, "Accounting for Forward Contracts and Purchased Options to Acquire Securities Covered by FASB Statement No. 115." Norwalk, CT: FASB, 1996.

————. EITF Abstracts: A Summary of Proceedings of the FASB Emerging Issues Task Force, EITF Issue No. 96-12, "Recognition of Interest Income and Balance Sheet Classification of Structured Notes." Norwalk, CT: FASB, 1996.

————. EITF Abstracts: A Summary of Proceedings of the FASB Emerging Issues Task Force, EITF Issue No. 96-13, "Accounting for Derivative Financial Instruments Indexed to, and Potentially Settled in, a Company's Own Stock." Norwalk, CT: FASB, 1996.

————. EITF Abstracts: A Summary of Proceedings of the FASB Emerging Issues Task Force, EITF Issue No. 96-14, "Accounting for the Costs Associated with Modifying Computer Software for the Year 2000." Norwalk, CT: FASB, 1996.

————. EITF Abstracts: A Summary of Proceedings of the FASB Emerging Issues Task Force, EITF Issue No. 96-15, "Accounting for the Effects of Changes in Foreign Currency Exchange Rates on Foreign-Currency-Denominated Available-for-Sale Debt Securities." Norwalk, CT: FASB, 1996.

————. EITF Abstracts: A Summary of Proceedings of the FASB Emerging Issues Task Force, EITF Issue No. 96-19, "Debtor's Accounting for a Substantive Modification and Exchange of Debt Instruments." Norwalk, CT: FASB, 1996.

————. EITF Abstracts: A Summary of Proceedings of the FASB Emerging Issues Task Force, EITF Issue No. 96-20, "Impact of FASB Statement No. 125 on Consolidation of Special-Purpose Entities." Norwalk, CT: FASB, 1996.

————. EITF Abstracts: A Summary of Proceedings of the FASB Emerging Issues Task Force, EITF Issue No. 96-22, "Applicability of the Disclosure Required by FASB Statement No. 114 When a Loan Is Restructured in a Troubled Debt Restructuring into Two (or More) Loans." Norwalk, CT: FASB, 1996.

————. EITF Abstracts: A Summary of Proceedings of the FASB Emerging Issues Task Force, EITF Issue No. 96-23, "The Effect of Financial Instruments Indexed to, and Settled in, a Company's Own Stock of Pooling-of-Interests Accounting for a Subsequent Business Combination." Norwalk, CT: FASB, 1996.

————. EITF Abstracts: A Summary of Proceedings of the FASB Emerging Issues Task Force, EITF Issue No. 97-3, "Accounting for Fees and Costs Associated with Loan

Syndications and Loan Participations after the Issuance of FASB Statement No. 125." Norwalk, CT: FASB, 1997.

————. EITF Abstracts: A Summary of Proceedings of the FASB Emerging Issues Task Force, EITF Issue No. 97-7, "Accounting for Hedges of Foreign Currency Risk Inherent in an Available-for-Sale Marketable Equity Security." Norwalk, CT: FASB, 1997.

————. EITF Abstracts: A Summary of Proceedings of the FASB Emerging Issues Task Force, EITF Issue No. 97-9, "Effect on Pooling-of-Interests Accounting of Certain Contingently Exercisable Options or Other Equity Instruments." Norwalk, CT: FASB, 1997.

————. Interpretation No. 9, "Applying APB Opinions No. 16 and 17 When a Savings and Loan Association or a Similar Institution Is Acquired in a Business Combination Accounted for by the Purchase Method." Norwalk, CT: FASB, 1976.

————. Interpretation No. 39, "Offsetting of Amounts Related to Certain Contracts." Norwalk, CT: FASB, 1992.

————. Interpretation No. 41, "Offsetting of Amounts Related to Certain Repurchase and Reverse Repurchase Agreements—An Interpretation of APB Opinion No. 10 and a Modification of FASB Interpretation No. 39." Norwalk, CT: FASB, 1994.

————. Statement of Financial Accounting Standards No. 5, "Accounting for Contingencies." FASB, Stamford, CT, 1975.

————. Statement of Financial Accounting Standards No. 15, "Accounting by Debtors and Creditors for Troubled Debt Restructurings." FASB, Stamford, CT, 1977.

————. Statement of Financial Accounting Standards No. 34, "Capitalization of Interest Cost." FASB, Stamford, CT, 1979.

————. Statement of Financial Accounting Standards No. 52, "Foreign Currency Translation." FASB, Stamford, CT, 1981.

————. Statement of Financial Accounting Standards No. 58, "Capitalization of Interest Cost in Financial Statements That Include Investments Accounted for by the Equity Method." FASB, Stamford, CT, 1982.

————. Statement of Financial Accounting Standards No. 65, "Accounting for Certain Mortgage Banking Activities." FASB, Stamford, CT, 1982.

————. Statement of Financial Accounting Standards No. 66, "Accounting for Sales of Real Estate." FASB, Stamford, CT, 1982.

————. Statement of Financial Accounting Standards No. 67, "Accounting for Costs and Initial Rental Operations of Real Estate Projects." FASB, Stamford, CT, 1982.

————. Statement of Financial Accounting Standards No. 72, "Accounting for Certain Acquisitions of Banking or Thrift Institutions (an Amendment of APB Opinion No. 17, an Interpretation of APB Opinions No. 16 and 17, and an Amendment of FASB Interpretation No. 9)." FASB, Norwalk, CT, 1983.

————. Statement of Financial Accounting Standards No. 77, "Reporting by Transferors for Transfers of Receivables with Recourse." FASB, Stamford, CT, 1983.

————. Statement of Financial Accounting Standards No. 80, "Accounting for Futures." FASB, Stamford, CT, 1984.

————. Statement of Financial Accounting Standards No. 91, "Accounting for Nonrefundable Fees and Costs Associated with Originating or Acquiring Loans and Initial Direct Costs of Leases (an Amendment of FASB Statements No. 13, 60, and 65 and a Rescission of FASB Statement No. 17)." FASB, Stamford, CT, 1986.

————. Statement of Financial Accounting Standards No. 95, "Statement of Cash Flow." FASB, Norwalk, CT, 1987.

————. Statement of Financial Accounting Standards No. 102, "Statement of Cash Flows—Exception of Certain Enterprises and Classification of Cash Flows from Certain Securities Acquired for Resale (an amendment of FASB Statement No. 95.)." Norwalk, CT: FASB, 1989.

————. Statement of Financial Accounting Standards No. 104, "Statement of Cash Flows—Net Reporting of Certain Cash Receipts and Cash Payments and Classification of Cash Flows from Hedging Transactions (an Amendment of FASB Statement No. 95)." Norwalk, CT: FASB, 1989.

————. Statement of Financial Accounting Standards No. 105, "Disclosure of Information about Financial Instruments Off-Balance Sheet Risk and Financial Instruments with Concentrations of Credit Risk." Norwalk, CT: FASB, 1990.

————. Statement of Financial Accounting Standards No. 107, "Disclosures About Fair Value of Financial Instruments." Norwalk, CT: FASB, 1991.

————. Statement of Financial Accounting Standards No. 114, "Accounting by Creditors for Impairment of a Loan (an Amendment of FASB Statements 5 and 15)." Norwalk, CT: FASB, 1993.

————. Statement of Financial Accounting Standards No. 115, "Accounting for Certain Investments in Debt and Equity Securities." Norwalk, CT: FASB, 1993.

————. Statement of Financial Accounting Standards No. 118, "Accounting by Creditors for Impairment of a Loan-Income Recognition and Disclosures (an Amendment of FASB Statement 114)." Norwalk, CT: FASB, 1994.

————. Statement of Financial Accounting Standards No. 119, "Disclosures about Derivative Financial Instruments and Fair Value of Financial Instruments." Norwalk, CT: FASB, 1994.

————. Statement of Financial Accounting Standards No. 121, "Accounting for the Impairment of Long-Lived Assets and for Long-Lived Assets to Be Disposed Of." Norwalk, CT: FASB, 1995.

————. Statement of Financial Accounting Standards No. 122, "Accounting for Mortgage Servicing Rights." Norwalk, CT: FASB, 1995.

————. Statement of Financial Accounting Standard (SFAS), 123R–"Share-Based Payment." SFAS 123R replaces SFAS 123–"Accounting for Stock-Based Compensation." Norwalk, CT: FASB, 2004.

————. Statement of Financial Accounting Standards No. 125, "Accounting for Transfers and Servicing of Financial Assets and Extinguishments of Liabilities." Norwalk, CT: FASB, 1996.

————. Statement of Financial Accounting Standards No. 126, "Exemption from Certain Required Disclosures about Financial Instruments for Certain Nonpublic Entities (an Amendment of FASB Statement No. 107)." Norwalk, CT: FASB, 1996.

————. Statement of Financial Accounting Standards No. 127, "Deferral of the Effective Date of Certain Provisions of FASB Statement No. 125 (an Amendment of FASB Statement No. 125)." Norwalk, CT: FASB, 1996.

————. "Financial Accounting Standards Board (FASB) of the Financial Accounting Foundation," SFAS-91, 114, 115, 133, 140. FASB, Norwalk, CT.

————. Statement of Position 92-3, "Accounting For Foreclosed Assets." AICPA, New York, 1992.

————. Statement of Position 94-6, "Disclosure of Certain Significant Risks and Uncertainties." AICPA, New York, 1994.

————. Statement of Position 95-2, "Financial Reporting for Nonpublic Investment Partnerships." AICPA, New York, 1995.

————. Statement of Position 97-1, "Accounting by Participating Mortgage Loan Borrowers." AICPA, New York, 1997.

————. Statement of Position 01-1, "Amendment to Scope of Statement of Position 95-2, Financial Reporting for Nonpublic Investment Partnerships," New York, 2001.

————. Financial Accounting Standards Board, EITF Abstracts: A Summary of Proceedings of the FASB Emerging Issues Task Force, EITF Issue No. 84-7, "Termination of Interest Rate Swaps." Norwalk, CT: FASB, 1984.

————. Statement of Financial Accounting Standards No. 157, *Fair Value Measurements* (SFAS 157). Norwalk, CT: FASB, 2006.

————. Technical Bulletin 85-2, "Accounting for Collateralized Mortgage Obligations." Norwalk, CT: FASB, 1985.

————. Technical Bulletin 94-1, "Application of Statement 115 to Debt Securities Restructured in a Troubled Debt Restructuring." Norwalk, CT: FASB, 1994.

Rezaee, Zabihollah. 2007. Corporate Governance Post–Sarbanes–Oxley: Regulations, Requirements, and Integrated Processes. Chapter 4. Hoboken, NJ: John Wiley & Sons, 2007.

Sarbanes–Oxley Act of 2002 (SOX). 2002. July 30. available at www.sarbanesoxleysimplified. com/sarbox/compact/htmlact/sec407.html.

Securities and Exchange Commission. "Regulation S-X, Article 9, Bank Holding Companies.

————. Federal Reporting Release No. 23, "The Significance of Oral Guarantees to the Financial Reporting Process." Washington, DC: SEC, 1985.

————. Federal Reporting Release No. 28, "Accounting for Loan by Registrants Engaged in Lending Activities." Washington, DC: SEC, 1986.

————. Federal Reporting Release No. 36, "Management's Discussion and Analysis of Financial Condition and Results of Operations; Certain Investment Company Disclosures." Washington, DC: SEC, 1989.

————. Federal Reporting Release No. 48, "Disclosure of Accounting Policies for Derivative Financial Instruments and Derivative Commodity Instruments and Disclosure of Quantitative and Qualitative Information About Market Risk Inherent in Derivative Financial Instruments, Other Financial Instruments." Washington, DC: SEC, 1997.

————. Securities Act Guide 3, Statistical Disclosure by Bank Holding Companies.

————. "Financial Reporting Policies, Section 401 Banks and Holding Companies," Financial Reporting Release No. 1, Section 404.03, "Accounting, Valuation, and Disclosure of Investment Securities," (Accounting Series Release No. 118, "Accounting for Investment Securities by Registered Investment Companies"). Boston: Warren, Gorham & Lamont, 1995.

————. Staff Accounting Bulletin No. 50, "Financial Statement Requirements in Filings Involving the Formation of a One-Bank Holding Company." Washington, DC: SEC, 1983.

————. Staff Accounting Bulletin No. 56, "Reporting of an Allocated Transfer Risk Reserve in Filings under the Federal Securities Laws." Washington, DC: SEC, 1984.

————. Staff Accounting Bulletin No. 59, "Accounting for Noncurrent Marketable Equity Securities." Washington, DC: SEC, 1985.

————. Staff Accounting Bulletin No. 60, "Financial Guarantees." Washington, DC: SEC, 1985.

————. Staff Accounting Bulletin No. 61, "Allowance Adjustments." Washington, DC: SEC, 1986.

————. Staff Accounting Bulletin No. 69, "Application of Article 9 and Guide 3 to Non-Bank Holding Companies." Washington, DC: SEC, 1987.

————. Staff Accounting Bulletin No. 71 and SAB 71A, "Financial Statements of Properties Securing Mortgage Loans." Washington, DC: SEC, 1987.

————. Staff Accounting Bulletin No. 75, "Accounting and Disclosures by Bank Holding Companies for a 'Mexican Debt Exchange' Transaction." Washington, DC: SEC, 1988.

————. Staff Accounting Bulletin No. 82, "Certain Transfers of Nonperforming Assets" and "Disclosures of the Impact of Assistance from Federal Financial Institution Regulatory Agencies." Washington, DC: SEC, 1989.

————. Staff Accounting Bulletin No. 89, "Financial Statements of Acquired Financial Institutions." Washington, DC: SEC, 1989.

————. Staff Accounting Bulletin No. 102, "Selected Loan Loss Allowance Methodology and Documentation Issues." Washington, DC: SEC, 2001.

————. Bank and Savings Institutions' Regulatory Guidance.

Selected guidance prepared by the federal bank and savings institutions regulatory agencies is contained in the following documents:

- *Bank Holding Company Supervision Manual,* Federal Reserve System
- *Comptroller's Handbook for National Bank Examiners,* OCC
- *Comptroller's Manual for National Banks,* OCC
- *Comptroller's Handbook for Fiduciary Activities,* OCC
- *Comptroller's Handbook for Compliance,* OCC
- *Federal Reserve Commercial Bank Examination Manual*
- *Thrift Activities Regulatory Handbook,* OTS
- *Instructions—Consolidated Reporting of Condition and Income,* FFIEC
- *Federal Deposit Insurance Corporation (FDIC)FDIC Division of Supervision Manual of Examination Policies*

- *FDIC Trust Examination Manual*
- *Federal Banking Law Reporter,* Commerce Clearing House, Inc.
- *OCC Bank Accounting Advisory Series,* Third Edition (June 1994)
- *The Dodd–Frank Wall Street Reform and Consumer Protection Act of 2010.* Dodd–Frank Act requires the development of over 240 new rules by the Securities and Exchange Commission (SEC), the Government Accountability Office (GAO), and the Federal Reserve to implement its provisions over a five-year period. In addition, the OCC, FDIC, FRB, OTS, and FFIEC regularly publish various bulletins, advisories, letters, and circulars addressing current issues.

CHAPTER 34

STATE AND LOCAL GOVERNMENT ACCOUNTING[†] (REVISED)

CYNTHIA PON, CPA
Macias Gini O'Connell LLP
KEVIN J. O'CONNELL, CPA
Macias Gini O'Connell LLP
ERNEST J. GINI, CPA, CGFM
Macias Gini O'Connell LLP

[†]   We would like to acknowledge the efforts of the contributors of the previous edition—Andrew J. Blossom, KPMG LLP; Andrew Gottschalk, KPMG LLP; John R. Miller, KPMG LLP; and Warren Ruppel, DiTomasso & Ruppel—and thank them for their undertaking. We also are indebted to Lynford Graham, whose thoughtful feedback helped raise our own understanding of governmental accounting.

34.1 INTRODUCTION

Governmental accounting has changed dramatically in recent years in response to changes in the state and local government environment. Subject to greater scrutiny by federal and state agencies and faced with budgetary challenges, governments must also negotiate an ever-increasing level of sophistication required to manage their operations—operations which are on par with the largest and most complex business organizations and are as diverse as airports, hospitals, schools, and fire protection. Add to that concerns involving deteriorating infrastructure, an aging workforce, public health care, and the spread of terrorism, and it is no surprise that governments are finding themselves addressing increasing demands for public accountability and transparency.

Before discussing the specifics of governmental accounting principles and practices, it is important to have an overall sense of the nature and organization of state and local government activities. The goal of this chapter is to provide insight on the current governmental accounting landscape and to shed light on future trends to explore. Continued examination is critical in light of the fact that governments are no longer able to be slow adopters, following behind business-related trends and regulations; they must be innovative and proactive in order to secure the quality of their service delivery, now and in the future.

34.2 THE NATURE AND ORGANIZATION OF STATE AND LOCAL GOVERNMENT ACTIVITIES

(a) STRUCTURE OF GOVERNMENT   For the most part, government is structured on three levels: federal, state, and local. This chapter deals only with state and local governments.

States are specific identifiable entities in their own right, but accounting at the state level is associated more often than not with the individual state functions, such as departments of revenue, retirement systems, turnpike authorities, and housing finance agencies.

Local governments exist as political subdivisions of states, and the rules governing their types and operation are different in each of the 50 states. There are, however, three basic types of local governmental units: general-purpose local governments (counties, cities, towns, villages, and townships), special-purpose local governments, and authorities.

The distinguishing characteristics of general-purpose local governments are that they

- Have broad powers in providing a variety of government services—for example, public safety, fire prevention, and public works
- Have general taxing and bonding authority
- Are headed by elected officials

Special-purpose local governments are established to provide specific services or construction. They may or may not be contiguous with one or more general-purpose local governments.

Authorities and agencies are similar to special-purpose governments except that they have no taxing power and are expected to operate with their own revenues. They typically can issue only revenue bonds, not general obligations bonds.

(b) OBJECTIVES OF GOVERNMENT   The purpose of government is to provide the citizenry with the highest level of services possible given the available financial resources and the legal requirements under which it operates. The services are provided as a result of decisions made during a budgeting process that considers the desired level and quality of services. Resources are then made available through property taxes, sales taxes, income taxes, general and categorical grants from the federal and state governments, charges for services, fines, licenses, and other sources. However, there is generally no direct relationship between the cost of the services rendered to an individual and the amount that the individual pays in taxes, fines, fees, and so on.

Governmental units also conduct operations that are financed and operated in a manner similar to private business enterprises, where the intent is that the costs of providing the goods or services be financed or recovered primarily through charges to the users. In such situations, governments have many of the features of ordinary business operations.

(c) ORGANIZATION OF GOVERNMENT   A government's organization depends on its constitution (state level) or charter (local level) and on general and special statutes of state and local legislatures. When governments were simpler and did not provide as many services as they do today, there was less of a tendency toward centralization. The commission and weak-mayor forms of governments were common. The financial function was typically divided among several individuals.

As government has become more complex, however, the need for strong professional management and for centralization of authority and responsibility has grown. There has been a trend toward the strong-mayor and council-manager forms of government. In these forms, a chief financial officer, usually called the *director of finance* or *controller*, is responsible for maintaining the financial records and preparing financial reports; assisting the chief executive officer (CEO) in the preparation of the budget; performing treasury functions such as collecting revenues, managing cash, managing investments, and managing debt; and overseeing the tax-assessment function. Other functions that may report to the director of finance are purchasing, data processing, and personnel administration.

Local governments are also making greater use of the internal audit process. In the past, the emphasis by governmental internal auditors was on preaudit—that is, reviewing invoices and other documents during processing for propriety and accuracy. The internal auditors reported to the director of finance. Today, however, governmental internal auditors have been removing themselves from the preaudit function by transferring this responsibility to the department responsible for processing the transactions. They have started to provide the more traditional internal audit function—that is, conducting reviews to ensure the reliability of data and the safeguarding of assets and to become involved in performance auditing (i.e., reviewing the efficiency and effectiveness of the government's operations). They have also started to report, for professional (as opposed to administrative) purposes, to the CEO or directly to the governing board. Finally, internal auditors are becoming more actively involved in the financial statement audit and single audit of their government.

(d) SPECIAL CHARACTERISTICS OF GOVERNMENT   Several characteristics associated with governments have influenced the development of governmental accounting principles and practices:

- Governments do not have any owners or proprietors in the commercial sense. Accordingly, measurement of earnings attributable or accruing to the direct benefit of an owner is not a relevant accounting concept for governments.
- Governments frequently receive substantial financial inflows for both operating and capital purposes from sources other than revenues and investment earnings, such as taxes and grants.
- Governments frequently obtain financial inflows subject to legally binding restrictions that prohibit or seriously limit the use of these resources for other than the intended purpose.
- A government's authority to raise and expend money results from the adoption of a budget that, by law, usually must balance (e.g., the estimated revenues plus any prior years' surpluses need to be sufficient to cover the projected expenditures).
- The power to raise revenues through taxes, licenses, fees, and fines is generally defined by law.
- There are usually restrictions related to the tax base that govern the purpose, amount, and type of indebtedness that can be issued.
- Expenditures are usually regulated less than revenues and debt, but they can be made only within approved budget categories and must comply with specified purchasing procedures when applicable.
- State laws may dictate the local government accounting policies and systems.
- State laws commonly specify the type and frequency of financial statements to be submitted to the state and to the government's constituency.
- Federal law, the Single Audit Act of 1984 and as amended in 1996, defines the audit requirements for state and local governments.

In short, the environment in which governments operate is complex and legal requirements have a significant influence on their accounting and financial reporting practices.

34.3 SOURCE OF ACCOUNTING PRINCIPLES FOR STATE AND LOCAL GOVERNMENT ACCOUNTING

Governmental accounting principles are not a complete and separate body of accounting principles, but rather are part of the whole body of generally accepted accounting principles (GAAP). Since the accounting profession's standard-setting bodies have been concerned primarily with the accounting needs of profit-seeking organizations, these principles have been defined primarily by groups formed by the state and local governments. In 1934, the National Committee on Municipal Accounting published "A Tentative Outline—Principles of Municipal Accounting." In 1968, the National Committee on Governmental Accounting (the successor organization) published *Governmental Accounting, Auditing, and Financial Reporting* (GAAFR), which was widely used as a source of governmental accounting principles. The American Institute of Certified Public Accountants (AICPA) Industry Audit Guide, "Audits of State and Local Governmental Units," published in 1974, stated that the accounting principles outlined in the 1968 GAAFR constituted GAAP for government entities.

The financial difficulties experienced by many governments in the mid-1970s led to a call for a review and modification of the accounting and financial reporting practices used by governments. Laws were introduced in Congress, but never enacted, that would have given the federal government the authority to establish governmental accounting principles. The Financial Accounting Standards Board (FASB), responding to pressures, commissioned a research study to define and explain the issues associated with accounting for all nonbusiness enterprises, including governments. This study was completed in 1978, and the Board developed Statement of Financial Accounting Concepts (SFAC) No. 4 for nonbusiness organizations. The Statement defined nonbusiness organizations, the users of the statements, the financial information needs of these users, and the information that is necessary to meet these needs.

(a) NATIONAL COUNCIL ON GOVERNMENT ACCOUNTING   The National Council on Governmental Accounting (NCGA) was the successor of the National Committee on Municipal Accounting reconstituted as a permanent organization. One of its first projects was to "restate," that is, update, clarify, amplify, and reorder, the GAAFR to incorporate pertinent aspects of "Audits of State and Local Governmental Units." The restatement was published in March 1979 as NCGA Statement No. 1, "Governmental Accounting and Financial Reporting Principles." Shortly thereafter, the AICPA Committee on State and Local Government Accounting recognized NCGA Statement No. 1 as authoritative and agreed to amend the Industry Audit Guide accordingly. This restatement was completed, and a new guide was published in 1986. Thus, NCGA Statement No. 1 became the primary reference source for the accounting principles unique to governmental accounting. However, in areas not unique to governmental accounting, the complete body of GAAP still needed to be considered.

(b) GOVERNMENTAL ACCOUNTING STANDARDS BOARD   In 1984, the Financial Accounting Foundation (FAF) established the Governmental Accounting Standards Board (GASB) as the primary standard setter for GAAP for governmental entities. Under the jurisdictional agreement, the GASB has the primary responsibility for establishing accounting and reporting principles for government entities. The GASB's first action was to issue Statement No. 1, "Authoritative Status of NCGA Pronouncements and AICPA Industry Audit Guide," which recognized the NCGA's statements and interpretations and the AICPA's audit guide as authoritative. The Statement also recognized the pronouncements of the FASB issued prior to the date of the agreement as applicable to governments. FASB pronouncements issued after the organization of GASB do not become effective unless the GASB specifically adopts them.

The GASB has operated under this jurisdictional arrangement since 1984. However, the arrangement came under scrutiny during the GASB's mandatory five-year review conducted in 1988. In January 1989 the Committee to Review Structure of Governmental Accounting Standards released its widely read report on the results of its review and proposed to the FAF, among other recommendations, a new jurisdictional arrangement and GAAP hierarchy for governments. These two recommendations prompted a great deal of controversy within the industry. The issue revolved around the Committee's recommended jurisdictional arrangement for the separately issued financial statements of certain "special entities." (Special entities are organizations that can either be privately or governmentally owned and include colleges and universities, hospitals, and utilities.) The Committee recommended that the FASB be the primary accounting standard setter for these special entities when they issue separate, stand-alone financial statements and that the GASB be allowed to require the presentation of "additional data" in these stand-alone statements. This arrangement would allow for greater comparability between entities in the same industry (e.g., utilities) regardless of whether the entities were privately or governmentally owned and still allow government-owned entities to meet their "public accountability" reporting objective.

This recommendation and a subsequent compromise recommendation were unacceptable to many and especially to the various public interest groups, such as the Government Finance Officers Association (GFOA), which, 10 months after the Committee's report, began discussions to establish a new body to set standards for state and local government. These actions prompted the FAF to consider whether a standard-setting schism was in the interest of the public and the users of financial statements. Based on this consideration, the FAF decided that the jurisdictional arrangement established in 1984 should remain intact.

In response to the jurisdictional arrangement just described, the AICPA issued Statement on Auditing Standards No. 69, "The Meaning of Present Fairly in Conformity with Generally Accepted Accounting Principles in the Independent Auditor's Report," which creates a hierarchy of GAAP specifically for state and local governments. SAS No. 69 raises AICPA Statement of Positions (SOPs) and audit and accounting guides to a level of authority above that of industry practice. As a result, FASB pronouncements will not apply to state and local governments unless the GASB issues a standard incorporating them into GAAP for state and local government. In September 1993, the GASB issued Statement No. 20, "Accounting and Financial Reporting for Proprietary Funds and Other Governmental Entities That Use Proprietary Fund Accounting."

Statement No. 20 requires proprietary activities to apply all applicable GASB Statements as well as FASB pronouncements, Accounting Principles Board (APB) Opinions, and Accounting Research Bulletins issued on or before November 30, 1989, unless those pronouncements conflict or contradict with a GASB pronouncement. A proprietary activity may also apply, at its option, all FASB pronouncements issued after November 30, 1989, except those that conflict or contradict with a GASB pronouncement.

The GASB subsequently issued Statement No. 29, "The Use of Not-for-Profit Accounting and Financial Reporting Principles by Governmental Entities," which amended Statement No. 20 to indicate that proprietary activities could apply only those FASB statements that were developed for business enterprises. The FASB statements and interpretations whose provisions are limited to not-for-profit organizations or address issues primarily of concern to those organizations may not be applied. These actions, along with the increased activity of the FASB in setting standards for not-for-profit organizations, have resulted in increasing differences in GAAP between nongovernmental entities and state and local governments.

These differences also highlight the importance of determining whether a particular entity is a state or local government. While it is obvious that states, cities, and counties are governments, other units of government are less clear. Is a university considered a government if it is supported 70 percent by taxes allocated by the state? What if the percentage is only 15 percent? If a hospital is created by a county but the county has no continuing involvement with the hospital, is the hospital a government? The GASB acknowledged these concerns in the Basis for Conclusions of Statement No. 29 in stating

> Some respondents believe that the fundamental issue underlying this Statement—identifying those entities that should apply the GAAP hierarchy applicable to state and local governmental entities—will continue to be troublesome until there is an authoritative definition of such "governmental entities." The Board agrees—but does not have the authority to unilaterally establish a definition—and intends to continue to explore alternatives for resolving the issue.

The decision as to whether a particular entity should follow the hierarchy for state and local governments or nongovernmental entities is a matter of professional judgment based on the individual facts and circumstances for the entity in question. The AICPA audit and accounting guide for not-for-profit organizations provides guidance to distinguish between governmental and nongovernmental organizations. It defines governmental organizations as

> Public corporations and bodies corporate and politic. . . . Other organizations are governmental organizations if they have one or more of the following characteristics:
>
> **a.** Popular election of officers or appointment (or approval) of a controlling majority of the members of the organization's governing body by officials of one or more state or local governments;
> **b.** The potential for unilateral dissolution by a government with the net assets reverting to a government; or
> **c.** The power to enact and enforce a tax levy.

Furthermore, organizations are presumed to be governmental if they have the ability to issue directly (rather than through a state or municipal authority) debt that pays interest exempt from federal taxation. However, organizations possessing only that ability (to issue tax-exempt debt) and none of the other governmental characteristics may rebut the presumption that they are governmental if their determination is supported by compelling, relevant evidence.

In 2006, the GFOA questioned the continued role of the GASB in response to its project on Service Efforts and Accomplishments (SEA) Reporting (see Section 34.4(b), Users and Uses of Financial Reports). However, in 2006 FAF reaffirmed that the GASB has the jurisdictional authority to include "service efforts and accomplishments" in its financial accounting and reporting standard-setting activities.

Recently Texas passed legislation that would give the state and any of its public entities permission to ignore GASB Statement 45, an accounting standard requiring state and local governments to disclose their liability for "other post-employment benefits," which include retiree health, dental, and vision benefits as well as some forms of life insurance. Texas CPAs are worried that this is a first step down a road where all 50 states will start developing their own set of accounting standards.

34.4   GOVERNMENTAL ACCOUNTING PRINCIPLES AND PRACTICES

(a) SIMILARITIES TO PRIVATE SECTOR ACCOUNTING   Since the accounting principles and practices of governments are part of the whole body of GAAP, certain accounting concepts and conventions are as applicable to governmental entities as they are to accounting in other industries:

- *Consistency.* Identical transactions should be recorded in the same manner both during a period and from period to period.
- *Conservatism.* The uncertainties that surround the preparation of financial statements are reflected in a general tendency toward early recognition of unfavorable events and minimization of the amount of net assets and net income.
- *Historical cost.* Amounts should be recognized in the financial statements at the historical cost to the reporting entity. Changes in the general purchasing power should not be recognized in the basic financial statements.
- *Matching.* The financial statements should provide for a matching, but in government it is a matching of revenues and expenditures with a time period to ensure that revenues and the expenditures they finance are reported in the same period.
- *Reporting entity.* The focus of the financial report is the economic activities of a discrete individual entity for which there is a reporting responsibility.
- *Materiality.* Financial reporting is concerned only with significant information.
- *Full disclosure.* Financial statements must contain all information necessary to understand the presentation of financial position and results of operations and to prevent them from being misleading.

(b) USERS AND USES OF FINANCIAL REPORTS   Users of the financial statements of a governmental unit are not identical to users of a business entity's financial statements. The GASB Concepts Statement No. 1 identifies three groups of primary users of external governmental financial reports:

1. *Those to whom government is primarily accountable—the citizenry.* The citizenry group includes citizens (whether they are classified as taxpayers, voters, or service recipients), the media, advocate groups, and public finance researchers. This user group is concerned with obtaining the maximum amount of service with a minimum amount of taxes and wants to know where the government obtains its resources and how those resources are used.
2. *Those who directly represent the citizens—legislative and oversight bodies.* The legislative and oversight officials group includes members of state legislatures, county commissions, city councils, boards of trustees, and school boards, along with those executive branch officials with oversight responsibility over other levels of government. These groups need timely warning of the development of situations that require corrective action, financial information that can serve as a basis for judging management performance, and financial information on which to base future plans and policies.
3. *Those who lend or participate in the lending process—investors and creditors.* Investors and creditors include individual and institutional investors and creditors, municipal security underwriters, bond-rating agencies (Moody's Investors Service, Standard & Poor's, etc.), bond insurers, and financial institutions.

The uses of a government's financial reports are also different. GASB Concepts Statement No. 1 also indicates that governmental financial reporting should provide information to assist users in (1) assessing accountability and (2) making economic, social, and political decisions by

- *Comparing actual financial results with the legally adopted budget.* All three user groups are interested in comparing original or modified budgets with actual results to get some assurance that spending mandates have been complied with and that resources have been used for the intended purposes.

• *Assisting in determining compliance with finance-related laws, rules, and regulations.* In addition to the legally mandated budgetary and fund controls, other legal restrictions may control governmental actions. Some examples are bond covenants, grant restrictions, and taxing and debt limits. Financial reports help demonstrate compliance with these laws, rules, and regulations.

  ○ Citizens are concerned that governments adhere to these regulations because noncompliance may indicate fiscal irresponsibility and could have severe financial consequences, such as acceleration of debt payments, disallowance of questioned costs, or loss of grants.

  ○ Legislative and oversight officials are also concerned with compliance as a follow-up to the budget formulation process.

  ○ Investors and creditors are interested in the government's compliance with debt covenants and restrictions designed to protect their investment.

• *Assisting in evaluating efficiency and effectiveness.* Citizen groups and legislators, in particular, want information about service efforts, costs, and accomplishments of a governmental entity. This information, when combined with information from other sources, helps users assess the economy, efficiency, and effectiveness of government and may help form a basis for voting on funding decisions.

• *Assessing financial condition and results of operations.* Financial reports are commonly used to assess a state or local government's financial condition—that is, its financial position and its ability to continue to provide services and meet its obligations as they come due.

  ○ Investors and creditors need information about available and likely future financial resources, actual and contingent liabilities, and the overall debt position of a government to evaluate the government's ability to continue to provide resources for long-term debt service.

  ○ Citizens' groups are concerned with financial condition when evaluating the likelihood of tax or service fee increases.

  ○ Legislative and oversight officials need to assess the overall financial condition, including debt structure and funds available for appropriation, when developing both capital and operating budget and program recommendations.

With the users and the uses of financial reports clearly defined, the GASB developed the following three overall objectives of governmental financial reporting:

1. Financial reporting should assist in fulfilling a government's duty to be publicly accountable and should enable users to assess that accountability by

   a. Providing information to determine whether current-year revenues were sufficient to pay for current-year services.

   b. Demonstrating whether resources were obtained and used in accordance with the entity's legally adopted budget and in compliance with other finance-related legal or contractual requirements.

   c. Providing information to assist users in assessing the service efforts, costs, and accomplishments of the governmental entity.

2. Financial reporting should assist users in evaluating the operating results of the governmental entity for the year by providing information

    a. About sources and uses of financial resources.

    b. About how the governmental entity financed its activities and met its cash requirements.

    c. Necessary to determine whether the entity's financial position improved or deteriorated as a result of the year's operations.

3. Financial reporting should assist users in assessing the level of services that can be provided by the governmental entity and its ability to meet its obligations as they become due by

    a. Providing information about the financial position and condition of a governmental entity. Financial reporting should provide information about resources and obligations, both actual and contingent, current and noncurrent, and about tax sources, tax limitations, tax burdens, and debt limitations.

    b. Providing information about a governmental entity's physical and other nonfinancial resources having useful lives that extend beyond the current year, including information that can be used to assess the service potential of those resources.

    c. Disclosing legal or contractual restrictions on resources and risks of potential loss of resources.

In April 1994, the GASB issued Concepts Statement No. 2, "Service Efforts and Accomplishments Reporting," which expands on the consideration of service efforts and accomplishments (SEA) reporting included in Concepts Statement No. 1. The GASB believes that the government's duty to be publicly accountable requires the presentation of SEA information. Concepts Statement No. 2 identifies the objective of SEA reporting as providing "more complete information about a governmental entity's performance that can be provided by the operating statement, balance sheet, and budgetary comparison statements and schedules to assist users in assessing the economy, efficiency, and effectiveness of services provided." The Concepts Statement also indicates that SEA information should meet the characteristics of relevance, understandability, comparability, timeliness, consistency, and reliability. In April 2007, the GASB started work on the SEA project, which will include future guidelines for SEA performance reporting issues and measures.

In April 2005, the GASB issued Concepts Statement No. 3, "Communication Methods in General Purpose External Financial Reports That Contain Basic Financial Statements," which provides a conceptual basis for selecting communication methods to present items of information within general-purpose external financial reports that contain basic financial statements. Preparers should select an appropriate communication method to convey information that enhances the consistency, comparability, and understandability of general-purpose external financial reports. The hierarchy for selecting communications methods is as follows:

    a. Recognition in the basic financial statements

    b. Disclosure in notes to basic financial statements

    c. Presentation as required supplementary information

    d. Presentation as supplementary information

In June 2007, the GASB issued Concepts Statement No. 4, "Elements of Financial Statements," which establishes definitions for the seven elements of historically based financial statements of state and local governments. These elements are the fundamental components of financial statements. The five statements of financial position elements are defined as follows:

- *Assets* are resources with present service capacity that the government presently controls.
- *Liabilities* are present obligations to sacrifice resources that the government has little or no discretion to avoid.
- A *deferred outflow* of resources is a consumption of net assets by the government that is applicable to a future reporting period.
- A *deferred inflow* of resources is an acquisition of net assets by the government that is applicable to a future reporting period.
- *Net position* is the residual of all other elements presented in a statement of financial position.

The two resource flows elements are defined as follows:

- An *outflow of resources* is a consumption of net assets by the government that is applicable to the reporting period.
- An *inflow of resources* is an acquisition of net assets by the government that is applicable to the reporting period.

Each element's inherent characteristics provides the primarily basis for these definitions. Central to these definitions is a resource, which in the governmental context is an item that can be drawn on to provide services to the citizenry. These definitions apply to an entity that is a governmental unit (i.e., a legal entity) and are applicable to any measurement focus under which financial statements may be prepared.

(c) SUMMARY STATEMENT OF PRINCIPLES   Because governments operate under different conditions and have different reporting objectives than commercial entities, basic principles applicable to government accounting and reporting have been developed. These principles are generally recognized as being essential to effective management control and financial reporting. In other words, understanding these principles and how they operate is extremely important to the understanding of governments.

(i) Accounting and Reporting Capabilities   A governmental accounting system must make it possible to both (1) present fairly the basic financial statements in conformity with GAAP, which include both government-wide and fund financial statements with full disclosure, and to provide adequately the required supplementary information, including the management's discussion and analysis (MD&A) and required budgetary comparison information; and (2) determine and demonstrate compliance with finance-related legal and contractual provisions.

(ii) Government-Wide and Fund Accounting Systems   Governmental accounting systems should provide information that permits reporting on a fund basis and provide conversion information that facilities reporting on a government-wide basis. A "fund" is defined as a fiscal and accounting entity with a self-balancing set of accounts recording cash and other financial resources, together with all related liabilities and residual equities or balances, and changes therein, which are segregated for the purpose of carrying on specific activities or attaining certain objectives in accordance with special regulations, restrictions, or limitations.

Under GASB Statement No. 34, government-wide financial statements should be presented in addition to fund financial statements. They should report information about the reporting government as a whole, except for its fiduciary activities. The statements should include separate columns for governmental activities, business-type activities, total activities, and component units, which are legally separate organizations for which the elected officials of the primary government (PG) are financially accountable, or other organizations for which the nature and significance of its relationship with a PG are such that exclusion from the financial statements of the PG would cause them to be misleading or incomplete. The government-wide financial statements should be prepared using the economic resources measurement focus and the accrual basis of accounting.

(iii) Types of Funds   The following three types of funds should be used by state and local governments.

(A) Governmental Funds (emphasizing major funds)

1. *The general fund.* To account for all financial resources except those required to be accounted for in another fund.
2. *Special revenue funds.* To account for the proceeds for specific revenue sources (other than expendable trusts, or major capital projects) that are legally restricted to expenditures for specified purposes.
3. *Capital projects funds.* To account for financial resources to be used for the acquisition or construction of major capital facilities (other than those financed by proprietary funds and trust funds).
4. *Debt service funds.* To account for the accumulation of resources for, and the payment of, general long-term debt principal and interest.
5. *Permanent funds.* To account for the resources used to make earnings, of which only the earnings may be used for the benefit of the government or its citizenry, such as a cemetery perpetual-care fund.

(B) Proprietary Funds

1. *Enterprise funds (emphasizing major funds).* To account for operations (a) that are financed and operated in a manner similar to private business enterprises, where the intent of the governing body is that the cost (expenses, including depreciation) of providing goods or services to the general public, on a continuing basis, be financed or recovered primarily through user charges; or (b) where the governing body has decided that periodic determination of revenues earned, expenses incurred, and/or net income is appropriate for capital maintenance, public policy, management control, accountability, or other purposes.
2. *Internal service funds.* To account for the financing of goods or services provided by one department or agency to other departments or agencies of the governmental unit, or to other governmental units, on a cost-reimbursement basis.

(C) Fiduciary Funds (and similar component units)

1. *Pension and other employee benefit trust funds.* To account for resources that are required to be held in trust for the members and beneficiaries of defined-benefit pension plans, defined contribution plans, other postemployment benefit (OPEB) plans, or other employee benefit plans.
2. *Investment trust funds.* To account for the external portion of external investment pools that the government sponsors.

3. *Private-purpose trust funds.* To account for all other trust arrangements under which the principal and income benefit individuals, private organizations, or other governments.

4. *Agency funds.* To account for resources held in a custodial capacity for individuals, private organizations, or other governments.

(iv) Number of Funds   Governmental units should establish and maintain those funds required by law and sound financial administration. Only the minimum number of funds consistent with legal and operating requirements should be established, since unnecessary funds result in inflexibility, undue complexity, and inefficient financial administration.

(v) Accounting for Capital Assets   A clear distinction should be made between proprietary capital assets and general capital assets. Capital assets related to specific proprietary funds should be accounted for through both the government-wide and proprietary funds statements. All other capital assets of a governmental unit should be accounted for only in the government-wide capital assets account, except for fiduciary fund capital assets that should be accounted for only in the fiduciary funds' statements.

(vi) Valuation of Capital Assets   Capital assets should be accounted for at cost or, if the cost is not practicably determinable, at estimated cost. Donated capital assets should be recorded at their estimated fair value at the time received.

(vii) Depreciation and Impairment of Capital Assets   While some assets are not depreciated, such as land, most assets are depreciated over their useful lives. An exception is also those assets accounted for using the modified approach, as outlined in GASB 34. Depreciation of capital assets should be recorded in the government-wide statement of activities; the proprietary fund statement of revenues, expense, and changes in fund net assets; and the statement of changes in fiduciary net assets. Capital assets should be evaluated for impairment when events or changes in circumstances suggest that the service utility of a capital asset may have significantly and unexpected declined.

(viii) Accounting for Long-Term Liabilities   Similar to reporting capital assets, a clear distinction should be made between proprietary fund and fiduciary long-term liabilities and general long-term liabilities. Long-term liabilities of proprietary funds should be accounted both in those funds and in the government-wide statement of net assets. All other outstanding general long-term liabilities should be accounted for in the government activities column in the government-wide statement of net assets, except for fiduciary funds' long-term liabilities that should be accounted for only in the fiduciary funds' statements.

(ix) Measurement Focus and Basis of Accounting   The modified accrual or accrual basis of accounting, as appropriate, should be used in measuring financial position and operating results.

- Governmental fund revenues and expenditures should be recognized on the modified accrual basis using the current financial resources measurement focus. Revenues should be recognized in the accounting period in which they become available and measurable. Expenditures should be recognized in the accounting period in which the fund liability is incurred, if measurable, except for unmatured long-term indebtedness and other obligations not due for payment in the current period, which should be recognized when mature or due.

- Proprietary fund revenues and expenses should be recognized using the economic resources measurement focus and the accrual basis. Revenues should be recognized in the accounting period in which they are earned and become measurable; expenses should be recognized in the period incurred, if measurable.
- Fiduciary fund revenues/additions and expenses/reductions should be recognized using the economic resources measurement focus and the accrual basis.
- Transfers should be recognized in the period in which the inter-fund receivable and payable arise.

(x) Budgeting, Budgetary Control, and Budgetary Reporting   An annual budget should be adopted by every governmental unit. The accounting system should provide the basis for appropriate budgetary control. Budgetary comparisons should be presented for the general fund and for each major special revenue fund that has a legally adopted annual budget.

(xi) Transfer, Revenue, Expenditure, and Expense Account Classification   The statement of activities should present activities accounted for in governmental funds by function and activities accounted for in enterprise funds by different identifiable activities.

Governmental fund revenues should be classified by fund and source. Expenditures should be classified by fund, function (or program), organization unit, activity, character, and principal classes of objects.

Proprietary fund revenues and expenses should be classified in essentially the same manner as those of similar business organizations, functions, or activities.

Contributions to term and permanent endowments, contributions to permanent fund principal, other capital contributions, special and extraordinary items, and transfers should each be reported separately.

(xii) Common Terminology and Classification   A common terminology and classification should be used consistently throughout the budget, the accounts, and the financial reports of each fund or activity.

(xiii) Interim and Annual Financial Reports   Appropriate interim financial statements and reports of financial position, operating results, and other pertinent information should be prepared to facilitate management control of financial operations, legislative oversight, and, where necessary or desired, external reporting.

A comprehensive annual financial report (CAFR) covering all funds of the governmental unit may be prepared and published, including appropriate government-wide financial statements; combined, combining, and individual fund statements; notes to the financial statements; required supplementary information; schedules; narrative explanations; and statistical tables.

Basic financial statements may be issued separately from the CAFR. Such statements should include the financial statements, notes to the financial statements, and any required supplementary information essential to a fair presentation of financial position and operating results and cash flows of proprietary funds.

(d) DISCUSSION OF THE PRINCIPLES   To enable readers to more fully understand the principles, a discussion follows.

(e) ACCOUNTING AND REPORTING CAPABILITIES

(i) Legal Compliance   *Principle 1* of governmental accounting (GASB Codification Section 1100.101) states

> A governmental accounting system must make it possible both: (a) to present fairly and with full disclosure the funds of the governmental unit in conformity with GAAPs; and (b) to determine and demonstrate compliance with finance-related legal and contractual provisions.

Several state and local governments have accounting requirements that differ from GAAP—for example, cash basis accounting is required, and capital projects must be accounted for in the general fund. Because of this situation, the legal compliance principle used to be interpreted as meaning that, when the legal requirements for a particular entity differed from GAAP, the legal requirements became GAAP for the entity. This interpretation is no longer viewed as sound. When GAAP and legal requirements conflict, governments should present their basic financial report in accordance with GAAP and, if the legal requirements differ materially from GAAP, the legally required reports can be published as supplemental data to the basic financial report or, if these differences are extreme, it may be preferable to publish a separate legal-basis report.

However, conflicts that arise between GAAP and legal provisions do not require maintaining two sets of accounting records. Rather, the accounting records typically would be maintained in accordance with the legal requirements but would include sufficient additional information to permit preparation of reports in accordance with GAAP.

(ii) Reporting Requirements   Under GASB Statement No. 34, the typical local government's set of basic financial statements consists of three components: (1) Government-wide financial statements; (2) Fund financial statements; and (3) Notes to the financial statements. Governments will also have other supplementary information in addition to the basic financial statements themselves. An example of how the various elements of a local government's financial statement are related is shown in Exhibit 34.1.

The table in Exhibit 34.2 summarizes the major features of the City and County of San Francisco's financial statements.

(f) GOVERNMENT-WIDE AND FUND ACCOUNTING SYSTEMS   Principle 2, fund accounting, is used by governments because of (1) legally binding restrictions that prohibit or seriously limit the use of much of a government's resources for other than the purposes for which the resources were obtained, and (2) the importance of reporting the accomplishment of various objectives for which the resources were entrusted to the government.

GASB Codification Section 1100.102 defines a fund for accounting purposes as

> A fiscal and accounting entity with a self-balancing set of accounts recording cash and other financial resources, together with all related liabilities and residual equities or balances, and changes therein, which are segregated for the purposes of carrying on specific activities or obtaining certain objectives in accordance with special regulations, restrictions, or limitations.

Thus, a fund may include accounts for assets, liabilities, fund balance or net assets, revenues, expenditures, or expenses. Accounts may also exist for appropriations and encumbrances, depending on the budgeting system used.

CAFR	Introductory Section		**INTRODUCTORY SECTION**		
			+		
			Management's Discussion and Analysis		
	Financial Section	**Government-Wide Financial Statements**	**Fund Financial Statements**		
			Governmental Funds	Proprietary Funds	Fiduciary Funds
		Statement of net assets	Balance sheet	Statement of net assets	Statement of fiduciary net assets
		Statement of activities	Statement of revenues, expenditures, and changes in fund balances	Statement of revenues, expenses, and changes in fund net assets	Statement of changes in fiduciary net assets
			Budgetary comparison statement	Statement of cash flows	
			Notes to the Financial Statements		
			Required Supplementary Information Other than MD&A		
			Information on individual nonmajor funds and other supplementary information that is not required		
			+		
	Statistical Section		**STATISTICAL SECTION**		

EXHIBIT 34.1   ORGANIZATION OF THE CITY AND COUNTY OF SAN FRANCISCO COMPREHENSIVE ANNUAL FINANCIAL REPORT

Source: City and County of San Francisco, California, Comprehensive Annual Financial Report for the Year Ended June 30, 2006, pp. 4–5.

A government should report separately on its most important, or "major," funds, including its general fund. A major fund is one whose revenues, expenditures/expenses, assets, or liabilities (excluding extraordinary items) are at least 10 percent of the corresponding totals for all governmental or enterprise funds and at least 5 percent of the aggregate amount for all governmental and enterprise funds. Any other fund may be reported as a major fund if the government's officials believe information about the fund is particularly important to the users of the statements. Other funds should be reported in the aggregate in a separate column. Internal service funds should be reported in the aggregate in a separate column on the proprietary fund statements. Separate fund financial statements should be presented for governmental and proprietary funds.

	Government-Wide Statements	Fund Financial Statements		
		Governmental	Proprietary	Fiduciary
Scope	Entire entity (except fiduciary funds)	The day-to-day operating activities of the City for basic governmental services	The day-to-day operating activities of the City for business-type enterprises	Instances in which the City administers resources on behalf of others, such as employee benefits
Accounting basis and measurement focus	Accrual accounting and economic resources focus	Modified accrual accounting and current financial resources focus	Accrual accounting and economic resources focus	Accrual accounting and economic resources focus; except agency funds do not have measurement focus
Type of asset and liability information	All assets and liabilities, both financial and capital, short term and long term	Current assets and liabilities that come due during the year or soon thereafter	All assets and liabilities, both financial and capital, short term and long term	All assets held in a trustee or agency capacity for others
Type of inflow and outflow information	All revenues and expenses during year, regardless of when cash is received or paid	Revenues for which cash is received during the year or soon thereafter; expenditures when goods or services have been received and the related liability is due and payable	All revenues and expenses during year, regardless of when cash is received or paid	All additions and deductions during the year, regardless of when cash is received or paid

EXHIBIT 34.2   SUMMARY OF THE MAJOR FEATURES OF THE CITY AND COUNTY OF SAN FRANCISCO'S FINANCIAL STATEMENTS

A government should present a summary reconciliation to the government-wide financial statements at the bottom of the fund financial statements or in a separate schedule. Fund balances for governmental funds should be segregated into reserved and unreserved categories. Proprietary fund net assets should be reported in the same categories required for the government-wide financial statements. Proprietary fund statements of net assets should distinguish between current and noncurrent assets and liabilities and should display restricted assets.

(g) TYPES AND NUMBER OF FUNDS   Because of the various nature of activities carried on by government, it is often important to be able to account for certain activities separately from others (i.e., when required by law). Principles 3 and 4 define seven basic fund types in which to account for various governmental activities. The purpose and operation of each fund type differs, and it is important to understand these differences and why they exist. Every fund maintained by a government should be classified into one of these three fund categories:

1. Governmental funds, emphasizing major funds:
   o   The general fund
   o   Special revenue funds
   o   Capital projects funds
   o   Debt service funds
   o   Permanent funds
2. Proprietary funds:
   o   Enterprise funds, emphasizing major funds
   o   Internal service funds

3. Fiduciary funds and similar component units:
   - ○ Pension and other employee benefit trust funds
   - ○ Investment trust funds
   - ○ Private-purpose trust funds
   - ○ Agency funds

The general fund, special revenue funds, debt service funds, capital projects funds, and permanent funds are considered governmental funds since they record the transactions associated with the general services of a local governmental unit (i.e., police, public works, fire prevention) that are provided to all citizens and are supported primarily by general revenues. For these funds, the primary concerns, from the financial statement reader's point of view, are the types and amounts of resources that have been made available to the governmental unit and the uses to which they have been put.

The enterprise funds and internal services funds are considered proprietary funds because they account for activities for which the determination of operating income is important.

The trust and agency funds are considered fiduciary funds. There are basically three types of trust funds: pension (and other employee benefit) trust funds, investment trust funds and private-purpose trust funds that operate in a manner similar to proprietary funds, and agency funds that account for funds held by a government entity in an agent capacity. Agency funds consist of assets and liabilities only and do not involve the measurement of operations.

Although a government should establish and maintain those funds required by law and sound financial administration, it should set up only the minimum number of funds consistent with legal and operating requirements. The maintenance of unnecessary funds results in inflexibility, undue complexity, and inefficient financial administration. For instance, in the past, the proceeds of specific revenue sources or resources that financed specific activities as required by law or administrative regulation had to be accounted for in a special revenue fund. However, governmental resources restricted to purposes usually financed through the general fund should be accounted for in the general fund, provided that all legal requirements can be satisfied. Examples include state grants received by an entity for special education. If a separate fund is not legally required, the grant revenues and the grant-related expenditures should be accounted for in the fund for which they are to be used.

Another way to minimize funds is by accounting for debt service payments in the general fund and not establishing a separate debt service fund unless it is legally mandated or resources are actually being accumulated for future debt service payments (i.e., for term bonds or in sinking funds).

Furthermore, one or more identical accounts for separate funds should be combined in the accounting system, particularly for funds that are similar in nature or are in the same fund group. For example, the cash accounts for all special revenue funds may be combined, provided that the integrity of each fund is preserved through a distinct equity account for each fund.

(i) Governmental Funds

(A) GENERAL FUND

The general fund accounts for the revenues and expenditures not accounted for in other funds and finances most of the current normal functions of governmental units: general government, public safety, highways, sanitation and waste removal, health and welfare, culture, and recreation. It is usually the largest and most important accounting activity for state and local governments. Property taxes are often the principal source of general fund revenues, but substantial revenues may also be received from other financing sources.

The general fund balance sheet is typically limited to current assets and current liabilities. The GASB Codification emphasizes this practice by using the terms *expendable assets* and *current liabilities* when describing governmental funds, of which the general fund is one. Thus, the fund balance in the general fund is considered available to finance current operations.

A governmental unit, however, often makes long-term advances to independent governmental agencies, such as redevelopment authorities or housing agencies, or provides the capital necessary to establish an internal service fund. The advances are recorded in the general fund as an advance receivable. Although in most cases collectibility is assured, repayment may extend over a number of years. The inclusion of a noncurrent asset in the general fund results in a portion of the general fund's fund balance not being readily available to finance current operations.

To reflect the unavailability of an advance to finance current activities, a fund balance reserve is established to segregate a portion of the fund balance from the general fund in an amount equal to the advance that is not considered currently available. Establishing this reserve does not require a charge to operations; rather, it is a segregation of the fund balance in the available general fund and is established by debiting unreserved fund balance and crediting reserved fund balance. The reserve is reported in the fund balance section of the balance sheet.

(B) Special Revenue Funds

Special revenue funds should be established to account for the proceeds of specific revenue sources (other than expendable trusts or major capital projects) that are legally restricted to expenditure for specified purposes and for which a separate fund is legally required. Examples are parks, schools, and museums, as well as particular functions or activities, such as highway construction or street maintenance.

A special revenue fund may have a definite limited life, or it may remain in effect until discontinued or revoked by appropriate legislative action. It may be used for a very limited purpose, such as the maintenance of a historic landmark, or it may finance an entire function of government, such as public education or highways.

A special revenue fund may be administered by the regularly constituted administrative and financial organization of the government; by an independent body or special-purpose local district, such as a park board or the board of directors of a water district; or by a quasi-independent body. In some cases, the fund may be administered by an independent board, but the government maintains the accounting records because the independent board does not have the necessary personnel or other facilities.

(C) Debt Service Funds

Debt service funds exist to account for the accumulation of resources for, and the payment of, long-term debt principal and interest other than that which is issued for and serviced primarily by an enterprise or similar trust fund. A debt service fund is necessary only if it is legally required or if resources are being accumulated for future payment. Although governments may incur a wide variety of debt, the more common types are described next.

Term (or sinking fund) bonds are being replaced by serial bonds as the predominant form of state and local government debt. For term bonds, debt service consists of annual additions of resources being made to a cumulative "investment fund" for repayment of the issue at maturity. The additions, also called *sinking fund installments,* are computed on an actuarial basis, which includes assumptions that certain rates of interest will be earned from investing the resources accumulating in the investment fund. If the actual earnings are less than the planned earnings, subsequent additions are increased; if the earnings are greater than planned, the excess is carried forward until the time of the final addition of the fund. Because term bond principal is due at the end of the bond's term, the expenditure for repayment of principal is recognized at that time.

Debt service on serial bonds, however, generally consists of preestablished principal payments that are due on an annual basis and interest payments based on either fixed or variable rates that are due on a semiannual basis. No sinking fund is involved in the repayment of serial bonds.

The revenues for a debt service fund come from one or more sources, with property taxes being the predominant source. Taxes that are specified for debt service appear as a revenue of the debt service fund. Taxes for general purposes (i.e., not specified but nevertheless used for debt service) are considered to be a transfer to the debt service fund from the fund in which the revenue is recorded, oftentimes the general fund.

Enterprise activity earnings may be another resource for servicing general obligation debt. In these instances, the general obligation debt should be classified as enterprise debt (a liability of the enterprise fund), and the debt service payments should be recorded in the enterprise fund as a reduction of the liability, not in the debt service fund. The debt service transactions would be recorded in the debt service fund only if the enterprise fund was not expected to be responsible for repaying the debt on an ongoing basis. Essentially, if the enterprise fund became unable to service the principal and interest and the general governmental unit assumed responsibility for servicing the debt, then the debt service fund would be used.

In addition, governmental units have been utilizing alternative financing activities, including lease-purchase arrangements and issuance of zero-coupon or deep-discount debt. The issues surrounding lease-purchase arrangements involve legal questions about whether such arrangements constitute debt of a government since they often do not require voter approval prior to incurring the debt. Zero-coupon and deep-discount debt issues center on the manner of presenting and amortizing the bond discount amount in the government's financial statements.

In other instances, governmental units have been securitizing specific receivables and future revenues in order to receive cash up front for current outlays. GASB recently issued Statement No. 48, "Sales and Pledges of Receivables and Future Revenues and Intra-Entity Transfers of Assets and Future Receivables," to address a divergence in practice as to whether these securitizations should be reported as a revenue or as a liability. For example, in January 2007 the County of Santa Clara, California, sold its future Tobacco Settlement Revenues scheduled to be earned in the years 2026 through 2056 and recognized $102 million as a source of funds in 2007 in its governmental funds prior to the effective date of GASB Statement No. 48. As a result, the county was able under prior guidance to record this as an inflow of resources in its governmental funds.

Recently, governments are examining the possibility of issuing debt to fund their unfunded actuarial accrued liability (UAAL) for their Other Postemployment Benefits (OPEB) as has sometimes been done with UAAL for their pension obligations. These are taxable debt issues that are used to fund all or part of a government entity's UAAL. This shifts the liability from one owed to the pension plan to one owed to bondholders and brings the liability onto the government's financial statements. The rationale for issuing this type of debt is to invest the proceeds in investments that provide a rate of return higher than the debt interest costs. Governments should exercise caution when evaluating the possibility of issuing OPEB or pension obligation bonds, given the volatility of the computation of the actuarial liabilities, the increase in the government's debt burden, and the dependence on a higher rate of earnings on investments.

Quite often, a refunding bond is issued to replace or consolidate prior debt issues. Determining the appropriate accounting principles to apply to refunding bonds depends primarily on whether the bonds are enterprise fund obligations or general obligations. GASB Statement No. 7, "Advance Refundings Resulting in Defeasance of Debt," outlines the appropriate accounting and reporting principles. For the refunding of debt, the proceeds of the refunding issue become an "other financing source" of the fund receiving the proceeds of the refunding bond (oftentimes a debt service fund created to service the original issue or a capital projects fund). Since the proceeds are used to liquidate the original debt, an "other financing use" is also recorded in the debt service or capital projects fund in an amount equal to the remaining principal, interest, and other amounts due on the original debt.

If, as a result of the refunding, the liability to the bondholders is satisfied, the refunding is referred to as a *legal defeasance of debt* or *current refunding*. However, refundings often do not result in the immediate repayment of the debt; rather, assets are placed in a trust to be used to repay the debt as it matures. These refundings are called *advance refundings* or *in-substance defeasances*. To qualify for an in-substance defeasance, the proceeds of the refunding bonds are placed in an irrevocable trust and invested in essentially risk-free securities, usually obligations of the U.S. Treasury or other government agencies, so that the risk-free securities, together with any premiums on the defeased debt and expenses of the refunding operation, will be sufficient for the trust to pay off the debt to the bondholders when it becomes due. The accounting for an in-substance defeasance is identical to legal defeasances except that payment is made to a trustee rather than to bondholders. The trustee then pays principal and interest to the bondholders based on the maturity schedule of the bond. In addition, the recording of payments of proceeds to the trustee as another financing use is limited to the amount of proceeds.

Advance refundings of debt follow the accounting principles outlined in GASB Statement No. 23, "Accounting and Financial Reporting for Refundings of Debt Reported by Proprietary Activities." Statement No. 23 requires that the difference between the reacquisition price and the net carrying amount of the old debt be deferred and amortized as a component of interest expense over the remaining life of the old or the life of the new debt, whichever is shorter.

In addition, GASB Statement No. 7 requires the disclosure of a description of the refunding transaction; the cash flow gain or loss, which is the difference between the total cash outflow of the new debt (i.e., principal, interest, etc.) and the remaining cash outflow of the old debt; and the economic gain or loss, which is the difference between the present values of the cash flows of the new and old debt.

For advance refundings, each year after the defeasance, the footnotes to the financial statements should disclose the remaining amount of debt principal that the trustee has to pay to bondholders.

(D) Capital Projects Funds

The purpose of a capital projects fund is to account for the receipt and disbursement of resources used for the acquisition of major capital facilities other than those financed by enterprise funds. Capital projects are defined as outlays for major, permanent fixed assets having a relatively long life (e.g., buildings), as compared with those of limited life (e.g., office equipment). Capital projects are usually financed by bond proceeds, but they can also be financed from other resources, such as current revenues or grants from other governments.

Capital outlays financed entirely from the direct revenues of the general fund or a special revenue fund and not requiring long-term borrowing may be accounted for in the fund providing such resources rather than in a separate capital projects fund. Assets with a relatively short life—hence not capital projects—are usually financed from current revenues or by short-term obligations and are accounted for in the general or special revenue fund.

Accounting for Capital Projects Fund Transactions. Bonds are issued and capital projects are started under a multiyear capital program. In some instances, it is necessary to secure referendum approval to issue general obligation bonds. Obligations are then incurred and expenditures made according to an annual capital projects budget.

When a project is financed entirely from general obligation bond proceeds, the initial entry to be made in the capital projects fund when the bonds are sold is as follows:

Cash	$XXX
Other financing source—	
Proceeds of general obligation bonds	$XXX

Whereas the proceeds of the bonds are accounted for in the capital projects funds, the liability for the face amount of the bonds is recorded in the government-wide statement of net assets.

If bonds are sold at a premium (i.e., above par value), the premium increases the other financing sources. Often, the premium is transferred—by a debit to "other financing sources" and a credit to "cash"—to the debt service fund established to service the debt for the project. If the bonds are sold at a discount (i.e., below par value), the discount reduces the amount recorded as other financing sources in the capital projects fund. Bond issuance costs either paid out of available funds or withheld from the bond proceeds usually are accounted as debt service expenditures in the capital projects or debt service funds operating statement.

Bond Anticipation Notes (BANs). Governments sometimes issue BANs prior to the sale of bonds, planning to retire the notes with the proceeds of the bond issue to which the notes are related. The reasons would include

- The governmental unit wants to accelerate initiation of a project, and issuance of the long-term bonds will require more time than is required to issue BANs.
- The governmental unit does not want to undertake long-term financing until the project is complete and ready for use. Hence BANs are used to provide construction financing.
- The current and projected interest rates make it prudent to issue short-term notes first and to defer issuance of long-term bonds.
- The individual capital projects to be financed from the proceeds of the bond sale are so small as to make the sale of bonds to finance each project impracticable.

The cash proceeds and the liabilities resulting from the sale of BANs should be recorded in the capital projects fund as follows:

Cash	$XXX
Bond anticipation notes payable	$XXX

When the long-term bonds are sold, an "other financing source" should be recorded and the BANs payable debited in an amount equal to the portion of the BANs redeemed as follows:

Bond participation notes payable	$XXX
Other financing source	$XXX

If the BANs are not redeemed with long-term bond proceeds or other funds by the end of the year, and the governmental unit has both the intent and the ability (as those terms are defined in Statement of Financial Accounting Standards (SFAS) No. 6, "Classification of Short-Term Obligations Expected to Be Refinanced," pars. 10 and 11) to redeem the BANs with long-term debt, the BANs payable account should be debited and an "other financing source" should be credited. If the governmental unit does not have the intent or ability to redeem the BANs with long-term debt, it is appropriate to leave the liability in the capital projects fund. The ability to redeem the BANs could be demonstrated by a post–balance sheet issuance of long-term debt or the entering into of a long-term financing arrangement for the BANs.

Project Budgets.   When debt is issued to finance an entire capital project, it is usually done at the beginning of the project in an amount equal to the total estimated project cost. Accordingly, a portion of the proceeds may remain unexpended over a considerable period of time. To the maximum extent possible, these excess proceeds should be invested in interest-bearing investments. However, consideration should be given to the federal arbitrage regulations that limit the amount of interest that can be earned from investing the proceeds of a tax-exempt bond issue. If certain limits are exceeded, the bond's tax-exempt status may be lost or severe penalties could be imposed on the issuer.

Project budgets are typically established for capital projects to control costs and to guard against cost overruns. All expenditures needed to place the project in readiness—that is, indirect as well as direct costs—should be recorded against this budget. The actual expenditures, however, will probably be either less or greater than the amounts authorized. Therefore, in the absence of any legal restrictions, any unspent balance should be transferred to the appropriate sources. If the project was financed only from bond proceeds, the transfer should be to the debt service fund from which the bond issue is to be repaid. If the resources were drawn from more than one source, such as bond proceeds and current revenues, the transfer should be split among the sources in proportion to their contributions. If the expenditures were greater than authorized and a deficit exists, sufficient funds must be transferred to liquidate any commitments.

As construction of the project is completed, the costs should be recorded in the capital account as Construction in Progress and then transferred to the final building account when construction is completed.

(E) PERMANENT FUNDS

Permanent funds should be used to report assets legally restricted so that only earnings, not principal, may be spent for the government's programs—that is, for the benefit of the government or its citizens.

(ii) Proprietary Funds

(A) ENTERPRISE FUNDS

Enterprise funds *may be* used to report any activity for which fees are charged to external users in exchange for goods or services. They are *required* to be used if *any one* of the following criteria is met in the context of the activity's principal revenue sources (insignificant activities, such as fees charged for frivolous small-claims suits, are excluded):

- The activity is financed with debt secured solely by a pledge of the net revenues from fees and charges of the activity. (This is met if the debt is secured in part by a portion of its own proceeds.)
- Laws or regulations require that the activity's costs of providing goods or services, including capital costs such as depreciation or debt service, be recovered by its fees and charges, not by taxes or similar revenues.
- The pricing policies of the activity result in fees and charges intended to recover the activity's costs, including capital costs such as depreciation or debt service.
- The primary focus of these criteria is on fees charged to external users.

Proprietary (enterprise) activities are frequently administered by departments of the general-purpose government—for example, a municipal water department or a state parks department. They can also be the exclusive function of a local special district, such as a water district, power authority, or bridge and tunnel authority.

User charges are one significant source of enterprise fund resources; revenue bond proceeds are another. Revenue bonds are long-term obligations, the principal and interest of which are paid from the earnings of the enterprise for which the bond proceeds were spent. The enterprise revenues may be pledged to the payment of the debt, and the physical properties may carry a mortgage that is to be liquidated in the event of default.

Revenue bond indentures usually also contain several requirements concerning the use of the bond proceeds, the computation and reporting of revenue bond coverage, and the establishment and use of restricted asset accounts for handling revenue bond debt service requirements. For instance, a revenue bond indenture may require the establishment of various bond accounts, including a construction account, operations and maintenance account, current debt service account, future debt service account, and revenue and replacement account. This does not necessarily mean establishing individual accounting funds for each bond issue. Instead, the accounting and reporting requirements can be met through the use of various accounts within an accounting fund.

The revenue bond construction account normally represents cash and investments (including interest receivable) segregated by the bond indenture for construction. Construction liabilities payable from restricted assets should be reported as "contracts payable from restricted assets." If there are significant unspent debt proceeds at year-end, the portion of the debt attributable to the unspent proceeds should not be included in the calculation of amounts invested in capital assets, net of related debt. Instead, that portion of the debt should be included as the same net assets component as the unspent proceeds.

A revenue bond operations and maintenance account often is established pursuant to a bond indenture. Resources for this account are provided through bond proceeds and/or operating income or net income. This account generally accumulates assets equal to operating costs for one month. Once this account has been established, additional proceeds from future bond issues generally are necessary only to the extent the costs associated with these expanded operations are expected to increase. This account is normally balanced by a restricted net asset account for revenue bond operations and maintenance.

Bond indentures may also include a covenant requiring the establishment of a restricted account for the repayment of bond principal and interest. Resources for this account also are provided through bond proceeds and/or operating income or net income. Normally, assets accumulated for debt service payments (i.e., principal and interest) due within one year are classified in the revenue bond current debt service account. This account is at least partially associated with the bonds payable—current account and the accrued interest payable account. Any difference between the revenue bond current debt service account and related current bonds payable and accrued interest payable should be reported as restricted net assets. When accounts are restricted for debt service payments beyond the next 12 months, a revenue bond future debt service account should be established.

The final restricted account typically established pursuant to a covenant within a bond indenture is the revenue bond renewal and replacement account. Net income is often restricted for payments of unforeseen repairs and replacements of assets originally acquired with bond proceeds. Provided that liabilities have not been incurred for this purpose, the revenue bond renewal and replacement account is balanced by net assets restricted for revenue bond renewal and replacement.

The following general rule should be considered when determining the amount of restricted net assets to record: Unless otherwise required by the bond indenture, net assets should be restricted only for amounts of restricted assets in excess of related liabilities and the balance of restricted assets funded by bond proceeds.

Another restricted asset often found in enterprise funds for utility operations is the amount resulting from the deposits customers are required to make to ensure payment of their final charges and to protect the utility against damage to equipment located on the customer's property. These funds are not available for the financing of current operations and, generally, the amount, less the charges outstanding against the account, must be returned when the customer withdraws from the system. Also, these deposits may, depending on legal and policy requirements, draw interest at some stipulated rate.

In some instances, revenue bonds are also secured by the full faith and credit of the governmental unit. This additional security enables the bonds to obtain better acceptance in the securities market. If the bonds are to be serviced by the enterprise activity, the cash, liability, principal, and interest payments should be accounted for in the enterprise fund. Even if the bonds are secured only by full faith and credit and not by a revenue pledge but the intention is to use enterprise revenues to service the bonds, they should be accounted for as if they were revenue bonds. If, however, general obligation bond proceeds are used to finance the enterprise activity and there is no intention to service the bonds with enterprise fund resources, the amounts provided to the enterprise fund should be recorded as a transfer from the fund recording the proceeds of the bond—typically, the general fund.

Other sources of contributions also provide significant resources for enterprise activities. Such resources include capital contributions by other funds or other governmental bodies; capital contributions by customers or other members of the general public; the aforementioned proceeds of a bond issue to be repaid from general fund revenues, federal grants, or state grants; connection charges to users of utility services; payments by real estate developers for installing utility lines; and similar receipts.

Another resource is the support provided by or to other funds of the government. For instance, an enterprise fund will frequently use the services or commodities of a central facility operated as an internal service fund. Conversely, the general fund departments will use the services of an electric utility fund.

It is important to handle these relationships on a businesslike basis. All services rendered by an enterprise fund for other funds of the government should be billed at predetermined rates, and the enterprise should pay for all services received from other funds on the same basis that is utilized to determine charges for other users. The latter will often include payments in lieu of taxes to the general fund in amounts comparable to the taxes that would have been paid by the enterprise were it privately owned and operated, or an "administrative charge" if the enterprise does not have its own management capacity and instead uses management services provided by the general government. Unless this is done, the financial operations of a government-owned enterprise will be distorted, and valid comparisons of operating results with those for a similar privately owned enterprise cannot be made. However, other considerations, such as the amount of planned idle capacity, have an impact on the comparability of public and private enterprise funds.

Interfund transfers may also occur between an enterprise fund and governmental funds. Operating subsidy transfers from the general fund or special revenue fund are possible. There may also be transfers from an enterprise to finance general fund expenditures.

Finally, there are the nonoperating income and expenses, which are incidental to, or by-products of, the enterprise's primary service function. Nonoperating income consists of such items as interest earnings, rent from nonoperating properties, intergovernmental revenues, and sale of excess supplies. Nonoperating expenses include items such as interest expense and fiscal agents' fees.

(B) INTERNAL SERVICE FUNDS

Internal service funds finance and account for special activities that are performed and commodities that are furnished by one department or agency of a governmental unit to other departments or agencies of that unit or to other governmental units on a cost-reimbursement basis. The services differ from those rendered to the public at large, which are accounted for in general, special revenue, or enterprise funds. Examples of activities in which internal service funds are established include central motor pools, duplication services, central purchasing and stores departments, and insurance and risk-management activities.

When an internal service fund is established, resources are typically obtained from contributions from other operating funds, such as the general fund or an enterprise fund, or from long-term advances from other funds that are to be repaid from operating income. The entry to be made when the fund is created varies depending on the source of the contributions.

The cost of services rendered and commodities furnished, including labor, depreciation on all capital assets used by the funds other than buildings financed from capital projects, and overhead, are charged to the departments served. These departments reimburse the internal service fund by recording expenditures against their budgeted appropriations. The operating objective of the fund is to recover costs incurred to provide the service, including depreciation. Accordingly, the operations of the fund should not result in any significant profit or loss. Whenever it uses the services of another fund, such as an enterprise fund, the fund pays for and records the costs just as if it had dealt with an outside organization.

Since exact overhead charges are usually not known when bills are prepared, the departments being served are usually billed for direct costs plus a uniform rate for their portion of estimated overhead. Any difference in actual overhead expenses may be charged or credited to the departments at fiscal year-end or adjusted for in a subsequent year. At the end of each fiscal year, net income or loss must be determined. The excess of net billings to the department over costs is closed to the net assets account.

(iii) Fiduciary Funds   The purpose of fiduciary (trust and agency) funds is to account for assets held by a governmental unit in a trustee capacity or as an agent for other individuals, private organizations, or other governmental units.

Usually in existence for an extended period of time, trust funds deal with substantial vested interests and involve complex administrative problems. The government's records must provide adequate information to permit compliance with the terms of the trust as defined in the trust document, statutes, ordinances, or governing regulations.

(A) PENSION (AND OTHER EMPLOYEE BENEFIT) TRUST FUNDS

In pension (and other employee benefit) trust funds, governments account for resources held for the future retirement and other postemployment benefits (defined benefit and defined contribution) of their employees. The resources of these funds are the members' contributions, contributions from the government employer, and earnings on investments in authorized securities. The expenses are the authorized retirement allowances and other benefits, refunds of contributions to members who resign prior to retirement, and administrative expenses. Professional actuaries make periodic actuarial studies of the retirement systems and compute the amounts that should be provided so that the benefits can be paid as required.

The proper accounting for pension trust funds has been on the GASB's agenda since its creation. The GASB initially allowed governments to choose from three different methods of accounting and financial reporting but required certain disclosures from all governments. The GASB has finally completed its consideration of pensions and other postemployment employee benefits (OBEB), and the current statements include: Statement No. 25, "Financial Reporting for Defined Benefit Pension Plans and Note Disclosures for Defined Contribution Plans," Statement No. 27, "Accounting for Pensions by State and Local Government Employers," Statement No. 43, "Financial Reporting for Postemployment Benefit Plans Other Than Pension Plans," Statement No. 45, "Accounting and Financial Reporting by Employers for Postemployment Benefits Other Than Pensions," and Statement No. 50, "Pension Disclosures—an Amendment of GASB Statements No. 25 and No. 27." Statements No. 25 and 43 address issues related to accounting by pension and other employee benefit plans along with pension and other employee benefit trust funds. Statements Nos. 27 and 45 address accounting and financial reporting for those employers who participate in a pension and other employee benefit plans.

Statements Nos. 25 and 43 describe two basic financial statements for pension (and other employee benefit) plans: the statement of plan net assets and the statement of changes in plan net assets. These two financial statements are designed to provide current information about plan assets and financial activities. Statements Nos. 25 (as amended by No. 50) and 43 have other requirements for note disclosure that include a brief plan description, a summary of significant accounting principles, and information about contributions, legally required reserves, investment concentrations, funded status of the plan as of the most recent actuarial valuation date, and the actuarial methods and significant assumptions used in the most recent actuarial valuation.

The accounting guidance is directed at employers who participate in a pension (and other employee benefit) plan and reflects two underlying principles. First, the pension or OPEB cost recognized should be related to the annual required contribution (ARC) as determined by an actuary for funding purposes. Second, the actuarial methods and assumptions used by employers should be consistent with those used by the plan in its separate reporting.

In implementing these basic principles. Statements Nos. 27 and 45 require the ARC to be recognized as pension or OPEB expense in government-wide financial statements and in the proprietary funds. Governmental funds will recognize pension expenditure to the extent that the ARC is expected to be liquidated with expendable available resources. If an employer does not contribute to the ARC (or has contributed in excess of the ARC), pension or OPEB expense/expenditure no longer equals the ARC. In these cases the ARC is adjusted to remove the effects of the actuarial adjustments included in the ARC and to reflect interest on previous under- or overfunding.

Although Statements Nos. 27 and 45 try to minimize the differences between accounting for pensions (and other employee benefits) and funding pensions (and other employee benefits), it does place certain limits or "parameters" on the actuary's modified calculation of the ARC. These parameters are consistent with parameters established for accounting for the plan itself in Statements Nos. 25 and 43. These parameters relate to the pension/OPEB obligation, actuarial assumptions, economic assumptions, actuarial cost method, actuarial valuation of assets, and amortization of unfunded actuarial accrued liability.

Statements Nos. 27 and 45 establish disclosure requirements that vary depending on whether the government merely participates in a pension (and other employee benefits) plan administered by another entity or includes a pension (and other employee benefits) trust fund(s). Disclosure requirements also vary for governments with a pension (and other employee benefits) trust fund based on whether the pension (and other employee benefits) plan issues separate publicly available financial statements. These disclosure requirements generally include a plan description, funding policy, pension cost components, actuarial valuation information, and trend data.

Resources accumulated for OPEB should be accounted for in a trust fund separate from resources accumulated for pension benefits.

(B) INVESTMENT TRUST FUNDS
Investment trust funds should be used by the sponsoring government to report the external part of investment pools, as required by GASB Statement No. 31, paragraph 18.

(C) PRIVATE-PURPOSE TRUST FUNDS
Private-purpose trust funds, such as one used to report escheat property, should be used to report all other trust arrangements under which principal and income benefit individuals, private organizations, or other governments.

(D) AGENCY FUNDS
Used by governments to handle cash resources held in an agent capacity, agency funds require relatively simple administration. The typical agency funds used by state and local governments include (1) tax collection funds, under which one local government collects a tax for an overlapping governmental unit and remits the amount collected less administrative charges to the recipient, and (2) payroll withholdings, under which the government collects the deductions and periodically remits them in a lump sum to the appropriate recipient.

(iv) Special Assessment Activities   Special assessment activities pertain to (1) the financing and construction of certain public improvements, such as storm sewers, which are to be paid for wholly or partly from special assessments levied against the properties benefited by such improvements, or (2) the providing of services that are normally provided to the public as general governmental functions and that would otherwise be financed by the general fund or a special revenue fund. Those services may include street lighting, street cleaning, and snow

plowing. The payment by the property owners or taxpayers receiving the benefit distinguishes these activities from activities that benefit the entire community and are paid for from general revenues or general obligation bond proceeds. Sometimes, however, a special assessment bond, which is often used to finance the special assessment improvement, also carries the additional pledge of the full faith and credit of the governmental unit.

It should be emphasized that whereas GASB Statement No. 6 eliminated the requirement to report special assessment funds in an entity's basic financial statement, accounting for special assessment activities is still an important part of governmental accounting.

Capital improvement special assessment projects have two distinct and functionally different phases. The initial phase consists of financing and constructing the project. In most cases, this period is relatively short in duration, sometimes lasting only a few months, and rarely more than a year or two. The second phase, which may start at the same time as, during, or after the initial phase, consists of collecting the assessment principal and interest levied against the benefited properties and repaying the cost of financing the construction. The second phase is usually substantially longer than the first.

There are many ways of financing a capital improvement special assessment project. Assessments may be levied and collected immediately. Funds will then be available to pay construction costs, and it will not be necessary to issue special assessment bonds. Alternatively, a project may be constructed using the proceeds from short-term borrowing. When the project is complete and the exact cost is known, special assessment bonds are issued to provide the exact amount of money, and the short-term borrowings are repaid. A third—and perhaps the most common—financing alternative is for the government to levy a special assessment for the estimated cost of the improvement, issue bonds to provide the funds, construct the improvement using the bond proceeds, and then collect the assessments over a period of years, using the collections to service the bonds.

Five basic types of transactions are associated with a capital-project type special assessment:

1. Levying the special assessment
2. Issuing special assessment bonds
3. Constructing the capital project
4. Collecting the special assessment
5. Paying the bond principal and interest

Because the special assessment fund has been eliminated for financial reporting purposes, the transactions related to special assessment activities are typically reported in the same manner and on the same basis of accounting as any other capital improvement and financing transaction. Transactions of the construction phase of the project should generally be reported in a capital projects fund, and transactions of the debt service phase should be reported in a debt service fund, if one is required.

At the time of the levy, the governmental fund should recognize the special assessments receivable with the deferred revenue; the deferred revenue should be reduced as the assessments become measurable and available in the fund financial statements.

The entry for the retirement of special assessment bonds and for the construction of the special assessment project would follow the accounting principles outlined in the discussion on capital projects. The usual entries are made for expenditures and for encumbrances, if such a system exists. At the end of the year, the revenues and expenditures should be closed to the fund balance to reflect the balance that may be expended in future periods.

Although the accounting for special assessment construction activities is quite similar to other financing and construction activities, the major issue relating to special assessment activities involves the definition of special assessment debt. Special assessment debt is often defined as those long-term obligations, secured by a lien on the assessed properties, for which the primary source of repayment is the assessments levied against the benefiting properties.

However, the nature and composition of debt associated with special assessment–related capital improvements is not always consistent with this definition. Rather, it can vary significantly from one jurisdiction to another. Capital improvements involving special assessments may be financed by debt that is

1. General obligation debt that is not secured by liens on assessed properties but nevertheless will be repaid in part by special assessment collections
2. Special assessment debt that is secured by liens on assessed properties and is also backed by the full faith and credit of the government as additional security
3. Special assessment debt that is secured by liens on assessed properties and is not backed by the full faith and credit of the government but is, however, fully or partially backed by some other type of general governmental commitment
4. Special assessment debt that is secured by liens on assessed properties, is not backed by the full faith and credit of the government, and is not backed by any other type of general governmental commitment, the government not being liable under any circumstance for the repayment of this category of debt should the property owner default

In some cases special assessment debt is payable entirely by special assessment collections from the assessed property owners; in other cases the debt may be repaid partly from special assessment collections and partly from the general resources of the government, either because the government is a property owner benefiting from the improvements or because the government has agreed to finance part of the cost of the improvement as a public benefit. The portion of special assessment debt that will be repaid directly with governmental resources is, in essence, a general obligation of the government. If the government owns property that benefits from the improvements financed by special assessment debt as in item 4 in the preceding list, or if a public benefit assessment is made against the government, the government is obligated for the public benefit portion and the amount assessed against its property, even though it has no liability for the remainder of the debt issue.

Because the special assessment debt can have various characteristics, the extent of a government's liability for debt related to a special assessment capital improvement can also vary significantly. For example, the government may be primarily liable for the debt, as in the case of a general obligation issue; it may have no liability whatsoever for special assessment debt; or it may be obligated in some manner to provide a secondary source of funds for repayment of special assessment debt in the event of default by the assessed property owners. A government is obligated in some manner for special assessment debt if (1) it is legally obligated to assume all or part of the debt in the event of default or (2) the government may take certain actions to assume secondary liability for all or part of the debt—and the government takes, or has given indications that it will take, those actions.

Stated differently, the phrase *obligated in some manner* is intended to include all situations other than those in which (1) the government is prohibited (by constitution, charter, statute, ordinance, or contract) from assuming the debt in the event of default by the property owner or (2) the government is not legally liable for assuming the debt and makes no statement, or gives no indication, that it will, or may, honor the debt in the event of default.

Debt issued to finance capital projects that will be paid wholly or partly from special assessments against benefited property owners should be reported in one of the following three ways:

1. General obligation debt that will be repaid, in part, from special assessments should be reported like any other general obligation debt.
2. Special assessment debt for which the government is obligated in some manner should be reported in the capital projects fund, except for the portion, if any, that is a direct obligation of a proprietary fund or that is expected to be repaid from operating revenues of a proprietary fund.
3. Special assessment debt for which the government is not obligated in any manner should not be displayed in the government's financial statements. However, if the government is liable for a portion of that debt (the public benefit portion, or as a property owner), that portion should be reported as previously stated.

(h) CAPITAL ASSETS REPORTING AND ACCOUNTING   The term *capital assets* includes land, improvements to land, easements, buildings, building improvements, vehicles, machinery, equipment, works of art and historical treasures, infrastructure, and all other tangible or intangible assets used in operations and that have initial useful lives beyond a single reporting period. Infrastructure assets are capital assets that are normally stationary and normally can be preserved for a significantly greater number of years than most other capital assets—for example, roads, bridges, tunnels, drainage systems, water and sewer systems, dams, and lighting systems. Buildings that are not ancillary parts of networks of infrastructure assets are not infrastructure assets.

Purchased capital assets should be reported at their acquisition costs, which should include ancillary charges needed to place the assets in their intended locations and conditions for use. Ancillary charges include costs directly attributable to asset acquisition, such as freight and transportation charges, site preparation costs, and professional fees. Donated capital assets should be reported at their fair values at their times of acquisition plus ancillary charges.

In general, capital assets should be depreciated. They should be reported net of accumulated depreciation in the statement of net assets, with accumulated depreciation reported on the face of the statement or in the notes. Capital assets not depreciated, such as land and infrastructure assets reported using the modified approach, discussed subsequently, should be reported separately if they are significant.

Capital assets, such as infrastructure, buildings and improvements, vehicles, machinery, and equipment may also be reported in greater detail. Capital assets should be depreciated over their useful lives based on their net costs less salvage values in a systematic and rational manner unless they are either inexhaustible, such as land and land improvements, or are infrastructure reported using the modified approach. Depreciation, reported in the statement of activities as discussed in the following text, may be calculated for (1) a class of assets, (2) a network of assets (all the assets that provide a particular kind of service for a government; a network of infrastructure assets may be only one infrastructure asset composed of many components—e.g., a dam composed of a concrete dam, a concrete spillway, and a series of locks), (3) a subsystem of a network (all assets that make up a similar portion or segment of a network of assets—e.g., interstate highways, state highways, and rural roads could each be a subsystem of a network of all the roads of a government), or (4) individual assets.

Eligible infrastructure assets—infrastructure assets that are part of a network or subsystem of a network—need not be depreciated but may be treated by a modified approach if both of the following are met:

1. The government manages them using an asset management system that has these characteristics:
    - It has an up-to-date inventory of eligible infrastructure assets.
    - It performs condition assessments of the eligible infrastructure assets and summarizes the results using a measurement scale. The assessments must be documented so they can be replicated and—based on sufficiently understandable and complete measurement methods so that different measurers using the same methods would reach substantially similar results—performed by the government or by contract.
    - It estimates each year the annual cost to maintain and preserve the eligible infrastructure assets at the condition level established and disclosed by the government.
2. The government documents that the eligible infrastructure assets are being preserved approximately at or above a condition level established and documented by administrative or executive policy or by legislative action and documented by the government. Adequate documentation requires professional judgment and may vary within governments for different eligible infrastructure assets. Nevertheless, documentation should include
    - Complete condition assessments of eligible infrastructure assets performed consistently at least every three years. Statistical sampling may be used, and eligible infrastructure assets may be assessed on a cyclical basis. A complete assessment on a cyclical basis requires all or statistical samples of all eligible infrastructure assets in the network or subsystem to be assessed.
    - The three most recent complete condition assessments provide reasonable assurance that the eligible infrastructure assets are being preserved approximately at or above the condition level established and disclosed by the government. The condition level could be measured either by a condition index or as the percentage of a network of infrastructure assets in good or poor condition.

All expenditures other than for additions and improvements made for eligible infrastructure assets that meet the two requirements and are not depreciated should be reported as expense in the periods incurred. Additions and improvements increase the capacity or efficiency of infrastructure assets; expenditures for them should be capitalized. A change from depreciation to the modified approach should be reported as a change in an accounting estimate.

When and if the requirements to report capital assets by the modified approach are no longer met, they should be depreciated in subsequent periods. The change should be reported as a change in accounting estimate.

Governments should in general capitalize individual or collections of works of art, historical treasures, and similar assets at their acquisition costs or fair values at the dates of acquisition or donation (estimated if necessary). They are encouraged but not required to capitalize a collection and all additions to the collection, whether donated or purchased, that meet all three of the following conditions (but collections capitalized by June 30, 1999, should remain capitalized and additions to them should be capitalized regardless of whether they meet the conditions):

1. The collection is held for public exhibition, education, or research for public service, not financial gain.
2. The collection is protected, kept unencumbered, cared for, and preserved.
3. The collection is subject to an organizational policy that requires that the proceeds from sales of collection items are used to acquire other items for collections.

Governments that receive donations of works of art, historical treasures, and similar assets should report revenues in conformity with GASB Statement No. 33. Governments should report program expense equal to the revenue reported on donated assets added to noncapitalized collections.

Capitalized collections or individual items of works of art, historical treasures, and similar assets that are exhaustible, such as exhibits whose useful lives decrease because of display or educational or research use, should be depreciated over their estimated useful lives. Depreciation is not required for collections or individual items of works of art, historical treasures, and similar assets that are inexhaustible.

(i) Methods for Calculating Depreciation   Governments may use any established depreciation method. It may be based on the estimated useful life of a class of assets, a network of assets, a subsystem, a network, or individual assets. Estimated useful lives may be obtained from general guidelines obtained from professional or industry organizations, information for comparable assets of other governments, or internal information.

A government may use a composite method, applying one rate, to calculate depreciation— for example, for similar assets or dissimilar assets of the same class, such as all the roads and bridges of the government. Depreciation is determined as the product of the total cost times the rate. The rate can be determined based on a weighted average or an unweighted average estimate of the useful lives of the assets included. Alternatively, it may be based on condition assessment or experience with the useful lives of the group of assets. It is generally used throughout the life of the group of assets, but it should be recalculated if the composition of the assets or the estimate of average useful lives changes significantly.

(ii) Subsidiary Property Records   The maintenance of subsidiary property records aids in the control of fixed assets. The subsidiary records should contain such information as classification code, date of acquisition, name and address of vendor, unit charged with custody, location, cost, fund and account from which purchased, method of acquisition, estimated life, and repair and maintenance data.

(iii) Disposal or Retirement of Capital Assets   In the disposal or retirement of a capital asset, the book value of the asset must be removed from the asset side and the gain or loss must be recorded in the statement of activities or the proprietary fund statements. If the asset is sold, the amount obtained in cash or by evidence of indebtedness should be recorded as another financing source in the appropriate governmental fund.

(iv) Impairment of Capital Assets   Governments should evaluate prominent events or changes in circumstances affecting capital assets to determine whether impairment of a capital asset has occurred. Indicators of impairment include physical damage, enactment or approval of laws or regulations or other changes in environmental factors, technological changes or evidence of obsolescence, changes in the manner or duration of use of a capital asset, and construction stoppage. A capital asset generally should be considered impaired if (1) the decline in service utility of the capital asset is large in magnitude and (2) the event or change in circumstance is outside the normal life cycle of the capital asset.

(i) REPORTING AND ACCOUNTING FOR LONG-TERM LIABILITIES   General long-term liabilities need to be clearly distinguished from fund long-term liabilities. General long-term liabilities are the unmatured principal of bonds, warrants, notes, or other forms of long-term

general obligation indebtedness. They may arise from debt issuances, lease–purchase agreements, and other commitments that are not liabilities properly reported in governmental funds. Other general long-term liabilities include capital leases, operating judgments, pensions and other postemployment benefits, special termination benefits, and landfill closure and postclosure care liabilities that are not due.

General long-term liabilities should be reported in the governmental activities column in the government-wide statement of net assets, not in governmental funds.

Typically, the general long-term debt of a state or local government is secured by the general credit and revenue-raising powers of the government rather than by the assets acquired for specific fund resources. Furthermore, just as general capital assets do not represent financial resources available for appropriation and expenditure, general long-term liabilities do not require current appropriation and expenditure of a governmental fund's current financial resources. Thus, to include it as a governmental fund liability would be misleading for management control and accountability functions for the current period.

(j) MEASUREMENT FOCUS AND BASIS OF ACCOUNTING   The accounting and financial reporting treatment applied to the government-wide financial statements and the fund financial statements is determined by its measurement focus. The measurement focus refers to what is being expressed in reporting an entity's financial performance and position. A particular measurement focus is accomplished by considering not only which resources are measured but also when the effects of transactions or events involving those resources are recognized (the basis of accounting). This principle describes the measurement focus and basis of accounting used by governments.

(i) Measurement Focus   The government-wide and proprietary funds financial statements should be prepared using the economic resources measurement focus and the accrual basis of accounting. Assets, liabilities, revenues, expenses, and gains and losses that result from exchange transactions and exchange-like transactions should be reported when the transactions occur. (In an exchange-like transaction, the resources or services exchanged, though related, may not be quite equal or the direct benefits may not be exclusively for the parties to the transactions. Nevertheless, the transactions are similar enough to exchanges to justify treating them as exchanges.) Assets, liabilities, revenues, expenses, and gains and losses that result from nonexchange transactions should be reported as discussed further on in this chapter.

(ii) Basis of Accounting   The basis of accounting determines when revenues, expenditures, expenses, and transfers—along with the related assets and liabilities—are recognized in the accounts and reported in the financial statements. Specifically, it relates to the timing of the measurements made, regardless of the measurement focus. For example, whether depreciation is recognized depends on whether expenses or expenditures are being measured rather than on whether the cash or accrual basis is used.

CASH BASIS
Under the cash basis of accounting, revenues and transfers in are not recorded in the accounts until cash is received, and expenditures or expenses and transfers out are recorded only when cash is disbursed.

The cash basis is frequently encountered, but its use is not generally accepted for any governmental unit. With the cash basis, it is difficult to compare expenditures with services rendered, because the disbursements relating to those services may be made in the fiscal period following that in which the services occurred. Also, statements prepared on a cash basis do not show financial position and results of operations on a basis that is generally accepted.

ACCRUAL BASIS

Under the accrual basis of accounting, most transactions are recorded when they occur, regardless of when cash is received or disbursed. Items not measurable until cash is received or disbursed are accounted for at that time.

The accrual basis is considered a superior method of accounting for the economic resources of any organization because it results in accounting measurements that are based on the substance of transactions and events, rather than merely on the receipt or disbursement of cash.

MODIFIED ACCRUAL BASIS

As indicated previously, the financial flows of governments, such as taxes and grants, typically do not result from a direct exchange for goods or services and thus cannot be accrued based on the completion of the earnings process and an exchange taking place. Governments have thus devised the "susceptible to accrual" concept as the criterion for determining when inflows are accruable as revenue. A revenue is susceptible to accrual when it is both measurable and available to finance current operations. An amount is measurable when the precise amount is known because the transaction is completed or when it can be accurately estimated using past experience or other available information. An amount is available to finance operations when it is (1) physically available—that is, collectible within the current period or soon enough thereafter to be used to pay liabilities of the current period, and (2) legally available—that is, authorized for expenditure in the current fiscal period and not applicable to some future period.

On the expenditure side, a government's main concern, for governmental funds at least, is to match the financial resources used with the financial resources obtained. This measure of whether current-year revenues were sufficient to pay for current-year services is referred to as *interperiod equity*. A measure of interperiod equity shows whether current-year citizens received services but shifted part of the payment burden to future-year citizens or used up previously accumulated resources. Conversely, such a measure would show whether current-year revenues were not only sufficient to pay for current-year services but also increased accumulated net resources.

This adaptation of the accrual basis to the conditions surrounding government activities and financing has been given the term *modified accrual*. Modified accrual is currently used in all governmental fund types (i.e., the general fund, special revenue funds, etc.) where the intent is to determine the extent to which provided services have been financed by current resources.

In proprietary funds the objective is to determine net income, and the accounting should be essentially the same as commercial accounting. Hence, proprietary funds use the economic resources measurement focus and the accrual basis without the need for modification described previously.

(iii) Revenue Transactions   The modified accrual basis of accounting is applied in practice for five different revenue transactions as follows:

1. Property taxes are recorded as revenue when the taxes are levied, provided that they apply to and are collected in the current period or soon enough thereafter to finance the current period's expenditures. The period after year-end generally should not exceed 60 days. The amount recorded as revenue should be net of estimated uncollectible taxes, abatements, discounts, and refunds. (Property taxes that are

measurable but not available—and hence not susceptible to accrual—should be deferred and recognized as revenue in the fiscal year they become available.)

2. Taxpayer-assessed income, gross receipts, and sales taxes should be recorded as revenues when susceptible to accrual.

3. Miscellaneous revenues such as fines and forfeits, athletic fees, and inspection charges are generally recognized when cash is received because they are usually not measurable and available until they are received.

4. Grants should be recorded when the government has an irrevocable right to the grant. If expenditure of funds is the prime factor for determining eligibility for the grant funds, revenue should be recognized when the expenditure is made.

5. Interest earned on special assessment levies may be accrued when due rather than when earned if it approximately offsets interest expenditures on special assessment indebtedness that is also recorded when due.

Escheat property, which consists of assets reverted to a governmental entity in the absence of legal claimants or heirs, should be reported in government-wide and fund financial statements generally as an asset in the governmental or proprietary fund to which the property ultimately escheats. If held for individuals, private organizations, or another government, it should be reported in a private-purpose trust fund or an agency fund, as appropriate (or in the governmental or proprietary fund in which escheat property is otherwise reported, with a corresponding liability).

Escheat revenue on escheat property reported in governmental or proprietary funds should be reduced and a governmental or proprietary fund liability reported to the extent that it is probable that escheat property will be reclaimed and paid to claimants. The liability should represent the best estimate of the amount ultimately expected to be reclaimed and paid, giving effect to such factors as previous and current trends and anticipated changes in those trends. The liability may differ from the amount specified in law to be held separately for payments to claimants.

Escheat-related transactions reported in the government-wide financial statements should be measured using the economic resources measurement focus and the accrual basis of accounting. Escheat transactions reported in private-purpose trust funds or in agency funds should be excluded from the government-wide financial statements.

(iv) Expenditure Transactions   Expenditure transactions under the modified accrual basis are treated as follows:

- If there is no explicit requirement to do otherwise, a governmental fund liability and expenditure should be accrued in the period in which the government incurs the liability. They include liabilities that normally are paid in a timely manner and in full from available financial resources, such as salaries, professional services, supplies, utilities, and travel. Unpaid, they represent claims against current financial resources and should be reported as governmental fund liabilities.

- Debt issue costs paid from debt proceeds, such as underwriter fees, should be reported as expenditures. Issue costs, such as attorneys' fees, rating agency fees, or bond insurance, paid from existing resources, should be reported as expenditures when liabilities for them are incurred.

- Inventory items may be considered expenditures either when purchased (the purchases method) or when used (the consumption method). Under either method, significant amounts of inventory at the end of a fiscal year should be reported as an asset on the balance sheet.

- Expenditures for insurance and similar services extending over more than one accounting period need not be allocated between or among accounting periods, but they may be accounted for as expenditures of the period of acquisition.
- Interest expenditures on special assessment indebtedness may be recorded when due if they are approximately offset by interest earnings on special assessment levies that are also recorded when due.
- Compensated absences, claims and judgments, special termination benefits, landfill closure and postclosure care costs, and "other obligations" should be recorded as a governmental fund liability when they are due for payment in the current period.

(v) Reporting on Nonexchange Transactions   As with a nonreciprocal transaction discussed in APB Statement No. 4, in a nonexchange transaction, a government of any level other than the federal government gives or receives financial or capital resources, not including contributed services, without directly receiving or giving equal value in exchange. Such transactions are divided into four classes:

1. *Derived tax revenues.* These result from assessments imposed by governments on exchange transactions, such as personal and corporate income taxes and retail sales taxes. Some legislation enabling such a tax provides purpose restrictions, requirements that a particular source of tax be used for a specific purpose or purposes—for example, motor fuel taxes required to be used for road and street repairs.
2. *Imposed nonexchange revenues.* These result from assessments on nongovernmental entities, including individuals, other than assessments on exchange transactions, such as property taxes, fines, and penalties, or property forfeitures, such as seizures and escheats. Such a tax is imposed on an act committed or omitted by the payor, such as property ownership or the contravention of a law or a regulation that is not an exchange. Some enabling legislation provides purpose restrictions; some also provides time requirements, specification of the periods in which the resources must be used or when their use may begin.
3. *Government-mandated nonexchange transactions.* These occur when a government, including the federal government, at one level provides resources to a government at another level and provides purpose restrictions on the recipient government established in the provider's enabling legislation. Transactions other than cash or other advances are contingent on fulfillment of certain requirements, which may include time requirements, which are called *eligibility requirements.*
4. *Voluntary nonexchange transactions.* These result from legislative or contractual agreements but are not deemed an exchange (unfunded mandates are excluded, because they are not transactions), entered into willingly by two or more parties, at least one of which is a government, such as certain grants, certain entitlements, and donations by nongovernmental entities including individuals (private donations). Providers often establish purpose restrictions and eligibility requirements and require return of the resources if the purpose restrictions or the eligibility requirements are contravened after reporting of the transaction.

Labels such as *tax, grant, contribution,* or *donation* do not necessarily indicate which of those classes nonexchange transactions belong to and therefore what principles should be applied. In addition, labels such as *fees, charges,* and *grants* do not always indicate whether exchange or nonexchange transactions are involved. Principles for reporting on nonexchange transactions depend on their substance, not merely their labels, and determining that requires analysis.

The following expense (or expenditure, for public colleges or universities) reporting principles for nonexchange transactions apply to both the accrual and the modified accrual basis, unless the transactions are not measurable or are not probable of collection. Such transactions that are not measurable should be disclosed.

Time requirements affect the timing of reporting of the transactions. The effect on the timing of reporting depends on whether a nonexchange transaction is an imposed nonexchange revenue transaction or a government-mandated or voluntary nonexchange transaction. Purpose restrictions do not affect the timing of reporting of the transactions. However, recipients should report resulting net assets, equity, or fund balance as restricted until the resources are used for the specified purpose or for as long as the provider requires the resources to be maintained intact, such as endowment principal.

Award programs commonly referred to as *reimbursement-type* or *expenditure-driven* grant programs may be either government mandated or voluntary nonexchange transactions. The provider stipulates an eligibility requirement that a recipient can qualify for resources only after incurring allowable costs under the provider's program. The provider has no liability and the recipient has no asset (receivable) until the recipient has met the eligibility requirements. Assets provided in advance should be reported as advances (assets) by providers and as deferred revenues (liabilities) by recipients until eligibility requirements have been met.

Assets should be reported from derived tax revenue transactions in the period in which the exchange transaction on which the tax is imposed occurs or in which the resources are received, whichever occurs first. Revenues net of estimated refunds and estimated uncollectible amounts should be reported in the period the assets are reported, provided that the underlying exchange transaction has occurred. Resources received in advance should be reported as deferred revenues (liabilities) until the period of the exchange.

Assets from imposed nonexchange revenue transactions should be reported in the period in which an enforceable legal claim to the assets arises or in which the assets are received, whichever occurs first. The date on which an enforceable legal claim to taxable property arises is generally specified in the enabling legislation, sometimes referred to as the *lien date*, though a lien is not formally placed on the property on that date. Others refer to it as the *assessment date*. (An enforceable legal claim by some governments arises in the period after the period for which the taxes are levied. Those governments should report assets in the same period they report revenues, as discussed next.)

Revenues from property taxes, net of estimated refunds and estimated uncollectible amounts, should be reported in the period for which the taxes are levied, even if the enforceable legal claim arises or the due date for payment occurs in a different period. All other imposed nonexchange revenues should be reported in the same period as the assets unless the enabling legislation includes time requirements. If it does, revenues should be reported in the period in which the resources are required to be used or in which use is first permitted. Resources received or reported as receivable before then should be reported as deferred revenues.

The following are the kinds of eligibility requirements for government-mandated and voluntary nonexchange transactions:

- The recipient and secondary recipients, if applicable, have the characteristics specified by the provider. For example, under a certain federal program, recipients are required to be states and secondary recipients are required to be school districts.

- Time requirements specified by enabling legislation or the provider have been met—that is, the period in which the resources are required to be sold, disbursed, or consumed or in which use is first permitted has begun, or the resources are being maintained intact, as specified by the provider.
- The provider offers resources on an "expenditure-driven" basis and the recipient has incurred allowable costs under the applicable program.
- The offer of resources by the provider in a voluntary nonexchange transaction is contingent on a specified action of the recipient—for example, to raise a specific amount of resources from third parties or to dedicate its own resources for a specified purpose, and that action has occurred.

Providers should report liabilities or decreases in assets and expenses from government-mandated or voluntary nonexchange transactions, and recipients should report receivables or decreases in liabilities and revenues, net of estimated uncollectible amounts, when all applicable eligibility requirements have been met (the need to complete purely routine requirements such as filing of claims for allowable costs under a reimbursement program or the filing of progress reports with the provider should not delay reporting of assets and revenues). Resources transmitted before the eligibility requirements are met should be reported as advances by the provider and as deferred revenue by recipients, except as indicated next for recipients of certain resources transmitted in advance. The exception does not cover transactions in which, for administrative or practical reasons, a government receives assets in the period immediately before the period the provider specifies as the one in which sale, disbursement, or consumption of resources is required or may begin.

A provider in some kinds of government-mandated and voluntary nonexchange transactions transmits assets stipulating that the resources cannot be sold, disbursed, or consumed until after a specified number of years have passed or a specific event has occurred, if ever. The recipient may nevertheless benefit from the resources in the interim—for example, by investing or exhibiting them. Examples are permanently nonexpendable additions to endowments and other trusts, term endowments, and contributions of works of art, historical treasures, and similar assets to capitalized collections. The recipient should report revenue when the resources are received if all eligibility requirements have been met. Resulting net assets, equity, or fund balance, should be reported as restricted as long as the provider's purpose restrictions or time requirements remain in effect.

If a provider in a government-mandated or voluntary nonexchange transaction does not specify time requirements, the entire award should be reported as a liability and an expense by the provider and as a receivable and revenue net of estimated uncollectible amounts by the recipients in the period in which all applicable eligibility requirements are met (applicable period). If the provider is a government, that period for both the provider and the recipients is the provider's fiscal year and begins on the first day of that year, and the entire award should be reported as of that date. But if the provider government has a biennial budgetary process, each year of the biennium should be treated as a separate applicable period. The provider and the recipients should then allocate one-half of the resources appropriated for the biennium to each applicable period, unless the provider specifies a different allocation.

Promises of assets including entities individuals voluntarily make to governments may include permanently nonexpendable additions to endowments and other trusts, term endowments, contributions of works of art and similar assets to capitalized collections, or other kinds of capital or financial assets, with or without purpose restrictions or time requirements. Recipients of such promises should report receivables and revenue net of estimated uncollectible amounts when all eligibility requirements have been met if the promise is verifiable and the resources are measurable and probable of collection. If the promise involves a stipulation (time requirement) that the resources cannot be sold, disbursed, or consumed until after a specified number of years have passed or a specific event has occurred, if ever, the recipient does not meet the time requirement until the assets have been received.

After a nonexchange transaction has been reported in the financial statements, it may become apparent that (1) if the transaction was reported as a government-mandated or voluntary nonexchange transaction, the eligibility requirements are no longer met, or (2) the recipient will not comply with the purpose restrictions within the specified time limit. If it then is probable that the provider will not provide the resources or will require the return of all or part of the resources already provided, the recipient should report a decrease in assets or an increase in liabilities and an expense, and the provider should report a decrease in liabilities or an increase in assets and a revenue for the amount involved in the period in which the returned resources become available.

A government may collect derived tax revenue or imposed nonexchange revenue on behalf of another government, the recipient, that imposed the revenue source—for example, sales tax collected by a state, part of which is a local option sales tax. The recipient should be able to reasonably estimate the accrual-basis information needed to comply with the requirements previously stated for derived tax revenue or imposed nonexchange revenue. However, if a government shares in a portion of the revenue resulting from a tax imposed by another government, it may not be able to reasonably estimate the accrual-basis information nor obtain sufficient timely information from the other government needed to comply with the previously stated requirements for derived tax revenue or imposed nonexchange revenue. If it cannot, the recipient government should report revenue for a period in the amount of cash received during the period. Cash received afterward should also be reported as revenue of the period, less amounts reported as revenue in the previous period, if reliable information is consistently available to identify the amounts that apply to the current period.

Revenue from nonexchange transactions reported on the modified accrual basis should be reported as follows:

- Recipients should report derived tax revenue in the period in which the underlying exchange transaction has occurred and the resources are available.
- Recipients should report property taxes in conformity with NCGA Interpretation No. 3, as amended.
- Recipients should report other imposed nonexchange revenue in the period in which an enforceable legal claim has arisen and the resources are available.
- Recipients should report government-mandated nonexchange transactions and voluntary nonexchange transactions in the period in which all applicable eligibility requirements have been met and the resources are available.

(k) BUDGETING, BUDGETARY CONTROL, AND BUDGETARY REPORTING ACCOUNTING

(i) Types of Operating Budgets Several types of annual operating budgets are used in contemporary public finance. Among the more common are the following:

- Line item budget
- Program budget
- Performance budget
- Zero-base budget

LINE ITEM BUDGETING

Listing the inputs for resources that each organizational unit requests for each line (or object) of expenditure is referred to as *line item budgeting*. This simple approach produces a budget that governing bodies and administrators can understand, based on their own experience. It provides for tight control over spending and is the most common local government budgeting approach, although this popularity is due primarily to tradition.

Line item budgeting is criticized because it emphasizes inputs rather than outputs, analyzes expenditures inadequately, and fragments activities among accounts that bear little relation to purposes of the government. However, all budgeting systems use objects for the buildup of costs and for execution of the budget.

Overcoming criticisms of a line item budgeting system can be accomplished by:

- Improving the budget structure to encompass all funds and organizational units in a manner that enables the total resources available to a particular organizational unit or responsibility center to be readily perceived
- Developing a level of detail for the object categories that permits adequate analysis of proposed expenditures and effective control over the actual expenditures
- Improving the presentation of historical data to stimulate the analysis of trends
- Providing a partial linking of outputs to the objects of expenditures

PROGRAM BUDGETING

Formulating expenditure requests on the basis of the services to be performed for the various programs the government provides is known as *program budgeting*. A program budget categorizes the major areas of citizen needs and the services for meeting such needs into programs. Goals and objectives are stated for each program, normally in relatively specific, quantified terms. The costs are estimated for the resources required (e.g., personnel and equipment) to accomplish the objective for each program. The governing body can then conduct a meaningful review of budget requests by adding or deleting programs or placing different emphasis on the various programs.

Program budgeting has existed for many years, but relatively few governments have adopted it, partly because line item budgeting is so familiar and comprehensible. Lack of acceptance also results from the difficulty of developing operationally useful program budgets that meet the governmental notion of accountability, that is, control of the number of employees and other expense items, rather than achievement of results in applying such resources.

The operational usefulness of program budgeting has also been questioned as a result of the complexity of the program structure, the vagueness of goals and objectives, the lack of organizational or individual responsibility for program funds that span several departments or agencies, and the inadequacy of accounting support to record direct and indirect program costs.

Nevertheless, program budgeting can be an extremely effective approach for a government willing to devote the effort. The steps that departments should take to implement the system are as follows:

- Identify programs and the reasons for their existence.
- Define the goals of programs.
- Define kinds and levels of services to be provided in light of budgetary guidelines (council- or CEO-furnished guidelines, e.g., budget priorities, budget assumptions, and budget constraints).

- Develop budget requests in terms of resources needed, based on the programs' purposes, the budgetary guidelines, the projected levels of services, and the previous years' expenditure levels for the programs.
- Submit budget requests for compilation, review, and approval.

PERFORMANCE BUDGETING

Formulating expenditure requests based on the work to be performed is the primary function of performance budgeting. It emphasizes the work or service performed, described in quantitative terms, by an organizational unit performing a given activity—for example, number of tons of waste collected by the Sanitation Department and case workload in the Department of Welfare. These performance data are used in the preparation of the annual budget as the basis for increasing or decreasing the number of personnel and the related operating expenses of the individual departments.

The development of a full-scale performance budget requires a strong budget staff, constructive participation at all levels, special accounting and reporting methods, and a substantial volume of processed statistical data. Primarily for these reasons, performance budgeting has been less widely used than line item budgeting.

The approach to developing a performance budgeting system is as follows:

- Decide on the extent to which functions and activities will be segmented into work units and services for formulation and execution of the budget.
- Define the functions in services performed by the government, and assemble them into a structure.
- Identify and assemble or develop workload and efficiency measures that relate to service categories.
- Estimate the total costs of the functions and services.
- Analyze resource needs for each service in terms of personnel, equipment, and so on.
- Formulate the first-year performance budget (for the first year, set the budget appropriations and controls at a higher level than the data indicate).
- Perform cost accounting for the functional budget category; initiate statistical reporting of the workload measures; match resources utilized to actual results.

ZERO-BASE BUDGETING

In the preparation of a budget, zero-base budgeting projects funding for services at several alternative levels, both lower and higher than the present level, and allocates funds to services based on rankings of these alternatives. It is an appropriate budgeting system for jurisdictions whose revenues are not sufficient for citizen demands and inflation-driven expenditure increases, where considerable doubt exists as to the necessity and effectiveness of existing programs and services, and where incremental budgeting processes have resulted in existing programs and their funding being taken as a given, with attention devoted to requests for new programs.

Zero-base budgeting can be used with any existing budgeting system, including line item, program, or performance budgeting. The budget format can remain unchanged.

The steps to implement zero-base budgeting are as follows:

- Define decision units—that is, activities that can be logically grouped for planning and providing each service.

- Analyze decision units to determine alternative service levels, determine the resources required to operate at alternative levels, and present this information in decision packages.
- Rank the decision packages in a priority order that reflects the perceived importance of a particular package to the community in relation to other packages.
- Present the budget to the governing body for a review of the ranking of the decision packages.

(ii) ***Budget Preparation***   The specific procedures involved in the preparation of a budget for a governmental unit are usually prescribed by state statute, local charter, or ordinance. There are, however, certain basic steps:

- Preparation of the budget calendar
- Development of preliminary forecasts of available revenues, recurring expenditures, and new programs
- Formulation and promulgation of a statement of executive budget policy to the operating departments
- Preparation and distribution of budget instructions, budget forms, and related information
- Review of departmental budget requests and supporting work sheets
- Interviews with department heads for the purpose of adjusting or approving their requests in a tentative budget
- Final assembly of the tentative budget, including fixing of revenue estimates and the required tax levy
- Presentation of the tentative budget to the legislative body and the public
- Conduction of a public hearing, with advance legal notice
- Adoption of final budget by the legislative body

Revenue and Expenditure Estimates

The property tax has been the traditional basic source of revenue for local government. The amount to be budgeted and raised is determined by subtracting the estimated nonproperty taxes and other revenues, plus the reappropriated fund balance, from budgeted expenditures. This amount, divided by the assessed valuation of taxable property within the boundaries of the governmental unit, produces the required tax rate.

Many jurisdictions have legal ceilings on the property tax rates available for general operating purposes. Additionally, taxpayer initiatives have forced governments to seek new revenue sources. Accordingly, governmental units have turned increasingly to other types of revenue, such as sales taxes; business and nonbusiness license fees; charges for services; state-collected, locally shared taxes; and grants-in-aid from the federal and state governments. Department heads, however, ordinarily have little knowledge of revenue figures. As a result, the primary responsibility for estimating these revenues usually lies with the budget officer and the chief finance officer.

Most governmental units, as a safeguard against excessive accumulation of resources, require that any unappropriated amounts carried over from a previous year be included as a source of financing in the budget of that fund for the succeeding fiscal year. Most controlling laws or ordinances provide for inclusion of the estimated surplus (fund balance) at the end of the current year, although many require that the includable surplus be the balance at the close of the last completed fiscal year.

Departmental estimates of expenditures and supporting work programs or performance data generally are prepared by the individual departments, using forms provided by the central budget agency. Expenditures are customarily classified to conform to the standard account classification of the governmental unit and thus permit comparison with actual performance in the current and prior periods.

PERSONAL SERVICES

Generally, personal services are supported by detailed schedules of proposed salaries for individual full-time employees. Nonsalaried and temporary employees are usually paid on an hourly basis, and the budget requests are normally based on the estimated number of hours of work.

Estimates of materials and supplies and other services, ordinarily quite repetitive in nature, are most often based on current experience, plus an allowance, if justified, for rising costs. Capital outlay requests are based on demonstrated need for specific items of furniture or equipment by individual departments.

In recent years, governmental units, particularly at the county, state, and federal levels, have disbursed substantial sums annually that are unlike the usual current operating expenditures. These sums include welfare or public assistance payments, contributions to other governmental units, benefit payments, and special grants. They are properly classified as "other charges." Estimates of these charges are generally based on unit costs for assistance, legislative allotments, requests from outside agencies or governmental units, and specified calculations.

In addition to departmental expenditures, the budget officer must estimate certain nondepartmental or general governmental costs not allocated to any department or organizational unit. Examples include pension costs and retirement contributions, which are not normally allocated, election costs, insurance and surety bonds, and interest on tax notes.

Although most governments still operate under laws that require the budget to be balanced precisely, an increasing number permit a surplus or contingency provision in the expenditure section of the budget. This is usually included to provide a reserve to cover unforeseen expenditures during the budget year.

The expenditure budget may be approved by a board, a commission, or other governing body before presentation to the central budget-making authority.

PRESENTATION OF THE BUDGET

To present a comprehensive picture of the proposed fund operations for a budget year, a budget document is prepared that is likely to include a budget message, summary schedules and comparative statements, detailed revenue estimates, detailed expenditure estimates, and drafts of ordinances to be enacted by the legislative body.

The contents of a budget message should set forth concisely the salient features of the proposed budget of each fund and will generally include the following: (1) a total amount showing amounts of overall increase and decrease, (2) detailed amounts and explanations of the increases and decreases, and (3) a detailed statement of the current financial status of each fund for which a budget is submitted, together with recommendations for raising the funds needed to balance the budget of each fund. It should identify the relationship of the operating budget to the capital program and capital budget, which are submitted separately.

ADOPTION OF THE BUDGET

Most states adopt the budget by the enactment of one or more statutes. Many cities require the formality of an ordinance for the adoption of the budget. In other cases, the budget is adopted by resolution of the governing body.

APPROPRIATIONS

Because appropriations constitute maximum expenditure authorizations during the fiscal year, they cannot be exceeded legally unless subsequently amended by the legislative body (although some governments permit modifications up to a prescribed limit to be made by the executive branch). Unexpended or unencumbered appropriations may lapse at the end of a fiscal year or may continue as authority for subsequent period expenditures, depending on the applicable legal provisions.

It may be necessary for the legislative agency to adopt a separate appropriation resolution or ordinance, or the adoption of the budget may include the making of appropriations for the items of expenditure included therein. Provision for the required general property tax levy is usually made at this time, either by certifying the required tax rates to the governmental unit that will bill and collect the general property tax or by enacting a tax levy ordinance or resolution.

(iii) Budget Execution   The budget execution phase entails obtaining the revenues, operating the program, and expending the money as authorized. The accounts are usually structured on the same basis on which the budget was prepared. Many governments maintain budgetary control by integration of the budgetary accounts into the general and subsidiary ledger. The entry is as follows:

Estimated revenues	$XXX
Appropriations	$XXX

If estimated revenues exceed appropriations, a credit for the excess is made to "budgetary fund balance"; if they are less the appropriations, the difference is debited to "budgetary fund balance."

Individual sources of revenues are recognized in subsidiary revenue accounts. A typical revenue ledger report is illustrated in Exhibit 34.3. This format provides for the comparison, at any date, of actual and estimated revenues from each source.

To control expenditures effectively, the individual amounts making up the total appropriations are recorded in subsidiary expenditures accounts, generally called *appropriation ledgers.* Exhibit 34.4 presents an example of an appropriation ledger. It should be noted that this format provides for recording the budget appropriation and for applying expenditures and encumbrances (see the following text) relating to the particular classification against the amount appropriated at any date.

When the managerial control purposes of integrating the budgetary accounts into the general ledger have been served, the budgetary account balances are reversed in the process of closing the books at year-end. Budgetary accounting procedures thus have no effect on the financial position or results of operations of a governmental entity.

ENCUMBRANCES

An encumbrance, which is unique to governmental accounting, is the reservation of a portion of an applicable appropriation that is made because a contract has been signed or a purchase order issued. The encumbrance is usually recorded in the accounting system to prevent

NAME OF GOVERNMENTAL UNIT
BUDGET VERSUS ACTUAL REVENUE
BY REVENUE SOURCE
FOR ACCOUNTING PERIOD JUNE 30, 20XX
FUND TYPE: THE GENERAL FUND

	REVENUES	BUDGETED	ACTUAL	VARIANCE
015	Real & per. revenue recognized			
0110	Real & per. prop rev. recognized	$ 459,449,213	$ 460,004,317	$ (555,104)
	Revenue class total	459,449,213	460,004,317	(555,104)
020	Motor vehicle & other excise			
0121	M/V taxes—current year	16,000,000	22,727,905	(6,727,905)
0122	M/V taxes—prior 2007	0	2,886,605	(2,886,605)
0123	M/V taxes—2006	0	32,051	(32,051)
0124	M/V taxes—2005	0	45,378	(45,378)
0125	M/V taxes—2004	0	85,393	(85,393)
0126	M/V taxes—2003 and prior	0	2	(2)
0127	Boat excise—cur yr 2008	15,000	40,414	(25,414)
0128	Boat excise—2007	0	155	(155)
0131	M.V. lessor surcharge	200	60	139
	Revenue class total	16,015,200	25,817,963	(9,802,764)
025	Local excise taxes			
0129	Hotel/motel room excise	13,500,000	13,580,142	(80,142)
0130	Aircraft fuel excise	12,400,000	12,960,966	(560,966)
	Revenue class total	25,900,000	26,541,108	(641,108)
030	Departmental & other revenue			
0133	Penalties & int.—prop. taxes	1,000,000	1,746,007	(746,007)
0134	Penalties & int.—M/V taxes	525,000	620,124	(95,124)
0135	Penalties & int.—sidewalk	0	115	(115)
0136	Penalties & interest/tax title	5,000,000	3,835,517	1,164,483
0138	Penalties & int./boat excise	0	3	(3)
3101	Data processing services	100	6,849	(6,749)
3103	Purchasing services	50,000	69,038	(19,038)
3104	Recording of legal instruments	150	291	(141)
3105	Registry division—fees	750,000	761,238	(11,238)
3107	City record/sale of publication	10,000	25,353	(15,353)
3108	Assessing fees	1,600	914	686
3109	Liens	400,000	373,410	26,590
3120	City clerk—fees	250,000	231,970	18,030
3130	Election—fees	12,000	10,633	1,367
3140	City council/sale of publication	200	310	(110)
3199	Other general services	35,000	18,691	16,309
3202	Police services	350,000	365,102	(15,102)
3211	Fire services	1,150,000	1,582,355	(432,355)
3221	Civil defense	40,000	161,835	(121,835)
3301	Parking facilities	3,350,000	3,775,810	(425,810)
	Revenue class total	$12,924,050	$13,585,565	$(661,515)

EXHIBIT 34.3 TYPICAL REVENUE LEDGER REPORT

NAME OF GOVERNMENTAL UNIT
BUDGET VERSUS ACTUAL EXPENDITURES
AND ENCUMBRANCES BY ACTIVITY
FOR ACCOUNTING PERIOD JUNE 30, 20XX
FUND TYPE: THE GENERAL FUND

EXPENDITURES		BUDGETED	ACTUAL [1]	VARIANCE
1100 Human services				
011 -384 -0384	Rent equity board	$1,330,977	$1,274,531	$56,446
011 -387 -0387	Elderly commission	2,534,005	2,289,549	244,456
011 -398 -0398	Physically handicapped comm	180,283	159,768	20,515
011 -503 -0503	Arts & humanities office	211,916	207,219	4,697
011 -740 -0741	Vet serv—veterans serv div	2,871,616	2,506,363	365,253
011 -740 -0742	Vet serv—veterans graves reg	158,270	146,392	11,878
011 -150 -1505	Jobs & community services	370,053	369,208	845
Activity total		7,657,120	6,953,030	704,090
1200 Public safety				
011 -211 -0211	Police department	116,850,000	117,145,704	(295,704)
011 -221 -0221	Fire department	80,594,068	79,587,423	1,006,645
011 -222 -0222	Arson commission	189,244	175,670	13,574
011 -251 -0251	Transportation—traffic div	13,755,915	13,707,890	48,025
011 -252 -0252	Licensing board	542,007	449,825	92,182
011 -251 -0253	Transportation—parking clerk	7,520,539	7,474,462	46,077
011 -261 -0260	Inspectional services dept	10,004,470	10,003,569	901
Activity total		229,456,243	228,544,543	911,700
1300 Public works				
011 -311 -0311	Public works department	64,900,000	60,281,837	4,618,163
011 -331 -0331	Snow removal	2,250,000	2,360,326	(110,326)
Activity total		67,150,000	62,642,163	4,507,837
1400 Property & development				
011 -180 -0180	RPD—general administration div	432,740	416,569	16,171
014 -180 -0183	Real property dept county	1,027,660	354,328	673,332
011 -180 -0184	RPD—buildings division	6,010,155	6,038,464	(28,309)
011 -180 -0185	RPD—property division	1,847,650	1,806,427	41,223
011 -188 -0186	PFD—code enforcement division	504,013	458,984	45,029
011 -188 -0187	PFD—administration division	4,677,365	4,697,167	(19,802)
011 -188 -0188	PFD—construction & repair div	3,063,637	2,808,266	255,371
Activity total		$17,563,220	$16,580,205	$983,015

[1] This example actual is presented as a non-GAAP budgetary basis that includes both expenditures plus encumbrances as a budgetary use of resources.

EXHIBIT 34.4   TYPICAL APPROPRIATION LEDGER REPORT

overspending the appropriation. When the goods or services are received, the expenditure is recorded and the encumbrance is reversed. The entry to record an encumbrance is as follows:

Encumbrances		$XXX
Reserve for encumbrances		$XXX

The entries that are made when the goods or services are received are as follows:

Reserve for encumbrances	$XXX
Encumbrances	$XXX
Expenditures	$XXX
Vouchers payable	$XXX

Many governments report encumbrances that are not liquidated at year-end in the same way as expenditures because the encumbrances are another use of budgetary appropriations. The total amount of encumbrances not liquidated by year-end may be considered as a reservation of the fund balance for the subsequent year's expenditures, based on the encumbered appropriation authority carried over.

ALLOTMENTS

Another way to maintain budgetary control is to use an allotment system. With an allotment system, the annual budget appropriation is divided and allotted among the months or quarters in the fiscal year. A department is not permitted to spend more than its allotment during the period.

The International City Managers' Association lists the following four purposes of an allotment system:

1. To make sure that departments plan their spending so as to have sufficient funds to carry on their programs throughout the year, avoiding year-end deficiencies and special appropriations
2. To eliminate or reduce short-term tax anticipation borrowing by making possible more accurate forecast control of cash position throughout the fiscal year
3. To keep expenditures within the limits of revenues that are actually realized, avoiding an unbalanced budget in the operation of any fund as a whole
4. To give the chief administrator control over departmental expenditures commensurate with the administrative responsibility, allowing the administrator to effect economies in particular activities as changes in workload and improvements in methods occur

INTERIM REPORTS

The last element in the budget execution process is interim financial reports. These are prepared to provide department heads, senior management, and the governing body with the information needed to monitor and control operations, demonstrate compliance with legal and budgetary limitations, anticipate changes in financial resources and requirements due to events or developments that are unknown or could not be foreseen at the time the budget was initially developed, or take appropriate corrective action. Interim reports should be prepared frequently enough to permit early detection of variances between actual and planned operations, but not so frequently as to adversely affect practicality and economy. For most governmental units, interim reports on a monthly basis are necessary for optimum results. With smaller units, a bimonthly or quarterly basis may be sufficient. With sophisticated data-processing equipment, it may be possible to automatically generate the appropriate information daily.

Governmental units should prepare interim financial reports covering the following:

- Revenues
- Expenditures
- Cash projections
- Proprietary funds
- Capital projects
- Grant programs

The form and content of these reports should reflect the government's particular circumstances and conditions.

PROJECT BUDGETS

When debt is issued to finance an entire capital project, it is usually done at the beginning of the project in an amount equal to the total estimated project cost. Accordingly, a portion of the proceeds may remain unexpended over a considerable period of time. To the maximum extent possible, these excess proceeds should be invested in interest-bearing investments. However, consideration should be given to the federal arbitrage regulations that limit the amount of interest that can be earned from investing the proceeds of a tax-exempt bond issue. If certain limits are exceeded, the bond's tax-exempt status may be lost or severe penalties could be imposed on the issuer.

Project budgets are typically established for capital projects to control costs and to guard against cost overruns. All expenditures needed to place the project in readiness—that is, indirect as well as direct costs, should be recorded against this budget. The actual expenditures, however, will probably be either less or greater than the amounts authorized. Therefore, in the absence of any legal restrictions, any unspent balance should be transferred to the appropriate sources. If the project was financed only from bond proceeds, the transfer should be to the debt service fund from which the bond issue is to be repaid. If the resources were drawn from more than one source, such as bond proceeds and current revenues, the transfer should be split among the sources in proportion to their contributions. If the expenditures were greater than authorized and a deficit exists, sufficient funds must be transferred to liquidate any commitments.

As construction of the project is completed, the costs should be recorded in the capital account as Construction in Progress and then transferred to the final building account when construction has been completed.

(iv) Proprietary Fund Budgeting   The nature of most operations financed and accounted for through proprietary funds is such that the demand for the goods or services largely determines the appropriate level of revenues and expenses. Increased demand causes a higher level of expenses to be incurred but also results in a higher level of revenues. Thus, as in commercial accounting, flexible budgets prepared for several levels of possible activity typically are better for planning, control, and evaluation purposes than are fixed budgets.

Accordingly, budgets are not typically adopted for proprietary funds. Furthermore, even when flexible budgets are adopted, they are viewed not as appropriations but as approved plans. The budgetary accounts are generally not integrated into the ledger accounts because it is considered unnecessary. Budgetary control and evaluation are achieved by comparing interim actual revenues and expenses with planned revenues and expenses at the actual level of activity for the period.

In some instances, fixed dollar budgets are adopted for proprietary funds either to meet local legal requirements or to control certain expenditures (e.g., capital outlay). In such cases, it may be appropriate to integrate budgetary accounts into the proprietary fund accounting system in a manner similar to that discussed for governmental funds.

(v) Capital Budget   Many governments also prepare a capital budget. A capital budget is a plan for capital expenditures to be incurred during a single budget year from funds subject to appropriation for projects scheduled under the capital program. The annual capital budget is adopted concurrently with the operating budgets of the governmental unit, being subject to a public hearing and the other usual legal procedures.

The capital budget should not be confused with a capital program or capital project budget. A capital program is a plan for capital expenditures to be incurred over a period of years, usually five or six years. The capital project budget represents the estimated amount to be expended on a specific project over the entire period of its construction. The capital budget authorizes the amounts to be expended on all projects during a single year. Controlling this amount is important for the proper use of available funds.

(vi) Budgetary Comparison Information   Under GASB Statement No. 34, the general fund's and the major special revenue funds' budgetary comparison schedules should present: (1) the original appropriated budgets; (2) the final appropriated budgets; and (3) actual inflows, outflows, and balances, stated on the governmental budgetary basis as discussed in NCGA Statement No. 1, paragraph 154. Separate columns may be provided comparing the original budget amounts with the actual amounts, the final budget amounts with the actual amounts, or both. The original budget is the first complete appropriated budget, which may be adjusted by reserves, transfers, allocations, supplementary appropriations, and other legally authorized legislative and executive changes made before the beginning of the reporting year. It also includes appropriation amounts automatically carried over from prior years by law. The final budget is the original budget adjusted by all legally authorized legislative and executive changes whenever signed into law or otherwise legally authorized. Governments may elect to report the budget comparison information in a budgetary comparison statement as part of the financial statements or as required supplementary disclosure as discussed in Section 34.4(m)(ii)(G), Required Supplementary Information (see Exhibit 34.5).

(l) CLASSIFICATION AND TERMINOLOGY   A common terminology and classification should be used consistently throughout the budget, the accounts, and the financial reports of each fund.

(i) Classification of Government Fund Revenues   Governmental fund revenues should be classified by fund and source. The major revenue source classifications are taxes, licenses and permits, intergovernmental revenues, charges for services, fines and forfeits, and miscellaneous. Governmental units often classify revenues by organizational units. This classification may be desirable for purposes of management control and accountability, as well as for auditing purposes, but it should supplement rather than supplant the classifications by fund and source.

(ii) Classification of Government Fund Expenditures   There are many ways to classify governmental fund expenditures in addition to the basic fund classification. Function, program, organizational unit, activity, character, and principal class of object are examples. Typically, expenditures are classified by character (current, intergovernmental, capital outlay, and/or debt service). Current expenditures are further classified by function and/or program.

	BUDGETED AMOUNTS		ACTUAL AMOUNTS (BUDGETARY BASIS) (SEE NOTE A)	VARIANCE WITH FINAL BUDGET POSITIVE (NEGATIVE)
	ORIGINAL	FINAL		
Budgetary fund balance, January 1	$3,528,750	$2,742,799	$2,742,799	$ —
Resources (inflows):				
Property taxes	52,017,833	51,853,018	51,173,436	(679,582)
Franchise taxes	4,546,209	4,528,750	4,055,505	(473,245)
Public service taxes	8,295,000	8,307,274	8,969,887	662,613
Licenses and permits	2,126,600	2,126,600	2,287,794	161,194
Fines and forfeitures	718,800	718,800	606,946	(111,854)
Charges for services	12,392,972	11,202,150	11,374,460	172,310
Grants	6,905,898	6,571,360	6,119,938	(451,422)
Sale of land	1,355,250	3,500,000	3,476,488	(23,512)
Miscellaneous	3,024,292	1,220,991	881,874	(339,117)
Interest received	1,015,945	550,000	552,325	2,325
Transfers from other funds	939,525	130,000	129,323	(677)
Amounts available for appropriation	96,867,074	93,451,742	92,370,775	(1,080,967)
Charges to appropriations (outflows)				
General government:				
Legal	665,275	663,677	632,719	30,958
Mayor, legislative, city manager	3,058,750	3,192,910	2,658,264	534,646
Finance and accounting	1,932,500	1,912,702	1,852,687	60,015
City clerk and elections	345,860	354,237	341,206	13,031
Employee relations	1,315,500	1,300,498	1,234,232	66,266
Planning and economic development	1,975,600	1,784,314	1,642,575	141,739
Public safety:				
Police	19,576,820	20,367,917	20,246,496	121,421
Fire department	9,565,280	9,559,967	9,559,967	—
Emergency medical services	2,323,171	2,470,127	2,459,866	10,261
Inspections	1,585,695	1,585,695	1,533,380	52,315
Public works:				
Public works administration	388,500	385,013	383,397	1,616
Street maintenance	2,152,750	2,233,362	2,233,362	—
Street lighting	762,750	759,832	759,832	—
Traffic operations	385,945	374,945	360,509	14,436
Mechanical maintenance	1,525,685	1,272,696	1,256,087	16,609
Engineering services:				
Engineering administration	1,170,650	1,158,023	1,158,023	—
Geographical information system	125,625	138,967	138,967	—
Health and sanitation:				
Garbage pickup	5,756,250	6,174,653	6,174,653	—
Cemetery:				
Personal services	425,000	425,000	422,562	2,438
Purchases of goods and services	299,500	299,500	283,743	15,757
Culture and recreation:				
Library	985,230	1,023,465	1,022,167	1,298
Parks and recreation	9,521,560	9,786,397	9,756,618	29,779
Community communications	552,350	558,208	510,361	47,847
Nondepartmental:				
Miscellaneous	—	259,817	259,817	—
Contingency	2,544,049	—	—	—
Transfers to other funds	2,970,256	2,163,759	2,163,759	—
Funding for school district	22,000,000	22,000,000	21,893,273	106,727
Total charges to appropriations	93,910,551	92,205,681	90,938,522	1,267,159
Budgetary fund balance, December 31	$2,956,523	$1,246,061	$1,432,253	$186,192

EXHIBIT 34.5   BUDGET-TO-ACTUAL COMPARISON SCHEDULE FOR THE GENERAL FUND IN THE BUDGET DOCUMENT FORMAT

Source: Illustration G1, GASB Statement 34.

- *Character classification*—reporting expenditures according to the physical period they are presumed to benefit. The major character classifications are: (1) current expenditures, which benefit the current fiscal period; (2) capital outlays, which are presumed to benefit both the present and future fiscal periods; and (3) debt service, which benefits prior fiscal periods as well as current and future periods. Intergovernmental expenditures is a fourth character classification that is used when one governmental unit makes expenditures to another governmental unit.
- *Function classification*—establishing groups of related activities that are aimed at accomplishing a major service or regulatory responsibility. Standard function classifications are as follows:
  - General government
  - Public safety
  - Health and welfare
  - Culture and recreation
  - Conservation of natural resources
  - Urban redevelopment and housing
  - Economic development and assistance
  - Education
  - Debt service
  - Miscellaneous
- *Program classification*—establishing groups of activities, operations, or organizational units that are directed at the attainment of specific purposes or objectives—for example, protection of property or improvement of transportation. Program classification is used by governmental units employing program budgeting.
- *Organizational unit classification*—grouping expenditures according to the governmental unit's organization structure. Organizational unit classification is essential to responsibility reporting.
- *Activity classification*—grouping expenditures according to the performance of specific activities. Activity classification is necessary for the determination of cost per unit of activity, which in turn is necessary for evaluation of economy and efficiency.
- *Object classification*—grouping expenditures according to the types of items purchased or services obtained—for example, personal services, supplies, other services, and charges. Object classifications are subdivisions of the character classification.

Excessively detailed object classifications should be avoided; they complicate the accounting procedure and are of limited use in financial management. The use of a few object classifications is sufficient in budget preparation; control emphasis should be on organizational units, functions, programs, and activities rather than on the object of expenditures.

(iii) Classifications of Other Transactions   Certain transactions, although not revenues or expenditures of an individual fund, are increases or decreases in the net assets of an individual fund. These transactions are classified as other financing sources and uses and are reported in the operating statement separately from fund revenues and expenditures. The most common other financing sources and uses are

- *Proceeds of long-term debt issues.* Such proceeds (including leases) are not recorded as fund liabilities—for example, proceeds of bonds and notes expended through the capital project or debt service funds.

- *Transfers.* These are flows of assets such as cash or goods without equivalent flows of assets in return and without a requirement for repayment. They include payments in lieu of taxes that are not payments for, and are not reasonably equivalent in value to, services provided. They should be reported in governmental funds as other financing uses in the funds making transfers and as other financing sources in the funds receiving transfers. They should be reported in proprietary funds after nonoperating revenues and expenses.

Other interfund transactions are

- *Interfund loans and advances.* These are interfund loans, which are amounts provided with a requirement for repayment. They should be reported as interfund receivables and payables. They should not be reported as other financing sources or uses in the fund financial statements. If repayment is not expected within a reasonable time, the interfund balances should be reduced and the amount not expected to be repaid should be reported as a transfer from the fund that made the loan to the fund that received the loan.

  If the advance is long term in nature and the asset will not be available to finance current operations, a governmental fund balance reserve equal to the amount of the advance should be established.
- *Interfund services provided and used.* These are sales and purchases of goods and services between funds at prices that approximate their external exchange values. They should be reported as revenues in the seller funds and expenditures or expenses in purchases funds, except that when the general fund is used to account for risk-financing activity, interfund charges to other funds should be accounted for as reimbursements.

  Amounts should be accounted for as revenues in the recipient fund and as expenditures in the disbursing fund.
- *Interfund reimbursements.* These are repayments from the funds responsible for particular expenditures or expenses to the funds that initially paid for them. They should not be displayed in the financial statements.

(iv) **Classifications of Proprietary Fund Revenues and Expenses**   Proprietary fund revenues and expenses should be classified in essentially the same manner as those of similar business organizations, functions, or activities.

(v) **Classification of Fund Equity**   Fund equity is the difference between a fund's assets and its liabilities. The equity reported in the government-wide statement of net assets is called *net assets* and should be displayed in the following three categories:

- *Invested in capital assets, net of related debt*—this category consists of capital assets, including restricted capital assets, reduced by accumulated depreciation and by any outstanding debt incurred to acquire those assets.
- *Restricted net assets*—this category reports those net assets with restrictions on their use, either by external or internal factors.
- *Unrestricted net assets*—this category consists of all other net assets.

INVESTED IN CAPITAL ASSETS, NET OF RELATED DEBT

The amount of this component equals the amount of capital assets, including restricted capital assets, net of accumulated depreciation and less the outstanding balances of bonds, mortgages, notes, or other borrowings attributable to acquiring, constructing, or improving the assets. The portion of debt attributable to significant unspent debt proceeds should be included in the same net assets component as the unspent proceeds—for example, *restricted for capital projects*.

RESTRICTED NET ASSETS

Net assets should be reported as restricted if constraints on their use are either

1. Imposed externally, by creditors, grantors, contributors, or laws or regulations of other governments.
2. Imposed by law by constitutional provisions or enabling legislation that both authorizes the government to assess, levy, charge, or otherwise mandate receipt of resources from external providers and includes a legally enforceable requirement to use the resources for only the purposes stated in the legislation.

Permanent fund's principal amounts included in restricted net assets should be presented in two components—expendable and nonexpendable. Nonexpendable net assets are those required to be retained in perpetuity.

UNRESTRICTED NET ASSETS

Unrestricted net assets are other than net assets invested in capital assets, net of related debt, and other than restricted net assets.

Net assets are often *designated* by the management of the government if they do not consider them available for general operations. Such constraints are internal and can be removed or modified by the management. They are not restricted net assets.

The equity reported in the proprietary fund statement of net assets or balance sheet should be labeled either *net assets* or *fund equity,* using the three net asset components discussed for government-wide net assets.

An important amount in the fund equity account for governmental funds is the amount available for future appropriation and expenditure (i.e., unreserved and undesignated fund balance). The equity reported in the governmental fund balance sheets should be labeled *fund balances* and should be segregated into reserved and unreserved amounts. NCGA Statement 1 notes that fund balance reserves report the portions of the fund balances that are (1) legally segregated for a specific use or (2) not available for expenditure because the underlying asset is not available for current appropriation or expenditure. Reserves are not intended as valuation allowances but merely demonstrate the current unavailability of the subject assets to pay current expenditures. Reserves and designations are established by debiting unreserved, undesignated fund balance and crediting the reserve or designation. The reserve is not established by a charge to operations.

Designations of fund balance identify tentative plans for or restrictions on the future use of financial resources. Such designations should be supported by definitive plans and approved by either the government's CEO or the legislature. Examples of such designations include the earmarking of financial resources for capital projects and contingent liabilities. Management designations for the use of resources should not be reported in the statement of net assets but may be disclosed in notes to the financial statements.

GASB Statement No. 34 requires reserved fund balances of nonmajor governmental funds to be displayed in sufficient detail to disclose the purposes of the reservations, and requires unreserved fund balances of the nonmajor governmental funds to be displayed by fund type. Management designations of fund balances should be reported as part of unreserved fund balances and disclosed as separate line items or disclosed in the financial statement notes. In response, the GASB is currently working on developing new guidance on fund balance reporting and governmental fund type definitions to mitigate the diversity in practice as it relates to this issue.

The equity reported in the fiduciary fund statement of fiduciary net assets should be labeled *net assets* but does not require net assets to be categorized into the three components. GASB Statements No. 25, "Financial Reporting for Defined Benefit Pension Plans and Note Disclosures for Defined Contribution Plans," No. 43, "Financial Reporting for Postemployment Benefit Plans Other Than Pension Plans," and No. 31, "Accounting and Financial Reporting for Certain Investments and for External Investment Pools," contain specific disclosure requirements for these types of funds.

(m) FINANCIAL REPORTING   Prior to 1979, governments traditionally prepared external financial reports by preparing financial statements for every fund maintained by the government. This often resulted in lengthy financial reports. External financial reporting has evolved to require the presentation of financial statements on a more aggregated basis and the inclusion of legally separate entities that have special relationships. Principle 12 relates to financial reporting and is discussed in the following text.

(i) The Financial Reporting Entity   GASB Statement No. 14, "The Financial Reporting Entity," establishes standards for defining and reporting on the financial reporting entity.

The statement indicates that the financial reporting entity consists of (1) the Primary Government (PG), (2) organizations for which the PG is financially accountable, and (3) other organizations that, if omitted from the reporting entity, would cause the financial statements to be misleading.

The Statement also outlines the basic criteria for including organizations in or excluding organizations from the reporting entity. All organizations for which the PG is *financially* accountable should be included in the reporting entity. Such organizations include

- The organizations that make up the PG's legal entity, and
- Component units—that is, organizations that are legally separate from the PG but
  - The PG's officials appoint a voting majority of the organization's governing board, and
  - Either the PG is able to impose its will on that organization or there is a potential for the organization to provide specific financial benefits to, or to impose specific financial burdens on, the PG.

A legally separate, tax-exempt organization should be reported as a component unit of a reporting entity if all of the following criteria are met:

- The economic resources received or held by the separate organization are entirely or almost entirely for the direct benefit of the PG, its component units, or its constituents.
- The PG (or its component units) is entitled to, or has the ability to otherwise access,[2] a majority of the economic resources received or held by the separate organization.

---

2.   *Ability to otherwise access* does not necessarily imply control over the other organization or its resources. It may be demonstrated in several ways. For example, the primary government or its component units historically may have received, directly or indirectly, a majority of

- The economic resources received or held by an individual organization that the specific PG (or its component units) is entitled to or has the ability to otherwise access, are significant to that PG.

Other organizations should be evaluated as potential component units if they are closely related to, or financially integrated[3] with, the PG. It is a matter of professional judgment to determine whether the nature and the significance of a potential component unit's relationship with the PG warrant inclusion in the reporting entity. Organizations not meeting the foregoing criteria are excluded from the reporting entity.

Reporting the inclusion of the various entities comprising the reporting entity can be done using one of two methods—blending or discrete presentation. Most component units should be included in the financial reporting entity by discrete presentation. Some component units, despite being legally separate entities, are so intertwined with the PG that, in substance, they are the same as the PG and should be "blended" with the transactions of the PG.

Certain other entities are not considered component units because the PG, while responsible for appointing the organization's board members, is not financially accountable. Such entities are considered related organizations. These related organizations as well as joint ventures and jointly governed organizations should be disclosed in the reporting entity's footnotes.

REPORTING COMPONENT UNITS

Discrete presentation of component unit financial information should be included in the statement of net assets and the statement of activities. However, information on component units that are fiduciary in nature should be included only in the fund financial statements, together with the PG's fiduciary funds. Information required by paragraph 51 of GASB Statement No. 14 about each major component unit can be given by

- Presenting each major component unit other than those that are fiduciary in nature in separate columns in the statements of net assets and activities,
- Including combining statements of major component units (with nonmajor component units aggregated in a single column) with the reporting entity's basic statements after the fund financial statements, or
- Presenting condensed financial statements in the notes.

The "aggregated total" component unit information, as discussed in paragraph 14 of GASB Statement No. 14, should be the entity totals derived from the component units' statements of net assets and activities. (Because component units that are engaged in only business-type activities are not required to prepare a statement of activities, this disclosure should be taken from the information provided in the component unit's statement of revenues, expenses, and changes in fund net assets.)

---

the economic resources provided by the organization; the organization may have previously received and honored requests to provide resources to the primary government; or the organization is a financially interrelated organization as defined by FASB Statement No. 136.

3. Financial integration may be exhibited and documented through the policies, practices, or organizational documents of either the primary government or the other organization. More than one column may be used to display components of a program revenue category. Governments may also provide more descriptive category headings to better explain the range of program revenues reported therein—for example, *operating grants, contributions,* and *restricted interest.*

If component unit information is presented in the notes, the following should be included:

- Condensed statement of net assets:
  - Total assets, distinguishing between capital assets and other assets (Amounts receivable from the PG or from other component units should be reported separately.)
  - Total liabilities, distinguishing between long-term debt and other liabilities (Amounts payable to the PG or to other component units should be reported separately.)
  - Total net assets, distinguishing between restricted, unrestricted, and amounts invested in capital assets net of related debt
- Condensed statement of activities:
  - Expenses by major functions and for depreciation expense if separately reported
  - Program revenues by type
  - Net program expense or revenue
  - Tax revenues
  - Other nontax general revenues
  - Contributions to endowments and permanent fund principal
  - Special and extraordinary items
  - Change in net assets
  - Beginning net assets
  - Ending net assets

The nature and amount of significant transactions with the PG and other component units should be reported in the notes for each component unit.

(ii) Basic Financial Statements   As discussed in Section 34.4(e)(ii), Reporting Requirements, the basic financial statements (BFS) include the financial statements of the governmental activities, the business-type activities, the aggregate discretely presented component units, each major fund, and the aggregate remaining fund information.

The two government-wide financial statements—the statement of net assets and the statement of activities—should report information about the reporting government without displaying individual funds or fund types. The statements should cover the PG and its component units, except for fiduciary funds of the PG and component units that are fiduciary in nature, which should be reported in the statements of fiduciary net assets and changes in fiduciary net assets.

The focus of the government-wide financial statements should be on the PG. The total PG and its discretely presented component units should be distinguished by separate rows and columns. A total column for the government entity and prior year information are optional.

Governmental and business-type activities of the PG should also be distinguished by separate rows and columns. (An activity need not be set out as a proprietary fund if it is not currently reported as such by the management of the government unless it is required to be reported as an enterprise fund, as discussed in Section 34.4(g)(ii)(A), Enterprise Funds.) Governmental and business-type activities are distinguished in general by their methods of financing. Governmental activities are generally financed by taxes, intergovernmental revenues, and other nonexchange-type revenues; they are generally reported in governmental funds and internal service funds. Business-type activities are financed in whole or in part by fees charged for goods or services; they are generally reported in enterprise funds.

These statements measure and report all financial and capital assets, liabilities, revenues, expenses, gains, and losses using the economic resources measurement focus and accrual basis of accounting.

Some amounts reported as interfund activity and balances in the funds should be eliminated or reclassified in aggregating information for the statement of net assets and the statement of activities.

Amounts reported in the funds as interfund receivables and payables should be eliminated in the governmental and business-type activities columns of the PG in the statement of net assets, except for the net residual amount due between the governmental and business-type activities, which should be reported as internal balances. (Amounts reported in the funds as receivable from or payable to fiduciary funds should be reported in the statement of net assets as receivable from and payable to external parties.) Internal balances should be eliminated in the total PG column.

The doubling-up effect of internal service fund activity should be eliminated in the statement of activities. Also, the effects of similar internal events, such as allocations of accounting staff salaries, which are, in effect, allocations of overhead expenses from one function to another or within a single function, should be eliminated so that the allocated expenses are reported by only the function to which they were allocated. (The effect of interfund services provided and used between functions should not be eliminated.)

(A) STATEMENT OF NET ASSETS
The statement of net assets should report all financial and capital resources and all liabilities, preferably in a format that displays *assets less liabilities equal net assets*, though the format *assets equal liabilities plus net assets* may be used. The difference between assets and liabilities should be reported as *net assets*, not *fund balance* or *equity*.

Governments are encouraged to report assets and liabilities in order of their relative liquidity (and subtotals of current assets and current liabilities may be provided). The liquidity of an asset depends on how readily it is expected to be converted to cash and whether restrictions limit the government's ability to use it. The liquidity of a liability depends on its maturity or on when cash is expected to be required to liquidate it. The liquidity of assets and liabilities may be determined by class, though individual assets or liabilities may be significantly more or less liquid than others in the same class, and some may have both current and long-term elements. Liabilities whose average maturities are more than one year should be reported by both the amount due within one year and the amount due in more than one year.

As discussed in Section 34.4(h)(v), Classification of Fund Equity, the three components of net assets are reported as (1) *invested in capital assets, net of related debt*; (2) *restricted*, distinguishing between major categories of restrictions; and (3) *unrestricted*.

Statement of Net Assets Format. The City and County of San Francisco's statement of net assets at June 30, 2006 in Exhibit 34.6 illustrates the statement of net assets format.

(B) STATEMENT OF ACTIVITIES
Some governments have a single function, program, activity, or component unit (together discussed as functions), as discussed subsequently. Most have more than one function. A government with more than one function should present a statement of activities that reports expenses by each function and revenues specifically pertaining to each function, arriving at net expense or net revenue by function. Net expense or net revenue is sometimes referred to as the *net cost* of a function or program and represents the total expenses of the function or program less its program revenues—that is, charges or fees and fines that derive directly from the function or program and grants and contributions that are restricted to the function or

program. That presentation indicates the financial burden (or benefit) each function places on the government's taxpayers and the extent to which each draws on the general revenues of the government or is self-financing. General revenues should be reported after expenses and revenues of the functions, together with contributions to term and permanent endowments, contributions to permanent fund principal, special and extraordinary items, and transfers reported separately, leading to change in net assets for the period.

CITY AND COUNTY OF SAN FRANCISCO
Statement of Net Assets
June 30, 2006
(In Thousands)

	Primary Government			Component Units	
	Governmental Activities	Business-Type Activities	Total	San Francisco Redevelopment Agency	Treasure Island Development Authority
ASSETS					
Current assets					
Deposits and investments City Treasury	$ 1,511, 936	$ 681,935	$ 2,193, 871	$ —	$ 1,268
Deposits and investments outside City Treasury	48,885	9,758	58,643	169,046	
Receivables (net of allowance for uncollectible amounts of $84,334 for the primary government):					
Property taxes and penalities	42, 586	—	42,586	—	—
Other local taxes	168,457	—	168,457	—	—
Federal and state grants and subventions	154,086	57,707	211,793	—	—
Charges for services	22,194	194,800	216,994	—	—
Interest and other	16,132	43,787	59,919	7,641	4
Loans receivable	7,025	132	7,157	12	
Capital lease receivable from primary government	—	—	—	14,460	
Due from component unit	782	—	782	—	—
Inventories	—	53,051	53,051	—	—
Deferred charges and other assets	10,423	3,531	13,954	—	—
Restricted assets:					
Deposits and investments with City Treasury	—	54,218	54, 218	—	—
Deposits and investments outside City Treasury	—	45,306	45,306	78,413	—
Grants and other receivables	—	36	36	1,206	
Total current assets	1,982,506	1,144,261	3,126,767	270,778	1,272
Noncurrent assets:					
Loans receivable (net of allowance for uncollectible amounts of $383,869 and $158,166 for the primary government and component units, respectively)	67,016	455	67,471	10,455	—
Advance to component unit	4,024	—	4,024	—	—
Capital lease receivable from primary government	—	—	—	175,636	—
Deferred charges and other assets	19,887	72,632	92,519	9,565	—
Restricted assets:					
Deposits and investments with City Treasury	—	617,925	617,925	—	—
Deposits and investments outside City Treasury	—	265,093	265,093	20,797	—
Grants and other receivables	—	61,670	61,670	—	—
Property held for resale	—	—	—	15,988	—
Capital assets:					
Land and other assets not being depreciated	504,527	1,208,435	1,712,962	119,965	—
Facilities, infrastructure, and equipment, net of depreciation	2,170,335	7,320,619	9,490,954	146,638	
Total capital assets	2,674,862	8,529,054	11,203,916	266,603	
Total noncurrent assets	2,765,789	9,546,829	12,312,618	499,044	
Total Assets	$ 4,748,295	$ 10,691,090	$ 15,439,385	$ 769,822	$ 1,272

(continued)

EXHIBIT 34.6   CITY AND COUNTY OF SAN FRANCISCO STATEMENT OF NET ASSETS (JUNE 30, 2006)

CITY AND COUNTY OF SAN FRANCISCO
Statement of Net Assets (Continued)
June 30, 2006
(In Thousands)

	Primary Government			Component Units	
	Governmental Activities	Business- Type Activities	Total	San Francisco Redevelopment Agency	Treasure Island Development Authority
LIABILITIES					
Current liabilities:					
Accounts payable	$ 178,765	$ 121,868	$ 300,633	$ 7,962	$ 3,207
Accrued payroll	64,377	46,498	110,875	—	—
Accrued vacation and sick leave pay	65,948	43,182	109,130	1,254	—
Accrued workers' compensation	41,803	35,466	77,269	—	—
Estimated claims payable	23,811	24,629	48,440	—	—
Bonds, loans, capital leases, and other payable	262,599	142,119	404,718	27,791	—
Capital lease payable to component unit	14,460	—	14,460	—	—
Accrued interest payable	7,764	18,472	26,236	27,207	—
Unearned grant and subvention revenues	2,421	—	2,421	—	—
Due to primary government	—	—	—	782	—
Internal balances	27,966	(27,966)	—	—	—
Deferred credits and other liabilities	125,111	91,061	216,172	750	664
Liabilities payable from restricted assets:					
Bonds, loans, capital leases, and other payables	—	17,393	17,393	—	—
Accrued interest payable	—	26,321	26,321	—	—
Other	—	38,331	38,331	—	—
Total current liabilities	815,025	577,374	1,392,399	65,746	3,871
Noncurrent liabilities:					
Accrued vacation and sick leave pay	66,576	36,381	102,957	1,553	—
Accrued workers' compensation	160,678	126,188	286,866	—	—
Estimated claims payable	45,666	53,154	98,820	—	—
Bonds, loans, capital leases, and other payables	1,690,096	5,438,803	7,128,899	700,942	—
Advance from primary government	—	—	—	4,024	—
Capital lease payable to component unit	175,636	—	175,636	—	—
Accrued interest payable	—	—	—	63,839	—
Deferred credits and other liabilities	—	46,757	46,757	6,117	—
Total noncurrent liabilities	2,138,652	5,701,283	7,839,935	776,475	—
Total liabilities	2,953,677	6,278,657	9,232,334	842,221	3,871
NET ASSETS					
Invested in capital assets, net of related debt	1,438,010	3,438,397	4,876,407	67,463	—
Restricted for:					
Reserve for rainy day	121,976	—	121,976	—	—
Debt service	53,076	256,055	309,131	54,821	—
Capital projects	10,589	148,957	159,546	—	—
Community development	71,207	—	71,207	—	—
Transportation Authority activities	23,727	—	23,727	—	—
Grants and other purposes	148,071	32,354	180,425	15,988	—
Unrestricted (deficit)	(72,038)	536,670	464,632	(210,671)	(2,599)
Total net assets (deficit)	$1,794,618	$4,412,433	$6,207,051	$(72,399)	$(2,599)

EXHIBIT 34.6 (*CONTINUED*)

At a minimum, the statement of activities should present

- Activities accounted for in governmental funds by function, as discussed in NCGA Statement No. 1, paragraph 112, to coincide with the level of detail required in the governmental fund statement of revenues, expenditures, and changes in fund balances.
- Activities accounted for in enterprise funds by different identifiable activities. An activity is identifiable if it has a specific revenue stream and related expenses and gains and losses that are accounted for separately.

Expenses.   All expenses should be reported by function other than special or extraordinary items, defined subsequently. At a minimum, direct expenses, those clearly identifiable with a particular function, should be presented. In addition, some or all indirect expenses of the functions may be reported by function, in columns separate from the direct expenses. A column reporting the total of direct and indirect expenses by function may also be presented. Governments that charge functions for centralized expenses need not identify and eliminate such charges. The fact that they are included in direct expenses should be disclosed in the summary of significant accounting policies.

Depreciation expense on capital assets specifically identifiable with functions should be included in their direct expenses. Depreciation expense on shared capital assets should be assigned ratably to the direct expense of the functions benefiting. Depreciation expense on capital assets that serve all functions, such as city hall, need not be included in the direct expense of the functions but may be reported as a separate line in the statement of activities or as part of the general government function. A government that reports unallocated depreciation on a separate line should state on the face of the statement of activities that this item does not include direct depreciation expenses of the various functions.

Depreciation expense for general infrastructure assets should be reported as a direct expense of the function that the government normally associates with capital outlays for and maintenance of infrastructure assets or on a separate line in the statement of activities.

Interest on long-term liabilities should generally be reported as an indirect expense on a separate line in the statement of activities, clearly indicating that it excludes direct interest expenses, if any, reported in other functions. The amount excluded should be disclosed on the face of the statement or in the notes. However, interest should be included in direct expense on borrowings essential to the creation or continuing existence of a program (e.g., a new, highly leveraged program in its early stages) if excluding it would be misleading.

Revenues.   A government obtains revenue essentially from four sources:

1.   Entities that buy, use, or directly benefit from the goods or services of programs, including the citizens of the government or others
2.   Entities outside the citizens of the government, including other governments, nongovernmental entities, or persons
3.   The government's taxpayers, regardless of whether they benefit from particular programs
4.   The government itself—for example, from investing

Type 1 is always a program revenue. Type 2 is a program revenue if restricted to specific programs. If unrestricted, type 2 is a general revenue. Type 3 is always a general revenue, even if restricted to specific programs. Type 4 is usually a general revenue.

Program revenues reduce the net cost of program function required to be financed by general revenue. They should be reported separately in three categories[4]: (1) charges for services, (2) program-specific operating grants and contributions, and (3) program-specific capital

---

4.   More than one column may be used to display components of a program revenue category. Governments may also provide more descriptive category headings to better explain the range of program revenues reported therein—for example, *operating grants, contributions,* and *restricted interest.*

grants and contributions. For identifying the function to which a program revenue pertains, the determining factor for charges for services is which function generates[5] the revenue. For grants and contributions, the determining factor is the function to which the revenues are restricted.

All other revenues are general revenues, including all taxes and all nontax revenues that do not meet the criteria to be reported as program revenues. General revenues should be reported after total net expense of the government's functions.

The following should be reported separately at the bottom of the statement of activities in the same manner as general revenues, to arrive at the all-inclusive change in net assets for the reporting period:

- Contributions to term and permanent endowments
- Contributions to permanent fund principal
- Special and extraordinary items (discussed in the following text)
- Transfers between governmental and business-type activities

Other financing sources and uses include face amount of long-term debt, issuance premium or discount, certain payments to escrow agents for bond refundings, transfers, and sales of capital assets (unless the sale meets the criteria for reporting as a special item).

Special and Extraordinary Items. Special items, significant events within the control of management that are either unusual or infrequent as defined in APB Opinion No. 30, should be reported separately at the bottom of the statement of activities. Extraordinary items, significant events that are both unusual and infrequent, should also be reported separately at the bottom of the statement of activities.

Statement of Activities Format. The City and County of San Francisco's statement of activities for the year ended June 30, 2006, illustrates the statement of activities format (see Exhibit 34.7).

(C) BASIC FINANCIAL STATEMENTS—FUND FINANCIAL STATEMENTS
Governmental Fund Balance Statement Format. Exhibit 34.8 presents the balance sheet presentation of the City and County of San Francisco's General Fund, the only major governmental fund of the City and County of San Francisco. Nonmajor funds are aggregated in an "Other" column. Note: the City and County of San Francisco's financial statements include optional partial or summarized prior year comparative information.

(D) REQUIRED RECONCILIATION TO GOVERNMENT-WIDE STATEMENTS
The amount of net assets reported for a PG in the government-wide statement of net assets usually will differ from the aggregate amount of equity reported in its fund financial position statements, because the fund statements are prepared using the funds flow measurement focus and modified accrual method (see discussion at Section 34.4(j), Measurement Focus and Basis of Accounting). There will also be differences between the changes in net assets reported in the various activity statements.

---

5.   It may sometimes be difficult or impractical to identify a specific function that generates a program revenue. For example, in many jurisdictions fines could be attributed to a public safety or a judicial function. If the source of a program revenue is not clear, the government should adopt a classification policy for assigning those revenues and apply it consistently.

CITY AND COUNTY OF SAN FRANCISCO
Statement of Activities
Year Ended June 30, 2006
(In Thousands)

| Functions/Programs | Expenses | Program Revenues | | | Net (Expense) Revenue and Changes in Net Assets | | | | |
| | | | | | Primary Government | | | Component Units | |
		Charges for Services	Operating Grants and Contributions	Capital Grants and Contributions	Govern-mental Activities	Business-Type Activities	Total	San Francisco Redevelopment Agency	Treasure Island Development Authority
Primary government:									
Government activities:									
Public protection	$ 780,642	$ 51,874	$ 103,358	$ —	$ (625,410)	$ —	$ (625,410)	$ —	$ —
Public works, transportation and commerce	272,397	113,861	30,223	37,411	(90,902)	—	(90,902)	—	—
Human welfare and neighborhood development	858,396	29,181	437,381	150	(391,684)	—	(391,684)	—	—
Community health	478,844	52,183	278,218	—	(148,443)	—	(148,443)	—	—
Culture and recreation	244,423	64,720	3,144	210,768	34,209	—	34,209	—	—
General administration and finance	167,490	55,799	2,400	—	(109,291)	—	(109,291)	—	—
General City responsibilities	49,054	31,647	5,195	—	(12,212)	—	(12,212)	—	—
Unallocated interest on long-term debt	94,923	—	—	—	(94,923)	—	(94,923)	—	—
Total governmental activities	2,946,169	399,265	859,919	248,329	(1,438,656)	—	(1,438,656)	—	—
Business-type activities:									
Airport	633,102	455,342	—	48,544	—	(129,216)	(129,216)	—	—
Transportation	695,593	210,692	122,057	58,399	—	(304,445)	(304,445)	—	—
Port	55,329	58,588	—	3,460	—	6,719	6,719	—	—
Water	213,584	201,833	—	—	—	(11,751)	(11,751)	—	—
Power	119,146	149,500	—	—	—	30,354	30,354	—	—
Hospitals	646,149	472,327	66,585	—	—	(107,237)	(107,237)	—	—
Sewer	160,701	164,703	30	—	—	4,032	4,032	—	—
Market	1,035	1,503	—	—	—	468	468	—	—
Total Business-type activities	2,524,639	1,714,488	188,672	110,403	—	(511,076)	(511,076)	—	—
Total primary government	$5,470,808	$2,113,753	$1,048,591	$ 358,732	(1,438,656)	(511,076)	(1,949,732)	—	—
Component units									
San Francisco Redevelopment Agency	$142,493	$25,345	$13,912	$—				(103,236)	—
Treasure Island Development Authority	9,188	8,208	—	—				—	(980)
Total component units	$151,661	$33,553	$13,912	$—				(103,236)	(980)
General Revenues:									
Taxes:									
Property taxes					1,016,220	—	1,106,220	65,826	—
Business taxes					323,153	—	323,153		—
Other local taxes					595,664	—	595,664	5,549	—
Interest and investment income					71,129	53,161	124,290	10,751	56
Other					56,022	272,873	328,895	9,722	527
Transfers—internal activities of primary government					(329,996)	329,996	—		
Total general revenues and transfers					1,732,192	656,030	2,388,222	91,848	583
Changes in net assets					293,536	144,954	438,490	(11,388)	(397)
Net assets (deficit)—beginning					1,501,082	4,267,479	5,768,561	(61,011)	(2,202)
Net assets (deficit)—ending					$1,794,618	$4,412,433	$6,207,051	$(72,399)	$(2,599)

EXHIBIT 34.7   CITY AND COUNTY OF SAN FRANCISCO STATEMENT OF ACTIVITIES (YEAR ENDED JUNE 30, 2006)

A government should present a summary reconciliation to the government-wide financial statements at the bottom of the fund financial statements or in a schedule. Brief explanations presented on the face of the statements often are sufficient. However, if aggregated information in the reconciliation obscures the nature of the individual elements of a particular reconciling item, a more detailed explanation should be provided in the notes to financial statements.

CITY AND COUNTY OF SAN FRANCISCO
Balance Sheet
Governmental Funds
June 30, 2006
(with comparative financial information as of June 30, 2005)
(In Thousands)

	General Fund 2006	General Fund 2005	Other Governmental Funds 2006	Other Governmental Funds 2005	Total Governmental Funds 2006	Total Governmental Funds 2005
ASSETS						
Deposits and investments with City Treasury	$ 443,102	$ 314,607	$ 1,060,891	$ 915,547	$ 1,503,993	$ 1,230,154
Deposits and investments outside City Treasury	1,465	355	22,287	45,745	23,752	46,100
Receivables:						
Property taxes and penalities	34,157	26,141	8,429	6,890	42,586	33,031
Other local taxes	154,505	148,744	13,952	12,788	168,457	161,532
Federal and state grants and subventions	63,843	61,412	90,243	89,559	154,086	150,971
Charges for services	17,117	7,416	5,077	6,832	22,194	14,248
Interest and other	6,184	4,406	9,035	3,726	15,219	8,132
Due from other funds	30,859	29,743	3,960	12,303	34,819	42,046
Due from component unit	3,848	2,416	958	959	4,806	3,375
Loans receivable (net of allowance for uncollectible amount of $383,869 in 2006; $165,336 in 2005)	—	1,174	74,041	241,728	74,041	242,902
Deferred charges and other Assets	7,243	6,797	1,729	1,570	8,972	8,367
Total assets	$762,323	$603,211	$1,290,602	$1,337,647	$2,052,925	$1,940,858
LIABILITIES AND FUND BALANCES						
Liabilities:						
Accounts payable	$ 84,710	$ 82,524	$ 88,151	$ 53,335	$ 172,861	$ 135,859
Accrued payroll	51,792	39,729	10,982	8,812	62,774	48,541
Deferred tax, grant, and subvention revenues	33,473	26,880	30,442	19,371	63,915	46,251
Due to other funds	821	1,857	61,964	77,614	62,785	79,471
Agency obligations	—	—	—	40	—	40
Deferred credits and other liabilities	130,251	144,541	94,755	267,899	225,006	412,440
Bonds, loans, capital leases, and other payables	—	—	150,000	150,000	150,000	150,000
Total liabilities	301,047	295,531	436,294	577,071	737,341	872,602
Fund balances:						
Reserved for rainy day	121,976	48,139	—	—	121,976	48,139
Reserved for assets not available for appropriation	10,710	9,031	20,202	17,683	30,912	26,714
Reserved for debt service	—	—	57,429	45,540	57,429	45,540
Reserved for encumbrances	38,159	57,762	423,120	97,920	461,279	155,682
Reserved for appropriation carryforward	124,009	36,198	294,340	549,571	418,349	585,769
Reserved for subsequent years' budgets	27,451	22,351	8,004	8,004	35,455	30,356
Unreserved (deficit), reported in:						
General fund	138,971	134,199	—	—	138,971	134,199
Special revenue funds	—	—	35,243	30,809	35,243	30,809
Capital project funds	—	—	13,662	7,193	13,662	7,193
Permanent fund	—	—	2,308	3,856	2,308	3,856
Total fund balances	461,276	307,680	854,308	760,576	1,315,584	1,068,256
Total liabilities and fund balances	$762,323	$603,211	$1,290,602	$1,337,647	$2,052,925	$1,940,858

EXHIBIT 34.8 CITY AND COUNTY OF SAN FRANCISCO BALANCE SHEET GOVERNMENTAL FUNDS

Exhibit 34.9 presents the reconciliation of the governmental funds balance sheet to the statement of net assets of the City and County of San Francisco. This reconciliation provides summarized explanations that do not describe the nature of the individual elements of these reconciling items. As a result, the City and County of San Francisco provides a more detailed explanation in the notes to financial statements.

Reconciling items between the Governmental Funds Balance Sheets and the Government-Wide Statement of Net Assets include the effects of

- Reporting capital assets at their acquisition cost and depreciating them instead of reporting capital acquisitions as expenditures when incurred.
- Adding general long-term liabilities not due and payable in the current period.
- Reducing deferred revenue for amounts not available to pay current-period expenditures.
- Adding internal service fund net asset balances.

CITY AND COUNTY OF SAN FRANCISCO
Reconciliation of the Governmental Funds Balance Sheet
to the Statement of Net Assets
June 30, 2006
(In Thousands)

Fund balances—total governmental funds	$ 1,315,584
Amounts reported for governmental activities in the statement of net assets are different because:	
Capital assets used in governmental activities are not financial resources and, therefore, are not reported in the funds.	2,670,387
Bond issue costs are not financial resources and, therefore, are not reported in the funds.	14,338
Long-term liabilities, including bonds payable, are not due and payable in the current period and therefore are not reported in the funds.	(2,161,461)
Interest on long-term debt is not accrued in the funds, but rather is recognized as an expenditure when due.	(6,459)
Because the focus of governmental funds is on short-term financing, some assets will not be available to pay for current period expenditures. Those assets are offset by deferred revenue in the funds.	164.015
Internal service funds are used by management to charge the costs of capital lease financing, fleet management, printing and mailing services, and information systems to individual funds. The assets and liabilities of internal service funds are included in governmental activities in the statement of net assets.	(201,786)
Net assets of governmental activities	$1,794,618

Exhibit 34.9 City and County of San Francisco Reconciliation of the Governmental Funds Balance Sheet to the Statement of Net Assets (June 30, 2006)

Reconciling items between the Governmental Funds Statement of Revenues, Expenditures and Changes in Fund Balances and the Government-Wide Statement of Activities include the effects of

- Reporting revenues on the accrual basis.
- Reporting annual depreciation expense instead of expenditures for capital outlays.
- Reporting long-term debt proceeds in the statement of net assets as liabilities instead of other financing sources.
- Reporting debt principal payments in the statement of net assets as reductions of liabilities instead of expenditures.
- Reporting other expenses on the accrual basis.
- Adding the net revenue or subtracting the expense of internal service funds.

For enterprise funds, (1) total enterprise fund net assets should be reconciled to the net assets of business-type activities (however, since both are on the accrual basis, there often are no differences) and (2) the total change in enterprise fund net assets should be reconciled to the change in net assets of business-type activities, provided there are differences that require reconciliation.

(E) Reporting Internal Service Fund Balances
Internal service funds are reported as proprietary funds. Nevertheless, their activities, financing goods and services for other funds, are usually more governmental than business type.

Therefore, internal service fund asset and liability balances not eliminated should normally be reported in the governmental activities column of the statement of net assets. However, if enterprise funds are the predominant or only participants in an internal service fund, that fund's residual assets and liabilities should be reported in the business-type activities column.

(F) Disclosure Requirements
Information essential to fair presentation in the financial statements that cannot be displayed on the faces of the statements should be presented in the notes to the financial statements, which should focus on the PG—its governmental activities, business-type activities, major funds, and nonmajor funds in the aggregate. Information about the government's discretely presented component units should be presented as discussed in GASB Statement No. 14, paragraph 63.

General Disclosure Requirements. Governments should provide the following added disclosures to the extent applicable in their summaries of significant accounting policies:

- A description of the government-wide financial statements, indicating that fiduciary funds and component units that are fiduciary in nature are not included
- The measurement focus and basis of accounting used in the government-wide statements
- The policy for eliminating internal activity in the statement of activities
- The policy for applying FASB pronouncements issued after November 30, 1989, to business-type activities and to enterprise funds of the PG
- The policy for capitalizing assets and for estimating their useful lives (A government that uses the modified approach for reporting eligible infrastructure assets should describe the approach.)
- A description of the kinds of transactions included in program revenues
- A description of the policy for allocating indirect expenses to functions in the statement of activities
- The government's policy for defining operating and nonoperating revenues of proprietary funds
- The government's policy on whether to first use restricted or unrestricted resources when an expense is incurred for purposes for which both restricted and unrestricted net assets are available

Required Note Disclosures about Cash and Investments. A government is subject to numerous GASB disclosures about cash and investments. The following are among the required disclosures:

- Description of how investments are valued, including the methods and significant assumptions used to estimate the fair value of investments
- The types of investments authorized by legal or contractual provisions
- The types of investments made during the period but not owned as of the balance-sheet date
- By type of investment, the investments' carrying amounts and fair values at year-end
- The custodial credit risk for uncollateralized deposits with financial institutions and investment securities that are uninsured and unregistered
- The credit and interest rate risks related to investments in debt instruments

- Terms of investments with fair values that are highly sensitive to changes in interest rates
- The concentration of credit risk for amount invested in a separate issuer (except investments held in or guaranteed by the U.S. government) when that amount is at least 5 percent of total investments
- The foreign currency risk of its investments denominated in a foreign currency
- Details about derivative instruments that are not reported at fair value
- The assignment of investment income between funds
- Specific information related to investment appreciation and income available for spending on donor-restricted endowments

Required Note Disclosures about Capital Assets and Long-Term Liabilities.   Details should be disclosed in the notes about capital assets and long-term liabilities of the PG, divided into their major classes and between those associated with governmental activities and those associated with business-type activities. Capital assets not being depreciated should be disclosed separately. The following information should be disclosed about major classes of capital assets:

- Beginning- and end-of-year balances, with accumulated depreciation presented separately from acquisition cost
- Capital acquisitions
- Sales or other dispositions
- Current depreciation expense, including the amounts charged to each of the functions in the statement of activities

Collections of works of art, historical treasures, and similar assets not capitalized should be described, and the reasons they are not capitalized should be given. Disclosures, as previously stated, should be given for collections capitalized.

The following information should be disclosed about long-term debt and other long-term liabilities, such as compensated absences, claims, and judgments:

- Beginning- and end-of-year balances
- Increases and decreases, presented separately
- The portions of each due within one year
- The governmental funds that typically have been used to liquidate other long-term liabilities

Debt service to maturity separated by principal and interest for each of the succeeding five fiscal years and in at least five-year increments thereafter for all outstanding debt should be disclosed. Interest on variable-rate debt should be calculated using the rate in effect at the financial statement date, and the terms that the interest rates change for variable-rate debt should also be disclosed.

Whether to make similar disclosures about capital assets and long-term liabilities of discretely presented component units is a matter of professional judgment, depending on each individual component unit's significance to the total of all discretely presented component units and the component unit's relationship with the PG.

Management Discussion and Analysis.   A management discussion and analysis (MD&A) is an overview and analysis of the government's financial statements. It should provide an objective and easily readable analysis of the government's financial activities based on facts, decisions, or conditions of which management is aware as of the date of the auditor's report. It should discuss the current-year results and compare them with the results of the prior year, including positive and negative aspects.

MD&A requirements are general to encourage effective reporting of only the most relevant information and to avoid boilerplate discussion. The information presented should be confined to the following eight items, including additional details pertaining to those items:

1. A brief discussion of the basic financial statements, including the relationships of the statements to each other and the significant differences in the information they provide. Analyses should be provided that help users understand why measurements and results reported in fund financial statements either reinforce information in government-wide statements or provide additional information.

2. Condensed financial information derived from government-wide financial statements comparing the current year to the prior year. Governments should present the information needed to support their analysis of financial position and results of operations.

3. An analysis of the government's overall financial position and results of operations, addressing both governmental and business-type activities as reported in the government-wide financial statements, to help users assess whether the financial position has improved or deteriorated as a result of the year's operations.

4. An analysis of balances and transactions of the individual funds, including the reasons for significant changes in fund balances or fund net assets and whether restrictions, commitments, or other limitations significantly affect the availability of fund resources for future use.

5. An analysis of significant variations between original and final budget amounts and between final budget amounts and actual budget results for the general fund or its equivalent, including any known reasons for such of those variations that are expected to have a significant effect on future services or liquidity.

6. A description of significant capital-asset and long-term debt activity during the year, including a discussion of commitments for capital expenditures, changes in credit ratings, and debt limitations that may affect financing of planned facilities or services.

7. A discussion by governments that use the modified approach to report some or all of their infrastructure assets.

8. A description of facts, decisions, or conditions of which management is aware at the date of the independent auditor's report that are expected to significantly affect financial position or results of operations—revenues, expenses, and other changes in net assets.

In addition to the information required to be presented as Required Supplementary Information (RSI) by GASB Statement Nos. 10, 25, 27, 43, 45, and other RSI required to be presented by GASB Statement No. 34 includes MD&A, budgetary comparison schedules for governmental funds, and information about infrastructure assets reported using the modified approach.

Budgetary Comparison Information.   Under GASB Statement No. 34, budgetary comparison schedules should present (1) the original appropriated budgets; (2) the final appropriated budgets; and (3) actual inflows, outflows, and balances, stated on the governmental budgetary basis as discussed in NCGA Statement No. 1, paragraph 154.

Information in a separate schedule or in notes to RSI should be provided that reconciles budgetary information to GAAP information. Notes to RSI should disclose excesses of expenditures over appropriations in individual funds presented in the budgetary comparison, as discussed in NCGA Interpretation No. 6, paragraph 4, as amended by GASB Statement No. 37. (If the budgetary comparison information is included in the basic statements, these disclosures should be in the notes to the financial statements rather than as notes to RSI.)

Modified Approach for Reporting Infrastructure.   A government with eligible infrastructure assets (for subsystems, if any) reported using the modified approach should present as RSI these schedules derived from the asset management systems:

- The assessed condition, based on assessments performed at least every three years, for at least the three most recent complete condition assessments, indicating the dates of the assessments
- The estimated annual amount calculated at the beginning of the year to maintain and preserve the assets at or above the condition level established and disclosed by the government compared with the amounts actually reported as expense for each of the past five reporting periods

The following should be disclosed with the schedules:

- The basis for the condition measurement and the measurement scale used to assess and report condition. For example, a basis could be distresses in pavement surfaces. A scale could range from zero for a failed pavement to 100 for pavement in perfect condition.
- The condition level at which the government intends to preserve its eligible infrastructure assets reported using the modified approach.
- Factors that significantly affect trends in the information reported in the schedules, including any changes in the basis for the condition measurement, the measurement scale, or the condition measurement methods used. Also to be disclosed is an estimate of the effect of a change in the condition level at which the government intends to preserve eligible infrastructure assets of the estimated annual amount to maintain and preserve the assets for the current period.

A government that has asset management systems for infrastructure assets that gather the information required under this subsection but do not use the modified approach is encouraged to disclose it as supplement information.

(iii) Comprehensive Annual Financial Report (CAFR)   Even though the GASB encourages each governmental entity to prepare a CAFR, the basic financial statement constitutes fair presentation of financial position and the respective changes in financial position and cash flows, where applicable in accordance with GAAP and could be opined on as such by an independent auditor. The statements would be suitable for inclusion in an official statement for a securities offering and for widespread distribution to users requiring less detailed information about the governmental unit's finances than is contained in the CAFR.

The CAFR differs from the BFS in the level of detail and the quantity of data presented. The additional data are *not* necessary for fair presentation of financial position or results of operation in accordance with GAAP, but they are useful and informative for certain readers of a government's financial report. Furthermore, the CAFR may be the vehicle for providing the necessary information for fulfilling the legal and other disclosure requirements of higher levels of government, bondholders, and similar groups. It is also useful in demonstrating management's stewardship responsibilities, since alongside the comparative budgets it presents in more detail the use of the available resources.

The recommended contents of the general-purpose government's CAFR include the following:

- *Introductory section*:
    - Title page. Contains the title "Comprehensive Annual Financial Report," the name of the governmental unit, the period of time covered, and the names of the principal government officials. Component units that issue separate statements should indicate the PG of which it is a component.
    - A title such as "City Hospital, a Component Unit of City, Any State" is recommended.
    - Table of contents. Identifies the presence and location of each item included in the report.
    - Transmittal letter. From the government's chief finance officer (or CEO), other information that is not included in the management's discussion and analysis that provides basic information about the government and how it operates along with other information useful in assessing the government's economic condition. The letter may include, for example, changes in financial policies; discussion of internal controls; significant elements of financial management; budget procedures and current budget; and a preview of the significant developments or changes contemplated in the coming year including economic conditions, outlook, and major initiatives.
- *Financial section*:
    - Independent auditor's report.
    - Basic financial statements. Includes all required financial statements and related notes as previously described.
    - Required supplementary information. Included when disclosure is required by the GASB.
    - Combining financial statements. Used when a governmental unit has more than one fund of a given type.
    - Individual fund financial statements and schedules. Used when this information is not provided in a separate column in a combining statement or it is desirable to present a level of detail that would be excessive for the BFS or the combining statements. Examples are detail comparisons to budgets that cannot be reflected on the combining statements, comparative data for prior years, or a demonstration of an individual fund's compliance with legal provisions.
    - Schedules necessary to demonstrate compliance. Included when such are required by state law or by a bond covenant.
    - Other schedules desired by the government. Used for reporting particular kinds of information that are spread throughout the numerous financial statements and that can be brought together and presented in greater detail than in the individual

statements, or that show the details of a specific amount or amounts presented in the BFS, the combining statements, or the individual fund financial statements.

- *Statistical section*:
  - Statistical tables cover a period of several years and contain data drawn from more than just the accounting records. Their purpose is to present social, economic, and financial trends, and the fiscal capacity of the governmental unit. The following titles indicate recommended statistical tables for a local general-purpose government's CAFR:
    - ◇ Net Assets by Components—Last Ten Fiscal Years
    - ◇ Changes in Net Assets—Last Ten Fiscal Years
    - ◇ Governmental Activities Tax Revenue by Source—Last Ten Fiscal Years
    - ◇ Changes in Fund Balances of Governmental Funds—Last Ten Fiscal Years
    - ◇ General Governmental Tax Revenues by Source—Last Ten Fiscal Years
    - ◇ Assessed Value and Estimated Actual Value of Taxable Property—Last Ten Fiscal Years
    - ◇ Property Tax Rates—Direct and Overlapping Governments—Last Ten Fiscal Years
    - ◇ Principal Taxpayers—Current Fiscal Year and Nine Years Ago
    - ◇ Property Tax Levies and Collections—Last Ten Fiscal Years
    - ◇ Ratios of Outstanding Debt by Type—Last Ten Fiscal Years
    - ◇ Direct and Overlapping Governmental Activities Debt
    - ◇ Legal Debt Margin Information Last Ten Fiscal Years
    - ◇ Pledged-Revenue Coverage Last Ten Fiscal Years
    - ◇ Demographic and Economic Statistics—Last Ten Fiscal Years
    - ◇ Principal Employers—Current Fiscal Year and Nine Years Ago
    - ◇ Full-time Equivalent City Government Employees by Function—Last Ten Fiscal Years
    - ◇ Operating Indicators by Function—Last Ten Fiscal Years
    - ◇ Capital Asset Statistics by Function—Last Ten Fiscal Years
- *Single Audit section*:
  Although it is not a required part of a CAFR, some governments include in a separate section the information, including auditor's reports, required by the Single Audit Act Amendments of 1996.

(iv) Certificate of Achievement Program   Governmental units may submit their CAFRs to the GFOA (180 North Michigan Avenue, Chicago, IL 60601) for evaluation in accordance with the standards of financial reporting established by the GASB and the GFOA. If the report substantially adheres to these standards, the government is awarded a Certificate of Achievement for Excellence in Financial Reporting. The certificate is valid for only one year. It may be reproduced in the government's annual report and should be included in the subsequent year's CAFR. Annually, the GFOA publishes a list of the governments that hold valid certificates.

Many governments endeavor to obtain the certificate. They realize that credit rating agencies and others familiar with governmental accounting and financial reporting recognize that governments holding a certificate typically maintain complete financial records and effectively report their financial information to permit detailed analyses to be performed. This characteristic can improve the government's bond rating.

(v) Popular Reports   Governments also prepare popular reports to communicate with persons who are neither interested in a complete set of financial statements nor able to review them. Popular reports are also called *condensed summary data*.

There are three types of popular reports. The first is an aggregation of the data from the financial statements that disregards the distinction among fund types and the different bases of accounting and presents the data as if all the assets, liabilities, equities, revenues, and expenditures (expenses) pertained not to the fund types but to the government as a whole. This results in a presentation similar to that made by corporations and their subsidiaries. In such cases, the government usually eliminates significant interfund transactions before arriving at totals.

The second approach is to visually present the entity's financial information—for example, by using pie charts or bar graphs. A common presentation is to present one pie to show the composition of revenue by cutting the pie into slices with each slice representing a major revenue source. The size of the slice would reflect the magnitude of the respective revenue source. Similar pie charts can be used to show the major categories of expenditures, the major categories of assets, and the major categories of liabilities.

The third approach is to issue consolidated government-wide financial statements. Such a consolidated approach replaces the funds and government-wide financial statements by a single "fund" that is used to report the financial position and results of operations of the entire oversight unit or reporting entity. Intragovernmental transactions are eliminated in the consolidation process, and a single basis of accounting (normally accrual) is used for all transactions.

Consolidated financial statements typically include a balance sheet and an operating statement. Because the accrual basis of accounting is normally used, capital assets are reported and depreciated. In addition, long-term obligations are reported.

34.5 BASIC FINANCIAL STATEMENTS REQUIRED FOR SPECIAL-PURPOSE GOVERNMENTS

Special-purpose governments are legally separate entities that are component units or other stand-alone governments, which are legally separate government organizations that (1) do not have separately elected governing bodies and (2) are not component units, plus joint ventures, jointly governed organizations, and pools.

A special-purpose government that is engaged in more than one governmental program or that has both governmental and business-type activities should meet the reporting requirements for governments that are not special-purpose governments. A special-purpose government is engaged in more than one governmental program if it budgets, manages, or accounts for its activities as multiple programs, such as a school district that provides regular instruction, special instruction, vocational education, and adult education.

(a) REPORTING BY SPECIAL-PURPOSE GOVERNMENTS ENGAGED IN GOVERNMENTAL ACTIVITIES   A special-purpose government engaged in a single governmental activity, such as some cemetery districts, levee districts, assessment districts, and drainage districts, may combine its government-wide financial statements and its fund financial statements in a columnar format that reconciles line items of fund financial information to government-wide information in a separate column on the face of the financial statements rather than at the bottom of the statements or in an accompanying schedule. Otherwise, the special-purpose government may present separate government-wide and fund financial statements and may present its government-wide statement of activities in a different format. For example, it may be

presented in a single column that reports expenses first followed by revenues by major sources. The difference, net revenue or expense, should be followed by contributions to permanent and term endowments, special and extraordinary items, transfers, and beginning and ending net assets.

(b) REPORTING BY SPECIAL-PURPOSE GOVERNMENTS ENGAGED ONLY IN BUSINESS-TYPE ACTIVITIES   A government engaged in only business-type activities should present only the financial statement required for enterprise funds, as follows:

- MD&A
- Enterprise fund financial statements:
  - Statement of net assets or balance sheet
  - Statement of revenues, expenses, and changes in fund net assets
  - Statement of cash flows
  - Notes to financial statements
- Applicable RSI other than MD&A

(c) REPORTING BY SPECIAL-PURPOSE GOVERNMENTS ENGAGED ONLY IN FIDUCIARY ACTIVITIES   A special-purpose government engaged in only fiduciary activities should present only the financial statement required for fiduciary funds, as follows:

- MD&A
- Statement of fiduciary net assets
- Statement of changes in fiduciary net assets
- Notes to financial statements

A Public Employees Retirement System (PERS) is a special-purpose government that administers one or more defined benefit pension plans and may also administer other kinds of employee benefit plans, such as defined contribution, deferred compensation, and postemployment health care plans. One that administers more than one defined benefit pension plan or postemployment health care plan should present combining financial statements for all such plans and, if applicable, required schedules for each plan. (A PERS that administers one or more agent multiple-employer plans applies these requirements at the aggregate plan level.) It should (1) present a separate column for each plan on the statement of fiduciary net assets and the statement of changes in fiduciary net assets or (2) present combining statements for the plans as part of the basic financial statements.

34.6 ACCOUNTING PRINCIPLES AND PRACTICES—PUBLIC COLLEGES AND UNIVERSITIES

Public colleges and universities should apply the principles discussed in this chapter. The primary guidance for public colleges and universities is GASB Statement No. 35, "Basic Financial Statements—and Management's Discussion and Analysis—for Public Colleges and Universities."

34.7 AUDITS OF GOVERNMENTAL UNITS

Audits of governmental units with financial statements can be performed in accordance with

- Generally accepted auditing standards (GAAS)
- *Government Auditing Standards* (the Yellow Book)

- The Single Audit Act Amendments of 1996 and Office of Management and Budget (OMB) Circular A-133

When performing an audit in accordance with GAAS, the guidance contained in the *AICPA Professional Standards* is followed. This is the same guidance followed by auditors when auditing the financial statement of commercial entities and typically results in the issuance of an opinion of the financial statements and perhaps a management letter. *Government Auditing Standards,* also known as the *Yellow Book* (U.S. Comptroller General, rev. 2007), establishes the concept of an expanded scope audit that includes both financial and compliance features. According to the Yellow Book, a financial audit can help determine whether

- The financial statements of an audited entity present fairly the financial position and the results of financial operations in accordance with GAAP.
- The entity has complied with laws and regulations that may have a material effect on the financial statements.

The Yellow Book incorporates the AICPA Professional Standards previously mentioned and sets forth additional standards and requirements, including the following six:

1. A review is to be made of compliance with applicable laws and regulations, as set forth in federal audit guides and other applicable reference sources.
2. The auditor reports on the entity's compliance with laws, regulations, contracts, and grant agreements and shall also include material instances of noncompliance and instances or indications of noncompliance or fraud found during or in connection with the audit.
3. The auditors shall report on their consideration of the entity's internal control over financial reporting as part of the financial audit.
   They shall identify as a minimum:
   a. Scope of auditor's work in obtaining an understanding of the internal control over financial reporting.
   b. The significant deficiencies including separate identification of material weaknesses identified as a result of the auditor's work.
4. Auditors performing government audits are required to obtain 80 hours of continuing education that directly enhance the auditor's professional proficiency to perform audits and/or attestation engagements every two years, of which 24 hours should be directly related to government. At least 20 of the 80 hours should be completed in each year of the two-year period.
5. Audit organizations performing government audits are required to establish an internal quality control system and participate in an external quality control review program.
6. The auditor communicates certain information related to the conduct of the audit to the audit committee or to the individuals with whom they have contracted for the audit.

(a) THE SINGLE AUDIT ACT AMENDMENTS OF 1996   Many state and local governments are required to obtain a periodic audit of the federal funds they receive, usually once a year. The audits are normally performed by an independent certified public accountant (CPA) or public accountant, or, in some states, by the government's internal audit personnel. A few jurisdictions have an independently elected or appointed auditor who conducts the audit. Single audits are conducted in accordance with GAAS, *Government Auditing Standards,* and the Single Audit Amendments Act of 1996 and its implementing regulation OMB Circular A-133, including its Compliance Supplement. These requirements have been updated for fiscal years beginning on or after July 1, 1997, by the Single Audit Amendments Act of 1996 (the Act).

The objectives of the Act are

- To improve the financial management of state and local governments with respect to federal financial assistance programs through improved auditing
- To establish uniform requirements for audits of federal financial assistance provided to state and local governments
- To promote the efficient and effective use of audit resources
- To ensure that federal departments and agencies, to the maximum extent practicable, rely on and use audit work performed pursuant to the requirements of the Single Audit Act

Though the single audit builds on the annual financial statement audit currently required by most state and larger local governments, it places substantial additional emphasis on the consideration and testing of internal controls and the testing of compliance with laws and regulations.

The Single Audit Act and OMB Circular A-133 require the auditor to determine whether

- The financial statements of the government, department, agency, or establishment present fairly its financial position and the results of operations in conformity with GAAP.
- The organization has internal and other control structures to provide reasonable assurance that it is managing federal financial assistance programs in compliance with applicable laws and regulations.
- The organization has complied with laws and regulations that may have a material effect on its financial statements and on each major federal financial assistance program.

Nonfederal entities that expend $500,000 or more in a year in federal awards are subject to a single audit unless they elect (if qualified) to have a program-specific audit conducted. If less than $500,000 is expended, the entity is exempt from federal audit requirements for that year, but records must be retained for review or audit by, for example, the General Accountability Office (GAO).

The Single Audit Act provides auditors with guidance on the focus of the audit by defining a level of audit work based on the concept of "major" federal programs. OMB Circular A-133 §___.520 provides specific guidance on how to determine what are major federal programs and outlines the three steps required in identifying "major" federal programs. These three steps are as follows:

1. Identify "Type A" and "Type B" programs. For most small- and medium-sized governments, a Type A program is defined as the larger of $300,000 or 3 percent of the total federal *expenditures* for all federal programs. For larger governments whose total federal expenditures exceed $100 million, a major federal financial assistance program is based on a sliding scale. All programs that are not categorized as a Type A program are "Type B" programs.

2. Identify "Low Risk Type A" programs by assessing all Type A programs. Typically, a Low Risk Type A program must have been audited as a "major" program within the last two years and must have no audit findings as defined in §___.510(a). All

Type A programs which are not low risk are high risk and must be audited as a major program.

3. Identify "High Risk Type B" programs if there are one or more Low Risk Type A programs identified. Auditors have two options in assessing risks in Type B programs:

   o *Option one.* Complete a risk assessment for *all* Type B programs that are greater than the Type B floor amount, then classify as major programs one-half of the Type B programs greater than the floor amount identified as high risk with a cap in the number of major programs at the number of Low Risk Type A programs.

   o *Option two.* Complete a risk assessment for *some* of the Type B programs that are greater than the Type B floor amount until the same number high-risk Type B programs are greater than or equal to the number of Low Risk Type A programs.

If a federal grantor agency formally designates a program to be major, this program must also be audited in addition to the major programs identified in previous steps.

The Single Audit Act and OMB Circular A-133 require the auditor to issue the following reports:

- A report on the audit of the basic financial statements of the entity as a whole, or the department, agency, or establishment covered by the audit
- A report on compliance and internal control based on an audit of the basic financial statements
- A report on compliance and internal control over compliance applicable to each major federal award program

In a single audit, the report on the audit of the basic financial statements is typically expanded to include an opinion on the fair presentation of the supplementary schedule of expenditures of federal awards in relation to the audited financial statements.

(b) OTHER CONSIDERATIONS   Most government officials and auditors of governmental units realize that a good audit should furnish more than an opinion on the financial statements. Other services a governmental auditor can provide are pinpointing the key information upon which decisions should be based and contributing to the presentation of this information in a manner that facilitates decision making; uncovering deficiencies in the accounting system and providing suggestions for improving the efficiency and effectiveness of the system; and obtaining and presenting information useful for marketing securities.

Obtaining a qualified auditor, particularly one who can provide the additional services described above, requires that the selection be based on qualifications and experience, and not solely cost. The National Intergovernmental Audit Forum, in its handbook *How to Avoid a Substandard Audit: Suggestions for Procuring an Audit*, indicates that

> Public entities should never select auditors without considering five basic elements of an effective audit procurement process:
>
> planning (determining what needs to be done and when),
> fostering competition by soliciting proposals (writing a clear and direct solicitation document and disseminating it widely),

technically evaluating proposals and qualifications (authorizing a committee of knowledgeable persons to evaluate the ability of prospective auditors to effectively carry out the audit),

preparing a written agreement (documenting the expectations of both the entity and the auditor), and

monitoring the auditor's performance (periodically reviewing the progress of that performance).

This handbook provides detailed information about the five elements of procurement previously listed as well as the use of audit committees in a government environment, along with other useful information about the auditor procurement process.

(i) Governmental Rotation of Auditors   The automatic rotation of auditors after a given number of years is a common practice in many governments; however, it is not always beneficial. Many governments have followed this policy, believing that they will (1) receive a fresh outlook from the audit, (2) spread the work among several firms, and (3) encourage lower fees. What the Government Accountability Office (GAO) found in its November 2003 *Required Study on the Potential Effects of Mandatory Audit Firm Rotation* is that mandatory audit firm rotation may not be the most efficient way to strengthen auditor independence and improve auditing quality, considering the additional financial costs and the loss of institutional knowledge. Automatic rotation may be harmful in that it could deprive the government of the extensive knowledge of the entity developed by the current auditor. It may also impair auditing effectiveness, given that a new auditor may need to spend considerable time learning the government's system. The government may actually incur more cost since its personnel will need to spend time explaining the organization, systems, and data to the new auditors, and the new auditors will need to spend valuable time reviewing information that is already part of the previous auditor's workpapers. Although a government should continuously monitor its auditor's performance to ensure that the service obtained is commensurate with the cost, the entity should normally change auditors only because of dissatisfaction with services and not for the sake of receiving a lower fee.

(ii) Audit Committees   In recent years, governments have started establishing audit committees similar to those in the private sector. Some appropriate tasks for a local government's audit committee include the following:

- Reviewing significant financial information for reliability, timeliness, clarity, appropriateness of disclosure, and compliance with GAAP and legal requirements
- Ascertaining that internal controls are appropriately designed and functioning effectively
- Evaluating independent audit firms and selecting one for approval by the appropriate body
- Overseeing the scope and performance of the independent audit function
- Ensuring that the auditors' recommendations for improvements in internal controls and operating methods receive management's attention and are implemented on a timely basis
- Providing an effective communications link between the auditors and the full governing board

The primary benefit of an audit committee is in assisting the full governing board to fulfill its responsibilities for the presentation of financial information about the governmental unit. There are also secondary benefits: The other parties involved in the issuance of financial information—management and independent and internal auditors—can perform their roles more effectively if an audit committee is involved in the process. Finally, there are advantages for the government's constituencies—in particular, the taxpayers and bondholders.

34.8 CONCLUDING REMARKS

Governmental accounting and reporting is changing and expanding at an increasing rapid rate. Coupling this with public accountability issues, the federal government's pressure for increased audit quality, and the penalties for substandard audit performance results in increasing levels of audit risk. Government audits, often considered low-risk engagements by many, are quickly becoming areas of extremely high risk. Auditing professionals need to recognize the risk associated with government engagements now and in the future before incurring severe penalties or embarrassment. The technical issues involved in government auditing are on a par with those in the commercial environment, but auditors have much less experience and less technical guidance to fall back on.

Dealing with these technical issues requires well-trained, highly motivated individuals and can no longer be left to less experienced members of the audit team. Dealing with the *real* issues governments are facing (e.g., infrastructure, terrorism, prison overcrowding, drugs, etc.) requires even more from the individuals in the profession. Like it or not, government accounting and reporting is being thrust into the spotlight and will be scrutinized by a multitude of individuals and groups. It is imperative that individuals in the industry realize this fact and begin now to prepare for the future.

34.9 SOURCES AND SUGGESTED REFERENCES

American Institute of Certified Public Accountants, "AICPA Audit and Accounting Guide: State and Local Governments." AICPA, New York, 2007.

———. "AICPA Audit and Accounting Guide: Government Auditing Standards and Circular A-133 Audits." AICPA, New York, 2007.

———. "AICPA Professional Standards." AICPA, New York, 2007.

City and County of San Francisco, California, "Comprehensive Annual Financial Report For the Year Ended June 30, 2006," 2006.

Financial Accounting Standards Board, "Classification of Short-Term Obligations Expected to Be Refinanced," Statement of Financial Accounting Standards No. 6. FASB, Stamford, CT, 1975.

———. "Accounting for Leases," Statement of Financial Accounting Standards Board No. 13. FASB, Stamford, CT, 1975.

———. "Objectives of Financial Reporting by Nonbusiness Organizations," Statement of Financial Accounting Concepts No. 4. FASB, Stamford, CT, 1980.

General Accounting Office, "Government Auditing Standards, July 2007 Revision." GAO, Washington, DC, 2003.

———. "Required Study on the Potential Effects of Mandatory Audit Firm Rotation." GAO, Washington, DC, 2003.

Governmental Accounting Standards Board, "Basic Financial Statements—and Management's Discussion and Analysis—for State and Local Governments." GASB Statement No. 34. GASB, Norwalk, CT, 1999.

———. "Codification of Governmental Accounting and Financial Reporting Standards." GASB, Norwalk, CT, 2007.

Government Finance Officers Association, "Governmental Accounting, Auditing and Financial Reporting." GFOA, Chicago, IL, 2005. (Study guide available)

Ives, Martin, "The Governmental Accounting Standards Board: Factors Influencing Its Operation and Initial Technical Agenda," *Government Accounting Journal*, Spring 2002, vol. 49 (1), pp. 22–27.

Mead, Dean Michael, "What You Should Know About Your Local Government's Finances." GASB, Norwalk, CT, 2007.

Office of Management and Budget, "Circular No. A-133, Audits of States, Local Governments, and Non-Profit Organizations, June 27, 2003 Revision." Office of Management and Budget, Washington, DC, 2003.

APPENDIX 34A PRONOUNCEMENTS ON STATE AND LOCAL GOVERNMENT ACCOUNTING

	Government Accounting Standard Board	Effective Date
Statement No. 1	Authoritative Status of NCGA Pronouncements and AICPA Industry Audit Guide	On issuance (7/84)
Statement No. 2	Financial Reporting of Deferred Compensation Plans Adopted under the Provisions of Internal Revenue Code Section 457	Superseded by GASB Statement No. 32
Statement No. 3	Deposits with Financial Institutions, Investments (including Repurchase Agreements), and Reverse Repurchase Agreements	Financial statements for periods ending after 2/15/86
Statement No. 4	Applicability of FASB Statement No. 87, "Employers' Accounting for Pensions," to State and Local Governmental Employers	Superseded by GASB Statement No. 27
Statement No. 5	Disclosure of Pension Information by Public Employee Retirement Systems and State and Local Governmental Employers	Financial reports issued for fiscal years beginning after 12/15/86
Statement No. 6	Accounting and Financial Reporting for Special Assessments	Financial statements for periods beginning after 6/15/87
Statement No. 7	Advance Refundings Resulting in Defeasance of Debt	Fiscal periods beginning after 12/15/86
Statement No. 8	Applicability of FASB Statement No. 93, "Recognition of Depreciation by Not-for-Profit Organizations," to Certain State and Local Governmental Entities	Superseded by GASB Statement No. 35
Statement No. 9	Reporting Cash Flows of Proprietary and Nonexpendable Trust Funds and Governmental Entries that Use Proprietary Fund Accounting	Fiscal periods beginning after 12/15/89
Statement No. 10	Accounting and Financial Reporting for Risk Financing and Related Insurance Issues	Pools—Fiscal periods beginning after 6/15/90
		Other—Fiscal periods beginning after 6/15/93

(Continued)

APPENDIX 34A *(Continued)*

Government Accounting Standard Board		Effective Date
Statement No. 11	Measurement Focus and Basis of Accounting—Governmental Fund Operating Statements	Fiscal periods beginning after 6/15/94
Statement No. 12	Disclosure of Information on Postemployment Benefits Other than Pension Benefits by State and Local Governmental Employers	Fiscal periods beginning after 6/15/90
Statement No. 13	Accounting for Operating Leases with Scheduled Rent Increases	Leases with terms beginning after 6/30/90
Statement No. 14	The Financial Reporting Entity	Fiscal periods beginning after 12/15/92
Statement No. 15	Governmental College and University Accounting and Financial Reporting Models	Superseded by GASB Statement No. 35
Statement No. 16	Accounting for Compensated Absences	Fiscal periods beginning after 6/15/93
Statement No. 17	Measurement Focus and Basis of Accounting—Governmental Fund Operating Statements: Amendment of Effective Dates of GASB Statement No. 11 and Related Statements	Immediately
Statement No. 18	Accounting for Municipal Solid Waste Landfill Closure and Postclosure Care Costs	Fiscal periods beginning after 6/15/93
Statement No. 19	Governmental College and University Omnibus Statement—An Amendment of GASB Statements No. 10 and 15	Superseded by GASB Statement No. 35
Statement No. 20	Accounting and Financial Reporting for Proprietary Funds and Other Governmental Entities That Use Proprietary Fund Accounting	Fiscal periods beginning after 12/15/93
Statement No. 21	Accounting for Escheat Property	Fiscal periods beginning after 12/15/94
Statement No. 22	Accounting for Taxpayer-Assessed Tax Revenues in Governmental Funds	Superseded by GASB Statement No. 33
Statement No. 23	Accounting and Financial Reporting for Refundings of Debt Reported by Proprietary Activities	Fiscal periods beginning after 6/15/94

	Government Accounting Standard Board	Effective Date
Statement No. 24	Accounting and Financial Reporting for Certain Grants and Other Financial Assistance	Fiscal periods beginning after 6/15/95
Statement No. 25	Financial Reporting for Defined Benefit Pension Plans and Note Disclosures for Defined Contribution Plans	Fiscal periods beginning after 6/15/96, Statement No. 26 must be implemented simultaneously
Statement No. 26	Financial Reporting for Postemployment Healthcare Plans Administered by Defined Benefit Pension Plans	Fiscal periods beginning after 6/15/96, Statement No. 25 must be implemented simultaneously
Statement No. 27	Accounting for Pensions by State and Local Governmental Employers	Fiscal periods beginning after 6/15/97
Statement No. 28	Accounting and Financial Reporting for Securities Lending Transactions	Fiscal periods beginning after 12/15/95
Statement No. 29	The Use of Not-for-Profit Accounting and Financial Reporting Principles by Governmental Entities	Fiscal periods beginning after 12/15/95
Statement No. 30	Risk Financing Omnibus	Fiscal periods beginning after 6/15/96
Statement No. 31	Accounting and Financial Reporting for Certain Investments and for External Investment Pools	Fiscal periods beginning after 6/15/96
Statement No. 32	Accounting and Financial Reporting for Internal Revenue Code Section 457 Deferred Compensation Plans	Earlier of fiscal periods beginning after 12/31/98, or amendment of the IRC Section 457 Plan
Statement No. 33	Accounting and Financial Reporting for Nonexchange Transactions	Periods beginning after 6/15/00
Statement No. 34	Basic Financial Statements—and Management's Discussion and Analysis—for State and Local Governments	[6]

(Continued)

---

6. In three phases, based on total annual revenue in the first fiscal year ending after June 15, 1999; Phase 1—governments with total annual revenues of $100 million or more, fiscal periods beginning after June 15, 2001; Phase 2—governments with total annual revenues of $10 million or more but less than $100 million, fiscal periods beginning after June 15, 2002; Phase 3—governments with total annual revenues of less than $10 million, fiscal periods beginning after June 15, 2003.

APPENDIX 34A *(Continued)*

	Government Accounting Standard Board	Effective Date
Statement No. 35	Basic Financial Statements—and Management's Discussion and Analysis— for Public Colleges and Universities: Amendment of GASB Statement No. 34	[7]
Statement No. 36	Recipient Reporting for Certain Shared Nonexchange Revenues: Amendment of GASB Statement No. 33	Simultaneously with Statement No. 33
Statement No. 37	Basic Financial Statements—and Management's Discussion and Analysis— for State and Local Governments: Omnibus	[8]
Statement No. 38	Certain Financial Statement Note Disclosures and Discussion and Analysis— for State and Local Governments	[9]
Statement No. 39	Determining Whether Certain Organizations Are Component Units	Periods beginning after 6/15/03
Statement No. 40	Deposit and Investment Risk Disclosures— An Amendment of GASB Statement No. 3	Periods beginning after 6/15/04
Statement No. 41	Budgetary Comparison Schedules— Perspective Differences—An Amendment of GASB Statement No. 34	Simultaneously with Statement No. 34
Statement No. 42	Accounting and Financial Reporting for Impairment of Capital Assets and for Insurance Recoveries	Periods beginning after 12/15/04

---

7.   Public institutions that are components of another reporting entity should implement the Statement no later than the same year as their primary government. For public institutions that are not components of another reporting entity, this Statement is effective in the three phases indicated in the preceding footnote.

8.   Simultaneously with Statement No. 34. For governments that implemented Statement No. 34 before Statement No. 37 was issued, Statement No. 37 is effective for periods beginning after June 15, 2000.

9.   In three phases, based on total annual revenue in the first fiscal year ending after June 15, 1999: Phase 1—governments with total annual revenues of $100 million or more, fiscal periods beginning after June 15, 2001; Phase 2—governments with total annual revenues of $10 million or more but less than $100 million, fiscal periods beginning after June 15, 2002; Phase 3—governments with total annual revenues of less than $10 million, fiscal periods beginning after June 15, 2003.

	Government Accounting Standard Board	Effective Date
Statement No. 43	Financial Reporting for Postemployment Benefit Plans Other than Pension Plans	Effective in three phases based on a government's total annual revenues in the first fiscal year ending after 6/15/99: for periods beginning after 12/15/05, 2006, and 2007
Statement No. 44	Economic Condition Reporting—The Statistical Section—An Amendment of NCGA Statement 1	Statistical sections prepared for periods beginning after 6/15/05
Statement No. 45	Accounting and Financial Reporting by Employers for Postemployment Benefits Other than Pensions	Effective in three phases based on a government's total annual revenues in the first fiscal year ending after 6/15/99: for periods beginning after 12/15/06, 2007, and 2008
Statement No. 46	Net Assets Restricted by Enabling Legislation—An Amendment of GASB Statement No. 34	Periods beginning after 6/15/05
Statement No. 47	Accounting for Termination Benefits	For termination benefits provided through an existing defined benefit OPEB plan, the provisions of this Statement should be implemented simultaneously with the requirements of Statement 45. For all other termination benefits, this Statement is effective for financial statements for periods beginning after 6/15/05.
Statement No. 48	Sales and Pledges of Receivables and Future Revenues and Intra-Entity Transfers of Assets and Future Revenues	Periods beginning after 12/15/06
Statement No. 49	Accounting and Financial Reporting for Pollution Remediation Obligations	Periods beginning after 12/15/07

(Continued)

APPENDIX 34A *(Continued)*

Government Accounting Standard Board		Effective Date
Statement No. 50	Pension Disclosures—An Amendment of GASB Statements No. 25 and No. 27	Periods beginning after 6/15/07, except for requirements related to the use of the entry age actuarial cost method for the purpose of reporting a surrogate funded status and funding progress of plans that use the aggregate actuarial cost method, which are effective for periods for which the financial statements and RSI contain information resulting from actuarial valuations as of 6/15/07, or later.
Statement No. 51	Accounting and Financial Reporting for Intangible Assets	Periods beginning after 6/15/09
Statement No. 52	Land and Other Real Estate Held as Investments by Endowments	Periods beginning after 6/15/08
Interpretation No. 1	Demand Bonds Issued by State and Local Governmental Entities	Fiscal periods ending after 6/15/85
Interpretation No. 2	Disclosure of Conduit Debt Obligations	Fiscal periods beginning after 12/15/95
Interpretation No. 3	Financial Reporting for Reverse Repurchase Agreements	Fiscal periods beginning after 12/15/95
Interpretation No. 4	Accounting and Financial Reporting for Capitalization Contributions to Public Entity Risk Pools	Fiscal periods beginning after 6/15/96
Interpretation No. 5	Property Tax Revenue Recognition in Governmental Funds	Fiscal periods beginning after 6/15/00
Interpretation No. 6	Recognition and Measurement of Certain Liabilities and Expenditures in Governmental Fund Financial Statements: an Interpretation of NCGA Statements 1, 4, and 5, NCGA Interpretation 8, and GASB Statement Nos. 10, 16, and 18	Simultaneously with Statement No. 34
Technical Bulletin No. 84–1	Purpose and Scope of GASB Technical Bulletins and Procedures for Issuance	None

	Government Accounting Standard Board	Effective Date
Technical Bulletin No. 2003–1	Disclosure Requirements for Derivatives Not Reported at Fair Value on the Statement of Net Assets	Financial statements issued after 6/15/03
Technical Bulletin No. 2004–1	Tobacco Settlement Recognition and Financial Reporting Entity Issues	6/15/04
Technical Bulletin No. 2004–2	Recognition of Pension and Other Postemployment Benefit Expenditures/ Expense and Liabilities by Cost-Sharing Employers	Pension transactions: for financial statements for periods ending after 12/15/04. OPEB transactions: applied simultaneously with the requirements of Statement 45
Technical Bulletin No. 2006–1	Accounting and Financial Reporting by Employers and OPEB Plans for Payments from the Federal Government Pursuant to the Retiree Drug Subsidy Provisions of Medicare Part D	On issuance (6/06) except for the portions of answers pertaining specifically to measurement, recognition, or required supplementary information requirements of Statement No. 43 or Statement No. 45. Those provisions should be applied simultaneously with the implementation of Statement 43 or Statement 45.
Concepts Statement No. 1	Objectives of Financial Reporting	None
Concepts Statement No. 2	Reporting Service Efforts and Accomplishments	None
Concepts Statement No. 3	Communication Methods in General Purpose External Financial Reports That Contain Basic Financial Statements	None
Concepts Statement No. 4	Elements of Financial Statements	None

	National Council on Government Accounting	Effective Date
Statement 1	Governmental Accounting and Financial Reporting Principles	Fiscal years ending after 6/30/80
Statement 2	Grant, Entitlement, and Shared Revenue Accounting by State and Local Governments	Fiscal years ending after 6/30/80
Statement 3	Defining the Governmental Reporting Entity	Issued 12/81; superseded by GASB Statement No. 14
Statement 4	Accounting and Financial Reporting Principles for Claims and Judgments and Compensated Absences	Fiscal years beginning after 12/31/82; 20 extended indefinitely by NCGAS 11
Statement 5	Accounting and Financial Reporting Principles for Lease Agreements of State and Local Governments	Fiscal years beginning after 6/30/83
Interpretation 1	GAAFR and the AICPA Audit Guide (Superseded)	Issued 4/86; superseded by NCGAS 1
Interpretation 2	Segment Information for Enterprise Funds	Issued 6/80; superseded by GASB Statement No. 34
Interpretation 3	Revenue Recognition—Property Taxes	Fiscal years beginning after 9/30/81
Interpretation 4	Accounting and Financial Reporting for Public Employee Retirement Systems and Pension Trust Funds (Superseded)	Fiscal years beginning after 6/15/82; superseded by NCGAS 6 and repealed by NCGAI 8
Interpretation 5	Authoritative Status of Governmental Accounting, Auditing, and Financial Reporting	Issued 3/82; superseded by GASB Statement No. 34
Interpretation 6	Notes to the Financial Statements Disclosure	Prospectively for fiscal years beginning after 12/31/82
Interpretation 7	Clarification as to the Application of the Criteria in NCGA Statement, "Defining the Governmental Reporting Entity"	Issued 9/83; superseded by GASB Statement No. 14
Interpretation 8	Certain Pension Matters	Fiscal years ending after 12/31/83
Interpretation 9	Certain Fund Classifications and Balance Sheet Accounts	Fiscal years ending after 6/30/84
Interpretation 10	State and Local Government Budgetary Reporting	Fiscal years ending after 6/30/84
Interpretation 11	Claim and Judgment Transactions for Governmental Funds	Issued 4/84; superseded by GASB Statement No. 10

FAIR VALUE MEASUREMENTS[†] (NEW)

Mark L. Zyla, CPA/ABV, CFA, ASA
Acuitas, Inc.

---

†   This chapter is adapted from the book *Fair Value Measurements: Practical Guidance and Implementation* (John Wiley & Sons, 2010), and is used with permission.

43A.1   INTRODUCTION

Prior to the implementation of Financial Accounting Standards Board (FASB) ASC 820, "Fair Value Measurements" (SFAS No.157), the application of fair value measurements in financial reporting varied among some three dozen or more of the pronouncements that required a fair value measurement. Since these statements referred to different accounting concepts, over time inconsistencies developed in applying fair value measurements under different statements. After the introduction of FASB ASC 805, "Business Combinations" (SFAS No.141), and FASB ASC 350-10-35, "Intangibles—Goodwill and Other—Subsequent Measure" (SFAS No.142), one of the most common applications of fair value measurements was in business combinations and the subsequent testing of goodwill and other long-lived assets. These statements required the fair value measurements of assets that were not readily measurable by the marketplace. Preparers of financial statements were concerned about measuring fair value in the absence of quoted market prices. FASB ASC 820, "Fair Value Measurements" (SFAS No. 157), establishes a framework for applying fair value measurements. The FASB believes that the implementation of FASB ASC 820, "Fair Value Measurements" (SFAS No. 157), will provide improvements to financial reporting as a result of increased consistency, reliability, and comparability.

FASB ASC 820 (SFAS No. 157) provides one standard definition of fair value that is required to be used throughout financial reporting. *Fair value* is defined as:

> the price that would be received to sell an asset or paid to transfer a liability in an orderly transaction between market participants at the measurement date.[1]

---

1.   Financial Accounting Standards Board, Statement on Financial Accounting Standard No. 157, "Fair Value Measurements," paragraph 5.

FASB ASC 820 provides consistent guidance as to measuring fair value in financial reporting.

43A.2 REGULATORY AND ECONOMIC BACKGROUND

(a) ECONOMIC ENVIRONMENT   Fair value has been a standard of measurement in financial reporting for some time, but recently the trend has been toward an increased use of fair value accounting. There are a number of factors that are influencing the trend from traditional rules-based accounting under U.S. generally accepted accounting principles (GAAP) to more principles-based measurements that include more fair value measurements in financial reporting. U.S. GAAP has been more historically cost based in its measurements than other international accounting standards, which are more principles based and have more of an emphasis on fair value accounting. However, certain economic trends are causing this emphasis in U.S. GAAP to shift toward a principles base of accounting with increased use of fair value measurement.

The first trend is the change in the general economic environment that has impacted the relevance of accounting measurements in certain transactions. Over the past 25 years, the overall enterprise value of many entities has become comprised of more intellectual property and other intangible assets, which have not been effectively measured under traditional GAAP. In addition, the entire global economy has become much more intertwined. Where once only the Fortune 1000 were able to conduct business internationally, the advent of the Internet has allowed any size company to establish an international presence.

The globalization of the economy is an important factor in the trend toward more fair value measurements in accounting. Globalization has increased the need for standardization in accounting across national boundaries. Consequently, the FASB and the International Accounting Standards Board (IASB) have begun a project to converge U.S. GAAP into international accounting standards. IASB accounting standards are considered principles based, which requires more fair value measurements. As the accounting standards converge, U.S. GAAP will require more fair value accounting measures.

The economy in the United States has undergone tremendous changes over the past 25 years. The first significant change in the economic environment during that time was brought on by the commercialization of the Internet, which resulted in what some call the "information revolution." The result was that a significant portion of the economy in the United States shifted from bricks-and-mortar–based businesses to ones that are more information based. These advances in information and technology that resulted from the commercialization of the Internet have had a tremendous impact on not only the U.S. economy but the global economy as a whole. By 2008, intangible assets comprised 75 percent of the S&P 500's market capitalization versus 17 percent in 1975.

The change in the economic environment both from the commercialization of the Internet and the globalization of the economy has created some challenges for the accounting profession. The relevance of financial statements became a concern of the FASB, as an increasing percentage of many companies' values are generated by intangible assets. The increasing transnational nature of business has created a need for consistent accounting standards across national boundaries as well.

(b) INCREASED REGULATION

(i) Sarbanes-Oxley and the PCAOB   The Sarbanes-Oxley Act of 2002 greatly increased governmental supervision and regulation of Securities and Exchange Commission (SEC) registered public companies. The Act also provided for the creation of the Public Company Accounting Oversight Board (PCAOB) to oversee auditors of public companies. The legislation is far-reaching and has had a significant impact on public companies that fall within its jurisdiction. The goal of Sarbanes-Oxley is to increase transparency in financial reporting. Some of the more significant provisions of the Act are:

- When financial statements are a part of an SEC report, a certification by the company's CEO and CFO must be included that states the report complies with securities laws and information contained within it fairly represents the financial condition and results of operations in all material respects.
- Management is also required to furnish a report about the adequacy and effectiveness of internal controls supporting financial reporting.
- Public companies must disclose material changes in their financial condition or operations on a "rapid and current basis" and not defer disclosure until their next quarterly or annual report.
- Financial statements must include all material correcting adjustments identified by outside auditors.
- Material off-balance-sheet transactions must be disclosed.
- Pro-forma financial statements must not contain material untrue facts or have omissions.
- Audit committees must have independent members and must disclose whether any members are considered financial experts.
- The CEO and CFO must disgorge any compensation or trading profits resulting from restated financial statements.
- Company loans to insiders are prohibited.
- Auditors are restricted in the nonaudit services they can provide.
- The lead audit partner and review partner for public company audits must be changed every five years.
- Public company personnel are prohibited from fraudulently influencing, coercing, manipulating, or misleading auditors.
- Criminal and civil sanctions are enhanced.[2]

(ii) Principles-Based Accounting   The increased level of detail and complexity found in rules-based U.S. GAAP led to concerns about the quality and transparency in financial reporting. An alternative principles-based approach to standards setting was seen by many as a solution to transparency problems. A principles-based approach to accounting standards setting would provide less interpretive and implementation guidance, encouraging an increased use of professional judgment in applying the standards. A principles-based system would have few exceptions and avoid situations where technical compliance could be achieved while evading the intent of the standard.

The Sarbanes-Oxley Act of 2002 required the SEC to conduct a study on the adoption of a principles-based approach to accounting standards. The SEC study recommended that the FASB should:

- Issue objectives-oriented standards
- Address deficiencies in the conceptual framework

---

2.   Corporate Department at Orrick, Herrington & Sutcliffe LLP, "Securities Law Update: Summary and Analysis of Sarbanes-Oxley Act of 2002," August 2002, www.orrick.com (accessed 6/23/09).

- Be the only organization setting authoritative accounting guidance in the United States
- Continue its convergence efforts
- Redefine the GAAP hierarchy
- Increase access to authoritative literature
- Perform a comprehensive review to identify standards that are more rules-based and adopt a transition plan to change those standards

The FASB agreed with the SEC recommendations and had already begun addressing some of the recommendations through a number of initiatives.[3,4] The Fair Value Measurement Project was one of these initiatives, and it eventually led to the issuance of FASB ASC 820, "Fair Value Measurements and Disclosure" (SFAS No. 157).

(c) FASB AND IASB CONVERGENCE   One issue that the FASB has heard from users of financial statements is that they are concerned about the differences in financial reporting in different countries. With the increase in the global economy and increasingly transnational businesses, investors and other users of financial statements require one standard set of financial information. "The FASB is committed to working toward the goal of producing high-quality reporting standards worldwide to support healthy global capital markets."[5] To address this concern, the FASB and the IASB have "acknowledged their commitment to the development of high-quality, compatible accounting standards that could be used for both domestic and cross-border financial reporting."[6]

Both the FASB and the IASB recognize that the users of financial statements would benefit from consistent standards. As a result, the two organizations have jointly created a framework to bring U.S. accounting standards in line with international standards. The Securities and Exchange Commission in the United States, which has been given the authority for setting standards by the U.S. Congress, has strongly signaled its support of the convergence of U.S. GAAP into international standards.

(i) The Norwalk Conversion Project   In September 2002 at a meeting in Norwalk, Connecticut, the FASB and IASB agreed to "use their best efforts to a) make their existing financial reporting standards fully compatible as soon as is practicable and b) to coordinate their work program to ensure that once achieved, compatibility is maintained."[7] The project has become known as the Convergence Project.

In February 2006, the FASB and the IASB issued what has become known as a Memorandum of Understanding (MoU). The MoU was based on three joint principles:

1. Convergence of accounting standards can best be achieved through the development of high-quality, common standards over time.
2. Trying to eliminate the differences between two standards that are in need of significant improvement is not the best use of the FASB's and the IASB's resources;

3.   Financial Accounting Standards Board, "FASB Response to SEC Study on the Adoption of a Principles-Based Accounting System, July 2004, www.fasb.org/response_sec_study_july2004.pdf (accessed 6/23/2009).
4.   Financial Accounting Standards Board, "Project Updates: Principles-Based Approach to U.S. Standard Setting," www.fasb.org/jsp/FASB/FASBContent_C/ProjectUpdatePage (accessed 6/23/2009).
5.   www.fasb.org/news/nr102902.shtml.
6.   FASB-IASB, Memorandum of Understanding, "The Norwalk Agreement," www.fasb.org.
7.   Id.

instead a new common standard should be developed that improves the financial information reported to investors.

3. Serving the needs of investors means that the FASB and IASB should seek convergence by replacing standards in need of improvement with jointly developed new standards.[8]

A goal set by the International Accounting Standards Committee Foundation (IASCF) is one of *harmonization*. Harmonization will be achieved when companies around the world follow one set of international accounting standards (IAS). In a step toward convergence, the FASB and the IASB have agreed to a time line for harmonization of GAAP into IFRS, the international standards. Part of the time line includes issuance of joint standards on an ongoing basis. The revised statement FASB ASC 805, "Business Combinations" (SFAS No. 141(R)), is the first statement that was jointly issued by both bodies.

(ii) Joint Projects   In April 2008 the FASB and IASB updated the Memorandum of Understanding to include milestones for 11 major joint projects in the convergence process. In seven of the 11 joint projects, the Boards either have issued common standards or are in the process of issuing common standards. The first common standard is "Business Combinations," issued by the FASB as FASB ASC 805 (SFAS 141(R)) and by the IASB as Revised IFRS 3. Another of the projects is "Fair Value Measurements," which was issued by the FASB in 2007 as FASB ASC 820, "Fair Value Measurements" (SFAS No. 157). The IASB issued a discussion paper in 2007, and after deliberations plans to issue a standard similar to Fair Value Measurements.

(d) SEC INITIATIVES   The U.S. Congress has given authority for establishing accounting standards to the Securities and Exchange Commission. The SEC in turn has delegated the authority for standards setting to the FASB. Even so, the SEC still maintains active influence over the setting of standards through its oversight of public company registrants. Therefore, the SEC has tremendous influence in the trend toward increased usage of fair value accounting.

As a result of the progress achieved by the FASB and IASB toward convergence, the SEC no longer requires reconciliation of IFRS-based financial statements to U.S. GAAP for non-U.S. companies registered to issue securities in the United States. The European Commission has a similar proposal for the European Union to eliminate the requirement to reconcile U.S. GAAP financial information to IFRS, or to provide other compensating disclosures when U.S. companies have securities registered in European capital markets.[9] These developments effectively create two sets of somewhat similar but not completely convergent standards in the United States and Europe. While these changes provide flexibility to foreign companies, domestic corporations registered in the United States and the European Union currently do not have the ability to choose between the two sets of standards.

(i) SEC Releases   As an example of this influence, the SEC has issued two releases that provide additional incentives for international companies reporting in the United States to report using international accounting standards.

---

8.   www.fasb.org/intl/MOU_09-11-08.pd.
9.   "Completing the February 2006 Memorandum of Understanding: A Progress Report and Timetable for Completion," September 2008, IASB, www.iasb.org (accessed April 21, 2009).

In July 2007, the SEC issued Release No. 33-8818, "Acceptance from Foreign Private Issuers of Financial Statements Prepared in Accordance with International Financial Reporting Standards without Reconciliation to U.S. GAAP." In conjunction with this release, the SEC voted unanimously to eliminate the reconciliation requirement for foreign issuers. The impact of this release is that in effect there is a dual reporting system in the United States. Foreign registrants can report under IFRS, whereas domestic companies are required to report under U.S. GAAP. On November 29, 2007, the EU commissioner called on the body to eliminate the reconciliation requirement for U.S. GAAP issuers.

In response to concerns by U.S.-based registrants, in August 2007 the SEC issued Release No. 33-8831, "Concept Release on Allowing U.S. Issuers to Prepare Financial Statements in Accordance with International Financial Reporting Standards." This release explores allowing U.S.-based registrants to choose between current U.S. GAAP and international accounting standards. Supporting this release, the AICPA issued a comment letter recommending that the SEC allow U.S. firms to report using IFRS. The impact on financial reporting of these two releases is that the SEC is furthering the emphasis on fair value accounting in U.S. financial reporting of publicly traded entities. The SEC is also demonstrating its support for the FASB and IASB's Convergence Project.

The SEC also recently proposed a "Roadmap" to the convergence of U.S. accounting standards with international accounting standards. The Roadmap identifies several milestones that if achieved would require U.S. issuers to use IFRS by the year 2014. The SEC recently extended the comment period for the Roadmap.[10]

(e) INTERNATIONAL AUDIT NETWORKS   One group advancing convergence of accounting standards is the accounting profession itself. The changes in the global economic environment have created challenges for the accounting profession. The Global Public Policy Symposium is a series of conferences that has an "objective . . . to provide an international forum for the exchange of views on how we can collaborate in maintaining healthy global capital markets and contribute to improvements in the quality, reliability, and accessibility of financial and other information that stakeholders need."[11] The symposia are sponsored by the six largest accounting and auditing firms, BDO International, Ernst & Young, Grant Thornton International, KPMG International, Deloitte, and PricewaterhouseCoopers. At one of the initial symposia, the CEOs of these international accounting firms issued a white paper, "Global Capital Markets and the Global Economy: A Vision from the CEOs of the International Audit Networks." The intent of the paper was to provide and "stimulate a robust dialogue about how global financial reporting and public company auditing procedures could better serve capital markets around the world."[12] The paper concluded that the accounting profession "has undergone a fundamental change from being largely self-regulated to regulated around the globe." That change will require that "all stakeholders look to the future and consider how investors' needs will change in a rapidly evolving global market."[13]

After the issuance of the initial white paper, the symposia conducted a series of roundtable discussions in various financial centers around the world. The discussions were held on a

---

10.   Regulatory Actions Proposed Rules 2009 First Quarter 33-9905, February 3, 2009, www.sec.gov.
11.   "Global Capital Markets and the Global Economy: A Vision from the CEOs of the International Audit Networks," November 2006, www.globalpublicpolicysymposium.com.
12.   Id.
13.   Id.

not-for-attribution basis in order to promote open discussion. In January 2008, a fourth symposium was held and another white paper was issued, titled "Global Dialogue with Capital Market Stakeholders: A Report from the CEOs of the International Audit Networks," summarizing the results from the roundtables. The discussions were organized into four categories in the white paper:

1. Global convergence: the need for consistency in financial reporting
2. Audit quality: the need for continuous improvement and greater consistency
3. Prevention and detection: a two-pronged approach to fraud
4. The future of business reporting[14]

One of the most discussed topics at the roundtables was the global convergence of accounting standards. The report concluded that there is "near-universal support" for one set of high-quality international accounting standards. However, the report noted that there is not a consensus about what the single set of standards should be or how it should be established. Nonetheless, the users of global capital markets agree that a goal of the accounting profession should be one set of common standards.

While agreeing on the need for one set of common accounting standards across international boundaries, the participants also had other concerns related to these standards. The participants expressed a strong preference for principles-based rather than rules-based standards. The view was that rules-based standards create a level of complexity that is not necessary for proper financial reporting.

Another theme resulting from the roundtable discussions related to accounting standards was the concern that there is not currently sufficient education and training in place to support the convergence to one set of standards. There was an acknowledgment that the convergence of standards would require a tremendous amount of training at every level for both preparers and auditors. Participants also noted that there will have to be a significant change in technology, particularly software that is currently used in financial reporting.

A final issue related to one set of auditing standards was that the participants recognized that small and medium-sized businesses have unique needs and may have more difficulty transitioning to international standards (IFRS). In order for convergence to be effective, the process has to include consideration of the needs of businesses of this size.

43A.3 FASB ASC 820, "FAIR VALUE MEASUREMENTS AND DISCLOSURES" (SFAS NO. 157)

(a) WHAT IT DOES AND DOES NOT DO   The FASB issued FASB ASC 820, "Fair Value Measurements and Disclosures" (SFAS No. 157), to clarify the concepts related to its measurement. According to the FASB, the purpose of the statement is to define fair value, establish a framework for measuring fair value, and expand disclosure about fair value measurements.[15] "Fair Value Measurements" does not intend to introduce any new accounting principles per se. "Fair Value Measurements" was issued by the FASB to provide one uniform statement under which the concept of fair value in all financial reporting is more fully explained.

---

14.   "Global Dialogue with Capital Markets Stakeholders: A Report from the CEOs of the International Audit Networks," January 2008, www.globalpublicpolicysymposium.com.
15.   SFAS 157, "Fair Value Measurements," paragraph 1.

(b) DEFINITION OF FAIR VALUE   FASB ASC 820, "Fair Value Measurements and Disclosures" (SFAS No. 157), provides one standard definition of fair value that is required to be used throughout financial reporting. Fair value is defined in SFAS 157 as:

> the price that would be received to sell an asset or paid to transfer a liability in an orderly transaction between market participants at the measurement date.[16]

This definition of fair value has introduced some interesting concepts that impact the measurement. Since fair value is the price to sell an asset, it is considered an exit price rather than an entry price. Exit price is what one could sell the asset for, not necessarily what one paid for the asset. This definition "presumes the absence of compulsion"[17] and that buyers and sellers are independent and knowledgeable, which is similar to the standard definition of fair market value for tax matters. Since fair value is a price at which an asset could be sold to a market participant, the statement further describes how fair value measurement is for a transaction assumed to occur in what is described as a principal market. A principal market is "the market in which the reporting entity would sell the asset or transfer the liability with the greatest volume and level of activity for the asset or liability."[18] If a principal market as just described does not exist, then fair value is measured by a sale to a market participant in the most advantageous market.[19] The statement describes the most advantageous market as one in "which the reporting entity would sell the asset or transfer the liability with the price that maximizes the amount that would be received for the asset or minimizes the amount that would be paid to transfer the liability."[20]

A fair value measurement under FASB ASC 820, "Fair Value Measurements" (SFAS No. 157), is for a particular asset or liability. The definition of fair value primarily relates to individual assets and liabilities. The reason provided by the FASB is that assets and liabilities are a primary subject of accounting measurement.[21] A common example of this concept is found in business combination. In a business combination the assets and liabilities of the acquired entity are measured at their individual fair values as of the date of the change of control in the acquisition. The definition of fair value is also applied to interests that are considered part of invested capital of the enterprise. Invested capital is commonly considered to be the shareholder's equity plus interest-bearing debt. Invested capital is how the enterprise is financed over the long term. An example of fair value measurement of this type of interest is the reporting unit described in FASB ASC 350 (SFAS No. 142) used for the testing of goodwill for impairment.

The statement notes that the measurement of fair value should consider attributes that are specific to that asset or liability. However, there are two alternatives in considering the specific attributes of the asset or liability. The first alternative is that the asset or liability may be recognized on a stand-alone basis. An example may be a building or a unique technology. The second alternative is that the measurement may consider the attributes of a group of assets and/or liabilities. An example would be customer relationships that are valued along with technology used in the production of goods sold to those customers. Another example of a group would be an entire reporting unit.

---

16.   Id., paragraph 5.
17.   Id., paragraph 6.
18.   Id., paragraph 8.
19.   Id., paragraph 10.
20.   Id., paragraph 8.
21.   Id., footnote 4.

Whether the asset or liability is measured on a stand-alone basis or as part of a group depends on what is sometimes described as its unit of account. The unit of account determines what is being measured by referring to the level at which the asset or liability is aggregated.[22]

One issue addressed by the statement is how to measure fair value when the business enterprise has a large number of units of an item. Suppose, in a business combination, the acquired corporation owns marketable securities, including 500,000 shares of a single corporation's publicly traded common stock. If the shares were to be sold at one time, the introduction of these shares to the market would likely depress the per-share price solely due to the change in the level of trading volume. Financial theory suggests that the value of the shares would decrease. However, paragraph 27 of FASB ASC 820, "Fair Value Measurements" (SFAS No. 157), states that the "quoted price shall not be adjusted because of the size of the position relative to trading volume."[23] Thus fair value measurements should not consider a so-called blockage factor. The FASB sometimes refers to this issue as the *aggregation problem* or as *specifying the unit of account*.[24]

(c) KEY CONCEPTS

(i) Price   FASB ASC 820, "Fair Value Measurements" (SFAS No. 157), describes the concept of price in the definition of fair value as follows:

> A fair value measurement assumes that the asset or liability is exchanged in an orderly transaction between market participants who wish to sell the asset or transfer the liability at the measurement date. An orderly transaction is one in which there has been exposure to the market for a period prior to the measurement date to allow for the usual and customary marketing activities involved in transactions for such assets or liabilities. An orderly transaction is not a forced transaction, such as a forced liquidation or a distress sale. From the perspective of a market participant that holds the asset or owes the liability, the transaction to sell the asset or transfer the liability is a hypothetical transaction at the measurement date. Therefore, the objective of a fair value measurement is to determine the price needed to sell the asset or that must be paid to transfer the liability at the measurement date (an exit price).[25]

Fair value measurement as described in the preceding paragraph is an exit price. An exit price is what the assets could be sold for or what must be paid to transfer liabilities to any market participant. Therefore, *fair value is not necessarily the value to the acquiring entity*. Nor is it necessarily, although it could be, the price that the acquiring entity actually paid for the asset. The same is true with liabilities. Fair value may not be the obligation for the liability of the specific entity itself.

The concept of "price" in the definition of fair value is an exit price. Fair value measurements may not necessarily be based on historical prices or even on expected future prices. Fair value is the price as of the date of measurement at which the asset could be sold or the liability transferred to a market participant.

The concept of exit value in the definition of fair value also assumes that both the buyer and the seller are independent and that both have all the relevant information to make a

---

22.   Id., paragraph 6.
23.   Id., paragraph 27.
24.   Id., paragraph 6.
25.   Id., paragraph 7.

prudent decision about buying and selling the asset or transferring the liability. The concept also assumes that the buyer and the seller are presumed to be independent, with equal knowledge; that the parties are unrelated; and that no party has a price advantage with respect to the transaction. The concept of exit price also assumes that the buyer and seller are willing, not compelled to either buy or sell.[26]

The concepts are similar to the definition of fair market value as promulgated in tax reporting under Revenue Ruling 59-60, which refers to

> the price at which property would change hands between a willing buyer and a willing seller when the former is not under any compulsion to buy and latter is not under any compulsion to sell and both parties have reasonable knowledge of relevant facts.

The FASB actually considered using this definition of fair market value as the definition of fair value in financial reporting, but noted the extensive tax case law relating to this definition and did not want to inadvertently introduce that case law into financial reporting. Even so, while similar, the definition of fair value introduced by FASB ASC 820, "Fair Value Measurements" (SFAS No. 157), has the additional concept of principal or most advantageous market and the concept of market participants, which create some differences in the two definitions.

(ii) Entry versus Exit Price   Under the definition of fair value as presented in FASB ASC 820, "Fair Value Measurements" (SFAS No. 157), fair value is again defined as "the price that would be received to sell an asset or paid to transfer a liability in an orderly transaction between market participants at the measurement date." Under this definition, fair value might not necessarily be the price at which the asset was acquired. Fair value is the price at which the asset could be sold to a market participant. This concept is referred to as an exit price. An exit price differs from an entry price, which is the price paid to acquire the asset or the price received to assume the liability. There are some important distinctions between entry prices and exit prices. Sometimes a business may pay more for an asset because it can utilize that asset in a way other businesses cannot. For example, a business may acquire some proprietary technology that it can use in conjunction with its own technology to develop a new product line. The acquired proprietary technology may be worth more to the acquirer in that circumstance and the acquisition price may reflect its potential use by the acquirer. Entities may not necessarily be able to sell assets at the prices paid to acquire them. Similarly, entities may not necessarily have the ability to transfer liabilities at the prices received to assume them.[27]

In many cases, the transaction price will equal the exit price and, therefore, represent the fair value of the asset or liability at initial recognition. In determining whether a transaction price represents the fair value of the asset or liability at initial recognition, the reporting entity must consider factors specific to the transaction and to the asset or liability. For example, a transaction price might not represent the fair value of an asset or liability at initial recognition if:

- The transaction is between related parties.
- The transaction occurs under duress or the seller is forced to accept the price in the transaction. For example, if the seller is experiencing financial difficulty, the seller might be forced to accept a lower price.

---

26.   Id., paragraph 10.
27.   Id., paragraph 16.

- The unit of account represented by the transaction price is different from the unit of account for the asset or liability measured at fair value.
- The market in which the transaction occurs is different from the market in which the reporting entity would sell the asset or transfer the liability; that is, the principal or most advantageous market.[28]

(iii) Market Participant   FASB ASC 820, "Fair Value Measurements" (SFAS No. 157), clarifies that "the transaction to sell the asset or transfer the liability is a hypothetical transaction . . . considered from the perspective of a market participant that holds the asset or owns the liability." Market participants are willing and able to transact in the most advantageous market. Fair value is defined as an exit price, which is based on a concept of market participant's, not necessarily entity-specific, assumptions. The FASB defines market participants as buyers and sellers in the principal or most advantageous market for the asset or liability who are:

- Independent of the reporting entity—that is, they are not related parties
- Knowledgeable, having a reasonable understanding about the asset or liability and the transaction based on all available information, including information that might be obtained through due diligence efforts that are usual and customary
- Able to transact for the asset or liability
- Willing to transact for the asset or liability—that is, they are motivated but not forced or otherwise compelled to do so[29]

The fair value measurement of an asset or liability is based on the assumptions that market participants would use in pricing the asset or liability, not the owner of the asset or the party responsible for the liability. As a practical measure, management does not have to identify specific market participants in measuring fair value. However, in measuring fair value, the reporting entity should identify characteristics of market participants, considering factors specific to (1) the asset or liability, (2) the principal or most advantageous market for the asset or liability, and (3) market participants with whom the reporting entity would transact in that market.[30] Market participants would likely include other potential buyers that also initially bid for the assets when estimating fair value in a business combination.

(iv) Principal Market or Most Advantageous Market   A natural question in thinking about the definition of fair value introduced by FASB ASC 820, "Fair Value Measurements" (SFAS No. 157), is that if fair value is an exit price to a market participant, what market should be considered? The FASB introduces two concepts to answer that particular question. First, the principal market as defined as the market that has the most volume or most activity for that particular asset or for the transfer of that particular liability. If there is no principal market, then the market would be where a prudent investor would obtain the highest price for the assets or best benefit for transferring the liability. FASB ASC 820, "Fair Value Measurements" (SFAS No. 157), refers to these concepts as follows:

> A fair value measurement assumes that the transaction to sell the asset or transfer the liability occurs in the principal market for the asset or liability or, in the

---

28.   Id., paragraph 17.
29.   Id., paragraph 10.
30.   Id., paragraph 11.

absence of a principal market, the most advantageous market for the asset or liability. The **principal market** is the market in which the reporting entity would sell the asset or transfer the liability with the greatest volume and level of activity for the asset or liability.

The **most advantageous market** is the market in which the reporting entity would sell the asset or transfer the liability at a price that maximizes the amount that would be received for the asset, or minimizes the amount that would be paid to transfer the liability, considering transaction costs in the respective market(s).

In either case, the principal or most advantageous market and, thus, market participants should be considered from the perspective of the reporting entity. This perspective allows for differences between and among entities with different activities. If there is a principal market for the asset or liability, the fair value measurement must represent the price in that market whether that price is directly observable or otherwise determined using a valuation technique. This is true even if the price in a different market is potentially more advantageous at the measurement date.[31]

Under the acquisition method, the fair value of assets acquired and that of liabilities assumed are measured on the balance sheet at each of their respective fair values as of the date of change in control in a business combination. As discussed earlier, fair value is not necessarily the price for which the asset was acquired or the liability assumed, but is an exit price at which the asset can be sold or liability transferred to a market participant. Market participants operate in either the principal market or, in the absence of a principal market, in the most advantageous market.

(v) Transaction Costs However, FASB ASC 820, "Fair Value Measurements" (SFAS No. 157), also says that the price in the principal or most advantageous market used to estimate the fair value measurement of the asset or liability should *not* contain any transaction costs for that particular asset or liability. Transaction costs are the direct costs that would be incurred to sell the asset or transfer the liability in the principal or most advantageous market for the asset or liability. The FASB decision not to include transaction costs is based on the idea that transaction costs are not a part of the asset or liability. Transaction costs are typically unique to a specific transaction and may differ depending on the transaction, not the asset or liability. However, fair value measurement may include the costs of transportation of the asset or liability to or from its principal or most advantageous market. FASB ASC 820, "Fair Value Measurements" (SFAS No. 157), notes that "the price in the principal or most advantageous market used to measure the fair value of the asset or liability must be adjusted for any costs that would be incurred to transport the asset or liability to or from its principal or most advantageous market."[32] As an example, in estimating the fair value of a piece of machinery that is used in a production line, one would consider the costs that would be incurred to transport the piece of equipment to the plant of the reporting entity. However, fair value would not include the cost of a machinery and equipment broker that may have been used to acquire the equipment.

---

31. Id., paragraph 8.
32. Id., paragraph 9.

(vi) Highest and Best Use   A fair value measurement as described by FASB ASC 820, "Fair Value Measurements" (SFAS No. 157), assumes "the highest and best use" of the asset by market participants. Highest and best use considers the use of the asset that is physically possible, legally permissible, and financially feasible. The highest and best use is the use that maximizes the value of the asset, or the group of assets within which the asset would be used by a market participant rather than by the reporting entity. As such, assumptions in the fair value measurements as to the highest and best use of an asset or group of assets are determined by how the asset or group of assets would be used by market participants, even if the intended use of the asset by the reporting entity is different.[33]

As an example, suppose a reporting entity acquires a telecommunications company in a business combination. The telecommunications company had developed some viable technology that is outside its core business. Consequently, the technology had not been implemented in the company's existing services. The acquiring reporting entity also does not have any intention of exploiting the technology. However, if the technology would be exploited by other market participants, the fair value of the technology would be based on its highest and best use. The fair value would be determined as though it would be utilized by other market participants and reported as such on the reporting entity's financial statements.

FASB ASC 820, "Fair Value Measurements" (SFAS No. 157), introduces the concept of valuation premise when discussing the highest and best use of an asset. The valuation premise can be the highest and best use as part of a group of assets, which is referred to in the statement as "in-use," or its highest and best use can be on a stand-alone basis, which is referred to in the statement as "in-exchange."

FASB ASC 820, "Fair Value Measurements" (SFAS No. 157), describes in-use and in-exchange as follows:

> The highest and best use of the asset is **in-use** if the asset would provide maximum value to market participants principally through its use in combination with other assets as a group, as installed or otherwise configured for use. That might be the case for certain non-financial assets. If the highest and best use of the asset is in-use, the fair value of the asset must be measured using an in-use valuation premise. When using an in-use valuation premise, the fair value of the asset is determined based on the price that would be received in a current transaction to sell the asset, assuming that the asset would be used with other assets as a group, and assuming that those assets would be available to market participants. Generally, assumptions about the highest and best use of the asset should be consistent for all of the assets of the group within which it would be used.
>
> The highest and best use of the asset is **in-exchange** if the asset would provide maximum value to market participants principally on a stand-alone basis. That might be the case for a financial asset. If the highest and best use of the asset is in-exchange, the fair value of the asset must be measured using an in-exchange valuation premise. When using an in-exchange valuation premise, the fair value of the asset is determined based on the price that would be received in a current transaction to sell the asset stand-alone.

---

33.   Id., paragraph 12.

Because the highest and best use of the asset is determined based on its use by market participants, the fair value measurement considers the assumptions that market participants would use in pricing the asset, whether using an in-use or an in-exchange valuation premise.[34]

The following examples illustrate the FASB's concepts of highest and best use "in-use" or "in-exchange." Additional examples can also be found in Appendix A of FASB ASC 820, "Fair Value Measurements" (SFAS No. 157).

(vii) Example of Highest and Best Use by a Market Participant A strategic buyer of a technology consulting company acquires another similar company in a business combination. Assume that the acquired entity has only three assets: developed technology, a trade name, and customer relationships. The developed technology was created by the acquired entity for its own use in conjunction with providing services to its customers. Under the acquisition method of accounting, the acquiring company measures the fair value of each of the assets individually, taking into consideration the specified unit of account for the assets. The acquiring company assumes that each of the three assets would provide the most value to market participants through its use in combination with the two other assets as a group. In other words, the highest and best use premise is in-use.

In a business combination, the acquiring company assumes that the market in which the assets could be sold is the same market in which it acquired the assets. The exit price under the definition of fair value (the price at which the assets could be sold to a market participant) may be the same as the entry price (the price at which the assets were acquired). However, the acquiring company would have to consider the most likely market participants to which the assets could be sold. The acquiring entity determines that there are two broad groups of potential market participants for these assets: financial buyers and strategic buyers.

The acquiring company performs an analysis to measure the fair value of each of these assets to both broad groups of market participants—strategic buyers and financial buyers. The results of their analysis are presented in Exhibit 43A.1.

Asset	Strategic Buyer	Financial Buyer
Customer Relationships	$1,250	$ 800
Developed Technology	2,000	1,750
Trade Name	500	750
Totals	$3,750	$3,300

EXHIBIT 43A.1 STRATEGIC VERSUS FINANCIAL MARKET PARTICIPANTS

The acquiring company determines that to a strategic buyer the fair value of the customer relationships is $1,250, the fair value of the developed technology is $2,000, and the fair value of the trade name is $500. To a financial buyer, the acquiring company determines that the fair value of the customer relationships is $800, the fair value of the developed technology is $1,750, and the fair value of the trade name is $750. The total fair value of the three assets to

---

34. Id., paragraph 13.

a strategic buyer is $3,750 but only $3,300 to a financial buyer. What is the fair value of the three assets that the acquiring entity should record on its balance sheet?

First, what would be the likely differences in fair values for each asset between the two groups of market participants? The fair value of the technology and customer relationships may be more to a market participant who is a strategic buyer, because any market participant within this group would likely integrate the technology and customer relationships with its own product lines, which would create more value for it in a business combination than it would for a market participant who is a financial buyer who may not have the opportunity to integrate those assets with others. However, the fair value of the trade name to a market participant who is a strategic buyer may not be as great as it would be for a market participant who is a financial buyer since the strategic buyer may already have an established trade name, whereas a financial buyer may not.

Second, what is the premise for the fair value measurement, in-use or in-exchange? The fair value of these particular assets is likely to be enhanced in conjunction with the use of the other two assets. For example, the value of customer relationships on its own would likely not be as great as it would be with developed technology and an established trade name. The acquiring company's analysis indicates that the fair value of these three assets is maximized by strategic market participants using an in-use premise of value.

The fair value of the three assets under the acquisition method and recorded on the balance sheet would be:

Customer relationships	$1,250
Developed technology	$2,000
Trade name	$ 500

Even though the fair value of the trade name is higher to a financial buyer market participant, the maximum value of these assets would be in-use to a strategic buyer market participant.

(d) INPUTS

(i) Observable versus Unobservable Inputs

FASB ASC 820, "Fair Value Measurements" (SFAS No. 157), provides an additional new term, *inputs*, to guide preparers in developing assumptions in measuring fair value. Inputs are the assumptions that market participants would use when pricing the individual asset or liability. For example, when estimating the fair value of a debt instrument, a risk-related input would be the yields on similar types of debt as observed in the marketplace. Another example of an input would be the growth rate in expected cash flows of a reporting unit over a particular forecast period. As with any other type of assumption, inputs vary greatly depending on the type of asset or liability.

Inputs can be either observable or unobservable:

- Observable inputs are those that market participants may use in pricing an asset and are derived from information in the marketplace. The inputs are therefore verifiable by independent market-based information. An example would be the yield on a similar debt instrument.
- Unobservable inputs are those that are unique to the entity itself. They are not observable by independent market-derived data. An example may be the growth in expected cash flows prepared internally by management described earlier.

Observable or unobservable inputs may be used in a fair value measurement. However, the FASB has expressed a strong preference for observable inputs over unobservable inputs whenever available.[35]

(ii) Fair Value Hierarchy   The FASB also provided additional guidance as to what it consider the relative reliability of the inputs by providing a fair value hierarchy in FASB ASC 820, "Fair Value Measurements and Disclosures" (SFAS No. 157). The purpose of the hierarchy is "to increase consistency and comparability in fair value measurements and related disclosures."[36] The fair value hierarchy prioritizes the inputs to valuation techniques used to measure fair value into three broad levels, with Level 1 having the highest priority and Level 3 having the lowest. The three levels within the hierarchy are as follows:

- *Level 1:* Observable inputs that reflect quoted prices (unadjusted) for identical assets or liabilities in active markets
- *Level 2:* Inputs other than quoted prices included in Level 1 that are observable for the asset or liability either directly or indirectly
- *Level 3:* Unobservable inputs (e.g., a reporting entity's own data)[37]

In many situations, more than one input is used to measure fair value. In these circumstances the inputs may fall into different levels within the fair value hierarchy. The level of the fair value hierarchy in which the fair value measurement is classified as a whole is based on the significance of the lowest level of the input of the measurement. The significance of the input to the fair value measurement is based on judgment. The classification of the level within the fair value hierarchy is important not only from a perceived reliability standpoint, but also because the classification impacts disclosures as to how the fair value was measured.

EXAMPLES OF MEASUREMENTS WITHIN THE FAIR VALUE HIERARCHY
Some examples of typical inputs within the fair value hierarchy include:

Level 1
- o   Prices for securities listed on the New York Stock Exchange
- o   Futures contract prices listed on the Chicago Mercantile Exchange

Level 2
- o   A rate on a debt instrument that is tied to a market rate such as the London Interbank Offered Rate (LIBOR)
- o   A dealer quote for a security that may not be traded on a public market, but the dealer is willing and able to transact

Level 3
- o   Inputs obtained from broker quotes that are indicative, such as a quote for certain machinery and equipment
- o   Valuation models that are based on management assumptions, such as cash flow forecasts that cannot be corroborated with observable market data

---

35.   Id., paragraph 21.
36.   Id., paragraph 22.
37.   Id.

(e) LIABILITIES   A fair value measurement may also apply to liabilities. Fair value of a liability assumes that the liability is transferred to a market participant at the measurement date. Fair value also assumes that the liability continues in existence to the counterparty. The liability is not assumed to be settled as of the measurement date. Since the liability is not assumed to be settled, the measurement of its fair value also assumes that the nonperformance risk does not change before and after its transfer. The statement defines nonperformance risk as the risk that the obligation will not be fulfilled. Nonperformance risk may affect the value at which the liability is transferred since the ability to fulfill the obligation may change. Nonperformance risk may include the reporting entity's own credit risk among the risk factors. The reporting entity must consider the effect of its credit risk (credit standing) on the fair value of the liability in all periods in which the liability is measured at fair value. Liabilities may be an obligation to deliver cash, which is referred to as a financial liability, or an obligation to deliver goods or services, which is referred to as a nonfinancial liability.

A common method to measuring the fair value of a particular liability is to adjust the discount rate to current market rates when computing the present value of the future cash flows related to the liability. The adjusted discount rate would be higher than the implied interest rate of the liability if nonperformance risk is judged to be greater. The impact on the fair value of the liability would be to lower the value of the liability to be recorded on the balance sheet. If nonperformance risk is judged to be lower, then the opposite impact occurs.

The accounting treatment of this measurement aspect of the fair value of liabilities seems a bit counterintuitive. As the credit risk of the reporting entity increases, the fair value of the liability declines. As the credit risk of the reporting entity decreases, the fair value of the liability increases. However, if one considers this treatment of fair value measurement from the perspective of the market participant, then it begins to make a bit more sense. If one is counterparty to a liability and that liability is transferred to another entity whose credit risk is greater than the original entity's credit risk, the likelihood of repayment decreases. If the likelihood of repayment decreases, then the value of the liability to the counterparty decreases. A higher credit rating would increase the probability of repayment and increase the value to the counterparty.

An example of a disclosure about the impact of a change in credit risk on the fair value of liabilities can be found in a recent financial report from Merrill Lynch.

> Merrill Lynch elected the fair value option for certain short-term and long-term borrowings that are risk managed on a fair value basis, including structured notes, and for which hedge accounting under SFAS No. 133 had been difficult to obtain. The changes in the fair value of liabilities for which the fair value option was elected that was attributable to changes in Merrill Lynch credit spreads were estimated gains of $91 million and $2.2 billion for the three and six months ended June 27, 2008, respectively. The changes in the fair value of liabilities for which the fair value option was elected that were attributable to changes in Merrill Lynch credit spreads were not material for the three and six months ended June 29, 2007. Changes in Merrill Lynch specific credit risk [are] derived by isolating fair value changes due to changes in Merrill Lynch's credit spreads as observed in the secondary cash market.[38]

---

38.   Merrill Lynch & Company Form 10-Q, for the quarterly period ended June 27, 2008, page 63.

As Merrill Lynch disclosed, a change in the credit spread (Merrill Lynch had become riskier) resulted in a gain of $91 million for the six months ended June 27, 2007, and a gain of $2.2 billion for the six months ended June 27, 2008. It is possible to make a couple of observations about this and similar disclosures. First, of course analysts knew that these gains were the result of the deterioration of Merrill Lynch's own financial position, which caused its outstanding financial instruments to become more risky. Second, the change in credit risk was from observations in the secondary market, thus a market participant assumption.

The FASB recently released Accounting Standards Update 2009-5, Measuring Liabilities at Fair Value, which clarifies the measurement of liabilities under FASB ASC 820, "Fair Value Measurements and Disclosures" (SFAS No. 157). It is discussed in section 43A.6 of this chapter, FASB Implementation Clarifications.

(f) VALUATION METHODS   FASB ASC 820, "Fair Value Measurements" (SFAS No. 157), identifies what is referred to in the statement as valuation techniques that are consistent with the market approach, the income approach, and the cost approach. Valuation specialists (also as indicated in "Fair Value Measurements") believe that in some circumstances a single valuation technique is appropriate. In other circumstances, more than one valuation technique will be more appropriate. If more than one valuation technique is used, the reporting entity should evaluate the indications of fair value for reasonableness. The fair value is the indication from the valuation technique that is most reasonable under the circumstances, whether it is one of the indications or some weighing of the indications within the range of indications.

FASB ASC 820, "Fair Value Measurements and Disclosures" (SFAS No. 157), highlights the three basic approaches or techniques that are commonly used to measure fair value: the cost approach, the market approach, and the income approach, as discussed next.

(i) Cost Approach   FASB ASC 820, "Fair Value Measurements and Disclosures" (SFAS No. 157), describes the cost approach to valuation as an approach "based on the amount that currently would be required to replace the service capacity of an asset (often referred to as current replacement cost). From the perspective of a market participant (seller), the price that would be received for the asset is determined based on the cost to a market participant (buyer) to acquire or construct a substitute asset of comparable utility, adjusted for obsolescence. Obsolescence encompasses physical deterioration, functional (technological) obsolescence, and economic (external) obsolescence and is broader than depreciation for financial reporting purposes (an allocation of historical cost) or tax purposes (based on specified service lives)."[39]

The notion behind the cost approach is that the fair value of an asset or even an entire business is estimated by the current replacement cost of the asset or the entire business less any adjustments for obsolescence related to the subject asset or assets that comprise the business. The replacement cost of the asset is what it would cost as of the measurement date to replace the asset or an entire business with an asset or group of assets of comparable utility. The cost approach is often used to estimate the value of specific assets, such as a building or machinery and equipment, or certain intangible assets such as customer relationships or an assembled workforce. Because of its nature, the cost approach is difficult to apply in estimating the fair value of an entire operating business; however, an example in financial reporting would be the estimate of the fair value of assets acquired in a business combination under FASB ASC 350, "Goodwill and Other Intangible Assets" (SFAS 142).

---

39.   SFAS 157, paragraph 18c.

(ii) Market Approach   FASB ASC 820, "Fair Value Measurements and Disclosures" (SFAS No. 157), describes the market approach as one that

> uses prices and other relevant information generated by market transactions involving identical or comparable assets or liabilities (including a business). For example, valuation techniques consistent with the market approach often use market multiples derived from a set of comparables. Multiples might lie in ranges with a different multiple for each comparable. The selection of where within the range the appropriate multiple falls requires judgment, considering factors specific to the measurement (qualitative and quantitative).
>
> Valuation techniques consistent with the market approach also include matrix pricing. Matrix pricing is a mathematical technique used principally to value debt securities without relying exclusively on quoted prices for the specific securities, but rather by relying on the securities' relationship to other benchmark quoted securities.[40]

The market approach estimates fair value by comparing a financial measurement such as cash flow or earnings or some other metric of the entity to a multiple or similar financial measurement or metric of a similar guideline entity whose shares are transacted in the marketplace. Commonly used financial measurements are multiples of prices to earnings (the P/E ratio) or multiples of invested capital to earnings before interest, taxes, depreciation, and amortization (EBITDA). The market approach conceptually is easily understood in that the approach estimates fair value through transactions of similar assets or business interests in the market. The difficulty in applying the market approach in measuring fair value, particularly in estimating the fair value of intangible assets, is in identifying guideline assets or business interests similar enough to support a determinative comparison.

(iii) Income Approach   FASB ASC 820, "Fair Value Measurements" (SFAS No. 157), describes the income approach as one using "valuation techniques to convert future amounts (e.g., cash flows or earnings) to a single present amount (discounted). The measurement is based on the value indicated by current market expectations about those future amounts. Those valuation techniques include: present value techniques; option-pricing models, such as the Black-Scholes-Merton formula (a closed-form model) and a binomial model (a lattice model), which incorporate present value techniques; and the multi-period excess earnings method, which is used to measure the fair value of certain intangible assets."[41]

Methods under the income approach can be equally applied to estimate the fair value of an entire entity or reporting unit, or they can be applied to estimate the fair value of a specific asset, particularly an intangible asset. The income approach is generally used to estimate the fair value of a business or an asset of the business such as an intangible asset through the risk-adjusted cash flows that the entity or specific intangible asset is expected to generate for the life of the entity or intangible asset. There are several common methods that can be used to estimate fair value under this approach. One method commonly used under the income approach is the discounted cash flow analysis. The discounted cash flow method estimates fair value through the sum of expected future cash flows that the entity or intangible asset will

---

40.   Id., paragraph 18a.
41.   Id., paragraph 18b.

generate, discounted to the present at a risk-adjusted rate of return commensurate with the risk of actually receiving the cash flows.

A version of the discounted cash flow method can also be used to estimate the fair value of a specific intangible asset by estimating cash flows that can be generated by the entire business and deducting fair returns on all of the other assets that contribute to the generation of the cash flow. This method is sometimes also referred to as the multiperiod excess earnings method. The residual cash flow after deducting returns on all of the other contributory assets is the cash flow generated by the specific intangible asset. The present value of this residual cash flow is then discounted at a rate reflective of the risk of the intangible asset in order to estimate the fair value of the specific intangible asset.

(g) EFFECTIVE DATES   When first issued, FASB ASC 820, "Fair Value Measurements" (SFAS No. 157), was to be effective for fiscal years beginning after November 15, 2007. However, on November 14, 2007, the day before the statement was to become fully implemented, the FASB delayed implementation of part of the statement. The reason for the partial implementation and partial delay was that preparers of statements felt they did not fully understand the implications of implementation of the statement. So the FASB agreed to a partial implementation. Therefore, FASB ASC 820, "Fair Value Measurements" (SFAS No. 157), was partially implemented for financial assets and liabilities, as well as for any other assets and liabilities that are carried at fair value on a recurring basis in financial statements. Examples of assets and liabilities carried at fair value on a recurring basis provided by the FASB include derivatives, loan-servicing assets and liabilities, and some loans and debt linked to business combinations.

The board provided a one-year deferral for the implementation of FASB ASC 820, "Fair Value Measurements" (SFAS No. 157), for nonfinancial assets and liabilities. These nonfinancial assets and liabilities are related to goodwill, business combinations, and discontinued operations, as well as to some nonfinancial intangible assets. The statement is now fully implemented for fiscal years beginning after November 15, 2008. While the FASB agreed to adopt the one-year delay, it had encouraged the earlier adoption of FASB ASC 820, "Fair Value Measurements" (SFAS No. 157), for nonfinancial assets and liabilities.

(h) REQUIRED DISCLOSURES UNDER FASB ASC 820, "FAIR VALUE MEASUREMENT AND DISCLOSURES" (SFAS NO. 157)   Under "Fair Value Measurements and Disclosures," the purpose of disclosures is to provide users of financial statements with information to assess the inputs used to develop the fair value measurement. Inputs to the measurement of fair value are categorized into Levels 1, 2, and 3 based on their relative marketplace observability. Assets and liabilities are measured either on a recurring basis or on a nonrecurring basis subsequent to their initial recognition. The required disclosures depend on whether the asset or liability is measured on a recurring or a nonrecurring basis. Trading securities would be an example of an asset measured on a recurring basis, whereas impaired assets would be an example of an asset measured on a nonrecurring basis.

(i) Recurring Measurements   In addition to providing financial statement users with information to assess the inputs to a fair value measurement, disclosures for Level 3 recurring fair value measurements serve the purpose of allowing users to understand how changes in the net assets' fair value are reflected in earnings. Required recurring disclosures for each interim and annual period for each major category of asset and liability are:

- The fair value measurements at the reporting date
- The level within the fair value hierarchy in which the fair value measurements in their entirety fall, segregating fair value measurements by level
- For fair value measurements using significant Level 3 inputs, a reconciliation of the beginning and ending balances, separately presenting changes attributable to:
  - Total gains or losses for the period (realized and unrealized), segregating those included in earnings (or changes in net assets), and a description of where they are reported in the income statement
  - Purchases, sales, issuances, and settlements, net
  - Transfers in and out of Level 3
- The amount of total gains or losses for the period included in earnings (or changes in net assets) that are attributable to the change in unrealized gains or losses relating to those assets and liabilities still held at the reporting date and a description of where those unrealized gains or losses are reported in the statement of income
- In annual reports, the valuation techniques used to measure fair value and a discussion of changes of valuation techniques, if any

(ii) Nonrecurring Measurements   For assets and liabilities measured on a nonrecurring basis after initial recognition, the following should be disclosed for each annual and interim period and for each major category of assets and liabilities:

- The fair value measurements recorded during the period and the reasons for the measurement
- The level within the fair value hierarchy in which the fair value measurements in their entirety fall, segregating fair value measurements by level
- For Level 3 measurements, a description of the inputs and the information used to develop inputs
- In annual reports, the valuation techniques used to measure fair value and a discussion of changes of valuation techniques, if any

Any quantitative disclosures for recurring and nonrecurring fair value measurements should be made in a tabular format.[42]

(iii) SEC Suggested Disclosures   In March 2008, the SEC sent letters to certain public companies with significant amounts of asset-backed securities, loans carried at fair value or the lower of cost or market, and derivative assets and liabilities reported in their financial statements. The letter requires that valuation models relying on significant unobservable inputs result in the classification of assets and liabilities as Level 3 measurements. When material, Level 3 inputs require further management discussion and analysis (MD&A) disclosure of:

- How Level 3 inputs are determined
- How changes to Level 3 inputs could change the fair values of assets and liabilities and how changes to those values would impact:
  - Results of operations
  - Liquidity
  - Capital resources

---

42.   Id., paragraphs 32–34.

- The amount of Level 3 assets and liabilities as a percentage of total assets
- The amount and reason for any material increase or decrease in Level 3 assets resulting from a transfer from or into Level 1 or 2
- If assets or liabilities are transferred into Level 3, discussion of the significant inputs no longer considered observable and any material gain or loss recognized
- Whether realized and unrealized gains (losses) affected the results of operations, liquidity, or capital resources and if so, how
- The reason for material declines or increases in fair value
- Whether the company anticipates fair values to diverge from anticipated amounts from settlement or maturity

For all assets and liabilities within the SFAS 157 hierarchy, disclose in MD&A:

- For all asset-backed security (all levels), the nature and type of any assets underlying the security, the years of issuance, the asset's current credit rating, and potential changes to the credit rating
- A description of the valuation technique or model, and material changes to the technique or model
- How relevant market indexes are included in the technique or model
- How the technique or model is validated
- How sensitive the fair values are to significant inputs (consider providing a range of fair values)
- How increases and decreases in fair value of assets and liabilities may affect liquidity or capital resources.[43]

43A.4 FASB ASC 825-10-25-2, "FINANCIAL INSTRUMENTS, RECOGNITION, FAIR VALUE OPTION" (SFAS NO. 159)

(a) KEY PROVISIONS   The FASB furthered the goal of eventually allowing the measurement of all financial assets and liabilities at their respective fair values in financial reporting through the issuance of FASB ASC 825-10-25, "The Fair Value Option for Financial Assets and Financial Liabilities—Including an Amendment of FASB Statement No. 115" (SFAS 159). SFAS 159, "Fair Value Option," expands the fair value measurements of financial instruments, both assets and liabilities, which is consistent with the FASB's long-term measurement objectives for accounting for financial instruments. The Fair Value Option permits entities to choose to measure most financial assets and liabilities and certain other items at their respective fair values. The FASB noted in the implementation of SFAS 159 that the objective of the statement is to improve financial reporting "by providing entities with the opportunity to mitigate volatility in reported earnings caused by measuring related assets and liabilities differently without having to apply complex hedge accounting provisions."[44]

The Fair Value Option is interesting from a financial accounting standpoint because it may be applied on an instrument-by-instrument basis, rather than to all financial assets or liabilities.

---

43.   Senior Assistant Chief Accountant of the U.S. Securities and Exchange Commission, "Sample Letter Sent to Public Companies on MD&A Disclosure Regarding the Application of SFAS 157 (Fair Value Measurements)," www.sec.gov/divisions/corpfin/guidance/fairvalueltr0308 .htm, accessed 6/22/09.

44.   SFAS 159, "The Fair Value Option for Financial Assets and Financial Liabilities—Including and Amendment of FASB Statement No. 115, 159-1."

The financial instruments covered by the statement are fairly broad, the one major exception being financial instruments that otherwise are accounted for by the equity method. The Fair Value Option is an election. Once an election is made to measure an instrument at its fair value under FASB ASC 825-10-25 (SFAS No. 159), the election is irrevocable (unless a new election date occurs). The fair value election is applied only to entire financial instruments and not to portions of an instrument.

(b) ELIGIBLE AND INELIGIBLE ITEMS   Under the Fair Value Option, the following financial instruments are eligible for election:

- A recognized financial asset or liability
- A firm commitment that would otherwise not be recognized and involves only financial instruments
- A written loan commitment
- The rights and obligations under an insurance contract
- The rights and obligations under a warranty

Those ineligible for election are:

- An investment in a consolidated subsidiary, including a variable interest entity
- Employer benefit plan obligations
- Financial assets and liabilities under lease agreements
- Deposit liabilities of bans, loan associations, and similar institutions
- Financial instruments that are classified as components of shareholders' equity[45]

43A.5 FINANCIAL CRISIS

(a) BANKING INDUSTRY POSITION: SUSPEND MARK-TO-MARKET   In recent testimony before the Senate Banking Committee, Federal Reserve Chairman Bernard Bernanke stated, "Accounting rules require banks to value many assets at something close to a very low fire-sale price rather than the hold-to-maturity price."[46] Mr. Bernanke's testimony echoed the views of many critics of fair value accounting. Critics believe that the credit crisis was made much greater by the so-called mark-to-market or fair value accounting of financial institutions that had invested in the securitized subprime debt. The criticism by many of fair value accounting is based on an apparent difference between the market value of certain securities in distressed markets and the value indicated by holding the securities to maturity.

(b) CFA INSTITUTE POSITION: EXPAND FAIR VALUE REPORTING   The CFA Institute Center for Financial Market Integrity (CFA Institute Center) represents the views of its members, including portfolio managers, investment analysts, and advisers, worldwide. Its mission is to promote fair and transparent global capital markets, to advocate for investor protection, and to promote high-quality financial reporting and disclosure. In a publication entitled *A Comprehensive Business Reporting Model: Financial Reporting for Investors*, the CFA Institute Center says, "Our views on fair value measurements are consistent with the

---

45.   Id.
46.   Federal Reserve Chairman Ben S. Bernanke testimony to the Senate Banking Committee on September 23, 2008.

principles laid out in FASB's recently issued Statement of Financial Accounting Standards (SFAS) No. 157, *Fair Value Measurement*."[47]

The CFA Institute Center's official position on fair value reporting is that all assets and liabilities should be reported at fair values based on market values for identical or similar assets or liabilities. The rationales for the position are:

- Fair value information is the only information useful for investment decision making.
- All investor decisions to buy or sell assets, or to lend or borrow money, are based on current fair market values.
- Thus, investors require up-to-date information on the fair values of assets held by a company and the claims against those assets.
- Where models are widely used in the markets for valuing financial instruments, the models should be applied using market inputs.
- Entity-specific or managers' estimates of fair values based on their own judgments do not qualify as fair values.
- At a minimum, all financial instruments should be reported at fair values.[48]

(c) CONGRESSIONAL STUDY The Emergency Stabilization Act of 2008 required the Securities and Exchange Commission to conduct a study on mark-to-market accounting applicable to financial institutions. Section 133 of the Act specifically called for the following:

a) STUDY.—The Securities and Exchange Commission, in consultation with the Board [of Governors of the Federal Reserve System] and the Secretary [of the Treasury], shall conduct a study on mark-to-market accounting standards as provided in Statement Number 157 of the Financial Accounting Standards Board, as such standards are applicable to financial institutions, including depository institutions. Such a study shall consider at a minimum:

1. the effects of such accounting standards on a financial institution's balance sheet;
2. the impacts of such accounting on bank failures in 2008;
3. the impact of such standards on the quality of financial information available to investors;
4. the process used by the Financial Accounting Standards Board in developing accounting standards;
5. the advisability and feasibility of modifications to such standards; and
6. alternative accounting standards to those provided in such Statement Number 157.

b) REPORT.—The Securities and Exchange Commission shall submit to Congress a report of such study before the end of the 90-day period beginning on the date of the enactment of this Act containing the findings and

---

47. CFA Institute Center for Financial Market Integrity Publication, *A Comprehensive Business Reporting Model: Financial Reporting for Investors*, July 2007, www.cfapubs.org (accessed 6/22/09).

48. CFA Institute Official Positions—Financial Reporting: Fair Value Reporting, www.cfainstitute.org (accessed 6/2209).

determinations of the Commission, including such administrative and legislative recommendations as the Commission determines appropriate.[49]

(d) SEC RESPONSE TO CONGRESS   On December 30, 2008, the Securities and
Exchange Commission's Office of the Chief Accountant and Division of Corporate Finance
delivered a report to Congress recommending against the suspension of fair value accounting
standards.

> Among key findings, the report notes that investors generally believe fair value
> accounting increases financial reporting transparency and facilitates better deci-
> sion making. The report also observes that fair value accounting did not appear
> to play a meaningful role in the bank failures that occurred in 2008. Rather the
> report indicated that bank failures in the U.S. appeared to be the result of growing
> probable credit losses, concerns about asset quality, and in certain cases, eroding
> lender and investor confidence.[50]

Other highlights of the report include:

- SFAS No. 157 applications should be improved, but not suspended. Other improvements would include better understanding of the impact of fair value through presentation and disclosure improvements.
- Existing fair values and mark-to-market requirements should not be suspended.
- Additional measures should be taken to improve the application of existing fair
  value requirements, particularly as they relate to Level 2 and Level 3 estimates. Such
  measures may include additional assistance in the form of guidance, education, and
  training for issuers and auditors in applying SFAS No. 157.
- The accounting for financial asset impairments should be readdressed. The FASB
  should reassess current impairment accounting models for financial instruments by
  narrowing the number of models that currently exist in U.S. GAAP.
- Further guidance to foster the use of sound judgment should be implemented. This
  is particularly directed to the SEC and the PCAOB as to whether statements of
  policy related to the application of judgment in making value measures would be
  appropriate.
- Accounting standards should continue to be established to meet the needs of investors. U.S. GAAP should not be established or modified to serve the needs of others
  (e.g., regulators) at the expense of investors.
- Additional formal measures to address the operation of existing accounting standards
  in practice should be established. Specifically mentioned are implementation of the
  SEC Advisory Committee on Improvements to Financial Reporting (CIFiR)'s recommendation for a Financial Reporting Forum; implementation by the FASB of a post-
  adoption review process, and establishment of a formal policy for standards setting
  in circumstances that necessitate near-immediate response.
- The need to simplify the accounting for investments in financial assets by continuing
  the joint work by the FASB and IASB should be addressed. The Boards should also

---

49.   www.sec.gov/spotlight/fairvalue/htm.
50.   "Congressionally-Mandated Study Says Improve, Do Not Suspend, Fair Value Accounting,"
       www.sec.gov/news/press/2008/2008-307.htm.

complete the measurement phase of the conceptual framework project in order to inform future decision makers about appropriate measurement attributes in accounting standards.[51]

(e) SEC AND FASB CLARIFICATIONS   In response to widespread criticism, the SEC Office of the Chief Accountant and FASB staff released a statement titled "Clarifications on Fair Value Accounting"[52] on September 30, 2008. The statement responded to several questions raised by the credit crisis.

*Can management's internal **assumptions** (e.g., expected cash flows) be used to measure fair value when relevant market evidence does not exist?*

Yes. When an active market for a security does not exist, the use of management estimates that incorporate current market participant expectations of future cash flows, and include appropriate risk premiums, is acceptable. FASB ASC 820 (SFAS 157) discusses a range of information and valuation techniques that a reasonable preparer might use to estimate fair value when relevant market data may be unavailable, which may be the case during this period of market uncertainty. This can, in appropriate circumstances, include expected cash flows from an asset.

Further, in some cases using unobservable inputs (level 3) might be more appropriate than using observable inputs (level 2); for example, when significant adjustments are required to available observable inputs it may be appropriate to utilize an estimate based primarily on unobservable inputs. The determination of fair value often requires significant judgment. In some cases, multiple inputs from different sources may collectively provide the best evidence of fair value. In these cases expected cash flows would be considered alongside other relevant information. The weighting of the inputs in the fair value estimate will depend on the extent to which they provide information about the value of an asset or liability and are relevant in developing a reasonable estimate.

Are transactions that are determined to be disorderly representative of fair value? When is a distressed (disorderly) sale indicative of fair value?

The results of disorderly transactions are not determinative when measuring fair value. The concept of a fair value measurement assumes an orderly transaction between market participants. An orderly transaction is one that involves market participants who are willing to transact and allows for adequate exposure to the market. Distressed or forced liquidation sales are not orderly transactions, and thus the fact that a transaction is distressed or forced should be considered when weighing the available evidence. Determining whether a particular transaction is forced or disorderly requires judgment.

---

51.   "Report and Recommendations Pursuant to Section 133 of the Emergency Economic Stabilization Act of 2008: Study on Mark-to-Market Accounting" Office of the Chief Accountant, Division of Corporate Finance, United States Securities and Exchange Commission, December 30, 2008.

52.   SEC Office of the Chief Accountant and FASB Staff, "Clarifications on Fair Value Accounting," 2008-234, September 30, 2008.

Can transactions in an inactive market affect fair value measurements?

Yes. A quoted market price in an active market for the identical asset is most representative of fair value and thus is required to be used (generally without adjustment). Transactions in inactive markets may be inputs when measuring fair value, but would likely not be determinative. If they are orderly, transactions should be considered in management's estimate of fair value. However, if prices in an inactive market do not reflect current prices for the same or similar assets, adjustments may be necessary to arrive at fair value.

(f) IASB AND FASB FINANCIAL CRISIS ADVISORY GROUP

In response to the current financial crisis, the FASB and IASB formed a Financial Crisis Advisory Group in early 2009. The group is comprised of senior business leaders both within and outside the accounting profession with broad experience in international financial markets. The purpose of the group is to advise both Boards about standard-setting implications of:

- The global financial crisis
- Potential changes to the global regulatory environment

The mission of the group is to provide recommendations as to how enhancing transparency and reducing complexity in financial reporting can serve the financial markets and restore investor confidence in those markets. The group conducted several advisory meetings during the first half of 2009 to address accounting issues pertaining to the credit crisis including:

- Areas in which financial reporting helped identify issues of concern, or may have created unnecessary concerns during the credit crisis
- Areas in which financial reporting standards could have provided more transparency to help anticipate the crisis or respond to the crisis more quickly
- IASB and FASB priorities and efforts to avoid future market disruptions
- The relationship between fair value accounting and the credit crises
- The findings and conclusions of the U.S. SEC study under the Emergency Economic Stabilization Act of 2008
- The need for due process and independence in accounting standards setting[53]

The Group published its recommendations on July 28, 2009. The report is organized into four main principles and contains recommendations to improve the functioning and effectiveness of global standard setting. In his comments about the report, Hans Hoogervorst, the co-chairman of the FCAG, emphasized the importance of broadly accepted accounting standards that are the result of thorough due process. He said, "The report highlights the importance but also the limits of financial reporting. Accounting was not the root cause of the financial crisis, but it has an important role to play in its resolution.[54]

---

53.   Financial Crisis Advisory Group (FCAG), Financial Accounting Standards Board, www.fasb .org/fcag/index.shtml.
54.   Financial Crisis Advisory Group, Press Release dated 28 July 2009, "FCAG publishes wide-ranging review of standard-setting activities following the global financial crisis," www. fasb.org/fcag.org.

43A.6 FASB IMPLEMENTATION CLARIFICATIONS

(a) FSP 157-3, FAIR VALUE IN NONACTIVE MARKETS (ASC 820-10-35)   On October 10, 2008, the FASB issued FASB Staff Position 157-3, "Determining the Fair Value of a Financial Asset When the Market for That Asset Is Not Active," (ASC 820-10-35) which further clarifies assumptions to be used in measuring fair value in circumstances where there may not be a market price. The statement's overview says, "This FASB Staff Position (FSP) clarifies the application of FASB Statement No. 157, *Fair Value Measurements*, in a market that is not active and provides an example to illustrate key considerations in determining the fair value of a financial asset when the market for that financial asset is not active." The important points of the FSP reinforce the concepts of fair value measurements introduced by SFAS 157, which include:

- Fair value measurement represents the price at which a transaction would occur between market participants at the measurement date (an exit price). Determining fair value in a dislocated market depends on the facts and circumstances and may require the use of significant judgment about whether individual transactions are forced liquidations or distressed sales.
- The use of the reporting entity's own assumptions about future cash flows and appropriately risk-adjusted discount rates is acceptable when relevant observable inputs are not available.
- Broker (or pricing service) quotes may be an appropriate input when measuring fair value, but are not necessarily determinative if an active market does not exist for the financial assets.[55]

The FSP provides an example of measuring the fair value of an asset in a circumstance where there may not be an active market for that particular asset. The example amends FASB ASC 820 (Statement 157) for paragraphs A32A to A32F.

(i) Example of Determining the Fair Value of a Financial Asset When the Market for That Asset Is Not Active   *Note:* The conclusions reached in this example are based on the assumed facts and circumstances presented. Other approaches to determining fair value may be appropriate. Also, this example assumes that the observable transactions considered in determining fair value were not forced liquidations or distressed transactions.

On January 1, 20X8, Entity A invested in an AA-rated tranche of a collateralized debt obligation security. The underlying collateral for the collateralized debt obligation security is guaranteed nonconforming residential mortgage loans. Prior to June 30, 20X8, Entity A was able to determine the fair value of the collateralized debt obligation security using a market approach valuation technique based on Level 2 inputs that did not require significant adjustment. The Level 2 inputs included:

- Quoted prices in active markets for similar collateralized debt obligation securities with insignificant adjustments for differences between the collateralized debt obligation security that Entity A holds and the similar collateralized debt obligation securities

---

55.   FASB FSP 157-3.

- Quoted prices in markets that are not active that represent current transactions for the same or similar collateralized debt obligation securities that do not require significant adjustment based on unobservable inputs

Since June 30, 20X8, the market for collateralized debt obligation securities has become increasingly inactive. The inactivity was evidenced first by a significant widening of the bid-ask spread in the brokered markets in which collateralized debt obligation securities trade and then by a significant decrease in the volume of trades relative to historical levels as well as other relevant factors. At September 30, 20X8 (the measurement date), Entity A determines that the market for its collateralized debt obligation security is not active and that markets for similar collateralized debt obligation securities (such as higher-rated tranches within the same collateralized debt obligation security vehicle) also are not active. That determination is made considering that there are few observable transactions for the collateralized debt obligation security or similar collateralized debt obligation securities, the prices for those transactions that have occurred are not current, and the observable prices for those transactions vary substantially either over time or among market makers, thus reducing the potential relevance of those observations. Consequently, while Entity A appropriately considers those observable inputs, ultimately Entity A's collateralized debt obligation security will be classified within Level 3 of the fair value hierarchy because Entity A determines that significant adjustments using unobservable inputs are required to determine fair value at the measurement date.

Entity A determines that an income approach valuation technique (present value technique) that maximizes the use of relevant observable inputs and minimizes the use of unobservable inputs will be equally or more representative of fair value than the market approach valuation technique used at prior measurement dates, which would now require significant adjustments. Specifically, Entity A uses the discount rate adjustment technique described in Appendix B of Statement 157 to determine fair value.

Entity A determines that the appropriate discount rate to be used to discount the contractual cash flows of its collateralized debt obligation security is 22 percent after considering the following:

- The implied rate of return at the last date on which the market was considered active for the collateralized debt obligation security was 15 percent. Based on an analysis of available observable inputs for mortgage-related debt securities, Entity A determines that market rates of return generally have increased in the marketplace since the last date on which the market was considered active for the collateralized debt obligation security. Entity A estimates that credit spreads have widened by approximately 100 basis points and liquidity risk premiums have increased during that period by approximately 400 basis points. Other risks (for example, interest rate risk) have not changed.

  Using this information, Entity A estimates that an indication of an appropriate rate of return for the collateralized debt obligation security is 20 percent. In making that determination, Entity A considers all available market information that could be obtained without undue cost and effort. For this collateralized debt obligation security, the available market information used in assessing the risks in the security (including nonperformance risk [for example, default risk and collateral value risk] and liquidity risk) includes:

  o Quoted prices that are not current for the same or similar collateralized debt obligation securities

- ○ Relevant reports issued by analysts and ratings agencies
- ○ The current level of interest rates and any directional movements in relevant indexes, such as credit risk indexes
- ○ Information about the performance of the underlying mortgage loans, such as delinquency and foreclosure rates, loss experience, and prepayment rates
- ○ Other relevant observable inputs
- Two indicative quotes (that is, nonbinding quotes) for the collateralized debt obligation security from brokers imply a rate of return of 23 percent and 27 percent. The indicative quotes are based on proprietary pricing models utilizing significant unobservable inputs (that is, Level 3 inputs), rather than actual transactions.

Because Entity A has multiple indications of the appropriate rate of return that market participants would consider relevant in estimating fair value, it evaluates and weighs, as appropriate, the respective indications of the appropriate rate of return, considering the reasonableness of the range indicated by the results. Entity A concludes that 22 percent is the point within the range of relevant inputs that is most representative of fair value in the circumstances.

Entity A placed more weight on the 20 percent estimated rate of return (that is, its own estimate) because (1) the indications of an appropriate rate of return provided by the broker quotes were nonbinding quotes based on the brokers' own models using significant unobservable inputs, and (2) Entity A was able to corroborate some of the inputs, such as default rates, with relevant observable market data, which it used to make significant adjustments to the implied rate of return when the market was last considered active.

In accordance with the requirements of Statement 157, Entity A determines that the risk-adjusted discount rate appropriately reflects the reporting entity's estimate of the assumptions that market participants would use to estimate the selling price of the asset at the measurement date. Risks incorporated in the discount rate include nonperformance risk (e.g., default risk and collateral value risk) and liquidity risk (i.e., the compensation that a market participant receives for buying an asset that is difficult to sell under current market conditions).[56]

(ii) Growing Concerns Financial statement preparers were concerned that FASB Staff Position No. FAS 157-3 (ASC 820-10-35) did not provide enough guidance on how to determine whether a once active market for a financial asset would be considered not active as of the measurement date, and, if the market is considered not active, whether a transaction that would normally occur in that market would be considered distressed. There was also a concern that the Statement 157 fair value hierarchy encouraged the use of an observable market transaction even when the transaction might be distressed or the market for that transaction might not be active. Finally, financial statement preparers and users believe that emphasis on using the so-called last transaction price as the sole or primary basis for fair value measurement has resulted in an inappropriate application of fair value measurement to certain financial assets.

In addition, the SEC study on mark-to-market accounting suggests that "additional measures should be taken to improve the application and practice related to existing fair value requirements (particularly as they relate to both Level 2 and Level 3 estimates)." This recommendation further notes that "fair value requirements should be improved through

---

56. Id., paragraph 11.

development of application and best practices guidance for determining fair value in illiquid or inactive markets."[57]

In response to the recommendations proposed by the Securities and Exchange Commission's study on mark-to-market accounting standards, the FASB issued two additional proposed staff positions, which were intended to provide further guidance on the implementation of fair value measurements, particularly in a distressed market. These proposed staff positions eventually became FASB Staff Position No. FAS 157-4, "Determining Fair Value When the Volume and Level of Activity for the Asset or Liability Have Significantly Decreased and Identifying Transactions That Are Not Orderly," and FASB Staff Position No. FAS 115-2, FAS 124-2, "Recognition and Presentation of Other Than Temporary Impairments." Both Staff Positions were issued April 9, 2009.

(b) FSP 157-4, DETERMINING FAIR VALUE WHEN VOLUME AND ACTIVITY HAVE SIGNIFICANTLY DECREASED AND IDENTIFYING TRANSACTIONS THAT ARE NOT ORDERLY (ASC 820-10-65)
When there has been a significant decrease in the volume and level of activity for an asset or liability, the objective of fair value measurement is to determine the price that would be received when selling the asset in an *orderly transaction* between market participants under *current* market conditions. The objective has not changed, even though market conditions may have changed. When weighing indications of fair value from multiple valuation techniques, the reasonableness of the range of values must be considered. The goal is to determine the point within the range of values that is most representative of fair value. The reporting entity's intention to hold the asset or liability is not relevant when estimating fair value, as it is a market-based measurement, not an entity-specific measurement. FSP 157-4 (ASC 820-10-65) applies to Level 2 and Level 3 assets and liabilities.

The first step in applying FSP 157-4 (ASC 820-10-65) is to determine whether there has been a decrease in the volume and level of activity in relation to a normal market. The following factors, while not all-inclusive, provide an indication as to the relative activity of the market for a particular financial asset.

- There have been few recent transactions (based on volume and level of activity in the market). Thus, there is not sufficient frequency and volume to provide pricing information on an ongoing basis.
- Price quotations are not based on current information.
- Price quotations vary substantially either over time or among market makers (e.g., some brokered markets).
- Indexes that previously were highly correlated with the fair values of the asset are demonstrably uncorrelated with recent fair values.
- There has been a significant increase in implied liquidity risk premiums, yields, or performance indicators (such as delinquency rates or loss severities) for observed transactions or quoted prices when compared with the reporting entity's estimate of expected cash flows.
- There is a wide bid-ask spread or there have been significant increases in the bid-ask spread.

---

57.   "Report and Recommendations Pursuant to Section 133 of the Emergency Economic Stabilization Act of 2008: Study on Mark-to-Market Accounting," SEC, December 30, 2008.

- There is a significant decline or absence of a market for new issuances (a primary market) for similar assets or liabilities.
- Little information is released publicly (e.g., a principal-to-principal market).

While the preceding list provides guidance about the characteristics of a market with a significant decrease in volume and activity, the preparer must still evaluate the relevance of the factors. If the preparer concludes that the market has experienced a significant decrease in volume and activity, then transactions or quoted prices may not be determinative of fair value, and the preparer goes to step 2 to determine whether the transaction is orderly. The circumstances that indicate a transaction is *not* orderly are:

- There was not adequate exposure to the market before the measurement date to allow for usual and customary marketing activities for the transactions involving such assets or liabilities under current market conditions.
- There was a usual and customary marketing period, but the seller marketed the asset or liability to a single market participant.
- The seller is in or near bankruptcy or receivership (distressed), or the seller was required to meet regulatory or legal requirements (forced).
- The transaction price is an outlier when compared to other recent transactions for the same or a similar asset or liability.

When determining whether a transaction is orderly, a reporting entity shall not ignore information that is available without undue cost and effort, but need not undertake all possible efforts.

FAS 157-4 provides the following guidance for using the transaction price depending on whether the transaction is orderly when there is a significant decrease in the volume and activity of a market.

- When the transaction is not orderly, the preparer should place little, if any, weight on that transaction price when estimating fair value.
- When the transaction is orderly, the preparer shall consider the transaction price when estimating fair value. Adjustments to the transaction price may be appropriate. The amount of weight placed on the transaction price when compared to other indications of fair value from multiple valuation techniques shall depend on the facts and circumstances, including the relative volume in the market and the proximity of the transaction date to the measurement date. Regardless of the valuation technique, the fair value measurement should include an appropriate risk adjustment reflecting a market participant's premium for uncertain cash flows.
- If there is insufficient information to conclude that the transaction is orderly, or not, then the transaction price shall be considered when estimating fair value. However, that transaction price may not be the sole or primary basis for determining fair value.[58]

---

58. FASB FSP 157-4, "Determining Fair Value When Volume and Activity Have Significantly Decreased and Identifying Transactions That Are Not Orderly."

(c) FSP 115-2, RECOGNITION OF OTHER THAN TEMPORARY IMPAIRMENTS (ASC 320-10-65)
FASB Staff Position FAS 115-2, FAS 124-2, "Recognition and Presentation of Other Than Temporary Impairments," amends current U.S. GAAP with respect to the recognition of other than temporary impairments for debt securities classified as available for sale and held to maturity. It also provides new guidance for determining when an other than temporary (permanent) impairment exists for debt securities.

A debt security is considered impaired if its fair value is less than its amortized cost. The impairment is considered other than temporary (permanent) if:

- The entity intends to sell the security.
- It is probable that the entity will have to sell the security before recovering its amortized cost basis.
- The entity does not expect to recover the entire amortized cost basis.
- A credit loss exists, which occurs if the present value of cash flows expected to be collected is less than the amortized cost basis.

FSP FAS 115-2 (ASC 320-10-65) prescribes new treatment for the recognition of other than temporary (permanent) impairments. The amount of the impairment recognized in earnings depends on the entity's intent and ability to hold the security and recover its amortized cost basis.

- If the entity intends to sell the security or will be forced to sell the security before recovering its amortized cost basis, the impairment shall be recognized in earnings. The amount of the impairment is equal to the difference between its amortized cost basis and its fair value on the balance sheet date.
- If the entity intends to hold the security and it is probable that the entity will be able to hold the security and recover its amortized cost basis (less current period credit loss), then the impairment should be separated and reported as follows:
  - The amount representing the current period credit loss shall be recognized in earnings.
  - The remainder shall be recognized in other comprehensive income (equity), net of taxes.

The new cost basis would equal the old cost basis less the impairment recognized in earnings. The new cost basis would not be adjusted for subsequent recoveries of fair value.[59]

(d) ACCOUNTING STANDARD UPDATE 2009-5, MEASURING LIABILITIES AT FAIR VALUE
Accounting Standard Update 2009-5, Measuring Liabilities at Fair Value was originally proposed as FSP FAS 157-c, and then as FSP FASB 157-f. This credit crisis issue has received a significant amount of attention and public comment. ASU 2009-5 clarifies the measurement of the fair value of liabilities under ASC Topic 820, Fair Value Measurement and Disclosures.

One issue related to liabilities that concerned preparers of financial statement is how the concept of exit price is impacted when there is a lack of observable markets or observable inputs to measure fair value in an assumed transfer. In many situations an entity would likely settle the obligation with the counterparty rather than pay for another entity to assume the obligation. In these situations, preparers are concerned that they are asked to assume a transfer that would not occur.

---

59.   FASB FSP FAS 115-2, FAS 124-2, "Recognition and Presentation of Other Than Temporary Impairments."

Another issue that the FASB seeks to clarify is how to measure the fair value of a liability when there is a contractual restriction on the liability's transfer. And finally, the FASB addresses whether the prices of debt instruments traded in the market place as assets represent the fair value of debt instruments from the issuer's perspective.

Under the Accounting Standard Update, the FASB reiterates that the quoted market price for an identical liability is the best evidence of fair value, and it would represent a Level 1 measurement. The Update further explains that in absence of a quoted price for an identical liability, fair value would be measured using an approach maximizing the use of relevant observable inputs and minimizing the use of unobservable inputs, and makes use of one of the following approaches:

- The quoted price of an identical liability when traded as an asset.
- The quoted prices for similar liabilities or similar liabilities when traded as an asset.
- Another valuation technique such as the income or market approach based on the amount the entity would receive if the entity were to transfer the liability or enter into an identical liability at the measurement date.

The FASB states that the fair value of liabilities measured using the price of the liability when traded as an asset also represents a Level 1 measurement. The board recognizes that quoted prices for liabilities traded as assets may require adjustments for factors specific to the asset that are not applicable to the liability. Those factors include the condition or location of the asset, the degree of comparability and the level of volume and activity in the market. Adjustments to the quoted price of the asset will cause the fair value measurement to be lower than Level 1.

The FASB also states that the contractual restriction on the transfer of a liability is already included in the transaction price because both creditor and obligor accepted the transfer price with full knowledge of the restriction. Therefore, an adjustment to inputs based on a contractual restriction is not warranted.[60]

43A.7 AUDITING FAIR VALUE MEASUREMENTS

The increase in the amount of fair value measurements in financial reporting creates a challenge for auditors. As discussed in previous chapters, fair value measurements often include inputs that are based on judgment and other assumptions made by preparers of financial statements. In many situations, the preparer of the financial statement may retain an outside valuation specialist to assist with the measurement. The judgment aspect of fair value measurement creates complexity in auditing those measurements. The role of the auditor is to obtain sufficient competent audit evidence to provide reasonable assurance that the fair value measurements are in conformity with GAAP.

An estimate is often the basis for a fair value measurement. AU Section 342, formerly the Statement on Auditing Standards No. 57 (SAS 57), "Auditing Accounting Estimates," provides guidance on auditing estimates in general.[61] According to "Auditing Accounting Estimates," management has the responsibility for making the accounting estimates incorporated in financial statements, including fair value measurements. The statement points out that

---

60. FASB Accounting Standards Update No. 2009-5, Measuring Liabilities at Fair Value, to Topic 820 Fair Value Measurements and Disclosures, August 2009, pp 1-7, www.fasb.org.

61. AU Section refers to the Codified Section of AICPA Professional Standards.

"estimates are based on subjective as well as objective factors and, as a result, judgment is required to estimate an amount at the date of the financial statements."

Auditing fair value measurements, however, requires more than just auditing management's estimates. When market prices are not available, management estimates fair value by using valuation techniques that require inputs that market participants would use in estimating value. The Auditing Standards Board (ASB) believed this added complexity required additional guidance in auditing management's fair value measurement beyond the guidance for just auditing estimates. The ASB provided this additional guidance through SAS No. 101, "Auditing Fair Value Measurements and Disclosures."

In particular, AU 328 (SAS 101) addresses audit considerations relating to the measurement and disclosure of assets, liabilities, and specific components of equity presented or disclosed at fair value in financial statements. These considerations are particularly relevant when fair value measurements change from period to period after the initial measurement of the asset or liability.[62] This standard, rather than SAS 57, applies today when auditing fair value measurements and disclosures.

AU 328 (SAS 101) is designed to provide a general framework for auditing all fair value measurements. The standard does not provide guidance as to auditing specific types of fair value measurement. The general framework begins with understanding management's process for developing the measurement of fair value. After understanding management's process, the auditor makes a determination whether the measurement conforms to GAAP. Audit procedures are used to assess management's assumptions, to assess the suitability of the valuation method, to test the inputs, and to test the valuation model itself.

When obtaining an understanding of the entity's process for determining fair value measurements and disclosures, the auditor should consider, for example:

- Controls over the process used to determine fair value measurements, including controls over data and the segregation of duties between those committing the entity to the underlying transactions and those responsible for undertaking the valuations
- The expertise and experience of personnel determining the fair value measurements
- The role that information technology has in the process
- The types of accounts or transactions requiring fair value measurements or disclosures (e.g., whether the accounts arise from the recording of routine and recurring transactions or they arise from nonroutine or unusual transactions)
- The extent to which the entity's process relies on a service organization to provide fair value measurements or the data that supports the measurement. When an entity uses a service organization, the auditor must consider the requirements of SAS No. 70, "Service Organizations" (AU Section 324) as amended.
- The extent to which the entity engages or employs specialists in determining fair value measurements and disclosures
- The significant management assumptions used in determining fair value
- The documentation supporting management's assumptions
- The process used to develop and apply management assumptions, including whether management used available market information to develop the assumptions
- The process used to monitor changes in management's assumptions

---

62.   Id.

- The integrity of change controls and security procedures for valuation models and relevant information systems, including the approval processes
- The controls over the consistency, timeliness, and reliability of the data used in valuation models[63]

Once the auditor gains confidence as to the reliability of the process used by management to determine fair value measurement, the next step is to test management's assumptions, the valuation model, and underlying data used in the model. Some considerations in auditing fair value measurements are:

- Management's assumptions are reasonable and are consistent with assumptions made by market participants.
- Management uses an appropriate valuation model to estimate the fair value measurement.
- Management uses known or knowable market participant assumptions that are available on the measurement date.

One simple indication of the reliability of management's processes is to compare the current fair value measurement to prior periods. Significant swings in value might be evidence that management's process is unreliable. However, the auditor should also take into consideration that the estimate of fair value may be impacted by market or economic changes from the prior period.

When testing management's assumptions, the auditor should evaluate whether significant assumptions used by management in measuring fair value provide a reasonable basis for the fair value measurements. Auditors should pay particular attention to the assumptions incorporated into a discounted cash flow model and evaluate whether those assumptions are reasonable and are consistent with market participant information. The auditor then focuses on the evidence that supports the significant assumptions that management has identified. Significant assumptions are those that materially affect the fair value measurement, such as:

- Those assumptions that are sensitive to variation or are uncertain in amount or nature. For example, assumptions about a discount rate may be susceptible to significant variation compared to assumptions about long-term growth rates in cash flow.
- Those assumptions that may be susceptible to misapplication or bias and can be easily manipulated in the fair value measurement. An example would be the selected royalty rate in the relief from royalty method used to estimate the fair value of a trade name.[64]

In considering the sensitivity of the fair value measurement to variation in significant assumptions, the auditor may ask management to use techniques such as sensitivity analysis to help identify sensitive assumptions. Assumptions used in fair value measurements should have a reasonable basis both individually and when used with other assumptions. AU 328 (SAS 101), "Auditing Fair Value Measurements," suggests that assumptions have to be consistent with these factors as well:

- The general economic environment, the economic environment of the specific industry, and the entity's economic circumstances

---

63. AU §328.12, www.aicpa.org.
64. AU 328.33.

- Existing market information
- The plans of the entity, including what management expects will be the outcome of specific objectives and strategies
- Assumptions made in prior periods, if appropriate
- Past experience of, or previous conditions experienced by, the entity to the extent currently applicable
- Other matters relating to the financial statements, for example, assumptions used by management in accounting estimates for financial statement accounts other than those relating to fair value measurements and disclosures
- The risk associated with cash flows, if applicable, including the potential variability in the amount and timing of the cash flows and the related effect on the discount rate[65]

In auditing the reasonableness of an assumption, the auditor should consider whether the assumption is consistent with management's plans and past experience.

In a fair value measurement based on a valuation model, the auditor should first review the model and evaluate whether the model is appropriate for the fair value measurement. Finally, if the auditor believes that the valuation model and the assumptions used in the model are appropriate, then the auditor should test the underlying data used in the valuation model. For example, if the guideline company method is used to estimate the fair value of a reporting unit, the auditor should test the data by comparing it to similar data from publicly traded guideline entities. The comparison should test data for "accuracy, completeness and relevancy."[66]

43A.8   CONCLUSION

The regulatory and economic environment in the United States and abroad has shaped financial reporting and fair value measurement. Increased globalization has created a need for consistent international accounting standards. Convergence of U.S.-based GAAP with international accounting standards is underway with support from the SEC, the FASB, and the accounting profession. Accounting standard setting is evolving from a rules-based to a principles-based system. The Sarbanes-Oxley Act of 2002 greatly increased governmental supervision and oversight of the SEC and the FASB and has led to increased emphasis on management's responsibility for maintaining effective internal controls and for better financial reporting.

FASB ASC 820, "Fair Value Measurements and Disclosures" (SFAS No. 157), establishes a framework for measuring fair value and expands related disclosures. It does not introduce any new requirements to measure assets and liabilities at fair value, but provides guidance for applying fair value measurement when required by existing pronouncements. *Fair value* is defined as "the price that would be received to sell an asset or paid to transfer a liability in an orderly transaction between market participants at the measurement date."

Key concepts are that fair value is an exit price to market participants who are willing and able to transact in the most advantageous market. Fair value measurement also assumes the highest and best use of the asset by market participants, which depends on the valuation premise (either in-use or in-exchange). Inputs to the fair value measurement are based on either observable market transactions or unobservable data. The input levels from the fair value hierarchy are the basis for disclosure using the fair value hierarchy. Level 1 inputs are

---

65.   AU 328.36.
66.   Id.

unadjusted quoted prices for identical assets in active markets, Level 2 inputs are directly or indirectly observable prices for the same or similar assets, and Level 3 inputs are unobservable inputs from the entity's own data.

In FAS 157, measuring the fair value of liabilities is based on the assumptions that the liability is transferred to a market participant at the measurement date and that the liability continues with the same level of nonperformance risk. Credit risk is a component of non-performance risk that must be considered at each measurement date. The entity must also consider its own credit standing when measuring the fair value of a liability. Ironically, an entity can report a gain from a change in the fair value of a liability when its own credit rating deteriorates.

The fair value measurement of liabilities under FAS 157 was a source of frustration for constituents. The recently issued ASU 2009-5, Measuring Liabilities at Fair Value provides guidance for applying the fair value hierarchy to liabilities. It states that the fair value of a liability measured using the price of the liability when traded as an asset represents a Level 1 measurement.

The measurement of fair value is generally accomplished by using one of the three valuation approaches—cost, market, or income—or by using a combination of two or more approaches. The cost approach is based on the amount that would be required to replace the service capacity of the asset. The market approach uses prices and other information from market transactions for identical or similar assets. And the income approach is a valuation technique that converts expected future cash flows to a present value by discounting the cash flows at an appropriate risk-adjusted interest rate.

Financial disclosures are required so that users can assess the inputs to the fair value measurement. The specific information required depends on whether the asset or liability is measured on a recurring or a nonrecurring basis after initial recognition. The SEC has also suggested that public companies with significant asset-backed securities, loans, and derivatives should disclose additional information in their management discussion and analysis.

Certain financial assets and liabilities may be eligible for fair value measurement under FASB ASC 825-10-25, "Fair Value Option." The option can be applied on an instrument-by-instrument basis, but once made, the election is irrevocable. The option allows entities to simplify the accounting for financial instruments, especially when those instruments are hedged.

Fair value measurement has been a central issue in the financial crisis. Many in the banking industry blame fair value measurement for exacerbating the crisis. Measuring assets at fair value during the market downturn caused many banks to fall below required reserve levels. In order to raise needed cash, banks were forced to sell other assets at low, fire-sale prices, placing further downward pressure on the markets. As a result, many in the banking industry called for a suspension of mark-to-market accounting (fair value measurement). Others, such as the CFA Institute, believe that fair value accounting did not cause the financial crisis and that the use of fair value measurement is in the best interest of investors and should be expanded. The debate made its way to Congress, and the Emergency Stabilization Act of 2008 required the SEC to conduct a study on mark-to-market accounting.

The SEC report recommended against suspending fair value accounting standards, saying that mark-to-market accounting did not play a meaningful role in the bank failures of 2008. The SEC cited increased transparency in financial reporting and better decision making as investor benefits from fair value measurement. The SEC and the FASB agreed to clarify some of the issues relating to fair value measurement. The SEC's chief accountant and the FASB staff released a joint statement clarifying several accounting questions. They said that

(1) management's internal assumptions about expected cash flow can be used to measure fair value in the absence of relevant market evidence, (2) a distressed or disorderly transaction is not indicative of fair value, and (3) transactions in inactive markets may be inputs when measuring fair value, but would not be determinative of fair value.

The FASB staff has also issued several positions to clarify fair value measurement. FSP 157-3 (ASC 820-10-35) provides guidance for determining fair value of financial assets when the market is not active. FSP 157-4 (ASC 820-10-65) provides criteria for recognizing when market volume and activity have significantly decreased and criteria for determining when a transaction is not considered orderly. When these circumstances exist, the staff position explains when and how the market transaction price should be used to measure fair value, and when it should not. FSP 115-2 (ASC 320-10-65) explains how to recognize and disclose other than temporary impairments of debt securities.

Auditing fair value measurements is challenging because many of the inputs are based on assumptions and rely on management's judgment. Auditing management's estimates requires the auditor to evaluate the reasonableness of the judgment in the context of the financial statements as a whole. AU 328 (SAS 101), "Auditing Fair Value Measurements and Disclosures," provides a general framework for auditing all fair value measurements. The auditor must assess management's assumptions, assess the suitability of the valuation method, test the inputs, and test the model itself.

CHAPTER 44

VALUATION OF ASSETS, LIABILITIES, AND NONPUBLIC COMPANIES (REVISED)

Neil J. Beaton, CPA/ABV, CFA, ASA
Grant Thornton LLP†

---

† The information contained in this chapter does not necessarily represent the views of Grant Thornton LLP.

44.1 INTRODUCTION

The current accounting environment is unprecedented in its need for accountants to be familiar with, and have a rudimentary understanding of, business valuation theory and implementation. The Financial Accounting Standards Board (FASB) has issued a number of pronouncements relating to business and asset valuation for financial reporting, including the latest comprehensive statement, FAS (Statement of Financial Accounting Standard) No. 157. This chapter focuses on the valuation of assets, liabilities, and nonpublic companies and must be viewed only as a primer since there are whole books, not just a chapter, devoted to the art and science of asset and business valuation.

(a) **DEFINITION OF *NONPUBLIC COMPANIES*** Unlike public companies whose common stock is actively traded and has readily ascertainable value, the common stock of a nonpublic company is typically concentrated in only a few individuals with infrequent trades (if any). As such, there is no objective means to quantify the value of such shares. Fortunately, a number of professional valuation organizations exist, including the AICPA, that provide training, education, and guidance for business valuation professionals. In addition, a number of excellent books have been written on the subject, allowing the curious accountant a means to dig deeper into valuation theory and practice.[1]

(b) **REASONS FOR A BUSINESS VALUATION** The need for valuing the stock of a nonpublic or closely held company is triggered by a number of circumstances. Among the more important situations requiring the valuation of nonpublic stock are estate planning, employee stock ownership plan transactions, granting employee stock options, buy/sell agreements, marital and corporate dissolutions, restructurings, sales, mergers, and divestitures, and litigation. In addition, financial reporting requires that valuations be performed to identify specific tangible and intangible assets in an acquisition (FAS 141R), for the testing of goodwill impairment (FAS 142), and for other listed assets and liabilities (FAS 144 and 157).

44.2 STANDARDS OF VALUE

The *International Glossary of Business Valuation Terms*[2] defines *standard of value* as the identification of the type of value being utilized in a specific engagement (e.g., fair market value, fair value, investment value). The common standards of value include the following:

- Fair market value
- Fair value, including *statutory* and *financial reporting* definitions
- Investment value
- Intrinsic value
- Book value
- Liquidation value
- Fair value in alternative contexts

Of the foregoing, fair market value and fair value are the most prevalent as these standards are promulgated primarily by the Internal Revenue Service and FASB, respectively.

---

1. See Appendix 44B.
2. *International Glossary of Business Valuation Terms.*

(a) FAIR MARKET VALUE DEFINED *Fair market value* is defined as the price, expressed in terms of cash equivalents, at which property would change hands between a hypothetical willing and able buyer and a hypothetical willing and able seller, acting at arm's length in an open and unrestricted market, when neither is under compulsion to buy or sell and when both have reasonable knowledge of the relevant facts.[3]

(b) FAIR VALUE DEFINED FAS 157 defines *fair value* as the price that would be received to sell an asset or paid to transfer a liability in an orderly transaction between market participants at the measurement date.[4] The definition of fair value is quite close to that of fair market value except for one key difference. The universe of potential buyers and sellers under fair value consists of "market participants," whereas under fair market value there is no limitation to the hypothetical buyer or seller. To increase consistency and comparability in fair value measurements and related disclosures, the fair value hierarchy prioritizes the inputs to valuation techniques used to measure fair value into three broad levels. The fair value hierarchy gives the highest priority to quoted prices (unadjusted) in active markets for identical assets or liabilities (Level 1) and the lowest priority to developing fair values from unobservable inputs (Level 3).[5] Quoted market prices in active markets are considered the best evidence of fair value of a security and should be used as the basis for the measurement, if available. If quoted market prices are not available, the estimate of fair value should be based on the best information available, including prices for similar securities and the results of using other valuation techniques.

44.3 AUDITING GUIDANCE

Fair values are estimates, and are frequently used in assessing the realizable value of assets and liabilities and indicating whether an allowance or write-down of the asset or liability might be required. SAS (Statement of Auditing Standards) No. 57, *Auditing Accounting Estimates*, defines the general responsibilities of management and the auditor with respect to accounting estimates and provides guidance to auditors in obtaining and evaluating sufficient competent evidential matter to support most significant accounting estimates in an audit of financial statements. For audits beginning after June 15, 2003, SAS No. 101, *Auditing Fair Value Estimates and Disclosures*, is effective, setting a higher standard for auditing fair value estimates than for other estimates. In broad terms it states:

- *Management* is responsible for making accounting estimates (including estimates related to a business combination or valuation of company stock).
- The *auditor* is responsible for evaluating the reasonableness of accounting estimates made by management in the context of the financial statements as a whole. In that context, the auditor should:
  - Obtain an understanding of the *events and circumstances* that result in an asset being valued.
  - Evaluate that the *methodology used* to estimate value is appropriate.
  - Evaluate that the *assumptions underlying* the methodology used are not unreasonable in the circumstances.

---

3. Id.
4. Statement of Financial Accounting Standards No. 157.
5. Id.

The AICPA Toolkit, *Auditing Fair Value Measurements and Disclosures,* contains substantial guidance to auditors on fair value issues in financial reporting, but predates the issuance of FAS 157. As such, although it provides excellent guidance on auditing fair value, its guidance is not as comprehensive as current accounting pronouncements.

44.4   BUSINESS VALUATION BASICS

A business valuation begins with an understanding of the business at the *micro* level (operations and finances) and then expands into more *macro* levels for context (industry, economy, competition). A thorough understanding of the company is required before any meaningful valuation analysis takes place. This knowledge is used to assess the "riskiness" of the company, which will impact implied discount rates and the selection of valuation multiples. Revenue Ruling 59-60, an oft-cited treatise on business valuation from the IRS, outlines the specific business areas an appraiser should consider in a valuation.[6] These include:

- The nature of the business and the history of the enterprise from its inception
- The economic outlook in general and the condition and outlook of the specific industry in particular
- The book value of the stock and the financial condition of the business
- The earnings capacity of the company
- The dividend-paying capacity
- Whether the enterprise has goodwill or other intangible value
- Sales of the stock and the size of the block of stock to be valued
- The market price of stocks of corporations engaged in the same or a similar line of business having their stocks actively traded in a free and open market, either on an exchange or over-the-counter

Analyzing a company's history can help identify past stability or instability, growth trends, operational diversity, and other facts needed to form an opinion of the degree of risk involved in the business. A historical analysis should include the nature of the business, its products or services, its operating and investment assets, capital structure, plant facilities, sales records, and management. Similarly, the economic and industry conditions in which a company operates can have a positive or negative impact on value. A historical financial analysis can provide insight into future growth potential, as well as place the company's current performance in context. Finally, an analysis of "comparable" or guideline companies is important to gauge the success of the company vis-à-vis its peers.

44.5   WHAT A VALUATION REPORT SHOULD CONTAIN

In general, a valuation report should articulate a clear understanding of the company, its industry, and the transaction(s) giving rise to the valuation assignment, and that understanding should be consistent with the circumstances. For example, the valuation of a 10 percent equity interest in a software development company for shareholder buyout purposes should indicate

---

6.   IRS Revenue Ruling 59-60.

the standard of value and premise of value under which the valuation is to be performed. The report should also set forth the methods and conclusions in a manner sufficiently comprehensive and clear to allow the reader to gain a clear understanding of the:

- Methods used and rationale for those methods
- Significant assumptions used and basis for selected assumption inputs

44.6 BUSINESS VALUATION METHODS

In its most fundamental form, the theory surrounding the value of an asset or an interest in a business depends on the future benefits that will accrue to the particular owner. The value of the asset or business interest, in short, depends on an estimate of the future benefits and the required rate of return at which those future benefits are discounted back to the valuation date.

The governing bodies of the major valuation credentialing organizations recognize three fundamental valuation approaches that prevail in the valuation industry and literature:

1. Income approach
2. Market approach
3. Asset-based, or cost, approach

Depending on the circumstance, any of the three approaches or some combination of the three approaches may be appropriate.

(a) INCOME APPROACH This is a general way of determining a value indication of a business, business ownership interest, security, or intangible asset using one or more methods that convert anticipated economic benefits into a present single amount.[7]

The income approach is at the very heart of valuation theory. It involves either capitalizing a single estimate of a company's future expected cash flows or discounting a stream of periodic future cash flows. In either case, events and circumstances internal and external to the company must be considered. *Economic income* can mean different things. In a valuation context, economic income is most frequently measured as *free cash flows* that ultimately inure to the benefit of the business owner. Another term sometimes used (particularly in a valuation prepared for gift and estate tax purposes) is *dividend-paying capacity*. Once economic income is forecast, it is then discounted using an expected rate of return that the market requires in order to attract funds to that unique investment opportunity. The result, in general terms, is the value of the enterprise.

So, valuation of an enterprise using the income approach requires two fundamental steps:

1. Measure the expected future free cash flows that inure to the benefit of the equity owners.
2. Convert those free cash flows to a present value using the appropriate cost of capital.

Exhibit 44.1 will help illustrate these concepts.

---

7. *International Glossary of Business Valuation Terms.*

Tech Co.
Valuation Analysis
Discounted Future Cash Flows

Inputs:
  Discount rate   25.00%
  Sustainable growth rate   3.00%

	YEAR 1	YEAR 2	YEAR 3	YEAR 4	YEAR 5
Discounted Future Earnings:					
Forecasted after-tax earnings	200	350	400	450	500
Add back depreciation	35	40	45	45	45
Deduct capital additions	(50)	(45)	(45)	(45)	(45)
Add (deduct) working capital Change	(55)	(75)	(75)	(75)	(75)
Add (deduct) LTD borrowings/ repayments	100	(25)	(25)	(25)	0
Net forecasted future cash flow	130	270	325	375	425
Discounted	123	204	197	182	165
Five-year sum					870
Terminal value	1,990				771
Implied Value of Equity Capital					1,641

EXHIBIT 44.1 ILLUSTRATION OF A DISCOUNTED CASH FLOW ANALYSIS

In this case, management is forecasting that Tech Co. will experience earnings increases for the next five years and then is expected to stabilize at a constant growth rate of 3 percent. Certain adjustments have been made to convert reported earnings to anticipated free cash flows to the equity owner. Typical adjustments include adding back noncash items (like depreciation), deducting capital expenditures, and adding or deducting changes in working capital during the growth years. The amount of cash forecast to be received by the enterprise from borrowings on long-term debt to sustain operations, or used to pay back borrowed amounts, are added or subtracted as they are part of free cash flows available to the equity holder.

Each year's cash flow is then discounted at the selected cost of equity, in this case 25 percent, back to the valuation date. Since a going-concern business does not have a defined life, a *terminal value* is computed at the end of year 5. This terminal value may be viewed as the hypothetical sale price of the business in the future based on a perpetual level of cash flow. The terminal value is also discounted back to the valuation date using the 25 percent discount rate and added to the sum of the discounted values of years 1–5 to arrive at the implied value of equity capital. Exhibit 44.2 shows a detail of how the terminal value is computed.

Tech Co.
Valution Analysis
Computation of Terminal Value

Inputs:	
Discount rate	25.00%
Sustainable growth rate	3.00%

	YEAR 5
Discounted Future Earnings:	
Forecasted after-tax earnings	500
Add back depreciation	45
Deduct capital additions	(45)
Add (deduct) working capital change	(75)
Add (deduct) LTD borrowings/repayments	0
Net forecasted future cash flow	425
Growth of year 5 cash flow (at sustainable rate)	438
Terminal value ($438/cap rate of 22%)	1,990
Discounted Terminal Value (to Valuation Date)	771

EXHIBIT 44.2 ILLUSTRATION OF TERMINAL VALUE CALCULATION

(i) Discount Rates   The term *discount rate* is used in this application interchangeably with *cost of capital* as they are similar in concept, and its derivation here is done to specifically reflect the appraiser's assessment of risk specific to this company. Under other circumstances, apart from the valuation of a company, a discount rate reflects the risk specific to a particular expected future cashflow such as interest on a loan or other debt instrument. In a business valuation, however, the cost of capital is the expected rate of return that the market requires in order to attract investment into a specific business. The fundamental building blocks for "building up" a discount rate in a business valuation are derived from a modified form of the Capital Asset Pricing Model (CAPM):

- *Safe rate of interest.* Valuators typically select U.S. Treasury obligations as these rates line up with the equity risk premium (discussed next) derived from studies performed by Ibbotson Associates, Inc. ("Ibbotson"). U.S. Treasury data can be found at www.federalreserve.gov under the "Economic Research and Data" link and then going to "Statistical Releases and Historical Data." Ibbotson is a commonly relied-upon source for empirical information that is used in building a discount rate. Ibbotson provides equity risk premium data in short-term, intermediate-term, and long-term forms based on data corresponding to the aforementioned Treasury maturities. The safe rate of interest provides for inflation and maturity risk. For most valuations, the consensus in the industry is to use the 20-year U.S. Treasury rate, which matches the Ibbotson data calculated in the annually published book, *Stocks, Bonds, Bills and Inflation.*

- *Equity risk premium.* Ibbotson data is also used to measure the increased risk of holding an equity security over a debt security. To accept this higher risk, an investor demands higher expected returns for investing in equities than for investing in U.S. Treasury obligations. Ibbotson tracks the historical average excess return of equities (broad stock market) over U.S. Treasuries as a measure of this risk. This premium is added to the safe rate of interest.
- *Small stock premium.* In addition, Ibbotson data is available that measures the increased risk of investing in a smaller company. Studies show that there is an additional return demanded by investors who invest in small-capitalization companies. This premium is added to the safe rate of interest and the equity risk premium.
- *Specific company risk premium.* Finally, many business valuation professionals add an additional premium for attributes present or lacking in a subject company. Examples include:

  - Size smaller than the smallest size premium group
  - Industry risk
  - Volatility of returns
  - Leverage
  - Other company-specific factors

This premium is added to the safe rate of interest, the equity risk premium, and the small stock premium.

Exhibit 44.3 shows the cost of equity measured for the Tech Co. example.

Tech Co.
Valuation Analysis
Discount Rate Buildup

Long-term U.S. Treasury Bond	4.00%
Equity risk premium (*Ibbotson Associates*)	7.50%
Equity size premium (*Ibbotson Associates*)	6.00%
Company-specific premium, including industry risk (judgmental)	7.50%
Discount Rate	25.00%
Sustainable Growth Rate	3%
Capitalization Rate	22.00%

EXHIBIT 44.3   ILLUSTRATION OF A DISCOUNT RATE BUILDUP

Many valuation analysts have refined the equity risk premium with current academic studies and other industry studies, such as the Duff & Phelps Cost of Capital Study, but the Ibbotson data is still widely used. Some professionals opt for the "pure" Capital Asset Pricing Model to estimate the cost of equity capital rather than the buildup method described earlier. Despite many criticisms, CAPM is still the most widely used model for estimating the cost of equity capital, especially for larger companies.

A third alternative discount rate methodology often used by valuation analysts is the *weighted-average cost of capital* (WACC). Here, the subject company's capital structure (equity and long-term debt) is taken into account. WACC is used to measure the value of the company's invested capital (equity and long-term debt), so the market value of long-term debt is subtracted from the implied value of invested capital to arrive at the equity value. This method is particularly useful when the subject's capital structure is different from other companies in that company's industry (more or less highly leveraged) or the valuation is being done on a control basis (from the perspective of a control owner who can change the capital structure to optimize the company's return).

(b) MARKET APPROACH   The market approach is a general way of determining a value indication of a business, business ownership interest, security, or intangible asset by using one or more methods that compare the subject to similar businesses, business ownership interests, securities, or intangible assets that have been sold.[8] Underlying the market approach to valuation is the economic principle of substitution: A prudent investor would not pay more for an investment opportunity than he or she would have to pay for an equally desirable alternative.

The market approach is commonly implemented by (1) selecting a group of peer or "guideline" public companies, (2) analyzing those companies, and (3) selecting one or more multiples from the guidelines to apply to the subject company's fundamentals. Using the example we started with under the income approach, through discussions with company management at Tech Co. and a review of several analysts' reports, five "guideline" companies were selected. Of course, these companies typically are not identical to Tech Co. because they may be many times its size or may have diversified operations. It is often difficult to find companies that are truly *comparable* companies, because most private company valuations involve companies that are relatively undiversified and small compared to companies that trade on public exchanges. This fact does not render the market method useless, but rather less compelling as the differences become larger.

Once guideline companies are selected, they are evaluated for comparability with the subject company. There are six common financial comparisons that are made:

1. *Size* (generally measured by revenues or assets)
2. *Growth* (generally measured as compound growth of sales, cash flow, or some other income statement measure)
3. *Leverage* (generally debt to equity)
4. *Profitability* (generally measured by gross margin, operating margin, or other intermediate income statement steps depending on the industry)
5. *Turnover* (generally measured as a percentage of sales to assets or sales to book equity; which also varies by industry)
6. *Liquidity* (generally measured by current, quick, or similar ratios)

---

8.   *International Glossary of Business Valuation Terms.*

This comparison assists in narrowing the group of selected guidelines and/or selecting an appropriate multiplier, or multipliers, from among them. A simple example of what this may look like is shown in Exhibit 44.4.

Tech Co.
Business Valuation Analysis
Guideline Public Company Analysis

($,000 except per share data)

	AGIL	CIMK.OB	ITWH	MANU	NCLM	Mean	Median
					Valuation Ratios Based on Peer Group		
Market Capitalization of Equity (MCE)							
Price per share	$ 7.31	$ 0.50	$ 13.75	$ 2.14	$ 13,77		
Shares outstanding (000)	22,990	7,294	7,550	83,600	34,500		
Market Cap. of Equity	$ 168,057	$ 3,647	$ 103,813	$ 178,904	$ 475,065	$ 185,897	$ 168,057
Financial Statistics							
Revenues—trailing 12 months	$ 48,431	$ 2,184	$ 157,292	$ 205,637	$ 71,762	$ 97,061	$ 71,762
Gross Margin—trailing 12 months	32,257	1,861	97,021	95,671	47,697	54,901	47,697
Net Income—trailing 12 months	Loss	Loss	Loss	Loss	19,462		
Implied Ratios							
MCE/Revenues	3.47	1.67	0.66	0.87	6.62	2.66	1.67
MCE/Gross Margin	5.21	1.96	1.07	1.87	9.96	4.01	1.96
MCE/Net Income	NA	NA	NA	NA	24.41	24.41	24.41

EXHIBIT 44.4   ILLUSTRATION OF MARKET MULTIPLES

In this instance, one might use the *MCE* (market capitalization of equity)/*gross profit* as a multiplier. A revenue multiplier would likely not be selected because revenue multipliers, while still prevalent in some industries, generally become less relevant as companies grow in size or have different cost structures from the guideline companies. The net income multiplier would likely not be selected because, in this case, four of the five companies reported a loss. Often, industries have specific multipliers that are commonly used, so try to be familiar with them and consider their application.

Selecting an MCE/gross profit multiplier from the range of observed multipliers to apply to Tech Co. requires judgment. In exercising this judgment, some of the selected companies may be weighted much more heavily than others, or some of the selected companies may be eliminated altogether because they are not very compelling once the financial and nonfinancial comparisons are made.

Assume an MCE/gross profit multiplier of 2.5 is selected based on an analysis of the guideline companies. Application of this multiplier to Tech Co.'s gross profit of $800 results in an implied value for Tech Co.'s equity of $2,000. The result from the application of the market approach is compared with the results of the income or other approaches used and conclusions about the value of Tech Co. can be reached.

(c) ASSET-BASED OR COST APPROACH   This is a general way of determining a value indication of an individual asset or business by quantifying the amount of capital required to replace the future service capability of that asset or business. On one hand, the theoretical underpinning of this method is simple: The value of the business enterprise is the value of the business assets (both tangible and intangible) less the value of the business liabilities (both recorded and contingent). On the other hand, the arduous task of valuing the separate intangibles in a business where the value is not contained in the hard assets makes this approach more costly and cumbersome to apply than the income or market approaches.

An example where the cost approach is used is in the valuation of a real estate holding company. In such a company, there may be very little value in the intangible assets, and the value of real properties can generally be ascertained with reasonable accuracy and cost.

The cost approach provides a systematic framework of estimating the value of an intangible asset also based on the economic principle of substitution. Accordingly, this approach does have its place in some of the analyses that take place in the valuation of separate intangibles under FAS 141R. For example, the determination of the value of an assembled workforce is typically done through the evaluation of the costs required to hire and train qualified people to do the task necessary in the company being acquired.

44.7 DISCOUNTS AND PREMIUMS

Depending on the purpose of the valuation and the source of information used to derive value, it may be necessary to adjust the concluded value. Most commonly, these adjustments would comprise a *discount for lack of marketability* (DLOM) (e.g., when public company guidelines are used to derive a value for a private company) or a *discount for lack of control* (e.g., when a group of acquired companies is used to derive a value for a minority interest in a private company). Under FAS 157, the concepts of discounts are rare since most valuations under FAS 157 are performed assuming control attributes. More commonly, a premium for control is encountered under FAS 157 whenever a minority interest valuation methodology is utilized, such as the public guideline company approach described earlier.

The concept underlying the DLOM is straightforward: The marketplace will pay more for an asset that can be liquidated quickly (such as a public company stock) than one that has limited near-term liquidity (such as a private company stock). Here, the differences in value are generally measured by empirical evidence that demonstrates discounts for lack of marketability between 0 and 90 percent but generally comes in between 35 and 45 percent.

Buyers will also pay more for an asset that is controlled by them than for an asset where they have little or no control. This can be readily observed in the marketplace when there is a buyout of a public company by an outside acquirer. Here, the whole is typically valued at greater than the sum of its parts (the individual holdings of the common shareholders). Here, too, the differences can be quantified by empirical evidence through reference to Morningstar's MergerStat Review or other data sources, such as Pratt's Stats.

44.8 INTANGIBLE ASSETS

(a) FAS 141R/142 ANALYSES   Intangible assets have become an important part of the economy in general, and for specific companies in particular. Intangible assets can be developed internally, acquired, or licensed. Each method of attaining those rights has a different approach to accounting associated with it. However, the economics underlying these assets are the same, and thus the valuation of these assets follows those principles that have already been discussed in this chapter. Identifying the intangible assets of a company begins with understanding the company itself. Intangible assets can be found in every area of a company, including operations, marketing, research, administration, distribution, and information technologies. Wherever a competitive advantage exists or rights have been established, you will most likely find intangible assets.

COMMONLY IDENTIFIED INTANGIBLE ASSETS

- Airport gates and slots
- Architectural drawings
- Assembled workforce
- Backlogs
- Blueprints
- Brand names
- Broadcast rights/licenses
- Certificates of need
- Contracts
- Cooperative ventures
- Copyrights
- Core bank deposits
- Customer contracts
- Customer lists
- Customer relationships
- Databases
- Designs
- Development rights
- Distribution networks
- Distribution rights
- Drawings
- Drilling rights
- Electronic media
- Employment agreements
- Exploration rights
- FCC licenses
- Film libraries
- Formulas
- Franchise agreements
- In-process research and development
- Insurance contracts
- Joint ventures
- Laboratory notebooks
- Landing rights
- Leasehold interests
- Licensing agreements
- Lyrics
- Management contracts
- Manuscripts
- Mask works
- Medical charts and records
- Mineral rights
- Musical compositions
- Noncompetition covenants and contracts
- Patent applications
- Patents
- Patterns
- Permits
- Processes
- Product designs
- Property rights
- Proprietary processes
- Proprietary products
- Proprietary technology
- Publications
- Retail shelf space
- Royalty agreements
- Service marks
- Schematics and diagrams
- Shareholder agreements
- Slogans
- Software
- Subscription lists
- Supplier relationships
- Technical documentation
- Technology rights
- Trade secrets
- Trademarks
- Trade names
- Trade dress

EXHIBIT 44.5   COMMONLY IDENTIFIED INTANGIBLE ASSETS

Generally, intangible assets are considered to exist as a separate asset of the company when they either stem from contractual rights or legally defined rights, or can be separated from the business in some form. If they do not have these attributes, they are generally grouped into an amorphous category commonly referred to as *goodwill*. Advances in the use of real option techniques now assist in the quantification of broader conceptual goodwill, including first-mover advantage, abandonment options, and expansion options.

(b) DETERMINE WHICH INTANGIBLE ASSETS ARE PRESENT   Intangible assets can be categorized according to their characteristics. This can be useful in the valuation process. For example, the category of *brand names* typically would include trademarks, trade names, trade dress (e.g., the shape of a container or color of the packaging), and slogans. A fundamental categorization of intangible assets is based on whether they have a limited life or an indefinite life. *Limited-life* intangible assets deteriorate due to some form of obsolescence brought on by either environmental changes or legally determined limits. *Indefinite-life* intangible assets can be renewed indefinitely or can last for an indeterminate period, depending on market factors or upkeep. Intangible assets can either indirectly support the business or directly generate revenue. *Supporting* intangible assets, such as an assembled and trained workforce or manufacturing processes, are necessary for sales to occur but do not drive sales. *Revenue-generating* intangible assets are directly associated with dollars in the door, such as customer contracts, production software, or charging a fee for using a franchised name. Exhibit 44.5 lists some of the most common forms of intangible assets.

(c) DETERMINE THE ACCOUNTING GUIDANCE   Whereas a number of GAAP pronouncements deal with intangible assets, there are three main pronouncements that give rise to intangible asset valuations: Statements of Financial Accounting Standards (FAS) Nos. 141R, 142, and 144. Application of these standards requires that both the appraiser and the auditor be familiar with the specifics in these pronouncements as well as the other relevant accounting pronouncements.

(d) DETERMINE THE APPROPRIATE METHODOLOGY TO ESTIMATE FAIR VALUE
Once a company's specific intangible assets have been identified (and the applicable GAAP and tax implications are understood), the next step is to value each one. The first step in that process is to determine the most appropriate methodology (or methodologies) to value a specific intangible. As was discussed in the foregoing section, there are generally three approaches to valuing intangible assets: the cost approach, the market approach, and the income approach. We will not go over those methodologies again, but instead we will focus on their application under FAS 141R and 142. The *cost approach* considers the cost to re-create a particular asset. It is typically used for intangible assets where there is no direct cash flow generation, such as an assembled workforce. The market approach considers information from sales of similar assets in the open marketplace. The market approach is difficult to utilize, because it is almost impossible to identify individual sales of intangible assets that are similar enough to the particular intangible asset to be relevant. The income approach is the most robust approach for valuing income-producing intangibles as it focuses on cash flow directly attributable to the intangible asset being valued. The following paragraphs discuss the general methodologies related to valuing intangible assets under FAS 141R.

Under the cost (or asset-based) approach, there are two general methodologies to valuing an intangible asset:

1. Directly estimate current cost to replace the asset at its current stage of obsolescence.
2. Adjust historical expenses to reflect current costs to create the asset.

When determining the current value of an asset under the cost approach, all historical costs must be reviewed and compared against the current state of technology. In addition, the effects of inflation and the time value of money need to be appropriately reflected.

Quantifying the impact of functional and technological obsolescence is challenging, but it can often be estimated after an understanding is obtained concerning the facts and circumstances surrounding the intangible asset and its environment. This often begins with discussions with the company's technical staff. For example, the cost approach might be used for valuing software code that is useful only in older computers. Another factor in the consideration of functional and technical obsolescence is quantifying the reduction in value attributable to historical benefits that are no longer available for the particular intangible asset. For example, a chemical plant that relied upon a state-of-the-art, two-step chemical process at the time of construction is now disadvantaged since current technology requires only a one-step process. The new, one-step process takes 10 percent less energy, thereby creating a cost savings over the older technology. This cost benefit, of course, reduces the value of the older facility by the present value of such anticipated benefits and can be quantified using a discounted cash flow model.

Finally, economic obsolescence must always be considered. Simply stated, an asset has become economically obsolete when no one will buy it because there are better alternatives. Whenever the cost of continued use exceeds the benefits, a downward adjustment in the value of the asset should be considered.

Although the cost approach is well recognized among valuation analysts, it does have shortcomings when used in the valuation of intangible assets. While the value of most intangible asset values is measured based on a future benefit that will be derived by that asset, the cost approach is rearward looking and, therefore, ignores future benefits. Furthermore, the duration of future economic benefits specific to the intangible asset is ignored by the cost approach. For example, a patent has a specific contractual life, but under the cost approach, value is not impacted whether it has only one year or five years left of protection. In addition, the expected trend of future potential economic benefits is lost under the cost approach. As with a photograph compared to a movie, under the cost approach one cannot tell whether the asset's past performance was up or down or which direction future performance will take. This is often critical when valuing intangible assets that are based on rapidly changing technology.

Given these shortcomings, the use of the cost approach is limited in valuing intangible assets. As is discussed shortly, the income approach is considerably more robust in capturing the value of intangible assets for purposes of FAS 141R.

The *market approach* has its own set of hurdles to overcome in valuing intangible assets. When applied to intangible assets, the market approach requires the valuation analyst to identify "guideline" transactions (similar to the identification of guideline public companies illustrated earlier). Although there are a number of sources where one can obtain market research, identifying relevant transactions is challenging, to say the least. Online databases such as www.royaltysource.com and publications such as *Licensing Economics Review* provide general data on various market transactions, but their relevance to a particular intangible asset may be difficult to establish. Careful analysis of each potential transaction must be made for relevance, for arm's-length determination, and for determination of relevant units for comparison.

Application of the market approach also requires that the valuation analyst identify the specific rights that attach to the asset that was transferred in the guideline transaction. These rights could include specified geographic territories, product or market exclusivity, sales channel access, or other unique attributes. Once the rights have been identified and analyzed, the valuation analyst will need to identify the full consideration paid in the transaction, including special financing terms that may mask the "real" price paid. If the transaction is dated, say over a year old, the analyst must also consider environmental changes from the time of the transaction, including economic conditions, industry trends, regulatory changes, and the possible existence of new substitute products. Another consideration that often muddles market transactions is the sale of a group of intangible assets rather than a single asset. If a group of assets is sold, adjustments will need to be considered if the subject asset is a single intangible asset. Unfortunately, adequate information to make such adjustments is often missing.

An example of bundled intangibles under the market approach may be helpful. In an engagement to value a manufacturing plant that utilized proprietary processes, licensed technology and publicly available components were combined in a unique way to produce some "widgets." We were able to identify a number of sales of similar plants within the prior two years of the valuation date, so we got excited. However, upon further inspection, key components of the sales were lacking, including the technology that was included in the sale, whether licenses for proprietary technology were obtained and when licenses were obtained, and the amount and duration of the licenses. Ultimately, we were unable to satisfy ourselves that we had adequate data points to apply the valuation metrics gleaned from these sales to our specific facility.

After discussing the cost and market approaches, it is no wonder the income approach is the most widely used valuation technique in the FAS 141R arsenal. Because most identified intangible assets can be individually addressed through application of the income approach, it is by far the most prevalent of the three approaches in valuing intangible assets.

Look at the *income approach* as it is applied to intangible assets. Unlike valuing an entire business using the income approach, as we saw previously, application of the income approach to a single intangible asset or a bundle of intangible assets requires that the economic benefit generated by each individually identified intangible asset be separately quantified. At the same time, in order to isolate the value of each intangible asset and to avoid double counting asset values, adjustments need to be made for *supporting assets*. Supporting assets include such things as working capital, plant, and equipment as well as the other separately identified intangible assets. The economic benefit streams so identified should be tested against the market whenever possible as long as the cost to do so is reasonable. Market forces also come into play in considering the duration of the income stream and the economic life of the asset. For example, the economic life of a current version of software will be limited if the company plans to issue new software versions on a periodic basis. In addition to the duration and economic life of the asset, the valuation analyst must identify the specific risks related to that asset's economic benefit stream and determine the appropriate rate of return for the risks associated with that benefit stream.

When assessing the useful life of an asset, determinants, when present, should include:

- Legal life
- Contractual life

- Judicial life
- Functional life
- Economic life
- Analytical life (based on analysis of available data)

These determinants allow for the specific measurement of the duration of cash flows generated by an identifiable intangible asset. Once duration is determined, the economic benefit can be modeled over its useful life and avoid overvaluing the asset by including future benefits that are contractually or otherwise limited.

Specific applications of the income approach that are commonly used in determining the value of intangible assets include:

- *Residual cash flow method*—focuses on the present value of cash flows after the consideration of returns for supporting assets (discussed previously). This method includes both the excess earnings and multiperiod excess earnings methods.
- *Differential cash flow method*—ascertains the difference between the value of the income stream with the asset in place and the value of the income stream without the asset in place.
- *Relief from royalty method*—quantifies the value of owning an asset as based on what it would cost to pay a royalty for use of the asset over the estimated benefit period (sometimes considered a market approach since royalty rates may be estimated from market data).
- *Options methodology*—focuses on contingent aspects of future value and ability to achieve those values.

Another unique factor that comes into play when applying the income approach to the valuation of intangible assets is commonly referred to as the *amortization benefit*. An amortization benefit arises as a result of the deductibility, over a 15-year term, of the intangible asset on the company's income tax return. Since most valuations are in consideration of the value if sold, the tax benefit of the 15-year amortization must be added back to capture the full economic benefit of ownership.

There are a number of ways to compute the amortization benefit, but we have found the following formula to be a simple and straightforward means to do so:

$$\text{TAB} = \text{VBA} * n/[n - ((\text{AF} * t * (1 + r)^{\wedge}0.5) - 1)]$$

where:

> TAB = Tax amortization benefit
> VBA = Value before amortization
> n = Number of amortization periods in years
>   (15 years in U.S., see IRC 197)
> AF = Annuity factor (AF = $1/r - 1/r(1 + r)^{\wedge}n$)
> t = Tax rate
> r = discount rate

As if the foregoing procedures were not enough, one must also assess the useful life of the asset in building a valuation model for specific intangible assets under the income approach. The useful life of an intangible asset to an entity is the period over which the asset is expected to contribute directly or indirectly to the future cash flows of the entity. Some factors set forth in FAS 142 that should be considered in such an analysis include:

- The expected use of the asset by the entity
- The expected useful life of another asset or a group of assets related to the intangible asset
- Any legal, regulatory, or contractual provisions that may limit the useful life
- Any legal, regulatory, or contractual provisions that enable the renewal or extension of the asset's legal or contractual life without substantial costs
- The effects of obsolescence, demand, competition, and other economic factors
- The level of maintenance expenditures required to obtain the expected future cash flows from the asset

Survivor curves are often employed to assist in determining the remaining useful life of an asset. Although a complete discussion of survivor curves is beyond the scope of this chapter, there are a number of books that discuss these techniques in depth, including *Financial Valuation: Applications and Models*, edited by James R. Hitchener, and *Valuing Intangible Assets*, by Robert F. Reilly and Robert P. Schweihs. Exhibit 44.6 captures the essence of such an analysis in valuing intangible assets.

Once all of the foregoing steps have been completed and the identifiable intangible assets have been valued, those values, along with any associated goodwill, need to be allocated to specific reporting units. The allocation process is prescribed by the FASB; however, it is anything but clear-cut in many instances. Although there have been a number of EITF bulletins addressing specific circumstances related to the attribution of intangible assets to reporting units, the following guidelines help in the allocation process:

- The asset will be employed in, or the liability relates to, the reporting unit's operations.
- The asset or liability will be considered in determining the reporting unit's fair value.
- All goodwill will be assigned to reporting units in a manner that is reasonable and supportable and consistent.

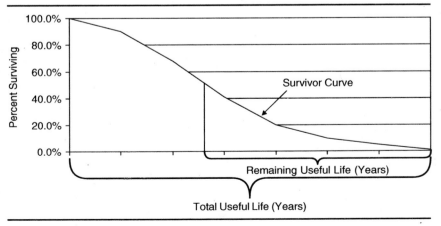

Exhibit 44.6 Illustration of a Survivor Curve

EITF Abstracts, Topic D-101, *Clarification of Reporting Unit Guidance in Paragraph 30 of FASB Statement No. 142*, provides additional guidance in the identification of reporting units. According to the abstract, a business segment must constitute a business, have discrete financial information, be reviewed by segment management, and have similar economic characteristics in order to be characterized as a separate reporting unit.

44.9   DOES IT ALL ADD UP?

Upon completion of the engagement, it is prudent to perform a reasonableness check of the underlying assumptions and valuation outputs. This also applies when reviewing the valuation analyst's work under an audit engagement for your particular firm. Some questions to ask are:

- Does the forecast correspond to internal budgets or external forecasts by stock analysts?
- Is the current forecast consistent with previous forecasts?
- Do the assumptions in the forecast appear reasonable in relation to historical performance?
- Do the assumptions in the forecast appear reasonable in relation to performance and structure of guideline companies?
- Do expectations for the industry and economy generally support management's assumptions?
- Does a discounted cash flow of the forecast reasonably tie out to the value of the reporting unit?
- Does the weighted average of the discount rates of the separate tangible and intangible assets (net of non-interest-bearing liabilities) aggregate to the discount rate for the entire business?

These questions should be addressed by the valuation analyst. They are also questions the reviewing party (auditor or their valuation resource) should ask in assessing the valuation analyst's work product.

44.10   CREDENTIALS OF A VALUATION ANALYST

In assessing the credentials of a valuation analyst, professional certifications are a starting point, but not a panacea. The AICPA has established the Accredited in Business Valuation (ABV) credential, whereas the American Society of Appraisers confers the Accredited Senior Appraiser (ASA) and Accredited Member (AM) designations. Other certifying organizations include the National Association of Certified Valuation Analysts, which confers a plethora of designations, and the Institute of Business Appraisers, which confers the Certified Business Appraiser (CBA) designation. A less specific, but highly respected, credential is the Chartered Financial Analyst (CFA) designation sanctioned by the CFA Institute. These credentials are a starting point; there is no substitute for experience. When assessing the expertise of any valuation analyst, always inquire as to the experience of the individuals performing the work.

In addition to professional certifications, it is important that any valuation be performed in accordance with applicable professional standards. The primary standards governing the valuation industry are the Uniform Standards of Professional Appraisal Practice (USPAP) and the newly issued Statement on Standards for Valuation Services (SSVS1) promulgated by the AICPA. A compliant valuation report will contain a list of "Contingent and Limiting

Conditions" as well as an appraisal certification expressing compliance with USPAP, SSVS1, or both. These standards can be found under the respective web sites of the issuing organizations, www.appraisers.org for USPAP or www.aicpa.org for SSVS1.

44.11   SOURCES AND SUGGESTED REFERENCES

The following reference materials have been reprinted with permission and are included as an aid to the participant.

Appendix 44A—International Glossary of Business Valuation Terms—a reprint from the *ABV Credential Candidates Handbook*

Appendix 44B—Additional Sources of Study—a reprint from the *ABV Credential Candidates Handbook*

INTERNATIONAL GLOSSARY OF BUSINESS VALUATION TERMS

To enhance and sustain the quality of business valuations for the benefit of the business valuation profession and the users of the services of its practitioners, the following-identified societies and organizations whose members provide business valuation services have adopted the definitions for the terms included in this glossary.

The performance of business valuation services requires a high degree of skill, and imposes upon the valuation professional a duty to communicate the valuation process and conclusion, as appropriate to the scope of the engagement, in a manner that is clear and not misleading. This duty is advanced through the use of terms whose meanings are clearly established and consistently applied throughout the profession.

If, in the opinion of the business valuation professional, one or more of these terms needs to be used in a manner which materially departs from the enclosed definitions, it is recommended that the term be defined as used within that valuation engagement.

This glossary has been developed to provide guidance to the business valuation practitioners who are members of the listed societies, organizations, and others performing valuations of business interests or securities by further memorializing the body of knowledge which constitutes the competent and careful determination of value and, more particularly, the communication of how that value was determined.

Departure from this glossary is not intended to provide a basis for civil liability and should not be presumed to create evidence that any duty has been breached.

Adjusted Book Value—the value that results after one or more asset or liability amounts are added, deleted, or changed from their respective financial statement amounts.

Appraisal—See **Valuation**.

Appraisal Approach—See **Valuation Approach**.

Appraisal Date—See **Valuation Date**.

Appraisal Method—See **Valuation Method**.

Appraisal Procedure—See **Valuation Procedure**.

Asset (Asset-Based) Approach—a general way of determining a value indication of a business, business ownership interest, or security by using one or more methods based on the value of the assets of that business net of liabilities.

Benefit Stream—any level of income, cash flow, or earnings generated by an asset, group of assets, or business enterprise. When the term is used, it should be supplemented by a definition of exactly what it means in the given valuation context.

Beta—a measure of systematic risk of a security; the tendency of a security's returns to correlate with swings in the broad market.

Blockage Discount—an amount or percentage deducted from the current market price of a publicly traded security to reflect the decrease in the per share value of a block of those securities that is of a size that could not be sold in a reasonable period of time given normal trading volume.

Business—See **Business Enterprise**.

Business Enterprise—a commercial, industrial, service, or investment entity, or a combination thereof, pursuing an economic activity.

Business Valuation—the act or process of determining the value of a business enterprise or ownership interest therein.

Capital Asset Pricing Model (CAPM)—a model in which the cost of capital for any security or portfolio of securities equals a risk-free rate plus a risk premium that is proportionate to the systematic risk of the security or portfolio.

Capitalization—a conversion of a single period stream of benefits into value.

Capitalization Factor—any multiple or divisor used to convert anticipated benefits into value.

Capitalization Rate—any divisor (usually expressed as a percentage) used to convert anticipated benefits into value.

Capital Structure—the composition of the invested capital of a business enterprise; the mix of debt and equity financing.

Cash Flow—cash that is generated over a period of time by an asset, group of assets, or business enterprise. It may be used in a general sense to encompass various levels of specifically defined cash flows. When the term is used, it should be supplemented by a qualifier (e.g. *discretionary* or *operating*) and a definition of exactly what it means in the given valuation context.

Control—the power to direct the management and policies of a business enterprise.

Control Premium—an amount (expressed in either dollar or percentage form) by which the pro rata value of a controlling interest exceeds the pro rata value of a noncontrolling interest in a business enterprise that reflects the power of control.

Cost Approach—a general way of estimating a value indication of an individual asset by quantifying the amount of money that would be required to replace the future service capability of that asset.

Cost of Capital—the expected rate of return (discount rate) that the market requires in order to attract funds to a particular investment.

Discount—a reduction in value or the act of reducing value.

Discount for Lack of Control—an amount or percentage deducted from the pro rata share of value of one hundred percent (100%) of an equity interest in a business to reflect the absence of some or all of the powers of control.

Discount for Lack of Marketability—an amount or percentage deducted from the value of an ownership interest to reflect the relative absence of marketability.

Discount Rate—a rate of return (cost of capital) used to convert a monetary sum, payable or receivable in the future, into present value.

Economic Life—the period of time over which property may generate economic benefits.

Effective Date—See **Valuation Date**.

Enterprise—See **Business Enterprise**.

Equity Net Cash Flows—those cash flows available to pay out to equity holders (in the form of dividends) after funding operations of the business enterprise, making necessary capital investments, and reflecting increases or decreases in debt financing.

Equity Risk Premium—a rate of return in addition to a risk-free rate to compensate for investing in equity instruments because they have a higher degree of probable risk than risk-free instruments (a component of the cost of equity capital or equity discount rate).

Excess Earnings—that amount of anticipated benefits that exceeds a fair rate of return on the value of a selected asset base (often net tangible assets) used to generate those anticipated benefits.

Excess Earnings Method—a specific way of determining a value indication of a business, business ownership interest, or security determined as the sum of (a) the value of the assets obtained by capitalizing excess earnings and (b) the value of the selected asset base. Also frequently used to value intangible assets. See **Excess Earnings**.

Fair Market Value—the price, expressed in terms of cash equivalents, at which property would change hands between a hypothetical willing and able buyer and a hypothetical willing and able seller, acting at arm's length in an open and unrestricted market, when neither is under compulsion to buy or sell and when both have reasonable knowledge of the relevant facts. **(NOTE: In Canada, the term *price* should be replaced with the term *highest price*.)**

Forced Liquidation Value—liquidation value at which the asset or assets are sold as quickly as possible, such as at an auction.

Going Concern—an ongoing operating business enterprise.

Going Concern Value—the value of a business enterprise that is expected to continue to operate into the future. The intangible elements of Going Concern Value result from factors such as having a trained workforce, an operational plant, and the necessary licenses, systems, and procedures in place.

Goodwill—that intangible asset arising as a result of name, reputation, customer loyalty, location, products, and similar factors not separately identified.

Goodwill Value—the value attributable to goodwill.

Income (Income-Based) Approach—a general way of determining a value indication of a business, business ownership interest, security, or intangible asset using one or more methods that convert anticipated benefits into a present single amount.

Intangible Assets—nonphysical assets (such as franchises, trademarks, patents, copyrights, goodwill, equities, mineral rights, securities, and contracts as distinguished from physical assets) that grant rights, privileges, and have economic benefits for the owner.

Invested Capital—the sum of equity and debt in a business enterprise. Debt is typically (a) long-term liabilities or (b) the sum of short-term interest-bearing debt and long-term liabilities. When the term is used, it should be supplemented by a definition of exactly what it means in the given valuation context.

Invested Capital Net Cash Flows—those cash flows available to pay out to equity holders (in the form of dividends) and debt investors (in the form of principal and interest) after funding operations of the business enterprise and making necessary capital investments.

Investment Risk—the degree of uncertainty as to the realization of expected returns.

Investment Value—the value to a particular investor based on individual investment requirements and expectations. (**NOTE: in Canada, the term used is *Value to the Owner*.**)

Key Person Discount—an amount or percentage deducted from the value of an ownership interest to reflect the reduction in value resulting from the actual or potential loss of a key person in a business enterprise.

Levered Beta—the beta reflecting a capital structure that includes debt.

Liquidation Value—the net amount that can be realized if the business is terminated and the assets are sold piecemeal. Liquidation can be either "orderly" or "forced."

Liquidity—the ability to quickly convert property to cash or pay a liability.

Majority Control—the degree of control provided by a majority position.

Majority Interest—an ownership interest greater than fifty percent (50%) of the voting interest in a business enterprise.

Marketability—the ability to quickly convert property to cash at minimal cost.

Marketability Discount—See **Discount for Lack of Marketability**.

Market (Market-Based) Approach—a general way of determining a value indication of a business, business ownership interest, security, or intangible asset by using one or more methods that compare the subject to similar businesses, business ownership interests, securities, or intangible assets that have been sold.

Minority Discount—a discount for lack of control applicable to a minority interest.

Minority Interest—an ownership interest less than fifty percent (50%) of the voting interest in a business enterprise.

Net Book Value—with respect to a business enterprise, the difference between total assets (net of accumulated depreciation, depletion, and amortization) and total liabilities of a business enterprise as they appear on the balance sheet (synonymous with Shareholder's Equity); with respect to an intangible asset, the capitalized cost of an intangible asset less accumulated amortization as it appears on the books of account of the business enterprise.

Net Cash Flow—a form of cash flow. When the term is used, it should be supplemented by a qualifier (e.g. *equity* or *invested capital*) and a definition of exactly what it means in the given valuation context.

Net Tangible Asset Value—the value of the business enterprise's tangible assets (excluding excess assets and non-operating assets) minus the value of its liabilities. (**NOTE: in Canada, tangible assets also include identifiable intangible assets.**)

Non-Operating Assets—assets not necessary to ongoing operations of the business enterprise. (**NOTE: In Canada, the term used is *Redundant Assets*.**)

Orderly Liquidation Value—liquidation value at which the asset or assets are sold over a reasonable period of time to maximize proceeds received.

Portfolio Discount—an amount or percentage that may be deducted from the value of a business enterprise to reflect the fact that it owns dissimilar operations or assets that may not fit well together.

Premise of Value—an assumption regarding the most likely set of transactional circumstances that may be applicable to the subject valuation (e.g., going concern, liquidation).

Rate of Return—an amount of income (loss) and/or change in value realized or anticipated on an investment, expressed as a percentage of that investment.

Redundant Assets (NOTE: In Canada, see Non-Operating Assets.)

Replacement Cost New—the current cost of a similar new property having the nearest equivalent utility to the property being valued.

Report Date—the date conclusions are transmitted to the client.

Reproduction Cost New—the current cost of an identical new property.

Residual Value—the prospective value as of the end of the discrete projection period in a discounted benefit streams model.

Risk-Free Rate—the rate of return available in the market on an investment free of default risk.

Risk Premium—a rate of return in addition to a risk-free rate to compensate the investor for accepting risk.

Rule of Thumb—a mathematical relationship between or among variables based on experience, observation, hearsay, or a combination of these, usually applicable to a specific industry.

Special Interest Purchasers—acquirers who believe they can enjoy post-acquisition economies of scale, synergies, or strategic advantages by combining the acquired business interest with their own.

Standard of Value—the identification of the type of value being utilized in a specific engagement (e.g., fair market value, fair value, investment value).

Sustaining Capital Reinvestment—the periodic capital outlay required to maintain operations at existing levels, net of the tax shield available from such outlays.

Systematic Risk—the risk that is common to all risky securities and cannot be eliminated through diversification. When using the capital asset pricing model, systematic risk is measured by beta.

Terminal Value—See **Residual Value.**

ADDITIONAL SOURCES OF STUDY BOOKS

- *Understanding Business Valuation: A Practical Guide to Valuing Small to Medium Sized Businesses*, by G. Trugman; 2nd Edition.
- *Valuing a Business*, by S. Pratt, R. Reilly, and R. Schweihs; 4th Edition.
- *Financial Valuation: Application and Models*, edited by J. Hitchner; 1st Edition.
- *CCH Business Valuation Guide*, by G. Hawkins and M. Pashall; updated annually.
- *Business Valuation Body of Knowledge: Exam Review and Professional Reference*, by S. Pratt; 2002.
- *Cost of Capital: Estimation and Applications*, by S. Pratt; 2002.
- *The Market Approach to Valuing Businesses*, by S. Pratt; 2001.
- *Competitive Strategy: Techniques for Analyzing Industries and Competitors*, by M. Porter; 1998.
- *Statistical Techniques in Business and Economics*, by R. Mason, D. Lind, and W. Marchal; 2005.
- *Fannon's Guide to the Valuation of Subchapter S Corporations*, by N. Fannon; 2007.

AICPA Publications and Pronouncements Related to Business Valuation

- Consulting Services Division, "AICPA Consulting Services Practice Aid—Valuing Private Equity Securities in Other Than a Business Combination," 2003.
- Consulting Services Division, "AICPA Consulting Services Practice Aid 96-3—Communicating in Litigation Services: Reports." New York: AICPA, 1996. Product No. 055000.
- Consulting Services Division, "AICPA Consulting Services Special Report 93-2—Conflicts of Interest in Litigation Services Engagements." New York: AICPA, 1993. Product No. 048563.
- Frank, Peter B., and Michael J. Wagner, "AICPA Consulting Services Practice Aid 93-4—Providing Litigation Services." New York: AICPA, 1993. Product No. 055145.
- Menelaides, Susan, Lynford Graham, and Gretchen Fischbach, "The Auditor's Approach to Fair Value," *Journal of Accountancy* (June 2003), pp. 73–76.

- Miller, Warren D., "Assessing Unsystematic Risk: Part I," *CPA Expert*, Vol. 5, No. 3 (Summer 1999), pp. 1–5.
- Miller, Warren D., "Assessing Unsystematic Risk: Part II—The Macroenvironment," *CPA Expert*, Vol. 6, No. 1 (Winter 2000), pp. 1–5.
- Miller, Warren D., "Assessing Unsystematic Risk: Part III—Market Structure," *CPA Expert*, Vol. 6, No. 3 (Summer 2000), pp. 1–5.
- Miller, Warren D., "Assessing Unsystematic Risk: Part IV—Industry Dynamics," *CPA Expert*, Vol. 8, No. 1 (Winter 2002), pp. 1–5.
- Trugman, Gary R., "AICPA Consulting Services Practice Aid 93-3—Conducting a Valuation of a Closely Held Business." New York: AICPA. Product No. 055148.

CHAPTER 46

FORENSIC ACCOUNTING IN LITIGATION CONSULTING SERVICES, INVESTIGATIONS, AND COMPLIANCE MATTERS (REVISED)

YOGESH BAHL, CPA, MBA
Deloitte Financial Advisory Services LLP[†]
FRANK HYDOSKI, PHD
Deloitte Financial Advisory Services LLP

[†]   The information contained in this chapter does not necessarily represent the views of Deloitte Financial Advisory Services LLP.

46.1   INTRODUCTION

Forensic accounting can be defined as the application of accounting principles, theories, and discipline to facts and hypotheses at issue in a legal or investigatory context. This legal context is generally litigation, but any dispute resolution proceeding (e.g., arbitration or mediation) is a candidate for the application of forensic accounting, as are a number of other contexts, including investigations involving accounting issues, information, or systems, and regulatory and corporate compliance matters.

Litigation consulting services can include forensic accounting, but also involve any professional assistance nonlawyers provide to lawyers in the litigation process in connection with pending or potential formal legal or regulatory proceedings before a trier of fact in connection with the resolution of a dispute between two or more parties. A trier of fact can be a court, regulatory body, or government authority; its agents; a grand jury; or an arbitrator of a dispute. Litigation consulting services also include the application of specialized disciplines to the issues involved in a matter in order to express an expert opinion that would help the trier of fact reach an informed conclusion.

Forensic accounting and litigation consulting services apply to both civil and criminal litigation. The principal focus of this chapter will be civil litigation because it is by far the most frequent dispute resolution proceeding in which the professional accountant will be involved. However, this chapter will also focus on corporate investigations, compliance, and other contexts in which forensic accountants are increasingly involved.

Although some may want to use the terms *forensic accounting, dispute analysis, litigation support,* and *litigation consulting* as synonyms, a distinction should be made. For purposes of this chapter, *forensic accounting* involves the exploration of accounting issues, information, or systems and refers to the disciplined process used in gathering facts and understanding issues prior to a dispute resolution proceeding, or in the course of an investigation, or in relation to the compliance matters this chapter describes. In addition, *litigation consulting services* refers to the assistance provided during a dispute resolution proceeding in the case, for example, of expert jury consulting.

(a) COMPARING LITIGATION CONSULTING SERVICES TO ATTEST SERVICES   The role of the practitioner in a litigation consulting engagement is different from that in an attestation engagement, where the certified public accountant (CPA) can express different levels of opinion about the reliability of a written assertion of another party. In a litigation consulting engagement, the practitioner provides his or her individual opinion around the facts at issue in the case, usually to opine on liability or damage amounts.

In an attestation engagement, the audience is composed of all persons relying on the accountant's report, whereas in a litigation consulting engagement, the audience for the litigation consulting practitioner's opinion and work product is generally limited to the trier of fact and the parties to the dispute who have the opportunity to evaluate and question the practitioner's conclusions, support for the conclusions, and methodology.

This chapter provides a brief description of litigation consulting matters relevant to accountants and explains their role in them. It also describes the role of accountants in a number of other contexts, including investigations, compliance, and technology. In this chapter, although the terms *accountant, practitioner, CPA*, and *litigation consultant* are used in various ways to describe an accountant who is providing forensic accounting and litigation consulting services, it should be noted that distinctions between service providers are often made, particularly with those who are licensed as CPAs and those who are not. The chapter includes a description of the types of cases in which accountants typically get involved, the types of services accountants usually provide, and a discussion of the professional standards relevant to litigation consulting services. Section 46.2(d)(iii) gives a brief overview of bankruptcy, while Chapter 45 discusses bankruptcy in detail. Section 46.2(g), "Testimony," provides examples of how to prepare and deliver deposition and trial testimony. Discussions of some of the issues related to expert testimony in this chapter are extended in Chapter 47, "Financial Expert Witness Challenges and Exclusions: Results and Trends in Federal and State Cases since Kumho Tire." Additionally, Chapter 48, "Introduction to E-Discovery," provides insight into the tools and techniques of modern forensic analysis. Finally, Chapter 49, "Detecting Fraud," provides an overview of the subject of fraud.

46.2 THE ACCOUNTANT'S ROLE IN DISPUTE RESOLUTION PROCEEDINGS

(a) U.S. LEGAL SYSTEM: GENERAL INFORMATION

(i) The Adversarial Process   In civil disputes, it is generally up to the parties (i.e., the plaintiff and defendant), not the court, to initiate and prosecute litigation, to investigate the pertinent facts, and to present proof and legal argument to the adjudicative body. The court's function, in general, is limited to adjudicating the issues that the parties submit to the court, based on the proofs presented by the parties.

(ii) Stages in a Civil Suit   Civil suits have four basic stages, barring appeal, which are the same for virtually all adversarial proceedings, whether in a federal, state, or administrative court:

1. *Pleadings.* A lawsuit is started by a complaint that is filed with the clerk of the trial court and served on the defendants. The complaint lays out the facts and causes of action alleged by the plaintiff. The defendants may file a motion to dismiss (arguing that the defendant is not legally liable even if the alleged facts are true) or an answer to the complaint. The answer may contain a denial of the allegations or an

affirmative defense (e.g., statute of limitations has expired). The defendant also may file a counterclaim that presents a claim by the defendant (counterplaintiff) against the plaintiff (counterdefendant).

2. *Pretrial discovery.* The purpose of pretrial discovery is to narrow the issues that need to be decided at trial and to obtain evidence to support legal and factual arguments. It is essentially an information-gathering process. Evidence is obtained in advance to facilitate presentation of an organized, concise case as well as to prevent any surprises at trial. This sharing of information often will result in the settlement of the case before trial.

    o   The first step in discovery typically involves the use of interrogatories and document requests. Interrogatories are sets of formal written questions directed by one party in the lawsuit to the other. They are usually broad in nature and are used to fill in and amplify the fact situation set out in the pleadings. Interrogatories are also used to identify individuals who may possess unique knowledge or information about the issues in the case. Requests for production of documents identify specific documents and records that the requesting party believes are relevant to its case and that are in the possession of and controlled by the opposing party. The opposing party is required to produce only the specific documents requested. Accordingly, when drafting these requests, care must be taken to be as broad as possible so as to include all relevant documents but narrow enough to be descriptive. It is not unusual for more than one set of interrogatories and document requests to be issued during the course of a lawsuit. The accountant is often involved in developing interrogatories and document requests on financial and business issues.

    o   Depositions are the second step in the discovery process. They are the sworn testimony of a witness recorded by a court reporter. During the deposition, the witness may be asked questions by the attorneys for each party to the suit. The questions and answers are transcribed, sworn to, and signed. The testimony will allow the party taking the deposition to better understand the facts of the case and may be used as evidence in the trial. The accountant may be heavily involved at this stage, both in being deposed and in developing questions for the deposition of opposing witnesses.

3. *Trial.* The third stage of the litigation/adversarial process is the trial. It is the judicial examination and determination of issues between the parties to the action. In a jury trial, the trial begins with the selection of a jury. The attorneys for each party then make opening statements concerning the facts they expect to prove during the trial. Then the plaintiff puts forth its case, calling all of the witnesses it believes are required to prove its case. Each witness will be subject to direct examination and then cross-examination by the opposing party's attorney. After the plaintiff has called all of its witnesses and presented all of its evidence, the defendant will then present its case in the same manner. The plaintiff then has an opportunity to present additional evidence to refute the defendant's case in a rebuttal. The defendant can respond in a surrebuttal. Finally, each party has the opportunity to make a closing statement before the court.

4. *Settlement.* At any time in the litigation process, the parties can attempt to settle the dispute without the intervention of the court. This can be accomplished by participating in settlement discussions or by using alternative methods of dispute resolution.

(iii) Alternative Dispute Resolution   Alternative dispute resolution can encompass mediation, arbitration, facilitation, and other ways of resolving disputes focused on effective communication and negotiation, rather than using adversarial processes such as the courtroom. Two basic types of alternative dispute resolution exist. There are nonbinding methods, such as mediation, negotiation, or facilitation, which assist in reaching, but do not impose, a resolution of the dispute. There are also more binding methods, such as arbitration or adjudication, in which a neutral decision maker rules on the issues presented. Combinations of these methods also exist. Alternative dispute resolution is often used because it is the vehicle prescribed in an agreement or contract for the resolution of a dispute.

The U.S. Constitution and most state constitutions provide for the right of trial by jury in most cases. This right does not have to be exercised, and many cases are tried without a jury (i.e., a bench trial where the judge is the trier of fact). In most states and in federal courts, one of the parties must request a jury or the right is presumed to be waived.

(iv) Required Proofs   In order for a plaintiff to succeed in a claim for damages, it must satisfy three different but related proofs: liability, causation, and amount of damages if applicable. If the burden of proof is not met on any one of these, the claim will fail:

1. *Liability.* The plaintiff must prove that one of its legal rights has been transgressed by the defendant. The plaintiff will present evidence attempting to prove that the actions of the defendant were in violation of the plaintiff's legal rights. Similarly, the defendant will present evidence in an effort to prove that the plaintiff's rights were not violated, or at least were not violated by the defendant.

2. *Causation.* If the plaintiff proves that the defendant has violated one of its legal rights, it must be shown that this violation resulted in some harm to the plaintiff. Here, attorneys for the plaintiff and defendant will try to prove or disprove the nexus between the defendant's actions and some harm to the plaintiff.

3. *Damages.* After presenting the evidence relating to the liability and causation issues, the parties' next step in most cases is to prove damages. Damages are one of a number of remedies that may be available to a prevailing plaintiff. Other types of remedies include specific performance (performance of the act that was promised), injunctions (an order by the court forbidding or restraining a party from doing an act), and restitution (the return of goods, property, or money previously conveyed). Damages are the only type of remedy discussed in this chapter. The general principle in awarding damages is to put the plaintiff in the same position it would have been in if its legal rights had not been transgressed. There are three main categories of damages: compensatory, consequential, and punitive. Compensatory damages compensate the injured party only for injuries or losses actually sustained and proved to have arisen directly from the violation of the plaintiff's rights. Consequential damages are foreseeable damages that are caused by special circumstances beyond the action itself; they flow only from the consequences or results of an action. Punitive damages are intended to penalize the guilty party and to make an example of the party to deter similar conduct in the future; they are awarded only in certain types of cases (e.g., fraud). The quantification of damages is primarily a question of fact. The burden of proving the damage amount normally falls on the plaintiff. Although accountants can be used in cases in which damages are not an issue, accountants are most frequently used in cases in which damages are an issue.

(b) THE ACCOUNTANT'S ROLE IN THE LITIGATION PROCESS   Typically the accountant is hired by attorneys representing either the plaintiff or the defendant. In some cases, however, an accountant may be engaged directly by one of the parties to the action. No matter who engages the accountant, a number of possible roles might be played. A litigation consulting practitioner can work as a testifying expert, a consultant, a trier of fact (e.g., an arbitrator), a special master (working for the court), or a court-appointed neutral party (an expert, not for the parties to the dispute, but to the court as a neutral party). A detailed discussion of the role of the testifying expert and the consultant follows.

(i) The Testifying Expert   Frequently, the accountant's purpose in the case will be to develop and render an opinion regarding financial or accounting issues. Ordinarily, only facts and firsthand knowledge can be presented by witnesses at trial. The only exception to this rule is the testimony of experts, which can include an expression of the expert's opinions.

According to the courts and the law, experts are those who are qualified to testify authoritatively because of their education, special training, and experience. A professional accountant can qualify as an expert in issues relating to accounting and financial data.

The accountant as expert may be asked to develop and present evidence in support of any or all of the required proofs. For example, the accountant can review and offer an opinion as to the adequacy of the work performed by another accountant in a professional liability suit (proof of liability). The accountant might review the financial records and the business environment of a company to determine whether a bank's withdrawal of credit caused the company to go out of business (proof of causation). Most commonly, the accountant will be asked to provide an opinion regarding the economic loss suffered by the plaintiff in the case or to rebut the damages alleged by the plaintiff on behalf of the defendant (proof of damages).

(ii) Nontestifying Consultant   In certain situations, the accountant will be asked to be a consultant rather than a testifying expert. The accountant will take on more of an advisory role and will not provide testimony. The work the accountant performs for the attorney as a consultant is generally protected by the attorney's work product privilege and as such is not discoverable by the opposing party. For this reason, accountants are often engaged initially as consultants. This enables the attorney to explore avenues and conduct analyses from which he might want to shield his testifying expert. However, once the accountant has been designated as an expert, all work products may be subject to discovery. It is critical for any accountant to work closely with the attorney to understand the processes that must be maintained to safeguard the consulting, as opposed to the expert, role. In certain circumstances, courts have pierced through the veil of the consulting role to suggest that the consultant's work, particularly in circumstances where the consultant has worked closely with the expert, should be made available.

(iii) Case Analysis and Planning   Whether in the role as testifying expert or nontestifying consultant, the litigation consulting practitioner can provide valuable assistance throughout the litigation process.

In many circumstances, the accountant can be of use to the attorney before the complaint is even filed. The accountant can help the attorney understand the accounting, financial, and economic issues involved in the case and can also help assess the potential value of the claim by providing an estimate of the amount of damages. In certain cases, the accountant may actually help to identify causes of action to be included in the complaint.

Once a case has been filed, the accountant can help the attorney understand and evaluate critical accounting, financial, and economic issues and assist with the formulation of an appropriate strategy. Strategy formulation is a continual process; as new information is received and additional issues uncovered, the overall strategy is revised. During the planning phase, the accountant will help evaluate alternative approaches and help the attorney determine the most reasonable approach to take based on all available information. At the same time, the accountant will assess the strengths and weaknesses of the opponent's case. The accountant's involvement in this phase will help the attorney to focus on those issues that have the greatest impact on proving the case.

(iv) Discovery   Discovery is the information-gathering stage of the litigation process. During discovery, each party attempts to identify and obtain all the information and documents necessary to prove its case. The accountant's initial assistance may be in formulating specific accounting and financially oriented questions to be included in interrogatories. The accountant will also assist in drafting document requests by identifying in a very specific manner the types of documents (particularly accounting records and reports) that would be of interest and that the opposing party is likely to have retained. The more specific the requests are, the more likely the response will be useful. The accountant will also be able to assist the attorney with the preparation of responses to the opposing party's interrogatories and document requests.

A significant role that the litigation consulting practitioner can play during the discovery phase is in the review and analysis of the documents. During this review, the litigation consulting practitioner can identify key documents that are helpful or harmful to the parties that have retained him. It is also during this phase that the litigation consulting practitioner identifies documents requiring further explanation that can be provided during deposition. Depending on the legal forum in which the case is being tried, expert reports are usually drafted, issued, and exchanged with the opposing party during or just after the discovery phase.

Depositions provide each side with an opportunity to elicit relevant facts and to identify weaknesses in an opponent's argument. The accountant can be helpful in this area by assisting the attorney in identifying subjects to be explored and in developing specific deposition questions, especially when financial executives or experts are being deposed. Frequently, an attorney will request the accountant to be present at these key depositions. Here, the accountant can help the attorney understand and interpret the deponent's responses and help formulate follow-up questions to probe more deeply into the subject area. Having the accountant present at the deposition will enable the attorney to better understand and consider the financial issues.

The accountant who will be a testifying expert may be subject to deposition by the opposing attorney. The opposition will attempt to gain a thorough understanding of the accountant's analysis and conclusions and, when possible, identify weaknesses and lay the groundwork for attack at trial. Section 46.2(g)(i) presents a description of the deposition process.

(v) Settlement Analysis   Settlement negotiations can occur at any point during the litigation process. They can be greatly facilitated by the use of an accountant. The accountant can be instrumental in helping evaluate existing alternatives and terms as well as in proposing other strategic approaches. The accountant's evaluation may involve analyses of (1) the economic value and feasibility of various strategies or (2) the strengths and weaknesses of the two sides' positions.

When assisting with the determination of value and evaluation of feasibility, the accountant can estimate potential damages under various scenarios and help assess the probability of occurrence for each, thereby giving the attorney a better understanding of the risks involved.

Just as important, the accountant can help evaluate the true economic value of various settlement alternatives and assist in determining possible tax effects of each. This will enable the attorney and client to make a more informed decision regarding settlement options and perhaps offer alternatives that benefit both parties. The accountant can also assist with an analysis of the relative strengths and weaknesses of both the plaintiff's and the defendant's positions, thereby helping the attorney strengthen his bargaining position and anticipate potential problems.

(vi) Pretrial   When preparing for trial, the accountant can assist the attorney with: (1) preparation of courtroom graphics, presentations, and exhibits; (2) preparation of witnesses for trial testimony; (3) preparation for the cross examination of opposing witnesses; and (4) fine-tuning the overall case strategy.

(vii) Trial   If the case does not settle, the final role of the accountant will be to assist during the trial itself. The accountant's testimony in court is a key part of this role. In testimony, the accountant, as expert, presents the opinions developed as a result of his or her information gathering, review, and analysis. It is imperative that the accountant present opinions in a straightforward, cogent, and concise manner. Section 46.2(g)(ii) describes the course of direct testimony and suggests ways that could enhance the effectiveness of the testimony.

Although opinion testimony is of paramount importance at the trial stage, the accountant can play other valuable roles. For example, the accountant can be of tremendous value to attorneys during the cross-examination of opposing experts and financial witnesses. The accountant can work with the attorney to prepare cross-examination questions in an effort to challenge the statements made during testimony or the credibility of the witness. The accountant will be important in this phase because of his or her ability to help formulate accounting and financially oriented questions designed to be difficult for the witness to evade or deflect. More important, the accountant will be able to assess the responses and provide follow-up questions to close the loop on important issues.

(viii) Credentials and Certifications   Experts or consultants in a litigation case bring their skills and past experience to the table. Increasingly, individuals are obtaining professional certifications to reflect those attributes. Along with increased societal and regulatory attention to fraud, as evidenced in the passage of the Sarbanes-Oxley Act of 2002 (SOX), various professional organizations are increasingly offering professional certifications in forensic and fraud-related subject matters. Fraud-specific specialty certifications, in most instances, are obtained as a supplement to the widely recognized designation of CPA, but holding a CPA designation may not be a prerequisite to holding other certifications.

One of the better-recognized certifications is the Certified Fraud Examiner (CFE) designation of the 40,000-member Association of Certified Fraud Examiners (ACFEs). The American Institute of Certified Public Accountants (AICPA) and ACFE have been working together for some years to leverage expertise and develop joint training programs. The American College of Forensic Examiners Institute (ACFEI) offers certifications such as the Certified Forensic Consultant (CFC) and Certified Forensic Accountant (Cr.FA), as well as specialized certifications in homeland security and certain aspects of forensic medical practice. The National Association of Certified Valuation Analysts (NACVA) supports the business valuation, litigation consulting, and fraud deterrence disciplines. It offers the Certified Forensic Financial Analyst (CFFA) and Certified Fraud Deterrence Analyst (CFD) credentials. The Forensic CPA

Society was founded in 2005, and offers a Forensic Certified Public Accountant certification to those CPAs passing an examination who also demonstrate relevant practical experience. There are other certification organizations other than those mentioned here.

Most certifications require candidates to pass a written examination and have prerequisite experience requirements and annual continuing education requirements as well as requiring adherence to a code of professional ethics.

(c) FEDERAL RULES OF EVIDENCE

(i) Federal Rule of Evidence 702   Many witnesses who testify during litigation are fact witnesses. A fact witness can provide testimony based on what she has seen, heard, or otherwise observed. A fact witness may not offer opinions. By contrast, an expert witness by reason of education or specialized experience possesses superior knowledge about a subject and as such may offer opinions at trial. An accountant may testify as an expert witness if his opinion will assist the trier of fact in understanding the evidence or determining the issues in a case.

Federal Rule of Evidence 702 governs the admissibility of expert opinion testimony. Rule 702 states that "if scientific, technical, or other specialized knowledge will assist the trier of fact to understand the evidence or to determine a fact in issue, a witness qualified as an expert by knowledge, skill, experience, training, or education, may testify thereto in the form of an opinion or otherwise."

(ii) Effect of Daubert v. Merrell Dow Pharmaceuticals   In *Daubert v. Merrell Dow Pharmaceuticals*, 113 S. Ct. 2796 (1993) (*Daubert*), the Supreme Court addressed the rules pertaining to the admission of expert testimony.

Since 1923, based on *Frye v. United States*, 293 F.1013 (D.C. Cir 1923), the federal courts applied a test (the general acceptance test) by which scientific expert opinions should be admitted into evidence. Under this standard, an opinion was admitted only if it was based on generally accepted methodology within the industry.

In the *Daubert* decision, the Supreme Court determined that in order for expert witness opinions to be admitted under Rule 702, they did not have to meet the *Frye* general acceptance test and clarified that Rule 702 does not establish general acceptance as a criteria for admissibility. The *Daubert* decision clarified the trial court's role in determining the admissibility of expert testimony. In doing so, the court need not determine whether the methodology meets the general acceptance test; instead the court must assess the validity of the methodology used and the applicability of that methodology to the specific facts of the case. Discussions of issues of expert testimony are extended in Chapter 47, "Financial Expert Witness Challenges and Exclusions: Results and Trends in Federal and State Cases since Kumho Tire."

(iii) Federal Rule of Civil Procedure 26   If the accountant has been engaged to serve as a testifying expert witness, he must become aware of the effect of Rule 26 of the Federal Rules of Civil Procedure, which deals with the procedure for written disclosure of expert testimony.

Pursuant to Rule 26, the identity of one side's potential testifying experts, as well as information about the expected testimony, must be voluntarily disclosed at the outset of a case, without receipt of a formal discovery request.

In addition, Rule 26 provides that the expert prepare and sign a written report. This report must be disclosed to the other parties before the expert will be allowed to testify at trial. Unless the date by which disclosure of the written report must be made is decided by the trial judge, rules of the local court, or agreement of the parties, the report must be disclosed at least 90 days before the date of trial. If an expert is retained solely to rebut the testimony of an opposing expert, the report of the rebuttal witness must be disclosed within 30 days of the disclosure of the other expert's report.

Generally, the expert witness will not be permitted to testify at trial to his opinions unless the opinions are contained in the expert witness's written report. Therefore, the content of the expert's report should contain all of his opinions and the bases for the opinions. In addition, once the expert's report is disclosed to the other side, any changes to the report must be disclosed before the commencement of trial.

Rule 26 requires that the expert's report contain:

- A complete statement of the opinion to be expressed and the bases and reasons therefore
- The data or other information the witness considered in forming the opinions
- Any exhibits to be used as a summary of or as support for the opinions
- Qualifications of the witness, including a list of publications the witness authored within the preceding 10 years
- The compensation to be paid to the witness for the study and testimony
- A list of all other cases in which the witness has testified as an expert at trial or in deposition within the preceding four years
- Signature of the expert

Pursuant to Rule 26, once the expert's written report required by Rule 26 has been disclosed, the opposing side has the right to take the deposition of any person who has been identified as an expert whose opinions may be presented at trial.

The accountant who is engaged as an expert witness in a matter to be tried in a federal court should ascertain the current status of Rule 26 in the applicable federal district and discuss compliance with Rule 26 with the counsel retaining him.

It is important to point out that the Federal Rules of Civil Procedure give local courts the option of not complying with certain provisions, including the provisions of Rule 26 discussed above. The accountant should consult with the retaining attorney to ascertain whether the case is to be tried in federal or local court and the local rules that apply to the case.

(d) TYPES OF SERVICES
(i) Damage Calculations

- *Patent infringement.* These cases typically involve unauthorized or unreported use or sale of licensed intellectual property, transfer pricing errors, inaccurate allocation of sales value to the patented components, and other erroneous deductions. Damages are in the form of lost royalties. Determining revenue loss may involve steps such as conducting interviews, examining sales records, pricing, freight, parts, and other types of deductions, and testing sales, production, and inventory for underreporting.
- *Breach of contract.* Typically, the plaintiff has a contract with the defendant that the defendant is accused of breaching. For example, the contract may call for the defendant to buy a certain quantity of product for a certain price. The defendant, however, fails to make the required purchases. Or the defendant may be accused of breaching a warranty on its goods or services. The accountant may be asked to quantify the damages suffered by the plaintiff as a result of the breach. Usually the damages are measured by lost profits, that is, the additional profits the plaintiff would have earned

but for the defendant's breach. Among the issues the accountant may address are lost revenues, avoided costs, available capacity, and possible mitigating actions, including sale of the product to others.

- *Business interruption.* A business interruption claim may arise from an accident, fire, flood, strike, or other unexpected event. It may even arise from a contract or warranty claim where the defendant's breach has caused the plaintiff to suspend operations. Typically, these claims are filed by a business against its insurance carrier, though a claim against the entity causing the event is possible. In a business interruption case, the plaintiff claims the event caused the business to suffer losses. Often the accountant is asked to quantify the loss. Elements to be considered may include lost profits, loss of tangible assets, loss of intangible assets (including goodwill), loss of an entire business or business line, cost to repair or reestablish the business, cost of downtime, or cost of wasted effort (time spent fixing the problem instead of generating operating profits).

- *Antitrust.* The plaintiff in antitrust litigation may be either the government or a private party. The government usually brings suit to oppose a merger or to break up a monopoly. Government suits are usually not for monetary damages. Experts in these suits, particularly in liability issues involving monopolistic practices, relevant market share, and the like, are often economists, not accountants. In a private suit, the plaintiff accuses the defendant of violating antitrust laws, resulting in injury to competition, including (or especially) injury to the plaintiff. The accountant's role again may be the computation of lost profits. A company may be accused of violating antitrust laws by selling the same goods at different prices to different parties in the same channel of distribution. This ostensibly discriminatory pricing may be refuted if the defendant can show that the price differences are justified by differences in cost of production, service, freight, and so on. An accountant may conduct these cost justification studies. Accusations of predatory pricing also fall under the antitrust laws. The defendant in a predatory pricing case is accused of pricing so low that competitors lose money and are driven out of business. Once the competition is eliminated, the defendant presumably raises prices and enjoys monopoly profits. One legal standard for predatory pricing is pricing below cost of production. Depending on the law, the standard may be either incremental costs or fully allocated costs. An accountant may help establish or refute this claim by studying product pricing and production costs and measuring the resulting profit margins.

- *Personal injury.* Personal injury cases stem from automobile accidents, slip-and-falls, and the like. Typically, damage components include medical expenses, pain and suffering, lost earnings, and loss of consortium to the injured party's spouse. The accountant is usually involved in the calculation of lost earnings and in calculations regarding the interest components of the judgment. For identification of the issues involved, see Section 46.2(e).

(ii) Arbitration   Arbitration is a form of alternative dispute resolution that is binding upon the parties involved. An impartial arbitrator listens to the evidence presented and renders a decision. Disputes in connection with a purchase and sale agreement are common candidates for arbitration. These can arise for a variety of reasons, such as disagreements related to purchase price adjustments based on a closing date balance sheet or some other financial measure; representation and warranty provisions involving financial information; transition services and related cost-sharing provisions; and earnout provisions or other deferred payment mechanisms that generally depend on future operations or earnings results. Many of these issues involve questions of fact and how those facts should be reflected in financial statements prepared in accordance with generally accepted accounting principles (GAAP) or another basis of accounting.

Buy–sell agreements may also contain a component of compensation to the seller in the form of an earnout that is typically based on future performance and attaining certain mutually agreed-on financial metrics. Disputes frequently result over the contractual wording and earnout measurement mechanisms when the company, according to the buyer's calculation, does not meet earnout targets and, therefore, the seller does not receive any or all of the potential earnout compensation that was anticipated. An accountant may be helpful in assisting both buyers and sellers in offering strategic advice during the drafting of earnout provisions as well as evaluating the relevant financial results to establish whether any or all of the earnout has been attained.

Because certain accounting issues disputed in a post-closing purchase price dispute may also be at issue in an earlier balance sheet that is subject to representations and warranties of the seller, these same issues might be disputed in a different forum under a breach of representation or warranty claim. While these disputes are often decided in a litigation context as opposed to private arbitration, the skills and experience of professionals are also highly applicable in these matters. The accounting issues in a dispute may or may not include some of the same issues involved in a post-closing purchase price adjustment. However, in addition to accounting and financial reporting, there are numerous other issues that can arise in a breach case, including:

- The manner in which the purchase price was established by the buyer
- The nature and extent of due diligence by the buyer
- The reliance and causation issues that may stem from any alleged accounting errors
- The damages alleged by the buyer

Addressing such issues may involve analyzing the underlying records, researching complex accounting questions, or interpreting contractual modifications of GAAP. The accountant may provide consultation to the buyer, seller, or the arbitrator himself, or may render expert opinions in breach of representation litigation matters. The accountant may be asked to assist with:

- Evaluating the accounting transactions and policies and practices that underlie a balance sheet transaction and assisting in identifying relevant and appropriate GAAP or other applicable accounting standards, including any contractual adjustments required by the buy–sell agreement.
- Identifying potential issues that a party may choose to pursue in an objection to a closing statement forming the basis of a purchase price adjustment.
- Helping guide the arbitration process in terms of the quantity and quality of documents to be shared, the extent of interviews of witnesses, or the number of submissions by the parties.
- Assisting the buyer or the seller in documenting their positions regarding the disputed issues and preparing one or more rebuttals. Although there is no standard format for these written submissions, professionals experienced with such disputes can help to convey the underlying issues and facts with clarity and express a party's view

with persuasiveness. Crafting submissions that are articulate, well organized, and responsive to the facts and circumstances is critical to success.

- Providing expert testimony as needed. Because many buy–sell agreement disputes are resolved in ad hoc arbitration where the arbitrator is also an expert in accounting, formal expert testimony is not always necessary to explain a party's position. However, expert testimony may be necessary in some disputes, particularly where parties have brought the issues before a court of law. The accountant may be called in to explain the nature of certain provisions, such as typical purchase price adjustment provisions, to distinguish unusual financial features of the contract, or to explain the nature of underlying evidence and related facts and help judges and juries understand complex accounting and industry issues.

(iii) Bankruptcy Bankruptcy matters may require an accountant's services for many different tasks. The role of the accountant and scope of services to be performed are influenced by the size of the company and by whether the accountant is working for the trustee, debtor in possession, secured creditors, or the creditors' committee(s).

Accountants for the debtor in possession may be asked to prepare analyses supporting the solvency or insolvency of the debtor, which may affect creditors' claims, recoveries, or security interests. Such accountants may also be involved in preparing prospective financial information filed with the U.S. Trustee's Office or used in negotiating plans of reorganization with the parties of interest. Another important role may require making analyses to support a debtor's use of cash collateral and analyses showing that adequate protection is available to the secured creditor.

An accountant for the creditors' committee, in addition to reviewing any analyses prepared for the debtor, will have additional responsibilities. The accountant may initially be asked to determine the cause for the business failure and may need to determine quickly whether the debtor's operation may be further depleting the assets available for creditors. The creditors' accountants may also need to investigate the conduct of the debtor. The scope and depth may vary significantly based on the relationship and confidence the creditors have with existing management. At a minimum, an analysis to determine possible preferential payments, fraudulent conveyances, and insider transactions is usually performed. The roles, definitions, and exceptions to preferences and fraudulent conveyances are detailed in the Bankruptcy Code as well as in Newton.[1]

The work required to establish liability in bankruptcy cases revolves around the question of whether the debtor is liable for debts and/or claims expressed by various parties and classes of claimants. However, liability issues in bankruptcy have the benefit of explicit rules in the Bankruptcy Code (Title 11 USC, more specifically, Subsections 543–549). These sections of the Bankruptcy Code detail the powers of a trustee to avoid transfers that defraud, hinder, or delay creditors, give preferential treatment to certain creditors, or do not give the bankrupt person or entity fair value for the transfer. Since these Code sections define the scope of the trustee's power, an accountant engaged by the trustee should first read and understand the relevant provisions before planning the work. In addition, an accountant should obtain an understanding of certain sections of the Uniform Commercial Code and in particular the Uniform Fraudulent

---

1. Grant W. Newton, *Bankruptcy and Insolvency Accounting* (New York: John Wiley & Sons, 1994).

Transfer Act of the state where the business is situated. The location of the business may influence the scope of the work since the time period under the bankruptcy statute only allows for recovery one year prior to the bankruptcy, whereas state laws vary from 3 to 10 years.

Once the appropriate time period and scope have been determined, the accountant needs to review all material transactions to gain an understanding of the economic benefit of the exchange to the bankrupt party, including all monetary and nonmonetary exchanges. In addition, the accountant needs to determine the timing and explanation for any liens or other security interest granted or recorded during the time period. This review should include any asset sales, purchases, foreclosures, and tax assessments. Transactions between related entities or commonly controlled entities or their affiliates must be reviewed. In a bankruptcy case, the accountant is trying to develop any evidence that might show fraud or fraudulent intent.

A preferential payment analysis covers a review of transactions within 90 days for non-insiders and one year for insiders prior to filing for bankruptcy protection wherein a creditor is paid for an antecedent debt at a time the debtor is insolvent and such payment is not in the ordinary course of business. The definition of insolvency for this purpose is the fair value of assets compared with the fair value of liabilities—a balance sheet approach. *Ordinary course of business* is not defined except by reference to case precedents. For example, if creditors are routinely paid in 90 days but certain creditors get paid just before bankruptcy within 30 days, such payments are probably not in the ordinary course of business.

Certain leveraged buyouts (LBOs) have encountered financial difficulty shortly after consummation, and some creditors have used various security law and bankruptcy law theories to unwind these transactions and seek recoveries from selling shareholders, secured creditors, and others.

The accountant's work in helping establish or defend liability is critical. Analyses that show the cash flow of the entity before and after the LBO help establish whether sufficient capital or working capital was available to the company. Changes in a company's borrowing, especially where a significant amount of assets have been recently pledged, also illustrate the potential damage to unsecured creditors. The accountant's ability to distinguish operating losses caused by the form and structure of the buyout from losses due to the economy or other competing companies will also assist counsel in determining whether the LBO can be attacked as a fraudulent transfer. For a more detailed discussion on bankruptcy matters and issues, please refer to Chapter 45 of this handbook.

(e) CALCULATING DAMAGES

(i) General Concepts   In proving liability, the plaintiff must demonstrate that the defendant's actions were in violation of the plaintiff's legal rights. In moving from liability to causation, the plaintiff must demonstrate that the illegal actions caused injury to the defendant; only then can damages be calculated. In discussing damages, we rely on the concept of the *but-for world*. The but-for world is the economic and physical environment that would have existed *but for* the actions of the defendant. In other words, it is the *undamaged* world, in contrast to the *actual*, damaged world that did occur and in which the defendant performed the alleged illegal acts.

(ii) Measuring Damages   Depending on the case, there are many different standards by which damages are measured, including the following four:

1. Lost profits (past profits, prospective profits, or both, including increased costs)
2. Lost asset value (the appraised value of identified assets, including goodwill, or other intangibles)

3. Lost personal earnings (wages, salary, etc.)
4. Lost royalties or licensing fees (amounts due for use of the plaintiff's assets or rights) or share of profits pursuant to participation agreements

In most cases, these approaches are all attempts to compute the difference between the but-for world and the actual world. That is, they attempt to measure the difference between what should have happened and what actually did happen.

Lost profits are the most common standard for business cases. Valuations are used in both business disputes and marital dissolution proceedings. Personal earnings are the damages standard for the economic component of personal injury suits. Other components are medical costs and pain and suffering. Reasonable royalty is used in intellectual property disputes, especially patent cases.

(iii) Mitigation   A plaintiff has the obligation to mitigate damages. This means that the plaintiff must take reasonable steps to minimize the damages suffered. More specifically, the courts (and damages experts or consultants) will compute damages as if the plaintiff mitigated, whether the mitigation really occurred or not.

In many cases, reasonable mitigation occurred, and the expert or consultant may look at the difference between what should have occurred and what did occur as the measure of damages. After all, the plaintiff's recovery through litigation is uncertain, and the plaintiff has every incentive to reduce their damages. However, if reasonable mitigation did not occur, the accountant should consider what adjustments may be necessary.

(iv) Present Value and Inflation   Time is a factor in most damage claims. A violation typically occurs sometime prior to the loss suffered by the plaintiff; the loss can continue into the future (e.g., lost earnings in a personal injury case); the trial can occur either after the entire loss has been suffered or prior to the full recovery from the effects of the violation; and the award may not be paid until sometime after the trial. Thus, a damage award must compensate the plaintiff for both past and future losses, but it must be made in full at the present time. This requires that the accountant accumulate both past and future lost profits to the present. This accumulation is accomplished by discounting the projected lost profits to the date of violation using a rate of interest and compounding the resulting amount to the present at some prejudgment interest rate. The choice of discount rate depends on the circumstances. A nominal discount rate (such as the Treasury bill rate, the prime rate, or any other market rate) includes both a real rate of interest and an inflation premium. If the damages into the future are computed in constant (uninflated) dollars, then discounting at a real rate (net of inflation) may be appropriate. If inflation has been built into the projected damage figures, a nominal interest rate is correct. In either case, the appropriate discount rate should include an adjustment for risk.

For more on determining the present value of a damage award, see Kabe and Blonder.[2]

(v) Income Taxes   Under the law, some damage awards are taxable to the recipient, whereas others are tax-free. In computing damages, the goal is to properly account for taxes so the plaintiff is in the same position as it would have been if the liability act had never occurred.

---

2.   Elo R. Kabe and Brian L. Blonder, "Discounting Concepts and Damages," in *Litigation Services Handbook,* 1996 Suppl., ed. Roman L. Weil, Michael J. Wagner, and Peter B. Frank (New York: John Wiley & Sons, 1986).

If the award is taxable, then the damages should be computed on a before-tax basis. The plaintiff then receives the damage award, pays taxes, and is in the proper after-tax position. If the amount is tax-free, only the after-tax amount should be assessed as damages.

Complications arise in two areas: (1) if prejudgment interest is due, and (2) if tax rates have changed from the damage date to the payment date. As discussed previously, prejudgment interest is computed on the after-tax amount, since that is the amount the plaintiff would have had to invest. However, if the award is taxable, the damages must be expressed in pretax dollars. A reasonable approach is to compute the entire award, including damages and interest, in after-tax dollars. Then gross up the award by the tax rate in the year of payment. When the plaintiff receives this amount and pays tax on it, plaintiff will be in the proper after-tax position. This approach, although accurate, has been relatively untested in court.

A similar situation arises if tax rates have changed. If pretax damages are used, the change in tax rates will result in an incorrect after-tax award. A reasonable approach is again to compute the after-tax amounts, then gross up the award for the current tax rate.

(f) SUPPORT FOR OPINIONS

(i) Sources of Information   The accountant acting as expert witness should have adequate data to authoritatively support opinions or conclusions. The data should be of high reliability since the accountant is subject to cross-examination.

There are two primary sources for data: the litigating parties (either the plaintiff or the defendant) and external sources, such as industry publications, economic statistics, and so on. The former is obtained through the discovery phase discussed previously. The latter is discussed here.

Many reference books list sources of business information. Also, computer databases are widely available and eliminate the need for data entry as the information can be downloaded into a computer file.

Often an accountant may need to call on other specialists or persons knowledgeable in the particular industry. These specialists may be found within a different practice area of the accountant's firm, or the accountant may need to obtain assistance from specialists outside his or her firm.

(ii) Reliance on Others   The accountant as an expert witness may rely on the work of employees as well as personal research or sources in forming his or her opinion. Federal Rule of Evidence No. 703 describes permissible bases on which expert testimony may be founded: (1) information acquired through firsthand observation, (2) facts observed by, or presented to, the expert witness at the trial or at the hearing, and (3) data considered by the expert witness outside of court. Rule 703 permits an expert to rely on facts that are not normally admissible in evidence if they are of a type reasonably relied on by experts in the field. *Reasonably relied on* means *trustworthy*. *Type relied on* is left to the discretion of the trial judge. In turn, the judge may question the accountant-witness as to the appropriate degree of reliance.

(iii) Documentation   All materials prepared, accumulated, or referred to by the accountant acting as an expert witness in a case may have to be made available to the opposing side. At the outset, the attorney and accountant should develop a clear understanding of exactly what the accountant will be preparing and retaining for the engagement. Then the accountant should carefully control the content of supporting documentation and collect relevant materials or avoid collecting materials that are irrelevant to forming an opinion. This should be an ongoing process, as the accountant may not be able to remove anything after receiving a subpoena. All work products of an expert may be discoverable and could be thoroughly scrutinized by the opposing party. Any errors, inconsistencies, and irrelevant materials may form the basis for an effective challenge to the testimony of the accountant.

(g) TESTIMONY

(i) Giving Deposition Testimony   A deposition of an expert witness is part of the discovery process in which counsel seeks to fulfill several major objectives. The most obvious objective is to find out what opinions the expert is going to offer at trial, and why. A deposition is also an opportunity to commit the expert to sworn testimony that can be later used for impeachment purposes, should the expert try to change his or her opinion. Additionally, counsel will use the deposition to assess the expert's effectiveness as a witness and the strength of the case for purposes of settlement negotiation and development of trial strategy. Consequently, expert depositions may be more important than the trial testimony and should be regarded with due respect.

Adequate preparation is crucial to giving an effective deposition. Naturally, a thorough review of the expert's opinions and underlying support is in order. The expert should also review any prior writings and testimony for previous positions that may be construed as contradictory. Being caught unaware in an apparent contradiction can have a debilitating effect on the credibility of a deponent's testimony. The expert should know the information and sources relied on, the various analyses performed, the opinions reached, and the strengths as well as the weaknesses of the case. Above all, the expert should tell the truth.

Finally, the expert witness should insist on a detailed predeposition briefing with counsel. This briefing should include a conclusion regarding disclosure strategy. If the objective is to cause a settlement to occur, a complete disclosure of all the strengths of the case should be made. If the case is likely to proceed to trial, then a restrictive approach may be called for. For example, counsel may instruct the expert to be careful to answer the questions asked by opposing counsel very directly and to avoid volunteering any related issues.

(ii) Giving Trial Testimony

- *Direct testimony.* The objective of direct testimony is to present an opinion in a manner such that it will be understood and believed by the judge and jury or other trier of fact. The testimony will begin by reviewing the witness's qualifications, which provide the prerequisite skill and training enabling the witness to provide the court with expert testimony. Opposing counsel will then have the opportunity to *voir dire* the expert and to challenge his qualifications as an expert. The judge will then decide whether the court will qualify the accountant as an expert. The expert's opinions then will be solicited. It is imperative that the expert not appear to be an advocate for the plaintiff or defendant but rather appear fair and unbiased. The job of advocacy should be reserved for the attorney. Violation of this precept will tend to undermine the expert's credibility. Finally, the basis for the expert's opinion will be presented. The engagement scope is reviewed, including who retained the expert and why, documents reviewed, interviews conducted, the engagement team, manner of supervision and time spent, compensation, and any engagement scope limitations imposed. Next, the methodology employed is explained, which leads to the conclusions and opinions reached. Typically, any weaknesses are acknowledged and explained in a preemptive fashion to reduce potential damage on cross-examination. The key to persuasive and effective testimony is communication. The expert's position may be a technical marvel, but it is worthless if the jury does not understand the testimony or is not convinced. Therefore, the expert should speak plain English and avoid technical accounting and financial jargon. Concepts should be explained by way of common, everyday occurrences. Condescending or patronizing speech is usually deemed inappropriate. The expert's job is to educate the jury and the court in an interesting fashion. This job can be facilitated by the use of and reference to trial exhibits. Trial exhibits are used to lead the jury, court, and the expert himself through the basis of the opinion, as well as to keep everyone's attention focused. As with the language used in testimony, the exhibits should be kept clear and simple so the point is clear and memorable. In many jurisdictions, the jury cannot take notes, and visual exhibits can be an effective way to impress the point or conclusion upon the jurors' memories.

- *Cross-examination.* The purpose of cross-examination is to cast doubt on or, if possible, undermine the expert witness's credibility and testimony. One of the simpler ways to accomplish this objective is through impeachment. Consequently, a thorough review of prior testimony, writings, and the deposition transcript is required. The expert must make sure not to be on record as holding a view that is or appears to be contrary to the one he is now presenting, or he must be able to provide an explanation.

- *Redirect examination.* The purpose of redirect examination is to rehabilitate points made by the witness and clarify responses and mischaracterizations. It is generally counterproductive to a witness's credibility to argue with opposing counsel or to resist answering questions that, to the jury, appear reasonable and straightforward. An evasive witness generally is a less credible witness. The expert is back in friendly hands during redirect, and this is the time to mitigate any real or perceived damage. During the redirect examination, the attorney will typically select two or three areas where additional explanation is necessary to counter the points made on cross-examination. This is the witness' opportunity to clearly explain why the points made during cross-examination are irrelevant and have no bearing on the expert's opinion.

46.3   THE ACCOUNTANT'S ROLE IN INVESTIGATIONS AND COMPLIANCE MATTERS

Forensic accountants are increasingly involved in a wide variety of client issues and projects that go far beyond litigation and litigation consulting. Most prominently, accountants have a key role in conducting corporate investigations and in using many of the tools developed in the litigation support context to do so. However, accountants are also involved in compliance investigations and compliance consulting. For example, forensic accountants are often involved in antibribery investigations, anti–money laundering investigations and consulting, and antifraud consulting. They are also deeply involved in other corporate issues, such as the protection of intellectual property. Finally, due to the penetration of technology in the corporate world, accountants have helped lead the way in developing the field of forensic technology. Today, forensic accounting and forensic technology are intertwined.

(a)   CORPORATE INVESTIGATIONS

(i) General/White Collar   This is a growing field within the area of forensic accounting and covers a wide range of cases. Examples of fraud and white-collar crime cases are schemes by executives, employees, and customers to siphon funds from financial institutions for their

personal use, check kiting, lapping, computer fraud, embezzlement, defense procurement fraud, costing fraud, schemes involving kickbacks, income tax frauds, charity and religious frauds, money laundering, insider trading cases, and fraudulent bankruptcy actions. Additional examples include investigations of *boiler-room* operations that solicit funds from investors based on promises of high investment return and Ponzi arrangements in which there are no real profits; instead, funds from new investors are used to pay investment returns to existing investors, giving the impression of profits.

The accountant's work in this area centers on investigating what happened and helping companies and their attorneys evaluate potential liability. After the investigation is completed, the accountant may be asked to quantify the amount of the loss attributable to the allegation.

The accountant will typically review and analyze many types of data, including correspondence, e-mail, journal entries, financial statements, and financial schedules. Many times, the accountant commences his or her investigation with little or no detail as to the extent of the situation and must put the pieces of a puzzle together. This involves developing and testing hypotheses throughout the investigation. Therefore, when reviewing documents and other data, it is important to keep an open mind and not dismiss any reasonable possibilities. Very often, an investigation in one area will lead to other problem areas.

Most corporate investigations take place in an adversarial environment. This is especially true in cases involving white-collar crime or fraud. The forensic accountant may conduct or assist the attorney in conducting interviews of relevant parties. Often the forensic accountant or attorney is attempting to obtain information from the persons who are the subject of the investigation and who may be attempting to conceal their activities. As such, the forensic accountant should maintain a high level of professional skepticism throughout the investigation.

Since the forensic accountant's investigation, work product, and findings may form the basis of evidence in a litigation case or prosecution, it is critical to understand the importance of obtaining and preserving evidence and seek guidance from the retaining attorney about such matters whenever necessary. In addition, the forensic accountant may have to coordinate his or her efforts with those of law enforcement officials who may have an interest in the matter.

The circumstances of each engagement are unique, and the forensic accountant or retaining attorney may need to engage other specialists or experts. Computer forensic specialists are frequently used in these types of cases to extract data from computer drives or to search the contents of computer disks using keyword searches. Private investigators can also be of great assistance in performing detailed background checks or surveillance of potential suspects.

In white-collar crime cases where Ponzi schemes are suspected, the accountant will want to document how the enterprise was structured and to develop organizational charts and flowcharts. Tracing transactions from the receipt of investor funds to their ultimate investment or disposition will be required. Analyses that illustrate the lack of any positive cash flow other than by raising additional investor funds can be useful to the attorney in proving liability. Documenting the flow of all cash transactions or custodial arrangements is within the accountant's scope.

The accountant should also analyze cash disbursements to see whether any patterns indicating self-dealing emerge and to help identify possible related entities or personal use or benefit of company assets. Unusual expenses should be vouched, and particular attention should be devoted to traditionally sensitive areas, such as travel and entertainment expenses. While some suspicious transactions are easily detected, such as employee fraud schemes involving payments to fake vendors, many illegal activities involve disguised transactions. Still, it is likely that things like paid bills and supporting evidence will be fairly self-explanatory.

In the case of a penny stock fraud scheme, the accountant may shift greater attention to the financial results and reports to shareholders, press releases, and the like to determine whether there is evidence that such public information is incorrect or inaccurate. Income recognition abuses or improper capitalization of expenses are typical categories of abuses used by penny stock promoters to misstate the operating results and mislead investors. In addition, the accountant should analyze key contracts, employment agreements, and other consulting arrangements. A timeline analysis that reflects all key "publicized events" should be developed and used to help determine whether such events did occur. The timeline can be used to analyze whether, in the same time frame, all acquisitions or dispositions of assets and other financial transactions were accounted for properly.

In recent years, forensic accountants have played a significant role in stock option investigations. Option-related issues arose principally with companies that were compensating their employees through stock—mainly companies in the high-tech industry and other start-up ventures. Stock option investigations generally involve looking into how companies have awarded, accounted for, and disclosed employee stock option grants. Improper *backdating*, in particular, carries substantial risk. An example of backdating is when the purported grant date of an award or the purported approval date is a date prior to the actual grant date or approval date. In addition to the investigation of whether potential problems with backdating existed, there was often a disconnect between those granting the options and how the options were being accounted for.

A company may choose to begin looking at its options activity with statistical analyses to see whether there are any indications of potential issues.

The accountant may be called in during this process to assist with one or more of the following:

- Performing preliminary analysis of historical data to see whether there is any indication that the company's stock price tends to rise following nonroutine grant dates or performing the now commonly used test of options backdating
- Quantifying grantee gains, often associated with backdating damages, to estimate the extent to which executives and the board may have actually benefited from any alleged backdating
- Analyzing alleged damages to understand alternative damage models
- Investigating liability by examining corporate communications and other records

In addition, a 2006 letter from the Chief Accountant of the SEC[3] is intended to provide guidance to assist companies in the determination of the appropriate measurement date in situations where indications of intentional backdating are not present. The letter addresses items such as:

- Administrative delays
- Validity of prior grants
- Uncertainty as to individual award recipients
- Documentation of option-granting activities incomplete or unable to be located
- Springloading

(ii) Securities Violations   Lawsuits in this area usually involve alleged violations of the federal acts, specifically Sections 11 and 12(2) of the Securities Act of 1933 and Section 10(b) of the Securities Exchange Act of 1934. These sections are concerned with making false or

---

3.   www.sec.gov/info/accountants/staffletters/fei_aicpa091906.htm.

misleading public statements about a company or omitting a material fact (either in a prospectus or in public statements, including financial statements), resulting in an alleged overvaluing of the company's stock. Plaintiffs claim that, but for the misleading statements, they would not have bought the stock or they would have bought the stock at a lower price. These lawsuits are often brought against officers, directors, investment bankers, lawyers, accountants, and others who may have been party to the misstatements.

Accountants may be accused of being involved in the liability, causation, and damages portions of securities cases. Involvement with liability issues is most common when there are allegations that the alleged fraud on the market was caused by the issuance of financial statements that were materially misstated or by the absence of important disclosures in the financial statements. On other occasions, an accounting firm may be a defendant accused of violating Section 10(b)5 by failing to perform an audit in accordance with generally accepted auditing standards (GAAS) and/or by giving a clean opinion to financial statements that do not conform to GAAP. Cases involving public company audits dated after the effective date of PCAOB[4] Auditing Standard No. 1, *References in Auditor's Reports to Standards of the Public Company Auditing Oversight Board*, will reference the standards of the PCAOB in lieu of GAAS. In these types of cases and investigations, the forensic accountant will review the auditor's workpapers and other relevant materials to analyze the adequacy of the audit of the financial statements within the context of the applicable professional standards.

The causation and damages phases of securities cases are closely linked. They consist of determining whether the information had any impact on the stock price and quantifying the losses suffered by the plaintiff investors as a result. Typically, the type of analysis performed by a forensic accountant involves determining what the stock price would have been if the proper information had been released at the proper time. The methods for doing this are beyond the scope of this chapter; see de Silva et al. for a treatment of this subject.[5]

(b) ANTI–MONEY LAUNDERING   Money laundering is the criminal practice of illegally filtering money (or lawfully derived money intended to be used for illicit purposes) through a series of transactions to break the trail of ownership. Money laundering is a diverse and often complex process and most often plays a fundamental role in facilitating the ambitions of drug traffickers, terrorists, organized criminals, insider traders, and tax evaders as well as many others who need to avoid the kind of attention that "sudden" wealth brings. A professional money launderer is typically limited only by the breadth of his or her imagination. No business, whether it takes cash or operates under a strict no-cash policy, is immune from becoming the unwitting accomplice of the money launderer.

Accountants' anti–money laundering (AML) and Bank Secrecy Act (BSA) responsibilities vary depending on the clients they serve and the services they perform. In general, accountants and auditors who serve the financial services industry are the most affected by the AML/BSA

---

4.   PCAOB is the Public Company Accounting Oversight Board (www.pcaobus.org), a non-profit organization created by the Sarbanes-Oxley Act of 2002 to oversee the auditors of public companies.

5.   Harinda de Silva, Nancy N. Low, and Tara N. Nells, "Securities Act Violations: Estimation of Damages," in *Litigation Services Handbook: The Role of the Accountant as Expert,* ed. Roman L. Weil, Michael J. Wagner, and Peter B. Frank (New York: John Wiley & Sons, 1995).

requirements of their respective clients. Accountants providing services for clients—acting in a fiduciary capacity, for example—also need to be concerned about not running afoul of the money laundering criminal statutes by unknowingly participating in a money laundering scheme. The *willful blindness* theory of criminal liability could apply as well, as noted below, but an attorney should always be consulted on these issues.

Financial institutions, and certain other businesses such as casinos, broker-dealers, and others, are required under the BSA and USA Patriot Act to implement and maintain a program of controls to deter and detect money laundering and terrorist financing. These programs can typically include:

- *Policies and procedures* to establish how an organization's AML controls are implemented, assigning responsibility for monitoring and maintaining controls, and helping ensure timely reporting of suspicious activity.
- *Know Your Customer (KYC) procedures and Customer Information Program (CIP) requirements* that establish the process for understanding who the organization's customers are, what information is required to adequately identify the customer, as well as assessing the customer's risk profile and risk to the organization.
- *Transaction monitoring*, a key component of an effective AML program. Transaction monitoring is typically automated, either on a real-time (i.e., as transactions are occurring), or batched (e.g., daily, weekly, monthly, etc.) basis. Transaction monitoring seeks to identify unusual and/or potentially suspicious activity by applying a set of defined AML scenarios or rules against the transaction activity for each customer.
- *Suspicious activity reporting (SAR)*. Once identified, suspicious activity must be reported within a specified number of days following identification. The Financial Crimes Enforcement Network (FinCEN), a department of the U.S. Treasury, is responsible for receiving and analyzing all SAR filings for all U.S. financial institutions.

In the course of providing accounting services to clients or in conducting an audit for a financial institution or a client, an accountant may find it necessary to:

- Exercise due diligence when performing client acceptance activities. Launderers may seek assistance from accounting professionals without the accountants fully realizing it. A client may ask an accountant to wire funds to and from various bank accounts without giving any reasonable explanation, to make cash deposits in different financial institutions with amounts just under the $10,000 reporting requirement, or issue checks to clients or their vendors in return for cash.
- Perform audit procedures pursuant to SAS 54, *Illegal Acts by Clients*, to determine whether money laundering has taken place and to obtain a more detailed understanding of the questionable transactions, the business reasons behind the transactions, and the parties involved.
- Analyze findings in previous examination reports, in areas other than BSA compliance, for adequacy of internal controls and audit procedures. If prior internal control audits have significant or a large number of findings, this may be indicative of deficiencies in the AML compliance program.
- Report money laundering activities to the client's Board of Directors (Board) if the accountant believes that money laundering has occurred under the Private Securities Litigation Reform Act of 1995. The Board is required to notify the Securities and Exchange Commission (SEC) within one day of being notified by the accountant. The Act further requires accountants to notify the SEC if the Board does not do so.

- Express a qualified or adverse opinion on the financial statements if the accountant believes the consequences of money laundering have not been properly accounted for or disclosed in the company's financial statements in accordance with SAS 54.
- Resign if a client refuses to accept the auditor's modified report.
- Advise clients who become subject to asset forfeiture.
- Provide remediation advice to clients regarding Internal Revenue Service (IRS) Form W-8, acceptance of and reliance upon which has been disallowed by the IRS due to incompleteness or lack of appropriate treaty status claimed. Additionally, accountants may be called on to advise clients who may have incorrectly filed or failed to appropriately file IRS Form 8300 (Currency Transactions). Such advice might involve counseling or consulting with the client's legal counsel (for internal auditors) or other specialists.
- Estimate increased contingent liabilities for clients who become subject to AML-related litigation, particularly criminal actions.
- Advise on accrual methods for presumptive legal and regulatory penalties and fines.
- Seek professional advice whenever appropriate and consult with the client's legal counsel (for internal auditors) or other specialists.

Accountants may become inadvertently exposed to potential money laundering activities through the processing and evaluating of their clients' financial records and activities. Accountants are often viewed as "gatekeepers" for their clients' financial transactions and need to conduct appropriate risk-based due diligence. Accountants should consider attending periodic training on money laundering–related issues, including preventive techniques, and courses of action in cases where the clients are suspected to be involved in money laundering. One of the most effective steps an accountant can take to understand how the accounting profession can work with clients to help prevent money laundering is to become familiar with the Bank Secrecy Act and the USA Patriot Act. Additionally, accountants and auditors who focus on the financial services industry should have an awareness of the AML self-regulatory mechanisms proposed by industry organizations,[6] previous enforcement actions, and regulatory penalties.

Accountants should also be aware of the *willful blindness* concept and should always consult an attorney on this issue. *Willful blindness* means attempting to avoid criminal or civil liability for a wrongful act by intentionally putting oneself in a position to be unaware of facts that would render one otherwise liable.[7] The government may charge accountants as accomplices to a money laundering crime. If the government is not able to prove the accountants' actual knowledge of criminal activities, the government may use the willful blindness argument sometimes employed by prosecuting attorneys.

(i) AML Technology   AML technology should be leveraged to support an organization's money laundering risk management undertaking. Such technology includes account behavior and transaction-monitoring software, systems that capture suspicious data, provide for analysis, investigation, and resolution, and produce SAR and currency transaction reports as well as monitor Office of Foreign Assets Control (OFAC) obligations and compliance with other sanctions programs.

---

6.   The New York Stock Exchange and the National Association of Securities Dealers, now collectively FINRA.

7.   http://en.wikipedia.org/wiki/Willful_blindness.

These technologies can provide organizations with the capability to effectively monitor the behavior of millions of client accounts and complex financial real-time and transactional activity, to identify potential unusual activity that may need further investigation, and to ensure the subsequent and timely reporting of suspicious activity to FinCEN or other jurisdictional regulatory authorities. In addition, these systems can provide an organization with the ability to define various types of potential suspicious activities based on customers' type of business, country of incorporation, transaction type, product, channel, time, and other dimensions that may be applicable to the business.

Because of the nature of the technologies in use, consultation with forensic technology specialists is generally required.

(c) FOREIGN CORRUPT PRACTICES ACT VIOLATIONS   In recent years, with the increasing globalization of business, U.S. regulators have focused on the conduct of businesses. Although an act dating back from the post-Watergate era, the Foreign Corrupt Practices Act of 1977 (FCPA) has been the focal point for investigations of companies and for actions being taken by the U.S. Department of Justice (DOJ) and the SEC. The increasing number of FCPA investigations has been considerable over the past several years, resulting in potentially high civil penalties. Official corruption investigations have also been spurred, during the latter part of 2007 and in 2008, by some foreign governments taking actions in antibribery matters that parallel the types of investigations coming from the United States.

The FCPA's most critical parts include the following:

- The *antibribery provision* covers a wide array of prohibited actions by any U.S. individual or organization, as well as non-U.S. persons and entities within U.S. jurisdiction, including paying, offering to pay, or authorizing payments to foreign officials in order to secure an improper business advantage. In other words, companies, their employees, and their agents are prohibited from offering or authorizing anything of value, directly or through third parties, to foreign officials for the purpose of obtaining or retaining business. The Act is both a criminal statute enforced by the DOJ and a civil statute enforced by the SEC.

- The *accounting requirements*—also known as the *books and records* provisions— apply to public companies that are "issuers" of securities under the Exchange Act of 1934. The accounting provisions require that issuers (including foreign issuers) accurately record payments in their books and records detailing their financial transactions. The accounting provisions apply to U.S. issuers' domestic and foreign majority-owned subsidiaries.

- The *internal controls provision* requires companies to establish and maintain a system of internal controls that provide reasonable assurances that transactions are properly authorized and recorded, and that companies do not make inappropriate payments to foreign officials. Companies must also make a *good-faith* effort to use their influence to cause entities (domestic and foreign) in which they hold a minority interest to devise and maintain an adequate system of controls.

Because the individuals involved with transactions that violate the FCPA often know the transaction is illegal, they will likely take precautions to hide the transaction, misrecord it, or move it off the financial records completely. Typical controls and processes rely on the accurate disclosure of the nature of a transaction, the truth of the underlying document, or primary approval. These assumptions may not be appropriate, and may not catch what is purposely hidden. A different focus from normal internal audit or investigatory procedures may be called for as a result. Sifting through transactions looking for bribes has a needle-in-a-haystack aspect and makes sampling less effective than it is in an audit context. Not only do transactions need to be reviewed more comprehensively, but the investigator also needs to be aware of the way in which bribes are often masked.

The forensic accountant's role in the course of an investigation into potential FCPA violations often includes analyzing electronic and hardcopy financial records and assisting counsel in conducting interviews of relevant personnel to help identify whether schemes exist and to understand how the schemes work, assess the scope of the violations, and report on findings. Accountants might also be called in to help their clients respond to specific allegations or requests that might not relate to wrongdoing on their part.

To review company records for the presence of schemes, accountants must inspect payable records, and especially journal entries regarding payables, including the text for such entries and words that mask the true purpose of the transaction (referring to a bribe as a *tuition payment*, for example), employee expense records and reimbursements, and e-mails and other forms of corporate communication. Forensic accountants who typically do this work have at their disposal a wealth of knowledge about how schemes work and therefore a number of specific tests they employ to determine whether instances of schemes are present in transactions. Because the records of most companies are electronic these days, the forensic accountant usually works closely with forensic technologists who have developed deep knowledge of the major accounting systems and techniques for exploring the data in these systems.

(d) ANTIFRAUD PROGRAMS AND CONTROLS With the advent of Auditing Standard No. 2 (AS 2), Auditing Standard No. 5 (AS 5), and the related SOX Section 404 (404) guidance, the need for companies to implement an effective Antifraud Programs and Controls Framework (AFPC) has been reemphasized, particularly for public companies. For example, it is now clear that management has a responsibility to assess fraud risks for their organization utilizing "sound and thoughtful judgments that reflect a company's individual facts and circumstances."[8] An overall risk assessment that does not appropriately consider specific fraud risks to the organization is not compliant with current legislation and regulation. Further, current legislation and regulations emphasize the use of a top-down risk-based approach in the design and implementation of entity-level controls, the intent being that appropriately designed entity-level controls can reduce process-level testing.

A focus of the accountant as AFPC consultant is to understand whether corporate management is fulfilling their responsibilities and duties in a manner that reflects the underlying spirit, guidance, and requirements under AS 2, AS 5, the Financial Accounting Standards Board Statement of Auditing Standards No. 99 (SAS 99), and SOX 404. Delivery of AFPC consulting services requires specialized training and experience. The practitioner must develop a thorough understanding of the client's antifraud program and make determinations as to the effectiveness of the program in terms of preventing and detecting fraud.

---

8. Securities and Exchange Commission, 17 CFR Part 241, *Commission Guidance Regarding Management's Report on Internal Control over Financial Reporting under Section 13(a) or 15(d) of the Securities Exchange Act of 1934*; Final Rule, page 15.

(i) AFPC Service Types   AFPC services generally fall into three broad categories that can be tailored to meet the needs of the engagement:

1. Assisting management with its design and implementation of an AFPC program or its components
2. Assessing the design and operating effectiveness of an organization's existing AFPC framework in order to aid management in meeting their responsibilities under 404
3. Assisting the audit engagement team in assessing the design and operating effectiveness of an audit client's AFPC framework, in connection with assurance services, as required under SAS 99 and AS 5

The accountant can add value to the AFPC process by assisting clients in several specific ways, including:

- Assessing the client's antifraud programs and controls in each of the five main COSO (Committee of Sponsoring Organizations of the Treadway Commission) areas, including:
  - *Control environment*—assessing the effectiveness of oversight provided by the Audit Committee and the Board, evaluating the Code of Conduct/Ethics, assessing the effectiveness of the whistleblower hotline and incident reporting within the entity, assessing the effectiveness of the entity's investigation and remediation processes, assessing the client's hiring and promotion procedures in terms of fraud risk, and other control environment considerations
  - *Risk assessment*—evaluating the client's approach and fraud risk assessment, assisting in the client's fraud risk assessment implementation, and providing training in the fraud risk assessment process
  - *Control activities*—considering the linkage of control activities the entity has identified as being antifraud in nature and assessing the effectiveness of those controls
  - *Information and communication*—assessing the client's approach to fraud training, assessing knowledge and records management around fraud, evaluating data and system security and antifraud measures
  - *Monitoring*—evaluating the effectiveness and extent of monitoring activities by management and internal audit
- Assisting in the company's fraud risk assessment
- Providing fraud awareness training to client personnel

For non-404 attest clients, especially those considering a future initial public offering, the AFPC team can also add value by conducting a formal assessment of the client's antifraud programs and controls with the goal of providing a road map of their required steps toward SOX readiness.

(e) LICENSING AND CONTRACT INVESTIGATIONS   Protecting company assets, particularly intellectual property, and securing the global supply chain has become a strategic initiative for companies entering into contracts with other entities through joint ventures, profit sharing, patent, trademark and copyright licensing, or distribution transactions. Corporations may have entered into production/distribution agreements with an international partner or into licensing contracts with global manufacturers of consumer products. In these situations, effective management of revenues and costs involving other entities can help protect a company's return on investment and bottom-line profits. In addition, specific industry knowledge is particularly important with respect to investigations involving contracts among the parties.

An accountant may be called in to assist in these matters by providing services, including:

- Conducting investigations to help clients evaluate whether they have been paid properly pursuant to their agreements, and if not, providing analyses to help quantify potential discrepancies
- Providing forensic services aimed at detecting and quantifying:
  - Unpaid royalties, understated joint venture profits, and unreported revenue streams
  - Inaccurate calculations of royalties payable
  - Overstatements of joint venture costs
- Helping clients understand financial implications related to licensing, co-promotion, and joint venture partners and the interpretations of financial calculations in the relevant agreements
- Assisting in evaluating business transactions, helping to identify potential transaction partners, and assessing the relative merits of various forms of compensation, including upfront payments, ongoing royalties, cross-licenses, and strategic partnerships
- Assisting in developing processes that could help reduce the risk of revenue loss and identify unauthorized use of licensed intellectual property
- Facilitating or assisting settlement negotiations regarding financial aspects of the agreements and damage calculations
- Helping develop the financial, accounting, and auditing provisions in licensing/profit sharing/distribution agreements
- Helping clients establish royalty rates for various technologies

(f) FORENSIC TECHNOLOGY Business records today are largely kept in electronic form. Corporate correspondence, corporate policies and procedures, compliance and governance records, records of transactions, manufacturing records, accounting ledgers, employee records, records of services, and so on, are generated and maintained in computerized format for most companies. The information forensic accountants need to do their work, whether the context is dispute resolution or investigations, is therefore increasingly electronic. An entire business dispute or multimillion-dollar litigation may hinge on identifying when a single piece of data was generated—or altered or deleted—by whom, and under what circumstances, or on a demonstration that no data was altered or deleted. Similarly, anti–money laundering investigations and investigations based on corruption allegations require the ability to sift through huge numbers of transactions to confirm or disconfirm the presence of money laundering transactions or bribes—the proverbial needle-in-a-haystack problem. Not only must various forms of computer technology be available to the forensic accountant to perform tests and develop opinions, but forensic accountants must be skilled in how they can most effectively be used as well. Simply put, the accountant must have the ability to acquire the information in a forensically sound manner and to analyze it. Lastly, forensic accountants and data management professionals need to take into account local and regional data security and privacy regulations at all times.

(i) *Computer Forensics* Computer forensics is the science of retrieving and chronicling evidence located on computers, disks, tapes, thumb drives, voicemail systems—any form of electronically stored information (ESI) for use as evidence in a court of law, or in an investigation, or in a compliance context. The practice of computer forensics includes the use of formal, accepted techniques for collecting, analyzing, and presenting suspect data in court, concentrating on rules of evidence, the legal processes, the integrity and perpetuity of evidence, reporting of facts, and the preparation and presentation of expert testimony. The same disciplined collection techniques are used in investigations where the key issues are the same—demonstrating that there was no bias in the collection of information, that the information was not altered in the collection process, and that the chain of custody was maintained.

A wealth of information may be recoverable from computer hard drives and backup tapes, including active, deleted, hidden, lost, or encrypted files, or file fragments. Even files that were created but never saved may be recovered. In addition to collecting information for litigation consulting and investigations, computer forensic specialists are also called on to analyze information technology (IT) systems for evidence of potential malfeasance, such as information deletion, policy violations, or unauthorized access. The process used by a computer forensic specialist often involves taking an image or exact replica of the hard drive, which is preserved in a locked, fireproof safe for evidentiary and chain-of-custody purposes. Diagnostic software tools are then run against copies of the image to search for the existence of relevant files. Paper documents still play a significant role in many litigation matters. Computer forensics may also be used to compare paper documents with their electronic counterparts to help determine whether the document has been altered.

After collecting information, computer forensics professionals can then look for e-mails, documents, spreadsheet files, Web downloads, and other electronic data that may have been deleted or encrypted, or may exist only in fragments. Such bits and pieces of data can have tremendous value in an investigation.

An accountant may be tasked with leading cases or investigations involving computer forensics or may assist counsel in the investigatory process of preserving, collecting, processing, and reviewing data. The accountant's role may include providing assistance with:

- Identifying the "trigger" that initiated the investigation (e.g., a document, an e-mail, a spreadsheet) and ensuring that the computer or IT systems involved are secured to prevent tampering or deleting evidence.
- Defining the scope and timeline of the investigation, considering complexities such as locations involved, global regions, type of accounting systems in use, language barriers, and the like. Because the very act of investigating can often reveal more layers of data and avenues to explore, *scope creep* is a common problem. Tightly defining the project parameters and specific tasks to be accomplished can help control "creep."
- Identifying and prioritizing individuals involved, particularly the custodians (i.e., owners or creators) of data in question, and interviewing them as needed.
- Engaging and consulting with computer forensics specialists to collect data and verify that the collection was done correctly and that a defensible chain of custody was maintained.
- Providing micro or macro financial analyses as needed, such as analyzing recovered files or assessing the situation in the context of the organization's broader financial picture.

(ii) Data Analysis   After data is collected, computer technology is also required to analyze it. Data analysis takes two principal forms: (1) Textual information is put into discovery databases so it can be explored by the forensic accountant and other members of the litigation or investigation team. The process and role of such databases is discussed fully in Chapter 48; (2) numeric information, such as accounting transaction data, is usually put into relational database management systems so that it can be ordered into patterns. Various analyses can be performed on the data, such as date analysis or analysis by type of transaction, or the database can be searched for particular types of transactions, such as those that may be in violation of the FCPA requirements. The data analysis component of litigation and investigations can often help put together pieces of the litigation puzzle by searching, analyzing, and modeling data obtained as part of the discovery process. Data can be obtained from various sources including accounting systems (such as SAP, Oracle Financials, etc.), manufacturing systems, human resource and payroll systems, billing systems, customer relationship management (CRM) systems, spreadsheets, and more. Individuals' personal files and folders are also open to scrutiny.

Leveraging data analysis to support the accounting investigation can yield several advantages, including the ability to:

- Extract and restore data from the original (native) format, which reduces the risk of working with potentially manipulated data.
- Maintain and process data in a secure environment.
- Summarize data for reconciliation to financial or system reports to check for completeness.
- Search and analyze the entire population of data for anomalies to identify a smaller set of exceptions for detailed review.
- Piece together data from different sources to create a coherent understanding of past transactions (e.g., bringing contract, payment, shipping, and banking records together to identify the full history of transactions).
- Obtain faster access to information by electronically processing large volumes of data, given that speed and accuracy are essential in a litigation case.
- Perform advanced keyword and pattern searches, including handling foreign languages.
- Compare data from various systems potentially in different formats (e.g., matching vendor names, addresses, bank accounts, etc. from the payables ledger to the employee master and payroll system).
- Reperform the analysis efficiently by changing the parameters.

The forensic accountant plays an active role in the data analysis process, particularly in defining tests, various forms of data reconciliation (such as reconciling general ledger data to the financial statements), assisting with the development of keywords for searching, developing anomaly detection tests in AML and FCPA contexts, and reviewing and interpreting analysis results for potentially responsive or hot transactions.

Given the specialized skills required to manipulate various database systems, understand the client's business processes, load the data into a platform for analysis, and develop and generate programs for analysis, it is advisable for the forensic accountant to work closely with a practitioner who specializes in data analysis. The background of such professionals typically includes an understanding of relational database systems, knowledge of financial information, and appropriate computer programming skills.

46.4   GLOBALIZATION IMPACT—IFRS

Increasingly, forensic accountants must focus on globalization, including in regard to accounting principles. IFRS is a single set of accounting principles that is more focused on objectives and principles and less reliant on detailed rules than U.S. GAAP. With more than 100 countries and approximately 40 percent of the Global Fortune 500 companies already using IFRS, and with the SEC expected to push for allowing U.S. multinationals to use IFRS by 2011, this will be an important challenge for the accounting profession. In addition, U.S. public companies will likely have the option of using either IFRS or U.S. GAAP. IFRS requires more use of professional judgment and provides less detailed, principles-based guidance. It focuses on reflecting "economic reality." Many U.S. public companies will face the challenge of converting their books and records and financial reporting obligations to IFRS and may face future litigation issues as a result. In addition, any other litigation issues currently accounted for under U.S. GAAP will translate into IFRS issues.

CHAPTER 50

COST-VOLUME-REVENUE ANALYSIS FOR NONPROFIT ORGANIZATIONS[†] (NEW)

JAE K. SHIM, PHD
California State University, Long Beach

[†] This entire chapter also appeared in the 2006 Cumulative Supplement to the *Accountants' Handbook*, Tenth Edition.

Managers of nonprofit organizations generally are not skilled in financial matters. They often are preoccupied with welfare objectives and ignore operations efficiency and operating cost controls. There are nine questions that nonprofit financial managers should address in connection with an organization's financial condition and activity:

1. Do we have a profit or a loss?
2. Do we have sufficient reserves?
3. Are we liquid?
4. Do we have strong internal controls?
5. Are we operating efficiently?
6. Are we meeting our budget goals?
7. Are our programs financially healthy?
8. Are we competing successfully?
9. Is our prioritizing of programs and activities reasonable?

By definition, the goal of a nonprofit entity is *not* to earn a profit. Its objective is to render as much suitable service as possible while using the least amount of human and physical services as possible. Ideally, breaking even should be the goal of a nonprofit organization. Breaking even occurs when revenues equal costs. If the nonprofit generates a surplus, it may not receive the same amount from the funding agency as last year. On the other hand, by operating at a deficit, the nonprofit may become insolvent or unable to perform the maximum amount of services. Chances are the nonprofit may not be able to borrow money from the bank as not-for-profit entities often have a weak financial stance. However, one thing is clear—over the long run, nonprofit entities cannot sustain persistent deficits unless they have large reserves. Even with large reserves, a nonprofit may have to operate below potential. This means the benefit of the nonprofit will not be maximized.

This chapter deals with many planning issues surrounding nonprofit organizations. Cost-volume-revenue (CVR) analysis, together with cost behavior information, helps nonprofit managers perform many useful planning analyses. CVR analysis deals with how revenue and costs change with a change in the service level. More specifically, it looks at the effects on revenues from changes in such factors as variable costs, fixed costs, prices, service level, and mix of services offered. By studying the relationships of costs, service volume, and revenue, nonprofit management is better able to cope with many planning decisions.

Break-even analysis, a branch of CVR analysis, determines the break-even service level. The break-even point (the financial crossover point at which revenues exactly match costs) does not show up in financial reports, but nonprofit financial managers find it an extremely useful measurement in numerous ways. It reveals which programs are self-supporting and which are subsidized.

50.1 QUESTIONS ANSWERED BY CVR ANALYSIS

CVR analysis tries to answer four questions:

1. What service level (or which units of service) is required to break even?
2. How would changes in price, variable costs, fixed costs, and service volume affect a surplus?
3. How do changes in program levels and mix affect aggregate surplus/deficit?
4. What alternative break-even strategies are available?

50.2 ANALYSIS OF REVENUES

Revenues for nonprofit entities are typically classified into the following categories:

- Grants from governments
- Grants from private sources
- Cost reimbursements and sales
- Membership dues
- Public contributions received directly or indirectly
- Donations and pledges
- Legacies, bequests, and memorials
- Program fees
- Other revenue, such as investment income (e.g., interest, dividends)

For managerial purposes, however, each type of revenue is grouped into its fixed and variable parts. Fixed revenues are those that remain unchanged regardless of the level of service. Examples are gifts, grants, and contracts. As an example, in a university setting, donations, gifts, and grants have no relationship to the number of students enrolled. In contrast to fixed revenues, variable revenues are the ones that vary in proportion to the volume of activity. Examples include cost reimbursements and membership fees. Continuing the example of a university setting, the total amount of tuition and fees received varies as the number of students enrolled increases or decreases. Different nonprofit entities may have different sources of revenue: variable revenue only, fixed revenue only, or a combination of both. In this chapter, we discuss all three cases in analyzing break-even and CVR applications.

50.3 ANALYSIS OF COST BEHAVIOR

For external reporting purposes, costs are classified by managerial function such as payroll, occupancy, office, and so on, as well as by programs and supporting services. See Exhibit 50.1 for a model functional classification.

For managerial purposes (i.e., planning, control, and decision making), further classification of costs is desirable. One classification is by behavior. Depending on how they react or respond to changes in the level of activity, costs may be viewed as variable or fixed. This classification assumes a known high and low volume of service activity called the *relative range of activity*. The relevant range is the volume zone within which the behavior of variable costs, fixed costs, and prices can be predicted with reasonable accuracy. The relevant range falls between the planned highest and lowest service level for the nonprofit. Within this level of normal activity the behavior of variable costs, fixed costs, and prices can be predicted with reasonable accuracy. Typical activity measures are summarized in Exhibit 50.2.

(a) VARIABLE COSTS Total variable costs change as the volume or level of activity changes. Examples of variable costs include supplies, hourly wages, printing and publications, and postage and shipping.

(b) FIXED COSTS Total fixed costs do not change regardless of the volume or level of activity. Examples include property tax, yearly salaries, accounting and consulting fees, and depreciation. Exhibit 50.3 shows the fixed-variable breakdown of IRS Form 990 functional expenses.

IRS Form 990 Line #	Functional Expense Category
26	Salaries and wages
27	Pension plan contributions
28	Other employee benefits
29	Payroll taxes
30	Professional fundraising fees
31	Accounting fees
32	Legal fees
33	Supplies
34	Telephone
35	Postage and shipping
36	Occupancy
37	Equipment rental and maintenance
38	Printing and publications
39	Travel
40	Conferences, conventions, meetings
41	Interest
42	Depreciation, depletion, etc.
43	Other expenses (itemize)

Exhibit 50.1   IRS Form 990 Part II—Statement of Functional Expenses

Nonprofit Types	Units of Service
Hospital or Healthcare	Bed days, patient contact hours, patient days, service hours
Educational	Number of student enrollments, class size, FTE (full-time equivalent) hours
Social Clubs	Number of members served

Exhibit 50.2   Measures of the Service Level

(c) TYPES OF FIXED COSTS: PROGRAM-SPECIFIC OR COMMON   Fixed costs of nonprofit entities are subdivided into two groups: (1) direct or program-specific fixed costs and (2) common costs. Direct or program-specific fixed costs are those that can be directly identified with individual programs. These costs are avoidable or escapable if the program is dropped. Examples include the salaries of those staff members whose services can be used only in a given program and depreciation of equipment used exclusively for the program. Common fixed costs continue even if an individual program has been discontinued. Examples include depreciation of the building and property taxes.

IRS FORM 990 LINE	EXPENSE CATEGORY
Fixed Costs	
26	Salaries and wages (not hourly employees)
27	Pension plan
28	Other benefits
29	Payroll taxes
30	Fund-raising fees
31	Accounting fees
32	Legal fees
36	Occupancy
37	Equipment rental/maintenance
41	Interest
42	Depreciation
43	Other
Variable Costs	
33	Supplies
34	Telephone
35	Postage and shipping
38	Printing and publications
39	Travel
40	Conferences, meetings
43	Other

EXHIBIT 50.3   FIXED-VARIABLE BREAKDOWN OF IRS FORM 990, FUNCTIONAL EXPENSES

50.4 CVR ANALYSIS WITH VARIABLE REVENUE ONLY

For accurate CVR analysis, a distinction must be made between variable costs and fixed costs. In order to compute the break-even point and perform various CVR analyses, the following concepts are important.

(a) CONTRIBUTION MARGIN (CM)   The contribution margin is the amount by which total revenue (R) exceeds the variable costs (VC) of the service. It is the amount of money available to cover fixed costs (FC) and to generate surplus. This is symbolically expressed as:

$$CM = R - VC \tag{1}$$

(b) UNIT CM   The unit CM is the amount by which the unit price (p) exceeds the unit variable cost (v). This is symbolically expressed as:

$$\text{unit } CM = p - v$$

(c) CM RATIO   The CM ratio is the contribution margin as a percentage of revenue:

$$CM \text{ ratio} = CM/R = (R - VC)/R = 1 - (VC/R) \tag{2}$$

or

$$\text{Unit CM} = (p - v)/p = 1 - (v/p) \qquad (3)$$

Note: Once you know the contribution margin ratio, then the variable cost ratio is 1–CM ratio. Similarly, if you know the variable cost ratio (VC/R), the contribution margin ratio is (1–VC ratio).

EXAMPLE 50.1

The Los Altos Community Hospital has the following data. This information will be used to illustrate the various concepts of contribution margin and contribution margin ratio:

Average revenue per day	=	$ 250	
Variable costs per patient day	=	$ 50	
Total fixed costs	=	$650,000	
Expected number of patient days	=	4,000	

	Total	Per Unit	Percentage
Revenue (4,000 days)	$1,000,000	$250	100%
Less: Variable costs (4,000 days)	200,000	50	20
Contribution margin	$ 800,000	$200	80%
Less: Fixed costs (annual)	650,000		
Net income	$ 150,000		

Note that unit CM = $p - v$ = $250 − $50 = $200 and CM ratio = unit CM/p = $200/$250 = .8 = 80%

50.5 BREAK-EVEN ANALYSIS

The break-even point represents the level of revenue that equals the total of the variable and fixed costs for a given volume of output service at a particular capacity use rate. Other things being equal, the lower the break-even point, the higher the surplus and the less the operating risk. The break-even point also provides nonprofit managers with insights into surplus/deficit planning. To develop the formula for the break-even units of service, we set:

$$R = TC \text{ (total costs)} \qquad (4)$$

$$R = VC + FC \qquad (5)$$

$$px = vx + FC \qquad (6)$$

Solving for x yields the following formula for break-even sales volume:

$$x = \frac{FC}{(p - v)} = \frac{\text{Fixed costs}}{\text{Unit CM}}$$

or

$$\text{Break-even point in dollars (R)} = \frac{\text{Fixed costs}}{\text{CM ratio}}$$

EXAMPLE 50.2

Using the same data given in Example 50.1, the number of break-even patient days and break-even dollars are computed as follows:

Break-even point in units   = FC/unit CM   = \$650,000/\$200 = 3,250 patient days
Break-even point in dollars = FC/CM ratio = \$650,000/0.8   = \$812,500

Or, alternatively,

Break-even point in dollars = 3,250 patient days × \$250 revenue per patient
                            = 3,250 × \$250 = \$812,500

The hospital therefore needs 3,250 patient days or \$812,500 dollars of revenue to break even.

(a) GRAPHICAL APPROACH IN A SPREADSHEET FORMAT   The graphical approach to obtaining the break-even point is based on the so-called break-even (B-E) chart as shown in Exhibit 50.4. Revenue, variable costs, and fixed costs are plotted on the vertical axis while service volume, x, is plotted on the horizontal axis. The break-even point is the point where the total revenue line intersects the total cost line. The chart can report surplus potentials over a wide range of activity and therefore can be used as a tool for discussion and presentation.

The surplus-volume (S-V) chart, as shown in Exhibit 50.5, focuses on how surplus varies with changes in volume. Surplus is plotted on the vertical axis while units of output are shown on the horizontal axis. The S-V chart provides a quick condensed comparison of how alternatives related to pricing, variable costs, or fixed costs may affect surplus (or deficit) as volume changes. The S-V chart can be easily constructed from the B-E chart. Note that the slope of the chart is the unit CM.

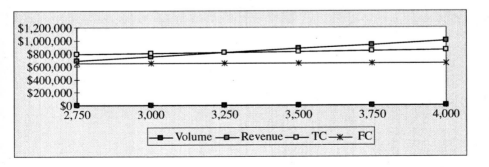

EXHIBIT 50.4   BREAK-EVEN (B-E) CHART—VARIABLE REVENUE

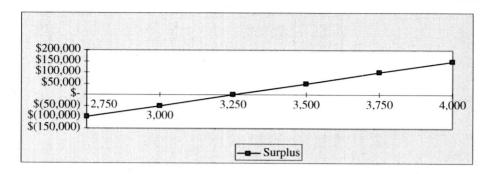

EXHIBIT 50.5   SURPLUS-VOLUME (S-V) CHART—VARIABLE REVENUE

(b) DETERMINATION OF TARGET SURPLUS VOLUME   Cost-Volume-Revenue (CVR) analysis can be used to determine the activity levels necessary to attain a target surplus (TS). Once the break-even level of activity has been computed, it is useful to determine the level of activity necessary to create a desired surplus. At the break-even point, all fixed costs have been covered.

Therefore, any additional revenue above the break-even level increases the surplus. To calculate the level of service needed to obtain our target surplus, we only need to expand our break-even formula—that is, expand the numerator of the break-even formula to include the amount of desired surplus in addition to fixed costs. In other words, to achieve our desired increase in surplus, not only fixed costs must be recovered but also the desired increase in surplus.

By expanding the break-even formula to obtain the level of activity for a desired target surplus, the formula becomes:

$$\text{Target income surplus level} = \frac{\text{Fixed costs} + \text{Target surplus}}{\text{Unit CM}} \qquad (7)$$

EXAMPLE 50.3
Using the same data given in Example 50.1, assume the hospital wishes to accumulate a surplus of $250,000 per year. Then the target surplus service level would be: $$\frac{\text{Fixed costs} + \text{Target surplus}}{\text{Unit CM}} = \frac{\$650,000 + \$250,000}{\$200} = 4,500 \text{ patient days}$$

(c) MARGIN OF SAFETY   The margin of safety is a measure of difference between the actual level of service and the break-even level of service. It is expressed as a percentage of expected service level. The margin of safety determines how far the estimated or expected level of service can decline and have the nonprofit still be profitable.

$$\text{Margin of safety} = \frac{\text{Expected level} - \text{Break-even level}}{\text{Expected level}}$$

The margin of safety is used as a measure of operating risk. The larger the ratio, the safer the situation since there is less risk of reaching the break-even point.

EXAMPLE 50.4

Assume Los Altos Hospital projects 4,000 patient days with a break-even level of 3,250. The projected margin of safety is:

$$\frac{4,000 - 3,250}{4,000} = 18.75\%$$

This means that the hospital's revenue can drop 18.75% before it suffers a deficit.

EXAMPLE 50.5

A nonprofit college offers a program in management for executives. The program has been experiencing financial difficulties. The dean of the school wants to know how many participants are needed to break even. Operating data for the most recent year are shown as follows.

Tuition per participant	= $ 7,000
Variable expense per participant	= $ 4,000
Total fixed expenses	= $150,000
Tuition revenue (40 participants @$7,000)	$280,000
Less variable expenses (@$4,000)	160,000
Contribution margin	$120,000
Less: Fixed expenses	150,000
Operating deficit	$ (30,000)

The break-even calculation is:

$$\$150,000/(\$7,000 - \$4,000) = 50 \text{ participants}$$

EXAMPLE 50.6

In Example 50.5, the dean of the school is convinced that the class size can be increased to more economic levels without lowering the quality. He is prepared to spend $15,000 per year in additional promotional and other support expenses. The promotional and other support expenses are additional fixed costs. If he spends the $15,000 on promotional expenses, the dean wants to know the new break-even number of participants and how many participants are needed to generate a surplus of $30,000.

If that is the case, the formula to calculate the new break-even point is

$$(\$150,000 + \$15,000)/\$3,000 = 55 \text{ participants to break even}$$

The formula to calculate the number of participants necessary to generate a target surplus of $30,000 is

$$[(\$150,000 + \$15,000) + \$30,000]/\$3,000 = 65 \text{ participants}$$

(d) SOME APPLICATIONS OF CVR ANALYSIS AND WHAT-IF ANALYSIS   The concepts of contribution margin and the contribution income statement have many applications in surplus/deficit planning and short-term decision making. Many "what-if" scenarios can be evaluated using these concepts as planning tools, especially utilizing a spreadsheet program. Some applications are illustrated in Example 50.7 using the same data as in Example 50.1.

EXAMPLE 50.7

Assume that the Los Altos Community Hospital in Example 50.1 expects revenues to go up by $250,000 for the next period. How much will surplus increase?

Using the CM concepts, we can quickly compute the impact of a change in the service level on surplus or deficit. The formula for computing the impact is

Change in surplus = Dollar change in revenue × CM ratio

Thus:

$$\text{Increase in surplus} = \$250,000 \times 80\% = \$200,000$$

Therefore, the income will go up by $200,000, assuming there is no change in fixed costs. If we are given a change in service units (e.g., patient days) instead of dollars, then the formula becomes:

$$\text{Change in surplus} = \text{Change in units} \times \text{Unit CM.}$$

EXAMPLE 50.8

Assume the Los Altos Community Hospital in Example 50.1 expects patient days to go up by 500 units. How much will surplus increase? From Example 50.1, the hospital's unit CM is $200. Again, assuming there is no change in fixed costs, the surplus will increase by $100,000, computed as follows:

$$500 \text{ additional patient days} \times \$200 \text{ CM per day} = \$100,000$$

EXAMPLE 50.9

Referring back to Example 50.5, another alternative under consideration is to hold the present program without any change in the regular campus facilities instead of in rented outside facilities that are better located. If adopted, this proposal will reduce fixed costs by $60,000. The variable costs will decrease by $100 per participant. Is the move to campus facilities advisable if it leads to a decline in the number of participants by 5?

	Present		Proposed
S(40 × $7,000)	$280,000	(35 × $7,000)	245,000
VC(40 × $4,000)	160,000	(35 × $3,900)	136,500
CM	$120,000		$108,500
FC	150,000		90,000
Surplus	$(30,000)		$ 18,500

The answer is yes, since the move will turn into a surplus.

50.6   CVR ANALYSIS WITH FIXED REVENUE ONLY

In many nonprofit activities, the objectives are not as clear-cut as the objective of profit in commercial business. Furthermore, the relationship between revenue and volume for a non-profit organization (NPO) is not nearly as well established as is the revenue–volume relationship in business. For example, some NPOs may have only one source of revenue, which is a lump-sum appropriation. This source does not change with changes in volume. Let FR be fixed revenue, or lump-sum appropriation. At break-even,

$$FR = VC + FC$$

$$FR = vx + FC$$

$$x = (FR-FC)\, v$$

$$\text{or break-even units} = \frac{\text{Fixed revenue} - \text{Fixed costs}}{\text{Unit variable cost}}$$

EXAMPLE 50.10

A social service agency has a government budget appropriation of $750,000. The agency's main mission is to assist handicapped people who are unable to seek or hold jobs. On aver-age, the agency supplements each individual's income by $6,000 annually. The agency's fixed costs are $150,000. The agency CEO wants to know how many people could be served in a given year. The break-even point can be computed as follows:

$$\text{Break-even units} = \frac{\text{Fixed revenue} - \text{Fixed costs}}{\text{Unit variable cost}} = \frac{750{,}000 - \$150{,}000}{\$6{,}000} = 100$$

The number of people that could be served in a given year is 100.

Exhibits 50.6 and 50.7 display the B-E and S-V charts for this situation.

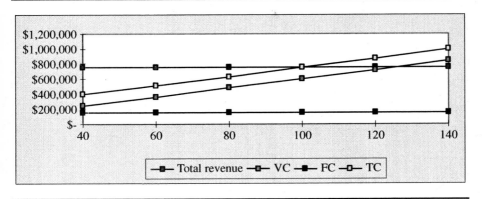

EXHIBIT 50.6   BREAK-EVEN (B-E) CHART—FIXED REVENUE

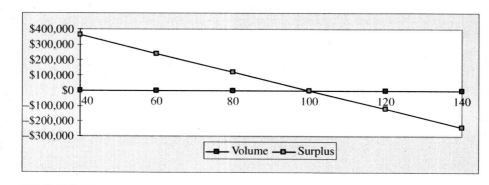

Exhibit 50.7 Surplus-Volume (S-V) Chart—Fixed Revenue

Nonprofits with a lump-sum appropriation have little incentive to increase their level of service. Doing so would either increase a deficit or reduce a surplus (see Exhibit 50.7). Either of these alternatives more than likely would result in a poorer performance evaluation for the program.

EXAMPLE 50.11

In Example 50.10, assume that the CEO is concerned that the total budget for the year will be reduced by 10 percent to a new amount of 90 percent ($750,000) = $675,000.
The new break-even point is:

$$\text{Break-even units} = \frac{\text{Fixed revenue} - \text{Fixed costs}}{\text{Unit variable cost}} = \frac{\$675,000 - \$150,000}{\$6,000} = 88 \text{ (rounded)}$$

The CEO's options facing budget cuts can be any one or a combination of three ways:
(1) cut the service level as computed previously, (2) reduce the variable cost (the supplement per person), and (3) seek to cut down on the total fixed costs.

50.7 CVR ANALYSIS WITH VARIABLE AND FIXED REVENUES

Many NPOs derive two types of revenue: fixed and variable. A lump-sum appropriation may exist to subsidize the activity, and a fee for services may also exist (e.g., state-supported colleges and universities). There are two cases in this situation, however.

Case 1: Lump-sum appropriation is less than total fixed costs; fee for service is greater than unit variable cost of service.

Note that $R = FR + px$

At break-even, $FR + px = vx + FC$, where $FR < FC$ and $p > v$

$$x = \frac{FC - FR}{pv}$$

$$\text{or break-even units} = \frac{\text{Fixed costs} - \text{Fixed revenue}}{\text{Unit CM}}$$

Case 2: Lump-sum appropriation is higher than total fixed costs; fee is lower than unit variable cost (subsidized activity) resulting in negative unit CM.

$$\text{Note that } R = FR + px$$

$$\text{At break-even, } FR + px = vx + FC, \text{ where } FR > FC \text{ and } p < v$$

$$x = \frac{FR - FC}{vp}$$

$$\text{or break-even units} = \frac{\text{Fixed revenue} - \text{Fixed costs}}{-\text{Unit CM}}$$

In this situation, the fixed revenue covers more than the actual fixed costs. However, the variable costs for service are already more than the nonprofit can charge. In this scenario the number of units that can be served is limited. There is a heavily subsidized unit with a small fee for service to discourage unnecessary use but still making the service available at low cost. This type of appropriate and unit pricing can be used for essential services such as community health services or mass transit.

EXAMPLE 50.12

ACM, Inc., a mental rehabilitation provider, has the following:

- $1,200,000 lump-sum annual budget appropriation to help rehabilitate mentally ill clients

- Monthly charge per patient for board and care = $600

- Monthly variable cost for rehabilitation activity per patient = $700

- Yearly fixed cost = $800,000

The agency manager wants to know how many clients can be served.

$$\text{Break-even number of patients} = \frac{\text{Fixed revenue} - \text{Fixed costs}}{-\text{Unit CM}} = \frac{1{,}200{,}000 - \$800{,}000}{-(\$600 - \$700)}$$

$$= \frac{\$400{,}000}{-(-\$10)} = \frac{\$400{,}000}{\$100} = 4{,}000 \text{ per year}$$

The number of patients that can be served is 4,000 per year.

Exhibits 50.8 and 50.9 display the B-E and S-V charts for variable and fixed revenue.

Note that at the level of service greater than B-E service (i.e., 4,000 units), the service is overused or underpriced (or both) (see Exhibit 50.9). We will investigate two "what-if" scenarios.

EXAMPLE 50.13

Using the same data as in Example 50.12, suppose the manager of the agency is concerned that the total budget for the coming year will be cut by 10 percent to a new amount of $1,080,000. All other things remain unchanged. The manager wants to know how this budget cut affects the next year's service level. Using the formula yields

$$\text{Break-even number of patients} = \frac{\text{Fixed revenue} - \text{Fixed costs}}{-\text{Unit CM}} = \frac{\$1,080,000 - \$800,000}{-(\$600 - \$700)}$$

$$= \frac{\$280,000}{-(-\$10)} = 2,800 \text{ Clients per year}$$

The service level will be cut from 4,000 clients to 2,800 clients.

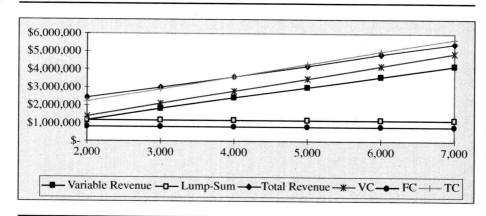

EXHIBIT 50.8   BREAK-EVEN (B-E) CHART—VARIABLE AND FIXED REVENUE (CASE 2)

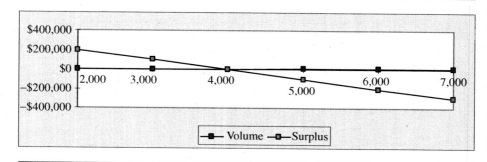

EXHIBIT 50.9   SURPLUS-VOLUME (S-V) CHART—VARIABLE AND FIXED REVENUE (CASE 2)

EXAMPLE 50.14

In Example 50.13, suppose that the manager does not reduce the number of clients served despite a budget cut of 10 percent. All other things remain unchanged. How much more does the manager have to charge clients for board and care?

Let v = board and care charge per year and x = 4,000 = number of clients served.

The following formula can be used to make this determination:

$$R = \$1,080,000 + 4,000p$$

$$VC + FC = \$700(4,000) + \$800,000$$

$$R + VC + FC$$

$$\$1,080,000 + 4,000p = \$700(4,000) + \$800,000$$

$$4,000p = \$2,800,000 + \$800,000 - 1,080,000$$

$$4,000p = \$2,520,000$$

$$p = \$630$$

Thus, the monthly board and care charge must be increased to $630.

50.8 PROGRAM MIX ANALYSIS

Previously, our main concern was to determine program-specific break-even volume. However, most nonprofit organizations are involved in multiservice, multiprogram activities. One major concern is how to plan aggregate break-even volume, surplus, and deficits. Break-even and Cost-Volume-Revenue analysis requires additional computations and assumptions when an organization offers more than one program. In multiprogram organizations, program mix is an important factor in calculating an overall break-even point. Different rates and different variable costs result in different unit CMs. As a result, break-even points and Cost-Volume-Revenue relationships vary with the relative proportions of the programs offered.

By defining the product as a package, the multiprogram problem is converted into a single-program problem. The first step is to determine the number of packages that need to be served to break even. The following example illustrates a multiprogram, multiservice situation.

EXAMPLE 50.15 (SHEET 1 OF 2)

The Cypress Counseling Services is a nonprofit agency offering two programs: psychological counseling (PC) and alcohol addiction control (AAC). The agency charges individual clients an average of $10 per hour of counseling provided under the PC program. The local Chamber of Commerce reimburses the nonprofit organizations at the rate of $20 per hour of direct service provided under the AAC. The nonprofit organization believes that this billing variable rate is low enough to be affordable for most clients and also high enough to derive clients' commitment to the program objectives. Costs of administering the two programs are given as follows:

	PC	AAC
Variable costs	$ 4.6	$ 11.5
Direct fixed costs	$120,000	$180,000

Example 50.15 (Sheet 2 of 2)

Other fixed costs are common to the two programs, including general, administrative, and fundraising costs of $255,100 per year. The projected surplus for the coming year, segmented by programs, follows.

	PC	AAC	Total
Revenue	$500,000	$800,000	$1,300,000
Program mix in hours	(50,000)	(40,000)	
Less: VC	(230,000)	(460,000)	(690,000)
Contribution margin	$270,000	$340,000	$ 610,000
Less: Direct FC	(120,000)	(180,000)	(300,000)
Program margin	$150,000	$160,000	$ 310,000
Less: Common FC			(255,100)
Surplus			$ 54,900

First, based on program-specific data on the rates, the variable costs, and the program mix, we can compute the package (aggregate) value as follows:

Program	P	V	Unit CM	Mix*	Package CM
PC	$10	$4.6	$5.4	5	$27
AAC	20	11.5	8.5	4	34
Package total					$61

*The mix ratio is 5:4 (50,000 hours for PC and 40,000 hours for AAC).

We know that the total fixed costs for the agency are $555,100. Thus, the package (aggregate) break-even point is:

$$\$555,100/\$61 = 9,100 \text{ packages}$$

The company must provide 45,500 hours of PC (5 × 9,100) and 36,400 hours of AAC (4 × 9,100) to avoid a deficit. To prove,

	PC	AAC	Total
Revenue	$ 455,000(a)	$ 728,000(b)	$1,183,000
Program mix in hours	(45,500)	(36,400)	
Less: VC	(209,300)(c)	(418,600)(d)	(627,900)
Contribution margin	$ 245,700	$ 309,400	$ 555,100
Less: Direct FC	(120,000)	(180,000)	(300,000)
Program margin	$ 125,700	$ 129,400	$ 255,100
Less: Common FC			(255,100)
Surplus			$ 0

(a) 45,500 × $10   (c) 45,500 × $4.60
(b) 36,400 × $20   (d) 36,400 × $11.50

EXAMPLE 50.16

Assume in Example 50.15 that 56,000 hours of PC services are budgeted for the next period. The nonprofit organization wants to know how many hours of AAC services are necessary during that period to avoid an overall deficit. The answer is 29,729 hours, shown as follows:

INPUT DATA	PC	AAC
Rates	$ 10	$ 20
Units of service (hours)	56,000	29,729
Variable cost per unit	$ 4.6	$ 11.5

CONTRIBUTION STATEMENT OF SURPLUS OR DEFICIT

	PC	AAC	TOTAL
Revenue	$560,000	$594,588	$1,154,588
Less: Variable costs	257,600	341,888	599,488
Contribution margin	$302,400	$252,700	$ 555,100
Less: Direct fixed costs	120,000	180,000	300,000
Program margin	$182,400	$72,700	$ 255,100
Less: Common fixed costs			255,100
Surplus			$ (0)

50.9   MANAGEMENT OPTIONS

Cost-Volume-Revenue analysis is useful as a frame of reference, as a vehicle for expressing overall managerial performance, and as a planning device via break-even techniques and what-if scenarios. Using CVR, many planning decisions, such as adding or dropping a service, outsourcing, answering special requests, and changing budget limits, can be made on a sounder basis.

In many practical situations, management will have to resort to a combination of approaches to reverse a deficit, including

- Selected changes in volume of activity
- Planned savings in fixed costs at all levels
- Some savings in variable costs
- Additional fund drives or grant seeking
- Upward adjustments in pricing
- Cost reimbursement contracts

All of these must be mixed to form a feasible planning package. Many nonprofit managers fail to develop such analytical approaches to the economics of their operations. Further, the accounting system is not designed to provide the information needed to investigate Cost-Volume-Revenue relations.

50.10   REFERENCES AND SUGGESTED READINGS

Shim, Jae K., *Cost Accounting for Managers: A Managerial Emphasis,* 6th ed. (Buena Park, CA: Delta Publishing, 2006).

Siegel, Joel, and Shim, Jae K., *Barron's Accounting Handbook* (New York: Barron's, 2005).

INDEX